THE OXFORD HISTORY OF
ENGLISH LITERATURE

General Editors

JOHN BUXTON *and* NORMAN DAVIS

Middle English Literature

J. A. W. BENNETT

Edited and completed by
DOUGLAS GRAY

CLARENDON PRESS · OXFORD

Oxford University Press, Walton Street, Oxford OX2 6DP
Oxford New York Toronto
Delhi Bombay Calcutta Madras Karachi
Petaling Jaya Singapore Hong Kong Tokyo
Nairobi Dar es Salaam Cape Town
Melbourne Auckland
and associated companies in
Berlin Ibadan

Oxford is a trade mark of Oxford University Press

Published in the United States
by Oxford University Press, New York

© Oxford University Press 1986

First published 1986
Reprinted 1990
First issued as a Clarendon Paperback 1990

British Library Cataloguing in Publication Data
Bennett, J. A. W.
Middle English literature.
1. English literature—Middle English,
1100–1500—History and criticism
I. Title II. Gray, Douglas
820.9'001   PR281
ISBN 0–19–812214–4 (Hbk)
ISBN 0–19–811970–4 (Pbk)

Library of Congress Cataloging-in-Publication Data
Bennett, J. A. W. (Jack Arthur Walter)
Middle English literature.
Bibliography: p.
Includes index.
1. English literature—Middle English, 1100–1500—
History and criticism. I. Gray, Douglas. II. Title.
PR255.B45 1986   820'.9'001   86–8741
ISBN 0–19–812214–4 (Hbk)
ISBN 0–19–811970–4 (Pbk)

Printed in Great Britain by
Richard Clay (The Chaucer Press) Ltd
Bungay, Suffolk

Preface

WHEN Jack Bennett died early in 1981 he left unfinished the Middle English volume of the Oxford History of English Literature, on which he had been working for many years. The period just before his death had been one of intense activity, during which sections and segments both large and small had been dispatched from Cambridge to the Oxford University Press, which had managed to find a typist who could decipher his notoriously idiosyncratic handwriting. When the surviving pieces were assembled it became clear that although they did not represent a complete book, they could be made into one with some effort and ingenuity. I was much honoured to be asked to undertake this task. I am grateful to Mr Edmund Bennett and to Professor Peter Heyworth, Jack Bennett's literary executor, for collecting the material and making it available. I owe a particular debt of gratitude to Professor Norman Davis for giving unsparingly of his time and for his constant encouragement, advice, and criticism.

It would be proper to give some indication of the nature and extent of my editorial work. It is difficult to do so in detail, since I have often had to expand draft manuscript notes, and to add link passages and matter whenever I thought it necessary (although I did not feel obliged to add a few words on *every* romance or piece of prose that he had left unmentioned). Of the longer additions, the sections on *Wynnere and Wastoure*, 'Robert of Gloucester', *Purity*, *The Peterborough Chronicle*, and the later sermons are mine, as is the whole of Chapter 8 and the Bibliography. (It was never intended that this book should contain chapters on Chaucer or the medieval drama; these will find their place in a new volume on the following period.) I have also had to do much trimming and revising, but I have tried to leave Jack Bennett's opinions (and his prejudices) untouched. I am responsible for the ordering of the chapters, and for the ordering of the material within each chapter. This has been a heavy responsibility, and sometimes as I struggled with the fragments I feared that that venerable white-haired figure might appear in a dream and begin to upbraid me with Holy Church's words, 'thow doted daffe, dulle arne thi wittes . . .'. Sadly, this book can never be the one to which he would have given his final approval. (Indeed, those of us familiar with his patterns of work know that for him the process of revision continued up to, and often beyond, the proof stage.) I can only hope that it does not differ too much from what he would have wished it to be. I am certain, however, that it shows in a remarkable way the immense range of his reading and scholarship, his characteristic humanity and piety, and the elegance of his thought and style. On behalf of those of us who benefited so much from his erudition and his example, I should like to dedicate the volume to the memory of this most humane of medievalists, in accordance with that Langlandian injunction which he quoted in dedicating his *Piers Plowman* to his own mentor, P. S. Ardern: *Redde quod debes*.

D.G.

Contents

Abbreviations

Aen.	*Aeneid*
AN	Anglo-Norman
Archiv	*Archiv für das Studium der neueren Sprachen und Literaturen*
AV	Authorized Version
B	G. L. Brook (ed.), *The Harley Lyrics* (3rd edn., Manchester, 1964)
BRUC	A. B. Emden, *A Biographical Register of the University of Cambridge to 1500* (Cambridge, 1963)
BRUO	A. B. Emden, *A Biographical Register of the University of Oxford to AD 1500*, 3 vols. (Oxford, 1957–9)
CA	*Confessio Amantis*
CB XIII	Carleton Brown (ed.), *English Lyrics of the Thirteenth Century* (Oxford, 1932)
CB XIV	Carleton Brown (ed.), *Religious Lyrics of the Fourteenth Century* (revised G. V. Smithers, Oxford, 1952)
CT	*Canterbury Tales*
E&S	*Essays and Studies by members of the English Association*
EETS	Early English Text Society (ES: Extra Series, SS: Supplementary Series)
EHR	*English Historical Review*
EMEVP	J. A. W. Bennett and G. V. Smithers (edd.), *Early Middle English Verse and Prose* (2nd edn., Oxford, 1968)
HF	*House of Fame*
HP	R. H. Robbins (ed.), *Historical Poems of the Fourteenth and Fifteenth Centuries* (New York, 1959)
JEGP	*Journal of English and Germanic Philology*
KnT	*Knight's Tale*
LGW	*Legend of Good Women*
LSE	*Leeds Studies in English*
MÆ	*Medium Ævum*
M&H	*Medievalia et Humanistica*
ME	Middle English
MED	*Middle English Dictionary*
Met.	*Metamorphoses*
MLR	*Modern Language Review*
MP	*Modern Philology*

MWME	J. B. Severs and A. E. Hartung (edd.), *Manual of the Writings in Middle English* (New Haven, 1967–)
NM	*Neuphilologische Mitteilungen*
NS	New Series
OE	Old English
OED	*Oxford English Dictionary*
OF	Old French
ON	Old Norse
PBA	*Proceedings of the British Academy*
PF	*Parlement of Foules*
PL	*Patrologia Latina*
RES	*Review of English Studies*
RS	Rolls Series
SATF	Société des Anciens Textes Français
Sisam	K. Sisam (ed.), *Fourteenth-Century Verse and Prose* (Oxford, 1921)
SL	R. H. Robbins (ed.), *Secular Lyrics of the Fourteenth and Fifteenth Centuries* (Oxford, 1952; 2nd edn. 1955)
SP	*Studies in Philology*
SRL	D. Gray (ed.), *A Selection of Religious Lyrics* (Oxford, 1975)
STS	Scottish Text Society
TC	*Troilus and Criseyde*
TLS	*Times Literary Supplement*
Tr. RHS	*Transactions of the Royal Historical Society*
W	E. Wilson (ed.), *A Descriptive Index of the English Lyrics in John of Grimestone's Preaching Book* (*Medium Ævum* Monographs, NS ii, Oxford, 1973)

Note on the Treatment of Texts

In the Middle English quotations i/j and u/v have been standardized according to modern usage; the letters þ, ð, ȝ have been transliterated into their modern equivalents; and one or two other spellings which might puzzle modern readers (such as silent *h* in forms like *hic* for *ic*, 'I') have been changed.

1

Pastoral and Comedy

The Owl and the Nightingale; The Fox and the Wolf; The Land of Cokaygne; Dame Sirith; De Clerico et Puella; The Man in the Moon

As the story of Anglo-Saxon literature opens with a masterpiece—'The Dream of the Rood'—that found no parallel in three hundred years, so, when in the late twelfth century English has its renascence, the first poet to be heard spoke in assured tones and showed a delicate humour, a rich humanity, and a sensitivity to nature that amounted to genius, and that will hardly be met with again before Marvell's time. The *Altercacio inter Filomelam et Bubonem*—the name given in the two extant manuscripts to the poem now called *The Owl and the Nightingale*—has been called miraculous by those who sense the change in English feeling that it displays when set alongside *Beowulf* or *Maldon*, *The Seafarer* or the *Riddles*—or even the Latin pastoral in which Alcuin laments the departure of the cuckoo, anticipating Arnold's 'too quick despairer, wherefore wilt thou go'; or the *Ecloga Theoduli*, in which the contestants challenge each other, prizes are promised, and a judge appointed: that title suggests a connection with Virgil's third eclogue, which Servius had called an *altercacio*. But 'miraculous' is merely a loose synonym for 'mysterious', 'unaccountable': a confession that we know nothing of the cultural conditions and little of the literary context out of which it grew. There is a springtime freshness about it, a *verve*, a sense of sheer fun.

There survive, to be sure, numerous earlier fragments of verse, pious, gnomic, or hortatory, in the old alliterative measure, even if debased or modified. They will merit attention later as links between the older literary culture and the school of verse that arose in the West Country about the same time that this bird-debate was being written. But the lively dialogue, poetic wit, the easy rhythms of its 830 octosyllabic couplets; the suppleness in sophisticated self-portraiture, with its humorous hyperbole—all these qualities link the author with the contemporary clerkly humanism of Walter Map and John of Salisbury. The disputants represent him as 'ripe and fastrede'—a man of mature wisdom who 'wot insight in eche songe'—is a shrewd judge of verse; and they give him a clerkly title: *Master* Nicholas. He is, then, a university man, the first of a long line of English clerks who had acquired from Abelard's example a relish for 'disputeison' (as distinct from the 'flytings' of an earlier age). *Piers Plowman* will proceed along much the same lines; and the 'Pleasant Conceited Comedie' called *Love's Labour's Lost* (which ends in a medieval *contentio* between Owl and Cuckoo) begins with an academic debate. Future lines of English literary development—as well as the English poet's foible for self-portraiture—are already to be discerned in this light-hearted poem that moves easily from the life of a country parish to the life of castle and manor, and naturalizes, seemingly at a stroke, the French octosyllabic couplet that was to remain popular till Gower's time, and after. The debate between the two birds may be read as expressing the conflict between traditional native mores and the French culture that was represented by a new poetic and that gave a new sweetness to love.

The Provençal *tençon*, or *tenso*, was a debate (sometimes scurrilous) between two speakers (sometimes fictive, sometimes actual *jongleurs*) on questions of love or politics or the virtues of a mistress; it might be entirely in couplets of identical form or in alternating strophes of attack and riposte, and would often conclude with a *tornada* or envoi voicing (as the English poem does) an appeal for judgement to a person (often a woman) of rank. In the late twelfth century it was perhaps the most fashionable form of court poetry.

The English poet's achievement consists in adapting some of the features of a *tenso*, fusing them with elements of quite different origin, and giving the disputants far more flexible roles than those they play in troubadour verse: an achievement in many ways similar to that of the masterpiece that will later mark the high point of the English romance, *Sir Gawain and the Green Knight*. It is really a tribute to the poet's powers that various critics have seen the debate between the birds as symbolizing so many different antagonisms: gaiety vs. gravity, worldly pleasure vs. spiritual asceticism, courtly love-poetry vs. didactic verse, conservative North vs. receptive South, or even, and more narrowly, the struggle between the simple type of music of the earlier Gregorian kind and the later type of highly varied secular music full of trills and runs, such as was used by the troubadours and was finding its way into the churches—the very kind that the Nightingale, for obvious reasons, wishes to justify. This last debate lasted into the time of Wyclif, who (or one of whose followers) disparages 'fleshly knacking and tattering' in good round terms, and still continues. If none of these antitheses fit the poem exactly, it is because the two contesting birds are much more than mouthpieces.

Certainly, the Owl is presented from the outset as almost literally sticking to the Old. Her dwelling-place (*earding-stowe*: an Anglo-Saxon term, by then archaic) (28) is an 'old stock', overgrown with ivy; and she never stirs from it; whereas the Nightingale, as her nature is, flies from bough to bough and her migratory habits mean that she can be represented as far-travelled: like a *clericus vagans* 'ho had ilorned wel aiware' (she* had gained her knowledge everywhere) (216). Yet such contrasts are never pressed to the point of conflict: ultimately each recognizes that there is some cogency in the other's argument; just as the Norman builders had come to make use of English craftsmen and churchmen, and English artists to assimilate some Norman patterns.

The setting of the debate neatly symbolizes the cultural situation. It is 'In one hurne of one breche' (14), a corner (OE *hyrne*) of a clearing: *breche* being a new toponym called for as the Normans began to break up and break into the ancient weald or woodland whilst, at the same time, creating the new royal forests (a French term for a French conception) that reached their greatest extent in the reign of the second Henry, whose death is noted in the poem.† It is in just such a sunlit clearing that nightingales (like primroses) are still to be found. Blossom hangs on the bough (16), so we must read *sumere* ('Ich was in one sumere dale') (1) as meaning spring. The poetry of southern England was constantly to evoke this season when, as both Chaucer and Langland noted, the sun is still 'soft' (mild) and the nightingale sings with full-throated ease. This first appearance of the nightingale in English verse thus betokens the taming and peopling of places formerly waste and wild. The Ovidian tradition that made Philomena's song one of sorrow (as in *Confessio Amantis*) had as yet made no impact. Milton's first sonnet will not only evoke just such a Maytime setting but plead with the nightingale to 'timely sing, ere the rude bird of hate / Foretell my hopeless doom, in some grove nigh'. Conformity to ornithological truth is no warrant for poetic felicity. Yet without it the poem would lose half its charm. If the nightingale goes on and on, it is because in early summer (beginning at dusk) it does sing all night long till the other birds gather for the dawn chorus:

> An sungen alswa vale wise
> An blisse was among the rise   (1663–4)

* Both birds are referred to by feminine pronouns.

† The extent of the change is indicated in W. G. Hoskins's chapter 'The English Landscape', in *Medieval England*, ed. A. L. Poole (Oxford, 1958), i. 1–36.

3

'singing joyfully in the branches in their different notes'. The owl's untidy nest, its mobbing by other birds, its mousing in churches, its intermittent hooting, penetrating like a great horn (318)—all these betray direct observation as does the owl's dismissive description of its rival as 'a lutel soti clowe' (a little sooty ball) (578) who as soon as it has 'trode' (generated) pipes

also as doth a mose[1]

Mid chokeringe mid stevne hose[2]   (503–4)

[1] *titmouse*   [2] *with squeaking, with hoarse voice*

and who dare not venture as far as Scotland or Ireland (907–8). The troubadours had cared nothing for such observations, and were content with bestiary sentiments. They pay only lip-service to Nature, whilst the Saxon poetry had told only of birds of the battlefield or the cuckoo that announces summer with foreboding. The Middle English poem has room for thrush and throstle, wren and 'wudewale' (?oriole) (1659). It abounds in glimpses of the English scene: teams of horses drawing loads of wheat or waiting at the mill door (775–8); pairs of wrestlers (795)—wrestling was the most popular sport of the time; a fox slinking along the hedge and so killing the scent (819 ff.)—a scene that will recur in every period of our poetry down to Masefield's *Reynard*; a carter shouting 'pull over' ('Drah to the') (1186).

The chief art of the poem lies in the adaptation of such patterns of behaviour to the critical, topical, and satirical points of debate, in providing them with a human dimension. Thus the reproach that the Nightingale does not sing in heathen lands (905 ff.) but wastes its music is answered by an allusion to an event of 1176: if a real missionary sent from Rome could do nothing with those devils, how could I? The Reynard story as taken over from the Latin *Ysengrimus* about the same time (see pp. 13–14 below) makes similar topical allusions, but not so deftly.

The poem concludes with an assembly of birds great and small that, like Chaucer's two hundred years later, evinces a sense of the rich plenitude of Nature.* Nature, *kind*, meaning 'the natural order of things' makes its first entrance into English thought. Not yet hypostasized as in *The Parlement of Foules*, it is the measure by which the disputants judge everything, and are willing to be judged. Thus the Owl claims that in using her sharp bill and long claws she is obeying

---

* Both owl and nightingale figure in Chaucer's assembly (*PF* 342, 351–2), taking roles similar to those they have here, just as Chaucer takes the poet's role of a silent auditor to the birds' colloquy. The simile in *Troilus and Criseyde* iii. 1233 recalls the opening lines of *The Owl and the Nightingale*.

natural law: 'Vor righte cunde ich am so kene' (276), whilst the Nightingale condemns unlawful love with the malediction:

> Wroth wurthe heom the holi rode
> The rihte ikunde swo forbreideth! (1382–3)

'May the wrath of the Holy Rood fall on those who so transgress the law of nature'—the kind thus invoked being concerned primarily with procreation.*

Constantly the author exploits the incongruity of birds talking as humans, if he strains it when alluding to adultery (1497 ff.) and in the later discussion of human mores (1515–602) when the Owl passes beyond the immediate topic of debate and even beyond the conventions of fable; though the situation, in which the birds are forgetting their disagreement in a side issue, remains not unhumorous—the Nightingale momentarily posing as a moralist and even something of a theologian, the Owl as a broad-minded man, or woman, of the world. We can perhaps detect here some pressure from the dominant social and literary concerns of the time: the emergence of 'amour courtois' or, to use the native phrase, 'derne luve'. In so far as such love is unlawful neither disputant will defend it. On the one hand, the Nightingale avers that

> Yef maide luveth dernliche[1]
> Heo stumpeth & falth icundeliche[2] (1423–4)

[1] *loves secretly* [2] *naturally stumbles and falls*

'it's only natural that young blood should sometimes outrun discretion'; but marriage can make all right (1427–8). On the other hand Owl argues that if a husband spends all his wealth on a woman not his wife (1527), she is hardly to blame if she forgets her vows. Whatever we make of this morality, it is clearly not one that puts a premium on passion. Rather, it suggests a characteristically English blend of moral principle tempered with pity. So Chaucer (or his poetic *persona*) would wish to have excused Criseide 'for routhe', if that had been morally permissible, and Gower would see that secret love always brings unease.†

* The phrase 'against kind' is first found in *The Peterborough Chronicle* in the entry for the year 1102. *The Owl and the Nightingale* provides examples of the older forms *ikunde* and *cun* (OE *gecynde* and *cynn*) which gradually disappear.

† The bird-debate on the weakness of women was to become a popular genre, of which an Anglo-Norman specimen is preserved in the Bozon MS (SATF xxxii) and a later English example is *The Thrush and the Nightingale*, CB XIII No. 52. The nightingale again takes the side of the weaker sex and again displays its *courtois* vocabulary: the lady described is compact of 'hendinesse and courtesye' (such synonyms help to naturalize French terms). She is the physician who can heal a lover's wound, but also the victim of

The world of 'amour courtois' is the world of Marie de France.
And from Marie's *lai* of *Laustic* (or a variant thereof), the poet takes
the tale of a suitor who assumes the shape of a nightingale to reach
his mistress (1050 ff.). Retelling it against her opponent, the Owl
asserts

> Thu naddest non other dom ne laghe*
> Bute mid wilde horse were todraghe[1]   (1061–2)
>
> [1] *torn apart*

The incongruity consists not in the punishment itself—Nequam
reports that a knight actually had a nightingale torn apart in this way—
but in the Owl positing that it had really befallen her antagonist. Yet it
must not be pressed: each bird is arguing as representative of its kind.
And this is the very point at which the poet indicates that he is aware of
the limitations of bird-fable:

> The nightingale at thisse worde
> Mid sworde an mid speres orde[1]
> Yif ho mon were[2], wolde fighte.   (1067–9)
>
> [1] *point*   [2] *if she had been a man*

For the most part the assimilation of natural attributes to human
behaviour (especially to human pettiness and pique) is deft and unobtrusive. We are told at once that the Nightingale is concealed in a
thick hedge ('in *shadiest* covert hid', says Milton) and it relishes its
security:

> Yif ich me holde in mine hegge
> Ne recche[1] ich never what thu segge[2]   (59–60)
>
> [1] *care*   [2] *say*

When the Owl would put herself on a level with the hawk (271–308), or
even with the raven and eagle (389–90), the poet is capitalizing at once
on the bird's self-importance and on the pretentiousness of owl-like
men.

The debate conducted with such brio savours as much of the court
as of the schools. Not surprisingly, since the development of legal
procedures had been a marked feature of the reign of Henry II. *Plait*
(legal suit) is the term used to describe it at the beginning (l. 5) and the
end (1737); and *tale* (3, 544) may be an English calque on this French
Wikke-tonge (to use the Chaucerian equivalent to the Malebouche of the *Roman de la
Rose*): the Thrush is accused of unduly blaming such ladies (107). The tone throughout
is light and gay; the poem is as much an exercise in verse-rhetoric as a serious *disputacio*.

* Editors have not noticed the technical sense of 'to have the law', used likewise as
regards (Guenevere's) adultery in Malory (*Works*, ed. Vinaver (2nd edn., Oxford, 1967),
1175; cf. also 374).

term; it certainly did duty for French *conte* (= the plaintiff's statement) in later times.* When the nightingale says her 'bare word' (547) can invalidate charges, she is using the plaintiff's right of *nude parole*; and when the Owl protests that she need not answer, she is within her rights as defendant. Less obvious, if more pervasive, is the influence of the new vogue for rhetoric, discernible in the way in which each bird, driven to present dubious arguments, pursues the recognized rhetorical device of *prosecutio cum proverbiis*, bolstering her case with gnomic lore, some drawn from old alliterative stock and ascribed to Alfred, even if with no greater warrant than Marie de France had for citing him as source for her Anglo-Norman fables.

The initial give and take is deceptively simple, holding no hint of later complexities. The Nightingale's complaint is wholly personal: she is upset because the Owl stops her from singing. Pejoratives (notably epithets and nouns in *un—ungode*, *unmilde*, *unorne*) are bandied about and the Owl repeatedly asks for open combat. Only after some 200 lines of this does argument begin in due form, with the Owl straining to upgrade herself socially and temporarily raising the tone of the dispute with pious allusions to a heaven where there is no satiety of song (335–62). The Nightingale has to take a new line, of moral censure: Owl is envious—and envy is a capital sin—of Nightingale's role as a harbinger of joy. Owl is thus forced to underline her religious role: if she sings only in winter, that is the time of Christmas; Nightingale's song belongs to the season of pride and wanton passion that does not last. The debate has become a *Conflictus Veris et Hiemis*, and Owl is moving over to the attack, with dismissive references to Nightingale's small size, and drab colour, and uncleanly habits. Her self-praise approaches smugness and is again given a pious colour:

> Vor me is lof to Cristes huse
> To clansi hit with fule muse   (609–10)

'the Church is dear to me and I like nothing better than to cleanse it of defiling mice'. Nightingale now resorts to the device of concession, covering weakness in argument by a display of apophthegms: *bihemmen* and *bilegge*, 'to trim and to glose over', are the terms the poet applies to the device, and the former is *hapax legomenon*. True, she knows only one song, but it is better than all the Owl's put together. True, she is small and weak, but cleverness is better than brute force. She too can be pious; by helping man to sing devoutly on earth, she

---

* F. Pollock and F. W. Maitland, *The History of English Law before the Time of Edward I* (revised edn., Cambridge, 1968), ii. 605 and n. 2.

prepares him for heavenly joys. But Owl sees through the ploy and calls a halt:

> Abid! Abid! the Ule seide,
> Thu gest al to mid swikelede[1]— (837–8)

[1] ? *you get to work wholly with treachery*

Nightingale's words are *bisemed* and *biliked* (specious, simulated—another nonce word). Getting to heaven involves more than song; repentance and tears are necessary: 'And that's where I come in', filling good men with longing to be hence ('and to depart and be with Christ' is the unspoken Pauline allusion). Fluffing the feathers of conscious virtue, Owl draws the contrast between the stay-at-home bird and her own habit of flying far and wide, sounding notes of warning.

At a loss for an immediate riposte, Nightingale is driven to pick up a taunt made some time earlier, when Owl twitted her with sitting near privies (592 ff.)—later described as adjoining men's 'bures' (dwellings). Nightingale recalls the description and converts Owl's jibe to a charge that she sits near the *bure*, in the narrower sense of bower, the parlour, or chamber where the lord lies with his lady-love. This (suppositious) impeachment she gladly admits: 'I needs must go towards the highest when I see it. . . . I do good with my song, bringing tidings of love'—a phrase not to be taken at its face value: for Nightingale at once forestalls criticism by glossing it as '*church*-song' (1036). No wonder the Owl, always prone to lose her temper (43), now loses it altogether. 'Yes, you sing in lovers' bowers, and so enticed a lady to sin.' Here comes in the summary version of Marie's *Laustic*. But Nightingale reads it differently: 'I merely hoped to amuse the imprisoned lady, it was the *jaloux* who was to blame, not me, and the late King Henry rightly punished him' (a teasingly cryptic allusion). Having turned the tale to her own advantage, Nightingale can now abuse her adversary—a wretched creature (*wrecche* implies outcast) useful only as a scarecrow, and as unpopular as a bedel that always brings bad news (1170)—'Curse him!' Owl seizes on the casual phrase: 'So you have powers of excommunication? I'm not to blame if I have foreknowledge of disasters; it sorts with my wide learning in biblical lore and symbolism [*tacning*, 1213].' There is some disproportion here, and scholastic preoccupations show through (as Chaucer's were to show through in *Troilus* and *The Knight's Tale*). Owl opines that she has won by sheer weight of words: 'Unless you can do better, you're disgraced' (1290).

Nightingale, again in a tight corner, keeps her wits about her, and counter-attacks. 'Your occult wisdom is all witchcraft.' Having scored this point, Nightingale is now confident enough to rebut earlier charges, in particular the charge that she sanctions adultery: 'True, I sing of love; but is it my fault if women love unwisely?' (Owl can hardly say so since she has taken the same line: her warning note was not the *cause* of disasters.) There is some speciousness here and Owl seizes on it: if Nightingale befriends *maidens*, ladies favour Owl, who solaces forsaken wives; which leads to another digression, if also to revealing glimpses of married domesticity, making it nonsense for her to claim that

> Thu me havest sore igramed
> That min heorte is wel neh alamed,
> That ich mai unneathe speke   (1603–5)

'You have upset me so much that my heart has almost failed, I can scarcely speak.' She has been speaking for 90 lines, and she now takes up the original charge that she is hateful to men, who hang her up as a lure or a scarecrow. With characteristic unction she claims that thus she sheds her blood for man (as if making a voluntary and Christlike sacrifice). Here she gratuitously overreaches herself, actually boasting, as Nightingale perceives, of her own shame. Rejoicing, the smaller bird bursts into a song that attracts all the birds of dawning, who delight that the Owl has lost the match. Owl, in her usual bad temper, claims that they have been mustered as an army (*ferde*, OE *fyrd*), and threatens to raise hue and cry (*utheste*). She ends by showing herself the hectoring bully that Nightingale had claimed she was at the start. Now the clever little Wren (who drew wisdom from her upbringing among men, 1725–6) steps in, saying 'shame! Would you provoke a breach of the peace [*grithbruche*]? Proceed instead to judgement, as you had agreed to do.' Nightingale, rather priggishly professing to be law-abiding, asks, 'But where is Master Nichole, who is to judge between us?' Wren replies that he is living in the village of Portesham, in Dorset, for the bishops won't give him better benefices. Even Owl agrees that they treat him scandalously and, more surprisingly, Nightingale agrees that Owl shall rehearse to Master Nichole the whole course of the *plait*. So they set forth peaceably to Portesham:

> Ah hu heo spedde of heore dome[1]
> Ne can ich eu[2] na more telle.
> Her nis na more of this spelle[3].   (1792–4)

[1] *but how they succeeded in their trial*   [2] *you*   [3] *story*

The *determinatio* is postponed.

This closing scene, with its humorous hyperbole, bland self-advertisement flavoured with blunt comment on the bishops and nobles who have proved indifferent patrons, is the high point of the poem. Unmistakably clerkly in tone, it indicates that the said Master Nichole, whom Nightingale has described as 'of Guildford', wise, discreet, and a skilled judge of song, and Owl as a once passionate man but now mature and steady (191–214), is the begetter of the poem, insinuating in these comments that a patron should overlook his youthful follies and reward his merits (and poetic skills). Such pleas for preferment—though none so deft—abound in medieval verse; Dunbar and Skelton will provide later examples. Here we are not far from the sophisticated world for which Walter Map's *De Nugis Curialium* was intended.

Critics, especially of medieval literature, are too fond of categories. They would pigeon-hole this poem as a *débat*. But it is also genuine pastoral, rooted in the actual life of field and forest. Provençal poetry provides similar springtime settings, *rossignol* included; but its descriptions are generalized and formulaic, its concerns entirely with emotions, real or feigned. *The Owl and the Nightingale* moves with colloquial ease, whilst on occasion using effectively the terms of law, learning, and chivalry. One senses in some passages the same scientific curiosity that gives Adelard of Bath's *Quaestiones Naturales* importance as a precursor of the Chartrain Renaissance. Of philosophers the poet may have read none except Boethius, but a passage on the effect of anger on the flow of blood from the heart and consequently on judgement (945–50) suggests an acquaintance, direct or indirect, with the new Arabic physiology which was based on Aristotle. Curiosity of the kind that Adelard had encouraged sorts with the evidence for direct observation found in the illuminations (as distinct from the texts) of English bestiaries in the late twelfth century; and our poet has not only watched birds, hares, and foxes, he has noticed that the owl's nest is hollow, roomy and 'plaited all abute' (645)—for the owl often takes over a crow's nest. Yet the poet's constructional and rhetorical skill is such that these details never obtrude; he is as much concerned to reveal the birds' personalities through their choice and use of rhetorical figures, and through their style of argument. The English poem points forward to the 'easy philosopher' of *Upon Appleton House*, conferring amongst boughs and trees. Already it shows Marvell's skill in touching lightly on serious topics.

It is proper to treat *The Fox and the Wolf* after this brilliant bird-pastoral, not only because they both represent animal fable in the broad sense, and share the same basic metre—the octosyllabics of most of the early rhymed verse—but also because they have some similarities of technique and patterns, though the fable (295 lines) is probably later than the longer poem, set as it is in the world of the friars, who did not begin to establish themselves in England till the 1220s. Joel Chandler Harris, with equal success, was to transplant to the world of Brer Rabbit this tale of the wolf who unwittingly rescues his rival from the well to his own detriment. Both poems, again, pit one creature against another: now, instead of Owl and Nightingale, we have, first Fox vs. Chauntecler and then Fox vs. Wolf. But here the opposition is expressed by deeds rather than words. We move into the harsher world of action. The proportion of dialogue diminishes, and description of action—concise, matter-of-fact description—plays a greater part. The very first line—'A vox gon out of the wode go'—signalizes the change.

The verbal patterning, however, remains much the same: repetition with variation is again frequent, indeed dominant. The liberal use of this device reminds us that poetry was still essentially oral, meant for recitation or reading aloud, whether in bower or cloister or on ale-bench. Repeated statement in such circumstances was essential to ensure that the outline of the narrative was clear to all comers—especially if the audience was large, at the beginning, when there would be a stir of people 'settling down'. Again, as in the *Owl*, the language is still essentially native English, with few foreign intrusions except for Anglo-Norman technical terms. Thus the poet preserves the Old English term for matins, *uhtsong*, in his *houssong* (265): the last example (missed by *MED*) of a word found elsewhere only in *Ancrene Wisse* and a few other early texts. Further, there is at least one instance of the proverbial 'stiffening' that characterized *The Owl and the Nightingale*: 'him is wo in euche londe / that is thef mid his honde' (101–2). But here the effect is not 'homely', but rather to indicate the Fox's sophisticated self-awareness. Still more striking is the metaphor describing the cold comfort the Wolf finds at the bottom of the well: 'Frogs have kneaded his dough' (256).

In colloquial vivacity the poem rivals the *Owl*, as when the Wolf asks what he shall do to get down to the delights in the well:

> Tho quod the vox, 'Ich wille the lere[1]:
> Isiist[2] thou a boket hongi[3] there?
> Ther is a bruche of hevene blisse[4]
> Lep thereinne, mid iwisse[5] . . .'   (231–4)

[1] *I will instruct you*   [2] *do you see?*   [3] *hang*   [4] *opening of (i.e., ? a means of reaching) heavenly joys*   [5] *certainly*

Some technical phrases (like the legal phrases in the *Owl*) have a special savour—notably in the confession scene, where 'underfon shrift' is the set formula and 'tel thine sunnen [sins] on and on' is identical with the priest Genius's instructions to Amans in Gower's *Confessio Amantis*:

> . . . telle it on and on
> Bothe all thi thoght and al thi werk.   (i. 194–5)

Again *Maister* (206) is the due form of address to a priest in the confessional (cf. *Confessio Amantis* i. 215); *clene live* (227) is the formula appropriate to a shriven penitent (cf. *Sir Gawain*, 1883); and the following line ('Ne recche ich of childe ne of wive') is expressive of the penitent's joy (like Gawain's) at receiving absolution—though here the intention is ironic. Irony, parody, and sardonic understatement are the chief verbal features of the beast epic genre as illustrated in the *Roman de Renart* from which the story comes. Ironic is the Fox's reference back to the Wolf's own words about 'clean life':

> 'Ich am therof glad and blithe
> That thou are nomen[1] in clene live';   (249–50)

> [1] *taken*

and the Wolf's plea to the Fox (193) that it of all beasts should 'for Cristes love be mi prest'. Almost everything Fox says is in fact double-edged—like the cryptic claim 'Ich have hem letten eddre blod [blood in the veins]' (44). But it is what he does *not* say that is most effective: he has no need to comment on the Wolf's gratuitous 'confession' that he had seen Fox in bed with his wife, for the Wolf admits that his eyes must have deceived him:

> Ich wende, also othre doth,
> That ich iseie were soth[1]   (217–18)

> [1] *that what I saw was true*

As for parody, we have, besides the confession scene, the parody of a typical twelfth-century sermon on the joys of Paradise (the theme of the century's greatest hymns):

> 'Her is the blisse of Paradiis—
> Her ich mai evere wel fare,
> Withouten pine, withouten kare,
> Her is mete, her is drinke;
> Her is blisse withouten swinke[1],
> Her nis hounger never mo,
> Ne none other kunnes wo[2]—
> Of alle gode her is inou[3]!'   (140–7)

> [1] *toil*   [2] *no other kind of misery*   [3] *plenty*

The poem as it survives consists of two parts, the first the tale of Chauntecler as Chaucer was to tell it, with a hiatus after l. 84. That something is missing here is certain, for ll. 65 ff. refer to the fox and imply that he is thirsty because he has eaten some of the hens (as in the *Renart*—doubtless the three that had not flown up to the roof: 32). But the two parts as they stand balance each other nicely enough: the Fox's hunger is counterpoised by the Wolf's thirst. The Cock's threat of pikes and stones and staves in part one (61–3) is carried out by the friars, when they attack the Wolf in part two (292). Both parts have a conventual setting in common: the hens are looked after by a cellarer (59); the well is in the garden of a friary. These two parts clearly derive ultimately from two episodes in the verse *Roman de Renart*—various branches of which were brought together about 1175–90, the approximate *terminus a quo* for the poem: in the *Roman*, the fact that the well is in the grounds of a Cistercian abbey is repeatedly stressed, but in the English version the Cistercians are replaced by friars. The first episode—here left incomplete—is found in Branch 'II' of the *Roman*, the source of the expanded versions in *The Nun's Priest's Tale* and Henryson's equally lively 'Taill of Schir Chantecleir'. The second part telescopes two elements: for in the *Roman* no mention is made *at this point* of the seduction of the Wolf's wife (it is a distinct episode in *Ysengrimus*), nor does the Fox insist on the preliminary (comic) confession. The basic story of the fox in the well is in Branch 'IV' of the *Roman*—one of the earliest.

The names in the poem—Renward, Sigrim (< Ysengrim), Chauntecler—point to a literary as distinct from a folklore origin: they are specifically English variants of the names in the *Roman*. And the description of the Wolf as neighbour and 'gossip' of the Fox also corresponds with lines in the *Roman*:

> Ja sui je vostre bon *voisin*
> Qui fui jadiz vostre *compere*   (iv. 236–7)

(In the Anglo-Norman version of the tale, found in the English manuscript (Digby 86), Renart is *le goupil* (godparent) of the Wolf.) But this very likeness shows that we are not dealing with a mere translation: for what is direct speech in the *Roman* has become authorial explanation in the English poem. And we may safely say that the force and verve of this poem is also the author's. He has not translated so much as transposed the wit of the *Roman* into his own mode. The change of *locus* from abbey to friary is further evidence of reshaping, as is the naming of the 'curtiler' (gardener) as Aylmer—possibly an allusion to a known member of the author's own house. The whole of the dialogue with Sir Chauntecler is evidently likewise of English invention. In the *Roman* the Fox slips in through a *guichet*, and seizes the fowls at once;

13

the English Chauntecler refuses to be taken in by Fox's assurance that he is good at blood-letting—the only possible occasion in the French for this ironic reference is the appearance of Reynard as a physician in Branch 'X'.* On the other hand, the English tendency to reduce the content of a French tale—as English romances will reduce the *matière* of French romances—shows in the omission of some details. Thus there is no indication as to how Sigrim the Wolf gets into the well-yard. The English version makes him more gullible than does the French, just as it makes Fox less cautious: in *Renard* he hesitates before using the bucket, but is deceived by his own reflection. Finally, the English poet has made a self-contained tale out of what were mere episodes in the *Roman*: so he gives no reference to further adventures, whereas Branch 'IV' ends with Isengrim meeting his son and plotting revenge.

Different as the general tone is from that of the *Owl*, the poem remains less harsh and sardonic than that of the continental beast epic or French fabliau. Yet the world described is one of purely malevolent motives, offering a purely material heaven not altogether different in its delights from the Land of Cokaygne. Greed and self-preservation are the strongest passions displayed, folly and deceit are recurring features. The baser sides of human nature are obliquely revealed. There is no trace of the religious values taken for granted in the *Owl*: on the contrary, the friars are characterized as *swith sley* (very crafty) (262)—a wholly gratuitous description, in the context, but premonitory of later anti-Minorite satire. And the clipped couplets and staccato style show a cutting edge that is consonant with the new realism.

In later verses geese as well as hens are the Fox's victims when, 'withouten cole or candlelight', he comes to the croft to find food for his cubs or ailing wife. One such poem retains the priestly figure of *The Fox and the Wolf*: the geese are 'shriven' and 'assoiled'; one of them, crying 'wheccumquek', prays 'take of my feders but not of my to' (*SL*, Nos. 48–9). *The Nun's Priest's Tale* was to immortalize the tradition.

Cokaygne is the first fully comic poem in our literature. Comedy is present in *The Owl and the Nightingale* and *The Fox and the Wolf*, but the comedy of Cokaygne is of the special, grotesque, medieval kind found in the figures that inhabit the margins of Gothic manuscripts: hares hunting men, mice hunting cats, the ass playing a harp: scenes

---

* The Middle English text as we have it is probably defective: e.g. at 73–4 we expect a mention of the *first* bucket as found in *Roman de Renart*, iv. 152–3:

> En ce puis si avoit deus seilles
> Quant l'une vient, et l'autre vait.

deliberately representing the world upside down, *impossibilia*. Caro-lingian Latin verse, suggests Curtius,* kept this classical topos alive and it flowered again in the *Carmina Burana*: 'stultus . . . incappatur'—the dunce takes a degree—says one Goliardic poem; and in another the Fathers, including St Benedict, are said to be found not in cloister but in alehouse, court, or market. The satiric thrust behind these verses, however, is bitter; the comic colour of *Cokaygne*, like its emphasis on sexual freedom, is only matched in the burlesque parodies of the Homeric journey to Hades in Lucian (and hence in Rabelais). And, like Lucian, the English poet is parodying style—the style of such descriptions of heavenly joys as are found in a pious work like *Sawles Warde*—as well as providing more obvious amusement. By adopting the *impossibilia* formula, he limits or sterilizes the satiric pos-sibilities implicit in an account of the solid joys and liquid pleasures known to monks and nuns. Yet the informing spirit remains unmistak-ably Goliardic. This distinguishes it from analogues in Old French, Old Irish, or Middle Dutch, from the account of the Muslim Paradise in the *Liber Scalae*, as from the numerous later variations beginning with the *Libro de Buen Amor* and ending with Heine.

The poem falls roughly into two parts: the first describing an Earthly Paradise, the second a New Jerusalem for monks and nuns. Stylistically, the first part is more limited: it is essentially a cata-logue, with items introduced by formulaic 'ther nis', 'ther be', etc. The basic formula in the second part is an introductory temporal clause. That we are to have expectations reversed is indicated in the opening couplet:

> Fur in see bi west Spaygne
> Is a lond ihote[1] Cokaygne.

> [1] *called*

Traditionally the happy paradisal land was set in the east: '*feor* heonan / *east* dælum' says the Old English *Phoenix*; but it was never associated with any known land. Traditionally, again, it is described by negatives. Says Lactantius:†

> Non huc exsangues morbi, non aegra senectus,
> Nec mors crudelis, nec metus asper adest . . .

And so here:

> Ther nis baret[1] nother strif,
> Nis ther no deth, ac[2] ever lif;

* E. R. Curtius, *European Literature and the Latin Middle Ages*, tr. W. R. Trask (London, 1953), 94–8.
† *Carmen de Ave Phoenice*, 15–16.

Ther nis lac of met³ no cloth,
Ther nis man no woman wroth ...   (27–30)

¹ *conflict*   ² *but*   ³ *food*

The Earthly Paradise is unpeopled: Enoch and Elias had gone not to this terrestrial paradise but to heaven. Here they are located in it to point the contrast between their loneliness and the joys of men and women living together in Cokaygne. The fair paradisal waters irrigating the land make a perpetual spring. Cokaygne's rivers run with oil, milk, wine, and honey, that compass about the New Jerusalem of Revelation 21. The emphasis upon the absence of stallions puzzles until we read the second part: the monk who is a good *stallion* has twelve 'wives' a year: the generative force is embodied not in horses but in monks, of all men.

Part Two describes a fair abbey. In the popular and much translated *Visio Pauli* (of the eighth century), the apostle views the heavenly Jerusalem and his vision is the basis of a twelfth-century Irish tale about St Patrick's Purgatory. One Owen or Owein, a knight, comes to a plain where stands a building like a cloister, whose monks warn him against temptation. Emerging from scenes of horror, Owen reaches a high-walled Paradise, which he enters through a gate adorned with precious stones and metals; they come out of the Apocalypse (chapter 21) like those on the bed of the stream of 'treacle', honey, balm, and spiced wine in *Cokaygne* (88 ff.). Through the streets moves a procession led by two archbishops. The ecclesiastical and cloistral allusions again link this Irish vision with *Cokaygne*; and an Irish provenance is further suggested by details in the legend of St Brendan, which was accessible in an Anglo-Norman version. There too we find streams with marvellous jewels, and an emphasis on crystal (cf. 68, 115); whilst in the Irish Vision of MacConglinne, a coracle of lard floating on a lough of milk reaches a fort of custard with a bridge of butter, a wheaten dyke, palisades of bacon, and so forth. A famous painting of Breughel's, and the modern song 'In the Big Rock Candy Mountains' testify to the perennial appeal of such highly edible constructions. But one detail in *Cokaygne* (found also in an Old French analogue) suggests a connection with the older Hellenistic tradition that flowered in Lucian: the roast geese fly about crying 'Gees, al hote, al hote', the cry of a street-vendor; Pherecrates (*fl.* fifth century BC) has roast thrushes 'flying round our mouths'.

A seventeenth-century engraver has attached to Breughel's 'Dutch Proverbs' the motto:

Par ce dessin il est montré
Les abus du monde renversé

and this pattern controls the final scenes in *Cokaygne*, where monks fly about not because they are angelic but because the genre requires that there be unnatural flight. It is folly to read these scenes as satirical or as alluding to a particular Irish abbey. The parody of theological language in the phrase used of the polygamous monk, 'Al throgh right and noght throgh *grace*' (171), is subordinate to the sexual fantasy of the young nuns 'slyly' swimming in the river on a hot summer's day: an erotic vein that emerges at the close of the Middle Ages in astrological miniatures that show naked maidens bathing in a fountain. For the penance of wading through swine's ordure there is perhaps some Freudian explanation; but a purgatorial element is part of many other-world visions.

The poem has been solemnly labelled as wish-fulfilment of a down-trodden peasantry, and as such found a place in an anthology of historical verse. Rather, it is burlesque, not fundamentally different from the deliberate parody of sacred ceremony at the Christmas Feast of Fools, when inferior clergy took over the cathedral, censed with pudding or sausage, and introduced an ass: a concession to the need for occasional relaxation which academic authorities still admitted in seventeenth-century Oxford. The parodic element persists to the end: 'Lordinges gode and hende' is a phrase of address used by a narrator of romances, a crier of a play—or a preacher: here the preacher is adjuring his hearers to strive for the heaven that he has described so glowingly.

Speed, verve, sophistication, characterize this *jeu d'esprit*. There is a similar briskness, a similar relaxation of the usual mores, a similar reversal of values, in the 450 lines of the earliest English fabliau, *Dame Sirith*, which reveals its continental origins and its genre in the heading of the manuscript: *Ci comence le fablet e la cointise de dame Siriz*. 'Cointise', stratagem, is a constant ingredient of fabliau: an element later visible in Chaucer's *Miller's Tale*, the frame of which is likewise an Old French fabliau. The English poem takes from this genre its amoral tone, its gusty comedy, its social setting, its range of characters: the merchant whose thought (like Chaucer's merchant's) is evidently ever on the increase of his winning; his fair wife whose come-hitherness goes along with outraged morality; and her seducer, a clerk, who in fabliau traditionally outwits a cuckolded husband. Bawds and procurers are common figures in this kind of literature, and our author seems to warm to his 'dame'. After protesting her holiness, she has

17

helped Wilekin to win the love of coy mistress Margery by telling her
the tale of a clerk who had transformed the witch's daughter into a
weeping bitch and threatens to do the same by Dame Sirith. Thinking
of her own plight, Margery urges her to comply with his desires and
seek him out: which is her warrant for bringing him to the now com-
pliant Margery. Dame Sirith leaves them to their play, saying in a
phrasal image that Shakespeare will use of Antony and Cleopatra:

> 'And loke that thou hire *tille*,
> And strek[1] out hire thes[2] . . .'   (440–1)
>
> [1] *stretch*   [2] *thighs*

This particular kind of sexual frankness, as we know from Chaucer's
'hende Nicholas', often goes along with tales of 'derne love', in which
'courtesy' is no more than a vogue word. The narrator evidently
relishes the situation and his curse on the dame (332) is no more than a
filler—a specious gesture to virtue. The vivid depiction of the dame as
she hobbles in, weak and faint and calling forth the young wife's sympathy, has no antecedent in the analogues. She is not otherwise
described, except ironically. Though she denies knowledge of witchcraft herself, her supposed fear of ecclesiastical censure (243–4) indicates her sinister side. We only know that she takes her dog with her
on her errand because she addresses it:

> 'Pepir nou shalt thou eten;
> This mustart shal ben thi mete,
> And gar[1] thin eien[2] to rene[3].'   (279–81)
>
> [1] *cause*   [2] *eyes*   [3] *run*

and later points to it:

> 'This is mi douter that ich of speke:
> For del of hire[1] min herte breketh.
> Loke hou hire eien greten[2].'   (355–7)
>
> [1] *sorrow over her*   [2] *run with tears*

Perhaps no fabliau depends so much on dialogue. There are only 36
lines of narrative in the whole poem, and these are confined to two
patches.

The basic exemplum is oriental. There are two earlier Latin
versions, one appearing in the *Disciplina Clericalis* of Petrus Alphonsus
and reappearing in Caxton's edition of Aesop,* another in a French

---

* Caxton translates the Fables of 'Alfonce' from a French version, in which the
woodcut for this tale properly shows a dog ('chienne'). But Caxton says 'the old bawd
makes her little *cat* weep by giving it mustard'. His depiction of the bawd is also different and he concludes by wishing that all such women were burnt alive.

conte moralisé of Nicole Bozon. It was probably circulating in oral as well as in written forms in England as well as France. The dramatic character of its dialogue is shown by the marginal letters in the manuscript that identify the speakers and mark off narrative from dialogue. But a skilled narrator (with a trained dog) could make all these differentiations by a change in stance or voice. Other such dramatic monologues are found in Old French, with a similar medley of verseforms, including the tail-rhyme stanza that here makes its first appearance in English—sometimes with three-beat lines ('As I com bi an waie'), sometimes with four ('So bide [enjoy] ich evere mete or drinke'). But we probably have to do with naturalization rather than translation. The action is localized—the husband goes off to Boston fair, in Lincolnshire; in much the same way Caxton in his *Aesop* will localize another tale that he takes from his Italian comtemporary Poggio whilst setting it in Oxford and introducing two Oxford MAs. Boston suggests an East Midland provenance, as does Wilekin, the Flemish name of the clerk: Flemish mercenaries began to settle in Eastern England in the twelfth century, and Wilekin is their generic name in a rhyme said to have been sung by them in 1173:

> Hoppe, hoppe Wilekin! Hoppe Wilekin!
> England is min and thin.

The medley of metres, which include four-beat lines in rhymed couplets, would at least serve to keep the audience alert. Otherwise all depended on mime and change of tone. The medieval narrator, whether a wandering minstrel, a *clerc déclassé*, or simply an amateur, must have depended a great deal on this versatility. Chaucer exploits it when he makes the Shipman mimic the Wife of Bath:

> 'The sely housbonde, algate he moot paye,
> He moot us clothe, and he moot us arraye'   (*CT* VII. 11–12)

as he later mimics the merchant's wife in his own tale:

> 'Who was so welcome as "my lord daun John"
> "Oure deare cosyn", "ful of curteisye"?'   (68–9)

The concluding stanza of *Dame Sirith*, though ostensibly an offer to be go-between, might equally well be delivered in such a way as to suggest that the reciter too could bring good luck to thwarted lovers, for a consideration (*mede*):

> And wose[1] is onwis[2]
> And for non pris[3]
> Ne con geten his levemon[4]

19

> I shal, for mi mede,
> Garen[5] him to spede[6].
> For ful wel I con[7].

| [1] *whoever* | [2] *unskilful* | [3] *price* | [4] *mistress* | [5] *cause* |
| [6] *succeed* | [7] *know how to* | | | |

The story of *Dame Sirith* forms the plot of the fragmentary *Interludium De Clerico et Puella*, the oldest secular play extant in English. The two works have several formulas, phrases, and rhymes in common, and the part the *clericus* plays in both doubtless gave the tale a special appeal to the young students who were beginning in the thirteenth century to swarm at Oxford and at Cambridge and some of whom may have had their taste for such plays sharpened by reading Terence. As the title indicates, the part of Margery is here taken by a girl who is no better than she should be; and the title also points to an actual dramatic presentation. The dramatis personae are clearly named throughout. The action of the extant scenes is brisk. The clerk's friend who, in the poem, advises him to consult the bawd finds no place here, and *clericus* goes straight to her. An *interludium* was by its very name a brief entertainment; the only other references to interludes (belonging to the fourteenth century) associate them with music and song. The play shares with the poem some forms of salutation, expostulation, and reproach. As Dame Sirith, professing to be old, sick, and lame, says:

> Ilke[1] dai mi lif I fede[2],
> And bidde[3] mi paternoster and mi crede   (208–9)

| [1] *each* | [2] *sustain* | [3] *pray* |

so her counterpart, Mome Elwis, avers:

> Wit my roc[1] y me fede
> Can I do non othir dede
> Bot my paternoster and my crede.   (69–71)

| [1] *distaff* |

The distaff is perhaps another token of her feigned sanctity: some French representations of the Annunciation show the Virgin Mary with a distaff. But whereas the clerk of the poem insinuates that the Dame could use secret craft, *Clericus* asks merely for 'thi help and thy cunsayle'. That the play—and so possibly the poem—had a French or Anglo-Norman predecessor is suggested by the names of the saints that one or other of the characters invokes (possibly as a mnemonic device or cue) at the beginning or end of a speech. St Michael was a saint of Northern France, St Denis of France, and the devotion to St

Leonard was introduced from Normandy; whilst Elwis is a form of Eloise, a name that after Abelard's time carried dubious connotations in Northern France. Whether Malkin (Marykin, Molly), the maiden's name, had such connotations at this date is not so certain.

The pace and ironic hints of the play presuppose a quick-witted audience. The women's parts were presumably taken by men—perhaps young *clerici* performing at a feast on Egg Saturday or after Christmas, occasions of merry-making at Oxford well on into the seventeenth century. It is students who would enjoy home-thrusts at a 'clerc fayllard' (good-for-nothing) (8) and at 'clerc of scole' who has seduced many a woman (29). The Goliardic tone was to survive until Skelton, and some of the verse itself has a Skeltonic rhythm:

> And myn Ave Mary
> For my synnes ic am sory
> And my *de profundis*
> For al that yn sin lys.   (73–6)

Skelton's Philip Sparrow will sing to the same tune, and play with liturgical phrases in the same way:

> And for all sparowes soules
> Set in our bede rolles
> *Pater noster qui*
> With an *Ave Mari*
> And with the corner of a Crede
> The more shal be your mede.

And his poem happens to be addressed to another Dame Margery.

The humour of every poem so far considered is largely literary humour, proper to the genre of each. Not all later comic poems have literary antecedents and some are in a very specific sense racy of the soil. Amongst these a poem that might be called, in the manner of Hugh MacDiarmid, 'The Drunk Man looks at the Moon' stands out in the early fourteenth-century miscellany, BL MS Harleian 2253. It is in five eight-lined stanzas, but is still almost entirely native English in its vocabulary, and traditional alliteration effectively reproduces the clumsy speech of the dull bemused peasant whose image it conjures up, and whose slow drunken gait is conveyed in a line like 'for doute leste he valle he shoddreth and shereth' and in alliterating monosyllables:

> Mon in the mone stond and strit[1]:
> On is bot-forke is burthen he bereth . . .

[1] *strides*

'Yef thy wed[1] ys ytake, bring hom the trous[2]!
Sete forth thyn other fot, stryd over sty[3]!'

[1] *pledge*   [2] *bundle of branches*   [3] *path*

This is the first roving English drunkard, and every line of the poem mirrors the life and labour—with 'twybyl' (two-edged axe) and 'bot-forke' (hay-fork)—of a rural scene that was not to change for six centuries. The man in the moon thus apostrophized (later addressed as 'Hubert, hosed pye') is, of course, the shadowy Cain of the legend that Dante alludes to in *Purgatorio* ii. The bundle of thorns Moonshine will carry, and it was regarded as every hedger's 'perk' only 40 years ago in Suffolk. Cain was thought to have degraded himself to the rank of churl, so there was no need to name him: the last line offers sufficient identification: 'the cherl nul nout adoun er the day dawe'. So when Henryson present Cynthia in his assembly of the gods who will judge Criseyde, she bears on her breast

> ane churl paintit ful evin
> Beirand ane bunche of thornis on his bak
> Quhilk[1] for his *thift* micht clim na nar[2] the hevin.

[1] *which*   [2] *nearer*

The same theft is the cause of the drunkard's concern as he gazes at the moon-figure in whom he recognizes a fellow-idler. He has cut his bundle of briar and the 'hayward' (hedgewarden) has made him give a pledge for it; but Dame Douce at the alehouse could wheedle it out of the manor's bailiff. He is perhaps a pilferer of unconsidered trifles like those Autolycus snatched off hedges: for only the hedge knows 'what weeds he wereth'.

In short, another ideal piece for a travelling reciter's repertoire, eminently suitable for the village green or tavern, and as actable as *Dame Sirith*.

2

Verse, Didactic and Homiletic

(i) Early Examples: *The Bestiary*; *Poema Morale*; The *Ormulum*; *Genesis and Exodus*

The direct observation of nature that distinguishes *The Owl and the Nightingale* will hardly be met with again before the time of Bewick and John Clare, except in poems like *Sir Gawain* or *Wynnere and Wastoure* that were written for audiences familiar with venery and responsive to descriptions of hunted deer, boars, or foxes. The melancholy Jaques would have been better pleased by a unique fifteenth-century poem on the plight of the hunted hare:

> Att wyntter in the depe snowe
>   Men wyl me seche for to trace,
> And by my steyppes[1] I ame iknowe[2]
>   And followyth me fro place to place.
> And yf I to the toune come or torne
>   Be hit in worttes[3] or in leyke,[4]
> Then wyl the wyffes also yeorne[5]
>   Flece[6] me with here dogis eyke[7].   (*SL*, No. 119)

[1] *steps*   [2] *recognized*   [3] *herbs*   [4] *leek*   [5] *eagerly*
[6] *skin*   [7] *also*

Shakespeare too will picture Wat on his hill. But as often as not Shakespeare (like Chaucer) saw Nature (*pace* Dryden) through the spectacles of books. The book they looked through was the Bestiary and its companion piece the Lapidary, which taught how to read sermons in stones. This is not to say that the Bestiary was always at hand; but its lore was so long and widely disseminated as to become indistinguishable from folk-belief, whilst at the same time it was absorbed into highly reputable encyclopaedias like Bartholomew the Englishman's *De Proprietatibus Rerum*.

The Latin *Physiologus* (oddly so called) is the basis of all vernacular bestiaries, and three short poems in the Old English Exeter Book, on the panther, the whale, and the peacock (or partridge) show that the Latin text had reached England long before the Conquest. They doubtless owe their presence in that collection to their usefulness as homiletic *exempla*. The Latin prose of *Physiologus* had been versified by one Thetbaldus or Theobaldus, possibly an abbot of Monte Cassino; and in the twelfth century English editors had greatly enlarged it and English artists in East Anglian scriptoria had greatly embellished it. No text is more typical of the medieval mentality: for it embodies the symbolic interpretation of scripture favoured by St Augustine, St Bonaventura, Hugh of St Victor—to name but a few— and given prestige by their approval. First was set forth the *natura* of a creature, much as Pliny might have described it, but then its *significacio*, its mystical or spiritual meaning, linked invariably if only implicitly with passages in scripture that name the creature in question. As Sir Thomas Browne realized when writing *Pseudodoxia Epidemica*, it was the moral and theological significance that counted, not the verifiability of the characteristics noted.

Clearly, the Middle English version was not intended as a faithful and full rendering of Thetbald. For one thing, it incorporates themes found only in the accompanying Latin prose gloss. What it did attempt was to reproduce the only notable feature of Thetbald's verse—its variety. His metres range from rhymed hexameters and leonine elegiacs to sapphics, adonics, and once to the catalectic dactylic tetrameter (in the section on the Spider). The English writer seems to have been deliberately emulating this variety. His skill in this kind is partly obscured by the corruptness of the only extant text: yet a genuine metrical sensitivity seeps through. His patterns vary from the basically alliterative, native measure to the rhymed syllabic, with several combinations of each. Elsewhere it approaches the pattern of the septenarius familiar to us from the Goliardic *meum est propositum*, familiar also in native form to readers of Orm the priest's verse homilies, which perhaps reflect—they are so pedestrian that they could scarcely have prompted—a new fashion for versifying homiletic material; new, but with some precedent in Ælfric's rhythmic prose sermons. The unique manuscript of the Bestiary comes from the same, East Midland, area as the *Ormulum*; and the comparable verse-paraphrase of *Genesis and Exodus* (which though based on Peter Comestor may have been influenced by the Old French *L'Estoire Joseph*) comes from a contiguous area. The illustrated Latin Bestiaries are a distinctive feature of Early English art. By the thirteenth century that art, having assimilated certain French techniques, was developing a style of its own, much as English verse was naturalizing the French technique of rhymed syllabic verse. Ælfrician sermons in rhythmic prose had perhaps never been current in Eastern England, where preachers would welcome presentations of traditional exempla when given moralizations in English dress and in easily memorized verse; with adjurations like 'hereth' and 'wulde ye nu listen' already built in.

The English versifier names his source as *Fisiologet*, a form suggesting that he knew a French or Anglo-Norman version of the *Physiologus*. At least three rhymed Anglo-Norman bestiaries were compiled in the twelfth and thirteenth centuries, of which one in octosyllabics survives in over twenty copies and includes topical and historical allusions as well as a mention of Reynard's exploits as hen-stealer. Some of the Anglo-Norman versions are illustrated. None derive from Thetbaldus's verse, but their metrical form may have encouraged the Englishman to choose verse as his medium. The oldest and fullest manuscript of Philippe de Thaon's Anglo-Norman version changes metre towards the end, shifting from six to eight syllables in the Lapidary section that frequently followed the Bestiary text. And that a homogeneous and unvarying metrical pattern was not considered mandatory in the thirteenth century is borne out by the metrical varieties of French semi-dramatic verse illustrated in the fabliaux that are congeners of *Dame Sirith*, as well as by the modulations of native alliterative metre visible in Layamon's *Brut*.

The Anglo-Norman versifiers of *Physiologus* are usually dismissed as rhymesters. But the English translator is not merely tagging verses; he constantly adds details or interpretations, some perhaps his own, others based on prose glosses. Of this process the lines on the Panther provide a clear instance. Only the English text says that this beast is 'blac so bro of qual' (white as a whale's brow), that its spots are 'trendled als a wel' (rounded as a wheel), and that Christ's beauty surpasses other men's 'so evensterre over erthe fen'—an image suggesting that the writer has often watched the evening star shining high above the flat and marshy fenlands of East Anglia. It is the Latin prose gloss which said that Christ at his resurrection gave forth *dulcissimum odorem* as he pronounced *Pax Vobis*. As often, the gloss became part of the text proper, to be linked with Ephesians 2: 17, 'he preached *peace* to you who were afar off'—like the animals drawn from afar by the Panther's sweet breath. This exegesis the English writer effectively fuses with a further Latin gloss which says that after the Ascension also Christ gave forth a *suavissimum odorem sc. sanctum paracletum* (the Holy Spirit, the comforter) *quem discipulorum cordibus infusit*. Hence comes the English couplet:

> Amonges men a swete smel
> He let her of his holi spel

—'he left the sweet fragrance of his holy teaching in the world.'

The Panther is the last beast in Thetbald's catalogue. The English poet adds the *Columba*, or dove, presenting it in novel fashion by moralizing each attribute as it is mentioned. Thus:

> With othre briddes ge doth as moder[1]
> So og ur ilk to don with oder[2]

[1] *she behaves like a mother*   [2] *so ought each of us to act towards the other*

The same *moralitas* is repeated in the exposition of the charming picture of the deer who follow their leader across a river, each supporting the other:

> Is non at nede[1] that other lateth[2]
> Oc leigeth his skinbon[3]
> On othres lendbon[4]

[1] *time of need*   [2] *abandons*   [3] *but lays his shin-bone*   [4] *on the next one's haunch*

So we should bear one another's burdens and thus fulfil the law of Christ:

> The hertes costes we ogen to munen[1],
> Ne og ur non other to sunen[2]
> Oc evrilc[3] luven other
> Also[4] he were his broder.

[1] *we ought to remember the hart's qualities*   [2] *shun*   [3] *everyone*   [4] *as if*

The depictions of elephant, lion, spider, and ant have different kinds of appeal, sometimes matched in the illustrated Bestiaries. This is the true art of the Bestiary—to convey theological truths in simple language and imagery. It is not the art of a *naïf* or pedestrian moralist.

Similarly, in describing the Eagle, this poet goes to Psalm 102 for warrant that it 'neweth his guth-hede' (renews its youth) and to Hugh of St Victor as authority for the claim that its beak grows twisted with age. A prose gloss on Thetbald says that the feathers are burnt away by the heat of the sun. But only the English poet identifies the waters into which the eagle falls with the baptismal font and applies the parable to a young child, already old in inherited sin. A colloquial tone and simple syntax make the lesson memorable: 'Buten a litel wat is tat / his muth is get untrewe' (there is still something not right—his mouth is twisted). An alert, humane intelligence has fleshed the bones of the traditional narrative. Alertness of another kind shows in the development of the brief reference to storms in the Latin *natura cetegrandie* into a dynamic metaphor of the seasons contending with each other in equinoctial gales:

26

Thanne sumer ond winter winnen[1]
Ne mai it [the whale] wunen[2] therinne.
So drovi[3] is te sees grund[4]
Ne mai he wunen ther that stund[5],
Oc stireth[6] up and hoveth[7] stille
Wiles that weder is so ille;

[1] *strive* [2] *stay* [3] *turbid* [4] *bottom* [5] *time* [6] *moves*
[7] *stays*

which leads into the picture of sailors landing on the whale's back with tinder for a fire—perhaps suggested by a miniature in an illustrated Bestiary. So too in *natura vulpis*, a single phrase, *rapit altilia*, is expanded into alliterative lines and couplets, and 'volatile sumit / Dentibus et tristem reddit edendo vicem' produces a sardonic couplet and lines describing tearing teeth, with strong echoic effect:

[She] gelt hem here billing[1]
rathe with illing[2].
tetoggeth and tetireth hem[3] mid hire teth sarpe[4].

[1] *repays them for their pecking* [2] *quickly with injury* [3] *pulls and tears them to pieces* [4] *sharp*

The reference is to the Fox's device of lying on its back and so effectively feigning death that ravens begin to peck at it (as verified in a Russian film).* This vignette, following on the description of the Fox's maraudings in the husbandman's *tun*, links the Bestiary with the world of Chauntecler and the vivid observation of *The Fox and the Wolf*. The terse, sardonic note is repeated in the onomatopoeic lines on the mermen whose song makes steersmen slumber and sleep so that

The sipes[1] sinken mitte suk[2]
Ne cumen he nummor up[3].

[1] *ships* [2] *with the sucking water* [3] *they never come up again*

Thus the technical expertise and experimentation evident in this poet's metrical innovations is matched by his skill in making the most of the material in his Latin source.

One of the two manuscripts that preserve *The Owl and the Nightingale* preserves also 400 rhymed lines markedly different in pattern and tone though metrically equally important; like the former poem, they may have been first written down in the South East (if not in London) and slowly transmitted to the West. Eighteenth-century scholars gave them the title *Poema Morale* or 'Moral Ode' (it was the century of odes), but neither is appropriate to a homiletic work that enjoins

* Stills from which are reproduced in K. Varty, *Reynard the Fox* (Leicester, 1967), plates 147–50.

Christian penitence and amendment of life. 'Conduct of Life' has
recently been proposed as a title; 'The Whole Duty of Man', or 'Ways
to Salvation' would be equally appropriate. If, as some think, it is an
early sermon in rhyme, it should, strictly speaking, be classed with
other sermons. Yet, if it is a sermon, it is a sermon without a text.
Instead, it begins with a self-condemnatory portrait:

> Ich em nu alder[1] thene ich wes · a wintre and a lare[2].
> Ich welde mare[3] thene ich dede · mi wit ahte bon mare.[4]
> Wel longe ich habbe child ibon[5] · a worde and a dede
> Thah ich bo a wintre ald · to yung ich em on rede[6] ...

[1] older [2] in learning [3] I have more responsibility [4] ought to be
greater [5] been [6] counsel

This is more like the Old English Exile's (or Penitent's) Prayer than
a sermon by Ælfric or Wulfstan. Certainly, its main themes are those
beloved of preachers: Hell, Heaven, Mortality, the Last Judgement;
and the clumsy line 'I wule nu cumen eft to the dome that ich er ow of
seide [that I told you of before]' (155), would have a function as a turning point in oral discourse. But it may simply reflect the habits of a
compulsive preacher, one acutely conscious of his responsibilities as
'lichame and sawle leche' (physician of body and soul) (302). The variants in the seven extant manuscripts may represent, in part, later
users' individual modifications.

Though the composer cites no texts directly, he shows some
acquaintance with scripture. His basic maxims are those of the Gospels,
in particular, 'love God, and thy neighbour as thyself'. He is shocked by
man's ingratitude to Christ: 'We yeveth unethe for his luve a stuche [bit]
of ure brede' (189). Our treasure should be in heaven, where neither king
nor reeve (sheriff) can take it away: a rendering of Matt. 6: 20 reflecting
the insecurities of the writer's own time. 'Lutel lac [gift] is Gode lof
[pleasing to God] that kumeth of gode wille.' Such gnomic sentiments
abound, and sometimes the aphorism runs to a couplet:

> Yif[1] we serveden God swa we doth erminges[2]
> Mare[3] we hadden en hevene thenne eorles her and kinges

(319–20)

[1] if [2] miserable mortals [3] more

And the couplets sometimes have a cutting edge:

> Swines brede[1] is swithe[2] swete, swa is of wilde dore[3]
> Alto dore he is abuh the yefth therfore his swore[4] (143–4)

[1] roast meat [2] very [3] animal [4] It is all too dear for the man who gives
his neck for it

28

But too often the pervasive admonitory sentiments sink into flat assertions, recurring with the inevitability of a hurdy-gurdy. 'Every man for
himself' is the main tenor of the message—though meaning, simply,
that each must look to his own salvation (and win it by deeds of mercy)
for both 'the fremede and the sibbe' (strangers and kin) will soon
forget him. The doctrine of self-knowledge that will bulk large in vernacular ethical writings appears in rudimentary form and gnomic
dress:

> Ech mon wat[1] him solve best · his werkes and his wille
> The the lest wat biseith ofte mest[2] · the hit al wat is stille[3].

(111–12)

[1] *knows* [2] *he who knows least has most to say about it* [3] *silent*

There is a heavy emphasis, as in the contemporary *Sawles Warde*
(see pp. 275–80 below) on the pains of hell, where the punishment is of
alternating heat and cold, and where the fire is unquenchable either by
'salt water or fresh of the burn' (248)—a phrase altered in some manuscripts to 'ne Avene strem ne Sture'; which has been taken as pointing
to a provenance in Hampshire or Wiltshire, near the confluence of the
rivers Avon and Stour, though the names are not peculiar to that
district. Otherwise the description is traditional, deriving ultimately
from Bede's *History* (v. 12). As in *Sawles Warde*, and in the first English
mural painting of the pains of hell, in the church of Chaldon, Surrey
(*c*.1200), punishment fits the sin. Whereas the path that leads to (an
unmaterial) heaven is the 'narrow way and green', because trodden by
few, the broad street, the too-well-trodden highway, slopes gently
down through a 'goodless wood' to a bare field. These locutions (not
found in a contemporary verse-sermon by one Guischart de Beaulieu
(? = Beaulieu, Hants), which has several likenesses to other passages)
recall the *tacitum nemus* and *lugentes campi* of *Aeneid* vi. That book of
Virgil's may well have been known to the versifier: it was early accommodated to Christian belief, in a way that Bishop Gavin Douglas was
to find acceptable.

Metrically the lines closely resemble the familiar septenarii of
Goliardic song, with a caesura after the fourth stress, and numerous
'trochaic' and 'iambic' variations.* The English line has normally
fifteen syllables, the last being invariably -*e* or -*en*. Formally, it is
identical with that in Orm's verse exegesis, written about the same
time, but is more varied, and less tedious, less mechanical in effect.
The regular verse-pattern, easily memorized, would commend the

* For a complete scansion of the first 30 lines see J. Hall, *Selections from Early Middle
English* (Oxford, 1920), ii. 327–8.

work to preachers; a writer or hearer accustomed to the alliterative pattern of Old English verse, or the looser pattern prevalent in Ælfric's sermons that were still being copied and used in the twelfth century, would not find it difficult to adjust his ear to this new rhythm. The poet's vocabulary is almost entirely English, and his stresses often fall on alliterating syllables (e.g. 'er déth and dóm come to his dúre he mei him sare adréden', 124); alliterating formulas and combinations still have a function: 'gamen and gleo' or 'for peni ne for punde'.

Eventually the line will break into the familiar ballad stanza. Dr Johnson, who cites from Hickes's (1705) text of the poem in his 'History of the English Language', which follows the Preface to his Dictionary, said with some truth that it 'contains the rudiments of our present lyrick measures'.

Nowhere is the continuity of English exegetical tradition and vernacular homily more clearly demonstrated than in the *Ormulum*, a work of which only about one fifth survives and that in the ugliest of manuscripts. 'Thiss boc iss nemmnedd Orrmulum forrthi that Orrm itt wrohhte' states the first line of the Preface. The title is probably modelled in part on Latin titles of the type *Speculum Ecclesie*, popular in the twelfth century; but the author's name is Scandinavian, and found chiefly in the Danelaw area; and his language reveals that blend of Scandinavian and English forms such as we might expect to find in north Lincolnshire: hence the plausible suggestion that he was an Augustinian canon of Elsham Priory.* He dedicates the work to his brother Walter, describing him as brother not only after the flesh, but also in God's house; and in view of the nature of the book one must assume that both brothers engaged in preaching to lay folk in English.

Orm's intentions were admirable, and his mode of exegesis and his choice of a metrical form align him with Ælfric, an earlier and greater homilist. But the numerous resemblances in exegesis of particular texts must not be taken to indicate that he had access to a text of Ælfric's homilies. Whereas Ælfric's homilies follow the sequence of a lectionary for the church year, the texts on which Orm commented are chosen on a quite different basis: they make up a continuum dealing with the life of Christ, in a chronological order (together with a series taken from the Acts of the Apostles). And his exhaustive, not to say tedious, commentary is based on the great twelfth-century glosses on Scripture: the *Glossa Ordinaria*, formerly attributed to Walafrid

---

* M. B. Parkes, in *Five Hundred Years of Words and Sounds: A Festschrift for Eric Dobson* ed. E. G. Stanley and Douglas Gray (Cambridge, 1983), 115–27, suggests that it was written in the Arroaisian Abbey at Bourne (Lincs.) early in the last quarter of the twelfth century.

Strabo, but probably directed by Anselm of Laon. They were doubtless found together in a great Vulgate Bible in Orm's monastery,
which would constitute 'the book', 'the holy book', to which he regularly refers. Such resemblances as there are to Ælfric arise from the
fact that the patristic sources on which Ælfric drew—in especial,
Gregory, Augustine, and Bede—were also drawn on for these two
Glosses. Some of the 'bisness' (examples) may well be his own: they
offer analogies rather than stories, and are not always self-evidently
illuminating. One or two derive from the *Physiologus*, a favourite resort
of preachers.

Like Ælfric, he chose a metrical form as easier for preachers to
recite or intone and for congregations to remember. But his metre is
very different from Ælfric's and far stricter. It is the jog-trot fif-
teener: isosyllabic, though marked by a strong stress rhythm—a
naturalized version of Latin syllabic metre. The quantitative cadence
would conduce to the lines being chanted or intoned; and Orm
devised a special spelling system to facilitate quick and regular
reading: the preachers for whom he intended the work may well have
been unfamiliar with the written vernacular in any form, and in need
of such guidance.

In thus adapting Latin syllabic metre Orm was anticipating other
early English poets, who tended to naturalize foreign syllabic metres
by combining them with a system of fixed stress. The general effect of
Orm's lines as we now read them on the page is undoubtedly
soporific—though we are occasionally startled by such a bold division
as *A / aronnes suness* (487–8) *metri causa*; yet a preacher with some
elocutionary training could doubtless have made them acceptable.
Campion, most deft and most versatile of lyricists, was to use the line
effectively, setting it in monorhymed triplets and varying rising with
falling movement.*

In the Dedication, the most engaging part of the work, Orm states
that he had undertaken to render into English, 'after the little wit that
God hath lent me' (a common humility formula) God's holy lore, at
the instance of his brother, who thought that it would be for the spiritual profit of English folk. He has collected texts from the Gospels as
they are read at Mass throughout the year, and added to each a
comment making clear their import. He admits that he has added
many words to fill out the verse, but avers that this will make the texts
better 'understanded of the people'; Walter is to scrutinize it carefully
and delete anything that might be misconstrued. It is intended for *all*

---

* See C. S. Lewis, *English Literature in the Sixteenth Century* (Oxford, 1954), 555.

English folk, who are to listen to it reverently, believe it in their hearts, declare it with their tongues, and follow it in their lives.

Tedious repetition of phrase, fact, and idea characterize the work as a whole. The Glosses on which it is based dictated the allegorical and typological reading of the Gospel texts (including a bizarre numerology (11248 ff.), and prompted the digressions, which are partly explicatory, partly the occasion of further allegorizing. Thus the discourse on Luke 1: 18 ('dixit Zacharias ad angelum, Unde hoc sciam? ego enim sum senex') is the occasion of long account of Jewish sacrificial ritual, in which the two goats represent the two Natures of Christ: his Divinity ('Goddcunndnesse'), which, alive and without pain, bore our sins away, and his Humanity ('Mennisscnesse')which drank Death's drink on the Rood Tree: all must be understood 'ghostly' (spiritually). The text itself is never transplanted literally but expanded and paraphrased, the characters being identified and described more than once:

> Thiss gode mann, thiss gode prest
> Thatt we nu mælenn offe[1]
> Wass, alls I seyyde[2] nu littlær[3]
> Yehatenn[4] Zacaryas.   (461–4)

> [1] *speak of*　　[2] *said*　　[3] *a little before*　　[4] *called*

In patristic fashion he offers variant interpretations of certain passages (e.g. 12000 ff.). Occasionally he falls into confusion (once identifying John the Baptist as Christ's 'darling'). The hearers are sometimes addressed in the singular, sometimes as 'laferrdinngess' (sirs). Thus the lamb brought by the Jewish mother on the day that 'Englishmen call Candlemas' (7705 ff.) betokens 'us who ought to recognize our Lord, as a lamb can recognize its mother among a thousand bleating sheep'. The sermon-divisions are only twice indicated by a concluding prayer. Once at least the divisions between the Gospel paraphrase and its application is clearly marked (12828 ff.). Sometimes the lesson is applied directly to himself (e.g. 2950).

Almost his only rhetorical device (apart from the occasional rhetorical question) is *repetitio*, and of that he avails himself continually; especially when setting forth theological mysteries he batters us with the Divine name:

> all thatt depe annd dærne witt[1]
> Thatt iss i Godes herrte
> Iss Godes Sune annd Godess Word
> Annd Godess dærne spæche.
> Annd forrthi wass the Laferrd[2] Crist

Off Godes aghenn kinde[3]
Forr Crist wass all soth Godess witt
All hiss dærne spæche . . .   (18493–500)

[1] *secret wisdom*   [2] *Lord*   [3] *own nature*

Only rarely does the note of direct speech sound sharp and clear, as when Christ addresses his mother at Cana:

'Abid, abid, wifmann[1], abid,
Ne comm nohht yet[2] min time'   (14020–1)

[1] *woman*   [2] *has not come yet*

Orm, traditional in his exegesis, is equally traditional in his language. It is less formulaic than Layamon's, but is wholly native, reflecting the blend of English and Scandinavian that had come about in the Danelaw area in the three centuries before Orm wrote, and that is exemplified in such fixed phrases as 'grith and frith'. The Virgin Mary is 'handfast' to Joseph—a Norse term and custom. Catechumens are 'prime-signed' (ON 'prím-signa' = marked with the sign of the cross, prior to instruction). Christ would not display his power 'alls iff he wollde leyyken' (ON 'leika', sport, play). The marriage feast at Cana is a 'brideale'. Most of the alliterative combinations are traditional and many will be found in more westerly texts: 'depe and dærne', 'trigg and treowe', 'flitten [ON] and farenn', 'biloken and bilappedd'. Basically, it is a homely language, free from French influences. John the Baptist feeds on grasshoppers and speaks of Christ's shoe-thong. He is sent like a beadle to prepare the way. Unleavened bread is 'therrflinng bred' ('tharfling bread': cf. tharf-cake in North-country use ('sourdough' in the Wycliffite Bible)). Theological terms are rendered in Old English forms, e.g. 'mennisscnesse' for (Christ's) humanity, or modifications of it (alongside 'rihhtwisnesse' is 'rihhtwisleyyc', with Norse suffix *metri causa*). The soul receives from God 'innsihht and minndignesse [memory]' (11507). Mary's name means 'sæsteorrne' ('sea-star', again with a Norse form).

The tedium that continuous reading of the *Ormulum* is apt to generate would not be felt by those who listened only to its expositions of the Gospel for the day. They would at least gain from it a pretty clear sense of the exact meaning of Scripture. No contemporary European commentary in the vernacular approaches it in fullness. The appearance of the manuscript may be rebarbative, but the work itself testifies to a conscientious consideration for the spiritual and doctrinal needs of the laity, twenty years before the Council of 1215 spurred the clergy as a whole into action.

The work known as *Genesis and Exodus* is both more and less than a presentation in verse of the opening books of the Bible: less, because it omits many passages not thought germane to the writer's purpose— which is to teach lay folk to love and serve God and live peaceably— more, because it covers parts of Numbers and Deuteronomy that relate to the wanderings of the Israelites under Moses. In fact it draws as much on Peter Comestor as on the Vulgate, and thus stands first in the line of extra-biblical paraphrases that culminates in Caxton's *Golden Legend*, which indeed also contains many of the supplementary details that appear in these verses. The 4162 lines in four-stressed couplets resemble those of *The Owl and the Nightingale*, though they include more trisyllabic feet and additional syllables. It is the extra-biblical details (some found also in the French *L'Estoire Joseph*, which also draws on Comestor) that now catch the eye: the two 'pilches' (coats of skin) made for Adam and Eve by angels; the tale of the love of an Egyptian princess for Moses, to whom he gave a ring of forgetful-ness; the tale of the burning coal that he chose instead of a royal signet ring; the account of Egyptian embalming—contrasted with Hebrew practice and with Christian anointing, alms-gift, and mass-song. The rainbow after the flood is said to betoken, in its blue band, destruction by flood, in its red, destruction by fire; the ark was not *pitched* but *limed*. The devil, we are told, was (according to Hebrew belief) made on Sunday and fell out on the next Monday. He is introduced with a verse from Isaiah, and given a monologue before he flies up to earth. The firmament was first enclosed with frozen waters. Adam was made in the field of Damascus. One Methodius, a martyr-bishop also cited in Higden's *Polychronicon*, is given as authority for some lines on the beginning and end of the world; Comestor is nowhere mentioned, though we are told that the work is drawn out of Latin 'with londes speche and wordes smale', which is certainly so. There are few rhetori-cal touches. Some alliterative phrases are not found elsewhere: 'flesses fremethe', 'rospen and raken' (diminish and scatter), 'sundring and samening'. Terms of Scandinavian origin ('ransaken', 'lages', etc.) belong to the East Midlands, to which the text must be assigned; forms and senses such as 'roke' (smoke), 'therknesse' (darkness), 'soren' (past participle of 'shear' in the sense 'reap') long survived in East Anglia. It is another testimony to the cultural mission of the Church in that area: the poem conveying not only biblical lore but some sense of the life of the ancient East. Moses emerges as a true leader of his people, and his plea for them is movingly rendered:

'Lorverd[1], merci' quad Moyses,
'Get ne let hem nogt[2] helpeles;

If he nu her wurthen slagen[3],
Egipte folc sal thorof ben fagen[4]
And seyen that he ben biswiken[5],
In the desert wel liderlike[6];
And thenk, loverth, quat ben biforen[7]
Abram and Ysaac and Jacob sworen'.　(3557–64)

[1] *Lord rejoice at that before to . . .*　　[2] *yet do not leave them*　　[5] *they are betrayed*　　[3] *If they are slain here now*　　[6] *vilely*　　[4] *will*　　[7] *of what has been promised*

His song of victory over the Egyptians, sung each day for a week, is commemorated in the seven visits to the font at Easter:

Thorof in Esterne be we wunen[1]
Sevene sithes[2] to funt cumen　　(3289–90)

[1] *accustomed*　　[2] *times*

Thus Jewish and Christian history become a continuum or rather, coalesce. The versifier, like a primitive Milton, prays that he may show the Creation ('Wrought with wit, wisdom and love') 'whether I read or sing' which suggests that he put it to use himself, and was a priest.

(ii) *Cursor Mundi*; *Handlyng Synne*; *The Prick of Conscience*; Devotional Pieces

Cursor Mundi, *anglice*, 'the over-runner of the world', is a dauntingly long work in 30,000 lines (chiefly rhymed octosyllabics) too often dismissed as a biblical paraphrase; in fact, it is often far from paraphrastic, and draws on several sources besides the Bible, notably Comestor's *Historia Scholastica*, which did for Western Europe as a whole what the *Cursor* did for Northern England at the end of the thirteenth century. Undoubtedly, it played a part in disseminating scriptural lore and scriptural narrative at a time when no translation of the Vulgate existed: that it survives in a number of manuscripts suggests that it was thought to be a more effective vehicle than, say, the *Ormulum*. It expands Scripture sufficiently to make its meaning clear to most intelligences. And indeed the author was more than a rhymester. He is very conscious of the appeal of secular literature—the romances that tell not only of Greece and Troy but of Gawain, Kay, Yonec, Tristram, Ysumbras, Amadas, and Ydoine, in 'selcuth rime, Englis, Frankys, and Latine'.* Love *paramour* is the folly of the

* ll. 1–26. On the passage, which is precious evidence for contemporary English literary taste, see *EMEVP*, 368–9. In two manuscripts Yonec is replaced by 'Kyng John' ('Ion(et)'): the only extant *Yonec* is that of Marie de France.

time. But his own paramour is Our Lady: to her the work is addressed, the legend of her life is throughout interwoven with the main themes, and it is in her honour 'for the love of English lede' that he undertook the work.

The passage just cited shows his acquaintance with verse romances, and the smoothness and flexibility of his verse doubtless owes something to the very works he professed to eschew. Like a popular poet, he repeatedly addresses his audience as 'louerdinges', adjuring them to 'herken to mi spell' or 'here nu quat Herodias did' (she salted down John the Baptist's head and hid it in a wall). Just as Chaucer was to do, he asks rhetorically 'Quat sal I sai yu lang sermoune?' Even transitions are managed in the romance way:

> Leve we nu Jesus a litil quile[1]
> And turn we to saint John ur stile[2] (13000–1).*

    [1] *time*   [2] *pen*

But other formulas are frequent, the most marked phrasal feature being alliterative combinations often including a distinctively northern word: 'sin and sake', 'wil of wane', 'grisly and grill', 'frith and fell', 'bak and bedde', '[to] stir of stedde'. What gives the work vividness and makes the narrative consistently readable is the deft use of lively dialogue, in a fashion more familiar from the later mystery plays, which treat the same themes (e.g. the Fall, the Flood, the Passion) in the same way.

When the narrative line diverges from scripture it is usually to follow such standard works as Comestor's *Historia Scholastica* (cf. *Genesis and Exodus*) or *The Golden Legend*. *Auctores* like Bede—doubtless accessible in a glossed Vulgate—are cited for such details as the duration of Lucifer's fall. From the beginning there are as many insertions as omissions: notable in the early pages are the account of the Earthly Paradise and of Seth's journey for the oil of Mercy—a passage that introduces the story of the Holy Rood Tree, which is recapitulated and continued at length in the later Passion narrative. Most of the commentary offered is of the standard teleological kind, but some enlivening details have no stated source: thus Abel is slain with the cheekbone of an ass, God tells Noah that he must not forget to put a wardrobe (privy) in the ark; when the deluge comes, the lion swims beside the hare, the sparrowhawk beside the starling, proud ladies beside their 'knaves'; Joseph casts chaff into the river so that it reaches Jacob's house as a sign that there is corn in Egypt. If these enlargements are due to Comestor, the topical comments on them are the

* Cf. 10931, 14126, 19601, 19747, etc.

writer's. He gives the tale of Noah's raven as the source of the phrase 'the raven's messenger' for a dilatory envoy (and uses it himself of Abraham's servant, 3333). Noah's nakedness shows that the primevals did not wear breeches; Isaac's decrepitude prompts a typical but not wholly banal passage (based on set presentations of *Senectus*) on the signs of death: it is not only that teeth rot (etc.) but that the old 'praise things that be gone'. More unexpected is an account of the siege of Troy and its origins (7059–82). Folk proverb finds a place: thus (of Esau)

> For hauke es eth[1], as I here say,
> To reclaime that has tint[2] his prai.   (3529–30)
>
> [1] *easy*   [2] *lost*

Amongst the major intercalations is the Dialogue of the Four Daughters of God, a dialogue that Langland was partially to re-enact in a notable passus. The *Cursor* draws it from 'Seynt Roberdes bok', i.e. the *Chasteau d'Amour* of Robert Grosseteste, and follows the French as well as the English version. *Cursor* gives us the full allegory including the castle (which Langland adapts in another place) with its barbicans and battlements ('red as rose in spring'). The story of the King's son who accords Justice with Mercy by taking the part of a thrall is feelingly presented as a 'sample' of our redemption:

> Mekil reuth[1] had he that time of man
> That wald liht[2] ute of that hie toure
> To lighten in a maydens boure
> That lefte sua many schepe alone
> To fett on[3] that wil[4] was gone   (9804–8)
>
> [1] *great pity*   [2] *descend*   [3] *to fetch one*   [4] *astray*

But for the *Cursor* poet the prime significance of the allegory is the place it gives to the Blessed Virgin Mary, and it culminates in his prayer to her which leads on to the story of her life:

> *Hereth* now that wol have mede[1]
> And I shal you the story *rede*
> Of the holy maydenes birthe
>
> (10123–4, Trinity Coll. MS)
>
> [1] *reward*

—where 'hear' and 'read' give an inkling of the way the poem was first presented. He begins with Joachim, who had stalwart herdsmen

> That miht agaynes the theves fight
> And that coude rise at time of niht
> And loke thair bestis ay in nede.   (10297–9)

That all this matter comes ultimately from the apocryphal gospels the poet nowhere reveals, though once, when describing Mary as the first woman to lift up the infant John, he remarks that this is 'as I found in some books' (11060). That Christ came 'as sun through glass' is too ancient and familiar a figure to need such a warrant. For stories of the Three Kings he draws—doubtless through some compendium—on 'John gilden mouth' (Chrysostom). And he treats the Nativity in terms that Lancelot Andrewes still found appealing: that bishop likewise presents Christ as born in a 'cratch'; which bespeaks 'no pride of coverlite, / Chamber, curtain, ne tapite [tapestry]':

> Of poverté na dedeigne[1] had he
> That biddis us love wel poverté.   (11309–10)

> [1] disdain

Some of the stories of the childhood of Jesus belong to folklore not to faith—though at least one of them, that of the restoring to life, at Mary's pleading, of the boy who had broken his toys, and of his birds of clay, is represented in an English church-mural at Shorthampton (Oxon.). Vivid colloquialisms are sprinkled here and there: Herod is assured that he will emerge from his bath of boiling pitch 'as whole as any trout'; when lions fawn on Jesus, they 'honurd him faunand thair taile' (12354). If some of the detail that fills out the spare narrative of the evangelists is curious—Christ begins his ministry in April, and 'thought it was too long to go without fellowship'—other additions are arresting: James and John are baiting their lines when Christ calls them; the Jews, displeased with the man born blind, 'schott him als a dog / right oute of thair synagog'. The Passion, as the final cause of the whole vast work, is prefaced by a new prayer for grace, and marked out by a change in metre:

> And resun es we ur rime rume[1]
> And set fra nu langer bastune[2]   (14922–3)

> [1] extend, enlarge   [2] verse

—to wit, an eight-line unit of alternating four- and three-stress lines, the second and fourth line rhyming: a stanza form undoubtedly effective in achieving poignancy and emotional tension, not least in the crowd scenes, with the Jews gathering, Pilate sitting with the burgesses, the mob playing games—'sitisot' or 'a bobet' (16623)—with Christ. This climactic narrative is amplified in several ways: by a hymn based on the Palm Sunday anthem *Gloria, laus et honor*; an imprecation on Judas and the tale of his assertion that the Resurrection is as impossible as that a cock that 'was skaldid yisternight' (15988) should crow (which it does forthwith, as in the late Greek text of the *Acta Pilati*). The Legend of the Holy Rood Tree furnishes the account of the burial of the three crosses. The Cotton manuscript of the *Cursor* inserts the tale of St Denis the Areopagite who sensed in distant Athens that God was suffering death 'in his kind' (? in his human nature). The sufferings prompt an appeal such as preaching friars would make. The poet as theologian introduces the ancient figure of Christ taking Satan with his own hook. As in contemporary books of devotion, the Saviour enters into a dialogue with Man. For the Resurrection the poet resorts to the traditional Bestiary *significacio* of the lion which sleeps three days after giving birth. The main narrative is rounded off with lines on the physical beauty of Christ's person.

The acts and sufferings of the Apostles occupy several thousand lines, with a characteristic intercalation on the Assumption derived from an earlier vernacular version of the account given by St Edmund 'of Pounteni' (Pontigny (and of Abingdon)):

> In suthrin Engliis was it draun
> And I have turned it till ur aun
> Langage of the northren lede[1],
> That can nan other Englis rede. (20061–4)

[1] *people*

The poet has his favourite rhetorical turns, like the repetition, or his reversal of the closing phrase of one line at the beginning of the next:

> Thai stod, bot all thas[1] other fledd,
> All other fledd, but yeit thai stod. (19486–7)

[1] *those*

References to patristic *auctores* (Ambrose, Gregory, Jerome—whose doubts about the Assumption are duly noted) indicate that he had been well trained as a cleric. But his overriding concern is that those who heard his *Cursor* read should turn from this little life, subject as it is to the revolutions of Fortune's Wheel (23719 ff.), and think of the Passion, rather than of 'hu Roland justed, and Olivere' (21910).

His chief fault is that he cannot bring himself to make an end. When we think he has done, he adds a heavily alliterative poem on the Sorrows of Our Lady in tail-rhyme verse that runs with fatal facility for some fifty pages. It testifies as much to the growth of devotions to the Virgin as to the author's own piety. He seizes the opportunity to add the story of the Feast of the Conception as told by Wace*—though he nowhere names that Norman poet—who had reported that when

* *La Conception Nostre Dame*, ed. W. R. Ashford (Chicago, 1933), ll. 39–156.

Elsey, abbot of Ramsey, was returning from the embassy to Denmark his ship was struck by a storm (described in twelve heavily alliterative lines, as if alliteration were the accepted medium for such sea-scenes); but an angel promised deliverance on condition that henceforth 18 December, formerly the feast of Our Lady's Nativity, should be the feast of her Conception. Later he returns to this tail-rhyme pattern in a long prayer to the Trinity, breathing a personal lament:

> ... luved I never rest ne ro[1] ...
> ...Ful leif me[2] was to cum in cri[3]
> Wid Magot and wid Margori
> Wid Mariot, Mald, and ma[4] ...
>
> Nu ask I nouther gra[5] ne grene
> Ne stede schrud[6] ne lorem schene[7]
> Ne purper pall[8] ne pride of pane[9]
> Ne riche robe wid veir and gris.[10]   (25452–66)

[1] *peace* [2] *dear to me* [3] *consort with* [4] *others* [5] *grey (clothes)* [6] *horse's caparison* [7] *fair bridle* [8] *robe of purple* [9] *skirt* [10] *vair and grey (fur)*

The piece moves on to the Hours of the Passion, and a descant (in a new stanza form) on the Five Joys of the Virgin. It is followed by a brief but densely alliterative prayer:

> Drightin[1] dere wid blisful beildes[2]
> That al this werld wid wisdom weildis[3] ...   (25684–5)

[1] *Lord* [2] *comfort* [3] *governs*

which leads into a long rhymed discourse on Shrift and Penance, with a composite model confession and such warnings as this about penances for incomplete confession:

> Thai sal yow up on balkes[1] lift
> Als suine[2] that ar to salting tift[3]   (26750–1, Cotton MS)

[1] *beams* [2] *swine* [3] *made ready for*

Part of this discourse is addressed to confessors, for whose benefit the poet cites Raymond (of Pennaforte); applying the formulaic questions 'Why, where, with whom, when, and how'. The Seven Sins are duly presented and analysed, perhaps with the help of the *Prick of Conscience* at one point (27641 ff.), certainly with that of Isidore (of Seville) (27626). Seneca is cited on the envious (27706), and Augustine on sodomy (27966 ff.). The confession of Pride—for which the remedy is meekness and self-knowledge—includes the admission: 'Caroles, jolites and plaies / Ic have behaldyn and ledde' (28146–7). Similarly, an idle priest admits *inter alia* that

> At wrestelyng, at wake, rengd[1] haf I
> And folud wit lust all luchery   (28526–7)

> [1] *reigned*

This lengthy section reminds us yet again that the prime purpose of this work, as of the bulk of medieval vernacular writing, was rectification of morals in Christian terms. Only occasionally are moral injunctions particularized to yield memorable images, as when the white-necked ladies are shown as studying

> Hu to dub[1] and hu to paynt
> And hu to mak yow semlé and quaint[2]
> Biletts[3] forbroiden[4] and colers wide
> For to sceu wit your quite hide[5]
> Wit curchefs crisp and bendes[6] bright
> Your scappes schins[7] to mans sight
> Thoru your trail[8] bath wide and side[9]
> Es nat at seke[10] to find your pride . . .   (28014–21)

> [1] *adorn*   [2] *elegant*   [3] *(?) ornaments*   [4] *embroidered*   [5] *to reveal your white skin*   [6] *ribbons*   [7] *shapes shine*   [8] *train*   [9] *long*   [10] *easily seen*

Foolish are the merchants who buy such wares. The follies of fashion will provide matter for a satiric genre in later verse. But the passage is hardly typical of a poet who did not recognize that logorrhea was an occupational hazard. Chaucer, Langland, Dante, were to make much, though never *too* much, of the Capital Sins. The author of the *Cursor*, like the author of *Handlyng Synne*, could never recognize his own fault: a failure to control his penchant for versifying.

Handlyng Synne is a version of a slightly earlier treatise in Anglo-Norman on the Sins, *Le Manuel des Pechiez* (*Péchés*), a confessional manual sometimes attributed to, but probably not composed by William of Wadington (of whom nothing is known). The adaptor calls himself Robert of 'Brunne'—usually taken to be Bourne in Lincolnshire, but possibly a 'Brunne' in Yorkshire;* elsewhere, in his *Chronicle of England* (see below, pp. 93–100), he gives his name as 'Mannyng'. He belonged to the Gilbertine order, which had been founded at Sempringham (Lincs.) in the twelfth century. He was at a Gilbertine priory nearby (possibly St Saviour's, the modern Bridgend) for fifteen years, during which time he wrote *Handlyng Synne*. He began his version in 1303, and, evidently, only after he had finished it did he turn to the *Chronicle*, which he completed in 1338. Members of the Gilbertine order were often sent from Sempringham to study at Cambridge; Mannyng asserts that he was there when Alexander Bruce

* See note below, p. 478.

gave a 'commencement' or degree feast. One might plausibly maintain that the poet had imbibed, and illustrates, the conception of 'gentle authority' which characterized the Gilbertine rule.

The framework of the *Manuel des Péchés* is similar to that of *Ayenbite of Inwit* (see below p. 292) and of several similar works (not to mention *The Parson's Tale*). It deals with the Ten Commandments, the Seven Capital Sins (and Sacrilege), the Seven Sacraments, the twelve parts, and graces, of Confession, the twelve articles of Faith. Mannyng follows this pattern (which had evident mnemonic value) except that he omits the last section (on the Creed). It may all appear too rigidly schematic, but as we read the dominant purpose shows through: to promote honest and holy living, responsible parenthood, the elimination of social sins (from backbiting to blasphemy). The *exempla* with their vivid dialogues would be a godsend to preachers in the English vernacular;* sermon formulas here and there (including appeals to an audience or a member thereof, e.g. 9311–12) suggest that Mannyng had in mind a homiletic use for the work. Sections of the poem like that on the Sacrament of the Altar (9891–902), expanded from four lines in the Anglo-Norman, read like the beginning of a self-contained sermon.

The *Manuel* and its English version must, however, still be seen primarily as manuals of confession, a product of that emphasis on regular auricular confession and Easter communion found in the Lateran canons of 1215. These decrees had been promulgated in England at the Council of Oxford (1222) and Bishops Poore, William of Blois, and Grosseteste had been energetic in implementing them. The growing emphasis on the manner of hearing confession and on enquiry into the nature and circumstances of sin involved a use of English by priest as well as people. The ultimate purpose of the work is to move hearers to make confession to their parish priest—even though the numerous *exempla* sometimes obscure this intention. It is addressed, now to 'ye wives', now to 'ye children', now to 'ye stewardes on benche', or 'thou baylé', to 'domesmen', midwives, customs men (2369), even to priests (11623 ff.). Readers as well as hearers are implied in such remarks as 'whedyr thou wylt opon the boke' (121) and in the assumption that some will be able to amend his 'foule Englyssh and feble ryme' (8625).

Like other works of the same genre, *Handlyng Synne* is a vehicle for

---

* And not only in the vernacular: Bishop Brinton uses one of them, showing the sinfulness of swearing by Christ's limbs, in a Latin sermon *ad cleros* (*The Sermons of Thomas Brinton, Bishop of Rochester* (1373–89), ed. M. A.Devlin (Camden Soc. ccliii (3rd Ser. 85), 1954), i. 191).

outspoken social comment and criticism: the purification of the soul through confession is to be achieved only when one's life has been adjudged by Christian standards as formulated in Canon Law and the standard penitentials. The curious, not to say confusing title, though a strained rendering of the French original, may be justified as a metaphor for the examination of conscience: 'Handyl thy synne yn thy thought...'. The social criticism (as in the 'Confessions' Passus in *Piers Plowman*, which embodies the same assumptions) must be read in this perspective.

Like the *Manuel*, *Handlyng Synne* is in octosyllabics. Verse, says Mannyng (following the French text), appeals to 'lewde men' (i.e. to lay folk, under which term we may include monastic lay-brethren, *conversi*):

> For many ben of swyche manere
> That talys and rymys wyl blethly[1] here   (45–6)
>
> [1] *gladly*

He will provide better pastime than the 'trotevale' that men listen to 'yn gamys, and festys, and at the ale' and that 'may falle ofte to vylanye'. His performance is as good as his promise. There is some art in the seemingly garrulous verse, a touch of poetic device, as in the repetition of a phrase or half-line but in inverted form, a pattern found also in the *Cursor Mundi* and the alliterative *Awntyrs of Arthur*. An early example is:

> At thy [God's] wurschyp shul we bygynne
> To shame the fende and shew[1] oure synne;
> Synne to shewe, us to frame[2],
> God to wurschyp, the fende to shame,
> Shameful synne ys gode to lete[3] ...   (3–7)
>
> [1] *reveal*   [2] *for our benefit*   [3] *give up*

When he comes to render (and elaborate) the hymn to Caritas in I Cor. 12, he does not fall below his original:

> Thogh y speke as weyl with tung,
> As any man or aungel hath song,
> And [if] y lyve nat with charyté,
> No thyng avayleth hyt to me ...   (7123–6)

Additional *exempla* apart, the work is not a mere translation. Several of the French tales are slightly altered, and there is frequent change of emphasis. In the French 'les fols' swear oaths 'par curteisie': the English gives a sarcastic twist to the couplet:

> Gentyl men, for grete gentry,
> Wene[1] that grete othys beyn curteysy.   (669–70)
>
> [1] *think*

43

Throughout Mannyng has his eye on lords who rob the poor (2224 ff.), or spend their substance on modern dress or on ornate tombs (8779 ff.), or who make a corner in wheat (5377 ff.)—criticisms that the fifteenth-century landowner Peter Idle will tone down when he adapts the work as a manual for his son. The tale of Dives and Lazarus, which was to provide the frame for the didactic *Dives and Pauper*, is extended. The age-old topic of the duplicity of executors, which goes back to Seneca, appears repeatedly. Essentially the tales display the life of feudal manor and county town, peopled by 'wykked legistres and false accountours', overbearing lords, worldly and unchaste priests. Some of the tales will now seem antifeminist, but Mannyng does not denigrate marriage:

> A gode womman ys mannys blys,
> There here love ryght and stedfast ys.   (1907–8)

A liberal sprinkling of gnomic sentiments with pragmatic force—some perhaps previously in octosyllabic form—helps to strengthen the folk-appeal of the work, as does Mannyng's alteration of the indirect speech of the French original into *vraisemblable* dialogue. Piers the Usurer in anger throws a loaf of bread at a beggar. When the beggar asks him for alms he glares at him 'felunlyche with yyen grym' (5612—a line that is also found in *Havelok*), but the beggar can still point to his loaf:

> 'Lo,' he seyde, 'what y have
> Of Pers yyft[1], so God me save!'
> 'Nay', they swore by here thryft[2],
> 'Pers yave[3] never swych a yyft!'   (5621–4)

> [1] *gift*   [2] *hope of salvation*   [3] *would give*

Piers, falling ill, dreams that the angels count the loaf as a gift, his sole good deed: 'They had noght elles, they mote nedys [they had to of necessity]' (5666). Mannyng's dry humour is part of his humaneness; it bespeaks his good sense, which shows also in his advice to parents not to oppose troths plighted by their children (1715–26).

He takes a rather severe view of sports and pastimes as occasions for sin. A notable example is his rendering of the tale of the Dancers of Colbek, for which he used a Latin version fuller than that in his French text: dancers who are cursed by a priest for dancing in his churchyard dance on for a whole twelvemonth, singing the carole that had wrought them woe, with its ironic refrain 'Why stonde we? why go we noght?' In fact the emphasis in Mannyng's version is as much on the priest's rash curse, which loses his daughter her arm, as on sacrilege. Of tournaments the Church had always been suspicious, and

Mannyng dwells realistically on the risks they involve: they are mentioned with regard to lechery and all the other capital sins. A young knight may be prompted to take part for love of his leman, but

> So ys he bete there for here love,
> That he ne may sytte hys hors above,
> That peraventure yn alle hys lyve
> Shal he never aftyr thryve.[1]   (4611–14)

> [1] *prosper*

Ladies' white kerchiefs may be the devil's sails:

> Wymples, kerchyves, saffrund betyde[1]
> Yelugh[2] under yelugh they hyde
> Than wete[3] men never, whether ys whether[4]
> The yelugh wymple or the lether[5].*   (3445–8)

> [1] *sometimes coloured saffron* [2] *yellow* [3] *know* [4] *which is which*
> [5] *skin*

Several of Mannyng's *exempla* do not seem to occur in the *Manuel*, and their insertion can probably be credited to him, though they are of the same kind as those in the French and usually prompted by similar matter there present. Amongst them are the tales of the witch with the leather bag that can milk a cow for her but not for the bishop because, as she wittily remarks, he does not believe; of the rich man addicted to swearing who is rebuked by Our Lady carrying a bleeding child (this 'lytyl tale', says Robert, 'y herde onys a frere spelle', and evidently others did too: it reappears in *Dives and Pauper* and still later in a Lincoln MS†); of the miserly Cambridge parson who on his death-bed tries to eat his hoarded money: friars break open his coffer, bring him the money on a silver dish, but take it away as he tries to cram the coins down his throat; of the Norfolk knight, whose manor being close to the churchyard (of which, 'as often falls', the walls are broken) lets his cattle graze there: when he brushes complaint aside, in a fashion not befitting a 'man gentyle', a bondman reminds him (as Piers Plowman will remind another knight) that

> 'Erles mygt, and lordes stut[1]
> As cherles shal yn erthe be put.'   (8697–8)

> [1] *(?) magnificent*

In a variant of the familiar Titivillus story, a deacon bursts out laughing as he watches, whilst reading the Gospel, a fiend busily

* The allusion is explained by reference to the colour yellow in German texts by Ruth Harvey, 'Gelwez Gebende', *German Life and Letters*, NS xxviii (1974–5), 263–85.

† J. W. Blench, *Preaching in England in the late Fifteenth and Sixteenth Centuries* (Oxford, 1964), 117–18.

noting down the abuse of two jangling women on a roll that grows longer and longer.* The need for faithful adherence to details of the Sacraments is illustrated by the tale of the midwife who misbaptizes with the formula 'God and St John'. At least two tales derive directly or indirectly from Bede's *History*, one that of the knight Jumna being released from his prison bonds when his brother, thinking him dead, says masses for his soul—replacing a similar tale in the *Manuel*.

Comic effects abound, and are clearly intentional. Plot and speech are presented so as to engage the sympathy of a rural audience; folk customs (e.g. that of laying food for 'shapers' (Fates) at the head of a new-born child, 9667 ff.) are given a Christian colouring; and several of the tales are set in Lincolnshire. Minstrelsy is held to be harmless because 'Seynt' Robert Grosseteste of Lincoln, 'so seyth the geste', loved harp-music; the assertion has a further interest in that it links the great bishop with a work which was an ultimate product of his attempts to propagate the confessional and disciplinary teaching of the Lateran Council. Mannyng represents a development in the whole technique of confession and the parish priest's role therein (cf. 11603 ff., 11430); it is not surprising that the original *Manuel* is ascribed to the Bishop in two manuscripts of Mannyng's version.

The number of the tales illustrating each 'branch' of the *Manuel* varies from three to seven. As in *The Canterbury Tales*, the great majority are not set in England, their sources often being biblical or patristic; almost a third belong to the category of visions that induce terror and so amendment of life. Some of them will reappear as sermon material in the Northern English Homily Collection and elsewhere. The book must be considered as one of the antecedents of Chaucer's far greater work, not only because it represents the type of narrative to which Chaucer's audience had chiefly been exposed—as his Pardoner remarks:

> Lewed[1] peple loven tales olde;
> Swiche[2] thynges kan they wel reporte and holde
>
> (*CT* VI. 437–8)

> [1] *ignorant*　　　[2] *such*

but also because Chaucer's own purposes included the didactic element that bulks large in his predecessor. By the same token, readers of *Confessio Amantis* would at once recognize it as a 'parody' of

---

* The devil Tutivillus appears in the play *Mankind* (15th century) and in a lyric (*SRL*, No. 78). See Margaret Jennings, *SP* (*Texts and Studies*) 1977 and M. D. Anderson, *Drama and Imagery in English Medieval Churches* (Cambridge, 1963), 173–7.

the work that had first made a similar vast collection of *exempla* accessible in English verse and in the metre that Gower chose.

The Prick of Conscience, or *Stimulus Conscientiae*, is a hortatory work of 9,600 rhymed octosyllabics, as popular in its time, to judge from the large number of manuscripts, as any poem of Chaucer or Langland. Its professed purpose is to stir the reader or hearer to meekness and fear of God—or rather fear of losing his love and the beatific vision: we should love God for himself, the writer insists at the end, though that is not the pervasive theme; his own meekness takes the form of a *captatio benevolentiae*:

> . . . haf me excused at this tyme
> If yhe fynde defaut in the ryme.   (9583–4)

It is meant for the 'lewed', the lay folk; he will gladly stand correction from clerks. We are to pray 'for hym specialy that it drew'; the verb implies compilation. And a compilation it largely is, done in some Northern scriptorium in the fourteenth century by a rhymer who had access to standard texts: Augustine, Haymo (4391), Innocent III (*De Contemptu Mundi*), a Compendium of St Thomas 'Alqwyn' (Aquinas), Bartholomaeus's *De Proprietatibus Rerum*. Innocent he quotes in the original Latin prose, alongside elegiacs attributed to St Bernard and a 'versifier in [Latin] metre' (897). John Chrysostom is drawn on at 5360. The 'Raymundus' cited on Purgatory (3946) is Raymund de Pennaforte. Only on this theme does the poet present variant opinions: some clerks say that the soul is 'the *air* of a body'; others that young innocents fly through purgatory like a bird, others that its pain is physical.

As verse it provides further evidence of the fatal attraction of the regular short-lined couplet, against which the variety and freedom of contemporary religious lyric stands out in sharp contrast. Yet it never grates on the ear as does later Tudor verse of the same order; and it offers a convenient, orderly, and easily memorized compendium of current belief and cosmology. Its seven parts cover the themes of the creation and later wretchedness of mankind, worldly instability, Death, Purgatory, Doomsday, the Joys of heaven, the Pains of hell.

The cosmology is essentially Chaucer's: God 'ordayned for mans behufe . . . heven and erth and the world brade'. But the earth is but a point 'imyddes a compase . . . / To regard of [in comparison with] tha hevens obout' (7586–8; cf. *The Parlement of Foules*, 57–8). The least star we see is greater than the earth, and a stone falling from the highest heavens would take a thousand years to reach it. By comparison with the broad country of heaven it is but a 'myddyng-pytt' (8770): a thought that for once prompts the writer to give a description 'on myn owen hede' (8874) of the wonders of heaven. In fact they are out of the last chapters of the Apocalypse; but he reaches out to an unexpected array of similes for the beauty of its denizens: fairer than Absalom, more noble than Augustus, and so forth. The joys of heaven are described much as they had been in *Sawles Warde* (see pp. 275–80 below), and so are the scenes of horrors and affright in hell, though the familiar Virgilian formula* is expanded: a hundred thousand men with a hundred thousand tongues of steel could not tell its terrors.

The dominant topos is that of man as a pilgrim engaged in 'gastly [spiritual] batayle', a wretched exile, whose first cry is of woe that he has come to a vale of tears. He is turned about on the wheel of Dame Fortune (1273 ff.). He dies daily: *Mors omnia solvit*. The platitudes are plentiful but they have classical as well as Christian components: Man is a lesser world, an inverted tree (as in Aristotle), and Cato is quoted (2169): 'Non metuit mortem / qui scit contempnere vitam.' Before death the nose becomes 'sharp' (like Falstaff's) and small. When Christ appears in judgement, the cross, the spear, the nails, the crown of thorns will show in the sky—a picture no more specifically 'medieval' than Michelangelo's. A passage on the fifteen accusers who will then confront the wicked—beginning with Conscience, and including the poor, and wronged subjects who accuse their sovereigns, is not without power.

Scriptural texts thread the narrative together and some renderings yield further evidence that many had settled already into fixed vernacular forms (as at 6190: 'I hungered and had defaute of mete / And yhe wald not gyfe me at ete'). Occasionally the Vulgate terms are expanded into a native formula; so *caro* becomes 'flesshe and felle' (739). The writer doubtless wrote for preachers, and was perhaps a preacher himself. He introduces one *exemplum* (5780): a King has a daughter whom he loves and entrusts her to his reeve—but requires a 'reckoning' (the proper term for a reeve's rendering of account); even so God entrusts the soul to man. We should not too easily dismiss all this as commonplace because the rhymes come pat. But we can at once dismiss the once-popular attribution of the work to Rolle, for which there is no foundation whatever.

As we have seen, a didactic poem like the *Cursor Mundi* often has a strongly devotional tone, particularly in its sections on the Passion, and it is not surprising to find this central topic of medieval devotion given separate treatment. Two such are the *Southern Passion*, a poem in

---

* see *EMEVP*, 423.

long lines in some manuscripts of *The South English Legendary*, and the rather more interesting *Northern Passion*. This latter (extant in no less than fourteen manuscripts) is an anonymous adaptation of an anonymous French original now called *La Passion des Jongleurs*, itself based on Latin gospel harmonies and such works as the Pseudo-Bernard *Vitis Mystica*. The English text omits some legendary details given in the French but inserts others, and rearranges part of the narrative in accordance with the Gospel sequence though it rewrites other parts with considerable freedom (a process continued in expanded versions found in three of the manuscripts). The French text already had such details as the stretching of Christ's hands and feet to reach the holes bored in the cross, and the bursting of his sinews. The English adds Christ's appeal to the passers-by (which had been adapted from Lam. i: 12); the setting of the cross into the pit is done to increase Christ's pains:

> That sunder rafe both sins[1] and vaynes
> And thai schogged it till and fra[2]
> On all manere to wirk him wa[3].

> (Harl. MS, 1646 f–h)

[1] *sinews*   [2] *shook it to and fro*   [3] *cause pain to him*

At the Last Supper Christ says of the sacramental bread that it 'shall save you from evil deeds', and in the Garden of Gethsemane, he tells the disciples that although they have slept well, 'Judas has sleped never a dele', and many other gratuitous though piquant details could be cited. However, the habit of loose paraphrase produces loose verse—no writer with his eye on the object could have said that the noontide darkness 'refte the sterres thair lyghte'.

Another central topic of medieval piety receives an enthusiastic treatment in forty alliterative stanzas in a Northern dialect called by their editor, Sir Israel Gollancz, *The Quatrefoil of Love*. This poem is essentially a devotional exercise in honour of the Virgin as a fourth element of the Godhead, linked with her son on earth and in heaven. The stanzaic form is that used in *The Pistill of Swete Susan*: eight lines with both rhyme and (somewhat cloying) alliteration, followed by a 'bob and wheel', as in *Sir Gawain*; and as in *Sir Gawain* (and *Pearl*) the last lines of the whole poem repeat the first. The setting is a conventional May morning; and the narrator reveals his vocation when he describes himself as walking through a 'merry orchard bidding my hours' (i.e. saying his Office). He overhears a Turtle Dove asking a fair maiden why she mourns. She is seeking a true love, for when she thinks she has found a constant love it flies away. The Turtle takes true love to mean the four-leafed clover (or, rather, Herb Paris, *Paris quadrifolia*), a symbol of faithful love, and so of the Godhead: the King of bliss, who wrought heaven, paradise, and 'all this merry middle-earth'; the Son of God; the Holy Ghost—there are three leaves. Stanzas on Creation and the Fall ('The first lefe was fulle woo / Whene his floures felle hym fro') are followed at once by an account of the Annunciation so that the fourth leaf can be named as the Virgin. Just as quickly the bird passes from the Massacre of the Innocents to the Passion, when the second leaf 'sulde falowe and falle', and 'alle the trewthe of this werlde was in a trewe may [maiden]'. The Harrowing of Hell is sketched in terms reminiscent of the Mystery Plays, with David playing his harp. The return of Christ's soul to his body is confusingly described in the lines: 'Unto the body agayne the haly gaste yode [went]'. Thomas at first doubts the news of the Resurrection because 'Women are carpand: it commes thame of kynde' (women are chatterers by nature). After the Assumption, Our Lady is crowned Queen of Heaven. 'Thus hase this faire trew-lufe made us alle fre': when we displease the three leaves the fourth kneels and weeps for our sake 'with hir eghne graye'. But at the Doom she will not dare to speak. To the Doom seven stanzas are devoted, including one describing the dress of fine ladies, with their 'bendys and botonys, felettis and fare' (fillets, buttons, ribbons and fine array) and another on 'thies galiarde gedlynges that kythes gentry' (those gay fellows who make a show of gentility). By this time the poem has become purely homiletic and exhortatory. Only the last stanza reminds us that a maiden was listening; it counsels us all to pray to the Fourth Leaf.* Though the symbolism may be defective if the notoriously rare quatrefoil clover rather than *Paris quadrifolia* is meant, it rests on more than folk-lore: correspondence between the natural and the divine was part of medieval belief.

(iii) Complaint and Satire: *The Parlement of the Thre Ages*; *Wynnere and Wastoure*; *Mum and the Sothsegger*

Confronted by the wickedness of this world, the medieval moralist found it hard not to be a satirist. The versifier who in *A Lutel Soth*

---

* In structure, theme and sentiment the verses resemble a shorter meditative refrain-poem with a similar *chanson d'aventure* opening: 'I passud thoru a garden grene' (*CBXV*, No. 78). Both poems seem flaccid to the modern reader. But that the *Quatrefoil* appealed to fifteenth-century taste is suggested by Wynkyn de Worde's (undated) printed edition; in which, though the text is modified for Southern readers, a good deal of the alliteration is retained (see N. F. Blake, *Archiv*, ccvi (1969–70), 189–200).

Sermon calls on us to give up our sins cannot refrain from an elaborate complaint on the wickedness of young people nowadays:

> Theos prude yunge men
> That luvieth Malekin
> And theos prude maidenes
> That luvieth Janekin

whisper together of 'derne [secret] luve' at 'chirche and at cheping [market]'. They ogle each other in church—'Heo [she] biholdeth Wadekin mid swithe gled eye'. Gilot will not give up her Robin in spite of her parents' threats, but goes with him in the evening shamelessly, swearing that no man has been near her—until her belly begins to swell. The most interesting examples, however, are to be found in alliterative verse.

The 665 alliterative lines headed *The Parlement of the Thre Ages* probably exemplify the kind of verse current in the North Midlands at the time when *Piers Plowman* and *Gawain* were composed, and acceptable to audiences who listened to the latter if not the former. The verse itself is not as accomplished as that of the longer and greater works: it abounds in weak fillers—the adverb *full* occurs over a hundred times, and there is an excess of copulatives. The descriptions of the dress of the three personified characters, though doubtless relished at the time, are cumulatively a little cloying. But the skill with which the technicalities of hunting (as seen through a poacher's eye in an age when poaching was almost respectable), of hawking, and of alchemy are accommodated to the alliterative line is impressive. We seem to be eyewitnesses as the narrator lodges his dog in the bole of a birch tree, gauges the direction of the wind from the light leaves of the young birch, and creeps under a crab-apple tree to take aim.

Like the Theseus of *The Knight's Tale*, he is hunting on a fine May morning, the occasion for a seasonal introduction more elaborate than that in *Piers Plowman*. As dawn breaks we watch hart and hind, fox, polecat, and hare scatter to their lairs, but not before the narrator has caught sight of a deer:

> With auntlers one aythere[1] syde egheliche[2] longe
> The ryalls[3] full richely raughten[4] frome the myddes,
> With surryals[5] full semely appon sydes twayne . . .   (28–30)

[1] *each*   [2] *wondrously*   [3] *second branches of the horn*   [4] *extended*
[5] *branches of the antler above the 'royals'*

The gnats are biting madly and stinging his eyes, but he brings down his prey, and grallochs it in the approved style: an intricate operation here described in even greater detail than in *Gawain*. Weary from this exertion, he falls asleep to dream the 'full dreghe swevyn' (long dream) that he proceeds to recount.

It is a dream of the encounter of three men: Youthe, Medill Elde, and Elde; a theme linked with the hunting prologue only in so far as Youth is depicted as an active man (aged 30) on a tall horse and with a hawk on his wrist; long-limbed and (like the Green Knight) narrow-waisted, he is dressed in green and wears a rich chaplet. All his garments are decked with precious stones. In the fourteenth century—witness *Gawain* once again—a man was judged by his horse. Youth's has a rich crupper and (painted) saddle of sycamore. Middle Age (aged 60) is figured by the abundance of his material goods and his concern with the increase of his winning:

> Of mukkyng[1], of marlelyng[2], and mendynge of howses
>
> . . . .
>
> Of purches of ploughe-londes, of parkes full faire.   (142 ff.)

[1] *muck-spreading*   [2] *fertilizing with marl*

Age (aged 100), dressed in black, is bald, blind, 'babberlipped' and lame, envious and angry, yet practising his devotions.

When Youth, sitting upright in his saddle, makes a complaint 'paramours' to his lady, and Middle Age reproaches him with squandering his wealth, he replies that he had sooner be a knight-at-arms 'and see a kene knyghte come and cowpe [contend at tourney] with myselven', or ride a-hawking by the river-side, or embrace fair damsels, or read knightly romances, or dance carols in hall than have any of Middle Age's wealth and property. His talk is as gay as his attire, and the only answer Middle Age can make is the gnomic 'Fole es that with foles delys' (264).

The 'flyting' concludes with Age rebuking both his predecessors, bidding them 'Make your mirror by me' (as Henryson's Cresseid adjures the women of Troy), and remember the *Neuf Preux*, the Nine Worthies. Which brings us to the true *raison d'être* of the poem: a detailed if inaccurate exemplary account of Hector, Alexander, Julius Caesar; Joshua, David, Judas Maccabeus; Arthur, Charlemagne, Godfrey of Bouillon. The theme was in vogue in the late fourteenth century and a splendid tapestry now in the Cloisters Museum, New York, bears evidence. That the poet drew on any one source cannot be shown, though his account of Alexander resembles that of Jacques de Longuyon's *Vœux du Paon* (early fourteenth century); the only *auctores* the poet himself acknowledges are the inevitable Dares and Dictys—the chroniclers of the Trojan war—and the *Brut*. The account degenerates into an elaborate exercise in name-dropping, among the names being that 'trewe knight' Troilus; Eli and Enoch (both shut up till the coming of Antichrist); Jason (and his fleece); Pharaoh, whose disaster at the Red Sea is confused with Joshua's crossing of Jordan; Uriah and Bathsheba; Merlin, Lancelot, and Galahad the good; Gawain, also 'good', here flings Arthur's sword into the mere—in some sources this is credited to Bedivere, Gawain having been killed in action—and sees Morgan and others steer off with Arthur in the boat. Many other knights of the Round Table are also named, as are Charlemagne's douzepers; Ganylon figures as Genyone—and other oddities (Arthur fights a dragon, not a giant at St Michael's Mount) suggest that the poet was not altogether at ease with this material.

The long roll call of the valiant is followed by a shorter catalogue of the wise: Aristotle (for his alchemy), Virgil (for his mirror), Solomon (for his biblical books), Merlin (for his necromancy). Finally comes a list of lover-knights: Amadas (and his Ydoine), Samson (and Dalilah), Ypomadon (and 'La Fere de Calabre'), Eglamour (and Cristabel), Tristram (and Iseut): all graven in earth. The parade is in fact an excuse to introduce the ancient *Ubi Sunt* motif.* Where is now Dame Dido, or Candace, comely queen of Carthage, Penelope or Gaynore (Guenevere) the gay? Nothing is certain but Death, uncertain only in his coming. *Vanitas Vanitatum*; *in Inferno nulla est redemptio*. But Age, not lingering over these commonplaces, exhorts his hearers to shrive themselves betimes. Though the central part of the poem forgets its beginning, Age's closing words are impressive: 'Deth dynges on my dore, I dare no lenger abide'. As the sun sets a bugle wakes the dreamer—as if it is echoing the dim horn of Death? He gets to his feet and hurries back to town. In this context the closing invocation (offering a very late example of the Old English traditional phrase 'deore dryhten') plays a more than conventional role:

> The dere Dryghten[1] the day dele[2] us of thi blisse
> And Mary, that is myld quene, amend us of oure mysse.[3]
>
>   Amen. Amen.

> [1] *Lord*   [2] *grant*   [3] *sin*

In the same manuscript is found another dream-vision in alliterative verse, *Wynnere and Wastoure*. A prologue laments the evils of the age in gloomily prophetic style:

> When wawes[1] waxen schall wilde, and walles bene doun,
> And hares appon herthe-stones schall hurcle in hir fourme[2],
> And eke boyes of [no] blode, with boste and with pryde,

* Traced by E. Gilson, 'De la Bible à François Villon' in *Les Idées et les lettres* (Paris, 1932).

VERSE, DIDACTIC AND HOMILETIC

Schall wedde ladyes in londe, and lede at hir will,
Thene dredfull domesdaye it draweth neghe aftir.   (13–17)

¹ *waves*   ² *cower in their lairs*

The poet relates how he once went wandering in the west, lay down beside a hawthorn (a tree often associated with magic), fell asleep, and dreamt a marvellous dream. In a fair green plain two hosts in full battle array confronted each other. As he prayed for peace 'till the prynce come, / For he was worthiere in witt than any wy [person] ells', he became aware of a 'caban' (? pavilion) adorned with English besants and garters, and the motto in the English tongue 'Hethyng have the hathell that any harme thynkes' (= *Honi soit qui mal y pense*). A king 'com- liche clade in kirtill and mantill' sends a messenger to forbid any warrior to strike a blow or to 'stir no nearer' with a host in his realm. The banners of the armies show that on one side are the pope, guardians of the law, Franciscans and Dominicans, Carmelites and Austin friars, and mer- chants, while on the other side are men of arms, bold squires, and many bowmen, who, if they begin to fight, will never stop until 'owthir here [either host] appone hethe be hewen to dethe'. The leaders of both sides are summoned before the king, who welcomes them as 'both servants of our house', and plead their case before him. One is called Winner

a wy that alle this werlde helpis,
For I ledes¹ cane lere, thurgh ledyng of witt.   (222–3)

¹ *men*

Unlike Waster, the other leader, he gathers and gleans, rather than opening the purse. Waster rejoins that there is little use in storing up 'wyde howses full of wolle sakkes', for hoarded wealth may rot or rust or feed the rats. The debate becomes heated, and colloquial in tone: 'Then es there bott "fille in" [pour out] and "feche forthe" . . . "Wee- hee", and "Worthe up", wordes ynewe.' Winner waxes sarcastic about Waster's sumptuous dinners:

. . . The bores hede schall be broghte with [bayes] appon lofte,
Buk-tayles full brode in brothes there besyde,
Venyson with the frumentes¹, and fesanttes full riche . . .

(332–4)

¹ *dishes of wheat boiled in milk*

and so on through a series of alliterating courses ('barnacle geese and bitterns and many billed snipes', etc.). But would you wish prelates to live just as ordinary priests in charge of parishes? (says Waster)—let the people have their part, 'sum gud morsell of mete to mend with their chere':

54

> If fewlis[1] flye schold forthe, and fongen[2] be never
> And wild bestis in the wodde wone[3] al thaire lyve
> And fisches flete[4] in the flode, and ichone [fr]ete[5] other
> Ane henne at[6] ane halpeny by halfe yeris ende,
> Schold not a ladde be in londe a lorde for to serve. (384–8)

[1] *birds* [2] *caught* [3] *stay* [4] *float* [5] *eat* [6] *i.e. would cost*

Whoever wins wealth must find a waster; for if it grieves one man it gladdens another. An incomplete manuscript robs us of a formal conclusion. In the last lines of the fragments, the king looks 'lovely' on his liegemen, and sends Winner abroad for a time to the Pope of Rome, where he will be well kept by the cardinals, whereas Waster is to go to Cheapside and pick clean any monied visitors—the more he wastes his wealth the more it will please Winner. Gollancz interpreted the poem, with its reference to the Garter, the Black Prince, and Edward III, etc. as a topical pamphlet (probably referring to the years 1352–3). But his identification of the two sides as representing the aristocracy and the merchant class does not seem to fit all the details of the poem. Others have seen in it a sharp attack on Edward III for his extravagance and his wars. There is probably a more general opposition of opposed vices of niggardliness and prodigality. There is something of the detachment of *The Owl and the Nightingale* in the way Winner and Waster put their points of view. Perhaps the lost ending (as in the case of that poem) would have been inconclusive; perhaps it might have suggested a balance to be found in a *largesse* tempered by *mesure* or moderation.

Mum and the Sothsegger, another alliterative poem, is primarily a moral discourse on the fatal faults of Richard II and his court: prolix, flaccid, repetitive, and poorly articulated. It shares a great many lines, alliterative phrases, and idioms with the earlier part of *Piers Plowman* but lacks that poem's moral and religious energy and control. Like *Piers*, it (or rather, one part of it: the two extant manuscripts are defective) is divided into a prologue and *passus*, but the divisions are arbitrary, corresponding to no breaks or new beginnings in the narrative. It is depressing to think that the older, longer, and greater poem did not inspire more worthy successors; but most epoch-making masterpieces—witness the history of Miltonic verse—are followed by inferior imitations. The conservatism of this versifier is of a different order from Langland's: jaundiced, and lacking a coherent social or political philosophy; and undiluted denunciation or exhortation soon grows tedious. Yet to judge it by Langlandian standards is perhaps unfair: it is essentially a topical poem that would be more pertinent and more appealing in Henry IV's day than in ours; and it apparently retained an appeal for 50 years or more, the extant manuscripts dating from c.1460.

It has no continuous allegory, but intermittently draws on natural history as presented in the Bestiaries or the encyclopaedias of Bartholomaeus Anglicus (which Trevisa had recently translated). Its ethic is traditional, though momentarily enlarged by appeals to the doctrine of *Scito te ipsum* —know thyself—that, thanks partly to St Bernard, had found earlier vernacular expression in the fourteenth century.* The King is told that he should choose as guides knights who 'knowe well hemself' (Fragment R, iii, 200): flatterers know 'ne God neither good man ne thaymself nothir' (Fragment M, 130: the appearance of this sentiment in both fragments is one reason for supposing that they are from the same pen). Shakespeare could have learnt nothing from the poem, but students of *Richard II* will find in it a salutary counterpoise to some Tudor versions of the usurpation.

The narrative as we now have it opens with the narrator learning as he passes through Bristol—most of such allusions including one to 'the chyders of Chester' are to the West Country, where the second fragment was found—that, whilst Richard was fighting 'the wild Irish', Henry Bolingbroke had landed in the East. The news emboldens him to speak out boldly. Richard's downfall is due to wilful waste, covetousness, and evil advice; he is *redeles*, lacking in good counsel: an alliterative epithet that sticks, as Unready (< OE *unræd*, 'of evil counsel') has stuck to Æthelred. The 'Mirrors for Princes' that are a feature of late medieval didactic literature must have encouraged such attention to a ruler's shortcomings. Richard's crown had once blazed with jewels—poets of the period, from Langland to the author of *Pearl*, never lose an occasion to include the topos of virtuous stones—but where are the pearls and rubies now? One might as well hunt a hare with a tabor as try to find them. Servants and masters are now alike, counsellors badly chosen (the allusion is to Bushy, Bagot, and Green, whose notoriety Shakespeare has confirmed). Unless Richard helps himself, 'his harvest is in'—one of the many colloquial phrases that lend some flavour to the work. But the chief complaint is against the evils of livery and maintenance. The badge of the white hart (worn by the angels in the Wilton Diptych) had become a symbol of his retainers' extortions. They had 'plucked the plomayle [plumage] from the pore skynnes'. But these harts are moulting now, fleeing to the forests, and they have lost ten score of homely *hearts*. Reason,

---

* See J. A. W. Bennett, '*Nosce te ipsum*: Some Medieval Interpretations', in *J. R. R. Tolkien, Scholar and Storyteller*, ed. Mary Salu and Robert T. Farrell (Ithaca, NY, 1979), 138–58.

taking up the tale as abruptly as he leaves it, endorses all this, with a few reservations, and the imagery of the hunt is now given another twist. Had Richard cherished his poor greyhound (Bolingbroke) and had pity on his lean deer ('rascaille'), he would have kept his 'head deer'.

For a time the image changes and the symbolic possibilities of Bolingbroke as an Eagle are exploited to the full: the eagle

> hasteth him in hervest to hovyn[1] his bryddis—
> And besieth him besely to breden[2] hem feedrin   (ii. 146–7)

[1] *brood over*   [2] *spread out his plumage for them*

('feedrin', OE *federhama*, is found only here in Middle English alliterative verse, though Gavin Douglas will revive it).

With Passus III we return to the properties of the hart, who, when a hundred years old, feeds on venom that prolongs his life. The role of Eagle (which like the partridge returns to its young) is then explained to Hick Heavyhead ('hard is thi nolle'). One of the faults of Richard's cronies is fine dress—sleeves that slide on the earth and slashed 'Duche' coats; a marginal note (presumably the poet's) applies Luke 7: 25: *qui mollibus vestiuntur in domibus regum sunt*). Seeing Witt (alias Wisdom) standing at the end of the hall (= Westminster):

> Well homelych yhelid[1] in an *holsum* gyse,
> Not overelong, but ordeyned in the olde schappe,
> With grete browis ybente, and a berde eke
>
> (iii. 212–14)

[1] *covered*

these dandies bid him pack off. Every kingdom 'under roof of the rainbow', the poet then avers, depends on the three orders of Counsellors (replacing the *Oratores* of the traditional trio), Warriors, and Labourers. It is as ridiculous for twenty-four year olds to be counsellors as for a cow (or chough?) to hop in a cage. Rulers should be no respecters of persons, not waste money on dancing and piping—and not stay up to all hours. The list of abuses that follows is of interest chiefly to historians.* The well-tried metaphor of the ship of state makes a brief appearance (iv. 72 ff.).

The second fragment, in which Mum appears, is equally discursive. His name bespeaks his character as a flatterer, reluctant, unlike the Sothsegger, to voice home truths. After a brief altercation with the poet, who has launched into a eulogy of Henry IV, witty and wise, cunning in war, trusting in the Trinity, Mum fades out and the poet

---

* On iv. 58 see K. B. McFarlane, 'Parliament and Bastard Feudalism', *Tr. RHS*, 4th series, xxvi (1944), 55 n.

resorts first to the works of Sidrac, Solomon, Seneca, then to the clerks of Cambridge, Oxford, and Orléans, and finally, to the Seven Sciences. Enthroned above these sits a 'Doctor of Doubts', but he has not much to say beyond recommending resort to clerks who

> walken fourth in the worlde and wonen[1] with lordes
> And with a covetous croke[2] Saynt Nicholas thay throwen
> And travaillen no more on the texte, but tournen to the glose
>
> (M 386–8)

> [1] dwell   [2] trick

i.e. they throw up study (St Nicholas being the patron saint of scholars) to flatter ('glose' = flattering gloss) patrons. In fact, the narrator goes to the friars, who assert that Mum is their friend. Their professions are then scrutinized and it is concluded that they are of Cain's kindred—an old taunt, here attributed to 'Armagh', i.e. Arch-bishop Fitzralph, who had preached against them in 1357—and joust against Jesus. Monks and seculars prove to be no better. The cata-loguing of their faults drags on drearily despite Mum's warning that it is of no avail. We glimpse Sothsegger dining with Dread in a private chamber having drunk 'dumb-seed' whilst Mum banquets with the Mayor. At last the poet, worn out, falls asleep, to dream (like *Piers*) that he is walking in a wilderness. Near a coomb (a hillside valley, a term evidenced only here in Middle English) he comes to the crest of a hill and looks out over new mown meadows, reaped cornfields, a fast-flowing river full of fish:

> The breris[1] with thaire beries bent over the wayes
> As honysoucles hongyng uppon eche half
> Chesteynes[2] and chiries that children desiren
> Were loigged undre leves ful lusty to seen   (M 898–901)

> [1] briars   [2] chestnuts

It is very much an ideal landscape, described without regard to the seasons. Hounds hunt the rabbit and the hare: 'For kisshyng of his croupe acauntwise he wente' (M 915) (i.e. for fear of having his rump 'kissed' he makes off with oblique runs). There are sheep and lambs, cows and colts, and, inevitably, harts and hinds, reindeer and roebuck; and birds babbling on every bush. The passage, though a catalogue, comes just in time to relieve the tedium of diatribe, and the sight—possibly owing something to the vision of Middle Earth in *Piers Plowman*—brings comfort to the dreamer. The glorious garden of a franklin's house catches his eye. An old man is tending a beehive, killing the drones as thick as they come. He explains that they are the worst enemies for they 'traveylen no twynte [jot] but taken of the beste'. The margin quotes St Bernard: *qui non laborat non manducet*, and the text itself acknowledges that the following discourse on the economy of the hive derives from Bartholomaeus (which is not to say that the poet himself knew nothing of bees or hives). Though the political application is obvious, the poet professes that it is 'too mystic for me'. But he is emboldened to ask the gardener whether Mum or Sothsegger should have the mastery. The inevitable answer is that Mum has been the master these many years: witness Parliament, where knights of the shire who should show the sores of the realm and 'berste oute alle the boicches and blaynes [boils and sores] of the hert' do nothing. Where does Sothsegger dwell? In man's heart and mind (as Truth did in *Piers Plowman*) which is of easy access, though Antichrist is ever on the watch to let in Covetise, and Dread to bar the Sothsegger. 'When you wake write down my words':

> lete no feynt herte
> Abate thy blessid bisynes of thy boke-making
> Til hit be complete to clapsyng[1]   (M 1280–2)

[1] *being given a clasp*

The dreamer wakes, to meditate once more on the veracity of dreams, in particular of Joseph's.

There follows an examination for the king's behoof of a bag full of books: a novel method of categorizing abuses and still of interest as the first venture into English bibliography. Here are many a privy 'poysé' ('in bokes unbredid [? opened] in balade-wise made'); a quire of acquittance; a visitation volume of fifteen leaves; a pair of pamphlets about bishops; 'a copie ... of culmes [contracts]'—a figure for false rumours, which unaccountably leads to the *exemplum* of Genghis Khan (from Mandeville) and how he came to be king; and that, equally unexpectedly, prompts the comment that the 'comun' (i.e. labourers) should not oppose the king; a scroll for squires; a writ 'of high wil [great purport] ywrite al newe'; a ragman roll made by Ragnal (a devil); a frayed 'forelle' (parchment book-cover); a 'librarie of [i.e. about] lordes'; a copy (writing) about covetise; a till (? box) of testaments; a 'cedule' (a slip of parchment attached to a roll) 'subtly indited'. On each term is hung a series of gnomic sentiments and topical warnings or exhortations, ranging from sceptical remarks about trust in Merlin's prophecies or astrology to traditional views on nefarious executors.

The text as we have it breaks off abruptly with a contrast between bishops of old time and of today. One has the sense of a writer who could have gone on for ever. He may have been a Sothsegger, but there are times when we wish that he had taken Mum's advice to heart.

(iv) *The South English Legendary*; *Scots Lives of the Saints*; *The Vision of Tundale*

To describe *The South English Legendary* as a collection of saints' lives is to deter a modern reader as well as to misconceive the purpose and appeal of a compilation that, to judge from the number of surviving manuscripts, was popular and well used. The reasons for the order and choice in the extant collection remain obscure; nor are the sources drawn on always identifiable. No compiler would presume to alter his authorities; but he would feel justified in elaborating detail or making it seem pertinent to an English audience. And though the Martyrologies provide a fixed sequence of events in a saint's life and passion, not all the saints in the *Legendary* were martyrs. Some (like St Dunstan, and St Wulstan of Worcester, native hero of the post-Conquest years) are here by virtue of their role in the development of the English Church; so that the collection served *inter alia* as a guide to Church and even to national history. It seems also to have served to popularize the biblical stories of the Apostles. The Life of St Luke provides the occasion for accounts of the other evangelists, and of their attributes, whilst the legend of St Michael leads to an excursus on planetary lore, cosmography, the causes of thunder and lightning, the nature of birth, and of the soul.

This is not the place to apply Bollandist criteria to such legends nor to justify the presentation of martyrs (*milites Christi*) who delighted to be tortured, and survived a series of torments until such time as Omnipotence allowed their death. We must rather consider the reasons for their popularity. It was not simply the appeal of the pious, but also of the marvellous and the remote, an element present in all medieval (and indeed much classical) literature. Like the Bible, saints' legends provided escape from insularity and the commonplace—a function that was later to be assumed by romance, and later still by film and television. But a feature of the *English Legendary* is the attention it gave to English saints and English history. It was something to learn that saints like Kenelm had walked these clouded hills not so many centuries ago, that the knife that killed Edward the Elder was yet to be seen at Caversham (and that some of the saints, like St Bridget in her diary, had lived homely, useful lives). Something patriotic was stirred by the tale of St Oswald, flecked with realism as it is when he is made bishop of York as well as of Worcester—'the godeman hadde inou to done to loky bothe to'. Here again such stories as 'non Angli sed angeli' receive popular form, even if the word-play in that phrase has to be lamely rendered as 'Englisse . . . englise iliche'. The saintly Chad is contrasted with later archbishops who ride on palfreys lest they stub their toe.

The compiler is hindered by no false sense of the dignity of history: the bad Pope who opposes St Hilary is 'taken short' and dies in a privy. He allows himself a smile over the priest in the Legend of St Benedict who miscounted Lent (Lenten fastings are in fact the theme of an unusually long, priestly comment). More typical is the writer's ejaculation when the waters make way for St Alban:

> Louerd muche[1] is thi mighte, woso[2] him wolde understande
> Woso hadde me thincth such an hine[3] to lede him aboute ilome[4]
> He ne dorste noght care worth a bene to wuch water he come.
>
> (p. 240)*

> [1] *great* [2] *whoever* [3] *servant* [4] *continually*

The conditions of a martyr's life are accommodated to contemporary understanding: so St Agnes's would-be lover is described in terms of *amour courtois*: 'for stille mornynge that he made he werth swuthe lene [became very thin]'.

The interest was as often in devils and hell as in heaven and martyrs; indeed in the tale of St Patrick's Purgatory and Knight Owein the account of hell and devils is fuller and more vivid than in any rendering elsewhere of celestial joys. But devils are sometimes presented as pathetic creatures, powerless against Christ. Belial pleads for pity when Juliana tortures him, and we see in him the sketch of the personality that was to become Screwtape. The reality of devils (and of false gods, 'the devil's chickens') constantly gives verve to the narrative. When Dunstan breaks the devil's nose, he flies off crying:

> Out! wat hath this calwe[1] ido[2], wat hath this calwe ido?'
> In the contreie man hurde wide how the ssrewe[3] gradde[4] so.
>
> (p. 207)

> [1] *bald man* [2] *done* [3] *fiend* [4] *cried*

When the devil leads Alphege over ditch and hedge 'and many a foul slade', the writer adds his own imprecation:

> Nou sorwe and sor him beo next fram toppe to the to
> And as wide him worthe wo as the sonne ssineth[1] aday . . . (p. 152)
>
> [1] *shines*

* Page references are to the edition of C. D'Evelyn and A. J. Mill (EETS ccxxxv–vi, ccxliv, 1956–9).

Similarly, of devils that afflict men in sleep:

'Daithat[1] such luther[2] chamberlein that awaketh men so sore
And God yive[3] hom sorwe inou and evere the leng the more.

(p. 409)

[1] *A curse on*　　[2] *wicked*　　[3] *give*

The long tale of St Brendan's voyages has fewer disquisitions and
reflections than its Latin original. Brendan himself comments to his
companions on the devils whose stench and smoke appal them: 'Hou
thincth yow? Was this a murie pas?'—rhetorical questions not found in
the stiffer and more prolix Latin. Here is the paradise of birds and the
island on which Judas, thanks to a casual act of charity in his former
life, gains some relief from torment, and the charming story of the
otter who brought tinder and a supply of fish. In Brendan's voyage we
pass beyond miracles and torments to *mirabilia*, the marvels of the
Lord, especially the marvels in the deep: 'Muche wonder me [one]
may iseo, wo-so wole abute wende.' It helped to create the taste for
travellers' tales that Mandeville, and the sixteenth-century voyagers,
were to satisfy. Wanderings of another kind figure in the narrative of
the Quest of Seth for the oil of life, which is told with feeling. Theophilus's pact with the devil, so illustrative of medieval religious and
feudal feeling, provides a simple and moving expression of the Mercy
of Christ. For—says the Virgin:

he [Christ] was ibore[1] of sunfol men, and for tham to dethe ido[2]
He mot nede[3] to tham beo milde, for righte kunde[4] it wolde so.

(p. 225)

[1] *born*　　[2] *put*　　[3] *must needs*　　[4] *nature*

Each life concludes with a prayer that we may come to heaven and to
the company of the saint commemorated.

The legends are told in journeyman's *septenarii*, chiefly self-
contained couplets, occasionally falling into verse-patterns later
found in *The Ancient Mariner*. They represent a popular equivalent to
the contemporary *Golden Legend* of Jacobus de Voragine. When that
ubiquitous Latin text was rendered into English prose in the fifteenth
century the writers sometimes drew on this earlier work. Caxton's
Golden Legend (which included additions of his own) made a much
longer book, yet it was reprinted five times before the Reformation:
evidence that the appeal of such works was perennial.

A Northern counterpart of *The South English Legendary* appears at
the end of the fourteenth century in Scottish dialect and octosyllabic
couplets. It seems to have developed by accretion. After a brief

prologue it begins with the lives of St Peter and Paul, followed by those of other Apostles, Mark, Luke, and Barnabas; Mary Magdalene and Martha are followed by Mary of Egypt; then comes a miscellaneous group, including the Seven Sleepers of Ephesus, more women saints, amongst whom Eustace and George are inserted, a sequence including John the Baptist, Cosmo, and Damian, and finally ten virgins. The absence of a liturgical pattern allows or encourages the inclusion of historical excursuses on (e.g.) Nero, Julian the Apostate (listed with the more respectable Julians), and (under James the Less) the destruction of Jerusalem; so that the work has more than pietistic or didactic interest. Simon Magus, whose tricks as a 'tregetour' Dunbar was to allude to, figures more than once. It seems likely that the compiler added to an original core as he found new material. He engagingly presents himself as searching in 'the goldine legende' for biographical details about Blaise; and on that work, which he once, if inadvertently, calls 'holy writ', he drew so often that one may regard his collection as the earliest English rendering of the book. Much of what strikes us today as novel or extraneous can be traced to the *Legend*: including the explication of the symbols of the Evangelists at the beginning of *Mark*, the astrological passage following a discourse on providence in *Clement* (xxi. 377 ff.), and the tale appended to *Andrew* of the Bishop whose patron the saint was, yet who was almost seduced by a fair virgin. The writer (or writers) also drew on Vincent of Beauvais, the '*Vitas Patrum*' ('fadris Lyfys': cf. xxv. 617), and biographies of particular saints. Thus the life of Mary of Egypt owes its unusual brio to the seventh-century *Vita* by Sophronius; and the long account of the Scottish Ninian vividly renders Ailred's *Vita*, to which is added 'a lytell tale . . . that in my tyme befel': viz. the healing of John Balormy whom 'I kend weile mony day' (xl. 1367). The *Vita* drawn on for the legend of Machor is now lost.

The compiler(s) evidently had some Latin (and Patristic) learning, and access to a monastic library that included *auctores* such as Cassian. The very first couplet translates a saying of Cato's—supported, surprisingly, by a reference to 'the Romance of the Rose'. The martyrdom of Paul provides excuse for adverting to the death of Seneca, 'thoct it be ypocrifa [apocryphal]'. The assertion found in *The South English Legendary* that Nero was prompted to burn Rome by memory of the destruction of Troy is here repeated, but there are no further allusions to secular literature. The writer's grasp of proper names in his sources is shaky: Gregory of Tours (Turonensis) becomes Gregory of Turin, Basil is confounded with Blaise (xxv. 659), Radegund with Cunegunda (xxii. 693).

The writer's professed motive is to eschew idleness himself and to stir other men to follow the example of the saint whose life he sets forth. Each legend concludes with an invocation, sometimes private, sometimes a general prayer that the saint will 'owre helpe be, now and ay'. The didactic or admonitory element varies markedly. It is absent in *Clement* (a life full of incident, including those illustrated in the mural cycle still visible in his church in Rome), but conspicuous at the close of *Paul*, in *Christopher* (few folk who look on his image as preserving them from an evil death know aught but his name), and in *Blaise* (about whom the writer himself knew nothing till he found the account in the *Legend*).

For stylistic, linguistic, and lexical reasons the view that John Barbour, the author of *The Bruce*, compiled this lengthy work is untenable. The writer himself tells us that he was a minister of holy church who could not work 'for gret eld and febilnes' but who finds solace in translation. One would think that 35,000 lines in rhymed couplets might be beyond the capacity of the man who at the close of the tenth legend complains that age and infirmity 'mare to sa [say] now lattis [prevent] me'. The author of Legend xxxvi (*John the Baptist*) refers to 'a buk I mad of the birth / Of Jesu Criste' (991–2) and to another in which he recorded the genealogy of Our Lady (1214–15). These themes indeed occur in the opening pages of the work, but the references may well be to books composed by a later writer who added this legend and others.

There is little that is distinctly Scottish in the compilation. Columba finds no place, though his disciple Machor appears. Margaret of Scotland is mentioned only incidentally (along with Elizabeth of Hungary). On the other hand, no distinctly English saints are included, unless one counts George; though in *John* is inserted a tale told by Ailred of Rievaulx of Edward the Confessor—here unpardonably confused with St Edmund.

A certain degree of 'naturalization' is achieved. The Knight who sent his ring to St Edmund (*sic*)

> had bene in landis syndry
> for til[1] haf lofe[2] of chevalry   (v. 611–12)

[1] *to*   [2] *praise*

A wreck in the days of Pilate is 'made escheat, goods and man'; the *telonium* of Matt. 9: 9 becomes, as in the Wycliffite rendering a 'tollbooth'. Occasionally a homely native apophthegm, such as 'ful harde is hungre in hale mawe [stomach]' adds salt to the narrative. Poetic tags are remarkably few and alliterative phrases like 'neither tongue nor tooth', 'brig nor bat' (bridge nor boat) are rare. The affective passages are the best: thus the grief of Alexis's mother is well conveyed in a lament beginning:

> Quhy[1] did thou this, my sonne dere,
> That of myne ene[2] suld be the lycht?
> Ful butlas bale[3] thou has me dycht[4] ... (xxiv. 457–60)

[1] *why* [2] *eyes* [3] *sorrow which cannot be remedied* [4] *brought*

St Andrew's notable invocation to the Cross on which he was to be martyred is movingly rendered from the version in his *Passio*. In general, passages in *oratio recta* are the most vivid; as when Mary Magdalene berates the prince of Marseilles in a vision (xix). The narrative parts flow almost too smoothly, in a monotone. Yet there is some variation in couplet structures. It is not always end-stopped, and the caesura may fall about anywhere, witness:

> Thane Josaphus, as a wicht[1] man
> And swepyr[2] alswa, a swerd gat; thane
> Bad his falow suthly chece ...

> (viii. 513–15)

[1] *strong* [2] *nimble*

Considerations of artistic economy did not weigh with the legendarists any more than with Orm or the compilers of *Cursor Mundi*. The longer the work the greater proof it gave of the writer's dedication; just as in a later century the more aureate the poem the more it bespoke the poet's devoutness.

With the fourteenth-century version of the twelfth-century Latin *Visio Tnugdali*—the vision of Tundal—we pass again into that Otherworld which in the Middle Ages was as real and as absorbing as the present one. The Latin text reflects varied spiritual, biblical, and allegorical patterns of thought, including those of Cistercian asceticism. It is correctly called a *Visio*, as distinct from a *somnium* or a *phantasma*; it cast its spell even over Matthew Arnold. The vision, recounted by one Brother Mark, befell a nobleman named Tundal as he lay for three days in what seemed the sleep of death, when his soul followed his guardian angel, first to a valley dark and terrible where souls lay burning, then to a great mountain of ice and fire. By a long plank, meant only for the elect, it crossed a deep valley, coming to a still narrower and longer bridge, blocked to Tundal because of his theft of a cow in his former life. Below it lay monsters, ready, like those in the much earlier *Visio Pauli*, to seize sinners as they fell.

The horrors of hell are counterbalanced by the sight of an earthly paradise, full of many-coloured flowers and fruit of all kinds such as Lactantius had described in *De Phoenice*, which had long before found its place in the English library. But the *Visio* (which Mark avers he has translated from the Irish) abounds in reminiscences of an earlier vision of the Irish Adamnán, the visit of Knight Owein to St Patrick's Purgatory—located in an island in County Donegal—as recounted in *The South English Legendary*. Amongst those Tundal meets are Donacus (Donough McCarthy), King of Munster in 1127, Conchobar, King of Thomond (Conor O'Brien), and Cormac, Tundal's lord.

In the paradisal garden are souls that have been cleansed by purgatorial pain:

> But yete hens may thai noght
> To the blisse aboven be brought.
> All yif[1] thai be clansed of alle ill
> Her mote[2] thai abyde Goddis wille . . . (1545–8)

> [1] *although*   [2] *must*

—a passage that has been taken to reflect the heresy proposed by John XXII who thought that some of the just do not enjoy the Beatific Vision before the Last Judgement.* The garden has a well of life-giving and rejuvenating water. Tundal and his angel come to a hall bright as the sun—the roof seems of carbuncle; door or windows there are none. On a richly enamelled chair sits Cormac:

> His clothyng was of ryche hewe,
> Tundale ful welle that kyng knewe. (1635–6)

The scene recalls Orfeo's visit to Pluto's palace (see pp. 143–7 below). The hall is furnished with cups and chalices richly dight, with 'boystes' (pyxes) and 'tabilles paynted richely'; crowds of singing people bring gifts to the king—the pilgrims to whom he has shown charity, and churchmen he has helped. But he has still to suffer; suddenly the house becomes dark as night and Cormac groans with anguish, as prayers rise up:

> 'Lorde God, yif hit thy wille be
> Have mercy on hym, and peté.' (1699–700)

The pair come next to a high wall of silver, and beyond that is one of gold and one of jewels. Their significance is not now clear. Friends of Tundal, chaste and holy, come up to embrace him, and call him by name. Within the wall of gold shines 'the grete bryghtnes of Goddis face'; crowned martyrs, those of Rev. 7: 14, sing Alleluia; others wearing 'purpur and byse' dwell in pavilions bedecked with

* G. Mollat, *The Popes at Avignon, 1305–1378*, tr. J. Love (London, 1963), 22.

'besandes', singing in 'trebull and mene, and burdowne': they are faithful monks, friars, nuns, and canons. Pious laymen also find a place. A tree that is compared to Holy Church bears flowers red, white, blue, and yellow—possibly alluding to the colours of Aaron's vestments. Beyond the jewelled wall

> Prevé wordes thay herde than
> That shuld be shewed to no man.   (2099–100)

We recall the 'things not lawful to utter' seen by St Paul. And they see the Trinity itself, a sight that is 'fode to angelles' and life to holy souls. Tundal can now look back and see 'alle thyng, both evell and goode', all pains and joys, all creation:

> He knewe what thyng that he wolde
> Wythoute ony boke to beholde   (2147–8)

The saints Tundal now meets are Irish saints—Ruadan and Patrick—and of the bishops the first is Celestine, bishop of Armagh (1106) and the next Malachy, his successor. There is a seat reserved 'For one of oure brether dere / That comes not yet' (2217–18)—perhaps St Bernard. Tundal would fain stay forever here, but must return to the body and cleanse himself from sin. At this injunction his soul waxes heavy, 'and feld hit charged with the body'. Crying for mercy, he begs a priest to hear his confession and give him communion. He narrates his experiences to the bystanders, gives all his goods to the poor, 'for hym to pray' and preaches the word of God. It is an unexpected conclusion, very practical, and literally down-to-earth. However we describe the *Visio*, we cannot call it 'escapist'.

The English translator evidently exercises a certain freedom, and perhaps did not perceive all the distinctions made in his original. There are some likenesses to the contemporary poem *Pearl*, but the *Visio* merits study in its own right, testifying as it does to the same concern that issued in the greatest poem of all poems, Dante's *Commedia*.

3

Layamon

Outside the literary histories Layamon (or, more properly, Laȝamon (Laghamon), that is 'Lawman') is almost unknown; not because he is a poor poet but because his *magnum opus* is lengthy, inaccessible, and for most readers today difficult or uncouth in appearance. His *Brut* (entitled 'Hystoria Brutonum' in the Cotton Caligula MS*) is the longest poem in English apart from *The Faerie Queene*, which in one sense it foreshadows, not only in giving Arthur an English context and an English value, but also in its archaic, not to say archaistic, language and spelling, which may have been intended to serve much the same purpose as do those features in Spenser and Doughty. His unique interest lies in the fact that though a literate poet, he continually shows signs and vestiges of an oral tradition that must have still operated in twelfth-century England in ways not distinctly different from those that Milman Parry has taught us to recognize in Homer: which is why Milman Parry's *The Making of Homeric Verse*, with its lucid and objective introduction by his son,† is a good starting point for any study of the *Brut*.

Size is never an index of quality. But the mere fact that a Worcestershire priest of no great intellectual pretensions could write 16,000 lines, about the beginning of the thirteenth century, on the history or pseudo-history of Britain is a pointer to the state and status of vernacular poetry a hundred years or so after the Conquest. Even a *remanieur* cannot work in a cultural void.

That Layamon is a *remanieur* is clear from his opening lines, in which he set down his intention to handle the noble deeds of Englishmen—'of Engle tha æthelæn tellen'; his search for sources; his discovery of an English version of Bede's History, of Latin books by 'Albin' (probably Alcuin—a reference intended presumably simply to add prestige) and 'the fæire Austin' (Augustine), and finally of the

---

* The poem survives in two composite manuscripts of the mid-thirteenth century. Various topical allusions indicate that it was composed in the reign of Richard I (1189–99). More than one scribe in some western scriptorium took pleasure in copying it. But until the Dissolution manuscripts often remained in their monasteries and it was Thomas Warton of Oxford in the eighteenth century who rediscovered the poem.

† Milman Parry, *The Making of Homeric Verse*, ed. A. Parry (Oxford 1971).

French book of Wace, a clerk who 'wel couthe [knew how to] writen'. In much the same way Geoffrey of Monmouth listed the 'sources' of his more famous *Historia Regum Britanniae* (*c*.1135) as Bede, Gildas, and 'jocund popular tales from Wales' (for his use of which—except as regards names—there is little evidence). Wace, who wrote not only a *Roman de Brut* but also a *Roman de Rou* (which covers the Norman Conquest as his *Brut* covers the British) is the first French poet who is more than a name; and Layamon is the first English poet plainly to put his name to his work and to tell us something of himself—as Wace does in the *Roman de Rou*.* Wace's *Brut*† is a verse expansion, 'French in form and feeling' of Geoffrey's *History*. Prosaic as much of Geoffrey's book is, it had an immediate and unprecedented popularity—Wace's work being one of the many signs of its impact. But Wace (as Layamon doubtless realized) had enlarged on Geoffrey by drawing on his own reading in Virgil, the Bible, contemporary English histories, and the French verse-chronicler Gaimar (from whom he probably took the tale of the fire-carrying sparrows that destroyed Cirencester).

We owe to Layamon the knowledge that Wace presented a copy of his *Brut* to Queen Eleanor, wife of Henry II; Wace would know that she was patron to other poets—including the Thomas who wrote the first *Tristram*, Marie de France, Benoit de St Maure. It is at the court of this English Queen that French literary history begins; and Layamon's epic chronicle is both a reflection of and a response to the poetic activity in French and Anglo-Norman that she encouraged.

Layamon's thumb-nail sketch of himself (like the tiny miniature inserted in the first capital of the Caligula MS) comes at the very beginning of his work. He is a priest, son of one Leovenath, and serves the 'noble church' (a modest Norman structure, still standing) of King's Areley, Worcs. In citing sources, real or supposititious, he is following, if unwittingly, the precedent of an Anglo-Saxon poet-priest, who writes stories 'swa ic on bocum fand'; and like a pious priest he beseeches the readers of these books (the phrase should strictly mean the books he consulted) to pray for his soul and his father's soul. Otherwise his work is bare of Christian sentiment. And he does not otherwise intrude upon his narrative. But from time to time he will announce his intentions, in a line like 'alse ich the wulle telle a [on] thisse bocspelle' (cf. 2635 and 2996), and he will comment on the story—sometimes as Chaucer does (of Arthur's parents, Uther and Ygaerne, he says 'I do not know whether she loved him')—and more often to indicate his sympathies and antipathies and to prompt ours.

* Ed. A. J. Holden, SATF xc (Paris, 1970–3), iii. 143–84, 5299–318, 11419–20.
† Ed. I. Arnold, SATF lxxx (Paris, 1938, 1940).

He engages us in another way, one familiar from later romances, when he marks breaks in the sequences of the narrative by the formula 'turn we again'. Occasionally he offers an explanatory gloss: the Roman forces 'that we call fyrds' 'were called in those days legions' (3002–3). Apart from the opening lines, he never refers to his *auctores* except in most general terms, like the *Gawain* poet's reference to his 'book' ('the bok as I herde say').

Layamon's professed purpose is to tell the noble deeds of English-men ('Engle'—a revealing term since the greater part of his poem concerns the 'Bruttes' or British whom the English kings eventually drove into Wales). We are to learn: 'Wat heo ihoten weoren and wonene heo comen' (what they were named and whence they came). The lines suggest a work of epic scope, such as the *Aeneid* or *Beowulf*.

There is no proof that Layamon knew *Beowulf* or like works, but his diction is undoubtedly redolent of the Old English epic and heroic verse. If he did in fact 'gon lithen wide yond thas leode' (journey far through this people) in search of authorities he must have visited the very places where manuscripts of Old English poetry were most likely to be found. In the West these would include the monasteries of Worcester, Pershore, Evesham, Wenlock, Tewkesbury (which certainly possessed a Wace in later times, as did Christ Church, Canterbury). His journey perhaps constituted the first 'voyage littéraire' of the kind that Leland the antiquary was to make in Henry VIII's time, and the Abbé Montfaucon later; and Layamon would have occasion to leaf through the contents of monastic libraries as no one before Leland did. In some of them (notably Worcester), Old English prose texts were being glossed or copied till late in the twelfth century. They probably possessed many more Old English texts than have survived. Henry of Huntingdon evidently knew and could read vernacular poems on historical themes, now lost; and such works would of themselves have stirred Layamon to emulation.

They may have shown greater metrical variety than the extant fragments of post-Conquest verse reveal. These fragments, however, are sufficient to show that the strict forms and rhythms of 'classical' verse had loosened. Thus 'The Grave', though alliterative, is in lines that fit no earlier pattern:

> Dureleas is thæt hus and dearc hit is withinnen
> Thær thu bist feste bidytt,[1] and dæth hefth tha cæye[2] . . .*

> [1] *shut in*   [2] *death has the key*

whilst the 'Soul's Address to the Body'† has lines with some rhyme

---

* Ed. A. Schröer, *Anglia* v. 289–90.   † Ed. R. Buchholz, *Erlanger Beiträge* vi (1890).

but with no alliteration at all. Layamon's metre, though later, is more conservative than this cloister verse, for reasons that will appear. Almost half of his verses follow the Old English pattern of two half-lines with two stresses in each, linked by alliteration, and with a varying number of unstressed syllables. The alliteration is sometimes double, sometimes crossed. To this structure Layamon sometimes adds rhyme (it may be inflectional rhyme only, or assonance), as an embellishment: 'Wace wes ihoten the wel couth writen' (he was called Wace, who well knew how to write). But many of his half-lines are linked only by rhyme and a shared stressed pattern: 'Nu biddeth Layamon alcne æthele mon.' This type probably results directly from Layamon's reading of Wace's rhymed couplets, but it is not an exact equivalent: Layamon is still under the influence of—and probably confused by—the native alliterative types, with their occasional rhyme. His most characteristic lines have both rhyme and alliteration, a combination that produces a wavering rhythm: 'Thus seide thet mæiden Cordoille and seothen set swithe stille' (1528).

The Old English alliterative line which makes its last appearance in Layamon—though modified versions will appear in the fourteenth century—was originally the vehicle of *oral* poetry. The division between oral and written poetry is not always easily drawn, especially in a period when verse was being written down to be recited, continuously or at intervals. The Norman Wace is writing for a listening audience—'ki vult *oir* et vult saveir' is his opening line. In England oral and written verse must have existed side by side for three or four centuries, and have interacted.

That Old English verse was originally oral the famous story of Cædmon, as told by Bede, sufficiently testifies. The slow diffusion of a literary culture by Church and monarchy in the time of Alfred and after is unlikely to have diminished the composition and dissemination of oral vernacular narrative or lyric verse. The roots of that verse were deep and there is little sign of any attempt to eradicate it. The form of composition and recital described in *Beowulf* must have been familiar to generations of hearers, pagan and Christian. At *Beowulf* 867 ff., the thegn is depicted as composing on the ride back from the mere new versions of the two familiar stories of Sigemund and Heremod. Being on horseback he must presumably have sung without benefit of harp. Later in the hall of Heorot, a poet sings the Finnesburh tragedy:

> þær wæs sang and sweg samod ætgædere
> fore Healfdenes hildewisan,
> gomenwudu greted, gid oft wrecen,

ðonne healgamen Hroþgares scop
æfter medubence mænan scolde . . .* (1063–7)

That is, he would tell or retell the story, keeping to a familiar outline, but doubtless varying his emphasis, his formulas, his figures from one telling to another: drawing on a stock of phrases, epithets, and half-lines, and seeking the most effective alliterative combinations of these. There are nine and sixty ways of constructing tribal lays. . . . In pre-Conquest England, in short, we are still not very far from the conditions that produced the oral poetry out of which the *Iliad* grew.

The implications of Milman Parry's work for students of Old English and Middle English poetry are not yet clear. As with Homer, 'it is still uncertain how far formulary means traditional and traditional means oral'. All one can do at this stage is to present a few of his findings, which seem to have some bearing on the poetry behind Layamon: that the oral poet is continuously subordinate to tradition; that he composes in traditional formulas (which depend on the metrical shape of the line), and also in traditional themes (which are basic and recurrent units of narrative—for instance, the single combat, the calling of an assembly, the arrival at a palace—or of description—of arms, feasts, etc.); and that his traditional oral forms are closely related to the way of life that surrounds them.

I suggest that though Wace and Layamon were literate poets, they had both inherited traditional usages. They preserve old forms and stances, but merely by writing down their verses they introduce new elements; the act spells the eventual death of oral traditon.†

In England, as in Homeric Greece, the recital of heroic or historical narrative was a recognized part of royal or noble entertainment. This is one feature that changed with the Conquest. The accustomed setting suddenly disappeared and the prestige of the gleeman doubtless declined. Saxon singers would not be *personae gratae* in Norman halls unless they changed their repertoire, their language, and their style. They may have come to rely more on their harp and less on their narrative skill. But in Layamon's mind, and perhaps in the popular

* 'There was singing and music together in accompaniment in presence of Healf-dene's warlike chieftain; the harp was played, and many a lay rehearsed, when Hrothgar's bard was to provide entertainment in hall along the mead-bench.' (Translations from *Beowulf* are from the version by J. R. Clark Hall (revised by C. L. Wrenn, London, 1950).)

† H. Ringbom, *Studies in the Narrative Technique of Beowulf and Lawman's Brut* (Åbo, 1968), 76, cited by A. C. Spearing, *The Gawain Poet* (Cambridge, 1970), 20 n., suggests that the inheritance of fixed formulas had disintegrated by Layamon's time, and that 'formulas' is therefore not a suitable term for Layamon's loosely structured phrases. But is not this to ignore Layamon's particular situation—the *given* text of Wace which con-stricts him? We cannot say what the state of *oral* poetry was in the eleventh and twelfth centuries.

imagination, they remained associated with the princely hall and with
noble entertainment. When he wishes to portray the delights of
Arthur's court he says:

> Birles[1] ther thrungen[2], gleomen[3] ther sungen
> Harpen gunnen dremen[4], dugethe[5] wes on selen[6] . . .
>
> (11419–20)

[1] *cupbearers*   [2] *went*   [3] *minstrels*   [4] *sounded*   [5] *company*
[6] *joy*

The scene hardly differs from that of *Beowulf*

> Leoð wæs asungen
> gleomannes gyd.   Gamen eft astah,
> beorhtode bencsweg   byrelas sealdon
> win of wunderfatum*   (1159–62)

Before Layamon, Wace, to be sure, had made much of the musical
powers of the British King Blegabret who:

> Mult sout de lais, mult sout de note . . .
>
> Il ert deus des jugleors
> Et deus de tuz les chanteors.   (3699–706)

But Layamon put his own interpretation on that passage by rendering
the lines: 'gleomen him weoren deore' (3491). For him the gleemen of
tradition must figure in any picture of a happy England. When Merlin
prophesies that all the inhabitants of Britain will submit to Arthur, he
also remarks: 'Of him scullen gleomen godliche singen.' And later
romances make 'gleemen' a feature of courtly entertainment in the
olden days; cf. the merry scene at the end of *Havelok*:

> Ther mouhte men here þe gestes singe
> The gleumen on the tabour dinge.   (2328–9)†

The conventions, style, diction, and metres of the native verse were
bound to alter as the prestige of the Norman-French increased, the
pattern of society altered, and the inflectional system of English was
modified. Old English epic verse (in our surviving copies) is sophisticated and artificial in its forms and language. It necessarily declined
with the diminishing of the audience that favoured it and the
dwindling numbers of clerks who could copy it. By the late twelfth
century, the new French rhymed syllabic verse was exerting a powerful influence on native writers: witness *The Owl and the Nightingale*. To

---

* 'The song, the gleeman's lay was sung. Then mirth rose high, the noise of revelry
was clearly heard; cup-bearers proffered wine from curious vessels.'

† Cf. also *Sir Ysumbras*, ed. G. Schleich (Berlin, 1901), l. 19. 'Glewmen he luffede
welle in haulle.'

'clerks' (men in orders) rhyme was no new thing: it was familiar from Latin hymns sung in the offices of the church. The hymns of St Godric (see p. 370 below), which antedate both Layamon and *The Owl and the Nightingale*, show clearly the influence of their Latin origins in rhythm and in rhyme, and Layamon might have employed rhyme to the extent that he does even if he had never read a line of Wace. But the discovery of a long poem on the history of his native land written in easy couplets would put him on his mettle. His motive in 'taking over' Wace would be patriotic in a double sense: he was providing Englishmen with an acceptable myth of their history, and he was proving that it could be made readable in his native tongue, and in a new form of what remains basically the native measure.

Certainly there is nothing slavish in his version of Wace—as there is nothing slavish in Wace's version of Geoffrey. Everything suggests that adaptation and amplification were always and everywhere taken for granted as part of a 'maker's' function.

The story he has to tell is largely of wars, conquests, and battles, and for description of these the diction and phraseology of Old English verse was wholly appropriate. The earliest poem of any length found in *The Anglo-Saxon Chronicle* is on the battle of Brunanburh, and Layamon's battle scenes are not far removed from it in spirit, even if the movement of the lines has altered. Yet comparatively few of Layamon's formulaic lines have exact precedents in Anglo-Saxon verse. Some of these combinations arose comparatively late from the admixture of the Norse element, first in the Danelaw, later in the North and West. Norse poetry, which is basically alliterative, was known—and composed—in pre-Conquest England; and Norse speech, so similar to English in structure, vocabulary, and consonant patterns, favours alliterative combinations. It strengthened the resistance to French by supplying doublets or variants of native words, in forms that fitted into alliterative patterns (as, for instance, the phrase 'gold and gærsume' (treasure), which is frequent in Layamon—'ne sculde him neother gan fore gold ne na gærsume' (11404)*). Verbal affinities with Old English verse appear in single words or phrases rather than in larger units: e.g. the word *blanken*, 'horses' (2924 in the Caligula MS; the Otho MS has *hors*), or *fetherhome* (1436), the term used in the Old English *Genesis B* for Lucifer's wings which is applied by Layamon to the wings with which King Bladud makes a fatal

---

* The word 'gersume' is first attested in English in *The Anglo-Saxon Chronicle*; it may well be an adoption from Old Norse. It survives in later Northern verse in such alliterative combinations. The idiom 'go for' (= avail) is found elsewhere in similar formulas; cf. *Havelok*, 44, 'for hem ne yede gold ne fee'.

experiment in flight (he crashes on the roof of Apollo's temple), or the phrase 'mid orde and mid egge' (2594).

Sometimes Layamon puts the elements of an Old English poetic phrase to new use. Thus 'dreamum bidæled' (used in *Beowulf* of Grendel) gives 'blissen . . . bideled' (with alliteration on different consonants). Other formulas with direct Anglo-Saxon antecedents or a recognizable Anglo-Saxon flavour cluster characteristically around certain traditional 'themes', with slight variations according to context, as is characteristic of oral verse. Typical scenes are:
(1) A leader's appeal to his followers. Thus Arthur cries:

> Nu cleopede[1] Arthur, athelest kingen[2]
> 'Whar beo ye mine cnihtes, ohte men and wihte[3]?
> To horse, to horse, halethes[4] gode!'   (10525–7)

[1] *cried out*   [2] *noblest of kings*   [3] *bold men and valiant*   [4] *warriors*

(2) Battles and their outcome. Here we sometimes find such phrases as 'feollen the fæie' (7005) or 'here tir [glory] wes at-fallen' (2114). Most of the regular ingredients are assembled in the account of Edwine's encounter with Cadwalan:

> 'Wurthe for nithing the mon the nule hine sturien![1]
> Habben bares heorte[2] and remes brede![3]
> Cuthen than kinge[4] that we quiken sunde![5]
> He lette blawen bemen and bonnien his verden[6].
> Forth he gon wende that he com to than ende[7]
> Ther the king Cadwathlan wunede on cumelan[8].
> Togadere gunnen resen theines swithe riche![9]
> Breken speren longe; sceldes brastleden[10] an honde;
> Heouwen heye helmes, scænden tha brunies[11].
> Feollen ærm kempes[12], æmteden[13] sadeles;
> Drem wes on volcke[14]: tha eorthe gon to dunien[15].
> Urnen tha brockes of reden blodes.[16]
> Feollen tha folckes; falewede nebbes[17];
> Bruttes gunnen breothen[18]; balu[19] wes on volken.   (15168–81)

[1] *Let that man who will not bestir himself be thought a worthless wretch*   [2] *boar's courage*   [3] *raven's cunning*   [4] *Make known to the king*   [5] *are alive*   [6] *He had trumpets blown and his hosts summoned*   [7] *place*   [8] *dwelt in his (?) encampment*   [9] *noble thanes rushed together*   [10] *shivered*   [11] *destroyed the corslets*   [12] *wretched warriors fell*   [13] *were emptied*   [14] *clamour rose in the host*   [15] *resound*   [16] *the brooks ran with red blood*   [17] *faces became pale*   [18] *perished*   [19] *woe*

Some of these phrases are found in Old English battle verse, but we find none of the carrion beasts and birds of Old English pieces; others are derived from Wace. The string of intransitive verbs is characteristic of Layamon, and 'nithing' is his favourite term of abuse. Noteworthy is the staccato effect, the piling up of half-lines that produce the sense of the tumult and noise of battle ('drem'). Here Layamon sets a pattern that recurs in Chaucer, though he writes in lines rather than half-lines:

> Now ryngen trompes loude and clarioun . . .
> In goon the speres ful sadly in arrest . . .
> The helmes they tohewen and toshrede;
> Out brest the blood, with stierne stremes rede.
>
> (*KnT CT* I. 2600–10)

And in describing the naval battle of Actium (*LGW* 635 ff.) Chaucer uses precisely the same technique, many of the same phrases, and the same alliterative patterns—'In goth the grapenel . . . he styngeth hym upon his speres ord.'

(3) A messenger's entry. In the society depicted a messenger's role is an important one. His arrival usually means disturbance, and it is often linked with scenes of rejoicing in hall, marked by formulas such as 'blisse wes an hirede' (1816), or variations of 'tha wes hit al stille that wuneden inne halle' (12463). Examples of the latter are used in the scene in Arthur's court when it is visited by the messengers of the Emperor Lucius, and it is repeated with dramatic effect when the news of Mordred's treachery is brought to Arthur in Italy:

> Tha sæt hit al stille in Arthures halle;
> Tha wes ther særinæsse mid sele than kinge[1];
> Tha weoren Bruttisce men swithe unbalde vor tham.[2]
> Tha umbe stunde stefne ther sturede[3] . . .
>
> (14052–5)

[1] *sympathy with the good king sound was heard*   [2] *very downcast because of that*   [3] *after a time a*

One senses the shock, then the subdued murmuring that grows gradually to a roar of anger.

Next in frequency are formulaic lines or half-lines that are fitted to recurring situations, e.g. 'Long bith ævere', a favourite opening for a speech. But not all such formulas are alliterative (cf. 'hoker and scarn' (derision and scorn) (8638)); some depend on rhyme ('ther wes wop, ther was rop [lamentation]' (11759)). In Layamon's kind of narrative, which assumes a listening audience, unable to turn back the pages to refresh the memory, reports of action already described are careful to repeat the essentials, and sometimes a phrase or more of the original account. Thus the summary of the fabulous tale of Cirencester emphasizes that the town was won 'mid swulcches cunnes ginnen' (with such kinds of tricks)—'Mid sparewen [sparrows] that beren that fur [fire] and sparewen heo forbarnden' (14643). Again, the account of Pellun, the 'clerk' from Spain who knew 'many crafts', and gazed on the sky, is repeated later when Cadwala is told about him (15218 ff., 15297 ff.). And frequently one speaker will repeat what another has said.

Phrasal repetition and parallelism, like antithesis, a feature of oral poetry, attracts a poet with a listening audience in mind, and clusters of phrases on the same pattern are obvious mnemonic aids, as well as being rhetorically effective. Wace makes regular use of such 'tirades lyriques' as Arnold calls them,* and Layamon extends or otherwise adapts them, employing alliteration and his own rhyme pattern, as in:

> Quelen[1] tha eorles, quelen tha beornes[2],
> Quelen tha theines, quelen tha sweines,
> Quelen tha lareden[3], quelen tha leouweden[4],
> Quelen tha aeldren[5], quelen tha yeongeren[6],
> Quelæn tha wifmen[7], quelen tha wanclen[8].   (15887–91)

| [1] *they kill* | [2] *warriors* | [3] *learned* | [4] *unlearned* | [5] *older* |
| [6] *younger* | [7] *women* | [8] *children* | | |

In similes Layamon, at certain points at least, is prolific, and many of them do not depend on Wace. Merlin promises to raise the stones that become Stonehenge 'as balls of feathers'; Julius Caesar fights 'like a wild boar'; hair is like gold wire—an image not found in Wace, but much favoured by later poets. The longer similes have parallels in Virgil, whom Layamon may have read, at least in extracts, rather than in *Beowulf*, and are striking partly because they suggest a more distinctively literary art than is found elsewhere. The best known is embedded in Arthur's speech about Childric (which again makes it notable, since epic heroes rarely indulge in such expansions):

> 'Ah[1] of him bith iwurthen[2] swa bith of than voxe[3],
> Thenne he bith baldest ufen-an than walde[4],
> And hafeth his fulle ploghe[5] and fugheles inoghe[6];
> For wildscipe[7] climbith and cluden isecheth[8];
> I than wilderne[9] holghes him wurcheth[10].
> Faren wha-swa avere [he] fare naveth he nævere nænne kare[11];
> He weneth to beon of dughethe[12] baldest alre deoren[13].
> Thenne siyeth[14] him to segges[15] under beorghen[16],
> Mid hornen, mid hunden mid haghere stefenen[17]:
> Hunten thar talieth[18], hundes ther galieth[19];
> Thene vox driveth yeond dales and yeond dunes[20].
> He vlih[21] to than holme[22] and his hol isecheth,
> I than firste ænde[23], i than holle wendeth.
> Thenne is the balde vox blissen al bideled[24];

---

* Wace, p. xc.

And mon[25] him to-delveth[26] on ælchere helven[27].
Thenne beoth ther forcuthest[28] deoren alre pruttest[29].
Swa wes Childriche, than strongen and than riche.'

(10398–414)

[1] But   [2] will become   [3] fox   [4] on the wooded country   [5] sport
[6] plenty of birds   [7] wildness   [8] seeks the clouds   [9] wilderness
[10] makes himself holes   [11] sorrow   [12] valour   [13] boldest of all animals
[14] follow   [15] men   [16] hills   [17] loud voices   [18] shout
[19] yelp   [20] hills   [21] flees   [22] hill   [23] part   [24] deprived of
joy   [25] one   [26] digs out   [27] every side   [28] most wretched
[29] proudest

Here we sense a spirit akin to that of the fox-hunt in *Sir Gawain and the Green Knight*. And it belongs to the tradition of the poetry of the chase that has its beginnings in *Beowulf*, and the description of the perilous mere:

Ðeah þe hæðstapa hundum geswenced,
heorot hornum trum holtwudu sece,
feorran geflymed . . .   (1368–70)*

Yet to remove this extended simile (longer than any in Milton, Virgil, or Dante) from its context is to lose part of its point. In the end Arthur does not destroy Childric but gives him 'grith' (peace, protection) and lets him sail away—to return and ravage the land. The most characteristic lines in the episode come in the poet's sharp concluding comment:

Her wes Arthur the king athelen bidæled[1];
Nes ther nan swa rehh[2] mon the him durste ræden[3].
Thet him ofthuhte[4] sære sone therafter.   (10428–30)

[1] deprived of noble men   [2] bold   [3] advise   [4] he repented

The hunt provides the basis for another elaborate simile, likewise applied to one of Arthur's fleeing foes—Colgrim:

Ther adruncke Sexes[1] fulle seove[2] thusend:
Summe heo gunnen wondrien[3] swa doth the wilde cron[4]
I than moruenne[5] thenne his floc is awemmed[6]
And him haldeth[7] after havekes[8] swifte;
Hundes in than reode[9] mid reouthe[10] hine imeteth;[11]
Thenne nis him neouther god no that lond no that flod;

*'Although, pressed by the hounds, the ranger of the heath, the hart strong in its horns, may seek the forest, chased from far' (he will give up his life . . . sooner than he will plunge in it).

Havekes hine smiteth, hundes hine biteth;
Thenne bith the kinewurthe foghel[12] fæie on his sithe[13].

(10060–7)

[1] *Saxons were drowned*   [2] *seven*   [3] *wander*   [4] *crane*   [5] *morning*   [6] *attacked*   [7] *pursue*   [8] *hawks*   [9] *reeds*   [10] *calamity*   [11] *find him*   [12] *noble bird*   [13] *doomed in his journey*

The most striking passage in the whole poem is the adjacent depiction of the slaughtered Saxons heaped up in the Avon till they made a bridge of steel across it: not content with this image Layamon adds another, putting it into Arthur's mouth, as if to enhance Arthur's prowess and dignity. The King pictures Baldulf looking down from a nearby hill on the 'steel fishes', lying in the stream:

Mid sweorde bigeorede[1]. Heore sund is awemmed[2];
Heore scalen wleoteth[3] swulc gold-faghe sceldes[4];
Ther fleoteth heore spiten[5], swulc hit spæren[6] weoren.

(10641–3)

[1] *begirt*   [2] *power of swimming is impaired*   [3] *float*   [4] *like gold-coloured shields*   [5] *fins*   [6] *spears*

'Sund is awemmed' is a typical Anglo-Saxon understatement.* But no Anglo-Saxon poet, and few later ones, can administer such a shock of recognition as this inverted image gives: the fins and scales of the gleaming fish are slowly 'realized' as the spears and shields of drowned warriors.

Finally Arthur, once more using the figure of the chase, shows Childric as the hunter hunted:

Nu he is bicumen hunte and hornes him fulieth[1];
Flihth over bradne wæld[2]; beorketh[3] his hundes;
He hafeth bihalves Bathen[4] his huntinge bilæfved[5];
Freom his deore[6] he flicth, and we hit scullen fallen[7] . . .

(10647–50)

[1] *follow*   [2] *broad plain*   [3] *bark*   [4] *beside Bath*   [5] *abandoned*   [6] *quarry*   [7] *kill*

The intensity of poetic feeling in these passages is unexampled in our early poetry. It owes little to traditional verse, and shows no signs of a training in a more formal rhetoric. But that Layamon had some acquaintance with *ars poetica* as it was beginning to be taught in the twelfth century is not impossible; and his reading of Wace must have made him aware of the value of metaphor and simile, if not of other rhetorical devices.

* Cf. 'He on holme wæs / sundes þe sænra, þe hyne swylt fornam' (*Beowulf*, 1435–6) (he was the slower at swimming in the mere, in that death had carried him off), where the last half-line illustrates the more deliberate Anglo-Saxon manner.

At least one of his similes has a Virgilian flavour, depicting Arthur rushing on his foes:

> ... swa the runie[1] wulf,
> Thenne he cumeth of holte, bihonged mid snawe,
> And thencheth to biten swulc deor swa him liketh[2]   (10041-3)

[1] *fierce*   [2] *such animals as he pleases*

And again Layamon intensifies the effect by an exclamation and a further simile:

> 'Forth we bilive, theines ohte[1],
> Alle somed[2] heom to! Alle we sculleth wel don.'
> And heo forth hælden[3], swa the hæghe[4] wude
> Thenne wind wode weieth hine mid mæine[5] ...   (10045-8)

[1] *Let us advance quickly, valiant thanes*   [2] *together*   [3] *advanced*
[4] *high*   [5] *when furious wind tosses it with violence*

It is the gale of the Marcher lands, that blows the sapling double, which comes to Layamon's mind, as it would to Housman's.

Layamon uses his formulaic style for various poetic purposes. The gnomic tags sprinkled over the text form part of authorial comment. Thus 'Gornoille [Goneril] was swithe wær, swa beoth wifmen wel ihwær [everywhere]' (1482), a *sententia* very similar to one later used by Chaucer:

> For wommen, as to speken in comune,
> Thei folwen alle the favour of Fortune.
>
> (*KnT CT* I. 2681-2)

Formulaic lines may be used to emphasize recurrent themes. The king or leader is continually giving orders to 'blow our trumpets and summon our fyrd', and when he is fighting against great odds his attitude will be similar to that of Byrhtnoth in *The Batlle of Maldon* or of the saga heroes:

> For leovere us is[1] here mid manscipe to fallen
> Thanne we heonne isunde farren[2] ure frenden to scare[3]
>
> (2909-10)

[1] *we prefer*   [2] *journey hence unharmed*   [3] *disgrace*

The good king is always characterized as the maker of good new laws and the preserver of good old ones: Belin promises that the Romans shall 'habben tha ilke læwen the stoden bi heore ældre dæwen' (2973), and in Britain he made 'lawen swithe gode'. At other times the formulaic style is used to intensify emotion. The response to fateful pronouncements or events is measured in physical images that have common features. When Cordoille (Cordelia) has spoken her true feelings, her father Leir

> iwerthe[1] swa blac[2] swlch hit a blac cloth weoren . . .
> Mid there wræthe he wes isweved[3] that he feol iswowen[4] . . .
> Tha hit alles up brac; hit wes uvel that he spac*
>
> (1533-7)

[1] *became*   [2] *pale*   [3] *stunned*   [4] *fell in a swoon*

So, when Leir flees to France and appeals in person to the daughter he has reviled:

> The quene Cordoille seæt longe swithe stille
> Heo iward reode[1] on hire benche swilche hit were of wine-
>   scenche[2] . . .
>
> (1761-2)

[1] *became red*   [2] *draught of wine*

Again, later, when the news is brought to Arthur of the death of Uther:

> Arthur sæt ful stille:
> Ænne stund[1] he wes blac[2] and on heuwe swithe wak[3];
> Anne while he wes reod[4] and reousede[5] on heorte.   (9923-5)†

[1] *at one time*   [2] *pale*   [3] *weak*   [4] *red*   [5] *grieved*

The poem is formulary in a larger sense. Like the *Iliad*, it is composed of set themes as well as of set lines and phrases. These themes are of course already present in Wace, but I would contend that the attractions of Wace for Layamon lay precisely in the fact that Wace had built his *Brut* out of traditional themes, which Layamon identified. The blocks out of which the narrative is built after the 'fortunate founding' are the reigns of kings, though they vary greatly in size. The inevitable monotony is alleviated by altercations or conflicts, often signalled by the arrival of a messenger, whose tidings are always set forth in measured phrase—whereas in Wace often the substance only is given. Sometimes the message only is written, and then it is more formal, as in Leir's to Cordoille's husband:

> 'The kinge of Bruttaine, the[1] Leir is haten[2],
> Greteth Aganippus, thene aldere[3] of Fraunce:
> Worthschepe have thu thire wel-deda[4].
> And thire feire sonde[5] that grete thu me woldest.

* Cf. Godlac's receipt of Dalgan's message (2254).
† And cf. the reaction to the news of Mordred's treachery, mentioned above, p. 76.

Ac I do the wel to witene[6], hær bi mine writ rith[7]
That mine drihliche[8] lond atwa ich habbe ideled[9].' (1576–81)

[1] *who*   [2] *called*   [3] *lord*   [4] *good offices*   [5] *message*
[6] *would have you know*   [7] *straightway*   [8] *noble*   [9] *divided*

And so forth for another thirteen lines.

Most of the speeches, in form and diction, directly reflect the situations out of which they arise. Thus the Romans' offer of submission to Belin (2659 ff.) is simple in language, suitably humble in tone. And it is at such points that we come closest in Layamon to a plain prose order, and the diction of common life. The first 'pillow conversation' in English* is between Gornoille (Goneril) and Maglaune her husband as they lie in bed. It flows easily, like intimate talk, free of formal phrasing:

'Seie me, mi laverd[1], monne[2] thu ert me leovest[3].
Me thuncheth[4] that mi fæder nis nowhit felle[5],
No he wurhscipe ne can[6], his wit he havet bileved[7].
Me thuncheth the alde mon wole dotie nou nan[8].
He halt[9] here fauwerti[10] cnihtes, daies and nihtes[11].
He haveth her thas theines, and alle heore swaines,
Hundes and havekes[12] . . .

Mi fader havet to monie of idele manne.
Ale tha feorthe dale lete we forth fuse[13].

Swa ich ævere ibiden are itholien nulle ich hit mare[14]!' (1642–59)

[1] *lord*   [2] *of men*   [3] *dearest*   [4] *seems to me*   [5] *clever*   [6] *is not capable of nobility*   [7] *lost*   [8] *is in dotage now*   [9] *maintains*   [10] *forty*   [11] *by day and night*   [12] *hawks*   [13] *let us expel the fourth part*   [14] *as ever I expect mercy I will not endure it longer*

Layamon is at his best in direct dramatic speech—as is shown when his Malgod persuades Brenne to attack Belin. The ring of the sentences is clear, the tone forthright, the argument cogent:

'Seie me mi laverd, leoust alre monne[1],
Whi tholest[2] thu that Belin, the[3] is thin awene[4] brother,
Havet swa mochel of thisse lande and thu havest swa lutel?
Nefde ye ba enne fader, and beie[5] enne moder?
Beiene of ane cunne[6], cuth[7] hit is on folke.
Nu stond al this muchele[8] lond a Bailenes awere[9] hond,
And thu eært his mon and his cniht, that is woh[10] and
nawiht[11] riht.

* E. Auerbach, *Mimesis*, tr. W. R. Trask (Princeton, 1953), ch. 10, discusses fifteenth-century French examples.

Eært thu thenne cheves-boren[12] that thu wult beon forloren,
Other thu eart swa eærgh[13] cniht that of londe ne rehchest
nawiht[14]?'

(2156–64)

[1] *dearest of all men*   [2] *sufferest*   [3] *who*   [4] *own*   [5] *Did you not*
both have one father and both ...   [6] *kin*   [7] *known*   [8] *great*
[9] *own*   [10] *wrong*   [11] *not at all*   [12] *born of a concubine*   [13] *cow-*
ardly   [14] *carest nothing*

In fact, a genuine speech rhythm is running through Layamon's head all the time—bringing the *Brut* nearer to *Piers Plowman* than to the more formalized Anglo-Saxon verse.

But whatever Layamon owes to unknown English (or Welsh) predecessors, the prime stimulus, the immediate model, lay in Wace's *Brut*. The poet who drew so largely on a French work can hardly have been insular in outlook. Many of the traits already discussed have their precedent in the *Brut*—parallelism, *sententiae*, pointed comment, the capacity for terse and simple statement. Wace's attractive treatment of the Arthurian story as he had found it in Geoffrey of Monmouth must have made for his popularity, evidenced by the survival of over twenty manuscripts. His *Brut* must have both whetted and catered for a growing appetite in the Norman ruling class for 'historical' lore concerning the country that every year—and not least in the reign of John—grew further apart from Normandy. And Layamon must have met a similar need, on a different level.

What the difference in level was we can guess from Layamon's omissions. He has no time, for instance, for the tournament where bright eyes rain influence—no time for *courtoisie*. The technical terms of French warfare are also ignored, perhaps because no vernacular equivalents could be found for them, perhaps because they lay outside the interest or experience of Layamon's audience. More surprisingly, he reduces passages of biblical names, biblical events, and biblical chronology. Wace's reference to Homer is omitted, and some but not all other classical references (e.g. to the temple of Concord, 2139 (Wace, 2309)). Other passages are presumably reduced for reasons of economy—and sometimes they become the more effective, as in the tale of Belin and Brenne, reconciled by their mother's tears:

A whet wult thu Brenne, whet wult thu balwe menge?[1]
Yif thu sleast thine brother, ne bistz thu never other[2]
Ne beon yit bute tweien[3], mine sunen yit[4] be beien.
Bithenc o thire monschipe[5], bithenc o thire moder,
Bithenc a mire lare[6], thu eært mi bærn deore[7].

Loka her the tittes that thu suke[8] mid thine lippes,
Lou war hire tha wifmon, tha the a thas weoreld ibær[9] . . .'   (2501–7)

[1] *stir up strife*   [2] *you will not live to see another*   [3] *you are but two*
[4] *you*   [5] *honour*   [6] *teaching*   [7] *dear child*   [8] *suckled*
[9] *woman who bore you into this world*

Layamon was unable to reproduce Wace's metrical smoothness, which fits so well his verve and vivacity. Yet Layamon's variations in rhythm and metre, the very looseness of his line, are assets inasmuch as a continuously smooth flow has ultimately a lulling, soporific effect. The narrative itself, often consisting of a roll-call of royal names and a bare recital of reigns, or bloody battles, makes for some monotony. But the opening theme—'The Matter of Britain'—is interesting enough, if only because it was to become one of the great topics of medieval literature; and its importance is indicated in the poem itself when Cassibellaune appeals to Julius Caesar on the grounds of their common origin:

'For ure ældere[1] of Troye flughen[2], and of anne kunne we beoth
    icumen.
Thine aldren and ure at Troye wuren ifeire[3].'

(3666–7)

[1] *ancestors*   [2] *fled*   [3] *comrades*

And in these early pages first appear names and stories that are to become the very stuff of later literature: Lear and Cordelia—a story with a happy ending for Lear, and no Edmund or Gloucester, in which Cordelia's suicide comes after Lear's restoration and death, and she is buried in Janus's temple 'as the book telleth'; Cymbeline (in whose reign Taliesin prophesied the birth of Christ); King Coel; Imogen; Gorboduc and his sons; Hengest and Horsa (Hengest figuring as a traitor); Merlin and Mordred. Place names too first mentioned here are to take on resonance later. Parts of the poem form a bizarre gazetteer: Leicester (Leircester), Logres (the land of King Locrine), Billingsgate (set up by Belinus), and Ludgate, named after the Lud who built Caerlud, which became London. Dover figures here (though not in Wace) as the haven that Caesar occupied on his first landing. To onomastic lore derived from Wace, Layamon may add details suggesting local knowledge—in particular as regards the South Coast. He evidently knew that Carmarthen was a likely place to find skilled armourers and that Caerleon had lost its erstwhile glories. Numerous references to Ireland and Irish customs—not to mention his naming of Irish saints (Brendan, Bridget, Columban) and Irish kings—suggest he may have visited that country. In telling the lively and romantic tale of Brian and Cadwalan (in which Brian carves off a piece of his own thigh to assuage his lord's hunger, 'the dearest roast that ever I set before any king' (15268–9), and later disguises himself as a merchant), he shows special knowledge of Southampton; having sailed thither from Barfleet, he wins over the citizenry by generously distributing part of his cargo (wine in tuns); the rest he stores in a cellar (an 'earth-house')—the earliest known reference to Southampton as an *entrepôt* for wine.*

Minor but regular expansions, possibly of biographical significance, are those relating to laws and justice. Mordred promises the citizens of Winchester 'free lawe'; Arthur establishes 'chireche-grith' (11138)—but Layamon's alliterative legal formulas like 'to sibbe and to some' (2045) come from the general English stock. Wace mentions laws named after Marcia, Guenclius's wife—'Marciene l'apela l'on sulunc le language breton'; Layamon insists that Alfred ('Englelondes deorling') merely put them 'on Englisc' (3153)—it is the only mention in the whole work of the Saxon hero-king. Equally notable is Layamon's penchant for matters marine and nautical. Two storm passages in particular are considerably expanded from Wace. The first describes the storm that overtook Godlac. In answer to Queen Dalgan's appeal to save her from an unwelcome match with Brenne, Godlac pursues and overtakes her ship (distinguished by its silken sails). When a storm arises and three and fifty ships founder, Godlac's seamanship saves him:

> He igrap ane wi-æxe[1] muchele[2] and swithe scærpe;
> He forheow[3] thænne mæst a-two riht amidden[4];
> He lette seil and thane meæst lithen mid uthen[5]. (2292–4)

[1] *battle-axe*   [2] *great*   [3] *cut*   [4] *in the middle*
[5] *go off among the waves*

Sea-weary, and driven by the storm, his crew seek shelter on the English coast (a scene repeated with variations in a later tale (cf. 3093)). Godlac tells his story at Belin's court, in racy direct speech (as against Wace's *oratio obliqua*) but is imprisoned until Brenne, Belin's brother, arrives in pursuit. Belin puts him to flight, and Godlac, having proffered gold and services to obtain his release, marries Dalgan: the tale resembles that in the Old English fragment known as *Finnesburh*; but, unlike that poem, has a happy ending.

The second storm scene describes the tempest that fell on the ships

* A diverting detail added by Layamon (14760 ff.) is an allusion to the oft-mentioned slander that Englishmen have tails, in which he plays on the words 'uncuth' and 'cued', 'tailes', and 'iteled' (reproached).

in which St Ursula and her virgin company left the shelter of the Thames for the German coast:

> Swurken[1] under sunnen sweorte weolcnen[2];
> Hayel and ræin ther aræs, the hit iseh him agras[3];
> Uthen ther urnen[4], tunes swulche ther burnen;
> Bordes ther breken; wimmen gunnen wepen.   (5974-7)

[1] *became gloomy*   [2] *black clouds*   [3] *whoever saw it was terrified*
[4] *waves surged*

This, like a similar passage in Barbour's *Bruce* (see below, p. 109) may have been suggested by the storm scene in *Aeneid* i. The heavily consonantal emphasis in Middle English alliterative patterns made the metre particularly suitable for descriptions of winter and rough weather.* The formulas in this scene, including the vivid comparison of weltering waves, recur elsewhere, and Layamon may well have had a literary model. Yet numerous graphic touches suggest that Layamon knew the importance of wind and tide and had a good weather eye. To these sea-scenes may be added the tale of the Grendel-like monster whom King Morpidus attacks (3211 ff.) with sword, spear, axe, and *hondsæx*, but all in vain. Layamon's comment on the valorous king's death: 'thus ferde [passed on] the king for he wes to kene [too valiant]' has yet again a ring of *Beowulf* about it.

Properly to assess Layamon's purpose, and his quality, we must consider his more substantial changes—the passages that can fairly be labelled additions to or expansions of Wace. The label must always be conditional, though no conclusive reasons have yet been adduced for the view that the French *Brut* had already been extended before Layamon found it. The passages in question belong almost wholly to the 'Arthuriad'; and even if they include Welsh or Breton elements, as some scholars have urged, they are fully integrated into the poem. Three of them are notable for the introduction of 'faerie', or magical, 'elvish' elements. This is from the first associated with Merlin, whose very birth is mysterious. It is Merlin who contrives the birth of Arthur, and Arthur's birth is signalized by gifts the *ælven* bestow on him by their magic. Arthur's mail-coat, again, was made by an elvish smith— 'he wes ihaten Wygar the Witege wurhte'—and his sword Calibeorne was likewise made by elves.

The Round Table (not called 'round' by Layamon) is the magical invention of a Cornish knight, as a result of a brawl over precedence. About the table, said Wace, 'Bretun dient mainte fable' (9752)—a phrase that Layamon takes to cover tales about Arthur himself; adding

---

* See N. Jacobs, 'Alliterative Storms: A Topos in Middle English', *Speculum*, xlvii (1972), 695-719.

sardonically that there was never a king so doughty that the British could not make up lies about him. There is no glamour in this Arthur. Both he and Guenevere lack the refinements, the courtesies—and the carnality—of later romance. In combat he is more savage than his French original—or than any king of Anglo-Saxon story. But the similes mentioned above make him more eloquent than any later Arthur: they suggest a monarch of the chase, and as such foreshadow the concern and settings of several Arthurian romances. 'Elves' are more loosely associated with Arthur in a passage describing his war with King Howel of Scotland. He comes upon a wondrous mere, in-habited by fish, fowl, eagles, and evil creatures:

> That water is unimete[1] brade, nikeres[2] ther bathieth inne;
> There is elvene ploghe[3] in atteliche pole[4].

(10851–2)

[1] *immeasurably* [2] *sea-monsters* [3] *sport* [4] *hideous pool*

This is a little suggestive of Grendel's mere in *Beowulf*, but that is far more eerie.

Layamon's most notable insertion into the Arthurian saga is the ominous dream on the night when the messenger arrives bringing news of Mordred's treachery.* The fact that it is to the messenger that Arthur tells his dream adds to its eeriness, for the messenger alone knows what it portends. The picture of Arthur 'riding' the roof of a hall (a motif found in Norse literature) scanning all his dominions; of Mordred and Guenevere hewing down the hallposts so that he falls and breaks his right arm, whilst Gawain breaks both arms; of Arthur in dream smiting off Mordred's head and hacking at his queen, then sud-denly finding himself in a waste-land, whence he is carried by a golden lion to the sea, where waves part him from the lion, and a fish brings him to land 'al wet and weri of sorwen and seoc'—all this has a grim intensity that we hardly meet outside the sagas, except perhaps momentarily in Gavin Douglas's later *Palace of Honour* where the poet dreams of fish shouting like elves as they race through water.

To the story of Arthur's last fight and death Layamon adds several apparently new touches, including the figure describing the approach of Mordred's army: 'ridinde and ganninde [marching] swa the rim falleth adune', and the mention of two women 'wunderliche idihte',

---

* As if fascinated by the poetic possibilities of dreams, he introduces another towards the close of the work (16006 ff.), when Cadwalader sleeps while at mass after praying that he be allowed to depart this life: a man wondrous fair (the description prepares us for an 'oraculum', or true vision) bids him awake and go to Rome whence, being shriven, he will depart to heaven.

who appear 'in a sceort bat sceoven mid uthen', and gently bear the
dying king away:

> Æfne than worden[1] ther com of se wenden
> That wes an sceort bat lithen[2], sceoven mid uthen[3],
> And twa wimmen therinne, wunderliche idihte[4],
> And heo nomen[5] Arthur anan and aneouste hine vereden[6]
> And softe hine adun leiden, and forth gunnen lithen . . .

> (14283–7)

[1] *immediately upon those words*   [2] *sailing*   [3] *moved forward among the waves*
[4] *arrayed*   [5] *took*   [6] *quickly bore him*

A minor but striking addition to the legend of Arthur's passing is a
comment about his return: though no one knows the truth,

> . . . while wes an witige[1] Mærlin ihate;
> He bodede[2] mid worde—*his quithes weoren sothe*[3]—
> That an Arthur sculde yete cum Anglen to fulste[4].   (14295–7)

[1] *prophet*   [2] *foretold*   [3] *sayings were true*   [4] *help*

Layamon's account of Merlin's prophecies may well owe something to
Geoffrey of Monmouth's *Vita Merlini*; but in these lines the indefinite
article is as noteworthy as the emphasis on the truth of the prophecies
and on the English (not the British, whose king Arthur was). It has
been plausibly suggested that we have here a guarded reference to
hopes that the young Arthur of Brittany might replace John as king:
Layamon, as distinct from Wace and Geoffrey, avers that King Arthur
('best of all youths') was sent for from Brittany to drive out the Saxons
(9896 ff.).*

Layamon's most important role lies in establishing the Matter (or
Myth) of Britain, and of Arthur. The myth was all the more potent
because it incorporated and extended genuine history, including
Caesar's invasion, the Saxon conquest, the reign of Athelstan: not to
mention the famous tale of *non Angli sed angeli*, perhaps Layamon's
only specific borrowing from Bede. By stopping at Cadwalader he
distances the whole sequence of events described, so that brave
British and cunning English become 'folded in a single party'. A random allusion to Norman 'nith-craften' (3547) is not sufficient to make
him a rebellious Englishman (or Welshman). His contribution to Englishry consists in providing native history (Wace's *romanz*) with a
dress, language, and colour that later romancers were to appropriate
for their own purposes.†

* J. S. P. Tatlock, *The Legendary History of Britain* (Berkeley, 1950), 504.
† The motives of the disguised hero, the prophetic dream, the storm at sea, the unexpected entry that silences merriment in hall, the sanctity of sworn brotherhood—all

To talk of Layamon's anachronisms is beside the point. For him a lord (British or Roman) is essentially a leader of a 'ferd' (OE *fyrd*); Brutus holds castles, Caesar is illiterate, Athelstan is credited with establishing moots, hustings, hundreds, even gaols, and making 'frith of deoren', i.e. preserving the game, though forest law did not in fact exist before the Conquest (if we except a bare reference in the Laws of Canute). The 'skycraft' attributed to Arthur's 'clerks' (12122–5) seems to belong rather to the twelfth century. The festivities of the Round Table blend Old English and Norman custom, with accompaniments of trumpets, gold ewers, silk towels—properties that will find a place in later romance.

If Layamon has little historical perspective, neither has Wace his predecessor. The society they describe remains static from century to century, corresponding neither to the Old English heroic age nor to the Normanized England of the twelfth century, yet with elements of both. The scene at the reception of Leir at the French court resembles that in which Beowulf arrives at Heorot. One king figures as a ring-giver ('bæges [rings] he dælde' 3701: not in Wace); another as a feudal lord ('thu art his mon and his cniht' (cf. Wace's 'porter homage'), 2162). In fact Layamon makes no absolute distinction between heroic and feudal society, whereas modern writers perhaps make the distinction too sharp. There is chivalry incipient in *Beowulf*, which has its own decorum, code of manners, formal greetings and courtesies, conventions of arming, pedigreed swords: the polished verse and firm tone of *Beowulf* suggest that it is the product of a long tradition, of which it is the sole, fortuitous relic. And the recurrence of so many of its themes and sentiments in Layamon is further evidence for the existence of a large body of unwritten verse on which he may have drawn. Madden, adopting the epithet favoured by early scholars, called the *Brut* a 'semi-Saxon' paraphrase. Although they meant it only in a linguistic sense, the epithet keeps its point.

these will be found in later verse. *King Horn* and *Havelok* have much in common in their tone and concerns with the *Brut*, and versions of them may well have been in embryo before Layamon died.

4

History in Verse

Short English Metrical Chronicle; 'Robert of Gloucester';
Mannyng's *Chronicle*; Barbour's *Bruce*

The tradition of verse-chronicle that began with *Brunanburh* shows signs of petering out in the anonymous couplets that go under the title of a *Short English Metrical Chronicle* but are better described (in one manuscript) as 'le brute d'Engleterre abrégé'. It is so short that it often degenerates into a mere list of regal names, though it has neither graces of style nor a care for verisimilitude that might make one wish it longer. In one manuscript it follows directly on the chronicle of 'Robert of Gloucester', in another (which includes an Anglo-Norman prose rendering of the English verse) it accompanies a text of Peter Langtoft's Chronicle.

The original text probably ran to no more than 900 lines, summarizing one of the numerous *Bruts* or the *Livere de reis de Brittanie** and finishing with Edward I; it was later extended to the early years of Edward III. More than one passage suggests a knowledge of 'Robert of Gloucester'. Some of the matter is common to Wace and Layamon. But to earlier accounts of Bath, city of Bladud, our versifier adds a mineralogist's analysis of the waters (saltpetre, salammoniac, etc., 'as the philosophres ['scientists'] us seggeth'). A few other passages have no known source: e.g. the account of the death of Vortigern at 'the castel of Aldewark'. The Lear story receives some embellishments; Hengist is credited with seven wives, 35 children, and with conjuring 'three hundred fiends of hell' to build a cross-channel bridge. Bladud inaugurates day-return trips (flights, in fact) from Bath to London. The account of the gifts of Hugh King of France to Athelstan—one of the rare passages of detailed description—includes, in one version, a line attributing to the precious stones in a rich cross of gold the virtue of turning foes into friends. St Kenelm's speaking head receives honourable mention. Alfred is said to have worked hard and slept little. One redactor has summarized Arthur's achievements, associating him with chivalry and 'gret aventures'. The texts as we have them

---

* Ed. J. Glover, RS xlii (1865).

testify to early fourteenth-century curiosity about national origins, but it was a zeal not according to knowledge, resulting in a strange medley of fact and fiction, and false onomastics; regal names and relationships are constantly confused: thus the legend of St Edmund of East Anglia is attached to King Edmund, in the time of Canute; and Edward the Confessor is called Canute's 'sone bastard'. The Danish king who attacks Alfred is in one version named as 'Havelok that was strong and stark' (430, cf. l. 729), a phrase evidently quoted from the romance of that name, a couplet of which is earlier applied to Arthur:

> He was the best knight at nede
> That myghte ride on eny stede   (245–6)

Cf. *Havelok*, 9–10 etc. The original writer evidently knew also the romance of *Richard Coer de Lion*, for the forty lines describing the king's stratagem of slinging hives of bees over the walls of Acre to discomfit the Saracens are taken almost word for word from the version of that romance in the Auchinleck manuscript, which contains a London text of the *Chronicle*. He probably drew at times on oral tradition, as in the story of the maiden Inge, an attempt to explain eponymously the name 'England' (275–330). Seven lines on Guy of Warwick (595–602) appear to be the first English reference to that hero, who in the Anglo-Norman prose text is said, moreover, to have killed the giant 'pur la nécessité d'Engletere', but the Anglo-Norman reference to the other English hero, Bevis of Hampton, and his 'destrere mult fort' is not found in the English verse.

Even in its fullest form the text was not too long to be memorized or recited. The opening couplet in one version runs:

> Herkeneth hiderward ye lordlynges
> Ye that wolen ihure[1] of kynges . . .

[1] *hear*

which in another is replaced by

> Here may men rede whoso can
> Hu Inglond first bigan
> Men mow[1] it finde in Englische
> As the Brout it telleth ywis.

[1] *may*

This reads like an appeal to a newly literate class by a cleric who sensed a growth in patriotic feeling. The author of the chronicle probably came from the same West Midland area as 'Robert of Gloucester', and Trevisa.

One version was probably made in Oxford; another shows acquaintance with local London traditions.

It will be clear that there is little in this humdrum chronicle to attract the modern reader. Yet it was by such means that a sense of English history spread in the fourteenth century and that the tale of Brutus's Albion became known to Chaucer and the author of *Sir Gawain and the Green Knight*. History, having taken something from romance, gave something back to romance; whilst Lydgate was to draw on this very text when compiling his verses on 'The Kings of England sithen William Conqueror'.

The 'Robert of Gloucester' just mentioned was long thought to be a monk of Gloucester, but it seems likely that more than one man had a hand in the making of the long verse chronicle in a 'measure'—according to Johnson—'which, however rude it may seem, taught the way to the Alexandrines of the French poetry'. It survives in two recensions, and was perhaps not completed much before 1325. Whoever the author or authors were, the work itself is not without interest, although Fuller's remark that antiquaries value 'Robert' more 'for his History than Poetry' has often been echoed. 'Robert' is interested not only in England (his poem opens: 'Engelonde is a well god lond—ich wene ech londe best') and in English historical events in his own times, but also in the English vernacular. His remarks on one linguistic effect of the Conquest—'bote a man conne [know] Frenss, me telth of him lute [he is little esteemed]' and that 'lowe men holdeth to Engliss, and to hor [their] owe speche yute [still]'. And he shows that he can use the vernacular with facility and some skill. He describes events in a plain and unpretentious style, but with a lively sense of incident (and sometimes it is clear that his account is based on first-hand information). If he is not moved by mystery or myth (he does not hold with the belief that Arthur will return—for his bones have just been discovered in Glastonbury), he is stirred by the violent scenes of his own day. He gives a vivid description of the rising of the supporters of Simon de Montfort at Gloucester in 1262–3, and of how the sheriff was seized:

> Hii[1] alighte with drawe suerd, with macis mani on,
> And with mani an hard stroc rumede[2] hor wey anon
> Vort[3] hii come up to the deis, and the sserreve[4] vaste[5]
> Bi the top hii hente[6] anon, and to the grounde him caste,
> And harlede him vorth villiche[7] with mani stroc among.
> In a foul plodde[8] in the stret suthe[9] me[10] him slong,
> And orne[11] on him mid hor hors and defoulede him vaste,[12]
> And bihinde a squier suthe villiche hii him caste,

And to the castel him ledde thoru out the toun,
That reuthe[13] it was vorto[14] se, and caste him in prison ...

(11072–81)

[1] *they*	[2] *cleared their*	[3] *until*	[4] *sheriff*	[5] *firmly*
[6] *they seized by the hair*		[7] *dragged him off ignominiously*		[8] *puddle*
[9] *then*	[10] *they*	[11] *ran*	[12] *trod him down thoroughly*	[13] *pity*
[14] *to*				

or of how at Oxford, in one of its many town and gown riots, the townsfolk came marching with banners 'to defouli alle the clerkis ar [before] hii iwar were', and how, warned by the ringing of the bell of St Mary's, these clerks 'up fram hor mete', and gave battle. In a few lines he can create a picture of the eerily grim weather before the battle of Evesham (1265), sent, he says, as a sign of Christ's displeasure:

... in the northwest a derk weder ther aros,
So demliche suart inou[1] that mani man agros[2]
And overcaste it thoghte[3] al that lond, that me mighte unnethe
ise[4],
Grisloker[5] weder than it was ne mighte an erthe be.

(11742–5)

| [1] *densely dark* | [2] *was afraid* | [3] *seemed* | [4] *one could scarcely see* |
| [5] *more terrible* | | | |

And he has an ear for colloquial expressions—the younger Simon de Montfort 'might say when he came':

'Lute ich abbe iwonne[1];
Ich mai honge up min ax, febliche ich abbe agonne[2].'

[1] *little have I won*   [2] *begun*

Different as are the matter and purpose of Robert Mannyng's *Chronicle* from those of *Handlyng Synne* (see above, pp. 41–7), in style the two works are not altogether disparate. Both reflect Anglo-French originals and the *Chronicle* perhaps benefited from his practice with the *Manuel des Péchés*. In the first part it follows the *Roman de Brut* of Wace, an accomplished versifier, not to say historian. Compared with him Mannyng comes off poorly. But he learned as he wrote, and the second part, based on the Chronicle of Peter Langtoft ('Peres bok'), shows increasing assurance, manifested in frequent authorial comment. He follows the 'romance', as he calls his source, even when marvelling at it for asserting that Edward the Confessor bequeathed his kingdom to Harold. For later events he drew on other sources as well—including Henry of Huntingdon who 'wrote the gestes olde'. Historical present helps to vivify the narrative:

> Henry is at his reste, his soule at Cristes wille,
> And Steven wille do his beste, in England leves he stille.
>
> (p. 109)*

Stephen in fact will fight the Battle of the Standard, which Mannyng describes as if it were yesterday: 'ther the Scottis misfore [fared badly], men telle the tale yit newe', followed by the remark 'the romance sais so there',—the 'romance' being his Anglo-French ('Romance') source to which he sometimes refers readers for details he omits.

Sometimes he goes back to Geoffrey of Monmouth's *Historia*, Wace's chief source, and even further back, to Bede. For some insertions no source can be found. His chronicle helped to confirm the manner of setting out history that was to be dominant for several centuries: his history is the reigns of kings, viewed from a moral standpoint. In the fourteenth century any history of Britain had to begin (witness the opening lines of *Sir Gawain*) with the tale of Troy and the descent of Brutus: hence Mannyng's allusions to Dares and to the story of 'the witches' Juno, Pallas, and Venus. His sense of identity with his native land shows through when he describes the events of the year 'whan the Romayns *us* forsoke'. He claims that the bishops of the time threw into wells crosses and bells 'that now men fynde on many half' (14562 ff.). We hear his own voice when St Anselm makes peace between Robert Curthose and the barons: 'I blisse Anselme therfore' (p. 97).

As in Layamon (and even as late as Camden), toponymy and onomastics play a large, sometimes a ludicrous, part: as when the 'fall' of Gogmagog is given as the origin of the name Falaise. In general Mannyng follows Wace both in matter and phrase, though adding tags and gnomic sentiments to fill out his lines and rhymes. And, as in Layamon, the narrative often proceeds by bouts of set speeches. Thus Corineus challenges the Poitevins, in terms a little crisper than Wace's:

> 'False folk! why fle ye?
> Fle ye alle for drede of me?
> I am al one, Coryneus,
> And for me one[1] ye fle thus?

* References to pages are from the edition of Thomas Hearne, *Peter Langtoft's Chronicle (as illustrated and improv'd by Robert of Brunne)* (Oxford, 1725), to lines from that part of the chronicle edited by F. J. Furnivall, RS lxxxvii (1887).

94

> Turn a-geyn! what have ye thought?
> Fende[2] your lord, and fles[3] nought!
> Turn a-gayn, and comes blyve[4],
> By two, by thre, by foure or fyve.
> And fende your land as men hardy;
> Ther folewes non bot onelyk y'[5].   (1571-80)

[1] *alone as I am*   [2] *Defend*   [3] *flee*   [4] *quickly*   [5] *only I*

Like Wace, Mannyng takes a dispassionate view of Arthur and has no doubt that he is dead; his confused encomium concludes:

> In Fraunce men wrot, and yit men wryte [his noble deeds]
> But herd have we of hym but lyte;
> There-fore of hym more men fynde
> In farre bokes, als ys kynde[1],
> Than we have in thys lond;
> That we have, there mon hit fond;
> Til Domesday men schalle spelle,
> And of Arthures dedes talke and telle.

> (10607-14)

[1] *natural*

These French books, we are told later, were written in a style that Englishmen cannot emulate, and in prose, for better understanding (10971-8).

There is not much subtle characterization in Wace, but still less in Mannyng: the incident in which the armies of Belyn and Brenne are reconciled by their mother Tonnewenne (3181-226) shows Mannyng adding touches of pathos that are hardly convincing. It is to Langtoft, his source for more recent events (up to the death of Edward I), rather than to the more rhetorical Wace that he pays tribute, in conventional style:

> Of his meninge y wot the weye
> But his fair speche can y nought seye;
> I am nought worthy open hys bok,
> For no conninge ther-on to lok ...   (16709-12)

Mannyng adds a preface to his Chronicle, addressed to 'Wites lewede', and animadverting, *inter alia*, on the varieties of French verse that he eschews:

> If it were made in ryme couwee[1],
> Or in strangere[2] or enterlace[3],
> That rede Inglis it ere inowe,
> That couthe not haf coppled a kowe[4],

95

That outhere in couwee or in baston[5]
Som suld haf ben fordon[6],
So that fele[7] men that it herde
Suld not witte how that it ferde[8].   (85–92)

[1] *tailed rhyme*   [2] *(a name for some stanza form)*   [3] *alternate rhyme*
[4] *coupled a tail = ?completed a couplet*   [5] *stanza*   [6] *come to grief*
[7] *many*   [8] *went*

(The relation between 'kowe' and 'couwee' is not altogether clear.) He professes that:

My witte was oure[1] thynne
So strange speche to travayle in . . .   (113–14)

[1] *over*

but the preface does not reveal what prompted Mannyng to undertake the task of translation; and it is not enough to say that he represents an interest in the English past, an interest that would be likely to grow as a sense of a new nation developed. He grasped the opportunity of extending his own as well as his readers' acquaintance with history, but it is clear that Mannyng also 'relished versing'. In his part of England there had been nothing of vernacular history since the last scribe of the Peterborough Chronicle (see pp. 259–63 below) had laid down his pen. And he may have consulted a version of that work: when he writes, of the Anarchy, 'som held with Stephen the kyng and som with Mald the quene' (p. 120), he is repeating almost word for word the earlier Chronicle (in its entry for 1140): 'sume helden mid te king, and sume mid themperice'. But his (or rather Langtoft's) version of the empress's escape from Oxford castle (p. 122) gives new details:

In the snowe for syght[1] scho yede out in her smok
Overe the water of Temse, that frosen was iys
Withouten kirtelle or kemse[2], save koverchef alle bare vis[3]

[1] *to avoid being seen*   [2] *shift*   [3] *with bare face*

To Langtoft Mannyng was doubtless attracted by his numerous references to his own county of Lincolnshire and events connected with it: they would suggest that a version in English would find at least a local response. A tale like that of the three monks of Lyndsay (Aldwyn, Elwyn, Reynfride) who went to build abbeys at Durham, York, and Whitby (pp. 80–1) would certainly stir local pride. But some of these Lincolnshire references are new, and reveal personal knowledge: notably his insertion of the tale of Havelok* (in the Lambeth continuation) in so far as it bears on the foundation of Grimsby:

* For the romance, see pp. 154–61 below.

Bot I haf grete ferly[1] that I fynd no man
That has writen in story, how Havelok this lond wan.
Noither Gildas, no Bede, no Henry of Huntynton,
No William of Malmesbiri, ne Pers of Bridlynton
Writes not in ther bokes of no kyng Athelwold,
Ne Goldeburgh his douhtere, ne Havelok not of told,
Whilk[2] tyme thé were kynges, long or now late,
Thei mak no menyng whan, no in what date.
Bot that thise lewed men upon Inglish tellis
Right story can me not ken, the certeynté what spellis.
Men sais in Lyncoln castelle ligges yit a stone,
That Havelok kast wele forbi everilkone[3],
And yit the chapelle standes, ther he weddid his wife,
Goldeburgh the kynges douhter—that saw is yit rife.
And of Gryme a fisshere men redes yit in ryme,
That he bigged[4] Grymesby Gryme that ilk[5] tyme.
Of alle stories of honoure that I haf thorgh souht[6],
I fynd that no compiloure of him tellis ouht.
Sen I fynd non redy, that tellis of Havelok kynde,
Turne we to that story, that we writen fynde . . .

(pp. 25–6)

[1] *wonder* [2] *at what* [3] *past everyone* [4] *founded* [5] *same*
[6] *searched*

The opening lines of this passage have their own interest as indicating that Mannyng did on occasion go to some trouble to consult authorities (and he mentions William of Malmesbury on at least one other occasion)—'compiloures' as he correctly calls them, whilst the later lines indicate beyond doubt that he knew of the English *Havelok* and sensed its value. Equally striking is his report that King John died not at Newark but at Haughe (Lincs.)—'so say men of that toun'—which, as Hearne noted (p. 212) is 'contrary to other Historians . . . but it seems Robert of Brunne . . . had it from tradition'. Other local references range from mention of Edward the Confessor's presence at Burgh in Lyndsey to the comment on the Lord Edward's presence at Netilham: 'it is the bishopes toun'. It is Mannyng the Gilbertine who notes that Hubert, John's Justiciar, translated St Gilbert 'in the hous of Sempryngham', and that the order arose in the time of Alexander Bishop of Lincoln. One event Robert can vouch for as an eye-witness. Speaking of Alexander Bruce, he writes:

Of arte he had the maistrie, he mad a commencyng*
In Cantebrige to the clergie, or[1] his brother were kyng.

* A. B. Emden's palmary emendation of MS 'corven kyng'. (*BRUC*, s.v. Bruce.)

Sithen² was never non of arte so that sped
Ne bifore bot on, that in Cantebrigge red.
Robert [the Bruce] mad his fest, for he was thore³ that tyme
And he sauh alle the gest⁴ that wrote and made this ryme.

(pp. 336–7)

¹ before   ² after   ³ there   ⁴ events

Mannyng himself, that is, was present at the Cambridge Commencement feast (analogous to the Oxford *Festum Ovorum*) of Alexander, paid for by his brother: our chronicler had not only seen the hero of Barbour's later epic, but sat at table with him and his more learned brother.

The chronicles Mannyng translates are national chronicles and in a special sense that they spell out the growth of nationhood. Arthur appears (if only incidentally) as a national hero and exemplar who had conquered thirty realms (p. 296); at the marriage of Edward of Warenne (p. 332) the feasting was the finest ever 'outtak [except] Carleon that was in Arthure tyme: / thare he bare the coroune therof yit men ryme'.

Mannyng's sense of Englishry emerges when he comes to the Conquest. It was a punishment for wickedness, and yet the Conqueror 'that we calle the Bastard'

. . . sette us in servage, *of fredom felle the floure*
The Inglis thorgh taliage¹ lyve yit in sorow fulle soure.   (p. 66)

¹ taxes

Of the pre-Conquest scenes the laconic account of the discovery of Harold's body in the Thames by fishermen at night is typical, with its concluding line: 'Som frendes he had that biried it in the kirke yerd' (p. 54). As we approach the thirteenth century the pace grows more lively, the verse takes on a jaunty swing. The Crusades bulk large and King Richard's adventures make as good reading here as they do in *The Talisman*. The poet now identifies himself with '*our* Englishmen', and, when he comes to the Lord Edward's exploits, he is deeply committed to the English cause and deeply hostile to Scotland and to Wales. Speeches freshen the narrative, and they are not always formal—' "O devel" said the king, "This is a foltid [foolish] man" ' (p. 164). Roger Lestrange addresses Llewellyn before his execution in emphatic measured phrase:

'Tuys ert thou forsuorn, and tuys thi feauté¹ broken,
'Tuys was thou doun born and for pes eft spoken.

98

'This is the thrid² tyme . . .
'Salle thou never thi lyve do Inglis man more wo.'   (p. 242)

¹ *fealty*   ² *third*

A liking for such turns shows in a sardonic comment:

Now of this olde monk, and this new kyng
That was not worth a fonk¹, don has his endyng.   (p. 172)

¹ *? spark*

In the first half the octosyllabics flow smoothly enough, and are occasionally diversified by unexpected shifts in the caesura; the second half, dependent on Langtoft, is in longer lines. Translation allows little room for rhetorical originality. Mannyng's verse is not excessively 'tagged'. A scattering of alliterative phrase is perhaps evidence of acquaintance with earlier verse, romance and other: 'he slouh alle riffe and raf' (p. 151); 'treie and tene' (p. 235); 'in mores and in medis' (p. 310); 'spied strete and strie' (p. 187). There is little distinctively local in vocabulary: though the seventeenth-century lexicographer Skinner noted that the term for herons—'heronsewes'—earlier than Chaucer's use—was still heard in seventeenth-century Lincolnshire. Narrative is fleshed with popular phrases and idioms. The comment on Stephen's perjury is that:

Thus he brak his avowe that he to God had suorn
For a buske or a bowe that he forgaf biforn.   (p. 112)

Occasionally a moral apophthegm is inserted, rephrased, or explained, and the work concludes with an *ubi sunt*, of ancient lineage:*

Where ere now alle thise, where ere thei bicomen,
Thise hardy men and wise? The Dede¹ has alle tham nomen²
. . . Now may men sing and say in romance and ryme
'Edward is now away, right has lorn his tyme'.

(p. 340)

¹ *Death*   ² *taken*

Besides *Havelok*, Mannyng knew the Tristan story and says that 'over gestes it has the steem [esteem]', though by his time it is partly unintelligible because 'of some copple [couplet] som is away'. From Langtoft he takes the abusive anti-Scots songs that enliven the account of Edward I's campaigns, extending the *incipits* as Langtoft gives them to such verses as these on the battle of Dunbar:

'The Scottis had no grace
To spede in ther space,

* See above, p. 53.

For to mend ther misse;
Thei filed[1] ther face
That died in that place'
(The Inglis rymed this).   (p. 277)

[1] dirtied

The English also rhymed this:

Jon the Baliol,
No witte was in thi pol[1],
Whan thou folie thouhtis,
To leve the right scole
Thou did als a fole,
And after wrong wrouhtis ...   (p. 279)

[1] head

These topical verses, whether anti-Scottish or anti-English, are in the same terse, interlaced 'rime couee'; which may indicate that they are literary reworkings of current popular verse. Whatever their origins, they bring a breath of 'flyting' into the main narrative, and Skelton, who loved to rail against the Scots, would have relished them. However, for the most exciting and dramatic verse chronicle of this period, it is to a Scottish writer—John Barbour—that we must turn.

Our knowledge of English verse composed north of the Border is fortuitous and its relics are fragmentary. Such as they are, they suggest that there early developed in the north a penchant for topical verse, satiric or elegiac. Wyntoun, the fifteenth-century chronicler, sets down a polished stanza lamenting the death of King Alexander I (*ob.* 1286):

Qwhen[1] Alexander our Kynge was dede
That Scotlande lede in luve and le[2],
Away was sous[3] of alle and brede,
Off wyne and wax, of gamyn and gle.
Our golde was changit into lede.
Crist, borne in virgynyte,
Succoure Scotlande and ramede
That stade[4] is in perplexité!   (vii. 3619 ff.)

[1] When   [2] peace   [3] abundance   [4] put

There is no reason to doubt that this stanza was contemporary; Wyntoun himself lacked the skill to write it. But, if genuine, it indicates that the stanza form which Dunbar adopted two hundred years later was already in common use; which would explain why another Northern poet, Laurence Minot (see p. 394 below), makes it the vehicle for comment on the taking of Calais (1347), though his lines, as befits their popular purpose, are more heavily alliterative. The siege of Berwick, exactly ten years after Alexander's death, was the theme of a jeering rhyme of rougher quality:

> What wenys[1] Kynge Edwarde with his long shankys
> To have wonne Berwyck all our unthankys[2]
>   Gaas[3] pykes him
> And when hath it . . .
>   Gaas dykis him.*

[1] *thinks*   [2] *against our will*   [3] *go*

The allusion here being to the part that King Edward had played in the siege by helping with the digging. Barbour, who evidently kept his ears open for such verses, and described the siege eighty years later, in another context refers to songs sung by young women 'ilke day' (xvi. 521–2). So events of Scottish history were the common subject of popular rhymes. Whether Barbour knew the flatter verse of English chronicle we cannot say: he chooses incidents of the kind that the 'Gloucester' chronicler relished, in particular the skirmishes which they both describe as 'bikkers'. Barbour's octosyllabics run so easily as to suggest that he was not the first Scots writer to practise them. He himself has been credited with a Scottish *Brut*, now lost; and a few of his formulas suggest acquaintance with older English epic (e.g. 'mony fey fell under feit', xv. 45). An abundance of similar alliterative phrases points to contact with some tradition of English verse narrative.

In his *exordium*, Barbour insists that the pleasure of narrative consists first in the actual act of composition ('the carpyng') and next in its veridicity: 'the suthfastnes / That schawys the thing rycht as it wes'; taking as his warrant the old stories already in writing that present the deeds

> Of stalwart folk that lyvyt ar[1]
> Rycht as thai than in presence war.

[1] *formerly*

The stories he has in mind, those that 'men redys', are evidently those of ancient history, for he soon compares his heroes to the Machabees who

> Fawcht into mony stalwart stour
> For to delyvir thar countré

* R. M. Wilson, *LSE* v (1936), 43.

Fra folk that, throw iniquité
Held thaim and thairis in thrillage.[1]   (i. 468–71)

    [1] *thraldom*

Yet at the same time he describes his work as a romance, and after a Prologue or, rather, Introduction of 444 lines begins afresh with a typical romance appeal to a listening audience:

Lordingis, quha[1] likis for till her
The Romanys[2] how begynnys her
Off men that war in gret distres
And assayit[3] full gret hardynes
Or[4] thai mycht cum till thar entent. . . .
Bot quhar God helpys quhat mai withstand?

                                               (i. 445–56)

    [1] *whoever*   [2] *romance*   [3] *underwent*   [4] *before*

This has the same appeal as *Havelok*, an earlier tale of a kingdom won after endurance of distress, because 'ther God wile helpen, nouht ne dereth [harms]' (*Havelok*, 647).

Barbour is writing in an age saturated in romance and sees history in romantic terms. Of Edward, Robert the Bruce's brother, he writes

Of his hye worschipe[1] and manheid[2]
Men mycht mony romanys make.   (ix. 491–2)

    [1] *honour*   [2] *manliness*

He describes his hero as himself familiar with romance: when the Bruce's force has to cross Loch Lomond in a boat that can take only three at a time, he reads aloud to his men the romance of *Fierabras*, who had overcome like perils before capturing the Crown of Thorns (iii. 437 ff.). Barbour sees himself as a *maker*, not simply a chronicler of the exploits of Bruce and James Douglas:

Off thaim I thynk this buk to ma[1]
Now God gyff grace that I may swa
Tret it, and bryng it till endyng
That I say nocht but suthfast[2] thing.   (i. 33–6)

    [1] *make*   [2] *truthful*

A maker was a wordsmith who might highlight adventures but did not invent them. Barbour, in fact, gives us continuous narrative that leaves the impression of authenticity. His version of Scottish history cannot often be faulted.* His discreet rhetoric helps to confirm one's

* See G. W. S. Barrow, *Robert Bruce and the Community of The Realm of Scotland*

impression of a well-read and well-balanced man, a 'clerk'; in fact he became Archdeacon of Aberdeen. But he was also a deeply committed poet, whose sympathies were entirely with his exemplary hero (*rex illustrissimus* runs the rubric of the Edinburgh manuscript of the *Bruce*). He early identifies himself with Bruce's party, and encourages his readers to do so, by such prayerful asides as:

> Der God that is off hevyn King
> Sawff hym and scheld hym fra his fayis[1]   (ii. 144–5)

[1] *foes*

(Douglas is making off with a bishop's horse.) It is as if he were putting Bruce forward as a Scottish rival to the British Arthur whom Layamon had made the epitome of valour. This would square with his 'romance' treatment of such events as Douglas's fulfilment of the Bruce's dying wish. After confessing that he had killed many an innocent man, Bruce says that he had hoped to show repentance by taking the Cross. Now he can only wish that his heart will go against the Saracens in token. So Douglas bears it with him when he fights them in Spain until at last he is slain, to the grief of his 'menyhe' (company), who lament his passing much as Beowulf's thegns had lamented their lord:

> For he wes swete and debonar
> And weill couth tret his frendis far
> And his fais[1] richt felonly[2].   (xx. 511–12)

[1] *foes*   [2] *fiercely*

Though small in stature, he 'lufit lawté'. Such physical detail is what repeatedly differentiates Barbour's narrative from conventional romance. But before describing, in most matter-of-fact terms, how Douglas's men boiled his corpse so that they could carry the bones back to Scotland, he inserts a learned comparison with Fabricius who in the wars against Pyrrhus refused a chance of pursuing his enemy, a tale he may have read in Valerius Maximus, on whom he certainly drew for a similar story. Barbour is thus elevating his epic heroes to the semi-mythical status of Havelok or Guy of Warwick. Of the young James Douglas he says:

> But wondirly hard thingis fell
> Till him or[1] he till state wes brocht.

(London, 1965), 431–2: Barbour emphasizes the chivalrous elements in Bruce and in his age, but nevertheless 'on the score of a general reliability ... must be reckoned a biographer, not a romancer, ... a most careful and exact recorder'.

Thair wes nane aventur that mocht[2]
Stunay[3] hys hert, ne ger[4] him let[5]
To do the thing he wes on set . . .

And nevir wald for myscheiff[6] faill
Bot dryve the thing rycht to the end,
And tak the ure[7] that God wald send.　(i. 296–312)

| [1] *before* | [2] *could* | [3] *terrify* | [4] *cause* | [5] *cease* | [6] *mis-* |
| *fortune* | [7] *fate* | | | | |

Yet he never obscures facts, never prettifies, never takes descriptions on trust. Of this same hero he says, as was said of Havelok, 'all hym luffyt that war him ner'; but—

Bot he wes nocht so fayr that we
Suld spek gretly off his beauté
In vysage wes he sumdeill[1] gray
And had blak har, as ic hard say
Bot off lymmys he wes weill maid,
With banys[2] gret and schuldrys braid.
His body wes weyll maid and lenye
As thai that saw him said to me

.　　.　　.　　.　　.　　.

And in spek wlispyt he sum deill.　　(i. 381–93)

[1] *somewhat*　　[2] *bones*

In his lisp, black hair, strength, and courtesy, the young Douglas resembled Hector—but of course Hector has never had his peer. Douglas sows his wild oats in Paris; but for this Barbour finds excuses that probably derive from some 'mirror for princes':

For knawlage off mony statis
May quhile[1] availye full mony gatis[2] . . .

.　　.　　.　　.　　.　　.

And Catone sayis us, in his wryt,
To fenyhe[3] foly quhile is wyt.[4]　　(i. 337–44)

[1] *sometimes*　　[2] *ways*　　[3] *feign*　　[4] *wisdom*

Barbour's rhetoric adds to the impression of romance. Like Malory and the French romance writers whom Malory read, he likes to follow one thread of narrative to a certain point, then to pick up another thread with a transition formula such as 'Nowe agayne to the king ga we' (ii. 49), or (iv. 1–3):

In Rauchryne[1] leve we now the king
In rest, forowtyn barganying[2],
And of his fayis[3] a quhile[4] spek we . . .

[1] *Rathein*　　[2] *without fighting*　　[3] *foes*　　[4] *while*

The rhetorical question that Chaucer uses at the close of Part I of *The Knight's Tale* ('Ye loveres axe I now this questioun . . .'), Barbour had already practised:

> Now demys quhethir[1] mair lovyng[2]
> Suld Tedeus haf, or the King?   (vi. 283–4)
>
> [1] *whether*   [2] *praise*

'Quhat sall I mair say of his mycht?' (x. 785) is a variant of this that Chaucer also will employ.

The work is propagandist in intent, and Barbour always keeps his audience in mind; writing to be read aloud, he uses the formulas of oral poetry: 'Lordingis, quha likis for till her': 'as ye hard me say', 'Now ye may her, if that ye will'. The device of *occupatio* is modified accordingly:

> But off thar nobleis gret affer[1]
> Thar service, na thar realté[2]
> Ye sall her na thing now for me.   (ii. 182–4)
>
> [1] *pomp*   [2] *royal dominion*

He frankly enlists his hearers' sympathies: 'God help him, that all mychtis may!' (iii. 366); 'Now, bot God help the nobill King / He is neir hand till his ending' (v. 583–4). At the outset Barbour insists that there are two elements in good narrative: (1) sheer skill in composition: 'the carpyng'; (2) verisimilitude: 'the suthfastnes / That schawys the thing rycht as it wes'. He takes as exemplars 'old stories' (he was evidently thinking of Greek and Roman historians) that described:

> the dedys
> Of stalwart folk that lyvyt ar[1]
> Rycht as thai than in presence war.   (i. 18–20)
>
> [1] *formerly*

Hence his search for evidence and citing of witnesses. When he affirms that on one occasion Edward Bruce with a mere fifty men discomfited fifteen hundred, he feels it necessary to quote his authority: 'That worthy knight Sir Allan of Cathcart told me this tale as I shall tell' (ix. 575–6). Similarly he knows intimately the terrain he describes: he can say of the north side of Kilmarnock water: 'The way [is] . . . sa ill, as it apperis today' (viii. 40). Many of the places referred to (like Edinburgh Rock) would be familiar to his audience. So he had every reason to be accurate.

In any given episode it is always his veridical detail and veridical language that are telling—as in the story of the haywain in which eight men hide at the time (August in Scotland) when, in ballad phrase, 'husbandmen winnis their hay' and halt it half way through the gate of Linlithgow Castle, cutting the 'hedesoyme' (traces) so that it cannot easily be withdrawn (x. 162 ff.). Barbour has no false sense of dignity of history. On one of the five occasions when three traitors attempt to kill the Bruce it is while he is going to the privy that he is attacked (v. 521 ff.). On another, when the three men invite him to partake of the wether they are carrying, the meal makes him sleepy and 'he winkit a littell we', as does his foster-mother, with fatal results.

Part of the vividness comes from the presentation of pithy talk: all the Scots leaders, and several of the English, are given something to say, and speak without resort to rhetoric—thus when Mowbray thinks he has captured Bruce, he shouts out in a provocative jeer: 'Help, help, I have the new-maid king!' (ii. 416). And all the talk is laced with terse proverbial wisdom (another feature found in popular romances like *Havelok*), phrases such as 'Ure [fate] helps hardy men'—Aymer de Valence's way of saying (when appraising Bruce's character) that Fortune favours the brave. Such apophthegms also crop up even in the middle of racy narrative. When the traitor Osborn throws a red-hot coulter into a heap of corn in the hall of Kildrummy Castle to set fire to it:

> . . . it full lang wes thar nocht hyd,
> For men sais oft that fyr, na pryd[1],
> But[2] discovering, may na man hyd.
> For the pomp oft the prid furth schawis[3],
> Or ellis the gret bost that it blawis.
> Na mar may na man fyr sa covyr
> Bot low[4] or reyk[5] sall it discovyr.
> So fell it heir; for fyre all cleir
> Soyn[6] throu the thik burd[7] can[8] appeir
> Ferst as a sterne[9], syne[10] as a moyne[11] . . .   (iv. 118–27)

| [1] pride | [2] without | [3] reveals | [4] flame | [5] smoke |
| [6] quickly | [7] board | [8] did | [9] star | [10] then | [11] moon |

Sententiae of this kind are constantly used as reminders of an over-ruling providence:

> Bot oft failyeis[1] the fulys thoucht;
> And wis mennis etling[2] cumis nocht
> Til sic end as thai weyn[3] alwayis.
> A litell stane[4] oft, as men sayis,
> May ger weltir a mekill wane.[5]
> Na manis micht may stand agane[6]

The grace of God, that all thing steris[7].
He wat quhat-to[8] all thing efferis[9]
And disponis[10] at his liking
Eftir[11] his ordinans, all thyng.   (xi. 21.30)

[1] *fails*   [2] *endeavour*   [3] *expect*   [4] *stone*   [5] *can cause a great*
wagon to be overturned   [6] *against*   [7] *rules*   [8] *knows to what*
[9] *belongs*   [10] *disposes*   [11] *according to*

Balliol's acceptance of the crown on Edward's terms provokes the cryptic authorial comment:

Quhethir[1] it wes throuch wrang or rycht
God wat[2] it, that is maist[3] of mycht.   (i. 177–8)

[1] *whether*   [2] *knows*   [3] *greatest*

Boethian overtones sometimes emerge: *determynat*, like the nonce-word *determinabilly* (iv. 677), first used by Barbour, has a philosophical colour:

For in this warld that is sa wyde
Is nane determynat that sall
Knaw thingis that ar forto fall;
But God, that is off maist powesté,[1]
Reservyt till[2] his majesté
For to knaw in his prescience
Off alkyn tyme the mowence[3].   (i. 128–34)

[1] *power*   [2] *to*   [6] *mutation*

Here *prescience* evidently predates Chaucer's use of the term (*TC* iv. 998), and *reserve* is not otherwise found in the required sense before Wyntoun, who is simply imitating Barbour.

It is to unpredictable human fortunes that these asides chiefly allude. *Weird* (fate) is invoked much as in *Beowulf*, or *Troilus*: 'Werd that to the end ay driffis / The warldis thingis' (iv. 148–9). With philosophy goes psychological perception. When Lennox joins Bruce they both weep for joy; but this was 'na greting properly', men can weep at will. True tears come from joy or pity springing from a tender heart (iii. 513 ff.). From Virgil, perhaps ('Forsan et hæc olim meminisse juvabit', *Aeneid* i. 203), Barbour had learnt that

Quhen men oucht[1] at liking[2] ar
To tell off paynys passyt by
Plesys to heryng wonderly.   (iii. 560–3)

[1] *at all*   [2] *at their ease*

The unheroic aspects of war are never glossed over: Englishmen caught unprepared for death 'rycht as bestis can rair [roar] and cry'

(iv. 418). 'Despitous' men can be slain unaware (v. 79 ff.). Bruce slays Comyn in church as he shows him the indenture:

> syne[1] with a knyff,
> Rycht in that sted,[2] hym reft the lyff. (ii. 35–6)

> [1] *then*   [2] *place*

When the English attack the Scottish *schiltrum* (the old *sceldtruma* formation used at Maldon and at Hastings (cf. p. 143)), they ride 'sarray' (viii. 296), in close order, 'with hedis stowpand and speris straucht [extended]'; they are repulsed when the Scots spear their horses, who trample down their riders in their flight. (Barbour notes also the psychological effect of this victory (viii. 387).) He never allows us to forget that it was usually a fight against odds—Douglas goes to recapture his inheritance with no more than two men. Whilst he can find room for didactic, or sententious, or eulogistic comment, he is economical in narrative, giving just those facts that bring life to the story. The method is beautifully exemplified in the account of Earl Randall's capture of Edinburgh Castle (Book x). The earl's father, Barbour tells us, had once been Keeper of the Castle, and Randall, as a youth 'sumdele volageous [somewhat flighty]', used to climb down by night to visit a 'wench' in the town, by a dangerous path known only to himself. Up this path on a dark night he offers to lead thirty men. The poet says, sardonically:

> I trow, mycht thai haf seyne cleirly,
> That gat[1] had nocht beyn undirtane,
> Thouch thai to let[2] thame had nocht ane. (x. 591–3)

> [1] *way*   [2] *hinder*

As it was, they were utterly winded by the time they reached the top, and the 'chak-wachis' (night patrol) assembled just above the place where they were resting:

> Now help thame God, that all thing may,
> For in gret perell ar they! (x. 614–5)

They were unnoticed, but one of the watch casually 'swappit doun a stane', shouting, 'Away, I see you well', on the off-chance that he would scare anyone in the neighbourhood. In the event their presence is betrayed by their talking and moving their weapons.

Similarly, when in the same book (x. 352 ff.) Douglas takes Roxburgh Castle, we learn the name of the man who made the hemp ladders ('Sym of the Ledows'), how he strengthened the rungs, and how the raiders wore black frocks over their armour so that in the dark they looked like cattle lying in the fields. They come so close to the watch that they hear one of them joking to his mate about the owner of these cattle whom they suppose to be making merry—it is the night of Shrove Tuesday—and beyond caring whether the Douglas takes off the cattle he has rashly left out all night. There is a 'plein-air' quality about the whole exciting story. In another encounter Bruce takes on and slays fourteen assailants by himself; when it is all over his men find him (like a knight refreshing himself after a tournament)

> sytand alane
> That of[1] his basnet[2] than had tane[3]
> To tak the air, for he wes hate[4].   (vi. 303–5)

[1] *off*   [2] *helmet*   [3] *taken*   [4] *hot*

We are put alongside the characters throughout, in their discomforts and perils as well as their feats of arms. When Lennox had to take to rowing:

> nevys[1] that stalwart war and squar
> That wont to spayn gret speris war[2]
> Swa spaynyt aris[3] that men mycht se
> Full oft the hyde leve on the tre[4]   (iii. 581–4)

[1] *fists*   [2] *were accustomed to span great spears*   [3] *oars*   [4] *the skin stick to the wood*

When his enemies gain on them, Lennox (following Jason's precedent) has goods thrown overboard so that his pursuers are delayed by stopping to pick them up. Barbour adds that the currents round the isle of Rathlin are as perilous as the Race of Brittany or the Straits of Morocco, but he localizes the action in native terms: the narrow place where the Macindrossers attack Bruce (iii. 109) is 'betuix a louch side and a bra'. The northern poets relished sea-scenes, and Barbour provides a splendid picture of Lennox entering the straits with a heavy sea running (iii. 697 ff.). Some ships slide down to the waves 'rycht as thai doune till hell wald draw', while others mount to the crest, and

> ay amang[1]
> The wavys reft thar sycht of land.

[1] *continually*

Vivid as this is, the vividness is perhaps Virgil: cf.

> Hi summo in fluctu pendent; his unda dehiscens
> Terram inter fluctus aperit.*
>
> (*Aen*. i. 106–7)

* 'Some of the seamen hang upon the billow's crest; to others the yawning sea shows ground beneath the waves' (trans. Fairclough).

The fact is that Barbour had a superb story to tell—a tale full of excitement and perils in 'the imminent deadly breach', of courage in adversity, and he had likewise a superb hero to commemorate, one who has so far escaped all attempts at 'debunking'. Robert the Bruce, as Barbour depicts him, is more human than Beowulf or *pius* Aeneas, more prudent than Roland. He has something of the cunning and alertness of an Odysseus, the strategy and generalship of an Alfred. All his qualities are harnessed to the cause of his country's liberation. His greatness, as Barbour perceived, lay not in his bravery but in his *mesure* or moderation:

> . . . he led hym[1] *with mesure* ay[2]
> And with gret *wit*[3], his chevelry
> He governit ay sa worthely
> That he oft full unlikly thing
> Brocht rycht weill to full gud ending   (ix. 667–71)

[1] *himself*   [2] *always*   [3] *wisdom*

It is the *deliberate* valour that inspires his men (vi. 316 ff.), the determination that is expressed so pithily in his comment when he is hunted down with hound and horn by Sir Aymer de Valence, like a wolf, or a thief: 'gif he cumis, we sall him se [we'll look after him]' (vi. 474). He shares with his followers all their hardships, but he also shares his own perilous adventures by recounting them in detail—evoking their praise and admiration (vii. 352 ff.). Before a battle he will hearten his men by a speech explaining his tactics (xi. 271 ff.). Withal he is a first-rate strategist, always choosing his terrain carefully and never missing a clue. He will detect a woman spy simply by reading her ugly countenance (vii. 553 ff.). He withdraws from Perth to the jeers of its defenders—only to come back with ladders on a dark night, wading through the moat up to his neck—to the astonishment of a French knight, who bursts out:

> 'A lord, quhat sall we say
> Of our lordis of France, that ay
> With gud morsellis farsis thair panch[1]
> And will bot et and drynk and dance,
> Quhen sic a knycht, sa richt worthy,
> As this is throu his chevelry,
> Into sic perill has hym set,
> To wyn ane wrechit hamlet!'   (ix. 396–403)

[1] *stuff their bellies*

The French knight crosses himself 'for the ferly [marvel]'—and follows Bruce's example. Like the poet, who occasionally uses French chivalric language—'avalye que valye' (ix. 147)—Bruce is not outside the chivalric code, and when Aymer de Valence challenges him to fixed combat on a fixed day he agrees—but at the same time cannily cuts dikes across the moors, and leaves gaps in them so that he can defend his position. He respects a valorous foe, and such a foe in turn respects him. When Macnaughton, a knight of Bruce's foe the Lord of Lorn, praises him as the 'starkest pundelan [warrior]' he ever saw (iii. 159–60), Lorn sneers, 'so you seem to like the way he kills off our fellows'. Macnaughton replies:

> 'Schyr', said he, 'sa our Lord me se'[1].
> To sauff your presence[2], it is nocht swa
> Bot quhethir sa he be freynd or fa[3],
> That wynnys prys off chevalry,
> Men suld spek tharoff lelyly[4].
> And sekyrly[5], in all my tyme,
> Ik hard[6] nevir, in sang na ryme,
> Tell off a man that swa smertly
> Eschevyt[7] swa gret chevelry!'   (iii. 172–80)

[1] *protect*   [2] *saving your presence*   [3] *foe*   [4] *loyally*   [5] *certainly*
[6] *I heard*   [7] *achieved*

When the Scots chase the English to the gates of York from Byland, one prisoner is ransomed in the usual style for twenty thousand pounds— 'As I haf herd mony men say' (xviii. 521). But two French knights are set free without ransom because Bruce sees that it is their 'worship' that has led them to fight and 'nouthir wrath na evil will' (534).

Throughout, Bruce is the embodiment of courage; but his confidence comes from a belief that heaven is on his side:

> '. . . thocht[1] thai [the foe] be fele[2]
> God may rycht weill our werdis dele[3]   (ii. 328–9)

> He that deis[4] for his cuntré,
> Sall herbryit[5] intill hevyn be'.   (ii. 340–1)

[1] *though*   [2] *many*   [3] *apportion our fates*   [4] *dies*   [5] *lodged*

Like the *Beowulf* poet, he thinks that praiseworthy deeds will bring lasting reward (cf. xvi. 523 ff. and *Beowulf* 24–5).

Robert's brother Edward is equally valorous, but differentiated in various ways: so much of a stoic that men marvelled when he actually showed grief for Neil Fleming:

> For he wes nocht custumabilly
> Wount for till meyne[1] ony thing
> Na wald nocht heir men mak menyng.   (xv. 236–8)

[1] *to lament*

Edward's bravery comes near foolhardiness and in the end costs him his cause and his life. Like Roland, he refuses to wait for reinforcements:

> 'Sall na man say, quhill[1] I may dre[2]
> That strynth of man sall ger[3] me fle!
> God scheld[4] that ony suld us blame,
> That we defoull our nobill name! (xviii. 53–6)

[1] *while*   [2] *endure*   [3] *cause*   [4] *forbid*

It is a stance that his Irish allies refuse to take: their custom being 'till follow, and ficht, and ficht fleand' (78).

Of Bruce's personal exploits, one of the most memorable was his stand against two hundred men of Galloway who traced him to a bog with a sleuth hound. He stops at a ford, and sends away the two men with him:

> 'Schir', said thai, 'quha sall with yow be?'
> 'God', he said, 'forouten ma[1];
> Pas on, for I will it be swa.' (vi. 88–91)

[1] *and no-one else*

The rest of the tale is equally terse (and equally typical). Bruce sees the enemy band coming up at speed, and debates whether he should go for help. He has to choose whether to flee or die:

> Bot his hert, that wes stout and he[1]
> Consalit hym allane to byde
> And kep thame at the furdis syde[2]
>
> .   .   .   .   .   .
>
> He did rycht as his hert hym bad
>
> .   .   .   .   .   .
>
> Met thame richt stoutly at the bra,
> And sa gud payment can thaim ma[3]
> That fiffsum[4] in the furd he slew[5] (vi. 116 ff.)

[1] *high, lofty*   [2] *ford's side* (i.e. *where they could only pass one at a time*)
[3] *make*   [4] *five in all*   [5] *slew*

—the kind of payment that the Byrhtnoth of *Maldon* had promised to the Danes in just such a situation:

> Hi willað eow to gafole garas syllan
> Ættrynne ord and ealde swurd*

The battle at Bannockburn is the climax of the whole poem and to it Barbour gives no less than three books (xi–xiii). Bruce's address before the battle can compare with Henry V's before Harfleur:

* 'They intend to give you spears as tribute, venomous point and ancient sword.'

> ... quhat sa evir man that fand
> His hert nocht sekir[1] for till stand
> To wyn all or de[2] with honour,
> For to maynteyme that stalward stour[3],
> That he be tyme suld tak his way ...   (xi. 398–402)

>   [1] *steadfast*   [2] *die*   [3] *conflict*

The poet reports it all like a modern commentator:

> I trow thai stalwardly sall stand
> And do thair devour[1] as thai aw[2].   (429–30)

>   [1] *duty*   [2] *ought*

The sight of the English army, one hundred thousand strong, awes Douglas and Sir Robert Keith, who are reconnoitring; characteristically Bruce tells them the facts and says that the enemy are in evil array—for often (Barbour explains) 'of ane word may ris / Discomfort and tynsall [damage] withall ...'. When battle was joined it grew so hot

> That all thair flesche of swat wes wete,
> And sic ane stew rais owth thame then[1],
> Of aynding[2], bath of hors and men,
> And of powdir, and sic myrknes
> Intill the ayr abovyn thame wes
> That it wes woundir for till se.   (xi. 613–18)

>   [1] *such a mist rose out of them then*   [2] *breathing*

Robert arrays his forces, riding on a pretty little grey palfrey, with a crown over his bascinet, a battle-axe in hand—which breaks when at the final onset he cleaves Henry de Bohun's head. The English vanguard is repulsed by Earl Randolph and his band, which bristled with spears like a hedgehog ('hyrcheoune'; xii. 353). Bruce consults his lords:

> 'For gif[1] ye think spedfull[2] that we
> Fecht[3], we sall fecht'.   (xii. 194–5)

>   [1] *if*   [2] *advantageous*   [3] *fight*

All agree that they will fight tomorrow:

> 'For dout[1] of ded[2] we sall nocht fale:
> Na nane payn sall refusit be
> Quhill[3] we have maid our cuntré fre'.   (204–6)

>   [1] *fear*   [2] *death*   [3] *until*

Then Bruce makes his longest speech—120 lines—deliberate and powerful: they are fighting for the right, for their wives, their children, their honour.

A general's address to his troops is a favourite topos in Tacitus, or Livy, and Barbour may have read Livy. But there are some authentic later examples (besides one in *Old Mortality*), which suggest that Bruce's speech before Bannockburn, like the Declaration of Arbroath (1320) sent by the Scottish barons to the Pope, was not poet's rhetoric—they too said that they fought against the English 'not for glory, or riches or honours, but only for liberty, which no true man would yield save with his life'.*

That night the English rest in the Carse (fen) of Stirling, bridging the pools with thatch, doors, and shutters. The next morning the Scots hear mass and the King makes knights

> as it afferis[1]
> To men that oysis thai mysteris[2]   (xii. 413–14)
>
> [1] *behoves*   [2] *use those crafts*

The English array themselves in a *schiltrum*—except the vanguard. Edward is advised to make a strategic withdrawal so that the Scots will be diverted by the spoil in their pavilions. But he scorns to retreat before such 'a rangale [rabble]'. He thinks that the Scots kneeling in prayer are praying for mercy, though a knight comments 'but nocht at [from] yow—yon men will wyn all or de'.

When at last the English give way the Scots army cries 'On thame! On thame! On thame! thai faill!' (xiii. 205); and the Scottish camp followers choose a captain from among themselves:

> And schetis, that war sumdeill[1] braid,
> Thai festnyt[2] in steid of baneris
> Apon lang treis[3] and on speris
> And said that thai wald se the ficht
> And help thar lordis at thar mycht.   (xiii. 236–40)
>
> [1] *somewhat*   [2] *fastened*   [3] *poles*

The English took them for enemy reinforcements and panicked, forcing Edward to leave the field, against his will. But one English knight, Sir Giles of Argentine, disdained flight. Barbour clearly approves; he gives the knight's own words, doubtless from some English source:

> 'Schir, sen[1] that it is swa—
> That ye thusgat[2] your gat[3] will ga,
> Haffis gud day! For agane[4] will I.
> Yet fled I nevir, sekirly.

---

* W. C. Dickinson, *Scotland from the Earliest Times to 1603* (3rd edn., revised and edited by A. A. M. Duncan, Oxford, 1977), 169.

And I cheis[5] heir to byde and de
Than till lif[6] heir and schamfully fle'. (xiii. 303–8)

[1] *since* [2] *thus* [3] *way* [4] *back* [5] *choose* [6] *to live*

The burn is heaped high with English dead, so that men could pass over their bodies dry-foot; the surviving English flee to Stirling and climb the crags there till they are so densely hung with men 'that it wes wonder for to se' (430). King Edward escapes by taking a boat to Bamborough Castle. The poet's final comment runs:

Lo! quhat falding[1] in Fortune is,
That quhile[2] apon a man will smyle
And prik[3] hym syne[4] ane otherquhile! (xiii. 632–4)

[1] *change* [2] *sometimes* [3] *wound* [4] *then*

The wheel of Fortune thus brings in its revenges. When Bruce is at the top of the wheel, Edward must needs be at the bottom.

Barbour not only loves his hero and his hero's cause. He loves the excitement of battle and of preparation for battle, the rising sun catching the shields and bascinets:

Thair best and browdyn[1] bricht baneris,
And hors hewit[2] on seir[3] maneris
And cot-armouris off seir colour,
And hawbrekis[4] that war quhit[5] as flour,
Maid thame glitterand, as thai war lik
Till angellis he[6], of hevinis rik[7]. (viii. 229–34)

[1] *embroidered* [2] *coloured* [3] *diverse* [4] *hauberks* [5] *white*
[6] *high* [7] *kingdom*

This is the very language of *Henry IV*, 'glittering in golden coats, like images'. The colours and motion of chivalry delight him, as they were to delight the writer of *The Knight's Tale*:

And armys that new burnyst wer,
So blenknyt[1] with the sonnys beyme
That all the land wes in ane leyme[2]
With baneris richt freschly flawmand,
And pensalis[3] to the wynd waffand[4]. (xi. 189–93)

[1] *shone* [2] *flame* [3] *pennons* [4] *waving*

Chaucer's picture of Theseus before Thebes in *The Knight's Tale* (*CT* I. 975 ff.) scarcely betters this.

Barbour delights in the deployment of forces, the details of action and of personal appearance. So he gives us innumerable vignettes like that of Ingram de Umfraville bearing a red bonnet on a spear as token of his 'height of chivalry' (ix. 508). He does not know the name of the man bribed to kill Bruce:

> But I herd syndir[1] men oft say
> Forsuth that his ane e[2] was out. (v. 506–7)

> [1] *various*   [2] *one of his eyes*

He likens the many pits dug at Bannockburn (for the English to fall into) 'till an waxcayme [honeycomb] that beis mais [make]' (xi. 368). When Douglas makes traps to catch fish, the fish are specified: 'geddis [pikes] and salmonys / Trowtis, elys, and also menounys [minnows]' (ii. 576–7). Scots poets have always been devotees of the creel. Douglas disguises himself, when going to kirk on Palm Sunday, in a mantle 'old and bare', and a flail 'as he a taskar [thresher] was' (v. 318). Entering a castle held by the English, and cutting down its defender, he broaches the nine casks so that

> Meill[1], malt, blude and wyne
> Ran altogidder in a mellyne[2]. (v. 405–6)

> [1] *meal*   [2] *medley*

Hence, says Barbour, the accepted phrase for such a mess is 'Douglas larder'. To this kind of local particularity Froissart, the only contemporary chronicler who can compare with Barbour, never attains. It shows in a different way in a night scene where Bruce's men are rowing towards a fire on a headland that they thought had been lit as a signal:

> Thai na nedill had na stane,
> Bot rowyt alwayis intill ane[1],
> Stemmand alwayis[2] apon the fyre. (v. 23–5)

> [1] *right forward*   [2] *steering straight*

The general pattern of Barbour's racy narrative, with its plenitude of incident, salted with vivid phrase, humorous and gnomic comment, resembles nothing so much as that of *The Canterbury Tales*, though Barbour had ceased writing before Chaucer had even begun to compose them, and his qualities are in fact inimitable. He speaks admiringly of Bruce as 'forsy' in fight, and he had himself a certain 'forsy' strength, kindled, one may suggest, by his ardent yet by no means uncritical devotion to the patriot adventurer who did ultimately win freedom for his country. His is an independent genius, an epic largeness comparable only to Scott's. He was a man after Scott's own heart, with the same gusto and 'spread', the same power to sustain a continuum of interest. Scott evidently relished the work; *The Lord of the Isles* is based on an episode in the *Bruce* and in some ways re-creates its ethos, even though transposing it into romantic terms, but more revealing is the likeness between Meg Merrilees and the hostess who tells the Bruce his fortune (iv. 632 ff.).

Barbour has affinities with other Scots poets. He set up the model of hero as king, to be followed in the *Wallace*, and later in *Squire Meldrum*. In his version of the Aesopian fable of the Fox and the Fisherman (xix. 648) he anticipates Henryson, in his seasonal transition-passage (Book v), Wyntoun, Douglas, Dunbar. Here he shows acquaintance with the romance-pattern that includes such passages as headpieces; of this *Kyng Alisaunder* and *Gawain* provide notable examples (see below, pp. 190, 214), and that Barbour is drawing on a convention is suggested by the presence of the nightingale which never sang in Scotland:

> This wes on vere[1], quhen wyntir tyde
> With his blastis hydwis to byde[2],
> Wes ourdriffin; and byrdis smale
> As thristill and the nychtingale,
> Begouth[3] rycht meraly to syng,
> And for to mak in thair synging
> Syndry[4] notis, and soundis sere,
> And melody plesande to here.
> And the treis begouth to ma
> Burgeonys[5], and brycht blumys alsua[6],
> To wyn the heling[7] of thar hevede[8]
> That wikkit wyntir had thame revede.   (v. 1–12)

[1] *spring* [2] *hideous to experience* [3] *began* [4] *various* [5] *buds*
[6] *also* [7] *covering* [8] *head*

The picture that emerges from over 12,000 lines is of a lively poetic mind, open to influence from vernacular as well as classical literature. Of Barbour's reading in Virgil there are several indications, including Bruce's justification for killing soldiers whilst they sleep:

> For weriour na fors suld ma[1]
> Quhethir he mycht ourcum his fa[2]
> Throu strynth or throu sutelté;
> Bot at gud faith ay haldin be   (v. 85–8)

[1] *make no account* [2] *foe*

—which echoes 'dolus an virtus, quis in hoste requirat? [whether deceit or valour, who would ask in war?]' (*Aen*. ii. 390). Statius (or more probably some prose abbreviation of the *Thebaid*) he draws on for the long digression in Book vi devoted to the tale of Tydeus, inserted there because it too includes a battle fought by moonlight. Comyn's treachery is paralleled by the betrayal of Troy, as told by those inseparable pseudo-historians, Dares and Dictys—but also by Mordred's betrayal of Arthur, 'as the *Brut* bears witness' (i. 560), an allusion that the authorities on the legendary history of Britain have overlooked. The tale of the 'leill Fabricius' at the end of Book xx doubtless comes from some common source-book. Of Bruce himself it is said that he told at length the story of Scipio freeing and arming slaves when Hannibal attacked Rome (iii. 220), and a quotation from the *Pharsalia* is applied to him (iii. 281–2): ('hym thocht he had doyne [done] rycht nocht / Ay quhill to do him levyt [remained] ocht'). One does not think of English kings of the period as prone to cite the classics, but Robert may well have had some learning: his brother Alexander incepted MA at Cambridge in 1301–2 and Robert Mannyng avers that Robert was present on that occasion (see above, pp. 97–8). Barbour presents him as literate, reading the 'Romanys off worthi Ferumbrace' aloud (iii. 437)—the twenty lines summarizing the romance do not allow us to say what version of it (probably French) Barbour had in mind. By the fourteenth century the exemplars of martial chivalry had been grouped as the Neuf Preux, the Nine Worthies, and it is to one of those, Alexander, that Barber compares the Bruce and his friends. Earl Randall's exploit in scaling the Edinburgh Castle Rock is likened to Alexander's in climbing the walls at Tyre, a digression manifestly based on the French *Roman d'Alisaundre* since it speaks, like the French, of Alexander leaping from a *berfrois* (tower on the wall) (x. 708). When the Lord of Lorn likens him to Golmakmorn, a hero from the Finn cycle (iii. 68–70), the poet remarks that a more apt comparison would be with Gaudifer in the Foray of Gadres.*

Octosyllabics are the ideal medium for this quick-flowing kind of narration, especially if (as often in Barbour) they are run on for two or three lines. But Barbour is doing more than tell a story; he is making a new kind of epic, in no less than twenty books. Within this scheme there is plenty of room for epic comment and generalization. And in several of the books, especially the early ones, he takes the earliest opportunity he can find of introducing generalizing comment on topics arising out of the narrative. Of these the famous paean to freedom is the first. It comes at the part where he is describing the miseries of the Scots under Edward's rule, when

---

* These allusions have been cited in support of the view that the Scots *Buik of Alexander*, which translates into octosyllabics three episodes from the great French cycle *Les Vœux du Paon* and *Les Fuerres de Gadres* was a work by Barbour himself, and that the date on the rhymed colophon thereto (1438) is a scribal error. But the *Buik* evidently belongs to the fifteenth century.

'their foes were their judges'—and 'Quhat wretchitnes may man have
mar?' Barbour sets forth the theme in an *exclamatio*:

> A! Fredome is a noble thing!
> Fredome mais[1] man to haiff liking[2].
> Fredome all solace to man giffis[3]
> He levys at ese that frely levys!
>
> . . . he that ay[4] has levyt fre
> Ma nocht knaw weill the propyrté[5]
> The angyr[6] nor the wrechyt dome
> That is cowplyt[7] to foule thyrldome[8]   (i. 223–36)

---

[1] *makes* [2] *happiness* [3] *gives* [4] *ever* [5] *distinctive quality*
[6] *affliction* [7] *linked* [8] *thraldom*

—which leads to a question posed in clerkly disputations in the
schools: whether a thrall should obey his lord rather than his wife if
she has asked him for her marriage debt. Of this, he says in a humility-
formula that anticipates Chaucer:

> I leve all the solucioun
> Till thaim that ar off mar renoun.   (i. 259–60)

In later books the eulogy of freedom is paralleled by a similar encomium of valour (vi. 325 ff.), valour being the mean between foolhardiness and cowardice. Against them should be set the strong
imprecations against treachery, notably the treason of Comyn, who
disclosed his pact with Bruce to King Edward, a trespass against the
moral law. But Bruce himself pays dearly for killing Comyn in church,
thereby breaking the *grith* that attached to the altar (ii. 44), and
earning the enmity of Comyn's friends.

The poem thus becomes an exposition of certain traditional values.
These values include Love, though love in Barbour is not *amour
courtois* as generally understood, even if described in similar terms:

> . . . luff is off sa mekill[1] mycht
> That it all paynys makis lycht
> And mony tyme mais tendir wychtis[2]
> Off swilk strenthtis and swilk mychtis
> That thai may mekill paynys endur.   (ii. 520–5)

---

[1] *great*   [2] *creatures*

These pains are not the pains suffered by a lover for his mistress, but
those of the wives of Bruce's followers, who shared their 'angyr and
pain' and are compared to the wives of the Seven Heroes who warred
against Thebes.

So there is nothing provincial about Barbour, as there was nothing
provincial about his hero. The poet was in fact a travelled man. As

archdeacon he was granted safe-conduct to go to Oxford to study in 1357 and 1364, and to go to Paris (like many Scots) for the same purpose in 1365 and 1368. His introduction of terms like 'solucion' and 'disputacion' and concepts like 'prescience' testifies to some scholastic training. One might justifiably claim him as the first Oxford poet to write in the vernacular.* But he has much stronger claims to attention. He belongs to the same company as Chaucer, Gower, and the *Gawain* poet, sharing with the two former poets the classical learning that is a new feature in fourteenth-century vernacular verse. There was some reason for his being unread south of the border in the fourteenth century, when there was still intermittent strife with Scotland, and northern English (not yet known as Scottish) sounded uncouth to southern ears. But neither indifference nor chauvinism should any longer be allowed to mask his unique qualities.

* A long excursus at the end of Book iv on the limitations of astrological prediction could be read as a comment on the Oxford clerk's addiction to that art in *The Miller's Tale*.

5

Romances

(i) Introductory

John Barbour calls his narrative of Robert Bruce's adventures, which were certainly historical, a romance, and the writer of the verse 'Laud' *Troy Book*,* based on the 'history' of Guido delle Colonne, speaks of himself as the 'maker' of his 'romance'. It is, in fact, to such classical or pseudo-classical narratives that the term *roman* is first applied in French: as in the *Roman d'Enéas* or the *Roman de Thebes*. In such titles it distinguishes the version written in the vernacular (*romanicé*) from the Latin original: Chaucer's Pandarus finds ladies of Troy listening to the *romance* of Thebes (appropriately enough, since it concerns a town besieged as Troy was besieged). But (like Barbour's *Bruce*) it is also described as a *geste* (< OF *geste*, L *gesta*, 'events'), a *geste* being a sub-species of romance; the term indicating that some historical truth is claimed for the narrative. So the narrator of the tale of *Havelok* calls it a *gest* (2984), and speaks of 'gestes' recited at a royal entertainment as well as of 'romanz reding on the bok' (2327-8).

A fourteenth-century romance, *The Earl of Toulous* is called both a 'geste' and a 'lay of Bretagne'. It is in rhymed stanzas, whereas the *Geste Historiale*, a rendering of the Troy story, is in alliterative measure. That *geste* sometimes indicated a narrative in that measure is suggested by the Host's words when interrupting Chaucer's own tail-rhyme romance:

> Lat se wher thou kanst tellen aught *in geeste*
> Or telle in prose somwhat, at the leeste
>
> (*CT* VII. 933-4)

—lines that should be read in the light of the Parson's avowal that he cannot '*geeste* rum ram ruf bi lettre'; a Southerner, he cannot offer an alliterative romance. But the 'geestours' whom Sir Thopas summons along with minstrels, to tell 'romances that been royales' whilst he is going through the tedious business of arming, would not be limited to the alliterative measure. In short, *geeste*, like *romance*, was an elastic,

* So called after the manuscript which contains it: MS Laud 595 in the Bodleian Library.

and often remains an elusive, term. We shall probably never know, for instance, what the author of *Sir Gawain and the Green Knight* had in mind when asserting that the honour of wearing a green baldric like his hero's was 'breved [recorded] in the best boke of romaunce' (2521).

Most romances, to be sure, like *Gawain*, narrate the adventures of some hero of chivalry. Yet the eponymous hero of *Havelok*, though of royal birth, can hardly be called such a hero. What such a tale has in common with the French romances from which so many English romances derive is the element of perilous adventure and feats of martial prowess. Love, which later ages were to associate with romance, plays a very minor part in *Havelok*.

When the dreamer in the *Book of the Duchess* asks for 'A romaunce . . . to rede and drive the night away' he is brought, of all things, a book that included Ovid's *Metamorphoses*. 'Romance' must here indicate some work in French verse with a strong 'story-interest' (Chaucer perhaps had in mind the version known as the *Ovide Moralisé*), and the lovelorn dreamer naturally turns to a tale of hapless love, that of Ceyx and Alcione. But they are husband and wife, not lover and mistress. The fidelity of husband and wife figures in English romances at least as often as 'courtly love', so-called, which is the dominant ingredient in so many French romances of the twelfth and thirteenth centuries. English taste had perhaps been conditioned by such works as the Old English translation of the Greek romance of *Apollonius of Tyre*, which has a plethora of adventures, though they are not knightly; and, though the expression 'to fall in love' first occurs in this text,* it is by no means courtly. Gower was to devote practically the whole of the eighth book of *Confessio Amantis* to this tale. It is hard to deny his rendering the title of romance, and like many romances it ends with husband and wife living happily ever after. It stands, however, apart from the main stream of development. The emphasis that chivalry placed on individual prowess resulted in the protagonist of tales of adventure being shaped in the mould of a knightly hero—even if (like Havelok) he could not be set in a knightly context. The attention paid in romance to the person and character of the hero is evident from the title that each bears, which in the vast majority of cases is simply the name of this hero.

The topographical and geographical settings of romances are not often, or consistently, particularized. Often they are second-hand, taken over wholesale from the French original. Untravelled audiences were hardly capable of visualizing scenes set often in the Medi-

* 'þa gefeol his agen mod on hyre luf', *The Old English Apollonius of Tyre*, ed. P. Goolden (Oxford, 1958), 2.

terranean world, a world threatened by onsets of the 'Saracens'. Yet Crusaders brought home some knowledge of this world, and romance-writers were catering for the new awareness, just as cheap novels of the Wild West were to cater for thousands of readers who had never seen the Rockies. Chaucer, always sensitive to literary climate, deliberately set his longest romance in the Greece of the crusaders that had by his time faded into history—so that his knight can begin his tale of 'old, unhappy, far-off things' with typical romance formulas: 'Whilom, as olde stories tellen us. . . .'

But the attraction of romance was never simply that of 'escapist' literature. The prince or knight had more than a decorative function in feudal society; even his pleasures—hunting, hawking, freebooting—had a part in feudal economy. As a romance-hero he could be presented only in terms of the civilization that audiences knew, or knew of. It is not that the Middle Ages lacked 'historical sense', rather, they were conscious that, as Chaucer puts it, 'ther nis no newe gyse that it nas not olde'. So the contemporary everyday world finds a place in the romances: sometimes we glimpse this world as clearly as we glimpse it in Chaucer's fabliau tales, as, for instance, in the scene in which the young Havelok, waiting for a porter's job on Lincoln bridge, and hearing the call 'bermen, bermen, hider forth alle!', thrusts his way forward, shoving down 'nine or ten' into the mud.

The very existence of manuscripts indicates that romances were read—which in the Middle Ages meant read aloud—as well as recited. Several passages suggest that some of them were sometimes sung. In the conclusion to *Troilus* Chaucer thus addresses his book:

> And *red* wherso thow be, *or elles songe*,
> That thou be understonde, God I biseche   (v. 1797–8)

—an old classical topic, given a new twist. The juxtaposition here of 'red' and 'songe' indicates that *read* means 'read aloud', a sense supported by several other examples;* 'sung' can hardly mean anything other than recited or intoned with the rhetorical dignity suggested by 'Arma virumque *cano*', the opening words of the *Aeneid*. Certainly some earlier tales and romances had been sung: in *Havelok* there is not only 'romance reading' but also singing—'ther mouhte men here the gestes singe'. In *Sir Cleges* a king is depicted listening to a harper who 'sange a gest by mowth' (l. 484). *King Horn* begins:

> Alle beon he lithe[1]
> That to my songe lythe[2];

[1] *Let them all be merry*   [2] *listen*

* See H. J. Chaytor, *From Script to Print* (Cambridge, 1945), ch. ii.

and the poet of *Emaré* assumes his poem will be sung—'As I here synge in songe'. But all these romances are in short-line couplets—or tail-rhyme stanzas (like Chaucer's *Sir Thopas*): couplets or rhymed stanzas could easily be set to a simple tune, or, possibly, intoned. (According to Masefield—who studied verse-speaking carefully— Yeats wanted poems to be chanted, set with musical notes, though not sung.) Some at least of the so-called Breton lays were associated with the harp. Works of more elaborate metrical form (like *Troilus*), or with long irregular stanzas (like *Sir Gawain and the Green Knight*) would not call for, or fit, musical accompaniment. But the 'bob and wheel'—the short rhymed verse at the end of each stanza in *Gawain*—may have been given such a musical rendering. Whatever the precise significance of 'sing' in the passages quoted, it reminds us that the romances were primarily *performances*—not books on a shelf.

For as long as the romances were read or recited *in public* they were surrounded by a sense of occasion. The importance of a social event would be marked by the number of *disours* (tale-tellers) present, along with the musicians and the jongleurs. Weddings and royal or knightly ceremonies were evidently the chief occasions for such entertainment. The *locus classicus* is in one of the lengthiest and most sophisticated Provençal romances, the thirteenth-century *Flamenca*, which gives us a list of all the romances recited at the wedding of a noble lord.* It occupies some 100 lines, and includes some tales that will turn up in English dress: some classical (Dido and Orpheus), others Arthurian (Ywain and Gawain, Percival, Libeaus Desconus). Though this catalogue gives us valuable evidence and information, we need not take it literally: the most voracious appetite for romances must have been appeased after a few days of these at courtly equivalents to modern 'pop' festivals. In fact, such listings seem to have become a recognized piece of romance 'furniture', to be introduced when appropriate. The Middle English romance *Richard Coer de Lion* lists seventeen romances on end (6723 ff.): these the narrator says he will not 'rede' (i.e. read aloud) since none of their heroes were as valiant as Richard; the names are introduced simply to serve as foils. Chaucer gives a similar catalogue in *Sir Thopas* (2087 ff.) where he is deliberately 'guying' the device, as Skelton does later in *Phyllyp Sparowe* (628 ff.). Yet when feasts went on for weeks there would certainly be plenty of opportunity for one or more *disours* to display the whole of their repertoire. In *Havelok* the 'romance-reading' and accompaniments go on for forty days—a conventional figure, but representing a good long time:

* *The Romance of Flamenca*, ed. and tr. M. J. Hubert and M. E. Porter (Princeton, New Jersey, 1962), ll. 618 ff.

people who had travelled several days along muddy tracks were in no hurry to go home. At the beginning of *Gawain*, Arthur is described as entertaining his knights at Christmas in just this fashion. We are told that he had the habit of not sitting down at such high feasts 'er him devised were / Of sum aventurus thyng an uncouthe tale' (92–3)—until some *disour* or *gestour* had come forward and entertained the company with a brand new *roman d'aventure*, fit for royal ears. The opening lines of the alliterative *Wars of Alexander* (a very readable work) affirm that folk are specially fain to listen to romances when they are 'festid and fed'. And a more didactic text, the *Speculum Vitae*, notes that minstrels and *gestours* perform 'namely [especially] whan thei come to festes' (l. 42).*

From the catalogues in various romances including the parodic *Sir Thopas* it would be easy to compile a list of consistently popular themes. The *Speculum Vitae* says that 'gestours' speak of Bevis of Hampton, Guy of Warwick, Octavian, Isumbras, and many other such 'gestes'. Some of these heroes remained popular, in degenerate chapbooks and blackletter ballads, till the seventeenth century. A long roll-call at the beginning of the 'Laud' *Troy Book* concludes with three names of particular interest:

> Off Havelok, Horne and of Wade,
> In romaunces that of hem ben made
> That gestoures often dos of hem gestes[1]
> At mangeres[2] and at grete festes.

> [1] *recite tales about them*   [2] *dinners*

Romances of Horn and Havelok are extant; but about a romance of Wade we know no more than the name. In *Troilus* (iii. 614) Pandarus 'tolde tale of Wade'. Unless this was or had become a purely proverbial expression it was probably a version of a story attached to a Norse hero of that name—a story that might seem appropriate to Pandarus at that juncture. Speght, an early editor of Chaucer, has the tantalizing comment: 'Concerning Wade, and his bote called Guingolet . . . as the matter is long and fabulous, I passe it over.' Speght may have been fudging (elsewhere Gringolet is the name not of a boat but of Gawain's horse), but a Franciscan who wrote a *Fasciculus Morum* in the fourteenth century refers to 'those mighty champions, Onewone [or Unewyn] and Wade, who now dwell in Elveland'.† Onewone must be Uneven, a known Teutonic hero (in Scott's time a castle bearing the name of Uneven stood near the Roman Wall), so Wade too may have had such an origin.

* J. Ullmann, 'Studien zu Richard Rolle', *Englische Studien*, vii (1884), 469.
† C. Brett, *MLR* xiv (1919), 1.

Another indication of popular taste—or rather of its diversity—is given in the opening of the alliterative *Wars of Alexander*. Some people, it says, like to listen to saints' lives; some have 'langing of lufe lays to herken / How ledis [men] for thaire lemmans [loved ones] has langor endured'; and some like to hear 'of curtaissy, of knighthode, of craftes or armys'. Here we have two categories of tales: (1) the love-story telling the ardours and endurances of love; what the lady in *Sir Gawain* cleverly calls 'the lettrure of armes'—the literature of knighthood, the nature of which she proceeds to identify:

> Hit is the tytelet token and tyxt[1] of her werkkez,
> How ledes[2] for her lele[3] luf hor lyvez han auntered[4],
> Endured for her drury[5] dulful stoundez[6]
> And after venged[7] with her valour and voyded[8] her care . . .

(1515–18)

| [1] inscribed title and very words | [2] men | [3] faithful | [4] ventured |
| [5] love | [6] grievous times | [7] avenged | [8] banished |

(2) the tales of knightly prowess, as such: the exploits of Guy of Warwick, Bevis of Hampton, and other champions. Two of the major fourteenth-century poets happen to provide us with more particular indications of favourite themes. The first is Chaucer. Parody always fixes on the familiar, and part of the parody of *Sir Thopas* lies in the fact that it compresses into small compass all the most obvious, and recurrent, features of romance. Thus: Sir Thopas figures as the valiant knight who is also a mighty hunter (in the romances, Arthur, Tristram, not to mention the Green Knight and others, frequently figure in hunts, described in detail); he rides through a forest, filled with love-longing—precisely as predicated in *The Wars of Alexander* (of a knight); he is threatened by a giant: as are all Arthurian heroes at some time or other—witness Gawain, Libeaus Desconus, and Arthur in the alliterative *Morte*; he is in love with an elf queen: she represents the element of faerie that occurs constantly—notably in *Sir Orfeo*—(and that is more powerful, and sometimes more sinister than its equivalent in modern children's stories or *A Midsummer Night's Dream*); finally, the general setting and situation gives opportunity to describe minstrelsy, feasting, arms, and armour, and the commonplaces of romancers, and excuse to 'lay it on' with both hands. Even the description of Sir Thopas sleeping in the open and lying in his *hood* is an allusion to the 'dole', the rough times, they might suffer: so Gawain on his way north slept with his 'yrnes' (armour) 'ner slayn wyth the slete' (729).

It is the author of *Gawain* who gives us another epitome of the incidents of romance—lines 691 ff. of that poem allude to several of the stock scenes of chivalric romance: knight-errantry in the strict sense, the fights at fords (715 ff.), strange adventures with dragons, and finally the reception at a mysterious castle. But what in other romances is the very stuff of the story is here quickly passed over. *Sir Gawain* is the greatest of the romances precisely because it is able to minimize, to subsume, the stock situations. It develops out of them but becomes something different in the process. And because it is so sophisticated, it demands an extended treatment which would swell this chapter inordinately. An account of it will be found in the following chapter (see pp. 202–17).

A listening audience made for some freedoms peculiar to oral narrative, as well as for some limitations. A listener cannot keep in mind every detail, or recall the appearances of every character—especially if the romance is long, and read or recited in sections, at day-long intervals. Chaucer could not have read the whole of his *Troilus* to any audience in a single day; it makes more demands on the listener than any play. Even *Gawain* probably took two or three sittings, and longer romances may have provided entertainment for a week or more. In these circumstances it was not consistency in detail that counted but the general effect, in particular the evocation of pleasingly familiar or traditionally acceptable scenes and settings—as in modern 'Western' films. Hence the abundance and recurrence of set-pieces or topoi: tournaments, chance encounters in a forest, challenges at a ford, descriptions of rich dress or armour, of choice menus, elaborate architecture, or entertainment.

The longer romances, and some of the short ones, are divided in extant manuscripts into sections, sometimes called 'fits' or *passus* that would allow for breaks or adjournments. Part of the 'manifest banter' of *Sir Thopas*, to use Hurd's term (he recognized that the parody exposed the 'impertinences only' of books of chivalry)[*] lies in the division of the incomplete work, brief as it is, into 'fits' (*CT* VII. 888–90)— and that at a point where it is not structurally called for; implying that such terms and divisions were sometimes introduced mechanically. *The Knight's Tale*, on the other hand, an epitome of English romance at its best and most sophisticated, is broken into four parts, the final *pars* making just over 600 lines. The four fits of *Sir Gawain* are shorter; but there the pause between the last two, indicated by 'And ye wyl a whyle be stylle', would have been brief.

In estimating an audience's powers of endurance we should remember that 'performances' would be comparatively rare, and that

---

[*] *Letters on Chivalry and Romance* (1762), ed. E. J. Morley (London, 1911), 147.

listeners would be keyed up for the occasion, not in the passive state of television-viewers. The endurance-powers of the reciter must also be considered. He would need, in Prynne the Puritan's phrase, to re-focillate his wasted spirits. After seven thousand lines of one version of the (distinctly prolix) *Guy of Warwick*, there occurs—somewhat abruptly—the couplet:

> For the gode that God made,
> Fylle the cuppe and make us glade.

Such pleas may have been supplied by a thoughtful 'maker', but in the stanzaic romances they are extra-metrical, which suggests that they may owe their place to the reciter. In the longer romances (*Kyng Alisaunder* has over 6,700 lines in one version, while *Arthour and Merlin* has nearly 10,000, and the Auchinleck *Guy of Warwick* 12,000 lines), it was sometimes necessary to provide a brief recapitulation of 'the story so far'. Thus, after indicating a break in the narrative of *Kyng Alisaunder* with the couplet:

> Now resteth Alisaunder in this siggyng[1]—
> Yhereth[2] now al other thing,

> [1] *siege*   [2] *Hear*

the poet reminds his hearers of earlier episodes:

> Herd yee habbeth, *ich wil reherce*,
> How the messagers comen from Perce[1]
> For trowage[2] and Philippe ennoyed[3]—
> How Alisaunder it hem withseide ...   (1661–6)

> [1] *Persia*   [2] *tribute*   [3] *angered*

Similarly major changes in the story-line, or returns to it, as well as digressions from the main theme, have to be clearly marked. When in *Libeaus Desconus* a knight is sent off as prisoner to Arthur, the poet signals clearly that he is 'out of the story':

> Now lete we Wylyam be,
> That went yn his jorné ...   (429–30)

using a formula which had been frequently used in earlier French romances.

There are less obvious means of indicating breaks, points of rest, or changes in the direction of the narrative. One is the seasonal or gnomic headpiece, usually lyrical in tone or heightened in expression. Of such verses *Kyng Alisaunder* offers no fewer than 27 examples, some of which constitute links as much as pauses. The realistic note struck in some of these (see pp. 190–1 below) would itself be sufficient to rouse a jaded audience. A similar series occurs in *Arthur and Merlin*, which follows the progress of the year:

> Mirie time is Averrille[1],
> Than scheweth michel of our wille[2];
> In feld and mede floures springeth,
> In grene wode foules singeth,
> Yong man wexeth jolif,
> And than proudeth* man and wiif.

(259–64; Auchinleck MS)

[1] *April*   [2] *desire*

It is also 'merry' in May, when the days draw out and 'Damisels carols ledeth' (ibid. 1714).

The *Gawain* poet who, like Chaucer, touches nothing that he does not transmute, offers a characteristic expansion of this device at the beginning of his second fit, devoting forty lines to the progress of the seasons, and framing them in gnomic sentiments that anticipate the melancholy Jaques:

> A yere yernes[1] ful yerne[2], and yeldes never lyke
> The forme to the fynisment[3] foldez[4] ful selden
>
> .   .   .   .
>
> Thenne al rypez and rotez that ros upon fyrst
> And thus yirnes[5] the yere in yisterdayez[6] mony,
> And wynter wyndez ayayn[7], as the worlde askez[8].

[1] *passes*   [2] *swiftly*   [3] *beginning*   [4] *matches*   [5] *speeds*
[6] *passing days*   [7] *returns*   [8] *requires*

The winter setting of Fit iv is sketched more briefly but no less effectively. The poet has in both places integrated the formal headpiece into the structure of the romance and at the same time made it a mirror of his hero's feelings. The opening lines of *The Canterbury Tales* show Chaucer achieving a similar effect, and the *incipit* of Malory's twentieth book—'In May, when every harte floryshyth and burgenyth . . .' has the same double function.

Critics have proposed to classify the romances as (to take one schema) biographical, homiletic, or verse-novel. But it is more important to indicate the importance of the listening audiences in shaping the structure and dictating the very medium of the genre. That medium is verse, because verse is easy to remember and easy to recite. And its beat was probably more regular, and so more appealing, than extant texts suggest. To a professional *disour* or *gestour*, whether

---

* Cf. 'Wymmen waxeth wounder proude' in the Harley lyric 'Lenten ys come with love to toune' (see below, p. 403), where the sense is evidently 'lively' or 'wanton'.

he was reader or reciter, keeping metre would count more than exact verbal reproduction; and this is the point of Chaucer's prayer that none should mismetre his *Troilus* 'for defaute of tonge' (*TC* v. 1796). The *disour* as much as the 'maker' of the romance was helped by the stock tags or *chevilles* that are an ingredient of most romances and trip lightly off the tongue—so lightly that their nuances easily escape the glossator faced with such a couplet as

> The fairest levedi[1], for the nones,
> That might gon on bodi and bones.

[1] *lady*

Listeners have to be given time to settle down, and opportunity to catch the gist of a passage if it has been blurred by extraneous noises. Opening lines are aimed at the curiosity, or the compassion, the common humanity of a potential audience. So the reciter will begin:

> The tale of Havelok is i-maked
> Hwil he was litel he yede ful naked

or (*The Earl of Toulous*):

> Leve lordys y schall yow telle
> Of a tale some tyme befelle
> Farre yn unkowthe lede:
> How a lady had grete myschefe[1]
> And how sche covyrd[2] of hur grefe

[1] *misfortune*   [2] *recovered*

The opening stanzas of *Sir Gawain*, whilst at once linking the promised tale with past British glories, promise *ferlyes* (marvels) and 'an outtrage awenture of Arthurez wonderez' (a story remarkable even amongst the many marvellous things associated with Arthur). The phrase 'if ye will a while dwell [stop, stay]' found in other romances indicates perhaps that passers-by must be persuaded to stop and listen. And such persuasion may be repeated at due intervals:

> And ye wyl a whyle be stylle
> I schal telle yow how thay wroght,

says the poet of *Gawain* at the close of his third fit, just before the climax of his story.

The size and nature of the audience for English romance cannot be accurately deduced from internal evidence. The reciter who asks for a pot of ale to wet his whistle may well be addressing a village clientele, a request for a cup of wine suggests a setting of castle or manor; but not many surviving manuscripts can have served as actual 'prompt-books'. Following the French habit, a romance-writer generally began with an address that would put the *disour* on good terms with his listeners. 'Herkenyth, lordynges, and yeveth lyst' is the opening line of *Sir Otuel*; here 'lordynges' stands for little more than the 'gentle reader' of early novels.

Large or miscellaneous audiences prescribed not only the range of themes and situations and techniques of narrative but also metrical form. Four-stress lines in rhyming couplets were evidently thought to be an excellent vehicle for a fast-moving narrative. The native alliterative mode evidently answered to something deep in the English sensibility; it had been the medium of poetic narrative in pre-Conquest times and was used again for this purpose—following Layamon's precedent—in the fourteenth century. The stanzaic forms adapted for romance renderings were generally simple and suited to recital, though Robert Mannyng complains of some that were too complicated.* Perhaps poems and patterns that appeal today because of their supposed originality were suspect then precisely because they seemed deviant: of early French romances *Aucassin and Nicolette* is probably now the best known, yet its form, a unique mixture of verse and prose, may have been considered daring in its time. *Sir Gawain and the Green Knight* with a stanza basically alliterative, but rounded off by a rhymed sequence, survives in one copy only, which may suggest that it was not well known in its day. There is not a single reference to it in medieval literature or medieval documents, unless we take 'the Greene Knyght' in the inventory of the books of John Paston II to refer to it rather than to the later romance of that name in tail-rhyme stanzas.†

But with the Pastons we come to the era of private reading, and when printers begin to cater for private readers we come to the end of romance in the forms that the Middle Ages knew it. Already in Chaucer's time there is evidence that listening audiences had grown small and select; and Gower can posit a reader with an audience of one—the lover's mistress, who wishes 'to rede and here of Troilus' (*CA* iv. 2795). Women of gentle birth are easily credited with this liking for private or semi-private readings. In one of the Harley Lyrics the poet describes his mistress's 'lefly [beautiful] rede lippes lele [true], romaunz forte rede'—as if reading romance aloud was a finishing-school accomplishment. The Iseult of *Sir Tristrem* was fond

* See above, pp. 95–6.
† *Paston Letters and Papers of the Fifteenth Century*, ed. N. Davis (Oxford, 1971), i. 517.

of hearing 'gle', and 'romance to rede aright' (1258). In *Ywain and Gawain* a girl* reads to a knight and his lady in an orchard:

> The mayden red at[1] thai myght here
> A real[2] romance in that place
> (But I ne wote of wham it was)—
> Sho was bot fiftene yeres alde.   (3088–91)

[1] *so that*   [2] *royal*

The role and status of the *disour* or minstrel who read or recited romances has been the subject of debate from the time of Thomas Warton and Joseph Ritson. With the term 'minstrel' we associate the harp, and doubtless many *disours* carried harps: Haukyn in *Piers Plowman* says that he cannot tell *gestes*, or harp. A harp would be a useful property in a recital of *Sir Orfeo*, which describes the king playing on this instrument. Miming and various degrees of impersonation must have added to the liveliness of what were in effect performances. The *disour* who begs his audience to keep still was casting his glance towards them; he would raise his voice for the speech of a haughty knight and modulate it to tones befitting a wife or maiden in distress. Even Chaucer's tales might have been enacted in this way (see above, p. 19).

It is the same Chaucer who temporarily assumes the role of a popular romancer when his Knight comes to describe such a tournament as formed a set piece in many a romance but was never described with such verve and conciseness:

> Ther shyveren shaftes upon sheeldes thikke;
> He feeleth thurgh the herte-spoon the prikke.
> Up spryngen speres twenty foot on highte,
> Out goon the swerdes, as the silver brighte,
> The helmes they tohewen and toshrede;
> Out brest the blood, with stierne stremes rede

(*CT* I. 2605–10)

where *sterne*, to be sure, seems an odd epithet; yet it occurs frequently, in a variety of senses, in alliterative romance. Chaucer is here adopting a favourite ploy of romance writers who would mass plosives and sibilants together to evoke the noise of conflict, and give *disours* an opportunity to dramatize the scene. In using native alliteration conjointly with inversion and repetition, as practised in Old French epic and later French romance, he is also providing us with a pretty instance of

* Of a (non-professional) male reader only one instance comes to mind—that of the doughty Robert Bruce encouraging his followers while crossing Loch Lomond (see above, p. 102).

contaminatio, the blending of literary forms and patterns, which is the horror of pedants but which is actually the key to his finest effects.

Only three English romances bear their authors' names. The composer of *Sir Launfal* gives his name at the end of his poem: 'Thomas Chestre made this tale'; he may also have written one of the romances of *Octavian*, and *Libeaus Desconus*. The author of *William of Palerne* names himself 'William'; and the fragmentary fourteenth-century *Apollonius of Tyre* (the story that Shakespeare adapts in *Pericles*) refers to its writer in its closing lines as 'a vicary' at Wimborne Minster in Dorset, where there was in fact a house of secular canons. A draft survives of some 400 lines of *Sir Ferumbras* (which is much the best English representative of the group of romances associated with Charlemagne)—a translation from French. It is written on the back of a document belonging to the diocese of Exeter; which suggests that it too may have been composed by a cleric.

The fact is that the French romances from which so many English romances derived were most likely to be found in the libraries of great monastic or religious houses: one at Canterbury had about a dozen before the end of the fourteenth century. And the literary career of a pious monk—like Lydgate in the early fifteenth century—shows that there is nothing inherently improbable in the notion of clerics writing romances. The secular settings and preoccupations of romance by no means rule them out. Most romances aim at profit as well as delight: a strain of piety shows through at one point or another—and regularly at the opening or close: witness the alliterative *Morte*, or the tail-rhymed *Avowing of Arthur*:

> He that made us on the mulde[1]
> And fare fourmet the folde[2] ...
> Giffe hom[3] joy that wille here
> Of dughty men and of dere[4].

    [1] *earth*   [2] *dry land*   [3] *them*   [4] *bold*

or *Havelok*:

> Krist late us evere so to do
> That we moten[1] comen him to;
> And with that[2] it mote ben so
> *Benedicamus Domino*

    [1] *may*   [2] *so that*

and *Orfeo* closes:

> Thus com sir Orfeo out of his care.
> God graunt ous alle wele to fare.

'Now that bere the croun of thorne / He bryng us to his blysse' concludes *Sir Gawain*. Chaucer respects and preserves this pattern not
only in the Knight's romance but in many of the other tales—incon-
gruous as it may now seem when it appears in the Miller's tale, or the
Merchant's. In fact it is all of a piece with the hearty, unforced—one is
tempted to say—Bellocian devotion that colours the most secular of
the romances. And it is not only the narrator but also the characters
who voice and reflect this piety. When the heroine in *Libeaus Desconus*
is rescued from a giant she is not content to say 'Thank God' but adds:

> 'Off hem I had be shent[1]
> Nade[2] God me socoure sent,
> That all the worlde wrought.
> He quyte the thy mede[3]
> That for us canne[4] blede
> And with his body us bought[5]'.   (700–5)*

[1] *destroyed*   [2] *had not*   [3] *May he settle accounts with you*   [4] *did*
[5] *redeemed*

Some of the romances are more consciously and consistently didactic or embody a deliberate moral purpose. *Guy of Warwick* enjoins
readers to

> Take ensawmpull be wyse men
> That have before thys tyme ben.   (7–8)

An exemplary, didactic purpose of this kind is indicated in romances
as various as *Sir Triamour*, *Sir Amadace*, *Sir Gowther*, *Kyng Alisaunder*.
Athelston begins:

> Lord, that is off myghtys most,
> Fadyr and Sone and Holy Gost,
> Bryng us out off synne
> And lene us grace so for to wyrke
> To love bothe God and holy kyrke
> That we may hevene wynne.
> Lystnes, lordyngys that ben hende,
> Off falsnesse, hou it wil ende
> A man that ledes hym therin.

Both the morality and the piety placed poet, *disour*, and audience all
within a stable framework of common values. There is never any question of listener looking askance at poet, and ribaldry, as distinct from
buffoonery, is relegated to the vastly different world of *fabliau*. Once
more Caxton shows himself the inheritor of the romance tradition.
When he defends Malory's moral purpose and tells his readers to

* *Ywain and Gawain* yields similar instances (2871 ff., 2998).

follow the good and eschew the evil, he is merely making explicit what the medieval audience took for granted. By the same token the 'happy endings' of romances are not a literary convention: when Chaucer piously concludes his romance with the prayer

> And God, that al this wyde world hath wroght,
> Sende hym his love that hath it deere aboght

(CT I. 3099–100)

he is as much in earnest as when writing the more notable invocation at the close of the pagan Troilus's tragedy. The medieval romance is ultimately a distinctively Christian form. It presents human action from the viewpoint of a world ruled by Providence (if Chaucer's Arcite seems to question this, it is because he too is a pagan) without blenching at evil, lust, pain, and slaughter, whilst 'Eastern' tales like that of Floris and Blancheflour could be fitted into this frame of reference without difficulty. The novel as it develops in the eighteenth century proceeds from different assumptions.

(ii) *King Horn*; *Floris and Blancheflour*; *Sir Orfeo* and other 'Breton Lays'

The oldest extant romance is probably *King Horn*: oldest both in its manuscript form and in date of composition. It runs to just over 1,500 short and rather jerky lines in a metre probably deriving—like Layamon's *Brut*—from the old English alliterative measure. The metre of both testifies to the tenacity of such verse-patterns at a time when the dominant culture was decidedly Norman. In this case, indeed, it may well be the Norman who borrowed or adapted the native English story, for the later and longer Anglo-Norman romance of *Horn* by one Thomas is clearly related to some version of this poem. Both poems are about the love of Horn and Rymenhild—a simple and intense love without a trace of the later sophistication of *courtoisie*—though the Anglo-Norman poem includes elaborate characterization lacking in the English. The dominant motifs link the romance with an earlier type of verse narrative—the French *chanson de geste*: e.g. the exchange of clothes with a palmer, the disguised hero who slips through the sentries, the revelation of identity (by sending a ring in a goblet), the fight with a giant, the exposure of the hero in a rudderless boat. Perhaps the most attractive passage in the whole story is Horn's address to the boat after it has drifted on to the shores of Westernesse:

> Schup, bi the se flode
> Daies have thu gode:

135

Bi the se brinke
No water the n'adrinke[1]
Yif thu come to Suddenne
Gret thu wel of myn kenne;
Gret thu wel my moder,
Godhild quen the gode.
And seie the paene[2] kinge,
Jesu cristes witherling[3]
That ich am hol and fer[4]
On this lond arived her
—And seie that he schal fonde[5]
The dent[6] of myne honde!   (139–52)

[1] *drown*   [2] *pagan*   [3] *adversary*   [4] *whole and sound*   [5] *feel*
[6] *blow*

The personalizing of the ship in this passage, erecting it almost into a character, bespeaks the same kind of culture that accepts the conception of a speaking cross in Old English verse. It enables the King of Westernesse to address the hero in terms that apply equally well to Horn the man and horn the instrument:

Horn thu go wel schulle[1]
Bi dales and bi hulle;
Horn, thu lude sune,
Bi dales and bi dune.
So schal thi name springe
Fram kynge to kynge!   (207–12)

[1] *piercing*

—a pun which the French version has to explain.

Floris and Blancheflour, translated and modified from a French original somewhere in the South East Midlands in the mid-thirteenth century—and soon copied in the South West—is as near as we come in English to the daintiness and charm of the more famous *Aucassin et Nicolette*, and has something of the perennial appeal, though little of the artistry, of that early masterpiece. The two tales have in common—probably—a Moorish source and a Spanish provenance; and the English poem (acephalous in the extant manuscripts) is undoubtedly derived from a twelfth-century French or Anglo-Norman version. Its tone is set in the very first incident. Blancheflour, daughter of a captive French widow, has been brought up with Floris, son of a Spanish queen, until they are seven years old. When Floris is sent to learn his letters, he bursts out weeping:

'Ne can y in no scole syng ne rede
Without Blauncheflour' he seide.

In a later effort to part the pair his father sells Blancheflour to merchants of 'Babylon' (i.e. Cairo)—and the Emir buys her for seven times her weight in gold. Floris is told that she has died for love of him, and shown her splendid grave. Only his mother's disclosure of the truth saves him from self-slaughter. With a rich train, a magic ring, and a goblet engraved with the story of Paris and Helen (and once given by Aeneas to Lavinia), he sets out in search of her, disguised first as a merchant, and later as a mason ('with squir and scantiloun [set-square and measure]'), who begs leave to inspect the wondrous tower in which Blancheflour is held with other maidens till a petal falling from the tree of love nearby shall mark her as the Emir's next bride. At the suggestion of a friendly burgess he wins over the cowardly but covetous porter during a game of chess, and is borne into the palace—by porters grumbling at the weight—in a basket of flowers. Clarice, one of the maidens, shrieks on discovering him, but touched by 'the treunesse of this treuthe' falls in with his plans and abets them, telling her friends that it was a butterfly brushing against her that had made her cry out. Soon the young pair are blissfully united in bed, where Blancheflour oversleeps, not once, but twice. When Clarice can no longer pretend to the Emir that it is Blancheflour's devotions in the night-watches that make her sleepy he learns the truth and condemns the lovers to execution. But whilst each begs to die for, or before, the other, the whole court bursts into tears of pity and a duke who has picked up Floris's magic ring persuades the King to pardon them. All ends in laughter, wedding, and feasting, and Floris sails home to rule over his father's kingdom.

So love conquers all. *Floire et Blancheflor* is an idyll that in France will have several successors, notably *Paul et Virginie*. It exploits the pathetic, it is generous almost to a fault in its descriptions. Yet it also finds room for the analysis of love that Chrétien had made mandatory. Almost all these features are removed from the English version, which runs to a little over 1,300 lines as against the three thousand of the French. The English *remanieur* strips the plot to its essentials, whilst slightly improving it here and there. Later, Boccaccio in *Il Filocolo* was to offer a freer adaptation of the tale, adding (e.g.) a reference to 'il sancto libro di Ovidio', but his version has no greater merits.

It was doubtless the Eastern magic and marvels—the gleaming carbuncle, Babylon of 140 gates and 700 towers, the brazen conduit, a stream that runs from Paradise over precious stones and tests chastity—that gave the poem its chief appeal, though they have less to do with the plot than such traditional romance elements as the disguisings of Floris and the sworn brotherhood that links two of his hosts. The erotic element of which Boccaccio was to make much in *Filocolo* is as marginal as the Christian. The octosyllabics run on smoothly enough, with here and there a standard couplet and a traditional alliterative phrase—'game ne gle', 'bale . . . bote', 'care ful cold', 'clippe and kisse'. Aristocratic as the French model may have been, and French as the stances (and swoons) of the lovers are, there is nothing that puts the tale beyond the sympathies of the citizenry who delighted in *Havelok* or *Horn*. Some of the repetitions of the French have been avoided. Much of the cloying sentiment of the extant French text has been stripped away (along with such Eastern delights as the metallic birds that sing in the wind, that Yeats was to enshrine in *Byzantium*), as if not acceptable to English audiences. If love is described in terms of 'lycoris' and galingale it is because of their rarity, not their sweetness: a later lyric poet was to make the same comparisons. 'Fin amour' here is the phrase used of Clarice's selfless love for Blancheflour. There is a salty flavouring of simple English phrases: the lovers lie 'neb to neb'; Death stabs 'under the ribbe' 'thilke [those] that bust [it would be fitting] best to libbe'; no servant 'that in his brech bereth the ginne'—no one, that is, save eunuchs, can wait upon the maidens of the tower. But chiefly the tale speaks of a warm Spain and an exotic East, bright with flowers: the flower motif being hidden in the names of the lovers as Floris himself is hidden in flowers; and Floris himself hides his purpose by saying his thought is 'mochel on mi marchaundise'—on the exchange he hopes to make for Blaunche-flour. If we miss the verve of *Aucassin*, there is something in this tale for most tastes of the time, and a foretaste of the *Arabian Nights*.

Of all the English verse romances, *Sir Orfeo* is the one that in grace and charm, lightness and neatness, comes closest to the twelfth-century lays of Marie de France, and to her conception of 'les granz biens', the goodness, of love. The prologue firmly associates it with lays made by Bretons—as if in deliberate imitation of Marie's general prologue to *her* collection of Breton stories. Marie gives these stories the name *lais*; and she tells us in her prologue that it was the recital of such *lais* by Bretons that prompted her to put them into French verse. No such lay has survived in the Breton tongue, and probably none was ever written down in it. Medieval Brittany (and in the remoter parts of Brittany today one still seems close to the Middle Ages) was a country of oral rather than of literary culture: a culture in which folk music evidently played a major part. The Jerseyman Wace tells us in his *Brut* (10545–9) that lays were of diverse kinds, denoted by the instruments to which they were sung—presumably by the travelling Breton jongleurs. There were, he says:

lais de notes
Lais de vieles[1], lais de rotes[2]
Lais de harpes, lais de frestels[3]

[1,2] *stringed instruments*   [3] *flutes*

Whether this means that the whole of a lay was sung to musical accompaniment we do not know: conceivably it was only the parts in direct speech. But we do know from later allusions what themes were thought proper for, and were associated with, these *lais*. In brief, they were stories with some supernatural element linked with a love story the basis of which might be chivalric or—more surprisingly—classical.

The appearance of classical story in the twelfth century and in a primitive land of wild cliff and shaggy wood is not so surprising when we find that such stories as those of Dido and Aeneas, Pyramus and Thisbe, Orpheus and Eurydice had been part of school reading for some centuries. Brittany had had some contact with Celtic Britain, where classical learning had flourished for a time; and there were schools enough in nearby Normandy to transmit such stories. The story of Orpheus in particular was widely known because of its appearance in metrical form with a moralized meaning in Boethius' *Consolation of Philosophy*, so influential in the twelfth century, as well as in the versions of Virgil and Ovid.

That a lay in Breton actually existed and was sung to a harp is inferred from allusions in two Old French verse romances: *Floire et Blancheflor* and the *Lai de l'Espine*, and from another reference in the Old French *Prose Lancelot*, in which King Baudemagus has a harper 'who played to him [*le notait*] the lai of Orfay and so pleased the king that no-one dared speak a word'. How closely that lay resembled the classical or Boethian version of the tale we cannot say—nor whether more than one version of the lay existed on the continent. On the other hand, it is easy enough to show that where the English poem departs from the classical tale it embraces elements that are specifically Celtic and hence presumably of Breton origin. These elements are those that relate to the other world and its inhabitants—in short to 'faerie' in its strict sense, which is 'the world of the supernatural', not whimsy creatures with wands at the bottom of the garden. That *this* kind of 'fairy story' was associated with Brittany we know from a story in the twelfth-century collection called *De Nugis Curialium* ('Courtly Triflings') by Walter Map, Archdeacon of Oxford. Map's book shows that he had a special appetite for such tales: he certainly travelled in France, and perhaps Brittany itself. In chapter viii of his fourth book he tells the tale of a man bringing back his wife from the dead:

A knight of Lesser Brittany lost his wife, and went on mourning for her long after her death. At last he found her by night in a great company of women in a valley surrounded by desert. Seeing her alive again he could not believe his eyes, and wondered what the fairies could be doing. But he snatched her away and enjoyed a union with her for many years, and had children by her whose descendants are numerous and are called the sons of the dead one.

In another version of the tale (II. xiii) Map adds that the knight snatched his lady out of *a dance*, a detail that links it with the story also told by Map of a hunter who sees a company of noble ladies 'clad in fair linen' and circling in airy motion and gay gesture as they sing in subdued harmony. To this last tale of the hunter Map gives a local English habitation (Ledbury North), and even provides a name for the hunter: Edric the Savage, a name actually connected in Domesday Book with the Ledbury district. These dancing ladies are obvious kin to the troops of midnight riders, sometimes known as the Wild Hunt or Hellwain, whose existence was vouched for by the sober-sided writer of the Peterborough Chronicle earlier in the twelfth century. This motif of the wild hunt is far more widespread than that of the recovered wife; but it too is firmly linked with the woods of Little (as well as with Great) Britain by the early thirteenth-century writer Gervase of Tilbury, who speaks of a company of warriors who hunt in them at noon and in the night with a great din of dogs and horns.*

It has been suggested that the tale as Map records it has already been 'contaminated' with the classical legend of Orpheus, but more probably Map misunderstood a Breton story about a woman who, in Celtic phrase, was 'taken' by the *sidhe* (a fairy folk) but eventually restored to the ordinary world. Perhaps one ought not to speak in this context of contamination, or even of fusion. And perhaps it was the existence of such Celtic beliefs that led a writer to reinterpret the Orpheus story. He substituted this Celtic concept of the 'taken' (persons who can be removed from their life, yet later restored) for the classical belief that the dead are indubitably dead, and in so doing he imparted new life and energy and particularity to the tale. The other-worldly women, who in *Sir Orfeo* dance in 'queynt atire' and ride on horseback, have no precedent in the classical tale; they are *sidhe*, who in Celtic lore are regularly associated with fine clothes and white horses. A second Celtic motif may be seen in the importance attached to Eurodis's sleeping under an orchard tree: apple orchards figure

* *EMEVP* 378.

frequently in Celtic romance, and there is evidence elsewhere in French and English romance for the danger of lying down in such a place. This re-reading of the Orpheus story we may reasonably credit to a Breton or Anglo-Norman poet on whose work the English author of *Sir Orfeo* presumably drew. But other, if minor, elements may well be the English poet's invention: perhaps, for instance, the adaptation of Orpheus to the role of the solitary man of the woods rendered wild by grief. This is 'invention' in the sense that it develops and magnifies a strand in the classical tale, but it may well have literary origins: the poet may have known, at first or second hand, Geoffrey of Monmouth's account in his *Vita Merlini* of the grief-stricken Merlin wandering in the woods in rags, and living by roots, grasses, and wild fruit. Again, the hollow tree in which Orfeo hides his harp—a nice touch— reminds one of other hollow trees: a hollow ash plays a part in *Lai le Freine*, another 'Breton' lay.

The relation of *Sir Orfeo* to the French poem may well be similar to that of two other Middle English romances, *Lai le Freine* and *Sir Launfal*, both of which clearly derive from extant Old French lays composed by Marie de France. But both are adaptations rather than close renderings, and *Sir Launfal* draws on an earlier English version. It is possible that *Sir Orfeo* likewise drew on such an English version of the story, made before the presumed Old French or Anglo-Norman original was lost. The occurrence of French objects, words, and phrases is not of course an argument for a French original: one might as well argue that French words and phrases in Chaucer's *Knight's Tale* prove a French source. The passages in *Sir Orfeo* most reminiscent of the French *lais* are in the prologue and conclusion, both of which may well have been added by a later *disour* or reciter. Some of the opening lines recall in their phrasing opening and closing lines used by Marie in one or other of her *lais*. But some sixty years later Chaucer uses very similar phrases to give his *Franklin's Tale* the status of a Breton lay, to which, strictly speaking, it has no claim. His knowledge of the genre was purely literary and second hand, possibly derived wholly or in part from *Sir Orfeo*.

Sir Orfeo begins, as most romances began, with an appeal to the audience and a brief indication of theme; and, as often, this preliminary sketch allows a small rhetorical variation on Orfeo's qualities as a harper, so that by the time the audience had settled down, the association of *Orfeo* and *harp* would have been driven home: it is a deliberate preparation for the climax of the tale. Queen Eurodis and her ladies sit down under a tree, but only the queen sleeps and takes her rest—to wake in such a frenzy that she has to be forcibly restrained. In ten short lines we pass from springtime sun and happiness to sadness and shadow: the queen is literally hunted ('reveyd' = driven) out of her senses. The case would evoke horror as much as pity—as did Dido's frenzies in *Aeneid* iv. 460–73, which is the probable prototype of all such scenes. Here the frenzy carries also with it the suggestion of an hallucination contrived by sinister powers.

Soon the shadows grow darker. First comes the king's piteous expostulation, with its climax, expressed in a series of carefully balanced rhetorical couplets:

> Allas! thi rode[1] that was so red . . .
> Allas! thi lovesom eyen to . . .

[1] *complexion*

the redness of the warm living features gives way to the effects of self-mutilation and the pallor of death: the queen's poignant announcement that they must part is similarly counterpointed by two more rhetorical couplets, perhaps deliberately echoing the scriptural phrases of the dialogue between Ruth and Naomi ('Whither thou goest I will go'). The dialogue suddenly becomes almost operatic in its intensity. Only at this point is the cause of the grief revealed to us—in a passage that eschews rhetorical variation in favour of swift clear narrative. That 'faerie' is involved, the medieval hearer would guess from the mention of snow-white steeds, damsels in white, and the king (wearing no earthly crown) who bears Eurodis away to his palace, shows her his kingdom—and then (she says):

> 'Me brought oyain[1] hom
> Into *our* owhen orchard'.

[1] *back*

The orchard that she had entered all unsuspecting only a few hours ago has now all the dearness of things long enjoyed in common but to be shared no more. That she is first abducted while, to her women's eyes, her body remains in the orchard sorts with the folk tales told of the *sidhe*, in which a wandering *soul* is thought of as both visible and tangible.

It is in the abduction scene here prefigured that a motif from another classical story may be traced. The real rape (*raptus*), when it comes, surely resembles the seizure of Persephone by Pluto more than the classical account of the death of Eurydice, which was by snakebite; and in the Middle Ages the story of Persephone was just as familiar as that of Orpheus, not only from Ovid but from the full-scale presentation of it in Claudian's masterpiece *De Raptu Proserpinae*. Pluto is not named in the present passage; but the omission of his name may well be due to some survival of the taboo on the name of the king of the underworld, the same taboo that led to fairies later being known only as the 'gude folk'. In fact Ovid himself makes the association of the stories of Orpheus and of Persephone when he describes Orpheus's visit to the shades (*Met*. x. 15–16), and he too avoids naming Pluto. The description of this king in ll. 150 ff. likewise suggests the Pluto of the Persephone story: the crown made of a jewel as bright as the sun fits Pluto's classic role as god of riches; and the king's invisible approach recalls the god's attribute of invisibility (which would easily merge with folk-belief that fairies were invisible). Claudian gives Pluto a helmet of invisibility which he could lend to mortals; and the king in *Sir Orfeo* seems to have similar powers, which he extends to his retainers; so that a thousand knights will be no more effective against him than the queen's two maidens were.

The role of the king of the underworld in these scenes is not unlike that of an incubus—the fairy or demon who seeks intercourse with a mortal woman; and in fact Dunbar, in his dream poem *The Golden Targe*, actually describes Pluto as 'the elrich incubus / In cloke of grene—his court usit no sable' (125–6)—where the word *incubus* must be a reference to his rape of Proserpina. Such an incubus, we deduce from *The Wife of Bath's Tale* (CT III. 879), sought women specifically under bushes or 'trees'. 'In King Arthur's days', says the Wife:

> Of which that Britons speken grete honour
> Al was this land fulfild of fayerye.
> The elf-queene, with her joly compaignye,
> Daunced ful ofte in many a grene mede.

And in *The Merchant's Tale* (IV. 2038), Chaucer directly associates the music and dancing that in *Sir Orfeo* accompany this king of power with Pluto and Proserpina 'and al hire fayerye'. The Middle Ages, demoting pagan deities, had made them demons or fairies.

But the poet of *Sir Orfeo* has thoroughly modernized—i.e. he has medievalized—the classical circumstances. His kings are medieval kings, with knightly retinues and feudal castles. He envisages King Orfeo's knights as arranged in a *scheltrom*, i.e. a formation with a defensive wall of shields (like the Roman *testudo*), such as Harold used at Hastings—indeed, one might take the *sceldtruma* as symbolizing the older English martial virtues and poetic preoccupations that proved as powerless against the *matière de (Petit) Bretagne* as Orfeo's men proved when pitted against the fairy king.

It is typical of the new romance sensibility represented, if not in-augurated, by Marie de France, that Orfeo (and everyone else in the poem) should give vent to emotion unrestrainedly. It is the same heightening of feeling that creates the difference between the heroic firmness of the Old English *Dream of the Rood*, and the weeping Virgin and the weeping John who by the thirteenth century have become so prominent in Crucifixion scenes. This expression of emotions in a version of classical legend has precedent in the *Roman d'Enéas*, the first Old French poem to illustrate the new sensibility on a large scale. The author of the *Enéas* betrays a fondness for the marvellous; and *Sir Orfeo* depends on a succession of marvels. Superficially, the marvel-lous or 'faerie' element is something light and intangible, mysterious, but enthralling: it is associated with the soft 'drowsihed' of high noon, dim cries in forest glades, visions of fair women. But, as with most medieval magic, there is also something ruthless and sinister about it. Consider Pluto's threat to Eurodis:

> 'And yif thou makest ous ylet[1],
> Whar thou be, thou worst yfet[2],
> And totore[3] thine limes al,
> That nothing helpe the ne schal;
> And thei[4] thou best so totorn,
> Yete thou worst with ous yborn[5].' (169–74)

[1] *hindrance be carried off*　　[2] *shall be fetched*　　[3] *torn to pieces*　　[4] *though*　　[5] *will*

It is in the light of this grim prediction that we must interpret the earlier scene in which the sleeping Eurodis scratched and tore her hands, feet, and face: she has been enacting in dream her response to the threat she now relates: in romance all dreams are fraught with significance.

But it is the essence of medieval romance that it never wholly loses sight of the quotidian world of reality. Hence the description of Sir Orfeo's grief after the queen is spirited away concludes with the finality of 'ther was non amendement' (200)—'Nothing could be done about it'. So later the 'barons' will remind his steward of the inevitable course of fate and tell him 'how it geth / It nis no bot [remedy] of mannes deth'—'That's how things are', a proverbial phrase that points up similar situations in other romances. But the real world also impinges on the territory of romance in the descriptions of everyday conduct. Thus Orfeo, like the good king he is, does not, for all his sorrows, forget his duties to his land and people: he summons his council, appoints his High Steward as his deputy, and arranges that, if need be, a 'parlement' shall choose a new king.

New too is the emphasis on the contrast in the completely changed status and condition of Orfeo: the king puts on a beggar's mantle. It is the kind of reversal of roles that had a deep fascination for the medieval mind—especially when it is deliberate. It is doubtless a product of Christian feeling, for the Incarnation itself involved such a reversal. Certain it is that the poet seizes the situation with both hands. The narrative now slows down for the first time, and we have some 33 lines of elaborate rhetorical structure (note the fourfold variation on the theme marked by the repetition of 'He that had'). Hence the poet is at his most conscious, with *figurae verborum*, iterations, and antitheses. The passage begins and ends with an *exclamatio* (234, 263–4). No further proof is needed that we are dealing with a highly literate 'maker'. Only at ll. 267 ff. do we return to the traditional picture of Orpheus in the woods. The scenes that ensue depict his misery and the new circumstances in a way which, whilst on the one hand recalling the occasion of Orfeo's grief—the hot 'undern-tides', the fearsome company of knights (ll. 291–2 echo ll. 135–6) who had borne away Eurodis, on the other hand slowly prepares us for a new stage. Orfeo is in these scenes at least in a kind of contact with the fairy troops that took Eurodis. But again the movement is very slow-paced, very deliberate. Each scene is carefully set and pointed with a temporal adverb—'oft' (282), 'other while' (289), 'and on a day' (303)— leading to a climax. He sees the king of faerie hunting, a strange fairy host in battle array, and then (297 ff.) a *third* company, a mixed troop of knights and ladies dancing to music (a 'carole'?): it is the first hint we have that Orfeo may find some solace. Finally come the sixty lovely women, skilled in hawking—that essentially courtly accomplishment. It is their perfect mastery of the art—'ich faucoun his pray slough'— that seems to rouse Orfeo from his dejection. The incident (and this is surely the English poet's invention) not only reminds him of departed joys but also prompts him, impulsively, to move towards the courtly company. The scene of silent mutual recognition (319–27) is as moving as that earlier one of enforced parting. Then comes the momentary struggle between despair and reckless determination: the despair expressed by his exclamatory 'wreche' (333), which retains some of the stricter sense of Old English *wrecca*—a solitary exile.

Following the troop, Orfeo enters the underworld through a rock— like other visitors in folklore. The beauty of this underworld is both natural and artificial, with an abundance of red gold and elegant pinnacles (cf. the ballad of *Child Waters*). The details here are not thrown in at random, but represent stages in the visitor's impression. First the outer walls, then the entrance arch or *voussoir* with its bright enamel insets, such as would be found in no earthly castle. The inner room, decorated with precious stones, hints at other Celtic traditions of the underworld, but they connote even more strongly the heavenly Jerusalem of the Apocalypse. No wonder that

> Bi al thing him think that it is
> The proude court of Paradis   (375–6)

—but 'him think' (it seems to him), is not a mere filler: it is Orfeo's idea, not the author's—the kind of distinction that Spenser makes time and again between appearance and actuality. The couplet may carry the hint that Orfeo feels himself on the verge of regaining former happiness, for in happier days Orfeo himself had made men think they were in Paradise (cf. 36–7). But that this is not the true Paradise we know from the source of its light—the rich stones (evidently carbuncles) that dispel the dark (*therk*, an East Anglian word that stands out sharply against all this glitter: another instance of the capacity of romance to juxtapose the splendid with the ordinary and local). So too the gate has an everyday lifelike porter—not the fell Cerberus of Ovid and Boethius—and in his presence Orfeo behaves true to his assumed craft and calling. It is a situation of which a *disour* reciting to a harp would take every advantage—doubtless omitting as superfluous that extra-metrical phrase 'quath he' (382).

Within the castle what Orfeo finds is not so pretty. Here the classical story, and the classical tradition of an underworld of gloom and sadness, reasserts itself. But the torments of Tartarus give place to painful deaths described in ten lines of rhetorical iteration (*anaphora*) that, like the earlier rhetoric of Orfeo's lament, is not strictly necessary to the story. But the catalogue is not merely decorative: these grim and gruesome scenes are shown to be an ineluctable part of 'faerie'; and that faerie still operates here is clear from the last category—persons not dead but wrapped in slumber (401–2), like those knights of Arthur that in some legends sleep below the earth till his trump shall sound again. In assimilating such beliefs to the classical story, the poet emphasizes at the outset that they seemed dead and were not. Many a folk-tale suggested that both the truly dead and those 'taken' could be won back to life: madness (cf. 'sum lay wode [mad], ybounde', 'sum awedde' (394, 400)) was regarded as a sign that a sick man's spirit was already with the fairies, and in particular those who died in childbirth or by drowning (398–9) were in this belief considered to be 'taken' rather than dead.

Within the hall sit king and queen in radiant apparel. Their posture is that favoured by thirteenth-century sculptors and artists, who regularly placed royalty in such crocketed tabernacles. They are first seen as figures of dazzling beauty. The brightness, and the ornament, are of a piece with the account of the underworld by Étienne de Bourbon (mid-thirteenth century).* A peasant sees the fairy company of Arthur's courtiers hunting, as so often, by night, and follows them. They enter a splendid palace where knights and ladies dance and play. The rustic gets as far as a royal bed on which lies a lady wondrously fair. He is surely but another embodiment of the belated peasant who, at the end of Book i of *Paradise Lost*, sees—or *dreams* he sees—just such a jocund fairy company. Milton knew the power of medieval legend, just as he felt the attraction of medieval romance.

The dialogue that ensues has a neat humour and an ironical undertone. Inasmuch as the king is Pluto—and whatever the original composer's conceptions, some fourteenth-century readers or hearers would doubtless identify him as such—the man who entered his presence without due summons was indeed foolhardy. To his question Orfeo humbly, but deftly, replies as if ignorant of the true nature of this particular 'lordes hous'. The sense of the god's cruel and inexorable power that informs the classical legend has in fact been transferred to the earlier part of the poem and largely confined to it.

It is only now that Orfeo plies his music, to captivate all the denizens of this place, and all the emphasis is, as in the opening scene, on its joyous quality. So we move into a lighter, brighter mood and a tone closer to the sunlit human world, to which we are soon to return. In due form the king promises whatever reward the minstrel shall ask, and the medieval reader would sense and savour the hint of a rash promise or careless bargain of the kind that gives spice to many a romance. Here, however, in conformity with the change of tone, nothing hangs on the promise but a broad jest (457–68), and there are no fatal conditions. Clearly at this point the poem has left the track of Ovid, Virgil, and Boethius.

The king's reply takes us another step nearer to the common-sensible actual world. The inexorable condition that gives pathos to the classical story has been ousted by the belief that the 'taken', or even the dead, can be retrieved; and the scene closes with the king wishing Orfeo joy—yet without any admission on Orfeo's side, or

* See E. K. Chambers, *Arthur of Britain* (London, 1927), 278.

apparently any awareness on the king's, that the harper has a special and intimate claim on the sleeping lady (whose role, as often in romance, will remain purely passive for the rest of the story).

From this point all is new invention—a welding together of a cluster of medieval motifs, namely: the king in disguise (like Alfred—who also played the harper) testing his subjects, an occasion for some unrefined humour (505–8); the faithful steward who earns his just reward; the lord who (like Horn and Havelok) enjoys his own again after much tribulation. Only now are we told that Orfeo has been ten years away—meaning a long and weary time. He goes to the outskirts of his capital, lodging in a hovel outside the city gates; all cities had such hovels, and the gates were the haunts of beggars.

It is a fine touch that makes the steward welcome Orfeo out of love of his erstwhile lord, another harpist, and a finer one, that depicts the hall crowded with musicians for the same reason: finer, this, because it makes the climax depend on Orfeo's mastery as a harper. Only at this point in the whole poem is the cæsura used to mark an emphatic rhetorical break:

> And Orfeo sat stille in the halle
> And herkneth; whan thai ben al stille. . . .

Finest touch of all is the steward's shock of recognition at the sight of Orfeo's very own harp. Now the roles are reversed. It is the steward's turn to swoon (cf. 197) and call himself a *wreche* (544), as Orfeo had once done; here, as before, the term has special point: the steward does think himself now a really lordless man.

The final explication is terse but complete. The world is quickly set right again, and all live happily. It is the proper, the almost inevitable end of romance, and the chief legacy of romance to the art of the novel as the great masters practised it.

A type of 'Breton lay' somewhat different from *Sir Orfeo* is evidenced in the longer tale of *Sir Launfal* (or *Launfal Miles*, 'Launfal the Knight', as it is called in the unique Cotton manuscript). It is 1,044 lines long, against the 580 of *Sir Orfeo*, and has in fact the better claim to the appellation 'Breton', since it is manifestly based—if at one remove—on an extant *lai* of Marie de France, who herself associates her own 'lai' of *Lanval* with Brittany, when she says of her hero (as the English poet does not) that 'en bretans l'apelent Lanval', and when she depicts him as riding away with his fairy mistress to Avalon 'as the Bretons say', whilst the 'maker' of the English lay—who names himself as Thomas Chester—evidently had independent access to Breton tradition, since for the name Avalon he twice substitutes the name

Olyroun, which must represent the Ile d'Oléron, off the coast of Brittany.

Between *Launfal* and *Orfeo* there are several obvious differences. Launfal is not in couplets but in the popular tail-rhyme stanza, which had an almost fatal fascination for fourteenth-century poets; and it is in the commonest form of the stanza: twelve lines in triplets that consist (usually) of two lines of four stresses followed by one three-stress line:

> The lady lep an hyr palfray
> And bad hem alle have good day—
> Sche nolde no lengere abyde.

Launfal is Arthurian, not classical, in setting and in reference. It involves all the trappings of chivalry and a good deal of *courtois* sentiment, in particular that convention which made happiness dependent wholly on a mistress's favour. The characters in *Launfal* are treated with less dignity and compassion than are those in *Orfeo*. Guenevere, in particular, as here presented, belongs to the primitive, pre-Chrétien stage of the Arthurian story. She is promiscuous, vicious, jealous, and unscrupulous (if we count as unscrupulous her late *profession* of love for Launfal, which is surely part of her ploy and not, as editors maintain, inconsistent with her earlier dislike of him). Of Launfal himself we are told at first no more than that he is too lavish, and so falls into poverty. The bankrupt knight is in fact a surprisingly frequent figure in medieval story: the prototype being the Theophilus of legend, who has to sell his soul to the Devil, much as Launfal has to redeem himself by his pledge to the Lady Triamour. It is one of the unexpected achievements of romance that from the sordid realities of Launfal's penury it can fashion a beautiful consolatory *exemplum*. The romance of *Sir Amadace* offers another variant of this theme. Strictly speaking it is religion rather than romance that works this change—in the Theophilus legend it is the power of the Virgin—but romance is always happy to accommodate religion. *Launfal* abounds in stock phrases and descriptions, conventional motifs and situations, all with obvious popular appeal. It is not surprising that the fairy lady's promise:

> 'Yf thou wylt truly to me take
> And alle wemen for me forsake,
> Ryche I wyll make the'   (316–17)

is parodied in *Sir Thopas*:

> 'Alle othere wommen I forsake
> And to an elf-queene I me take'   (VII 794–5)

for it is precisely these declarations that are the butt of Chaucer's satire. Amongst other motifs found elsewhere are (for instance) the giant of monstrous size (he is fifteen feet high—though a pigmy compared with the giant in *Libeaus Desconus*, who reaches forty feet); the feasting that goes on for forty days; the peerless qualities of Sir Launfal himself. Add to these themes the year's time-limit for his search for his 'leman' (compare the year's limit in *Gawain* and the 'twelve month and a day' in *The Wife of Bath's Tale*); the listing of the names of Arthurian Knights in ll. 13–24, and the rash promise (cf. *Sir Orfeo*)—in *Launfal* the hero rashly promises never to mention his leman. The description of rich and rare accoutrements or settings (888 ff.) and of tournaments (433–504) are also common form. The terminology of love and fighting in the romance is unremarkable—the two occupations are closely bound up, and the verb 'to play' is (as elsewhere) used of both (cf. 'for play, lytyll they sclepte that nyght')—and the imagery is no more unusual. Triamour's hair 'schon as gold wyre', and she is 'whyt as lylye yn May, or snow that sneweth on wynterys day'; and the more extended description of her charms at 927 ff. is only the elaboration of a stereotype, which would be relished for that very reason. Again, Launfal's grief when he realizes that Triamour has vanished is expressed in terms much like those of Orfeo's woe at the loss of Eurodis. But Launfal's grief has less warrant.

What Launfal chiefly has in common with *Orfeo* is the element of faerie. But even that element is less powerful, and less pervasive. Only at the point at which the two richly-decked damsels sent by the daughter of the King of Faerie approach Launfal as he sits, at noon, under a tree does the fairy action much resemble that of the better poem; and even in this passage the supernatural is accepted as matter of fact. Elsewhere, too, the magic has a certain flatness. The crude 'poetic' justice which requires Triamour to blind the envious Guenevere with a single breath belongs to the world of folk-tale as much as to magic; and so perhaps does the belief that every year upon a certain day Launfal comes back from fairyland ready to do combat. But Chester makes these closing lines memorable by adding that on these occasions one 'may here Launfales stede nay'—an effective adaptation of a detail found in the Old French *lai* of *Graelent*, in which the horse neighs for grief.

This kind of adaptation is typical of Chester: he is a *remanieur*, a refashioner, not a mere translator. He evidently drew on *Graelent* for several other scenes and minor details, which are woven into his tale with some care; and he evidently had access to some version not now extant of Marie de France's short *lai*. The Middle English version of this *lai* that does survive and that goes under the name of *Landevale* runs to 538 lines of short rhymed couplets, and differs from Marie's tale at several points. Chester has apparently introduced at least two episodes of his own accord and uses them to help to bind the three sections of the story together: Arthur's courtship and wedding, and the action that Valentine the giant takes out of envy. Chester seems also to have invented Launfal's visit on his way home, at the beginning of the tale, to the self-interested mayor who is quick with excuses for not providing accommodation as soon as he realizes Launfal's predicament. The closing scenes are at least as effective in the English as in Marie's French. There is neat suspense as Launfal's life hangs in the balance: his friends assure him that his mistress is approaching; yet she is not in the first company of maidens that arrive, nor yet in the second; and Guenevere is resuming her plea to Arthur to punish Launfal with death, when Triamour rides in on her milk-white palfrey with greyhounds with collars of gold, to vindicate her knight.

Admittedly there are a few discrepancies, loose ends and, what is worse, loose beginnings: the dwarf Gyfre slips into the tale rather oddly. But Chester's audiences probably troubled little about such things. And Chester manages to anchor the tale in contemporary society. One of the few things he says of Arthur is that he 'held Engelond yn good lawes'; which is precisely what is said in *Havelok* of Athelwold, the semi-historical King of England; and it is borne out, in a sense, when Arthur later turns Launfal over to knightly jurors, who carefully deliberate, and take sureties (the original scene in Marie's *Lanval* was evidently modelled on an actual contemporary trial for felony). Launfal's penury, again, is portrayed in uncompromisingly prosaic terms: he lacks even shirt and breeches (undergarments) and his horse gets all mucked up in the fen. The mayor of Caerleon is a recognizable *nouveau riche* bourgeois type: he has turned Launfal away in his poverty, but fawns on him when he comes into money. Launfal's call at the mayor's house, at the beginning of the poem, and the trial, with the return of Triamour at the end, are vivid and memorable. As a tale—and it is as a tale that we should judge it, for it is not highly-wrought and polished verse—it has more merit than the critics usually allow; and its closing stanzas do convey something of faerie's mystery, even if Chester cannot suffuse this through the work as a whole, as the nameless poet of *Sir Orfeo* could.

The poem called *Lai le Freine* illustrates how tentative and fragile must be definitions of 'romance' or 'the Breton lay'. Here is nothing of refined love or *courtoisie*, nothing of chivalry (save for cursory mention of a tournament that does not take place), nothing of magic or faerie.

The action springs from the envy of a woman, jealous because the wife of her husband's friend has borne two male children at a birth. She invokes the belief that such a woman must have had intercourse with two men. The charge rebounds on her when in due course she too bears twins—both girls. To avoid slander she resolves to kill one of them; but a maid persuades her to expose the child instead. She wraps it in a rich mantle 'from Constantinople', places a ring on its arm, and the maid leaves it by night in a hollow ash (*freine*) near a convent. Found by the abbey porter, and duly named 'La Freine', she is fostered by the abbess. Years pass, and word of her beauty reaches a knight, Sir Guroun, who abducts her to make her his mistress. But his retainers persuade him that he must have a lawful heir, and he becomes betrothed to another girl. Here the Middle English fragment ends. Marie de France's *lai*, from which it derives, continues the story. She is in fact twin to La Freine. On the eve of the wedding the mantle and the ring reveal the relation to the repentant mother, and all ends happily, with La Freine married off to another, accommodating knight. The coincidence is unforced, and the motivation of the action realistic.

Only two passages in Marie's *lai* link it with Brittany: the opening reference (reproduced in the English) to the scene of the tale, and a later allusion to the ancient archbishopric of Dol in Upper Brittany (not reproduced). The English version follows the sense and even the phrasing of the French. Thus:

> Sone after sche gan herk
> Cokkes crowe and houndes berk   (153–4)

echoes almost word for word

> . . . aveit oi
> Chiens abaier et coks chanter.   (144–5)

But there are numerous minor variations, including omissions, additions, changes from direct to indirect speech, or vice versa. Sometimes a phrase is added simply to supply a rhyme, but some changes affect characterization and story. Thus the English poem omits the picture of the envious wife smiling falsely at her husband when he receives the news of the double birth, but has her slander the friend's wife before a messenger, not before her household. It introduces a midwife who refuses to have part or lot in child-murder, but omits the description of the ring that will later lead to identifying the foundling. Marie places the convent in 'une vile riche et bele', the English poet removes it to a desolate spot. He discards other details that make for verisimilitude, but is careful (unlike Marie) to have the babe christened. The knight's ruse for gaining access to the convent by endowing it with lands and rents and thus gaining the right to membership of its fraternity is accommodated in the English version by rendering the French legal term *retur* ('to seek refuge in a vassal's house') by the equally technical *recet* (284). At such points we seem to be worlds away from 'romance'. One glimpse of the workaday world we owe to the English poet. As the maid who has laid the child in the ash tree turns homeward

> it gan to dawe[1] light
> The foules up and song on bough
> And acre men[2] yede[3] to the plough.   (180–2)

> [1] *dawn*   [2] *field labourers*   [3] *went*

The remaining short romances which can make some claim to the title of 'Breton lay' reveal at once some similarities with these stories and some pleasing diversity. *Emaré* (of just over 1,000 lines) is a piteous tale of the patient sufferings of a beautiful heroine. Like Chaucer's Constance, she is persecuted and betrayed, cast adrift on the sea in an open boat (twice), and falsely accused, but is eventually reunited with her contrite husband. She is an exemplary figure of patient virtue. *Sir Degaré* is set in Brittany. The hero is the son of a princess ravished (while sleeping under a tree in the forest) by a knight of fairyland. His father disappears, leaving a sword without a point, and his mother abandons him, leaving treasure, a letter telling of his noble birth, and—the equivalent of Cinderella's slipper—a pair of gloves which will fit only the girl he is to love. When he grows up, he goes off in search of his parents. He has adventures (including a battle with a dragon), and is knighted, but can find no one that the gloves will fit. He wins the hand of the daughter of a king, only to find (when the gloves are produced) that he has married his own mother! She confesses the secret of his birth; he sets out once again on a quest for his father. In the forest where he was begotten, he falls in love with a maiden in a magic castle on an island. At last he finds his father, and, after the marriage with his mother is dissolved, sees them reunited, and, accompanied by them, returns to the maiden of the island. *Sir Gowther*, a slightly shorter poem, deriving—it claims—from a 'lai of Breyten' is much less like a 'fairy-tale'. It has a magic birth, but here the father who visits the wife of a duke in her garden is a devil. The romance is related to the widespread exemplary story of Robert the Devil, which was still popular in sixteenth-century England. Gowther grows up to be an unholy terror, but a series of violent and sacrilegious deeds comes to an end when, after having been called 'a devil's son',

Gowther learns from his mother the circumstances of his birth. Confession and severe penance follow—he is instructed to eat only the
remnants of dogs' food and to remain silent until a sign comes to him
from heaven. He lives as 'Hob the Fool' in the court of Almayne, but
secretly takes arms to defeat the Saracens and to defend the emperor's
daughter, who is dumb. The sign is given when the daughter is able to
speak and to declare that she has been saved by this unknown
champion.

From the North-East Midlands at about the middle of the fourteenth century comes *The Earl of Toulous*, a vigorously told romance of
1,224 verses in an unusual twelve-lined stanza. The conclusion claims
that

> Yn Rome thys geste cronyculyd ywys;
> A lay of Bretayne callyd hyt ys,
> And evyr more schall bee.

But this, like similar claims for Breton origins, need not be taken
seriously. It is another tale of a falsely accused queen, in this case the
fair Empress Beulybon, wife of the Emperor Diocletian, on whom the
Earl Barnard makes war to recover lost territory. She is accused of
adultery to the emperor by two knights enamoured of her. She is
destined for burning but the Earl of Toulouse intervenes, arranging
with a merchant 'of Almayn' to take him, with seven steeds, to her
rescue. *En route* they lodge with an abbot, her uncle, who assures the
Earl that she is innocent. He clothes the knight in a monk's habit, and
so disguised sends him to shrive her on the fatal day. Assured by her of
her innocence, he challenges her accusers, strikes down one, and
causes the other to yield. The abbot reveals his identity to the
Emperor, whom in due course he succeeds, duly marrying the fair and
virtuous widow. They had no less than fifteen sons, all doughty
knights. A simple, run-of-the-mill tale; but many films that satisfied
audiences of the 1930s were no more subtle, and it is with them that it
should be compared.

(iii) *Havelok*; *Gamelyn*; *Athelston*; *Sir Amadace*; *Libeaus Desconus*

In naming *Havelok* a 'lay' its editors have treated it as an English
equivalent to the Anglo-Norman *Lai d'Haveloc*. That poem, to be sure,
is called a *lai* in its opening lines, but there is no reason at all to think
that 'the Bretons' did make a 'lai' about this Danish prince. The
Anglo-Norman poet is trying, like Chaucer with his *Franklin's Tale*

much later, to pass off his poem as a Breton lay though in fact he based it on a known literary work, Gaimar's *Histoire des Engleis*. The only excuse for this device is the fact that, following Gaimar, the Anglo-Norman poet introduces the story with a reference to Arthur's supposed conquest of Denmark. Grim is not a fisherman but a baron. In short, the Anglo-Norman poem is entirely aristocratic in its terms of reference, and to that extent, but to that extent only, comparable to Marie de France's *lais* (and similar Old French works): the magic elements are not specifically or characteristically 'Breton'. We should not, then, call the English poem a *lay* but rather a *gest*: which is what the poet himself calls it:

> Nu have ye herd the *gest* al thru
> Of Havelok and of Goldeborw (2984–5)

—it is the *gesta*—the doings, the history of these two. And it differs from the Anglo-Norman *Lai d'Haveloc* in a dozen ways, not least in its names. The phraseology of the opening lines of the Anglo-Norman work, the allusions to 'nobles fez', 'les pruesses', and 'l'aventure d'un riche rei / E de plusurs altres baruns' indicate clearly enough that it is intended for a courtly audience; whereas the prologue to the English poem is addressed at once to 'wyves, maydens, and alle men'.*

The tale itself opens in the most leisurely fashion, but in a firm and forthright tone that is to be consistently maintained. It is at once apparent that we shall be dealing in blacks and whites, virtues and villainies; but it is equally apparent that the story is to be solidly planted in a workaday England in which peace and justice were the prime desiderata. If the poem was (as some think) composed during or just after the reign of John, the appeal of the opening description of the exemplary King Athelwold would be particularly strong. His Saxon name in itself would speak to the nostalgia for the supposedly good times gone, the good old Saxon days 'thanne was Engelond at ayse' (59) as thirteenth-century England certainly was not; though Athelwold himself is not actually named for a hundred lines (such delayed identification is frequent in romances). It is noteworthy that this Athelwold is said to have died and been buried at Winchester (158)—the West-Saxon capital—and in Winchester the king's daughter Goldeboru is brought up (313), so that the association of the Saxon

---

* Not that the prologue was necessarily composed by the writer of the poem proper—'him that haveth the ryme maked / And therfor fele [many] nihtes waked' (2998–9). It is journeyman's work, repetitive, using clichés or couplets borrowed from the poem: an advertisement compiled by a reciter who knew the poem by heart; here telling just enough to attract listeners who might be willing to give him a pint of 'right good ale'.

line with the old Wessex capital is doubly strong. The pious motive for the king's actions stated at l. 74 'so was he his soule hold'—so concerned was he for his own spiritual welfare—and the detailed accounts of ecclesiastical ceremonies—running to some sixty lines in all (184–247)—imply a trust in traditional values and the stable elements of society. Contrariwise, the typical courtly romances, be they English or French, show little of this concern for the commonalty and the condition of England. *Havelok* gives us the first glimpse of ordinary life in post-Conquest literature—the lives of the labouring people who were to be a concern of Langland. But it is not a dissident England, nor is the poet a dissident poet. Like Langland, he accepts the status quo, and in particular the conception of ordered estates of the realm, each with its own function.

It is consistent with this conception that the king should prescribe that the heroine Goldeboru is to be brought up by Godrich her guardian until

> She couthe of curtesye
> Don, and speken of luve-drurye   (194–5)

—i.e. till she could go through the accepted stages of courtship. The poet takes this for granted, but does not make 'luve-drurye' a major element: the hybrid character of the word 'luve-drurye', a compound in which the native form *love* glosses its French synonym, is itself revealing. He goes out of his way to distinguish it from *mariages de convenance*: Goldeboru is not to marry

> til that she loven mouhte
> Hwom so hire to gode thouhte.   (196–7)

It is not easy now to respond to the relevance, the immediacy of the poem as it goes on to describe the due processes of summons, the fear of oathbreaking (e.g. 578 ff.), the promise of freedom to Grim the thrall. The double repetition of this promise (527 ff., 628 ff., 676) is not inept: in thirteenth-century England thraldom was a weighty matter.

The first movement of the poem finishes with the revelation of Earl Godrich's treachery. He is given the first of the interior monologues that are a feature of the poem, though hardly as complex as the monologues of French courtly romance; and his reference to Goldeboru as 'a fole, a therne' (298)—a mere serving-maid—sufficiently indicates where our sympathies are to be directed, just as his soliloquy, couched in everyday idiom laced with a popular saw—'Hope maketh fol man ofte blenkes' (307)—is meant for common, uncourtly ears; there is no trace of noble accents.

The general point of Godrich's malice is driven home by oblique appeals for sympathy for his victim:

> The castel dede he yemen[1] so
> That non ne mihte comen hire to[2]
> Of hire frend, with hir to speken
> That evere mihte hire bale wreken[3].   (324–7)

[1] *control*   [2] *to her*   [3] *revenge her suffering*

'Say we now forth in our spell' (338) signalizes a pause for breath, and beer, and the picking up of a new thread—the parallel Danish story of the good King Birkabein and the treacherous Godard, involving the entry of the King's son Havelok. Parallelism is a marked feature of the structure of *Havelok*, as of other romances. It provided a convenient broad mnemonic pattern for both audience and reciter. Here the author soon brings the Danish story of Birkabein and his 'riche' but villainous kinsman Godard alongside that of Athelwold and Godrich, telling it in much the same terms. Havelok and his sisters are put in a dungeon just like Goldeboru: 'ther non mihte hem comen to' (413). It is the same tale of a villain being taken for a true man, and is followed by the same imprecations—or rather more: the twenty lines of invective (422–46) display a fine taste for commination. But it is not mere rhetoric; the sharpest denunciation is kept for Godard as oathbreaker (423) and traitor (443), and *trayson* (444) has the specific feudal sense of an injury done by a vassal to his lord.

This vehement outburst creates a certain intensity of feeling; and the characters now begin to speak in terms that have the ring of actuality:

> And Godard seyde: 'Hwat is you?[1]
> Hwi grete[2] ye and goulen[3] nou?'   (453–4)

[1] *what is the matter with you*   [2] *weep*   [3] *cry*

and the children cry:

> 'Weilawei! Nis it[1] no korn
> That men mihte maken of bred[2]?
> Us hungreth so[3] we aren ney[4] ded.'   (462–4)

[1] *Is there no …?*   [2] *could make bread with*   [3] *we are so hungry*
[4] *almost*

Here as elsewhere the prevalence of short monosyllables or disyllabic forms is striking: it produces the effect of sharp crisp interchange—and the vocabulary is throughout native English or naturalized Norse. There are a few tags—like 'kniht ne knave', 'speke ne fnaste', 'gold ne fe'—but even these belong to popular speech, even though they may occur in narrative passages. By the same token proverbial expressions occur in dialogue and narrative alike: the authorial comment 'ther God wile helpen, nouht ne dereth [harms]' (648) is typical. The phrasal texture of the whole poem is strikingly consistent; and this kind of utterance fits naturally into the scansion of the couplets. The art is simple, but it *is* art. The poet can evoke pity at the projected murder of Havelok and the actual murder of his sisters without resort to tear-jerking. We see the actual killings through Havelok's eyes and feel his sense of the consequences: 'Ful sori' (477) indicates wretchedness, not mere sorrow in the modern sense. The interior monologue that was developing in French romances like *Enéas* now serves a new function when at 509–22 it shows the working of enlightened self-interest, a kind of popular equivalent to the more intellectual self-analysis of Chrétien's characters. The thoughts of Grim the fisherman are expressed in the same way and at some length (790–810). Indeed this is one of the most striking features of the poem, and provides a marked contrast to the flat narrative sequence of the Anglo-Norman *lai*.

The scene of the discovery of Havelok's identity by means of two favourite folk motifs—the supernatural flame and the royal birthmark—makes excellent drama. To be sure, the flame is found in Gaimar's version of the tale, but here it has attracted to it the similar token of the birthmark—which leads to Grim's prophecy that Havelok will come to his own again and all shall be well—another authorial device for keeping the audience alert (606 ff.). And Grim's wife adds just the right familiar domestic touch, dashing off for bread and cheese, pastries, and cakes to feed the famished boy (641–4).

Here as elsewhere there is an instinctive sense of the right balance between speech and action. Speech rarely goes beyond six lines, action is swift. Grim's dismissal by Godard, and his departure from Denmark to set up his little earthen house on the Lincolnshire coast is all compassed in fifty lines, including six of minstrel pattern promising more excitements to come—'Yf that ye wilen therto here' (732).

The description of Grim's life as a Lincolnshire fisherman gives a unique glimpse of East Coast life. If the Crabbe of *Peter Grimes* was a Pope in worsted stockings, here is Crabbe's predecessor in no stockings at all, but familiar with men who caught and sold the fish and set 'weirs' (traps) in the sea: a term and a practice well evidenced in East Anglia. Into this plain, peasant life comes the spectre of hunger—'a ful strong dere [dearth] . . . of korn of bred' (824–5). Famine was never far away in this part of England, so Grim might well send Havelok to Lincoln to seek his own fortune—whereas in the Anglo-Norman *lai* he leaves simply because he is unskilled at fishing. Still more vivid is the

scene showing Havelok on the bridge at Lincoln, looking out for a job
as porter; and there is other evidence that the bridge was precisely the
place where the fisherfolk brought their catch, and catered for the
castle that then as now dominated the town: 'berman' being the local
term for such a porter. Other local terms appear at this point—like
'rippe' (basket) later found in Norfolk (a 'ripper' being the porter who
brought fish in baskets from the coast). We are in the Old Danelaw
area and by and large the poem reflects its mores and manner of
speech. Havelok's manner of speech, however, here begins to be more
formal, more rhetorically balanced as if betokening his princely
future. The motive of the disguised prince is being steadily developed,
even whilst he pauses in his errands to play with children by the way-
side. He is 'gentle' in both senses, with nothing of a proud Norman
baron about him, and too modest to enter the national shot-putting
contest until his lord enjoins him to. The wicked Godrich forces this
supposed thrall to marry Goldeboru. The notion of an enforced
marriage is not original, but the wording of their separate yet similar
objection is. Finally she yields to what must be the Divine will. This is
not trite or fatalistic piety. God (and the Cross of Christ) soon appears
in the tale, speaking through his angel to explain the significance of
Havelok's birthmark; and Havelok's prayer before the Rood is so
intense that it is no surprise to find that

> His leve at Jesu Crist he tok,
> And at his suete moder ok,
> And at the croiz that he bi lay. (1387-9)

Havelok's fervent prayers follow Goldeboru's interpretation of his
prophetic dreams suggested, but only suggested, by the dream which
Argentille (Goldeboru's counterpart) has in the *lai*, and in which
sundry animals attack the hero, and the sea rises to terrifying heights,
and the pair climb into a tree to avoid two lions, till the beasts submit
to them. The dream that the English poet gives us is more original,
and more dramatic in its imagery: castles fall at Havelok's knee and
yield up their keys. It determines Havelok to return to Denmark with
his wife and the sons of Grim. It is an index of the appeal of traditional
fidelities that Grim's sons have joyfully acknowledged him as their
lord on his return to Grimsby with Goldeboru (1207 ff.) and have even
offered him all their possessions. The emphasis on such loyalties sorts
with that on oath-keeping—especially in respect of 'trewage', a recurrent theme in *Havelok*.

If tension weakens at this midpoint in the narrative it is in part
because some 200 lines describing Havelok's return to Denmark have

been lost; to an East Coast audience who knew ships and men that often made the crossing they would have special interest. In Denmark Havelok meets Earl Ubbe, once a friend of his father, to whom he gives a gold ring as a kind of surety. The gnomic comment 'he was ful wis that first yaf mede [gave reward]' (1635) turns out to be ironical. Ubbe recognizes Havelok's worth but not, as yet, his ancestry. He entertains the pair on a princely scale. That night the house in which the couple are lodged with Bernard, a reeve, is attacked by thieves. The appeal here is to the bourgeois interest in order and security; and burgesses actually figure in these town scenes (2012, 2049), which have no parallel in Arthurian romances: the disguising as monks was a device actually used by robbers in the time of Edward III;* and the fight described with such relish is a bourgeois equivalent to Lancelot's epic defence of the door in the last books of Malory. It reveals Havelok's prowess, for he drives out the thieves like dogs from a mill-house, and slays three with a single blow from the door bar.

> Havelok lifte up the dore tre
> And at a dint[1] he slow hem thre;
> Was non of hem that hise hernes[2]
> Ne lay therute ageyn the sternes[3]   (1806–9)

[1] *one blow*   [2] *brains*   [3] *exposed to the stars*

Later Hugh Raven joins in, seizing an oar, an appropriate and probably a common weapon. From this lively scene Ubbe and Bernard his reeve emerge as generous, and ingenuous, characters. To ensure the safety of Havelok and his wife Ubbe lodges them in a bower next to his own, with nothing between

> 'But[1] a fayre firrene wowe[2]—
> Speke y lowde or spek I lowe
> Thou shalt ful wel heren me
> And than[3] thou wilt, thou shalt me se'.   (2078–81)

[1] *except*   [2] *wall made of fir*   [3] *when*

The detail may seem otiose. But it means that when Havelok's birth-mark shines miraculously for the third time the light can penetrate the wall. Thus Ubbe comes to recognize Havelok as the long-lost heir; and not only does he forthwith do homage himself, he has all the members of the estates do the same, dubs Havelok knight and makes him King. The 150 lines given to the rendering of oaths and homages testify to the importance of the scene. From this point the pace slackens and the poet flags; formulas and gnomic remarks bulk larger.

---

* See G. O. Sayles (ed.), *Select Cases from the Court of King's Bench under Edward III* (Selden Society lxxxii, London, 1965), vi, p. 95.

The retribution meted out to a Godard abandoned by his associates is described in good set terms and legal phrase. A king—this seems to be the moral—cannot take the law into his own hands. Havelok, the poor boy who had made good, now goes back to his home town, to found a priory in Grim's memory. He has scarcely landed when Godrich (Godard's English counterpart) raises the 'ferd' (the army, an Old English term) against him, claiming that Havelok has seized this priory and strangled monks and nuns (as pre-Conquest Danes doubt-less did). The gory details of the fight are the folk-equivalents of those that figure in descriptions of battles and tourneys in more courtly romances.

As the end approaches other features of popular romance are packed together. Havelok marries off Grim's daughter Gunnild to the Earl of Chester, and they have five strapping sons. The Earl of Corn-wall's cook becomes himself an earl, and marries Grim's other daughter, who is described more lyrically than Goldeboru herself (2916–21). Havelok reigns as an ideal king, dignified, magnanimous, and loving his queen with a requited love. Once they have reached this topmost position in the feudal scale they can be described in terms befitting an aristocratic Palamon and Emily, and it is not impossible that Chaucer had them in mind as he concluded *The Knight's Tale*, where Theseus plays the reconciling role here taken by Havelok when he weds Gunnild to Chester. The difference between 'courtly' and 'popular' romance was never absolute or divisive.

It happens that one tale of this popular type was once—and quite early—associated with Chaucer. In no less than ten manuscripts of the Canterbury Tales the 58 lines of *The Cook's Tale* are followed by the tale of *Gamelyn* in loose and variable rhymed couplets. Thomas Lodge later found the story and based on it part of his novel called *Rosalynde or Euphues Golden Legacy*—on which Shakespeare, in turn, based *As You Like It*. In some of the manuscripts of the *Tales*, this tale is actually headed or rubricated as 'The Cook's Tale'—partly because of its position but partly also, perhaps, because at one point in the tale Gamelyn, the hero, is treated as a cook by his wicked brother, who asks him: 'Is our mete yare [ready]?'

> Tho wrathed him Gamelyn, and swor by Goddes book
> 'Thou schalt go bake thiself. I wil nought be *thy cook*'. (91–2)

Chaucer may possibly have known the tale but cannot conceivably have written this text of it: metre, language, treatment all forbid it.

Gamelyn is the story of a younger son of a knight done out of his rights by his brothers. Its emphasis is on his virtues and his valour.

Like Havelok he excels in popular sports—such as wrestling—but his status in society is different; he is not a ruler in the ordinary sense though he does eventually become 'king' of a band of outlaws like a Robin Hood. In fact the plot was later made the basis of a ballad ('Robin Hood newly revived', Child 128). Essentially popular in appeal, it fulfilled the function of early 'Westerns', and as in such films all the emphasis is on action—chiefly in the shape of brawls. 'Gone, the merry morris din, / Gone the song of Gamelyn' wrote Keats in 'Robin Hood', identifying Gamelyn with 'the tough-belted outlaw' of the next verse in his poem. In fact there is nothing of the morris din in Gamelyn—the noise is, chiefly, the cracking of bones and pates, varied by the carousals: Gamelyn, with typical generosity, dispenses five tuns of wine to 'alle maner men': like Havelok he is 'no chiche' (niggard).

We are left in no doubt of the author's sentiments: 'evel mot he thee [prosper]!' he exclaims when Gamelyn's false brother tricks him. The religious orders in the persons of abbots and priors (480 ff.; cf. 780 ff.) are given unsavoury sentiments, and the sheriff's role is similar to that in the Robin Hood story. The outlaws fit into the same pattern, and their king is 'hende' (courteous) and 'come of gentil blood' (663); there are hints of the Duke in the Forest of Arden: 'Yonge men', says the master outlaw as he spies Gamelyn and Adam 'under the woodshaw', 'I am war of gestes [visitors]; God sende us non but goode.'

Like all popular romances it ends with everybody living happily ever after and Gamelyn coming to his own again, having revenged himself on his enemies. The King (unnamed) makes Gamelyn his Chief Justice 'of all his fre forest' (892) and forgives his followers. To suit the conventions, Gamelyn weds 'a wife both good and fair'—but that is all we hear of her. The most surprising feature of the tale is the use of technical legal terminology—surprising, because it suggests that the audience would appreciate its force: thus Ote, Gamelyn's better-disposed brother, says:

> 'I bidde him to maynpris that thou graunt him me
> Til the next sittyng of delyverance.'   (744–5)

(i.e. 'I ask that he be granted to me on bail till the next sitting of the assize for gaol delivery.')*

In general the language is lively and idiomatic. The images are fresh, the talk is terse, even sardonic. When Gamelyn sets to work with his stave on the guests who are feasting on his substance he 'sprengeth

---

* Cf. 789 ff. and 798, where Gamelyn is indicted and cried a 'wolfshead' (as in pre-Conquest times).

[sprinkles] holywater with an oken spire [bar]' (503). His companion Adam says in the same scene:

> 'Er they ben *assoyled* there schal noon passe ...
> They ben men of holy chirche. Draw of hem no blood
> Save wel the croune and do hem non harmes,
> But brek *bothe* her legges—and sithen here armes.'
>
> (516–24)

And later he says:

> 'we schul so welcome the scherreves men
> That som of hem schul make here beddes in the fen[1].'
>
> (587–8, cf. 596)

[1] *mud*

There is here a touch of the grimmer humour we find in Norse and Old English narrative. The wisdom of the tale is that of the folk—'He moste needes walke in woode that may not walke in towne' (672)—and so is its rough justice: sheriff and evil judge are hanged high 'to weyven with ropes and with the wynd drye' (880). This narrator was probably versed in popular tales and rhymes that were never committed to paper or parchment.

Athelston may serve as a third example of a popular romance because its appeal is clearly to popular feeling. But the action concerns people who, if not highly born, are all highly placed. Athelston himself is nephew to the King of England, whom he succeeds. He makes his three sworn brethren Earl of Dover, Earl of Stone, and Archbishop of Canterbury respectively. The action, which is developed largely by dialogue, concerns the plot by Wimund Earl of Dover against the Earl of Stone and his wife, whom he falsely accuses of treason. The King angrily and brutally rejects the entreaties of his pregnant wife—the 'garland of cherries' that she casts away perhaps was a pregnant woman's longing—striking her with his foot and so killing his stillborn son. He is equally fierce with the Archbishop, threatening him with death—a scene reminiscent of Henry II's conflict with Becket. The counter-threat of excommunication of the whole country (as effected in John's day) brings the King to heel; says the Archbishop:

> 'I schal gar crye thorwgh ylke toun
> That kyrkys[1] schole be broken doun,
> And stoken[2] agayn with thorn;

And thou schal lygge in an old dyke
As it were an heretyke.
    —Allas, that thou were born!'

   ¹ *churches*   ² *stopped up*

Even so, the Earl of Stone, his wife, and all his children are put to the ordeal by fire—though all survive unharmed. The Archbishop forces the King to reveal the name of his slanderer, who fails the test of ordeal and is hanged and drawn asunder by horses; this is the punishment for a traitor in *Havelok* and points the moral of the story:

Now Jesu, that is hevene-kyng
Leve¹ nevere traytour have betere endyng!

   ¹ *allow*

This tail-rhyme romance has in common with *Havelok* a curious mixture of pre-Conquest and post-Conquest allusion. The trial by fire is traditionally one that Emma, wife of Canute, passed through unscathed; and her story was evidently still known in Langland's day. The son born to the innocent countess is christened Edmund—after St Edmund, King of the East Saxons (who figures in the contemporary Wilton Diptych); and Athelston of course is the name of the tenth-century Saxon king commemorated in the Old English poem on the battle of Brunanburh. All these names suggest that a sense of national history remained strong despite the Norman Conquest. The most vivid part of the poem is the account of a messenger's desperate journey from the King at Westminster to the Archbishop of Canterbury—via Charing Cross, Fleet Street, London Bridge, Stone, Sittingbourne, Ospringe, and Blee—the very route of Chaucer's pilgrims. On his return journey he gallops so fast that his horse ('worth an hundred pound') understandably drops down dead. The Archbishop follows, riding post on palfreys picked up at his various manors *en route*, using no less than nine to get to Westminster. Next morning the King goes to prayers in the Abbey and, looking up to the choir, sees the seated Archbishop who he thought was sixty miles away. The prelate, in fact, emerges as the dominant character; and he is not beyond telling a barefaced lie to entice the Earl of Dover to town. This involves the description of another journey to Westminster (the seat of justice), this time via Gravesend (755). As in *Havelok*, the frame of the tale is two sets of parallel actions. And as in *Havelok*, the action and the interest are firmly English and the story itself probably owes little to foreign romance. It may be seen as a miniature of the age-old conflict between Church and State, or a reflection of the romance belief in the power of innocence and poetic justice. But it is not all black and white. Athelston is not merely 'bull-headed' passion personified; he tries hard to keep his pledge of secrecy—and eventually tells the truth—'in shrift' (686 ff.).

Of the tail-rhyme romances, *Sir Amadace* (or *Sir Amadas*) is one of those furthest removed from the eighteenth-century conception of the romantic. It is commonly classed as a story of the Grateful Dead, a motif to which a whole book has been devoted;* but its essential theme is the dangers, and rewards, of generosity, the theme also found in Chester's *Sir Launfal*; it is an *exemplum* with an appeal to all who find it difficult to make both ends meet.

The story opens with the hero faced with the embarrassment not only of an empty purse but of his consequent inability to play the generous donor. In this plight he will not stay where 'I am so wele kennit': better said sorrow than seen. He mortgages his lands, shares most of the money thus produced among knights, squires, and the poor, and with three servants goes away to make good. As he rides through a forest he sees a light burning in a chapel that gives off a foul stench. His servant, having stopped his nose with his hood, approaches the chapel to find a woman keening over a decaying corpse. It is her dead husband, a rich merchant who had squandered his wealth on lavish gifts: like a fool 'he clad more men at Yule than did a noble knight'. He thus provides a mirror-image of Sir Amadas. He had justified his action by saying that 'God sent it every deal' and so it was not his to keep. At his death neighbours seized his horses and cattle, sheep and swine, but though his widow had sold her dowry there was still £30 owing, and one creditor, fierce as a boar, would not allow the corpse to be buried till he had his money. Amadas, seized with remorse for his own reckless lavishness, rides off to the nearby town, changes his clothes, and invites the cruel creditor and his wife to a fine feast. Preoccupied with his recent experience, he at last reveals it. But the creditor's only response is 'Serve him right! The fellow owed me £30.' When Amadas urges him to be charitable, this Shylock is obdurate. Amadas had kept £40 of his own; now, despite his steward's grumbles, he settles the debt himself, and lays out the rest on funeral expenses for the corpse and a fine funeral feast for all comers, especially the poor.

Now Amadas sets off again. Three miles out of town he dismisses his three men, saying that God may yet succour him and giving them

---

* G. H. Gerould, *The Grateful Dead* (London, 1908).

their horse and gear. This movement of the poem concludes with his comment:

> 'Nowe may wise men sitte at home
> Quen[1] folus[2] may walke ful wille of wone[3]
> And, Christ wotte[4], so may I'   (406–8)

¹ *when*   ² *fools*   ³ *destitute*   ⁴ *knows*

and with his acknowledgement that his kindness has hitherto been misplaced; it should have been directed to the poor. Suddenly a knight clad in white rides up. Amadas, though distressed, does not forget his courtesy, and salutes him. The knight bids him take heart: he is in God's hands:

> 'A mon that hase allway bynne kynde
> Sum curtas mon yette may he fynde'.   (463–4)

This weighted couplet, in which 'courtas' carries the sense 'conscious of his obligation to *gentilesse*' reads like a comment on the episode of the corpse, and so it proves to be. The stranger bids him seek out a nearby king and win his fair daughter by prowess in the field. The two knights will meet again, but Amadas must promise to share with the stranger whatever he acquires by the marriage.

Things turn out as the White Knight had foretold. Amadas equips himself with clothes, gold, and a fine steed from a ship he finds wrecked on the shore, wins lands and honour and the king's daughter, and distributes his new wealth like his old. In due course a son is born. All goes happily till one day 'this felau come to the gate', clad in white like an angel. He sends a pregnant message to Amadas: 'tell him that my suit is white and say we have together been'. He has come for his promised share, which must include half of Amadas's child and half his wife. She insists that Amadas should keep the compact: 'Thou wan me and I am thine'. The White Knight asks Amadas which he loves more—his wife or his children. This is to be kind only to be cruel, for when Amadas chooses his wife he is ordered to cut her in two. Meekly she awaits the fatal stroke. But as Amadas, like another Abraham, lifts his sword the Knight cries 'Stop'. He hands back both wife and children, saying: 'Now is time of peace. You were not to blame if you were loath to kill such a lady. I am the man for whose burial cost you gave all you had. I prayed then that God would reward you. Farewell, and love this lady as your life.' Then 'he glode [glided] away as dew in towne'. Amadas and his wife kneel down to thank God and 'Mary fre'. They live happily ever after. The poet comments that there are nowadays few ladies who would have served their lords in this way—'sum wold have sayd nay'. Amadas (soon to succeed as king) recalls his old retainers and bestows largesse as of yore.

The closing invocation of divine blessing on the listening company sets the Christian seal on the story. All hangs on acceptance of God's will and his beneficent purpose. The hero, like Gawain, is put to the test, but unlike Gawain he does not flinch from it. The testing of the hero is the real pivot of this romance, and it is the test that highlights the wife's role. Passive as a maiden to be wooed, she is positive and unflinching as a wife. We have here glimpses of married life, its stresses, fidelities, and consolations, that romance rarely gives us.

In its language, technique, and pious tone, if not in theme, *Sir Amadace* is typical of the better tail-rhyme romances. But criticism must take account, in Chekhov's terms, of the minuses as well as the pluses. And we shall not appreciate the parodic spirit that pervades Chaucer's *Sir Thopas* unless we have watched a journeyman *remanieur* at work on a larger scale. *Libeaus Desconus*, by some critics unkindly credited to the Thomas Chester who wrote *Launfal*, has an Arthurian theme, with some resemblance to the *Tale of Sir Gareth* as we find it in Malory. The six copies that survive, and the textual evidence indicating that there must have been several earlier texts of it, suggest that it was in demand. By the end of the fourteenth century such romances could be bought for a shilling or two, when wages were a few pence a day and ale twopence a gallon. The extant copies of *Libeaus* are cheap and bad, as if hastily turned out to meet a demand.

It is a version of the ever-popular story of the young man who makes good by his own endeavour. With his inner development there is little concern; the emphasis is on his prowess. It evidently derives in part from the first half of Renaut de Beaujeu's *Li Biaus Descouneus*, the superior subtlety of which some critics have exaggerated. But many of the motifs found in it may also be found in earlier English romances.

'Libeaus Desconus' is the name that Arthur gives the hero when he comes to seek knightly service. In fact he is an illegitimate son of Gawain, begotten 'under a forest side'; the opening scene of *The Wife of Bath's Tale* suggests the probable circumstances. His mother calls him 'Bewfis' (*beaufils*). His chance comes when a fair maid called Ellen rides into Arthur's court escorted by a dwarf, saying that her 'Lady of Synadoun' had been seized and imprisoned. She wants a knight to rescue her, and the unfledged Libeaus begs for the honour. Ellen, hoping for a knight of greater renown, at first spurns the offer. But Arthur says bluntly 'Thou getest non other knyght'. The veterans, including Gawain, rig him out with weapons and armour. He rides off with the dwarf and Ellen (who is still in a foul temper), and they come to a ford guarded, as is *de rigueur* in Arthurian romance, by a formidable knight whom Libeaus soon unhorses. They hack away on foot till the knight pleads for mercy and is sent off to Arthur. On his way he meets three of his nephews, who vow vengeance. That night Ellen and Libeaus sleep out. She apologizes, and they make 'game and great solace' together which may or may not imply love-making. Next day he takes on the eldest brother, breaking his thigh, and then the other two, who soon cry mercy and are dispatched to the court. Libeaus and the lady spend the night in a leafy arbour, but are roused by the dwarf, who smells roast meat: it is a boar being roasted by two giants who are about to wrong a fair damsel. One of these Libeaus runs through with his spear, and the other, who strikes his horse dead with the boar, he decapitates. The damsel (Violet) explains that they had besieged her father's castle. In gratitude he predictably offers to Libeaus Violet, a cluster of castles, and succession to his kingdom. But Libeaus is not ready to settle down. He and Ellen set out again and come to a fine castle. Ellen explains that its owner (Gyfroun) has the custom of challenging all comers to show a fairer mistress than his: prize, a white gerfalcon. The battlements are decorated with the losers' heads. Libeaus duly produces Ellen decked out in all her finery, but she is rated a mere washerwoman (and that is a euphemism; the story seems to get temporarily out of control here, the judgement being based on differences in dress). Gyfroun and Libeaus fight and Libeaus sends off the gerfalcon as trophy to Arthur, who rewards him with one hundred pounds sterling (Arthurian romances retain that relish for material rewards that characterizes Anglo-Saxon epic). Libeaus, having spent his prize on a great feast, sets out again, and runs across the hunt of Sir Otes de Lyle, a fugitive in the Wirral. At Ellen's instance Libeaus takes one of the dogs, and rudely refuses to relinquish it. Otes, having collected his friends, ambushes Libeaus, who is soon 'besette as deer ys yn a nette'. Libeaus is worsted, yet Otes not only surrenders, but he hands over treasure, land, and rents—at an agreed valuation ('be sertayne extente'), a curious intrusion of workaday legal practice—and he joins the procession to Arthur. Evidently Libeaus is to be judged as much by his gratitude to Arthur for befriending him as by his prowess, or ferocity: his winnings are his lord's.

We need a break at this point—the half-way point in the tale—and the poet provides one in the form of a seasonal headpiece:

> Hyt befell yn the month of June,
> Whan the fenell hangeth yn toun
> Grene yn semely sales.[1]   (1225–7)

[1] *halls*

Libeaus, who has set off for further adventures in Ireland and Wales, comes to the fine city of Yle d'Or, where a great giant holds a maid in thrall. This is meat and drink to Libeaus, who announces:

> 'I have yseyn[1] grete okes
> Falle for wyndes strokes,
> The smale han stonde[2] stylle.'

> [1] *seen*   [2] *stood*

The giant has no sense of fair play and, while Libeaus is taking a drink in his helm, knocks him into the river—as if he needed rebaptizing, quips Libeaus. Off comes the giant's head, Libeaus enters the city in triumph, the lady at once begs him to be her lord, and he rashly agrees. He stays for a year, literally enchanted, and forgetting all about the Lady of Synadoun and even Ellen, until she reproaches him with being false to Arthur. Stung to the heart, he rides off to Synadoun, where the citizens are busy carrying filthy rubbish out to the fields to throw at any knight beaten in joust with the constable of the castle. Soon, of course, the constable is rocking in his saddle 'as child doth in a cradle'. He recognizes Libeaus as a true son of Gawain and a Knight of the Table Round, and explains that the Lady is held by necromancers. And so it proves. When Libeaus enters 'la cité gast', as it is called in the French, he finds none but minstrels playing by torchlight. Suddenly the torches are quenched, the minstrels vanish, the earth shakes and two knights with poisoned swords thunder in. One he slays, the other mysteriously vanishes. As Libeaus reaches for him a window falls out of the hall, and a dragon with a woman's face emerges, kisses him on the mouth, and forthwith turns into a fair naked woman. She has been under a charm that could be dispelled only by kissing Gawain or one of Gawain's blood. She at once offers him marriage, if Arthur will consent. Arthur graciously agrees and

> The joye of that bredale
> Nys not told yn tale
> Ne rekened yn no gest.   (2107–9)

Long drawn-out as the romance is, it represents a considerable shortening as well as a slight refashioning of the French. The result is to magnify the role of Arthur as the *fainéant* lord on whom everything depends and for whom everything is done. It is full of clichés of phrase and incident; clichés that a *disour* might vary or even extemporize as he went along. It is romance going down hill; the last weird scenes take us into the world of Huon of Bordeaux, the long and intricate tale that Lord Berners was to translate for the delight of Tudor readers. By comparison, *Libeaus* is concise and its dialogue crisp. But part of

Malory's appeal in his own time must have been that instead of this ragged and monotonous verse in corrupt texts he offered clean and nervous prose.

(iv) *Arthur and Merlin*; *Ywain and Gawain*; *The Avowing of Arthur*; *The Awntyrs of Arthur*; The Stanzaic *Morte Arthur*; The Alliterative *Morte Arthure*

In an incomplete romance probably originally written down towards the end of the thirteenth century, and headed in one manuscript *Of Arthour and of Merlin* (9,938 lines), Arthur makes his first appearance in English verse since Layamon finished his *Brut*. The poem is closely dependent on a French prose text now known as *Merlin*, to which the poet refers as 'this romaunce' or 'the Bruyt'. That his source is French he leaves to be inferred from the somewhat clumsy introduction:

> Mani noble ich have yseiye[1]
> That no Freynsche couthe seye.
> Biginne ichil for her love
> Bi Jesus leve that sitt above
> On Inglische tel mi tale. . . .

[1] *seen*

This suggests also that he had a 'gentle' audience chiefly in mind, and indeed the narrative is replete with genealogical and 'historical' lore.

The story falls into two distinct parts: the first, running from the death of Constance to the crowning of Arthur, shows the translator's awareness of other versions of the story as it had developed out of Geoffrey of Monmouth; the second follows the French *Merlin* more closely. Modern readers may prefer to read this British history in Malory's prose, but they should remember that Malory in his adaptation of French narrative was doing much the same thing as the author of this poem (of which he was evidently unaware), though the earlier *remanieur* identifies himself and his readers more closely with the ancient British chivalry, more than once speaking of 'our men' and 'our knights'—'And our gred [our men cried] "Sle! lay on! / Kepe [look] there! Kepe here! Lete passe none!"' (9323–4.) Like Malory he reorders, conflates, digresses—and occasionally misunderstands his source. In general his omissions make for a straightening of the narrative line, and perhaps we have here a sign that the English liked a plainer narrative than did the French.

The chief interest lies in Merlin the mystery man. By turns shapeshifter, strategist, master of statecraft, he has the dominant role: his disguises are always intriguing, his appearances always dramatic, not least when he stings Arthur into martial action by his reproaches. The traditional stories of Arthur's birth and recognition—now familiar to readers of Malory—are here recounted, but he rarely becomes the centre of the action, and his mores are primitive: he lies with Liganor as soon as he sees her (4185 ff.); 'fin amour', a concept long established in France, plays little part. True, Vortigern, 'for love fin', takes 'to fere and to wive' the daughter of King Anguis (Auchinleck version, 478 ff.) but in so doing he sets a fearful example since she was a 'Saracen' (a synonym for pagan, applied to all Norse marauders in English romance). In fact both the French original and the English renderings reflect the themes, formulas, and preoccupations of earlier French epic. Traditional themes, topoi, and formulas here appear repeatedly, sometimes for the first, but by no means for the last, time in English. Amongst them are: the arming of a warrior; the assembly of named notables; the noise and dust of battle in which arrows are as thick as motes in a sunbeam and javelins as dense as gnats; variant formulas for death and destruction in battle—'sum gras gnowe [bite the grass]'; processional entries; formal feastings. If some of these are traditional 'oral' formulas, others suggest a poet improving on or deliberately varying such formulas. Nor are they limited to externals. A picture of inner preoccupations is more than once suggested by such a couplet as

> The king at his mete[1] sat
> Michel[2] he thought and litel he at[3]:

> (2267–8; cf. 6527–8)

> [1] *food*   [2] *much*   [3] *ate*

Rhetorical formulas are not abundant, but two recur: the rhetorical question addressed to a supposed audience, as later in Chaucer 'What helpeth it make tale long?' (3055, etc.); and *repetitio* (the re-use of a word or phrase in the same (usually the initial) position—as in the lines describing the destruction of battle:

> Ther was sone leyd adoun
> Mani wel bright gonfaynoun[1]
> The schaftes tobroken[2] and cloth torent[3]
> And mani a gret lording yschent[4]
> Mani knight other[5] slough
> Mani hors her guttes drough[6]. . . .   (439–44)

[1] *banner*   [2] *broken*   [3] *rent apart*   [4] *destroyed*   [5] *another*
[6] *dragged*

The expressiveness of some phrases clearly owes little to the French.
One Gogenar (or Goinar) remarks to Leodegan

> ' "He nath non heved that nil it defende"
> Lete be, sir, thi precheing,
> And oyain[1] tho houndes fling.'   (9214–16)
>
> [1] *back*

—'. . . Stop your chatter, and get at these heathen dogs'. The Devils (in a
passage of devout synopsis of the Christian *credo*) are described as falling out of heaven 'Al fort Our Dright seyd "Ho"' (till Our Lord said
'Stop' (645)). Gnomic or sententious comment, often put in Merlin's
mouth, relieves the monotony of the narrative tone:

> Men seyt yere and other to[1]
> Wrong wil an hond go[2]
> And ever at the nende[3]
> Wrong wil wende.[4]   (1895–8)
>
> [1] *for years*   [2] *be present*   [3] *end*   [4] *go*

Merlin warns of the unexpectedness of death by a curious parable of a
man who buys shoe leather, shoes, and grease to oil them, expecting
he will wear them out, but dies before he gets back to his own door
(1303–10).

The romance is pleasantly punctuated by a series of brief descriptions of months and seasons (see above, p. 128)—beginning with April
that 'merrytime'. 'Mirie' is the word linking most of these passages,
though it can have no place in winter when

> The leves fallen of the tre
> Rein alangeth[1] the cuntré
> Maidens leseth[2] here hewe
> Ac[3] ever hye[4] lovieth that be trewe.   (4201–4)
>
> [1] *makes dreary*   [2] *lose*   [3] *but*   [4] *they*

There is no great particularity in these 'nature-passages'. June is
characterized as the time 'when fenel hongeth abrod in toun' (3060);
but fennel is also the plant of summer in *Libeaus Desconus* (see above,
p. 168) and the Harley lyrics. Some are suggested by passages in the
French, which are more closely related to the action. The device is
developed in *Kyng Alisaunder*, and its reappearance there has been
claimed as a sign of common authorship.

Ywain and Gawain is more directly dependent than any other
English Arthurian romance on Chrétien de Troyes (it is based on his
Yvain); yet no other romance is so markedly native in its briskness, not
to say brusqueness, and its northern idiom. It opens, unconven-

tionally, with an amusing domestic scene: Guenevere issuing from her bedroom and sitting with the knights of the Round Table. The traditionally abrasive Kay tries to pick a quarrel with Colgrevance, who has jumped up at the queen's approach: 'Ful light of lepes has thou ben ay', he jeers. To Guenevere's reproof Colgrevance adds his own:

> 'Na more manes[1] me thi flyt[2]
> Than it war a flies byt.'

> [1] *troubles*   [2] *scorn*

—'you have treated better men than me thus'. Eventually the company settles down to hear an 'aventure' of Colgrevance.

'Six years ago' he says,

as I was riding I came to a parapet with a drawbridge on which stood a knight with a falcon on his wrist. He took me into a splendid palace where a beautiful damsel unlaced my armour and led me down to supper. Next day I set out again and in a forest full of wild beasts met an ugly giant with ears like an elephant's, which the beasts dread. The giant directed me to a magic basin hanging by a well: 'if water from the well is thrown on the basin it will raise thunder and lightning, sleet, and rain'.

All had happened as foretold. As the storm ceased came a burst of bird song and a company of horsemen and a knight who, in a brief encounter, wounded Colgrevance and rode off with his horse. Colgrevance had returned to his hosts, who said that none who had made the journey had ever returned before.

Ywain and the irrepressible Kay are disputing the matter when Arthur enters. He suggests that he and the others should go to see all this on St John's Eve, but Ywain rides off immediately. He engages in the same enterprise, but pursues the knight as far as his castle, where the portcullis is let down to cut through his horse and saddle—a scene that caught the fancy of some medieval artists.* He is succoured by a damsel called Lunet, who warns him of the dangers of his situation— the knight is dead and his widow bent on vengeance—but promises him help and proffers a ring with a stone of invisibility:

> 'Als the bark hilles[1] the tre
> Right so sal my ring do the'   (741–2)

> [1] *protects*

As the pursuit draws near she hides him in her bed. The knight's funeral follows, with the armour of the dead man carried on his horse

---

* The scene appears in a number of English misericords. See M. D. Anderson, *Misericords* (Harmondsworth, 1954), 20 and plate 9.

(as in *The Knight's Tale*, but not as in Chrétien). Ywain, glimpsing his widow, promptly falls in love:

> Luf, that es so mekil[1] of mayne[2],
> Sare had wownded Sir Ywayne   (871–2)
>
>   [1] *great*   [2] *power*

—the prudent English poet adding:

> He wroght ful mekyl ogayns[1] resowne
> To set his luf in swilk[2] a stede[3].   (904–5)
>
>   [1] *against*   [2] *such*   [3] *place*

Lunet sees at once what the trouble is and prepares Alundyne, her mistress, who is unexpectedly amenable, and becomes Ywain's wife. Ywain rides off to bring back Arthur and his knights. All pleasure themselves with hawking and hunting till Gawain reproves Ywain as a slugabed knight, though admitting that he too would leave chivalry for a wife like Alundyne:

> Bot yit a fole that litel kan
> May wel cownsail another man   (1477–8)

—a touch of proverbial stiffening added by the English poet. Ywain leaves her, 'with teris trikland on hir chekes'; he wears her ring as keepsake and promises to return in a year. When he forgets his promise a messenger, who calls him traitor and 'losenger' (deceiver), snatches the ring and disappears. Mad with grief he runs to the forest and lives on roots and venison. Years later three ladies find him sleeping under a tree. It seems to one of them that she has seen him before. With a magic ointment of Morgan la Fée's they cure him of his madness, and soon he is strong enough to resume his knightly adventures. Finding a dragon attacking a lion, he rescues the lion, who fawns upon him and at night keeps watch and ward for him. When one day Ywain visits again the perilous well and stone, he swoons, his sword pierces his neck, and the lion would willingly have killed himself. A maiden (none other than Lunet) who has been immured nearby on a charge of treason stirs Ywain to her defence. With the lion's help he first fells a dragon in a nearby castle, then returns just as she is about to be burnt, saying to himself:

> Yf thai be many and mekil of pryse
> I sal let[1] for no kouwardise;
> For with me es bath God and right,
> And thai sal help me forto fight,

And my lyon sal help me;
Than er we foure ogayns tham thre.' (2517–22)

[1] *give up*

His opponents object to the lion, though Ywain says it is present merely as his page. In the event the lion intervenes and Lunet's foes are burnt in the fire prepared for her. Ywain's wounds, and the lion's, are healed in a nearby castle, scene of a series of tedious episodes redeemed for the modern reader only by a few touches such as the maidens set to sewing:

> For al that we wirk in this stede,
> We have noght half oure fil of brede;
> For the best that sewes here any styk[1]
> Takes bot foure penys in a wik[2]. (3051–4)

[1] *stitch*   [2] *week*

Eventually, Ywain sets out to gain Alundyne's grace, once more visiting the well and wetting the stone. Lunet devises a reconciliation. The pair live and love happily ever after, and

> So did Lunet and the liown
> Until that ded[1] haves dreven[2] tham down.

[1] *death*   [2] *driven*

The romance, though it retains 'courtois' elements, lacks the psychological interest (and *entrelacement*) of the original. Chrétien's preoccupations with the values of love and chivalry do not appeal to this adaptor. The English poet, evidently relishing the tale, never takes it (or himself) too seriously. Granting the marvels and improbabilities, the dialogue is all credible and vivid. Additions and corrections (e.g. *Cardiff* for *Carlisle*) show that the Englishman was reading his text carefully: he clarifies the incident of the trapping of Ywain at the entrance to the castle, though introducing some discrepancies at other places. Ywain becomes very much an English knight, courageous but lacking in sentiment.

The Avowing of Arthur belongs to the northern group of Arthurian romances but is novel in its materials and its tone. Its seventy-two tail-rhyme stanzas are not markedly 'courtly'. Chrétien might never have written for all this poet cares. The interest here focuses on hunting rather than on love. The north and north-west have always provided good hunting tales, for mountain and fell offer both a home for the beasts of the chase and the excitement of danger. Scott's Dandie Dinmont was to hunt in Lidderdale. The setting of the *Avowing*, as of several cognate romances, is Inglewood Forest; and the occasion is a series of vows made by Arthur, Gawain, Kay, and Baldwin—who stands somewhat apart from the rest and introduces a decidedly non-courtly, even cynical element.

The Knights of the Table Round are first presented as preoccupied with the chase of buck and boar, hart and hare. News comes to Carlisle—traditionally a seat of Arthur's court—that a savage boar, higher than a horse, is roaming Inglewood. The four named knights set out in search of it, but it proves as formidable as that pursued by the Green Knight. When they withdraw for the night, Arthur vows to bring it down unaided the next morning, while the others make their own vaunts, homely equivalents to the more famous *Vœux du Paon*. Gawain vows to watch by Tarn Wadling all night, Kay to kill anyone who accosts him in the forest, but Baldwin's brag is of a different kind: he will never be jealous about any woman, never refuse food to any, and never fear the threat of death.

'Furst to carpe of oure kinge', in the poet's phrase: Arthur finds his boar (its tusks are three feet long) and attacks with sword and spear. His brows grow as black 'as kiln or kitchen', and he is almost overcome by its smell and fumes. At last he cuts off its head—the proper end to a boar-hunt—but, after giving due thanks to Mary, falls asleep exhausted. Meanwhile Kay has found his 'adventure' in the form of a knight, Menealfe, leading a damsel in distress. Predictably he has the worst of the encounter, but his opponent spares his life on condition that he leads him to Gawain. So they both go to the tarn, where Kay identifies himself with unusual frankness as the knight who 'out of time' (i.e. inopportunely) 'boasts and blows' (i.e. brags). Gawain runs a course with Menealfe, who is soon swooning. With characteristic courtesy Gawain removes his helm and 'lets the wind blow on him'—it is the usual form of first aid: so Arthur in the alliterative *Morte* 'Keste upe his umbrere and . . . caughte of the colde wynde to comforte hym selven' (943-4). Kay, incorrigible, taunts Menealfe with his fall—'and thi wenche lost withalle'. But Gawain, begging him to ignore Kay, sends him off to Guenevere, who praises Gawain, 'my knight', for delivering the maiden. Menealfe, having heard the rules (they produce a book with the 'laws' in it), joins the Round Table.

Now comes Baldwin's turn. A band of knights, including Kay, go off to find him, dressed in green gowns 'To hold thayre armur clene / And were [keep] hitte fro the wete'—a pleasantly prudential touch. Over these gowns they wear cloaks by way of disguise. Challenged, Baldwin brushes off Kay, and as he falls prostrate asks 'Do you want any more?' He makes for the court where Arthur, privy to the plot, asks: 'Did anything befall you as you came through the woods?': 'No,

I heard nor saw but good.' Only when Kay returns announcing their discomfiture does Arthur learn the truth. He proceeds to test Baldwin's second vow by sending a minstrel to see if anyone goes meatless at his table. He finds that in fact all comers are liberally fed, down to pilgrims, palmers, and the poor: 'cooks in the kitchen swithly [hard] did sweat'. When Arthur later expresses surprise at this lavish entertainment, Baldwin smilingly replies:

> 'Sir, God hase a gud plughe[1]
> He may send us all enughe[2],
>   Qwy schuld we spare?'   (778–80)

> [1] *plough*   [2] *plenty*

Such is the value attached (as in *Sir Amadace*, found in the same manuscript) to *largesse*. But there is a touch here too of the Northern hospitality of the Green Knight, and Dandie Dinmont.

It remains to test Baldwin's other brag—that he is incapable of jealousy. There follows a 'temptation scene' reminiscent of those in *Sir Gawain and the Green Knight*. At night Arthur sends him off with the royal huntsman: with or without venison, he is to come back early. Arthur amuses himself amongst the ladies and, when evening falls, goes with a knight to the bedroom door of Baldwin's wife, calling 'open'. The scene is drawn with a rough, unsubtle humour. 'What do you want?' says she. 'I've come for some fun' ('In derne [secret] for to play'). 'Haven't you got your own queen?' But when Arthur promises that he will do no real mischief, the lady lets him in and he explains that he wishes the knight to lie by her, to keep a wager. He bundles his companion into bed, sitting down himself to play chess with one of the women. Torches and lights are brought, presumably so that the king can see that the knight does not grow amorous, though in fact the knight is fearful of what Baldwin will do when he returns, as he does early in the morning, with a good bag. He makes straight for the kitchen, as if to show that he is more concerned about food than about his wife. Arthur says that he has tracked his knight to the wife's bedroom and kept watch on him. 'You need not have troubled', replies Baldwin coolly. 'I trust my wife.' Arthur is astonished at this indifference (which recalls the Green Knight's complaisance at Gawain's bedside encounter).

The explanation lies in a tale within the tale. When fighting a Sultan in Spain, Baldwin had been in a castle with five hundred men and only three women as servants. Out of envy two of these had drowned the third, and when threatened with death themselves promised to 'serve you by day and pleasure you by night'. When one of the pair kills the other out of jealousy, Baldwin argues, 'let's share her, as we did the pair'. He had learnt that it is not worth being possessive when 'each earthly thing hath end'. Arthur takes the point but is still baffled by Baldwin's lavishness, and stoic indifference to death: 'thi yatis [gates] are evyr yare [open]', he says in wonder. Again an experience in a besieged Spanish castle provides the clue: 'Some of us broke out, but one timorous knight hid himself in a barrel and was blown to pieces by an enemy gun': 'no man shall dree before his day except through want of wit' (a variant of the Beowulfian axiom that Fate oft saves the undoomed man). The rest of us, says Baldwin, vowed never to be afraid of death:

> For dede[1] nevyr to be drery,
> Welcum is hit
> Hit is a kyndely[2] thing.   (1043-5)
>
> [1] death   [2] natural

At this same siege he had learnt his third lesson. They had almost run out of food when a messenger from the enemy called on them to surrender. Instead Baldwin asked him to stay to luncheon, ordering all the provender remaining to be set forth in lavish array. The messenger returns to report that the enemy are in good heart and make as merry as if it were Christmas. The siege was raised that night. The moral of which is:

> Mete laynes mony lakke[1]
> And there mete hor[2] sege brake
> And gerut hom to giffe us the bake[3].   (1113-15)
>
> [1] food covers many a fault   [2] their   [3] caused them to turn their backs on us

'God give sorrow to the man who refuses food.' Arthur and the Round Table agree that Baldwin is right, and that he has kept his vow.

Though rather gauchely told, these *exempla* and apophthegms introduce a novel element into a romance that is in itself markedly different in tone and ethos from any of its congeners. The Baldwin who depicts women as sensual and complaisant does not wholly square with the husband who trusts his wife's fidelity; and his largesse seems to be disguised self-interest. But the mere presence of such *exempla*, placed as they are at the climax of the poem, has the effect of making Baldwin rather than Arthur or Gawain the key character, with a unique and fully-formed philosophy.

The Arthurian romance that comes closest to *The Avowing of Arthur* in its pattern, its allusions, and its location (Cumberland and the south west of Scotland) is the *Awntyrs of Arthur at the Tarne Wathelyne* (Tarn

Wadling, Cumberland, also mentioned in the *Avowing*). This text is found in the same manuscript as the *Avowing* and in three other manuscripts as well; so it evidently had a sort of popularity. It is another product of that local North Western culture that flowered in *Sir Gawain and the Green Knight* (and it was probably composed shortly after it). Like *Gawain* it is alliterative and stanzaic and has bob and wheel, but the lines are rhymed as well as alliterative. The verse is less supple than *Gawain*, and the alliteration heavier. The stanzas are linked by alliteration, as in *Pearl* (i.e. the last line or phrase of one stanza is repeated as the first of the next). It consists only of 715 lines in all; but it shows the influence of *exempla*—like those that Baldwin tells in the *Avowing*. And like the *Avowing*, it begins with a royal hunt. Gawain is acting as escort to Guenevere on this hunt when they are suddenly caught in a storm, during which a fiendish spirit rises from the tarn—a 'lowe' (flame) on the loch, it is called: exactly the same phrase is used of the weird sights at Grendel's mere in *Beowulf* ('fyr on flode'); both emanations being doubtless will-o'-the-wisps. Gawain tries to explain away this mysterious presence as an effect of the eclipse of the moon*—always associated with supernatural occurrences:

> 'It es the clippes of the mone, I herde a clerke saye',
> And thus he comforthede the qwene with his knyghtehede.

But Guenevere is not the only one to be terrified; even the great hounds are afraid. It is in fact the spirit of Guenevere's mother who is suffering for breaking her marriage vows: 'Qwene was I whilome', she says, 'bryghtere of browes than Beryle or Brangwayne.' This reflects a version of the *memento mori* motif, the simple theme of 'as I am now so you shall be' that figures in the legend of the Three Living and the Three Dead—the three skeleton-kings that suddenly accost three live kings as they ride in the forest. 'Take example by me' is the spirit's message: 'This es it to luffe paramoures'; she pleads that thirty trentals may be said to save her soul.

Both Guenevere and Gawain take the opportunity to put some pertinent theological questions. Guenevere asks what is the sin most grievous to God and what deeds most please him. Pride is the answer to the first question, measure and works of mercy (the gifts of the Holy Spirit) the answer to the second. Gawain is anxious to learn 'how shall we *knights* fare who fight and win worship by wightness [strength, valour] of hands?' An unexpected question to find in the middle of an Arthurian romance, since it implies doubts about the whole chivalric

---

* In one version the sun.

system. The prophetic answer to Gawain is that 'Arthur salle lighte fulle lawe appone the see sandis'; the Round Table is to lose its renown near Romsey; Gawain is to be 'slayne in a slake [ravine]'; and Arthur will be wounded near Cornwall—treacherously surprised by a subject (presumably Mordred). In Arthur's hall at this very moment:

> 'The childe playes hym at the balle
> That salle owtraye[1] yow alle.'   (310–11)

[1] *undo*

Then the spirit glides away 'with a grysely grete [cry]'; the sun comes out again, and life goes on happily as before.

That night, while Arthur and his court are at supper, a lovely lady leads into the hall a knight of great *noblesse* wearing fine armour and a rich mantle. He is Sir Galeron of Galloway, looking for someone to fight, and claiming that Arthur has wrongly given away his lands to Gawain. Gawain with unruffled courtesy leads him to a bedroom fitted up in the latest style, while Arthur takes counsel as to who shall answer this challenge. The king is loth that it should be Gawain, but he insists: 'Late gaa ... God stond with the right!' After mass next morning the combat begins, Galeron's lady shrieking whenever he is hurt, Guenevere 'greeting' (weeping) with 'bothe her gray ene'. Gawain is furious when his horse Grissell is beheaded, and grieves (there is a similar scene in *Guy of Warwick*) 'for doel of the dumbe best' (554). Finally Arthur stops the fight; Galeron admits that he knows no one 'half so wight as Gawain'; Arthur dubs them both dukes; Gawain gives Galeron the land that is rightly his; he is made a Knight of the Table Round and weds his lady. The two branches of the poem—the didactic episode of the spirit and the tale of Gawain's prowess—are rather crudely grafted together when Guenevere decrees that all religious orders shall say a million of masses (meaning the maximum possible number) for her mother's soul. 'Thus this ferlyes byfelle in a foreste' says the last stanza, linking it by partial echo to the first in the manner of the poet of *Sir Gawain and the Green Knight*.

The worst thing about the romance is its misleading title: nothing whatever happens to Arthur at the Tarn. The oddest thing is the adaptation to an Arthurian context of the well-known story of the Trental of St Gregory (of which a fourteenth-century version exists, probably known to the poet). In that story Gregory's mother appears to him in similar circumstances, begging him to have a trental (thirty requiem masses) said for her soul—and they prove effective. In the romance the spirit specifies thirty trentals. The point of the scene depends on knowledge of Guenevere's sin of adultery—her 'lufe paramoures'—

which is evidently also conceived of as a sin of Pride. The prophetic answers to Gawain's questions have no bearing on the rest of the poem beyond making us aware that his chivalry, and Arthur's, have their limitations; and our sense of this is strengthened when Galeron accuses Arthur of unjust dealing. The manner of the spirit's manifestation suggests too that there is something not altogether innocent in Guenevere's association with her favourite knight. In short, there is more in the tale than at first meets the eye. It is as though a cloud, as yet no bigger than a man's hand, is rising in the clear sky of Arthurian romance. The cloud will grow to blot out the sun and signal the *Morte*.

One verse-romance stands out as a genuine and a worthy precursor of Malory's Arthur: the stanzaic *Morte Arthur*. Its verse-form (eight four-stressed lines rhyming ababbab), markedly different from the fashionable tail-rhyme, imposes its own discipline, yet it is equally suitable for narrative, *oratio recta*, or dialogue; and the iambic pattern favours simple disyllabic rather than polysyllabic words. It is a supple verse, into which much can be compressed.

The romance falls into two clearly defined parts, the first corresponding roughly to Malory's Book of Lancelot and Guenevere (Caxton's books xviii–xix), the second to his 'Most Piteous Tale of the Morte Arthur Saunz Guerdon' (Caxton xx–xxi). Both derive ultimately from the French *Mort Artu*, the last branch of the Arthurian Prose Cycle. But the English poet, as the English habit was, has compressed and simplified the French story. It is rewarding to read the poem alongside Malory's better-known recension, not least because one then sees how much his treatment of details may have been based on the English poem. That Malory drew on the second half of it, as ancillary to his French source, is certain; whether he used the first half remains doubtful.

The story begins with the great tournament which King Arthur proclaims at Winchester. At this tournament, Lancelot (who has gone to it in disguise) receives such grievous wounds that the leech despairs of his life, but he eventually recovers and is able to send back messages to Guenevere (and Arthur):

> 'Grete welle my *lorde* I yow pray,
> And telle my *lady* how I fare,
> And say I wylle come whan I may.' (508–10)

That message briefly adumbrates the fatal dichotomy between his obligations to Arthur his liege and Guenevere his mistress: for here as everywhere we must read between the lines—the story would be familiar enough for the writer not to feel it necessary to enlarge. When Lancelot does return to court he refrains from speech with the Queen; and when they eventually embrace she reproaches him for loving the Maid of Astolat, with that mixture of art and self-pity that we find in Malory too. If this has to be, she says, at least keep secret our former love, and continue your feats of arms so that I may hear news of you:

> 'But, Launcelot, I beseche the here,
> Sithe[1] it nedelyngis[2] shall be so,
> That thou nevir more dyskere[3]
> The love that hathe bene betwyxe us two,
> Ne that she nevir be with the so dere
> Dede of armys that thou be fro[4],
> That I may of thy body[5] here,
> Sithe I shalle thus beleve[6] in woo.'   (752–9)

[1] *since*   [2] *necessarily*   [3] *reveal*   [4] *abandon*   [5] *you*
[6] *remain*

It is the arrival of the maiden's corpse in the little boat that signalizes the new and sinister rift in the Arthurian fabric. As Arthur himself foretells:

> 'I darre savely[1] say therto
> Bygynne wille auntres or ought yare[2]'.   (982–3)

[1] *safely*   [2] *something will come of this, and soon*

The rift begins with Gawain's false charge that Lancelot had taken this maiden as his mistress. When Lancelot appears as the Queen's champion and the squire who has poisoned the apple is hanged, drawn, and burnt (as a traitor) harmony is temporarily restored, and Lancelot is honoured more than ever (1671).

The second movement of the poem opens with Agravayn's suggestion that Arthur must be told of Lancelot's continuing intrigue with the Queen. While the talk is going on, Arthur enters and wants to know what it is all about. No one will say; but Agravayn remains behind when the rest leave. It is the cue for the second premonition:

> Welle they wyste that all was shente[1];
> And syr Gawayne by God than swere[2]:
> 'Here now is made a comsemente[3]
> That bethe not[4] fynysshed many a yere.'   (1724–7)

[1] *ruined*   [2] *swore*   [3] *commencement*   [4] *will not be*

Eventually the Queen 'has the law'—and is for burning. Lancelot is able to collect a strong force, and offers to prove that the charges against Guenevere are false, sending this message by a maid richly apparelled in green samite, with a dwarf for escort—'so were the manerys in that tyde / when a mayde on message went' (2060–1)—a 'distancing' touch that reminds us that romances had their own time scale: it is borne out by a scene in *Libeaus Desconus*, where Ellen goes on a message accompanied by a dwarf.

From this point on the tale becomes what Caxton was to call it—the *piteous* history. Lancelot carries Guenevere off to Joyous Gard, and war breaks out:

> Grete pyté was on eyther syde
> So fele goode ther were layd doun.   (2156–7)

Arthur himself is unhorsed by Bors; after the battle there is 'sore weeping' on each side—'No chyldys play', as the poet says (2245). Only the pope's intervention, in the person of the Bishop of Rochester, brings Lancelot grudgingly to conclude a peace. But the truce does not hold, and when Lancelot returns to France, Arthur too crosses the channel and harries his lands:

> Withstode hem neyther stone ne tre
> Bot brent and slow on iche a syde.   (2536–7)

It is at this point that Malory's dependence on the poem becomes continuous, and the dependence extends to phrases and even words. Thus Lionel says to Lancelot:

> 'Lett hem pryke with all ther pryde
> Tylle they have caught both hungre and colde.
> Than shall we oute uppon them ryde
> And *shredde* them downe as shepe in folde.'   (2560–3)

Malory uses this same alliterating phrase—indeed it sticks out like an excrescence in his narrative. Meanwhile at home the treacherous Mordred spreads the rumour that Arthur is dead; and the fickle people agree that 'Arthur lovyd noght but warynge, / And suche thynge as hymselfe soght' (2975–6). The final scenes are now familiar from Malory's rendering. Thus when Sir Bedivere comes back from the mere to the dying Arthur without casting away Excalibur, and Arthur asks what he has seen: 'Nothynge but watirs wap [lapping] and wawys wanne', says Malory, echoing 'Nothynge / But watres depe and wawes wanne'. The scene of the final meeting—and parting—of Lancelot and Guenevere shows the poet at his finest—and some would say that it is finer than Malory's equivalent. It is a comparatively late interpolation in the French versions of the *Mort*: a romanticizing of the earlier, more austere story. It was perhaps at this point rather than in the Grail books that Malory gave the tale a twist that wrenched it from its original religious pattern. But the stanzas deserve attention in their own right. They eschew the tone of easy assurance that Malory attributes to Guenevere when she says 'as synfull as ever I was, now ar seyntes in hevyn'. The poet shows his awareness of the climactic nature of the scene by carefully intertwining stanza with stanza, the last line of one being echoed in the first of the next. Malory subtly (or accidentally? one can never tell with him) alters the emphasis here. His Lancelot says 'Wherfore, madame, I praye you kysse me, and never no more.' 'Nay,' sayd the quene, 'that shal I never do, but absteyne you from such werkes.'

Malory early reached print because Caxton was looking for a big fat book to show what his new press could do. The stanzaic poem looked old-fashioned by that time, and remained unread for 400 years. Caxton's *Morte* had the advantage, too, of a known author, with a mysterious prison history. Of the stanzaic poet we know nothing save that he came from the North West Midlands—from the *Gawain* country, in fact. He wrote at the same time as the Gawain poet, and is a further witness to a local culture which burst forth mysteriously and as mysteriously disappeared.

The other vernacular version of the tragedy of Arthur is contained in the much longer alliterative romance of the same name. Malory drew on this work too—or rather on the account of Arthur's wars with the Emperor Lucius that occupies the first 3,400 lines. But it is quite different in style, character, and feeling from the stanzaic poem—and comes from a different area—Lincolnshire or thereabouts. It is some 4,350 lines in all, and indeed it is almost epic in its scope; one might call it an epic impregnated with romance motifs. But its author would not have understood the term epic, whereas he does think of the Arthur of his poem as the fit subject for romance: in the course of the action Arthur has a dream of the wheel of Fortune which would provide a splendid opportunity for introducing the concept of 'tragedy'. Instead the philosopher who interprets the dream says that Arthur 'sall in *romance* be redde with ryall knyghtes' (3440). To be sure an ingenious critic called a book on the poem *The Tragedy of Arthur*.* But he both overrated and misread the work, which he saw as essentially a criticism of Arthur, and as presenting his fall as a retribution for the sin of prosecuting imperialist wars. Now imperialist wars were criticized in the fourteenth century, and sharply—in particular by Gower and by Langland. But no reader of the poem can doubt that the author relished describing the fighting and the forays, just as Froissart did; and it is Froissart who provides the clue to the pattern of the

* W. Matthews, *The Tragedy of Arthur: a Study of the alliterative 'Morte Arthure'* (Berkeley and Los Angeles, 1960).

poem, and its appeal in its own day. It belongs wholly to the period of the Hundred Years War; episodes like Arthur's withdrawal to Saxony, and redeployment of his forces with archers on either flank and a strong rearguard (1972), or the vigorous naval engagement (3600 ff.) would have all the immediacy of the French campaigns. Despite the rhetoric, the details of shipping, channel crossings, and the like, are precisely observed. Husbands and wives parted by the wars would know too well how Arthur felt on leaving Guenevere—who swoons when he asks for his sword. We are in the presence of a new kind of actuality, which pushes aside the adulterous Guenevere for the moment and makes her a fond wife. The French wars came home to men's business and bosoms. The best way to understand the ebullient and rather bloody chivalry depicted in the poem is to delve into Froissart, in Berners's translation. Froissart was a godsend to the war-artists of the next generation, but we must not be misled by their glamour. It is true that Froissart thinks of the war not so much as a natural conflict as a chivalric enterprise, a kind of international tournament—so that he can treat each side in combat more or less impartially. But even Froissart cannot hide the horror, the carnage, and the waste. Professor Matthews's assumption that the English poem is based on a lost French work of the early fourteenth century prevented him from seeing its topicality.

Arthur's role in the poem is much fuller, and more dynamic, than in any earlier Arthurian text. He is presented as one of the Nine Worthies, a world conqueror, on the scale of an Alexander, closer to a Beowulf than to the courtly king of *Libeaus* or *Gawain*; and his humour is like the grim humour of *Maldon* (46–7, 60–1). So Arthur's final answer to the Emperor Lucius's demands for tribute is to send back to Rome in leaden chests the bodies of Lucius himself and his senators (whom Arthur has killed in battle) with the message that this is

> The taxe and the trebutte of tene schore[1] wynteres
> That was tenefully[2] tynte[3] in tyme of oure elders.   (2344–5)

> [1] *score*   [2] *painfully*   [3] *lost*

Rather cruder, but equally traditional, is Arthur's quip as he fights with the giant Golapes, and cuts off his legs at the knees:

> 'Come down', quod the kynge, 'and karpe[1] to thy ferys[2]
> Thowe arte to hye by the halfe, I hete[3] the in trouthe,
> Thow salle be handsomere in hye[4], with the helpe of
>   my Lorde!'

> (2126–8)

> [1] *speak*   [2] *companions*   [3] *assure*   [4] *quickly*

—'you'll soon look prettier'—and at that he strikes off his head. So in one of the sagas a swordsman says as he cuts off a tall opponent's legs 'Now are we of a size'. Again, the vaunting speeches (e.g. 2342 ff.) are much like the *beots* or heroic brags in *Beowulf* or *Maldon*: consonantal alliteration lends a special force to such utterances. In counterbalance there are amused understatements: as Arthur sets out to find his giant he says that he is going on pilgrimage to seek a saint; and Bedivere later comments 'If all saints are like that, saint shall I never be' (1269). It is a pleasant change from the heroics of chivalry, and probably as 'true-to-life' as they.

The ruthlessness of the poem is the ruthlessness of the French—and Spanish—wars. It belongs to the time of Pedro the Cruel and 'cruel' is one of the commonest epithets, though that term bespeaks fierceness, resolution as much as cruelty. So it is misleading to say that Arthur is here presented as a cruel king. Rather, he appears as a some-what complex character. Like Byrhtnoth in *Maldon* and Roland in the *Chanson*, like Beowulf himself, he is subject by virtue of his very emi-nence to pride or *démesure*, *ofermod*. In so far as at the outset he is shown considering the welfare of his people during his absence he is laudable; when (like Athelwold in *Havelok*) he distributes treasure selflessly, he displays the great medieval virtue of generosity. But he is limited by human blindness, failing to divine Mordred's secret inten-tions. And he attacks not only pagans but fellow-Christians: in Tuscany he overthrows towers, afflicts the populace, ravages blindly, destroying even the vines (3159) and the churches; yet he can promise that widows shall be safe, and threaten with death anyone who forces a woman—lady, virgin, or citizen's wife (3080 ff.)—in the conquered city. It is the puzzling medieval mixture of ruthlessness and restraint. In one breath he boasts 'We salle be overlynge of alle that on the erthe lengez' (3211), in the next vows to take the crusader's cross. At the same time there emerges the comparatively new doctrine of the sanc-tity of the monarch's person, from which not all the waters of the rough rude sea could wash the balm, or as Arthur himself here says:

> Sall never harlotte[1] have happe[2], thorowe helpe of my Lorde
> To kyll a corownde kynge with krysome[3] enoynttede.'

> (2447–8)

[1] *rascal*   [2] *fortune*   [3] *chrism*

This assertion removes him as far from Layamon's Arthur as from Tennyson's. The manner of his dying is equally distinctive. Whereas Layamon had noted the belief that he went to Avalon, whence he will yet return to help the English, in this poem he dies and is duly buried;

and thus, adds the poet, ends the cycle that began with the landing of Brutus. The colophon later added—*hic jacet Arturus rex quondam rexque futurus*—does not sort with this conclusion, and has no place there.

The closing allusion to the Brut recalls the setting of *Sir Gawain* in the same broad framework. If *Sir Gawain* is a peace-time poem concerned with the delights of the chase, it is those delights that in the *Morte* represent the acme of knightly activity. It opens, to be sure, with a chronicle of Arthur's conquests. But no sooner has he rested and held the Round Table than he is off to Wales with his swift hounds

> For to hunt at the hartes in thas hye lanndes,
> In Glamorgan with glee, thare gladchipe was evere. (58–9)

And at the end of the poem his vow to revenge Gawain is made in hunting terms:

> 'I sall never ryvaye[1] ne racches uncowpyll[2]
> At roo[3] ne rayne-dere that rynnes apponne erthe;
> Never grewhownde late glyde ne gossehauke latt flye
> Ne never fowle see fellide that flieghes with wenge;
> Fawkon ne formaylle[4] appon fiste handille
> Ne yitt with gerefawcon[5] rejoyse me in erthe
> Ne regne in my royaltez ne halde my rownde table,
> Till thi dede[6], my dere, be dewly revengede . . .'

$$(3999–4006)$$

[1] *hunt by the river*   [2] *unleash hounds*   [3] *roe*   [4] *formel (female hawk)*
[5] *gerfalcon*   [6] *death*

These common contexts bring into relief the criticisms implicit in both poems of the chivalric code as embodied in their protagonists. In both are hints of its fatal concomitant of pride and self-sufficiency—whereas a king properly owes his 'worship' to his knights—but also of a new self-awareness. In his morning lament over Gawain the Arthur of the *Morte* acknowledges that 'He es sakles [innocent] supprysede for syn of myn one'. And as Gawain was shown as more than a stock hero in his encounter with the half-giant Green Knight, so, in the *Morte*, Arthur's fight with the giant of St Michael's Mount reveals him as pleasingly human, ready to pose as one of his own knights.

(v) *Kyng Alisaunder*; *Alexander and Dindimus*; The 'Laud' *Troy Book*; *The Siege of Jerusalem*

Like Arthur, Alexander was in the Middle Ages one of the Nine Worthies, a great chivalric hero, whose legendary conquests gave romancers an opportunity to describe the wonders of the East as well as battles on an epic scale. The whole history of Alexander as the Middle Ages knew it, from his remarkable birth to his death by poison and his burial in the city he had founded, is the 'matière' of the 8,000-line romance that editors call *Kyng Alisaunder*. It is based primarily on the *Roman de Toute Chevalerie*, a thirteenth-century romance in Anglo-Norman verse composed, or rather compiled, by one Thomas of Kent (and profusely illustrated in three manuscripts by three different English artists). It is indeed a notable witness to the fusion of native and Norman cultures. The occasional use of the most impressive and most popular of all medieval Latin epics, the *Alexandreis* of Gautier de Châtillon (*alias* Gautier de Lille)* indicates that the translator's learning was not purely insular; and from Latin or vernacular versions of episodes in the legend he probably drew such passages as the charming story of the Flower Maidens, who have no food but flowers (like the 'maiden in the moor' of a mysterious contemporary song) and no drink but the dew on violets and roses (6474–95).† On the other hand, the episode in which Alexander fixes a spear on the summit of Taurus, not to be removed, has been thought to derive from the English *Arthur and Merlin* (see p. 170 above) and even to show that the two works are from the same hand. The occasional occurrence of traditional alliterative phrases ('kyng and ek kaysere', 'Kaymes [Cain's] kynrede', 'wiis and war', etc.) and of some not so traditional—'there was kytt many a cod' (2409), '[many a knight] gnouw [bit] the gras' (2370)—suggests contact with the stream of alliterative romance.

There is some evidence that, like Chaucer, this poet knew the *Roman de Thebes*; and his style suggests that he was steeped in works belonging to the same genre as that historical romance. He is by no means a slave to his original—he follows Gautier's example in providing, and sometimes inventing, names that add particularity to the narrative; and though occasionally careless or incoherent, in general he displays the skill and fluency of a writer familiar with the rhetorical arts as applicable to a work devised for oral delivery.

Thus in rendering the French exordium he contrives within 24 lines to insert a simile, an *exemplum*, and a *sententia*—as if to impress a discerning audience with his credentials. In describing Alexander's exploits against Darius, he remarks:

> This bataile distincted[1] is
> In the Freinsshe, wel iwis[2].

---

* For this, and for the whole development of the Alexander legend, see G. Cary, *The Medieval Alexander* (Cambridge, 1956).

† Line references are to manuscript B (Laud Misc. 622) in the EETS edition.

> Therefore I habbe hit to coloure
> Borowed of Latyn a nature³,
> Hou hightten⁴ the gentyl knyghttes,
> Hou hii contened hem⁵ in fighttes,
> On Alisaunders half and Darries also.
> Yif yee willeth listnen to,
> Yee shullen yhere geste of mounde⁶,
> Ne may non better ben yfounde.   (2195–204)

¹ *? set apart*   ² *assuredly*   ³ *? method of representation*   ⁴ *were named*
⁵ *acquitted themselves*   ⁶ *worth*

Here 'coloure' apparently has the unique sense of 'add rhetorical colour' (those 'colours of rhetoric' in which Chaucer's Franklin professed to be unversed), and the following line is perhaps a scribal corruption of 'the Latin auctour' (viz. Gautier). The 'colours' of *simile* and *repetitio* are in fact employed in the very next passage:

> Now telleth this gest, saunz faile,
> So on the shyngel¹ lithe the haile
> Every knighth so liith on other.
> Many man so lees² his brother,
> Many lefdy hire amy,
> Many maiden her drury³
> Many childe his fader lees   (2205–11)

¹ *roof-tile*   ² *lost*   ³ *loved one*

—where the last line is an epic formula as old as the *Chanson de Roland*; in an account of a later conflict the pattern of initial 'Many' + noun is repeated no less than fourteen times in so many lines (3200 ff.), and recurs internally in most of them.

In such contexts it is the variety of similes drawn from workaday life that enlivens the narrative: a butcher hacking his pig on his stall, a mason hammering at stone, a shipwright at a nail. There are a dozen different ways of killing knightly foes and every one of them is illustrated in this poem. Like comparisons of a different order, illustrated in

> [Alexander] lep on his rygge¹
> So a golfynche² dooth on the hegge³   (781–2)

¹ *back*   ² *goldfinch*   ³ *hedge*

and the account of fleeing knights who

> . . . ferden so dere in halle
> And floteden¹ so fyre in felde.   (2436–7)

¹ *wavered*

They had precedents in French and Latin epic; hence it is not surprising that they are also found in *Arthour and Merlin*. The ironical

189

metaphor of paying tribute in the form of deadly blows is also found in Old English heroic poetry and in the alliterative verse of *Morte Arthure* (see above, p. 185), as well as in Old French. Touches of what might be called primitive novelistic psychology in the depiction of character (e.g. 'more she thought than she said', 231) are also prompted by French practice.

More directly traceable to French *laisses* (the sequences of asson-anced lines characteristic of the *chansons de geste*) is the device of a series of monorhyming couplets, found notably in some of the head-pieces and most often (as most easily devised) with the suffix *-yng*, one passage with this ending running on for fourteen lines (911–24). The seasonal or sententious headpieces in which some of these *laisses* occur sometimes prelude a change in direction of the narrative and may have followed a pause in the recital at what a television producer would today call a 'natural break'. It is these lyrical interludes (twenty-seven in all, many linked by an emphatic 'Merry') that illustrate most forcefully the writer's capacity to adapt and extend elements of Old French style. Typical is the preface to the account of the ruse by which Alexander causes Darius to move his position to the bank of the river Estrage:

> Mery it is in the day graukynge[1],
> Whan the foules gynneth synge,
> And jolyf herte so gynneth sprynge.
> To sone it thencheth[2] the slow gadelynge[3]!
> In mychel love is grete mournynge;
> In mychel nede is grete thankynge.
> A ferly thoughth[4] is with the kyng.
> Erly he riseth. . . .   (4056–63)

[1] *dawning*   [2] *seems*   [3] *wretch*   [4] *extraordinary plan*

Others provide vignettes of the courtly society to which the poem is ostensibly addressed, and reflect the sensibility of that society; others again jolt us in their realism:

> Noyse is gret with tabour[1] and pype,
> Damoyseles playen with peren[2] rype.
> Ribaudes festeth[3] also with trype;
> The gestour[4] wil oft his mowthe wype.   (1573–6)

> Good it were to ben knyghth,
> Nere[5] tourneyment and dedly fighth.
> With marchaundes to ben it were hende[6],
> Neren th'acountes at bordes[7] ende.

> Swete is love of damoysele,
> Ac it asketh costes fele[8]. . . .   (7352–57)

[1] *small drum*   [2] *pears*   [3] *menials feast*   [4] *minstrel*   [5] *were it not for*   [6] *pleasant*   [7] *table's*   [8] *demands many payments*

Such a passage reveals a serious purpose, which is never far from the surface of the narrative. The *Distichs* of Cato are quoted at the outset, where the poet points scornfully at those whose thoughts are set 'in the gut and in the barel' and would rather hear ribaldry than of God, or St Mary, more than once invoked later as the best 'amy'. Later we are reminded of feminine vanity and see a lovely woman as she stoops to folly, caught 'so in the lyme is the fleiye' (420). The description of the marvels of the East as viewed by Alexander brings the book within the compass of the cyclopaedic. Solomon is cited as an authority for these marvels; and Alexander is presented sometimes as a Christian (who sends souls to 'Belzabuk', 2702), sometimes as a pagan. His empire is described in medieval terms: the Athenians refuse him 'trowage'. His destruction of Thebes would recall to readers who followed the fortunes of the French in medieval Greece its destruction in the fourteenth century. It is depicted as containing a High Street as fine 'As is Chepe that is in Lounde' (2652).

The steady flow of narrative is broken from time to time by pregnant and evocative couplets. We see Olympyas on her bed:

> In a chaysel[1] smok she lay,
> And in a mantel of Doway[2].
> Of the brighthede of her face
> Al aboute schoon the place.
> Selde[3] she spaak, and noughth loude,
> And so don wymmen that ben proude.   (279–84)

[1] *of fine linen*   [2] *Douai cloth*   [3] *seldom*

Neptanabus, the magician who has promised her that the god Amon will come to her room:

> hymself was knighth and swayn,
> And boure-mayde and chaumberlayn   (377–8)

but he came to a bad end:

> A pytt he [sc. Alexander] dude sone[1] make
> And broughth hym in his longe hous,
> And thus ended Neptanabus.   (748–50)

[1] *quickly*

Alexander rides out secretly to catch a sight of Darius:

> In a morowen-tyde it was,
> That dropes hongen on the gras,
> And maidens loken in the glas
> Forto atyffen her faas.[1]   (4101–4)

> [1] *to titivate their faces*

As in most English romances, the direct speech is generally lively and convincing, and much of it is in the form of 'gabs', akin to Old English 'flyting':

> 'Fy, vyle ateynt hores sone!
> To mysdon was ay[1] thi wone[2],
> Quyk tak[3] me thi wed[4] for this disray[5].'   (879–81)

> [1] *ever*   [2] *custom*   [3] *give*   [4] *security*   [5] *outrageous behaviour*

But, after so many conquests, like other great conquerors, Alexander is brought down by death. He is given a poisoned cup, and after he has drunk it

> Away he sette that golde red:
> 'Allas!' he seide, 'Ich am neigh ded!
> Drynk ne shal nevere efte more
> Do to this werlde so mychel sore
> As this drynk hath ydo. . . .'   (7852–6)

His body is 'richly kept' in a temple in Egypt, but his empire is divided, and soon torn by strife:

> Thus it fareth in the myddelerde[1],
> Amonge the lewed and the lerde[2]!
> Whan the heved[3] is yfalle,
> Acumbred[4] ben the membres alle.

> [1] *world*   [2] *the uninstructed and the learned, i.e. all men*   [3] *head*   [4] *in distress*

The other surviving complete romances of Alexander belong to the fifteenth century, and, in the case of the *Alexander Buik* and Hay's *Buik of King Alexander*, to Scotland. Three fragments of alliterative Alexander poems survive. The third and longest of these (*The Wars of Alexander*) is usually thought to be a fifteenth-century work, but the other two are earlier. Fragment A (of just over 1,200 lines) tells the beginning of Alexander's life. Fragment B, called *Alexander B* or *Alexander and Dindimus* (1,139 lines) describes some of the wonders seen by the conqueror (in a rather less lively manner than in *Kyng Alisaunder*), but the bulk of the fragment consists of an epistolary debate between the king of the Greeks and the king of the Brahmans. It is a text of cultural rather than poetic interest. That this fragmentary Middle English text found its way into what is now MS Bodley 264, one of the great French Alexander books, is a curious circumstance, which provides it with more gorgeous illustrations than are to be found accompanying any other fourteenth-century English poem. The fragment itself scarcely merits such ornament. It follows closely the Latin text on which it is based, the style of which is plain, not to say undistinguished. Each statement of the Latin is represented by a line or two lines of monotonous alliterative verse, and the general effect is diffuse. For the most part the vocabulary of the fragment is as plain as that of the Latin. Some of it belongs to the old alliterative deposit (notably synonyms for 'man'—'seg', 'gome'—and collocations like 'swet othur swink' (310), 'greden your grace' (606)). A convention of oral narrative intrudes unexpectedly when the poet appeals to an audience in such terms as:

> And yif ye ludus[1] have list[2] the lettrus to knowe,
> Tendeth[3] how this tale is titeled[4] therinne.   (189–90)
>
> [1] *people*   [2] *desire*   [3] *take heed*   [4] *?arranged*

But the dislocation of normal accentual patterns suggests that he is writing for the eye rather than the ear. When the English expands the Latin it usually adds little, but one such expansion is illuminating. Where the Latin has 'nos nostra et nostrorum predecessorum facta perlegimus', the English runs:

> We raiken[1] to oure romauncus and reden the storrius[2]
> That oure eldrene[3] on erthe or[4] this time wroute[5].   (467–8)
>
> [1] *go*   [2] *stories*   [3] *ancestors*   [4] *before*   [5] *made*

Occasionally the English particularizes, with advantage. Thus to the Latin 'varia genera piscium contemplamur' it adds:

> There maken dolfinus dine, and diverce fihches,
> That there swimmen ful swithe and swangen[1] aboute.   (492–3)
>
> [1] *dart*

There remains something appealing in the picture of the Brahmans' simple life—they plough not, neither do they hunt; and they die (325) 'bi cominnge of kynde [nature] as hevene king demus [ordains]'—and something impressive in their censure of a conqueror whose armies lower the level of the Nile by drinking at it. The narrative requires that Alexander should learn the shortcomings of the classical gods from Gymnosophists to whom they are but names; the English text says more at this point about Juno and Apollo (697–704) than does the

Latin, and corrects the Latin when it makes Cupid female. The insistence of the Gymnosophists on God as a spirit of purity—

> He clameth[1] nouht but clennesse and clepeth[2] to his joie
> Clene-mindede men that meke ben founde
>
> (625–6)

[1] *claims*   [2] *calls*

—would doubtless commend the work to right-thinking readers.

The siege of 'Troy the great' provided one of the great subjects for medieval story-tellers. The material comes from what were then the standard sources—the 'histories' of Dares and Dictys; the long and elegant twelfth-century romance of Benoit de Sainte-Maure (the *Roman de Troie*), which gives us the first extended treatment of the story of Troilus and Criseyde; and the thirteenth-century 'history' of Troy's destruction by Guido delle Colonne. Our English romancers are more at home with the destruction and the battles that led to it than with stories of doomed lovers. The alliterative *Gest Historiale of the Destruction of Troy* in 14,044 lines is the longest. It follows Guido's account through thirty-six books. The verse moves forward rapidly (sometimes exhaustingly so), and there are a number of vivid scenes (notably a description in book xxxi of a storm which wrecked the Greek fleet). *The Seege or Batayle of Troye* (*c.* 2,000 lines in couplets) sounds rather like a 'minstrel' romance; the style is heavily formulaic. But this too has some fine vivid and dramatic scenes.

However, the most interesting of the Troy romances is that now known as The 'Laud' *Troy Book*. This is a librarian's title, and not one that a medieval reader would have understood. The unique manuscript bears no title, but the Prologue, after the customary pious invocation, at once announces the theme. It is the Romance of Hector, worthy to rank with those of Bevis, Guy, Gawain, Havelok, Horn, and Wade.

No earlier romancer had made a hero of Hector. But Dares, Dictys, and 'Master Guy' had set down the doom of Troy: Guy (i.e. Guido delle Colonne), the alleged translator of Dares and Dictys from Greek to Latin, had found them 'with-oute lesyng or variaunce / In siker prose, and no romaunce' (6356–7). These are the English poet's sole authorities, named intermittently or cited as 'the romaunce' throughout the work—Dares in particular when he departs from him (as in not giving the names of the Greeks' ships (3318)); though Statius is cited as saying that the Greeks delayed the attack on Troy for fear of Helen (4138). That the poet's knowledge is second-hand is evident from his references to Dares's *verse* (4830); he knows him as 'the heraud' (4859).

Like his authorities, the Englishman begins with the story of Jason, who, with Hercules, sets out from the strand of Colchis:

> Thei sailen many a day and nyght
> With many stormes lyght,
> Til thei were weri of the see.   (391–3)

The adventure has the perennial appeal of the stranger on the beach, and at the feast. Medea at once engages our interest, as Jason engages hers:

> 'For I se wel [she says] and have in mynde
> That thow art comen of gentil kynde,
> And art a lovely creature. . . .'   (705–7)

Soon he is 'my derlyng', and events follow their well-known course. The verse rattles along in easy style till, thanks to the Trojan horse of brass, 'the toun of tounes to noght gos' (18374). It is Laomedon's initial enmity to Jason and Hercules that proves to be the occasion of war (its beginning is marked with the rubric: *his incipit bellum*). The central scenes are re-created vividly, as is the wrath of Achilles, in a reportorial style. From time to time the reporter addresses his audience—perhaps after a break for refreshment: at 3243 ff. an exhortation to listen is followed by an epitome (some fifty lines) of the main action to come.

Hector is the hero, and if he fails it is Fortune's fault, not his own. He is given his place with Alexander, Caesar, Arthur, the Great Worthies (5893 ff.). But Fortune (foe to Troy as well as to Hector) is led by Destiny, which thwarts men's purposes just when they are most confident. No poem shows better how medieval men possessed, and were possessed by, the tale of Troy in a way that their Renaissance successors never were. In reading into it Fortune's malignancy, the *remanieur* follows the Chaucer of *Troilus* and the Dante of *Inferno* xxx. 13–15. The long *planctus* for Hector (10987–11016) bespeaks some acquaintance with rhetorical modes and bears comparison with the lament for Gawain in the alliterative *Morte* and for Lancelot at the end of Malory's book.

In this tale of classical Greece, Agamemnon speaks of Adam and Eve, Calcas, like Amphiarax in the romance of Thebes that Criseyde read (*TC* ii. 1045), is a bishop. A thunderstorm (vividly described) is so fearful that the Greeks think Noah's flood is come again (7265–6). Episcropus ('that ape and owle') calls Hector a 'fitz-a-putayn' (7447). The epic tale has been transposed into the military modes and manners of the fourteenth century. The warriors bear medieval coat-armour. Jason wears 'his trewe and trusti' basinet, Nestor a 'coyfe and ketil-hat' (1499)—as they are accoutred in miniatures and tapestries. The appeal must have been chiefly to a knightly audience that would respond to the sharply realized scenes, so like those that Froissart was at this very time setting down in the chronicles of the Anglo-French wars, which come to mind when King Hupon says that 'him hadde ben better to have ben at Gaunt [Ghent]' (7368) than to have met Achilles. In this updated language Antenor swears by the Rood and Hector by St Denis. Troilus laughs to scorn Elenus the pacifist:

> 'Lete him go, if he be aferd[1],
> To the temple, and schave his berd,
> And helpe the clerkes belles to rynge,
> And make him a prest a masse to synge!'   (2563–6)

[1] *afraid*

The narrative sometimes shifts to the historic present; the speeches are energetic and dramatic. Cassandra's warning of coming woe strikes fearfully on one's ears. Agamemnon argues forcibly against the dangers of Pride. The language is homely, the similes are unhackneyed; when Troy is first destroyed

> Ther nys nought stondende an hous
> In al the toun to hide a mous,
> That hit nis downe and overthrowen,
> Ther may the wynd wel colde blowen. . . .   (1757–60)

The Trojans flail the Greeks 'as don herdes / On weri bestis that drow in the plow' (9162–3). Achilles strikes 'as men smeten atte balle' (9218). Hercules rides after the foe 'as a fulmard [polecat] doth afftir the hennes' (1658).

> So mery was nevere nightyngale
> Syngand in no hasel-crop,
> Ne no child playing with his top

—as was Ajax when the King of Cassedone comes to his rescue (5548–50).[*] The plethora of battles and hand-to-hand encounters produces a crop of such *ad hoc* similes. Hector cleaves a body 'as it hadde ben a cloven calff' (4572). About him lie

> hondes and knockeles
> As thikke as any honysocles
> That in somer stondes in grene medes.   (5381–3)

Achilles is 'as hole as any pykerel' (14628; cf. 14008).

* Cf. Agamemnon's 'A! Ector, thin ere aught to glowe!' (6541).

The days of battle are marked off by braces of couplets that have a touch of nature:

> Night is went and gon a-way,
> Day is dawed and is day,
> It was a lovely morn,
> And Agamenon blew his horn. (4191–4)

The work leaves one with the sense of a poet thoroughly *engagé*. A few allusions (e.g. to service-books, 9368) suggest a priestly training. He does not disdain details like the victualling of an army, or its ordnance (4670 ff.), yet can render Andromeda's prayer to Hector in affecting terms (10070 ff.). The narrative style is as crisp as Barbour's, or Gower's:

> Thei drow ther sayl unto the top;
> Here schippis sayled gay and prop[1],
> Til thei were comen in-to Troye listes.   (3597–9)

> [1] *?handsome*

But Gower would not have added the authorial address:

> A, Priamus, if that thow wistes[1]
> The sorwe that comes to the and thine . . .   (3600–1)

> [1] *knew*

nor would he have reproached the false Greeks with cowardice:

> If ye ben ought[1], now yow a-wreke[2]! . . .
> For al the gold of Galilee
> He wol not fro yow flee.   (5394–400)

> [1] *of any worth*   [2] *avenge*

Unusual alliterative combinations ('plasch and polk [pond and pool]', 6226; 'chavel and choppe [jaw and jawbone]', 5538), and the flavouring of Northerly words ('tythand', 'beck', 12667) add something to the picture that emerges of a resourceful poet. The alliterative couplings are the more effective for being sparsely used:

> Thei leffte ther nother pot ne panne,
> Dische ne dobler[1], cuppe ne kanne.   (5871–2)

> [1] *large plate*

The unusual similes ('thei lay ston-stille as two cattes', 6788) are complemented by unusual metaphors: Achilles 'hadde yeven up his dische' if Hector had maintained his attack (8957). Earlier, 'he yaff the duk a cruste of brede' (5431) indicates a blow that knocks a man off his horse. Some of the scenes have the richness of tapestry, but others are matter-of-fact: the grim details of warfare like the loss of 'many a leg and many a thye, / Many an hond and many a kne' (4387–8) are constantly particularized. At one point a horse runs about with 'half a man' on its back (6264). Yet it is perhaps in this poem that the English sense of what is done and not done first emerges:

> Thei seyde: 'it was but folye';
> Thei seyde: 'it was not so done'. (8500–1)

In our final romance we move from an ancient scene to a modern one. *The Siege of Jerusalem* is an historical romance—a 'geste'—though more historical and less 'romantic' than any of Scott's historical romances, which it in some way adumbrates. Though in one of the seven extant manuscripts it is divided, like *Piers Plowman* (which accompanies it in one collection), into *passus*, it runs to no more than 1,334 lines, and could be recited at a sitting. For the most part it is plain straightforward narrative. There is no preliminary appeal to an audience, and the only authorial comments are in the nature of fillers: 'Now blesse us our lorde' (440), 'Now of the cité and of the sege wolle I sey more' (949) which signal the conclusion of a section of the narrative. The apparent digression at the outset on the Passion—that theme so prominent in devotion and verse of the period—has its *raison d'être* in the tortures perpetrated by the Jews, who had scourged Christ with 'whips of cuirbouilli' till he ran with red blood as rain runs in the street, blinded him like a bee (a favourite medieval figure for blindness), and hunted him—'umbecasten hym with a cry' (18) as hunters surround their quarry. Christ had not avenged this villainy. That task was reserved for Titus and Vespasian.

In peril after a violent storm, that begins when 'cloudes clateren gon as they cleve wolde' and 'the racke myd a rede [? violent] wynde roos on the myddel', and mounts until

> The brode sail at o brayd tobresteth atwynne[1]
> That on ende of the schip was ay toward heven, (66–7)

[1] *breaks asunder in a moment*

a ship is driven into Bordeaux harbour. There one Nathan, messenger of the Jews who had brought word that they would no longer pay tribute to Nero, and (like another Jonah) had 'hidden under hatches' during the storm, tells them of a possible salve for their afflictions; Titus having a cancerous lip and his father Vespasian (Waspasiun) suffering from 'a biker [swarm] of waspen bees' on his head and leprosy. But he tells Titus first of the Nativity (Mary is as 'clene as a clef [cliff] ther cristalle sprynges'), the Trinity, the Miracles, Judas's treachery, Pilate's complicity. It is Veronica's veil bearing the image of Christ that can heal them, and does, as soon as Titus has voiced his anger at Pilate: a psychosomatic effect that has a parallel when Josephus cures a later illness of Titus by confronting him with a man he bitterly hates: his blood boils, and his palsy forthwith departs. His first response is a prayer to 'corteys Crist' to bring trouble on Nero. Once Titus has been baptized he sets out to exact a (somewhat unchristian) retribution for Christ's death.

The account of the siege itself derives largely from Higden's *Polychronicon*, which Trevisa translated about the time our poet was writing (see below, p. 355). But there is some episodic extension from the *Golden Legend*, whence comes the concluding description of the suicide of Nero, by a fruit-knife. An account of the succession of the emperors, deftly tipped in, shows that medieval knowledge of the Roman empire was far from negligible. All the material is handled freely. New artifices are added, and some passages, like the account of idols falling (as in the apocryphal Infancy Gospels) and the setting of the night-watch (725–36), closely resemble passages in the *Troy Book*. But possibly these, like the sea-storm, which recalls that in *Patience*, should be regarded as so many variants on favourite topoi. The romancers' liking for themes likely to evoke a quick response in an audience we have already noted. The arming of Vespasian is such a theme, and resembles that of Sir Gawain. So is the depiction of heavy slaughter. Here Jews, falling thick as hail, cover the battlefield so that

> Myght no stede doun stap[1] bot on stele wede[2],
> Or on burne[3], other on beste, or on bright scheldes.   (601–2)
>
> [1] *step*   [2] *steel garments*   [3] *man*

Less common are scenes of first aid: here leeches, working by torch-light, wash wounds with wine, stopping them with wool, and saying charms over them, just as in *The Knight's Tale*. Eulogy of a valiant leader is another such element ('This is a comlich kyng knyghtes to lede', 764), as is the description of dawn before battle:

> Whan schadewes and schir[1] day scheden[2] attwynne,
> Leverockes upon lofte lyften her stevenes.[3]   (737–8)
>
> [1] *bright*   [2] *separated*   [3] *Larks raised their voices*

Again we recall *The Knight's Tale*. But this dawn is the more welcome because Vespasian has passed a sleepless night: he

> walwyth[1] and wyndith[2] and waltreth[3] aboute,
> Ofte tourneth for tene[4] and on the toun thynketh.   (735–6)

[1] *rolls*   [2] *turns*   [3] *tosses*   [4] *vexation*

The tone here is more realistic than romantic.

Vespasian is an earlier Coeur de Lion. The battle scenes suggest both the zeal and the cruelty of the Crusaders. The account of the siege itself is modernized, or rather made topical, so that it resembles a crusading enterprise rather than a Roman; it is also a chivalric 'layk' (sport): when off duty the knights go hunting and hawking by day, and dance by night. The appeal would be to audiences who knew at first or second hand of the siege of foreign towns, including those in France that Froissart was describing at this very time. Titus's soldiers solemnly swear allegiance to a feudal lord (1005–6). Their tents, like those of the Crusaders, are 'stoked ful of storiis [paintings] . . . kerneld [crenellated] alofte' (330–1). They make a siege engine called a sow, as the English had done at the siege of Berwick. Their enemies are reduced to eating the leather of shields and shoes (and even to cannibalism).

The diction, though often formulaic, and like that in such similar works as *The Wars of Alexander*, sometimes goes beyond the usual: one rare Old English verb (*houshed*, 'heaped scorn on') here makes a unique appearance (976), and the rare *fethyrhames* (wings): 'no freke in might fonde [enter] withowttyn fethyrhames' (679) has an equally ancient origin. The alliterative mode proves equal to such mundane themes as naval outfitting (cf. 283–4), and the bustle of night-time preparations:

> Was noght while the nyght laste bot nehyng of stedis
> Strogelyng[1] of stele wede[2] and stuffyng of helmes.   (421–2)

[1] *polishing*   [2] *armour*

Such touches suggest an author deeply involved in his theme. Indeed, most of the alliterative poets, whatever their vocation may have been, seem to have been thoroughly at home on the field of Mars. In general the language and diction show affinities with the alliterative *Morte Arthure* and the *Troy Book*, perhaps because all three works have a northerly provenance. There is little rhetoric, beyond an authorial apostrophe to the towns of Judea (295 ff.). Similes are rare: Jews flee as fowl before the falcon (310); burgesses once big-bellied as barrels grow thin as greyhounds (1247–8); the Jews shrink (or shriek?) as a woman swoons when water rises (528). The effect of such similes is reinforced by vivid phrases: the fire that sweeps over Syria is a 'red laschyng lye [flame]' (304). When 'bishop' Caiaphas and his clerks are burnt their ashes blow over the city wall:

> 'Ther is doust[1] to your drynke' a duke to hem [sc. the Jews] crieth
> And bade hem bible[2] of that broth for the bischopes sawle.
>
> (719–20)

[1] *dust*   [2] *drink*

Everything suggests that when this poem was set down the alliterative measure was still strong and in good heart.

6

The Poems of the Gawain Manuscript

Sir Gawain and the Green Knight; *Patience*; *Purity*; *Pearl**

With the alliterative poem that we call *Sir Gawain and the Green Knight*, English medieval romance reaches its peak—though that phrase is misleading if it suggests a gradual development to perfection: the gulf between the poem and its congeners is as great as that between the novels that Jane Austen read and her own. Its author has mastered all the poetic techniques and narrative devices of his predecessors, but he has also taken elements from various genres of romance, including chronicle, and welded them to form a vehicle for new values and more subtle suggestions. Love and combat have their place, but in a fresh context and perspective. In its own kind, the Arthurian kind, the work is as refined as the *Troilus and Criseyde* that developed out of *Il Filostrato*, and it bears the marks of the same kind of transforming intelligence. The Arthurian hero here takes on a new aspect and a new interest. In some ways the work is more courtly than *Troilus* and the poet evidently had in mind a courtly audience. Descriptions of rich feasts, of a castle built in the latest style, of elegantly ornamented armour, of choice furnishings in the best contemporary design, of conversations replete with polite phrase and elegant allusion, of hunts conducted in accordance with the elaborate laws of venery: all these show familiarity with the correct French—which is to say European—terms of art that were current at the court of Richard II and in the households of his nobility. On the other side of the picture are scenes of wild and rugged country, winter and rough weather, boisterous humour with some grim touches, plain-spoken comment by characters whose language is localized and colloquial. The combination of the romantic and the real, of humour and high tone, of lyrical delicacy and verbal wit, is one that is hard to find elsewhere.

The poem opens, not with the usual appeal for a hearing, but with

* These four poems are found in a manuscript (now MS Cotton Nero A.x in the British Library) from the end of the fourteenth century. They are all in the North West Midland dialect and share some phrases and images; it is often assumed that they are by the same poet, but this cannot be conclusively proved.

a deliberate deployment of rhetoric and learning to link the poet's tale with the traditions of high romance that harked back to Troy. The appetite for Arthurian tale had grown in the fourteenth century, when Arthur took his place firmly as one of the Nine Worthies. But equally strong was the appetite for 'ferlies' (marvels). Hence the summary of the weal and woe of British history is quickly followed by promise of a lay to outdo all Arthurian *aventures*. And it will be with 'lel letteres loken / In londe so hatz ben longe'—which is probably not 'testimony to the continuity of alliterative tradition' but an assertion of authenticity. To Arthur's Round Table the poet now devotes a whole stanza; portraying a court at its gayest and most splendid, recalling that of Edward III or John of Gaunt. Guenevere is there, and Gawain, and Arthur himself, eager for an 'adventure'. Suddenly there rushes in a great green horse bearing a great green knight. The account of this unnamed stranger occupies three full stanzas of vivid description, not least remarkable for their colour effects. He bears not only a green visage and a green axe but a branch of green holly: axe and holly will turn out to symbolize his dual nature, whilst his stature will come to betoken his ultimate moral superiority. (Each part will offer a similar display of such precise description, with a deliberate purpose.) Arthur's courtesy is soon put to the severest test. In a speech full of delicate nuances the stranger asks the King to grant him on this New Year's day a 'gomen'—a sport: he will stand and take from any of the knights present a blow from his own great axe provided the striker agrees to take a blow himself a year hence. His taunts when no one steps forward sting Arthur to action, but Gawain decorously and modestly forestalls him, takes the axe and in due course neatly strikes off the green head. The tension over, the courtiers vent their suppressed fears by kicking out at it—only to see the stranger stoop, pick it up and, lifting up its eyelids, voice a reminder of the promise to meet at his Green Chapel next New Year. It is not quite the kind of *aventure* that Arthur had hoped for; and though he passes it off as an interlude, his words to Gawain are double-edged: 'Now sir, heng up thyn ax, that hatz innogh hewen', and the first fit closes in the same premonitory tone. As in the succeeding parts, action develops in a crescendo then moves from the climax to a weighted diminuendo. From seeming mirth we move to meditation:

> Now thenk wel, Sir Gawan
> For wothe[1] that thou ne wonde[2]
> This aventure for to frayn[3]
> That thou hatz tan on honde.   (487–90)

[1] *danger*   [2] *shrink from*   [3] *make trial of*

Fit Two picks up this note. Arthur has got his 'hanselle', both a New Year gift, and a prognostic—but, as *Handlyng Synne* remarks:

> Many havyn glad hancel at the morw[1],
> And to hem or[2] evyn comth mochyl sorw.   (373–4)

[1] *morning*   [2] *before*

The seasonal headpiece that follows is cued in to point the transience of the seasons and human joys. On the feast of All Saints Gawain asks his liege lord permission to depart, putting himself in God's hand ('as God wyl me wysse [guide]') and arming himself and his horse Gringolet with special care. The closing lines of each successive stanza, as elsewhere, both summarize and point forward. In one set (563–5) Gawain asks 'what can one do but face whatever fate offers?'; in the next (587–9), he is 'gurde wyth a bront ful sure / With silk sayn [girdle] umbe [around] his syde': his later decision not to trust to this sword and to don a different silken girdle will promote the catastrophe. Most significant is his adoption of a new coat-of-arms—a pentangle, thought to be effective against evil spirits, but here primarily 'in bytoknyng of trawthe'—the 'trawthe' (fidelity and truth) that is to be tested in unexpected ways. The English, says the poet, call this figure 'the endless knot'; he lists the five virtues that it represents (*Fraunchise*, or grace, liberality; *Felawschyp*, or goodwill; *Clannes* or (spiritual) purity; *Cortaysye*, or knightly decorum; and *Pité*, or compassion, 'that passes all points'—all virtues). This most economical of poets is well aware that the forty lines given to the pentangle delay the narrative but he is 'intent yow to telle, thof tary [delay] hit me schulde': the symbolism of the blazon is crucial. It is all of a piece ('withouten ende at any noke [angle]'); painted with gold because Gawain is said to be 'as golde pured'; and he is described as 'voyded of [free from] uche vylany' because 'voided' is heraldically (empty, because cut out in the middle) the proper term for the pentangle. Once Gawain has assumed these arms he is presented as a knight dedicated to God's and Mary's service, for whom even the wild country and wilderness of the Cheshire Wirral, through which he is to pass, will have no terrors. His primary concern becomes to reach a place where he might hear Our Lady's Matins and assist at Christ's Mass. Soon after making his own devotions he passes from wilderness to forest, and there gleaming through the frosted oaks shines a castle impressive even to a knight at home in the splendour of Camelot and replete with servants, knights, and squires who receive him cordially. For the six days of feasting and fun that follow he is relaxed to the point of dropping his guard in the presence of his (still unnamed) host and hostess, whilst the former grows so exuberant that he can scarcely be contradicted when, having promised that Gawain shall reach his goal in time, he proposes jovially and as if in afterthought that Gawain, still travel-worn, should lie in for another day or so and swap his winnings with the Knight who is now bent on hunting. Now the concluding comment is 'the olde lorde of that leude / Cowthe wel hald layk alofte': he well knew how to keep a game up; 'layk' hinting not only at his 'tricksomeness' but at his extrovert northern character—like so many terms in his utterance ('barlay', 'spenne', 'swap', 'wap').

Fit Three takes us through three sets of sharply contrasting scenes of manly outdoor sport and silken dalliance, beginning with the Lord's hunting of the great deer—described, like the later 'gralloching', in detail that would quicken the interest of all true lovers of venery—while Gawain lies snug in his sunlit chamber. As he dozes the door creaks and, peeping through the curtain, he sees the Lady of the castle approaching his bed. He plays for time, feigns astonishment, and crosses himself—a sign both of his devotion and of his suspicion. She speaks with laughing lips and playful metaphor: 'Caught! You're my prisoner, unless we come to terms.' Gawain adopts the same tone, begging for quarter ('grace', which is part of the vocabulary of the religion of love, in which lovers are love's prisoners). Even while she talks, the Lady literally hems him in and in an ambiguous phrase offers 'her cors'—full possession and complete submission. She soon alters her key a little, as does Gawain as he perceives that he is in jeopardy. In a speech of elaborate construction and high-flown sentiment he deflects the flow and force of the Lady's advances, whilst deftly turning the talk to virtue. She is not easily foiled, she keeps up a running fire of amorous glances (1281). But Gawain remembers his fateful enterprise and does not yield. The eagerness with which he grants her leave to go provokes her to a momentary outburst of pique, real or simulated, before she bestows a farewell kiss and steals away as quietly as if they *were* secret lovers, whilst Gawain goes at once to mass, and dines later between the Lady and her chaperone.

The hunt has lasted all day, and the huntsmen make their way home by moonlight, blowing the 'prys' as they approach the warmth and bright fire of the hall, where the Lord resumes his bantering line with his guest as he displays his quarry. 'Have I prys [praise] wonnen? Have I thryvandely [abundantly] thonk thurh my craft served [deserved]?' Gawain, embracing him and kissing him, avers that what *he* has worthily *won* 'with as god wylle hit worthez to [shall become] yourez'—an indefinite phrase that in no wise involves the Lady. Nor will he go further, despite the Knight's insinuations. After another night of mirth and 'dainties', they renew their covenant and the next morning the Lord is off before daybreak, and a fierce boar will occupy him all day. His Lady has risen just as early, and is soon 'at' Gawain again (1474), intent now not so much on changing his mind as on touching his heart. But again it is she who is forced to give the kiss. She takes up again the role of teacher in an unexpectedly long, coiled, and ambiguous sentence to the effect that in chivalry the thing most praiseworthy is the game of love—'the *lel layk* of luf'. Since Gawain is the most famous knight of his day he *must* know what love is. Is he really ignorant, or does he think me too stupid? Again Gawain parries so skilfully that no sign of fault appears on either side as they talk and laugh. At last the Lady gets in her second kiss, but nothing more. Meanwhile the Lord is pursuing his boar, with equal determination, more danger, and more success. At last while the white water of the burn swirls around them he thrusts his sword into it and hurries home eager to show his trophy. Gawain comes to receive his 'feez' (1622—the boar's head is technically the lord's 'fee' since he slew it, but also the payment due), in return for which Gawain kisses him as before. 'Thrid time throwe [turn out] best' he bids Gawain remember.

The third hunt is a fox-hunt, described with the vividness that was to characterize the best later accounts of this English sport, from Scott's in *Guy Mannering*, to Surtees, to Somerville and Ross, and to Masefield's *Reynard the Fox*. Again the Knight makes his kill; this time the Lady finds Gawain dreaming that his fatal day has already come. To wake and see her beside him lovelier than ever is to be for once captivated by her allure, and in peril of betraying his soul, and his host's trust. Insinuating that he must have another mistress, she now plays the role of a love-sick Elaine, and asks but for a keepsake, like the ring she offers him. Refusing it (for it would be regarded as a love-token) he finds it impossible to refuse her next proffer of a 'simple' green girdle, a talisman that she claims will preserve his life. Once he has accepted it he is in a cleft stick. And just as her Lord had done, she adds a condition fraught with danger: *for her sake* he is to conceal it from her Lord. It is his promise to do this that in the event will count against him: fear will lead him to *suppressio veri*. In this scene, in fact, he has been tested as regards all the pentangular virtues and been found wanting. The three kisses the Lady bestows as she leaves signify to us the accomplishment of her ulterior purpose.

The next scene, of Gawain's immediately asking to be shriven by a priest, has its puzzling features, and it is not possible to pronounce whether Gawain is to be thought of as making his supposedly complete confession with a good conscience: certainly, the sense of *détente* that Gawain manifests during the rest of the day suggests that he feels in a state of grace (or at least of confidence). The last stage of the fox-hunt finds the fox devious to the last. That the killing has its parallel with the third temptation scene is suggested as the hounds raise a kind of chanted office for Reynard's *soul* (1916). Certainly the balance in the last exchange of winnings is markedly different from those on the first and second days. Now the three savorous kisses are better than a 'foule foxe felle [skin]'; and the imprecation accompanying it is deeply suggestive ('the Fende haf the godez!'). The account the Lord gives of the fox's capture must have seemed to Gawain to apply to his own plight. He has not revealed the gift of the girdle.

It is New Year's Eve, always something of a Saturnalia. As they say good night, with much French gracing Gawain goes so far as to proffer allegiance. Once again the fit modulates to a quiet close, but now for the first time the poet expresses his own involvement deftly with an appeal, and a promise, to his listeners:

> Yif he ne slepe soundyly, say ne dar I,
> For he hade muche on the morn to mynne[1],
> Yif he wolde, in thoght.
> Let hym lyye there stille,
> He hatz nere that he soght.
> And[2] ye wyl a whyle be stylle[3]
> I schal telle yow how thay wroght.[4]   (1991–7)

[1] *think of*   [2] *if*   [3] *quiet*   [4] *acted*

The last fit opens on a bleak and gloomy morning. Gawain lies listening as one dawn cock answers another. Our sympathies move to him as he jumps up to arm and face the dreadful business of the day. He winds the lady's 'lace' twice about him 'for gode of himselven'—a phrase richly ironic. Escorted by a guide he sets off on a meandering track through rugged country. They travel for two hours or more before sunrise, when the guide can point out to him the location of the Green Chapel in the valley below. It is a queer kind of chapel, a hollow mound, with a hole in each side overgrown with grass, more suitable—it seems to Gawain—for the Fiend. From a nearby cliff comes the noise as of a grindstone sharpening a blade. Soon the Green Knight comes vaulting across a stream, using the handle of a great axe for a pole. From now on he appears as attractively human, even humorous, if ambiguously so. Gawain, though prepared to meet the promised blow, flinches involuntarily as the blade descends—to incur the same reproach as the Lady had made: 'You surely aren't Gawain the good if you move before you're touched.' Stung, Gawain bids him strike again. This time he is nicked in the neck, and sees his blood bright against the snow. The ordeal is over and with a great leap he draws his own sword. But the Green Knight is leaning casually on his axe. Gawain's courage appeals to him, and he proceeds to explain the purpose of the test, in an explanation revealing that he is the Lord of the Castle in disguise. The 'tap' was to show that 'trwe mon trwe restore'—an honourable man must pay back honestly: Gawain should have given up the girdle.

He now subtly divines Gawain's inmost thoughts and purposes, recognizing that it was not out of desire to deceive, or out of love for the Lady that he had taken the girdle, 'bot for ye lufed your lyf'. Yet nothing can mitigate the taste of Gawain's shame. Just as the Lord had thrown down the foul fox-skin, Gawain now throws down the worthless girdle condemning his own covetousness as much as his cowardice. A year ago he had professed that the loss of his life would be the 'smallest' (355); now it is love of his own life that has led him astray. The Green Knight has now assumed the role of confessor, and accepts his confession: the nick in his neck becomes a sign of penance done. With the Knight's genial laugh (2388), a new and happy note is heard, and is held to the end. Gawain is now verily restored to innocence. He now picks up the girdle as a shameful symbol of his pride, of the weakness of his flesh. Gawain's determination, despite the Knight's invitation to return with him, to go back to Camelot represents his return to mundane realities. When the wound heals he is 'al in sounde' (2489), sounder than ever before: he has learnt his own frailty. The girdle worn as a knotted baldric will show that one cannot unfasten ('unhap') the moral 'harme' that one does to oneself. But it is not to be counted against Arthur and his court that they cannot share his traumatic experience which transforms the badge of shame into a sign of honour. The poet draws no moral. As Hawthorne said,* romance effects its aims subtly, indirectly, unobtrusively.

The two points round which the poem revolves have been labelled the Beheading Game—in which the stranger knight offers his neck to a blow from his own axe on condition that the striker should meet him on his own ground a year later—and the Exchange of Winnings—a game proposed by Gawain's unnamed host when the year comes round. Whether the anonymous poet found these two themes, which have their French and Celtic analogues (one is the Irish *Fled Bricrend* from which Yeats took the beheading tale for *The Green Helmet*), in a lost French work, or was the first to fuse them, is still disputed. To

* See his Preface to *The House of the Seven Gables*.

pursue the speculation is less profitable than to note the fine economy of the poem as we have it; the links provided by Gawain's rash promises—the first, to meet his host, the second, to exchange his gains.

The poet professes to be telling a tale that he has heard 'in toun', and later appeals to 'the book' as authority for Gawain's itinerary (690) and to 'the best boke of romaunce' (2521) for the honourable associations that his baldric took on. But such references are hardly to be taken more seriously than are Chaucer's to 'myn auctour' Lollius, or Malory's to his 'French book'. They are merely asseverations of credibility, though that he did know books of romance (the phrase probably implies French romance) is very likely. He writes as if his audience was at least familiar with the name and exploits of Arthur and his Table Round.

This poet, however, tells his tale with originality and superb narrative skill. The division into four parts convenient for continuous recital allows him to enfold one theme in the other while binding the whole further together by minor thematic links between fits one and two (which give parallel descriptions of Arthur's Camelot and of Sir Bertilak's castle and its customs), and between fits one and four (the appearance and reappearance of the Green Knight with a great axe; the appeal to literary authority on the matter of Britain, pursued as far as the destruction of the citadel ('borgh') of Troy itself; the presentation of Arthur's knights, once as fearful, later as amused beholders). The exchanges of 'winnings' link parts two and three, whilst the Lady who first appears in fit two is the centre of the three bedroom temptation scenes that in fit three counterbalance the three hunting adventures. All four parts share in every sense a common climate. The season is midwinter, with its cold and discomfort kept at bay by the bright fires and fine array of a Christmas season, the vigorous pastimes of healthy men and lively ladies.

Mystery and magic surround the central tale. The green stranger appears soon and suddenly, as if from the land of Faerie, though Arthur, to reassure the ladies, suggests that he is but part of a Christmas game. The entry recalls that of the knight on the steed of brass who in Chaucer's *Squire's Tale* enters 'in at the halle dore al sodeynly', and the illusions credited to 'subtile tregetoures' in *The Franklin's Tale* and actually presented at the French court in 1378 and 1389. Yet the sense of 'faerie' is confined—save for the very faintest suggestion at the point where Gawain wakes to find the Lady sitting on his bed, and crosses himself as if she were an evil spirit—to the opening scene and to the mention of Morgan la Fay at the close.

Interlacing of two or more stories was a device that the poet would find in French romances, but his interlacing displays the same economy as his descriptions. The pattern is not intricate, though every incident, almost every phrase, has its point of connection or contrast with another scene. Guenevere 'ful gay' sits in the place of honour at Camelot, the nameless Lady in the other castle—even 'more beautiful than Guenevere, as it seemed to Gawain' (945), who, as he sat next to the Queen in the first scene, in the northern castle sits next to the Lady. Arthur's retinue turns out to bid Gawain farewell, Bertilak's to bid him welcome. The Christmas revelry in the north matches in its many particulars that in Camelot the year before. The effect of such differenced repetitions or contrasts, and of weighted terms or phrases repeated in new contexts, within a brief compass of 2,530 lines is to add to the impression of density, of rare excellence, that the opening stanzas prepare us for with their insistence that Arthur was the 'hendest', his court the hardiest, his queen the comeliest.

The stock-in-trade of romances, the adventures that might be expected to befall a wandering knight—challenges by giants, meetings at fords, encounters with dragons and wild beasts—these are all recounted, but almost dismissively in less than a dozen lines (715–23). The passage is simply the prelude to a radically different kind of adventure, and points to a new emphasis on the harsh actualities of knight-errantry, first hinted at when the Michaelmas morning brings a foretaste of winter and forces Gawain to think of his 'anious vyage'— his troublesome journey—and developed in the account of drenching rains and freezing sleet, and nights spent in cold armour; conditions that make the sudden glimpse of a beautiful castle on a sunny morning on Christmas Eve seem an almost miraculous answer to a devout penitent's prayer (753–62) and that make the genial welcome given there to Gawain so much surpass his expectation that it temporarily dispels not only his fears for the outcome of his tryst but also his anxiety to keep his word.

The originality of the conduct of the narrative is matched by an extraordinary attention to verbal detail. It is the subtle shading of speech and dialogue that first alerts us to the poet's skill in exploiting the limitations imposed by a firm alliterative line and a stanza that includes a rhymed element with a formal conclusion. French and English (including long-naturalized Scandinavian word and phrase) are here on amicable terms, and in harmony with each other. The hero is both '*tulk* [ON] of tale most trewe / And *gentylest* [OF] knyght of *lote* [ON]'. If the Green Knight at first appears as brusque and hostile, ignorant of Arthur's court, and even of Arthur himself, that King does

not fail to address him as 'sir *cortays* knight'. His 'gere', his accoutrements, are described in French terms; but he carries a bob of holly
from an English wood. The knights in Arthur's court bear the names
of French romance; but Camelot with its carols and Christmas games
is indubitably English. Gawain's north-country guide will speak in
plain countryman's terms: 'Come ye there, ye be kylled . . . let the
gome one [leave the fellow alone] / And gotz away som other gate.'
Gawain's traditional courtesy is revealed, not in description but in his
plea to his liege lord for permission to take up the stranger's challenge;
the plea is couched in elaborately oblique sentences, tinged with
French phrases and modest allusions that bespeak his sense of the
delicacy of the situation. He takes the very same tone when first confronted with the advances of the seductive Lady whose own deftly
shaped clauses reveal her undoubted skill in 'luf-talkyng' (which is
'lovers' talk' rather than 'loving talk') and in the rhetoric of persuasion;
whilst Gawain's reply shows him fencing in phrases that hint at the
puzzlement he is too polite to express. At the next encounter, however,
the Lady's tactic is quite different: she professes to doubt whether this
can really be Gawain if he is reluctant even to kiss her. When he wins
the round, her disappointment, if not her temper, shows in the longest
speech in the poem (1507–34). At the last meeting she tries still
another ploy, first insinuating that Gawain has another love and then
angling for his sympathy by depicting herself as so forlorn that he
would be cruel not to take the keepsake she offers. Again, Sir Bertilak,
bluff extrovert as he appears, chooses his words with care, and can
give them an edge as sharp as an axe: as when his polite 'graunt merci'
is followed by

> Hit [sc. the kiss] may be such hit is the better and ye me breve
>   wolde[1]
> Where ye wan this ilk wele *bi wytte of yorselven*.

> (1393–4)

[1] *if you would tell me*

Irony and deliberate ambiguities of this kind flavour much of the talk.
   We find the same care and precision in the choice of words
throughout the narrative. When, at the beginning of the poem, the
Green Knight's entry is described—in contrast to the music ushering
in the first course—as 'another noyse ful newe'—the last two words are
pregnant. The description of him as *half etayn* (140) comes to signify
that he is precisely part giant (and to that degree 'elvish') and, as host,
human. His lady, when first foiled by Gawain, does not betray herself
but 'such *semblaunt* to that segge [man] semly ho [she] made' (1658):

'semblaunt' (demeanour) and 'semly' conveying just the shades of intention that are involved: in company she will not slip beyond decorum, but acts deliberately to keep him 'on the hook'; and he will later refer to this *sembelaunt* (1843). His airy promise to 'lelly layne' (loyally conceal) her gift involves a breach of 'lewté' (loyalty). Assonance will sometimes point a contrast: whilst the lord '*laykez* [plays] ... by lyndewodez evez [borders]', Gawain '*lurkkez* ... under covertour ful clere, cortyned aboute' (1178–81). Indeed, in his choice of alliterative words, the poet's skill is so unobtrusive that it is likely to pass unregarded. His deft yet sparing use of local words or idioms is obvious enough. It is rather in the weight given to familiar terms that his verbal art lies: exemplified in the force of 'fonge' (taken) in the pointed summing-up of:

> Watz never freke[1] fayrer *fonge*
> Bitwene two so dyngne dame   (1315–16)

[1] *man*

or in the Lord's use of 'craft' in his question: 'Have I thryvandely thonk thurgh my craft served?' (1380). Such a well-established word as 'costes' ranges, glossarially, through at least seven senses. Many such terms 'look before and after'. The Lady begins by professing that she needs must be Gawain's 'servant' (1240); he ends by avowing that he is hers. 'Wordplay' in this poem involves more than the humour of 'now are we even, in this eventyde' (1641). When Arthur bids Gawain 'heng up thyn ax', he adds, because the blow has committed his knight to a perilous adventure, 'that hatz innogh hewen' (477): applying a common figurative phrase literally and understating his unease. The New Year with which this *hansel* is associated is called 'young', as Arthur himself is. It is his liking for 'yelpyng' (vaunt, challenge) (492), that has been more than met: the term is drawn from the same Old English poetic deposit that Layamon worked, and carries the perilous implications of a 'beot' in *Beowulf*. And when a year later the Green Knight, wielding another such axe, fails to frighten Gawain, he comments 'thou hatz thi hert holle' (2296): not just because Gawain has not flinched but because—as we soon learn—he knows that he has duly 'paid over' his wife's kisses. Even phrases that elsewhere function as tags are often in this poem given full weight. The alliteration in a line like 'I am at your comaundement, to kysse quen [when] yow lykez' (1501) seems deliberately spare, to indicate Gawain's compunction, his careful politeness. His remark that in his land 'threte is unthryvande' (1499)—'force is of no avail'—has the air of a proverb, the effect of a *sententia*. On the other hand, 'druryes greme and grace' (love's grief and grace) a few lines later extends the courtly notion of 'love's grace' (cf. *Troilus and Criseyde* i. 42, and Gower's *Confessio Amantis* iv. 1620–1). Few writers in this period besides Gower and Chaucer can survive the dissection of such phrases. But we undervalue the art of this poet if we dismiss them as conventional.

He is, finally, a thoughtful and thought-provoking poet, interested in ethical dilemmas and questions of moral choice, a profoundly moral poet, but not a moralizer. His story of the testing of Sir Gawain shows how an exemplary knight's piety has been given a deeper, firmer base. Piety characterizes Gawain from the outset. He trusts that God will direct him to the Green Man. His faith as displayed in the Pentangle is in the Five Wounds (a favourite devotion of his century) and in the Virgin whose image is painted on his shield and to whom he prays. When first the Lady accosts him he instinctively crosses himself for protection (1202), and no less than nine lines are devoted to his confession. On the fatal day, the nearer he comes to the trysting place the greater grows his trust in God, expressed at the close of two succeeding stanzas:

'Ful wel con Dryghtyn[1] schape[2]
His servauntez for to save' (2138–9)

. . . .

'To Goddes wylle I am ful bayn[3]
And to hym I haf me tone[4].' (2158–9)

[1] *the Lord* [2] *contrive* [3] *obedient* [4] *committed*

It is only a knight of such devoutness that can plausibly be made to cite Scripture to his purpose (2416–19). More important, it is only a knight who practises compassion and penitence who can be presented as 'crying for his misdeed' (760), pondering in his 'conscience' (inmost thought) (1196), deliberating, groaning and blushing 'for gref and grame' (mortification) (2502). By the same token, Sir Bertilak, though as the Green Knight he retains traces of Celtic and Other-World origins, is here as Christian a lord as Arthur himself. Christmas is solemnized as devoutly in his castle as at Camelot, his chaplains and priests are well in evidence, credibility is not strained when he assumes the role of confessor and when he and Gawain commend each other to 'the prynce of paradise' (2473).

It is this fusion of chivalry, magic, and a firmly-held orthodoxy that gives *Gawain* its special flavour. If in one direction it points to the novel of character, in another it points to *The Faerie Queene*; but Spenser will take longer to achieve his effects. Everything here is expressed economically and dramatically, through visual detail. With a mere line or two the poet can light up a northern landscape, showing us a castle that 'schemered and schon thurgh the schyre [bright] okcz' (772) or a cold winter morning when

> Ferly[1] fayre watz the folde[2], for the forst clenged[3];
> In rede rudede upon rak[4] rises the sunne,
> And ful clere costez[5] the clowdes of the welkyn[6].   (1694–6)

[1] *wondrously*   [2] *earth*   [3] *frost clung (to the earth)*   [4] *fiery red against the drifting clouds*   [5] *coast*   [6] *heaven*

What distinguishes these impressionist pictures is their subtle association with the mood or temperament of the characters involved. The climate and region in which the Green Knight hunts sort with the Dandie Dinmont aspects of his personality. The hostile Wirral, the freezing fells through which Gawain travels, the snow that 'snitered ful snart' (came shivering down bitterly) and 'snayped the wylde' (cruelly nipped the wild creatures) (2003) on the morning of his departure for the chapel—these correspond to his own feeling that he is summoned by a formidable adversary, a knight of 'furious fancies', to a journey through unfamiliar and hostile country.

The outdoor scenes are described in distinctive terms that have the effect of localizing them, hazardous though it is to attempt to identify features of the landscape today. The boar is found near a 'ker' (a thicket on marshy ground) and driven between a 'flosche' (pool) and a 'foo cragge' into a 'knot' (rocky knoll) (1421–31). He turns at bay in a hole or cave 'of a rasse [? ledge] by a rokk ther rennez the boerne [swift stream]' (1570), evidently just above a small 'force' down which the stream tumbles into foam. It is near just such falls that Gawain makes out the chapel: a mound beside a burn that foams 'as it boyled hade' (2174). The din of the crashing waters matches the sound of a 'grindel-stone'—a term last recorded in a Chester Glossary and the Three Jovial Huntsmen. Each hill nearby had a hat, 'a myst-hakel huge' (2081)—'hackle' as a term for a beehive cover survives in northern dialect, like the expressions 'Pendle's got her cap on' and 'nobbut' (cf. 'nobot' = only, 2182). Words like 'skwez' (clouds) or 'gryndel' (fierce) in these scenes all represent Old Norse elements in north-country speech; 'breme' (loud, 2200), from Old English, survives as an element in Cumberland place names. The effect of such concentrations of local terms and idioms is to sharpen the contrast between the landscape and the 'Frankish fare' of the castle. A poet so sensitive to landscape will treat the traditional seasonal headpiece found in several of the romances (see above pp. 172, 190–1) as more than an occasion for rhetorical display. It is no coincidence that a later novelist equally concerned with sentient and suffering humankind should evoke the progress of the year, the great clockwork of Nature, in just such terms:

Daisies and buttercups give way to the brown waving grasses ... the waving grasses are swept away ... the tawny-tipped corn begins to bow with the weight of the full ear ... then, presently, the patches of yellow stubble lie side by side with streaks of dark-red earth.... And this passage from beauty to beauty, which to the happy is like the flow of a melody, measures for many a human heart the approach of foreseen anguish—seems hurrying on the moment when the shadow of dread will be followed up by the reality of despair.

(Mr. Gilfil's Love-Story, ch. v)

Even as the summer seemed cruelly hasty to George Eliot's heroine, so in the poem when 'hyyes hervest [autumn hastens] and hardenes hym [encourages it, i.e. the plant] sone, / Warnez hym for the wynter to wax ful rype' (521–2) we share Gawain's sense that the year is hurrying him relentlessly to redeem his pledge.

We have to do, then, with a romancer whose psychological subtlety is equal to that of Chrétien. As Chrétien plots the growth in moral stature of 'the great man slowly wise', so the English poet pictures a knight compact of all chivalric virtues and boasting the Christian virtues that his blazon denotes, who has yet to face the supreme test of 'trawthe'; who fails the test yet, in failing, learns self-knowledge and the most Christian of all the virtues—humility. In retrospect, his constant care for fine dress and accoutrements, though in no sense dandiacal, shows as a flaw: at the castle it is the furred robe he chooses that makes him seem the comeliest knight that ever Christ made. 'Pride' (and 'proud') as applied to a chevalier does not necessarily carry moral connotations. But at the close Gawain himself applies it thus:

> quen pryde schal me pryk for prowes of armes
> The loke to this luf-lace shal lethe[1] my hert. (2437–8)

[1] *humble*

In the *Parlement of the Thre Ages*, Gawain appears as a model of knightly virtue. Here we see him as the reflective hero, liable to fear and foreboding, and painfully learning self-knowledge. From St Bernard onwards, ascetical writers had expatiated on the classical *Nosce te ipsum* and diffused the technique of self-scrutiny. The knight of history, the knight-errant of romance—even of Chrétien's romances, and even when love-lorn—was of necessity an extrovert who must ever be on guard against external perils. Love-soliloquies, to be sure, are commonplace in Chrétien. Chaucer gives us a Criseyde privately pondering on Pandarus's words (*TC* ii. 599) and Diomede's (v. 1024), a Troilus who 'in his thought gan up and down to wynde / Hire wordes alle' (iii. 1541). But Gawain meditates at the same time as he preserves his wonted courtesy: lying silent while the Lady sits on his bed and finally saying to himself, 'the proper thing is to ask what she wants'. It is the first test of his 'trawthe' to his host. Till it comes to the last one we can gauge his inner motives only from his behaviour and his ripostes. But with the offer of the 'luf-lace' (a compound the more ambiguous because it is never used by the Lady)—'Then *kest* the knyght, and hit come to his hert / Hit were a juel [jewel] for the jopardé'—then *pondered* the knight (1855–6). Reflexion of another kind is suggested in the account of his last, sleepless night in the castle: 'he hade muche on the morn to mynne [think on], yif he wolde / *In thoght*' (1992–3).

In the light of such passages we must regard the careful account of his formal confession and absolution (1876–84)—in the same chapel in which he had first met the Lady—as deliberately placed; and must assume that he did not consider possession of the girdle to be sinful. And only a man so open to self-examination would react so violently to the Green Knight's charge made with the utmost politeness ('here yow lakked a lyttel, sir' (2366)) that the failure to disclose the gift to him was a failure in *lewté*. That he who had always despised treachery and 'untrawthe', whose arms marked him as 'tulk of tale most trwe' (man most true in his speech) (638), should have yielded to the temptation to ensure his life—this is what shames him for ever in his own sight. Worn baldricwise, the lace will be for him 'the token of untrawthe' (2509).

The pattern of moral maturation is hardly different from that of the Grail Quest: a journey, a test, confession of pride and self-sufficiency, return to Arthur's court. It lacks the tragic tones of the Grail story as we know it in Malory because there is no fatal enamourment. Guenevere is just a beautiful queen, the Lady a decoy. The scribe who added as an *explicit* the Garter motto 'Hony soyt qui mal pence' saw that it was as appropriate to the girdle (*mutatis mutandis*) as to the Lady's garter which a King had made a symbol of knighthood. Some who wore it might take Gawain's words to heart, others might not. In any event, his espousal of the badge makes the last two lines of the poem more than a conventional *finis*:

Nou *that bere*[1] *the croune of thorne*
He bryng vus to his blysse!

[1] *he who bore*

There is nothing heavy, nothing moralistic about this conclusion. And it is in keeping with the delicate balance of tone throughout the romance. The depiction of the other characters has been similarly balanced, though the contrasts are never crude. If Arthur is the comeliest king, lord of the most renowned knights and loveliest ladies, he is also somewhat 'childgered' (boyish), 'wylde' with the exuberance of youth. His challenger, at Camelot contemptuous and almost rude, on his own ground is too polite to ask Gawain his name yet shows his genial boyishness by catching his hood on his spear as he holds it aloft as a Christmas prize. If he is more vivid and concrete than Arthur it is because of his crucial role. He changes not only in shape and colour but in tone and role—emerging at the close as a beneficent and benevolent knight-confessor. The only sharp personal contrast is that between his fair Lady and her attendant 'auncien', yellow, wrinkled, muffled, sour-lipped, and blear-eyed: combining elements from Age as pictured in the *Roman de la Rose* and the Loathly Lady that figures in *The Wife of Bath's Tale* and Gower's story of Florent. We can hardly guess at her function till the Green Knight discloses that she is his aunt, and none other than Morgan la Fay; then the significance of her presence alongside Gawain at his arrival and at later merry-making becomes apparent and she emerges as a sinister all-controlling goddess. We cannot dismiss her as machinery. Morgan had once been a Celtic divinity: *dea quaedam phantastica* as Giraldus Cambrensis puts it in his *Speculum Ecclesie* (ii. 9). Such shapes kept something of their ancient power in the poet's time and region. But her sinister arts do not avail. The predominant note of the poem, for all the perils, moral and physical, that it discloses, remains one of comedy—merriment, games, laughter. In no romance, French or English, is the joyous sense so abundant. The perils and risks merely add spice to the fun. Even Gawain's shame, which he is to wear for life, is subsumed in laughter that can hardly have been intended as cruel or ironic. The last word of the poem is 'bliss'.

The poem we call by the name of *Patience*—but which I prefer to call *Jonas*—is distinct in style, size, and form from its neighbours in the Cotton manuscript, and in my view the occasional similarities in the poetic stance and diction to one or other of them are not striking enough to prove common authorship. Its presence in the same manuscript is not a forceful argument. Medieval manuscripts were often as not 'omnibuses', compiled by a scribe or bookseller rather than a poet or a minstrel. As well argue that the romances of the Auchinleck manuscript were composed by one man as argue that *Patience* must come from the same hand as *Sir Gawain*.

Admittedly *Patience* does in one (minor) feature of construction resemble its companions. The first line—'Pacience is a poynt, thagh [though] hit displese ofte'—recurs, with a slight variation, as the last line, just as do the opening lines of *Gawain* and *Pearl*. But this device or variants of it can be found in other poems of the period, and even if it could not we should have to accept the possibility that the *Patience*-poet learnt its effectiveness from a study of such poems when they came to his hands or his ears, and that he was adapting another man's patterning. This return to the opening phrases of the poem is, if anything, more effective in the present case since the poem is short enough for anyone to retain them in the memory.

In *Patience*, the first line is epigrammatic enough to arrest attention at once. We must pause on *poynt* long enough to discern that a 'poynt' here means a virtue—as it does in *Gawain*, where *pité* 'passez alle poyntez'. To the modern reader it will not at once be evident that the matter of the poem is congruent with this meaning, even taking into account the gloss provided in the following seven lines. But those lines do indicate that *Patience* is to be regarded as a more positive quality than modern usage suggests and modern ethics affirms. It is worth noting at the outset that patience held a place of honour in *medieval* ethics. It is the main theme of Chaucer's *Clerk's Tale*, bulks large in Chaucer's own tale of *Melibee*, and has its place in *Piers Plowman*. When, in *The Knight's Tale*, Arcite bids Palamon 'for Goddes love, [to] taak al in pacience' (*CT* I. 1084) he is recalling him to a standard of ethical behaviour, not simply saying 'grin and bear it'. There is, of course, a biblical *locus classicus* for the demonstration of this virtue—the story of Job,* not the story of Jonah, in which the virtue is never touched on. But in Job, the poetry, the philosophy, the theology reduce the story itself to a frame.

The medieval conception of patience can be understood only if we bear in mind its etymological root in the Latin word *patior* and its value as the antithesis to action.† *Actio* and *Passio* are the opposite ends of a single pole. Hence in the present poem the concern with Jonah's impulsive and self-centred actions is part of the development of the opening theme, part of a necessary movement towards a proof of the theorem stated. But in the ethical sphere, Patience is opposed to another entity—the vice of Ira, or Anger. And the poet soon suggests that it is better 'to abyde the bur [blow]' than 'ay throw forth my

---

* In Prudentius's *Psychomachia* Job is the escort of Patientia.

† Cf. G. R. Crampton, *The Condition of Creatures: Suffering and Action in Chaucer and Spenser* (New Haven and London, 1974).

thro'—than continually give vent to *anger* (7–8). Later he will note repeatedly Jonah's proneness to peevish anger; indeed it becomes his dominant trait, though scripture nowhere alludes to it. It is soon associated with impatience again (48).

Patience is essentially a Christian virtue. The poet's way of reminding us of this is to cite the Beatitudes in which it is enshrined—the utterances of Our Lord himself, and given special importance by the inclusion of Matt. 5: 1–12 as the Gospel lesson in a festal mass; hence the poet can say that he heard it 'on a halyday at a hyghe masse'. It is in fact the lesson for All Saints' (as well as two other feasts). As a holy day of obligation, All Saints' would be celebrated with a High Mass, as the poet says. In paraphrasing this passage he rearranges it slightly—putting the second Beatitude after the third; he makes the *pacifici*, the peace-makers, 'those who hold their peace'—i.e. the long-suffering—and those who are persecuted for righteousness's sake become those that 'con her hert stere'—a marked deviation from the dominical utterance, for the phrase can only mean 'those able to restrain themselves, to suffer, to endure'. The Beatitudes as thus presented provide an array of all the seven Christian virtues as personified in medieval art and literature: Poverty, Pity, Penance, Meekness, Mercy, 'Clannesse' (i.e. Chastity or Purity), Peace, and Patience. It is with such companions that Patientia (Long-Suffering) appears in Prudentius's *Psychomachia*, the *fons et origo* of medieval allegory, in which she does battle with Ira and conquers her (110–76) ('No virtue, [says Prudentius] enters the struggle without this virtue's aid. . . .')

But Patience is nowhere named in the Gospel. The poet has derived it from the verse just cited and from verse 2, which he does not allude to at all, 'blessed are ye when men shall revile you and persecute you'. Again, Poverty is not ranked among the virtues nor is it linked with Patience in the Gospel text. In saying that these two virtues are 'fettled in on forme, the forme [first] and the laste', the poet is envisaging the virtues as forming a circle, in which the end is joined to the beginning—as well as suggesting that (spiritual?) poverty involves patience. The switch from 'poverty in heart' to the poverty that inflicts itself willy-nilly is at first puzzling; and there is something sardonic even if light-hearted about the punning description of them as '*nedes* playferes' (of necessity play-mates)—though it may suggest a ring-dance of the Virtues in which first and last join hands. The poet is indeed 'playing' (36) with both terms, and with the two senses of poverty—spiritual and material. This emphasis on play prepares us for the benign and humorous approach to the chief figure of the poem and it is repeated at l. 46 'Sythen I am sette with hem samen [both], *suffer me byhoves*'—with its quip on 'suffer'.

We seem to be descending by degrees from the spiritual heights of the Beatitudes to the mundane world in which 'poverty oppresses' and a lord may order a liegeman to do his bidding without gainsaying (51 ff.). The poet puts this in the first person, perhaps rather to identify himself with the type of audience he is addressing than to define his own status. The direct appeal to the audience that immediately follows—'Wyl ye tary a lyttel tyme'—is the traditional device of a *disour* (and a *disour*, like a minstrel, might well belong to the retinue of a liege lord). He is presenting Jonah as such in a similar situation: 'Did not Jonas in Jude suche jape sum-whyle?' The rhetorical question, the sense and texture of which is perhaps deliberately tight, presupposes some knowledge in his audience of the biblical story. The prologue, having begun with an exploration of the New Testament Beatitudes, concludes with a promise to expound the tale of Jonah as told in the Old. But the twenty lines that establish an authorial presence and 'opinion' (l. 40) are noteworthy. Other authors of the period, if they present themselves at all, adopt more obvious means. They do not begin by applying to themselves the text they intend to expound.

The narrative proper (introduced with a formula—'Hit bitydde sumtyme ...'—that fits the tale from holy writ into the broad 'romance' genre) begins very briskly. And at once the poet begins to add his own flavour to the biblical narrative, adjusting, interpreting, and filling it out. We learn at once that God's message that he is to go to Nineveh will make Jonah 'unglad', and that it is unwelcome. Scripture tells us simply that Jonah rose up to flee from the presence of the Lord. The poet depicts him as more angry than fearful (74) and as nursing his anger and grumbling ('ay janglande for tene'). His dread is not of God but of such punishment as might be visited on a stranger in an English town: the stocks or loss of his eyes (79–80). He develops these fears in an interior monologue, a device new to English poetry of this kind. Here the unconscious self-revelation is devastating in its naivety, nowhere more visible than in his concluding words: 'and lyghtly [perhaps], when I am lest [lost], *he letes me alone*' (88). The character of Jonah is thus pin-pointed. This is no inspired prophet but a very ordinary self-interested grumbler. Such a character, whatever its religious role, positively invites a light, not to say satirical, treatment. At this stage Jonah resembles no one more than the pathetic and pusillanimous Don Abbondio of Manzoni's *I Promessi Sposi*, the cleric who for dread of local overlords refuses to perform his religious duties. The peevish tone of l. 81—'this is a mervayl message a man for

to preche!'—will be found in many of Manzoni's pages on that unheroic priest. The further Jonah goes the more stubborn and pessimis-
tic he becomes: he is sure he will be not only stripped but crucified
(96). But we know that we are not to regard him as a mere figure of low
comedy when the poet has him avow that he would not go to Nineveh,
'thagh the fader that hym formed were fale [? good, ? unheeding] of his
hele' (92). This is a weighted line reminding us of Jonah's status, and
of his dependence on his creator, which far outgoes that of a subject on
his liege lord. Its nexus is with the following line—in which self-pity
rises almost to a reproach directed at a remote deity, untouched by
human distresses—'Our syre syttes', he says, 'on sege [throne] so
hyghe, / In his glowande glorye and gloumbes [will look displeased]
ful litel' if I am taken and killed. This juxtaposition highlights a
phrasal feature of the poem that actually embodies its final meaning.
The two lines contain two different periphrases for the deity; and the
poem will hereafter be punctuated, rhetorically and thematically, by
similar periphrases. They are more than kennings or synonyms. They
are so many allusions to the manifold attributes of God as manifest
even within the narrow confines of this poem. The periphrases occur a
dozen or more times between ll. 92 and 530, but are never repeated in
the same form, so that each variation serves as an alerting signal. Thus
when Jonah is soon foolishly thinking that

> ... that wygh¹ that al the world planted
> Has no maght² in that mere³ no man for to greve   (111–12)
>
> ¹ *being*   ² *might*   ³ *sea*

he is being presented as pitiful in his limited perception, in believing
that he can escape God's eye. The case calls for a comment based on
Psalm 93: 8–9: O fools, do you think that 'he heres not that eres alle
made? / Hit may not be that he is blinde that bigged [made] uche
[each] eye'—a passage that certainly resembles another reference to
that Psalm in *Purity* (581–6). Jonah must surely be in his dotage (125) if
he forgets that the 'welder [ruler] of wyt' (129) neither slumbers nor
sleeps (130).

If we ask why the poet chose this little book as an *exemplum* of
patience and whether he *could* count on general knowledge of the
story, we must consider the second question first. The story of the
whale or great fish appears in the earliest Christian iconography.
Scenes of the ship, of Jonah being dropped into the fish's mouth, and
of him landing on a tree-lined shore, are found from the Catacombs to
the Gothic cathedrals of Bourges and Chartres. The central miraculous fact of Jonah's survival in the whale's belly is cited by Christ

himself in the Gospels, and that passage (Luke 11: 29–32) would be very familiar. To our poet the appeal lies in the opportunity presented by the dialogue between man and his maker to present the prophet as a type of erring, sinful, and selfish mankind. If we are to look for affinities with *Pearl* beyond those of diction it is with this aspect we must begin. Jonah, like the dreamer in *Pearl*, means well. But like the Dreamer he has almost no understanding of the ways of God, and like the Dreamer he reveals this by his persistent questioning of them.

The vivid account of Jonah's embarkation for Tarshish springs from a single brief matter-of-fact phrase in Scripture—'so he paid the fare thereof'. Seemingly incidental, it alerts the poet to the narrative possibilities in the story. He visualizes the scene as if Joppa were Gravesend or Hull to give us the brilliant bustling narrative of ll. 101 ff.:

> . . . thay her tramme ruchen[1],
> Cachen up the crossayl[2], cables thay fasten;
> Wight at the wyndas[3] weghen her ankres . . .

> [1] *adjust their gear*   [2] *hoist the mainsail*   [3] *quickly at the windlass*

—'But the lord sent a great wind into the sea'. That the wind was aimed in wrath at Jonas the poet has no doubt (133). This would justify him in making two winds out of one and dignifying them by the classical names Eurus and Aquilon—as it is later Zefirus that at God's command dries up the woodbine (470).

These touches reveal that the poet had at least a little learning, but the names are not merely decorative. These personified winds are God's creatures and for them to hear is to obey (135–6); and meetly do they deal out punishment on the reluctant prophet. The storm scene that follows is done with astonishing brio, although it is a topos favoured at the time (see above, p. 86). These clouds have an underbelly of sullen red, these winds wrestle with each other as in an equinoctial gale. Ropes and masts are broken and the sea rushes in:

> The sayl sweyed on the see; thenne suppe bihoved[1]
> The coge[2] of the colde water, . . .   (151–2)

> [1] *had to drink*   [2] *small boat*

Scripture at this point has 'the mariners cast forth the wares that were in the ship to lighten it'. The English poet adds a deeper motive—'for be monnes lode [life's journey] never so luther [wretched], the lyf is ay swete'. The sentiment is one that lies beneath the surface in *Gawain*. It will recur like a gleam of sunshine in an inconstant sky throughout this poem: it is its distinctive note. The writer to whom life is sweet will naturally particularize the merchandise—bags, chests and coffers, 'bryght wedes' and casks, and feather beds. The scene is that of the wreck in Scott's version of the ballad of *Sir Patrick Spens* in which 'ankers brak and topmast laps' and 'Mony was the featherbed / That flotterd on the flaem'. But it is all to no avail—'ever wrother [angrier] the water, and wodder [more fierce] the stremes'. Jonah is to be paid in his own coin.

In Scripture the seamen pray in desperation to their several gods. Here the gods are specified like the winds: Vernagu, Diana, Neptune, Mahoun, Mergot, the Sun, and the Moon. It is as if the poet were consulting some handbook of popular mythology. Yet he allows one mariner to say 'He that rules the rak [storm-cloud]' (176), whilst another angrily rouses Jonah as he snores and dreams below deck— 'the freke [man] hym frunt [kicked] wyth his fot and bede hym ferk [get] up' (187). The rude awakening presages all the later development. They question him about his country and his errand, and also— another pointed and ironic insertion of the poet's—about his God: 'Hatz thou, gome [man], no governour ne god on to calle?' (199). It is a stinging question, and it is shown as acting like a sudden prick of conscience, a sudden illumination of his guilt. Reluctantly they cast him overboard. But before considering his plight the poet goes out of his way to note that the ship survived: a *sweeter* current drove it and its crew to land, where they duly sacrificed to Jonah's *merciable* God. Again the epithets are carefully chosen.

In the scene of Jonah's immersion, however, the Lord of Scripture has no place. The gale or hurricane is so strong that it forces up to the surface a 'wylde walterande [rolling] whal'. The *Bestiary* tells us that in the equinoctial gales, when wind and wave *wrestle* together the whale lies snug on the sea bottom. The poet ignores the scriptural verse which says that the Lord prepared a great fish to swallow up Jonah, or rather, he substitutes the impersonal phrase, 'as *wyrde* then schaped'. It swallows the prophet before the seamen have even let go of his feet. The resulting situation is presented as being less unpleasant for the whale than for Jonah. But never was the phrase 'cold comfort' (264) used more aptly. For Jonah is conscious throughout—from the time that he glided down the great mouth 'as mote in at a munster dor'— like a speck of dust in at a minster door—tumbling head over heels till he finds footing 'in a blok [enclosed space] as brod as a halle' but stinking like the devil. Here, as it happens, the poet seizes on the same feature as Prudentius (in his version of the story in the *Cathemerinon*), who has Jonah escape the futile stroke of the teeth and wander here and there in the darkness of the inward parts round and round the tortuous winding of the guts, his breath choking. In this stink, 'ther watz bylded [set up] his bour, that wyl no bale suffer'. It is the first stage of his punishment.

'. . . Bot ever is God *swete*.' His first cry for mercy is answered when he finds a nook ('hyrne', 290) out of reach of the slobber of the entrails, though much to the whale's discomfort. In his distress he recognizes the might, the mercy, and the *mesure*—or moderation—of the Lord as he had never done in happier circumstances. He is safe against the raging waves that he hears beating on the back of the whale (301–2).

The third 'fit' or passus begins precisely where the second chapter of the Old Testament book begins, with Jonah praying to his Lord out of the whale's belly—here, with clear allusion to the analogy of Matt. 12: 40, described as 'hellen wombe'. The prayer is expanded by variation, producing a new emphasis on the mercy and pity of 'my riche lorde'—a note developed in the narrative (cf. 'oure fader', 337). This is not the despair of a man 'cast by comfort out', and God is quick to accede to the petition; the whale spits him out 'spakly' (at once), though in *sluchched* clothes. Jonah is landed in the very regions he had fled from. The point is not made in Scripture, but for the poet it is part of the divine purpose, even part of the divine comedy (and it is not improper to think of the poem in these terms, however reluctant modern critics may be to do so. Nowadays we are at once too senti-mental and too austere). The new note of gentleness persists as the scriptural command 'Arise go into Nineveh' is converted into a ques-tion, with a sardonic touch, and a verbal play: 'Nylt thou never to Nineve *by no kynnes waye*?'—'Now won't you do what I say?' Jonah's answering 'Yisse' denotes an emphatic affirmative, reinforced by his appeal for 'grace' (347). He departs forthwith to warn the Ninevites that within forty days 'Upsodoun schal ye dumpe depe to the abyme'. It is as if Jonah is consciously drawing on his own recent experience, just as his final warning that they will lose the *swete* of life puts them on a par with the storm-tossed seamen for whom life was 'ay swete'. Here the poet is again going beyond Scripture—as he does also when he shows the Ninevites dropping dust on their heads and the king hoping that God may find mercy for them.

Whereupon Jonah, in a phrase that Langland uses, 'wex wroth as the winde'. So says the first verse of the fourth and last chapter of the biblical book. But again the poet underlines the anger, by devoting no less than four lines to it (409–12), before presenting Jonah's prayers to his 'high prince' in a cluster of polished French terms that are the more striking because hitherto the diction has been noticeably plain and native of the soil. Now it is God's mercy, not his rigour, that provokes the prophet—and to such a degree that he thinks it '*swetter* to swelt' (better to die) (427). His perverseness is part of the comedy, and blind to the meaning of God's question, 'is this ryght so *ronkly* [exceedingly] to wrath?', he flings 'joyles and janglande' out of the city, to build a little bower of hay and fern.

But as he could not hide from God's judgement, neither can he hide from God's grace—for which indeed he had before appealed (347). It is this grace that provides overnight a beautiful woodbine (where the Vulgate has *hedera* (ivy), and the Authorized Version 'a gourd') the change to the sweet-smelling vine emphasizes the contrast with the bower in which Jonah had earlier found himself—in the stinking belly of the whale.

Jonah's delight as he lies 'loltrande' (lolling) (458) in its cool shade develops into a kind of nostalgia for his 'ain countree', the hills of Effraim or Hermon, and it diverts his (and our) thoughts from Nineveh. Once more God has to intervene—He causes the vine to wither—and once more Jonah gives vent to his spleen and his grief as he openly and childishly upbraids the maker of man for depriving him of *his* woodbine (the possessive pronoun is used thrice in 17 lines). 'Why so angry for so little?' asks the Lord; it is the use of the interrogative rather than the imperative that gives the poet his cue for the personal, colloquial interchange that follows. 'It is *not* a little thing', pouts Jonah, 'and I wish I were dead.' The two scriptural verses which give God's reply become 35 lines. The tone is first dismissive—'thy wodbynde'—but soon it displays his tender concern for all creatures of his handiwork—amongst whom are to be reckoned the women and children, and the dumb beasts of the city: 'the sor [grief] of such a swete place burde [must] synk to my hert' (507). The divine compassion is here voiced in touchingly human terms. It is not enough, it is not even profitable, to say that they are not found in the original. The passage is a distillation of *all* those scriptures that reveal a God who will have mercy and not sacrifice (including the God who will weep over Jerusalem). Jonah had addressed Him as 'maker of man'. He now learns the true meaning of that phrase—that there is no malice in God. The note of benignity is maintained to the end: 'Be noght so *gryndel* [angry], god-man, bot go forth thy wayes' (526).

The coda, corresponding to the eight lines of introduction, offers a summarizing commentary on the main action. Here the poet provides a homely figure of general application: the man who tears his clothes in anger will have hard work sewing them up again—he, 'mote eft sitte with more unsounde to sewe hem togeder'. And then, because at the outset he had presented himself as one whom it behoves to suffer in poverty, he rounds off the work with an application to himself:

> *Forthy*[1] when poverte me enprecez[2], and paynez innoghe[3],
> Ful softly with suffraunce saghttel[4] me bihovez.

[1] *therefore*   [2] *oppresses*   [3] *greatly*   [4] *become calm*

This return to a personal application makes it not improper to say that this terse and neatly fashioned little masterpiece presents the story of Jonah as seen through an unusual poetic temperament, one that combined a humorous appreciation of human follies and predicaments with a rare understanding of the deeper purport of Scripture. This poet is never pompous or derivative; his didactic purpose never obtrudes. Each line is pointed and spare, in rhythm and diction close—especially in dialogue—to ordinary speech. The plainness is part of the economy. All is said and done in under 530 lines. Even when departing from his biblical original, the poet has taken something of its brevity, and of its architectonic.

In presenting God as a father pitying his children the poet uses human terms that never detract from or minimize his majesty and his otherness. He commands and reproves, but he also talks with his creatures. Jonah can address him in human terms—'haf here my trauthe', he says (336). This is the God with whom Abraham can plead for Sodom, and there is a likeness between the two as they parley with God (though these roles are reversed) which goes some way—but not far—to explain why *Purity* and *Patience* have been taken to be by the same hand. One must regret that Melville, who presents Jonah's story with such gusto, never saw the poem. As it is, the only later work that compares with it is Stella Benson's *Tobit Transplanted*, but that is a full length story and in prose.

The poem variously called *Purity* or *Cleanness* (from its first word) by its modern editors is almost certainly the least known work in MS Cotton Nero A.x. It is sometimes said to be excessively didactic and poorly constructed. But this is to underestimate it. It has not the complexity of *Gawain* nor the formal perfection of *Pearl*, but a closer inspection will reveal a genuine poetic talent. The opening lines state the theme:

> Clannesse whoso kyndly cowthe comende[1],
> And rekken up alle the resounz that ho by right askez[2],
> Fayre formez myght he fynde in forthering his speche,
> And in the contrare kark[3] and combraunce[4] huge.

[1] *could praise*   [2] *justifications that are rightly hers*   [3] *trouble*   [4] *distress*

It is no coincidence that the word 'contrare' appears so early in the poem. The very next line refers to the terrible wrath of God that is shown to those whose lives exhibit the opposite of 'cleanness', what the poet calls 'unclannesse' or simply, 'filth'. More schematically than in *Patience* the central virtue is illustrated by its opposite, but *Purity* shares with that poem the central technique of exemplary narrative. Here, however, we find a number of stories linked together. That three of them are of particular importance for the poet's purpose is clearly indicated by the final lines: 'Thus upon thrynne weyss I haf yow ... schewed', says the poet, that 'unclannes' arouses the ire of God, while 'clannes is his comfort'. To call what comes between the introduction of the theme and the concluding 'thus . . .' an *exposition* of 'cleanness' is perhaps to make it sound too much like a sermon, while to call it an *exploration* of the virtue is to suggest something more intellectually rigorous than it in fact is. It is rather a loosely constructed meditation with a series of *foci* in the dramatically conceived and executed *exempla*. Dramatic narrative and meditative analysis are carefully woven together. The characteristic techniques and attitudes of the poet can be seen in the first lines. There is an alternation, often an abrupt alternation, between the 'positive' and the 'negative' aspects of his presentation of the virtue. There is, too, an intricate system of verbal and thematic 'motifs' which are introduced—often allusively— and later echoed—as allusively—or expanded.

The poet first remarks on the need for purity in the priests who serve in God's temple. If they are sinful, they arouse his wrath. Already one or two words carry hints of themes which are to be important later—'if thay conterferte crafte and *cortaysye* wont . . .' says the poet (13), and four lines later refers to the 'courte' of God: 'courtesy' and 'cleanness' will be associated later in the poem. Even such an apparently unconsidered word as 'gere' in a remark that sinful priests pollute 'both God and his gere' (16) may conceal an allusion to the sacred vessels of the temple that are to play such an important role in the final story of Belshazzar's feast. What emerges here most powerfully, however, is the poet's intense sense of the awesome power of God, of the absolute perfection of his purity, and of the absolute demands that he makes on his followers. He sits in perfect purity:

> He is so clene in his courte, the kyng that al weldez[1],
> And honeste in his housholde, and hagherlych[2] served
> With angelez enourled[3] in alle that is clene
> Bothe withinne and withouten, in wedez[4] ful bryght.　(17–20)

---

[1] *rules*　　[2] *fittingly*　　[3] *steeped in*　　[4] *garments*

He can be approached only by those who are pure in heart—as
Matthew 'records'

> The hathel[1] clene of his hert hapenez[2] ful fayre,
> For he schal loke on oure lorde with a loue[3] chere   (27–8)

> [1] *man*   [2] *fares*   [3] *humble*

while those whose hearts are not 'clene' cannot endure the blow (the
'burre') that the wrathful God will deal them. A direct address to his
readers—'hygh not to heven in haterez totorne' (do not hasten to
heaven in tattered clothes)—introduces a sermon-like similitude: if an
earthly lord sitting in dignity would be enraged by a wretch with 'his
tabarde totorne', how much more true will it be of the omnipotent
King of Heaven? Thus we 'slide' (this is a characteristic technique)
into the New Testament parable of the wedding feast, the story of the
king who held a great feast for his son's marriage, and who, when the
invited guests excused themselves (herein some lively speeches), sent
out to bring in strangers ('be thay fers, be thay feble . . . / Be thay hol,
be thay halt, be thay on-yyed . . .'). The poet has skilfully woven
together the accounts of Matthew (22: 2–14) and Luke (14: 16–24),
shaping his narrative to give it the emphasis he requires. For all his
intellectual austerity, there is nothing puritanical about the poet's
description of this feast—it is served

> Bothe with menske[1] and with mete and mynstrasy noble,
> And alle the laykez[2] that a lorde aght in londe schewe.
>
> (121–2)

> [1] *honour*   [2] *entertainments*

The austerity returns when the Lord finds a man in 'fowle wedez' at
the feast. The scene before he is angrily dismissed is tense and
dramatic, and the poor wretch's fear and shame are memorably
caught:

> That other burne[1] watz abayst[2] of his brothe[3] wordez,
> And hurkelez[4] doun with his hede, the urthe he biholdez;
> He watz so scoumfit[5] of his scylle[6], lest he skathe hent[7],
> That he ne wyst on[8] worde what he warp[9] schulde.
>
> (149–52)

> [1] *man*   [2] *abashed*   [3] *angry*   [4] *hangs*   [5] *confused*   [6] *wits*
> [7] *should suffer harm*   [8] *one*   [9] *utter*

The judgement is severe: he is handed over to the 'tormenttourez', fet-
tered, and thrown into prison. The moral has already emerged, and it

is underlined—but not too heavily—by the poet ('war the wel . . . thy wedez ben clene, / And honest for the halyday, lest thou harme lache [receive]'). This episode is a 'figure' of what will happen later in the poem, and the writer expands his *moralitas* in a more general way— God's wrath is provoked by sin. If at this point we might think that his depiction of God is boldly humanized—he forgot 'alle his fre thewez [noble ways] / And wex wod [became furious] . . . for wrath at his hert'—the episodes that follow show that the poet's imagination is stirred by the extreme and 'primitive' Old Testament demonstrations of the terrible wrath of God.

The first extended narrative section (ll. 203–544) begins with two brief examples from the book of *Genesis* of the ways in which God's wrath was visited upon sinful creatures: Lucifer's fall as a result of the 'fyrste felonye' (a breach of the 'trouthe' and 'courtesy' properly due to one's lord), chiefly notable for the remarkable lines which describe the falling of the 'thikke thowsandez' of rebel angels:

> Fellen fro the fyrmament fendez ful blake,
> Sweved[1] at the fyrst swap[2] as the snaw thikke,
> Hurled into helle-hole as the hyve swarmez.   (221–3)
>
> [1] *?fell*   [2] *blow*

This is followed by an account of the fall of Adam ('thurgh the eggyng of Eve') which is the cause of the uncleanness now characteristic of men. These are preludes to the elaborately told story of Noah. The biblical account is vividly and dramatically expanded. God becomes aware of the total corruption of the world ('me forthynkez [I repent] ful much that ever I mon made') and sends his warning to Noah (the pattern of a divine warning followed by divine vengeance is one which is repeated, with increasing power, throughout the poem—the mystery plays, too, made dramatic use of the warning); here God speaks to him with 'wylde wrakful wordez'. The building of the Ark is done with the detail characteristic of these alliterative poems. An exchange between God and Noah briefly introduces a more familiar tone:

> 'Now Noe', quoth oure lorde, 'art thou al redy?
> Hatz thou closed thy kyst[1] with clay alle aboute?'
> 'Ye, lorde, with thy leve', sayde the lede[2] thenne . . . (345–7)
>
> [1] *Ark*   [2] *man*

before the terrible Flood which is to 'wasch alle the worlde of werkez of fylthe'. The horror of this episode is finely imagined; the poet manages to convey a sense of the way in which it builds up from the early surges of the water:

> Then bolned[1] the abyme[2] and bonkez[3] con ryse;
> Waltes[4] out uch walle-heved[5] in ful wode[6] stremez   (363–4)

[1] *swelled*   [2] *depths*   [3] *slopes of the earth*   [4] *gushes*   [5] *each spring*
[6] *furious*

to the scenes of terror as all creatures try to flee:

> The moste mountaynez on mor thenne were no more dryye,
> And theron flokked the folke for ferde[1] of the wrake[2].
> Sythen[3] the wylde of the wode on the water flette[4];
> Summe swymmed theron that save hemself trawed[5],
> Summe styghe[6] to a stud and stared to the heven,
> Rwly[7] wyth a loud rurd[8] rored for drede;
> Harez, herttez also, to the hyghe runnen,
> Bukkez, bausenez[9], and bulez to the bonkez hyghed,
> And alle cryed for care to the kyng of heven. . . .
>
> $\qquad\qquad\qquad\qquad\qquad\qquad\qquad$ (385–93)

[1] *fear*   [2] *vengeance*   [3] *then*   [4] *floated*   [5] *believed*
[6] *climbed to a (high) place*   [7] *pitifully*   [8] *noise*   [9] *badgers*

It is of no avail, for as the poet sombrely remarks, God's mercy 'watz passed / And alle his pyté departed fro peple that he hated'. But the poet's own 'pyté' shows itself in a marvellous moment of true pathos when he imagines the fate of human friends and lovers in this grim scene:

> Frendez fellen in fere[1] and fathmed[2] togeder
> . . . .
> Luf lokez to luf, and his leve takez,
> Forto ende alle at onez and for ever twynne[3]. . . .   (399–402)

[1] *together*   [2] *embraced*   [3] *part*

There is no place in this stark version of the story for the comedy of Noah's recalcitrant wife of which the dramatists were so fond, but the very starkness of the treatment intensifies the emotional relief at the end, when God makes his solemn promise and gives his blessing to his surviving creatures, bidding them go forth and multiply. This is 'pointed' by a splendid scene—a kind of lyrical praise of the plenitude of Nature—when the inhabitants of the Ark disperse:

> Uche[1] fowle to the flyght that fytherez myght serve,
> Uche fysch to the flod that fynne couthe nayte[2],
> Uche beste to the bent[3] that bytes on erbez[4].
> Wylde wormez[5] to her won[6] wrythez in the erthe,

The fox and the folmarde[7] to the fryth[8] wyndez,
Herttes to the hyghe hethe, harez to gorstez[9],
And lyounez and lebardez[10] to the lake ryftes[11].
Hernez and havekez[12] to the hyghe rochez,
The hole-foted[13] fowle to the flod hyghez[14],
And uche best at a brayde[15] ther hym best lykez;
The fowre frekez[16] of the folde[17] fongez[18] the empyre. . . .

(530-40)

[1] each	[2] could use	[3] pasture	[4] grass	[5] reptiles	[6] their
[1] dwelling	[7] polecat	[8] wood	[9] scrublands		[10] leopards
[11] ? river valleys		[12] eagles and hawks		[13] web-footed	[14] hasten
[15] quickly	[16] men	[17] earth	[18] take		

The usual brief *moralitas* follows, urging each man to 'be war' that he is never found 'in the fylthe of the flesch' and that he who would appear before the sight of God in the 'bright houses' of heaven must be as pure as the beryl, or as the 'margerye-perle'.

It is not long before we return to another stretch of narrative, to the Old Testament stories of God's visit to Abraham, of the angel's warning visit to Lot, and of the destruction of the cities of Sodom and Gomorrah. The remarks of the author at the end of the poem suggest that he thinks of these episodes from chapters 18–19 of Genesis as forming one unit. Certainly the Abraham story forms an appropriate prelude to the longer story of Lot and the cities, and serves to remind the reader that God shows great mercy as well as great anger. The treatment of 'olde Abraham' is familiar and homely. We see him sitting 'byfore his hous dore, under an oke grene'—not *in ostio tabernaculi sui* ('in the tent door')—when the three strange visitors arrive. Abraham gets Sarah to provide food for them while he goes to his 'cow-house' to get a calf and they sit down to a picnic on the 'green'. The poet develops the hint in the biblical story into a charming scene, full of light and merriment (it is worth recalling that *Patience* calls the personified Purity 'miry Clannesse'). In this 'pure' feast, God shows his courtesy:

God as a glad gest mad god chere,
That watz fayn[1] of his frende and his fest praysed
Abraham, al hodlez, with armez upfolden,
Mynystred mete[2] byfore tho[3] men that myghtes al weldez[4].

(641-4)

| [1] glad | [2] food | [3] those | [4] wield |

In the background, Sarah 'the madde' is laughing behind the door 'for busmar' (in scorn) when she hears the promise that she will conceive.

The threat of God's terrible vengeance is not far away, however, because the inhabitants of the cities have 'scorned nature'. We follow the biblical story with Abraham's question—'wilt thou also destroy the righteous with the wicked?'—and the sending of the two angelic messengers to Lot with God's warning. The Bible's plain *duo angeli* are nicely transformed into images of physical purity:

> Bolde burnez wer thay bothe, with berdles chynnez,
> Royl rollande fax[1] to raw sylke lyke,
> Of ble[2] as the brere-flour[3], whereso the bare schewed[4].
> Ful clene watz the countenaunce[5] of her cler yyen[6];
> Wlonk[7] whit watz her wede, and wel hit hem semed;
> Of alle feturez[8] ful fyn[9], and fautlez[10] bothe;
> Watz non aucly[11] in outher[12], for aungels hit wern[13]. . . .
>
> (789–95)

[1] *splendid flowing hair* [2] *complexion* [3] *briar-rose* [4] *wherever the bare skin could be seen* [5] *expression* [6] *eyes* [7] *splendid* [8] *features* [9] *perfect* [10] *without fault* [11] *blemish* [12] *either* [13] *they were*

The visitors are made welcome. Lot's injunction to his wife not to serve them with 'sour ne no salt', and her consequent bad behaviour—a motif derived from a legendary source—could have been turned into a comic episode like that of Noah's wife in the plays, but again our author prefers to take it seriously—'Why watz ho [she], wrech so wod [mad]? Ho wrathed oure lorde'—and as a premonition of her fate. There is a very lively scene (837 ff.) when the unregenerate Sodomites wish to seduce the beautiful angels, and Lot has to try to calm the crowd with 'mesurable wordez'. The pattern of a solemn warning of disaster to come is repeated, and Lot and his family flee (the family needing to be hurried along by the angels). The disaster itself is described as vividly as that in the story of Noah:

> Clowdez clustered bytwene, kesten up torres[1],
> That the thik thunder-thrast[2] thirled[3] hem ofte.
> The rayn rueled[4] adoun, ridlande[5] thikke,
> Of felle flaunkes[6] of fyr and flakes of soufre[7],
> Al in smolderande[8] smoke, smachande[9] ful ille,
> Swe[10] aboute Sodamas. . . .   (951–6)

[1] *hill-like masses* [2] *bolt of lightning* [3] *pierced* [4] *tumbled* [5] *falling* [6] *sparks* [7] *sulphur* [8] *smothering* [9] *smelling* [10] *fell*

Lot's wife is turned to 'a stiffe ston, a stalworth image, / Also salt as ani se—and so ho yet standez'. All that remains of the cities is the Dead Sea, 'drovy [murky] and dym . . . Blo [livid], blubrande, and blak'. The poet seems to have taken some of the details of his description—e.g.

the fruit growing there which when cut apart or bitten in two proves full of swirling ashes—from Mandeville's *Travels* (see pp. 359–63 below).

Lines 1049–148 are a reflective passage on man's need to imitate the purity of God, and present Christ's life on earth as the pattern of purity, love, and courtesy (there is even a reference to Jean de Meun, 'Clopyngnel', and his 'clene Rose'). The poet gives us a final lyrical evocation of the joy of the Nativity scene:

> . . . aungelles with instrumentes of organes and pypes
> And rial[1] ryngande rotes[2], and the reken fythel[3],
> And alle hende[4] that honestly moght[5] an hert glade[6],
> Aboutte my lady watz lent[7], quen ho delyver[8] were.
> Thenne watz her blythe barne[9] burnyst[10] so clene
> That bothe the ox and the asse hym hered[11] at ones;
> Thay knewe[12] hym by his clannes for Kyng of nature. . . .
>
> (1081–7)

[1] *splendid*   [2] *stringed instruments*   [3] *noble fiddle*   [4] *gracious men*
[5] *could*   [6] *rejoice*   [7] *placed*   [8] *delivered*   [9] *child*
[10] *burnished*   [11] *worshipped*   [12] *recognized*

To this 'courteous one' come the lepers, the lame, the diseased, and the blind, and are made clean. But the poet's mind is already moving ahead to the final section of narrative. He remarks on the danger of lapsing again into uncleanness after having been cleansed by the water of penance, and adds a significant detail—God is so 'scoymus' (fastidious) that he forbids even the defouling of a basin, 'a dysche other a dobler [platter] that dryghtyn [the Lord] onez served'.

The last *exemplum*, told by Daniel 'in his dialokez', begins with Nebuchadnezzar's capture of the sacred vessels of the temple. As a punishment for the uncleanness of idolatry, God raised up an enemy against the Jews. The author evidently is excited by the possibilities of martial scenes. A sally by the Jews—'Loude alarom upon launde lulted [sounded] watz thenne . . . / Hard hattes thay hent [seized] and on hors lepes; / Cler claryoun crak cryed on lofte . . .'—leads only to the capture of king Zedekiah, and to the sacking of the city of Jerusalem. The horror of this scene is close to what might have happened in the wars of the poet's own day:

> Thay slowen of swettest semlych burdes[1],
> Bathed barnes[2] in blod and her[3] brayn spylled.
> Prestes and prelates thay pressed to dethe,
> Wyves and wenches her wombes tocorven[4]
> That her boweles outborst aboute the diches. . . .   (1247–51)
>
> [1] *ladies*   [2] *children*   [3] *their*   [4] *cut open*

Nebuchadnezzar carries off the sacred vessels in triumph, and is prudent enough to keep them safely in his treasury ('and ther he wroght [acted] as the wyse, as ye may wyt [learn] hereafter'). His successor Belshazzar, however, is an idolator, and proud and arrogant to boot. If his idols (made of 'stokkes and stones') do not produce what he wishes, 'he kleches to [seizes] a gret klubbe and knokkes hem to peces'. He rules his empire 'in pryde and olipraunce [arrogance] . . . in lust and in lecherye and lothelych werkkes'; for the poet these vices, together with the wickedness of idolatry, are clearly interconnected, and subsumed under the general idea of 'uncleanness'. The Old Testament story of Belshazzar's Feast is, although briefly told, a highly dramatic story (in our century it has been given a fittingly dramatic musical setting by William Walton). As we should expect, this poet responds with enthusiasm to its possibilities. He carefully builds up the tension to a climax in the great feast which the king orders. An innumerable company of kings, emperors, and other lords congregates in Babylon, where, in a magnificent and huge palace (seven miles long on each side), the feast is served. It is a rich and elaborate scene: the knights and barons fill the side tables, while Belshazzar, with his 'clere concubynes in clothes ful bryght', sits on the dais. The dishes in which the food is served are described with loving detail, and all the while there is great melody:

> . . . the nakeryn[1] noyse, notes of pipes;
> Tymbres[2] and tabornes[3] tulket[4] among,
> Symbales and sonetez[5] sware[6] the noyse,
> And bougounz busch[7] batered so thikke. (1413–16)

[1] _of drums_   [2] _tambourines_   [3] _tabours_   [4] _? beaten_   [5] _bells_
[6] _answer_   [7] _beating of drumsticks_

It is a more exotic and more barbaric version of the entertainment given at Arthur's feast in _Sir Gawain_. The climax comes when in a remarkable passage the poet shows us Belshazzar transported by ecstasy:

> . . . hit warmed his hert,
> And breythed[1] uppe into his brayn and blemyst[2] his mynde,
> And al waykned[3] his wyt, and wel-neghe he foles[4];
> For he waytez[5] on wyde, his wenches he byholdes,
> And his bolde baronage aboute bi the woghes[6]. . . .

(1421–4)

[1] _rushed round_   [2] _fuddled_   [3] _was enfeebled_   [4] _becomes mad_   [5] _gazes_
[6] _walls_

A 'dotage' comes upon him (he is clearly one of those whom God wishing to destroy makes mad), and he orders the sacred vessels to be brought before him. They are elaborately described by the poet, because they are the images of heavenly rather than earthly splendour. The great candlestick

> watz not wonte[1] in that wone[2] to wast no serges[3],
> Bot in temple of the trauthe[4] trwly to stonde,
> Bifore the sancta sanctorum[5]. . . .   (1489-91)

[1] *accustomed*   [2] *dwelling*   [3] *candles*   [4] *truth*   [5] *Holy of Holies*

These sacred vessels become the centre of a scene of orgy:

> Now a boster on benche bibbes therof
> Tyl he be dronkken as the devel and dotes ther[1] he syttes . . .
>
>   (1499-500)

[1] *where*

punctuated by the roars of Belshazzar—'bede [serve] us therof!', 'Pour out the wine', 'Wassayl!'. Once again, God first sends a warning. These lords glorying in their uncleanness and their 'golden gods' are stunned into an eerie silence as the hand appears and writes the words upon the wall. The effect it has on Belshazzar (we may think of similar scenes in Layamon; see pp. 76, 80-1 above) is memorably caught:

> When that bolde Baltazar blusched[1] to that neve[2],
> Such a dasande[3] drede dusched[4] to his hert
> That al falewed[5] his face and fayled the chere[6];
> The stronge strok of the stonde[7] strayned his joyntes.
> His cnes cachches to close[8] and cluchches his hommes[9],
> And he with plattyng his paumes displayes his leres[10]. . . .
>
>   (1537-42)

[1] *looked*   [2] *fist*   [3] *numbing*   [4] *struck*   [5] *grew pale*
[6] *composure*   [7] *blow*   [8] *he seizes his knees very tightly*   [9] *legs*
[10] *with beating his palms (i.e. fists) tears his cheeks*

As in the biblical story, it is only the prophet Daniel who can interpret the writing. He does this in a long and eloquent speech. It is a testimony to the narrative art of the poet that he works in at this dramatic moment the story of the earlier punishment of Nebuchadnezzar, Belshazzar's father. God, says Daniel, drove him to madness so that he ate grass and 'counted him a cow'; his hair grew to immense length—'twentyfolde twynande [twisting] hit to his tos raght [reached]'. The poet elaborates the grotesque appearance of the unfortunate man:

> His berde ibrad[1] alle his brest to the bare urthe,
> His browes bresed[2] as breres[3] aboute his brode chekes;

Holwe[4] were his yyen[5] and under campe hores[6],
And al watz gray as the glede[7], with ful grymme clawes,
That were croked and kene[8] as the kyte paume[9].
Erne-hwed[10] he watz. . . .   (1693–8)

[1] *spread over*   [2] *bristled*   [3] *briars*   [4] *hollow*   [5] *eyes*
[6] *rough hairs*   [7] *kite*   [8] *sharp*   [9] *talon*   [10] *coloured like an eagle*

The grotesque description matches that of the ugly gigantic herdsman in *Ywain and Gawain*. This punishment lasted, says the prophet, until he came both to the knowledge of God's power ('til he *wyst* ful wel who wroght alle myghtes') and to self-knowledge (till 'he com to Knawlach and kenned hymselven'). After repentance he was restored—'but *thou*, Baltazar' says Daniel, 'thou hast ignored the warnings and set them at little'. He expounds the terrible meaning of the words on the wall. With grim dramatic irony, the grateful king clothes the prophet of doom in fine robes. That very night vengeance comes swiftly, heralded by a sinister change in the weather ('mourkenes the mery weder, and the myst dryves'). A sudden and effective night attack by the Medes (using scaling ladders) brings them into the city. They go straight to the palace and slaughter its inhabitants:

Baltazar in his bed watz beten to dethe,
That bothe his blod and his brayn blende[1] on the clothes.

(1787–8)

[1] *mingled*

and his body is thrown into a ditch, like a dog's. The final *exemplum* of the punishment of 'unclannes' is brought to a sudden and grim close. The poet simply adds a succinct and pointed ending ('Thus upon thrynne wyses . . .') which is appropriately 'courteous' and 'clene' for this subtle and interesting work.

Dante's *Comedy* apart, no medieval poem can rival *Pearl* in brilliance of surface, tightness of texture, and complexity of construction, range of language and freshness of metaphor and spiritual vision. It is this last quality, and the capacity to embody theological truths in untechnical speech that chiefly set it off from Chaucer's greatest work. But it also has a wit born of unexpected collocations: the kind of wit that we associate with the Metaphysicals, though it is not as self-conscious or as coruscating as Donne's or Marvell's—no deliberate cleverness for cleverness's sake—it is the wit of *caritas*. And in fact the authors of *The Collar* and *The Anniversaries* share the same themes and attitudes as the fourteenth-century poet. Herbert's *Collar* (like others of his poems) shows the same movement from self-concern to submission:

> But as I rav'd and grew more fierce and wilde
> At every word,
> Me thoughts I heard one calling, *Child*:
> And I reply'd, *My Lord*.

Again William Drummond, in *A Cypresse Grove*, will speak of the soul as a pearl:

Thinke then ... that thou arte a Pearle, raised from thy mother, to bee enchaced in gold, and that the death-day of thy bodie is thy birth-day to eternitie ...

—which is the prime theme of our poem.* As for the dexterous concatenation of stanzas that is such a marked feature of *Pearl*, Donne's *Corona*, though less complex, offers the nearest parallel.

Donne's admirers saw him as bending stubborn language to the rule of his imperious wit. In like manner the *Pearl* poet bends meaning and form, syntax, dialect, idiom to fit his tight verse-pattern, itself essentially a new construction, even if fourteenth-century verse had earlier shown itself hospitable to linked stanzas employing both rhyme and alliteration—as in the topical verses of Minot (see below, pp. 394–5). All that we miss in *Pearl* are the clusters of formulas that had become rather too marked a feature of the standard fourteenth-century alliterative line. The short octosyllabics of *Pearl* do not favour such *chevilles*, and yield only a handful—'grymly grounde', 'stok other ston', 'comly on-under cambe' (beneath her comb). And several of the alliterative combinations that we do find—like 'mokke and mul', 'slente other slade', 'stout and styf'—may come directly from popular spoken use. The terse line and the rhymed stanza encourage deployment of the semantic riches of a vocabulary in which Norse, Anglo-Saxon, and French were now thoroughly fused and of a great variety of rhythm. The poet is skilled in presenting theological truths in bold compounds—'angel-havyng', 'luf-daungere', 'doel-doungoun'. He has a genius for the unexpected epithet: 'the maynful mone' (powerful moon) (1093) or 'yor worlde *wete* [? rainy, ? misty]' (761). He is sparing of similes, but two are memorable: pebbles glitter in water like stars, and the virgins before the Lamb are 'as mylde as maydenez seme at mas' (1115)—fitly so, since the Mass symbolizes that same Lamb.

The scenes set forth are largely biblical, but biblical language is actualized and Anglicized. The 'shearer' (*tondens*) of Isa. 53: 7 becomes the 'clipper', the *procurator* of the Parable of the Vineyard a 'reeve'. The jeweller of another parable sells all his goods, 'bothe

---

* In a typically 'metaphysical' way, Drummond seems to be playing on two senses of *mother*: (1) mother earth/grave; (2) *mother* as in 'mother of pearl', from French *mère perle*—the oyster.

wolen and lynne' (731). The Apocalyptic 'voice of a great thunder' (*vocem tonitrui magni*) becomes 'as thunder throwez in torrez blo' (875) (like the rumbling of thunder in the lowering hills—of Cumberland?). The renderings of Scripture are racy and idiomatic. When the poet does preserve a Latinate term he uses it carefully: 'property' in 446 is expanded by 'in itself being' to give the learned sense of *proprietas*. French terms are used as carefully as jewels:

> For synglerty o hyr dousour[1],
> We calle hyr Fenyx of Arraby.   (429–30)
>
> [1] *uniqueness of her sweetness*

Never had English been so rich and supple, so hospitable as in the later fourteenth century, and of this condition the poet took every advantage. And never had English art or manners been so elegant; the spiritual refinement of the poem has its secular counterpart in *Troilus and Criseyde* and *The Knight's Tale*, and can be thought of as mediating between the two worlds. The wars had strengthened rather than weakened cultural ties with France (just as the Augustans went on admiring Montesquieu and Montaigne). A poem about a Pearl inevitably draws on lapidary language; and the associations of lapidary lore were predominantly French, as Chaucer witnesses by citing the *Lapidaire* in *The House of Fame*. French too was the language of architecture, painting, gardening—an art as highly esteemed in the fourteenth century as landscaping was to be in the eighteenth. Our poet draws on each of these arts, indeed blends them: his trees with blue trunks bear silver leaves, and the gravel he treads on consists of 'orient pearls'. Tapestry was the most 'prestigious' art of his time, and one can best picture the scenes of the poem, not in terms of the crude illustrations in the unique manuscript, but as a sequence of frames or designs such as would be supplied to the weaver of a tapestry series. The poet himself hints at the likeness when he says of the rocky 'paradisal' forest that

> Wern never webbez[1] that wyyes weven[2]
> Of half so dere adubbemente[3].   (71–2)
>
> [1] *tapestries*   [2] *men weave*   [3] *splendour*

Such a simile would not occur to Dante, who thinks rather of painting and sculpture as the richest arts. Of English tapestries made at this time no substantial pieces survive. But French specimens are plentiful. The great Apocalypse series at Angers may well be exactly contemporary with *Pearl*, and originally may have equalled in number the 101 stanzas of the poem. The appeal of this series is distinctive: it lies

in its verve and variety, which with its technical mastery induce something of the same sense of awe and wonder that is evoked by *Pearl*,
which is itself so deeply indebted to the Apocalypse,*—in us and in
the dreamer that the poem depicts.

Indeed, as the artists of the Angers tapestries represent St John as
both narrator and observer—experiencing variously curiosity or per-
plexity, stupor or fear, joy or serenity, so the poet takes his dreamer
through a gamut of similar emotions: his desolate grief (51) is forgotten
in wonder (99 ff.) and astonishment (156). Now he stands 'as hende
[quiet] as hawk in halle', now 'as stylle as dased quayle'. Now he is
'rasch and ronk' (eager and impetuous) (1167), now 'baysment [amaze-
ment] gef myn hert a brunt [blow]' (174). It is these changing emotions
that overrun the fixed stanzaic pattern, and engage our interest, even if
our concern with the argument flags.

And in a wider sense the vision that St John saw 'in gostly drem'
(790) provides a model for this more personal narrator. The dreamer
whose spirit goes in a dream 'in Godes grace / In aventure ther
mervaylez meven' (on a quest where marvels take place), at one point
actually associates himself with the Apostle:

> As John the apostel hit sygh[1] wyth syght
> I syghe that cyty of gret renoun. . . .   (985–6)

> [1] *saw*

The taut metrical texture, the linguistic wit, the sheer craft of the
poem, prepare us for an allusive and complex mode of reference, and
should guard us against over-literal reading. That the poet should
never tell us more of his relationship with the Pearl than that 'Ho watz
me nerre [nearer] than aunte or nece' (233) is typical of this mode.
English religious alliterative verse had sometimes previously favoured
the enigmatic and the oblique. In *The Dream of the Rood*, for example, it
is but slowly that we identify the 'beacn', 'treo', and 'beam' with the
Cross. The whole of *this* poem is devoted to exploring the meaning of
its very first line: its 'perle' will grow in meaning and richness. The
traditional glossing of Scripture encouraged symbolic or allegorical
reading—especially of 'vision' texts, which took on something of the
value of Scripture itself, since Scripture gave a high place to the vision,
whether that of Ezekiel, of Isaiah, of St Paul, or of St John, or the
Transfiguration vision of Matt. 17.

* In presenting the Apocalyptic scenes the poet could count on some effect of recognition. A number of illustrated Apocalypses of English provenance survive, and there
were doubtless many more. One series adorned the Chapter House at Westminster, but
there is now only a fragment of the Judgement scene. (See E. W. Tristram, *English Wall
Painting of the Fourteenth Century* (London, 1955), 47.)

Further, any conscientious parish priest would translate at least the Sunday Epistle and Gospel (as well as the readings for feast days). The poet evidently writes for an audience steeped in Scripture, and assumes that the merest flicker of an allusion will be noted. The dense cluster of such allusions in the second part of the third stanza sets a pattern for the whole work, indicating emphatically that the poem is to be read in a New Testament context—which is to say (as the Maiden herself says) in a liturgical context:

> As Mathew melez[1] in your messe
> In sothfol[2] gospel of God almyght.   (497–8)

> [1] *declares*   [2] *true*

The New Testament parable was the prototype of the medieval *exemplum*, and in *Pearl*, but still more in *Purity*, scriptural narrative, parabolic or other, is expanded and vivified by the very same means that a fourteenth-century homilist would employ. It is to the *exemplum* that we owe such touches as the lines that in the Parable of the Vineyard render 'cum sero . . . factum esset':

> Sone the worlde bycom wel broun;
> The sunne watz doun and hit wex[1] late.   (537–8)

> [1] *grew*

That third stanza holds promise of many of the allusive conceits that will be deployed later:

> For uch[1] gresse mot[2] grow of graynez dede[3];
> No whete were ellez to wonez wonne[4].
> Of goud[5] uche goude is ay bygonne.
> So semly a sede moght fayly not[6],
> That spryngande spyces up ne sponne[7]
> Of that precios perle wythouten spotte.   (31–6)

> [1] *each*   [2] *must*   [3] *death*   [4] *brought to [men's] dwellings*   [5] *good*
> [6] *could not fail*   [7] *would not spring up*

The pearl is here identified with a seed because of the association of the two in the term *seed-pearl*, which doubtless was current long before the first recorded instance (1553), and which Donne uses in precisely the same context: '[where man's buried flesh hath brought forth grass . . .] God that knows in which Boxe of his Cabinet all this *seed-Pearle* lies . . . shall recollect that dust and recompact that body. . . .'*

The medieval reader was as conscious of genres as his Renaissance counterpart, and would attend carefully to those opening stanzas for

---

* *The Sermons of John Donne*, ed. E. M. Simpson and G. R. Potter, vii (Berkeley and Los Angeles, 1954), 115.

signals announcing the nature of the work—especially as the elaborate rhetoric of the first movement (*descriptio*, 5–8; *apostrophe* ('O moul', 23); *circumlocutio*, 14; *expolitio*, 52–3) bespeaks a conscious craftsman delighting to 'expoun in speche' (37).

The initial presentation of the narrator's plight:

> Ofte have I wayted[1], wyschande that wele
> That wont watz whyle[2] devoyde[3] my wrange[4]
> And heven[5] my happe[6] and al my hele   (14–16)

[1] *watched*   [2] *formerly*   [3] *cast out*   [4] *? sorrow ? sin*   [5] *increase*
[6] *well being*

suggests a 'courtois' lover bereft of his love—echoes, in fact, the Black Knight's 'Myn hap, myn hele, and al my blesse' in *The Book of the Duchess* (1039); and *luf-daungere* (11) might seem to belong to the same idiom. But the *moralitas* of 'uch gresse mot grow of graynez dede . . .' (31 ff.) soon modifies this impression. The 'erber' next described is the fragrant flower-garden where the pearl had 'trendeled down' and where the odours bring sleep to ease his anguish: this to be sure suggests such a place of delight as Machaut pictures in his *Le Dit du Vergier* where the sweet scents speak of the lady. In fact the 'gilofre' (gillyflower) and the 'gingure' (43) have been transplanted from the garden of the *Roman de la Rose*; the fragrance that flows from it may have been borne by the south wind invoked by Solomon's Song: 'blow upon my garden that the spices thereof may flow out' (4: 16). But the 'pleasaunce' is at once associated with loss of delight (as the Garden of Eden will be; cf. 642). The following stanza (the last of the first movement or proem) darts between suggestions of *debate* (Reason and Kynde are set in opposition to Will), of *complaint*—'I *playned* my perle that ther watz spenned [imprisoned]'—and of *consolation*—'thagh kynde of Kryst me comfort kenned'. All of these motifs will recur and develop in the vision that follows. And if 'kynde of Kryst' seems to need a gloss, the poem itself will supply it. Indeed it is an extended exposition of the phrase.

All this testifies to the poet's knowledge of genres but testifies also to an intention to go beyond traditional framework—somewhat as in *Gawain* the poet moves beyond the stock themes of romance. Likewise, at the beginning of the second movement in *Pearl*, we have all the usual signals of a dream poem, resembling (for instance) those at the beginning of *Piers Plowman*—a 'marvellous' dream of a wilderness 'wiste I never where' (cf. l. 65). But here there is a difference: 'In sweven / My goste is gon *in Godes grace*'. The last phrase picks up and emphasizes 'kynde of Kryst'—and, like it, announces a dominant theme: Grace is to be identified with Christ himself (425): 'We leven on Mary that grace of grewe [from whom grace grew]'.

We sense that the 'mervaylez' mentioned (64) will not be of the romance kind; and when they are specified they turn out to be unearthly: gleaming cliffs of crystal, trees with boles of 'Indian blue', savorous fruits, scents, birds of brilliant hue that sing melodiously to the beating of their wings. The details conspire to make us glance again at the first movement.

Though formally that opening may recall a courtly French poem, we note in retrospect that the expression of grief was quickly counter-poised by a sense of sweet song from an unknown source (19–20), lines that are matched in the vision by the birdsong of 90 ff. As often, the *locus amoenus* of the dream-setting conditions to some degree the nature of the *locus amoenus* in which the poet will find himself in the dream itself.

That the pearl is only figuratively a pearl is already suggested by the phrasing of l. 6—'so smal, so smothe her sydes were'—this is the vocabulary of encomiasts of feminine beauty. By the third stanza it has the quality of a decayed body that fertilizes the earth to bring forth flowers, fruits, and spices. The 'erber', then, must contain a grave. The narrator entered it

> In Augoste in a hygh seysoun
> Quen[1] corne is corven[2] wyth crokez kene[3].

[1] *when* [2] *cut* [3] *sharp sickles*

Reaping is indeed the labour identified with August in all English calendars prefaced to Books of Hours. But it is also associated with Death—not only in common phrase, but specifically in the Apocalypse (14: 13–16) where the heavenly voice says first 'blessed are the dead which die in the Lord' and then 'thrust in thy sickle and reap'. Thus the attentive reader is already prepared for a vision that must be read 'spiritually'—and for the poet's admission that 'kynde of Kryst me comfort kenned' (55). The opening stanzas are heavy with variation, and line 55 glances back at the doctrine underlying 30–6: the doctrine that Christ's divinity and power is evidenced in the general Resurrection.

Thus we can hardly avoid reading the crystalline landscape in this vision vouchsafed by God as unearthly if not paradisal. And we soon learn that it borders on Paradise itself; at least, as the dreamer says, 'I thoght that Paradyse / Watz ther over gayn [on the other side of] tho bonkez brade' (138)—an intimation repeated as soon as the dreamer sees his pearl in this new setting. The birds of 'flaumbande hwez' and

unearthly song who fly about there are not those earthly birds that in
The Parlement of Foules sing with 'voys of aungel' but rather resemble
the Phoenix, itself a symbol of Resurrection. Are these birds, 'smale
and grete', symbols of rejoicing souls? Marvell, in his *Garden*, figures
his soul as such a bird:

> There like a Bird it sits, and sings,
> Then whets, and combs its silver Wings;
> And, till prepar'd for longer flight,
> Waves in its Plumes the various Light.

Of the delights that the dreamer, his griefs forgotten, finds in these
vales he cannot tell a tenth: he is an 'urthely herte' (135). And lovelier
still is the paradisal land that lies beyond the deep brook that he is following. He searches for a ford. But something tells him that he must
not venture across (153–4). On the further shore sits a maiden, 'debo-
nair' and in mantle of gleaming white. Conviction that he knows her
grows as he gazes; he is stunned at seeing her in 'so strange a place'.
He thinks that something 'gostly' (? spiritual, ? supernatural) is
toward, yet is terrified lest she escape him. That this 'precios pyece
[being] in perlez pyght [adorned]' is his own lost pearl is suggested by
the phrase 'so smothe, so smal' (190) earlier used of the jewel. Like the
pearl 'clanly clos [set] in golde so clere' (2), she perfectly befits her
setting. The embodiment of all excellences so far figured, she out-
shines all earthly beauty. Not only is she decked in pearls but she
wears a royal crown of pearls on the unbound golden hair that
betokens maidenhood (213), and on her breast a wondrous pearl,
immaculate. Patristic tradition spoke of the soul in grace as adorned
with precious stones. But the poet's emphasis on the white pearls of
her robe and the flawless pearl on her breast seems wholly personal;
he is bringing home to us the metamorphosis that left him dumb. It is
she (now cryptically described as 'me nerre then aunte or nece') who
first speaks and makes her own glad gesture of recognition, doffing her
crown as she greets him, as if to put him at ease. The scene strikingly
recalls Dante's meeting with Matilda (*Purgatorio*, xxviii) in the
Paradiso Terrestre where the deep but narrow stream of Lethe separates
the forest from her flowery glades: Matilda likewise smiles at the
traveller's approach and answers his questions. But unlike Pearl, she
is not in 'araye ryalle' (191); and this royal array will prove to be more
than decorative.

Now the dreamer takes the stance that is to characterize him for
most of the vision—puzzlement and resentful self-regard. Fate
('wyrde', 249)—a term that the maiden will repeat (273)—has put her in

bliss whilst he (he speaks of his working life) is in 'del [distress] and gret daunger' (250) (a courtly term to which the poet has early (11) given a special twist). He is in fact, as the link lines of three stanzas deftly indicate, joyless, when if he were a true 'jeweller', he should be 'gentyle' and 'kynde'—a weighted word, conveying in the context more than the (acceptable but insufficient) sense of 'courteous'; he who claimed to set her 'sengeley in synglere' (8) is not experienced enough in his craft to see that his pearl has simply been put in a richer coffer, which gives permanence to what was fleeting as a rose. The cherished rose is subject to sublunary nature ('kind'). But the law here is quite other: the gem is proved to be 'a perle of prys' 'thurgh kynde of the kyste [chest]' which encloses it (271–2). The operative phrase here stands parallel to the equally cryptic 'Kynde of Kryst' of l. 55. The two 'kinds' are in fact one, as the dreamer seems to realize when he vows to 'love my Lorde and all his lawez' (285). The lines resume the theme adumbrated in the Proem—'so semly a sede moght fayly not': the seed sown (says St Paul in 1 Cor. 15: 37–8) is bare grain, but God gives to each its proper body (*unicuique seminum proprium corpus*). Thus St Paul figures the transition from the natural to the spiritual at the Resurrection. The emphasis on the role of the dreamer as a jeweller who has lost a cherished gem has already called up associations with the similitude of the Kingdom of Heaven to the man who sells all that he has to buy one pearl of price (Matt. 13: 45 ff.)—which follows hard upon the parable of the man who sells all to buy a field in which he has found hidden treasure (a phrase that Langland in *Piers Plowman* (C text vi. 98–100), citing the same parable, associates with the gift of *grace*).

The maiden's stern reproaches (267–8) suggest that the dreamer has still to learn the lessons of these parables, though he answers in terms of the very parable with which *Piers Plowman* links that of Matt. 13: 44—the woman who finding the lost coin, calls her friends to rejoice with her (Luke 15: 8–9): 'Now haf I fonde hyt, I schal ma feste [rejoice]' (283), a line that is perhaps also coloured by the other parable of loss and recovery—the story of the prodigal, whose return is celebrated with feasting (Luke 15: 11–32). But characteristically the dreamer assumes too much in implying that he has sought out his pearl, whereas the sight has been gratuitously vouchsafed him. Instead of treating this glimpse as a grace he yearns only for private union with her; the 'schyr wodschawes' are reduced to the setting of a *pastourelle*. The avowal of love for his Lord is prompted only by the renewal of his private hopes.

It is a human enough response. But the maiden's purpose is to strip the dreamer's mind of the merely human. In her world all values will be as different from earthly values as the paradisal landscape is from the garden of the Rose. Essentially, the doctrine she represents is the Pauline doctrine of the Resurrection. When he expounds this to the Corinthians the Apostle roundly rebukes the doubter as *insipiens* — 'thou fool'. Pearl is equally downright:

> 'Jueler', sayde that gemme clene
> 'Wy borde[1] ye men? So madde ye be!
> Thre wordez hatz thou spoken at ene[2]:
> Unavysed[3], for sothe, wern alle thre.'   (289–92)

> [1] *jest*   [2] *once*   [3] *thoughtless*

So does the Virgin Mary in many a Miracle rebuke a sinner; so does Holy Church, as fair a Lady, berate Langland's dreamer in Passus i of *Piers Plowman*. The poet is not concerned to depict the merely winsome, the merely faultless, the merely loving and lovable. One is reminded of Proust: 'des incarnations vraiment saintes de la charité active . . . avaient généralement un air allègre, positif . . .'.

But her *exclamatio* betokens a change of presentation. As if engaged in a formal academic *disputatio*, the maiden brings three charges against her interlocutor. Firstly, he has not shown faith:* it has required a vision to assure him that his pearl is safe. Secondly, he assumes that he has a right to share her joys (on this she brusquely comments: 'You might ask permission first' (316)). Thirdly, he has not realized the distinction between the two 'kinds' and still believes that he can reach his pearl by crossing the stream. The most sombre lines in the whole poem are directed at this misconception, and they gain force from their echo of a phrase in his own earlier exclamation ('to thenke hir color so clad in clot!' (23)):

> Thy corse in clot mot calder keve[1]
> For hit was forgarte[2] at Paradys greve[3]   (320–1)

> [1] *must sink in the earth more coldly*   [2] *made corrupt*   [3] *grove*

(where the last phrase looks back to 'Paradys erde' (248)). The loss in Eden was the archetypal loss: man lost life itself in that paradisal garden, of which the 'erber' is but a symbol or reflection.

---

* He is 'uncortayse' (303), believing that God would 'make a lie'. 'Uncortayse' conveys something more than 'discourteous'—rather, 'ignorant of the very basis of the heavenly *kingdom*'. This is the first allusion to the conception of *courtesy*, which will play a large part later. The introduction of major themes in this casual, surreptitious fashion is characteristic.

To these points the interlocutor has no direct answer, though the 'humanness' of his reply is touching:

> 'Now haf I fonte[1] that I forlete[2],
> Schal[3] I efte[4] forgo hit er ever I fyne[5]?' (327–8)

   [1] *found*   [2] *lost*   [3] *must*   [4] *again*   [5] *cease*

But in the perspective of Paradise this is mere raving, 'doel-dystresse',* impatience of Divine purpose. Until he learns submission he can learn nothing. The maiden's words here are stinging and emphatic:

> '. . . anger gaynez the not a cresse
> Who nedez schal thole[1], be not so thro[2]
>
> .   .   .   .   .   .
>
> Thou moste abyde that he schal deme[3].
> Stynt[4] of thy strot[5] and fyne to flyte[6].' (343–53)

   [1] *endure*   [2] *stubborn*   [3] *endure what he will apportion*   [4] *cease from*
   [5] *wrangling*   [6] *cease to chide*

There and then the tone changes, and he is reminded of the Divine pity, mercy, comfort—that very comfort of Christ that he had acknowledged before he fell asleep (55). But he still looks to the Pearl rather than to Christ for comfort, still reproaches her for having made him grief's companion. In fact he is torn between two emotions, and, in the very act of acknowledging his own unworthiness and his trust in Christ's mercy, reveals the selfishness of his sorrow: 'You are in bliss and pay no heed to my distress'.

But it is enough that he shows pleasure in her state of happiness (393–4). Now for the first time the maiden says 'bliss betide thee' and speaks the word of welcome. He has shown the first signs of that meekness which all who appear before 'My Lord the Lamb' must show.

In using this title, which in this conjunction indicates that meekness is the very condition of the place, the maiden gives the dialogue a new turn and the poem a new theme—*Agnus Dei* (the eucharistic implications are not to be missed). In saying that the Lamb 'thurgh hys godhede' took her, though tender of age, 'to hys maryage' (413–14), the maiden is not only specifying the action of 'the kynde of Kryst', but pointing to the apocalyptic marriage supper that will provide the climax to the vision. The maiden's coronation reflects the coronation of the Virgin herself, which is sometimes conceived of as likewise honouring the Church, the Bride of Christ. But here the crowning,

---

* The compound pairs with *doel-doungoun*, the dreamer's final description of the sorrowful sublunary world (1187).

like the endowing with an inheritance (417), is a feudal image. She has made the best possible match, with a lord of the highest lineage ('parage')—the figure of the royal tree of Jesse was never far from the sight of the medieval Christian. And she develops the figure deliberately (415–20) as if to assure her interlocutor that she has 'done' far better than any earthly father could have contrived—a further confirmation of our sense that the relationship is filial.

The dreamer's puzzlement here is natural and inevitable. In heaven surely only Mary, from whom Grace grew (in the person of Christ), can bear the crown? At the mention of this name the maiden kneels in reverence—the passage approaches the Dantesque—to invoke her in the time-honoured paradox 'Makelez Moder and myryest May' but also in a phrase that echoes the dreamer's affirmation: 'blessed bygynner of uch a [every] grace!'. This term is repeated as if to indicate in what sense she is the 'queen of courtesy' (a concept that the maiden herself embodies in her address and demeanour).

The dreamer, it appears, is still thinking in mundane terms, whereas the court of the kingdom of the living God has a unique inherent property: all here are crowned, and all acknowledge Our Lady as 'queen of courtesy'. It is because courtesy means grace that the Pearl can here supply the Pauline figure of the body and its members (1 Cor. 12), for St Paul introduces it by saying *divisiones gratiarum sunt* (AV 'there are diversities of gifts'). And she applies it in a new and vivid way: the head is not annoyed 'though you wear a rich ring on arm or finger'. Yet again the interrogator strains at the gnat, misses the main point; he not only thinks that the Pearl has made *herself* queen, but argues that rewards should be proportionate, whereas she had not even learnt her Creed or Pater Noster (this emphasis implies however that she has been baptized; the efficacy of infant baptism is never in question). Here the poet is pushing the case to the extreme limit, while still presenting the dreamer as illogical, over-literal, thinking in mundane terms: it would be all very well if she were made *countess*, 'but a quene'—his protest rings out in a blunt phrase—'hit is to dere a date' (492).

The phrase provides a new link-line for a sequence of stanzas that lift the exposition to another plane. God's goodness is as limitless as his justice. In evidence the maiden cites the Parable of the Vineyard (Matt. 20: 1–16), deliberately amplifying it as a preacher might (it was, as she reminds the dreamer by the phrase 'in your Mass' (496), the Gospel for Septuagesima Sunday) so that it becomes the formal and dramatic centre of the whole poem. The scene is visualized like a miniature from the labours of the Months in a Book of Hours: the labourers 'kerven and caggen and man hit clos' (cut and tie up and secure it)—the task assigned to March. A few other touches unify and localize the scene: the lord's steward is an English reeve, paying the 'meyny', when 'the world bycom wel broun'.

But it is the interpretation of the Parable that counts—or rather, the rendering of *multi sunt enim vocati, pauci autem electi*, 'many are called but few are chosen': *electi* becomes 'mykez' (*amici*, 'friends'), 'pore men' who were 'lyttel' (of little esteem)—as if to bring home the truth to a rich jeweller. In heaven, the lesson is, earthly values have no place; rich and poor, unworthy and meritorious, are alike. So this Pearl can reach heaven before those who had toiled on earth and even passed years in Purgatory (588).

Like some academic disputant, the dreamer denies the conclusion. As if still smarting at her earlier charge that he has erred in *his* tale (257), he claims that *her* 'tale' is unreasonable. He opposes her quotations from Scripture with another. His 'poynt determinable' smacks of the schools (to *determine* was to maintain a thesis). But in maintaining the supremacy of God's justice (595) he cites only that part of a verse that suits his purpose: Psalm 61 (12–13) speaks not only of the power but also of the mercy of God: 'quia potestas Dei est, et tibi, Domine, *misericordia*' (power belongeth unto God. And also unto Thee, O Lord, belongeth mercy). The tangled or at least obscure phrases that conclude his argument (599–600) suggest, though by no means admit, his bafflement and frustration.

The maiden, at once recognizing the disputatory form (cf. 613) argues from the very *misericordia* that the dreamer ignores: 'the gentyl Cheventayn is no chyche [niggard]'—his grace is 'gret inough'. 'Gentyle' is again the epithet for the Lord at 632; and here (alone) the maiden is 'gentyl', bespeaking the *courtoisie* of heaven, one aspect of which the Lamb will embody. But the poet's chief purpose is to explain the nature of this divine grace. We are living under the New Covenant, not the Old. And she is thus able to apply the parable to all who like her have received this grace by baptism at birth. The efficacy of this sacrament is such that it saves those on whom the dark night of death—the evensong of their brief day—falls before they had done ill (and who could thus be said to have served in the vineyard). The careful spelling out of this lesson doubtless reflects the sharpness of contemporary controversy on the nature of salvific baptism.

The mention of this sacrament leads naturally to what necessitates all sacraments: the Fall, first cause of all 'doel' (642), only to be cancelled by the water and blood that flowed on the Rood. A deliberate firmness, and *repetitio*, here make for due solemnity. Yet the weight depends on allusion: the pains and death of Christ are reserved for a later stage (804 ff.); the poet can count on allusions like that to 'the glayve [lance] so grymly grounde' being mentally expanded by readers trained in habits of devotion, while the cryptic mention of the 'deth secounde' (652) will be clarified in the closing Apocalyptic vision.*

With the twelfth section we reach the most nakedly doctrinal part of the poem. The maiden affirms that sinners have access to grace through that other sacrament of penance (662–3), and distinguishes between the righteous and the innocent. She counters the Dreamer's quotation from the Psalms with one from Psalm 14, suggesting that the verses cited cover two categories: the righteous and the innocent. In the scholastic manner, Solomon is brought in to support David, and the verse cited from *Wisdom* is construed in the light of the traditional gloss, which allows the maiden to render it in a form that might apply to the Dreamer himself: 'Lo, yon lovely yle! / Thou may hit wynne if thou be wyghte [valiant]' (694–5)—suggesting the land from which the stream divides him. Text is piled on text; it is the very same tactic that Conscience employs in the third Passus of *Piers Plowman* and it doubt-less mirrors scholastic practice. But the maiden is concerned as much for the salvation of her interlocutor as for a debating victory: hence her prayer that he may 'pass' (over the stream?) at the final judgement (707), saved 'by innocens and not by ryghte'. The personal emphasis is striking here. Taking her cue from the Psalmist ('Lorde, thy servaunt dragh never to dome', 699), the Pearl throughout the stanza applies David's lines to the Dreamer, and at one point to herself as well ('the corte ... ther alle *oure* causez schal be tryed', 702). We have moved from apologetic to something like prayer. If the prescription 'by innocens and not by ryghte' is notably different from that at the close of the other stanzas in this *corona*, in which 'innocence' and 'right' are linked, not distinguished, this is perhaps because the Dreamer has to be warned that his hope must be wholly in the innocence that the sacraments confer. Only thus can he become like the innocent chil-dren who enter the Kingdom.

From the Old Testament, the Old Covenant, the Pearl appeals to the New, from David to Jesus. In citing Luke 18: 15–17 ('Suffer little children ...')—and deliberately emphasizing it by amplitude—she brings her argument back to the starting point, rounds it off with an affirmation of childhood's saving innocence, and reduces the

* It is usually referred to Rev. 20: 14, 21: 8, but the poet will make something different of those verses; he must have noted the earlier reference in Rev. 2: 10–11—he that over-cometh, will be given 'a crown of life' and 'shall not be hurt of the second death': it is the crown of life that Pearl is wearing.

Dreamer's claim of 'reasonableness' to the level of the disciples' foolish rebukes when they tried to dissuade those who brought the children by 'many reasons' (716). To all those with such faith as the children's and without spot of sin shall the Gate of Heaven be opened 'tyt' (quickly) (728). Here once again Vulgate language is transmuted into terse and homely vernacular and accommodated by noteworthy combinations of phrase into the formulaic pattern of the verse.*

Taking up this theme of spotlessness, and pointing to the pearl upon her breast (the Dreamer had remarked at the outset that it was 'wythouten wemme [stain]', 221), the maiden now widens the contours of her thought to include the figure of the pearl considered as symbol of purity rather than richness, invoking the parable of the merchant seeking goodly pearls (Matt. 13: 45). It is the perfection and purity of the stone that are now underlined: it is round and endless (738), and so the proper symbol ('token') of the endless joy and peace of heaven. But in some phrases of this stanza (the pearl 'boght is dere') there are hints of an analogy with Christ, who dearly bought with his blood (741) heaven for mankind, so that the pearl will also betoken the peace, the reconciliation thus made (cf. Col. 1: 20). And a note of urgency enters when the maiden heightens the language of the parable as she offers it to the 'jeweller' whom she had upbraided as 'mad':

> I rede the forsake the worlde wode[1]
> And porchace *thy* perle maskelles[2].   (743–4)
>
> [1] *mad*   [2] *spotless*

The contrast between earthly and heavenly values that Langland makes in the sixth Passus of the C-text, and Chaucer at the end of *Troilus*, is here set down in two taut injunctions. That the 'worlde' is 'wode' needs, from the maiden's perspective, no proving.

Yet once more the Dreamer shies away from the professed truth, the clear lesson. His gaze is still fixed on the outward beauty of form and garment. Despite the maiden's striking allusion to the creator (she claims that the Father 'of folde and flode' had told the parable of the merchant (736)) he now enquires: 'Quo formed the thy fayre fygure?' Traditionally it was Nature who as God's vicegerent created lovely women. The *locus classicus* in the *Roman de la Rose*, like the notable adaptation of it in Chaucer's *Physician's Tale*, indicates that allusion to Pygmalion in this context was common form (the Ovidian story of the

---

* Line 726—'wythouten mote other mascle of sulpande synne'—primarily renders *non habentem maculam aut rugam* (Eph. 5: 27) but it also looks back to the *sine macula* of Ps. 14: 2, and prepares us for the apocalyptic presentation of purity (Rev. 19: 7, 8; cf. 1 Peter 1: 19, 2 Peter 3: 14).

sculptor who brought marble beauty to very life was disparaged in an age that put Nature above Art). By adding a similar allusion to Aristotle the Dreamer takes up the stance of a puzzled schoolman. But he speaks better than he knows when he says that her beauty was not bestowed by Nature, that her colour and qualities ('thyn angel-havyng, so clen cortez', 754) are beyond Aristotle's conceiving: we remember that the resurrected body is not *corpus humilitatis nostrae* ('our vile body') but *configuratum corpori claritatis suae* ('fashioned like unto his glorious body') (Phil. 3:21). Yet he still (755) regards the breast-pearl as a badge of rank.

When in reply she speaks (almost possessively) of '*her* spotless Lamb' and her 'dere destyné' (757-8) she is consciously pointing up the total difference between her present place and his 'worlde wete'. She phrases a familiar verse from the Song of Songs as if it were a love song: 'Cum hyder to me, my lemman swete'; this is a verse which was sometimes applied to Christ or to the Church, and the maiden most meetly cites it here because it was applied also to the Virgin Mary. Her beauty, she is saying, belongs to all the Redeemed, but to them only. Her garments are spotless because they were washed in the blood of the Lamb (766).

Still clinging to the notion that she has ousted or surpassed other claimants 'comly on-under cambe'—a phrase that belongs to secular lyric and so suggests that the speaker thinks still in terms of the mundane beauty of the 'worlde wete'—the Dreamer has directed his restless curiosity to this Lamb: why has he chosen her above all others? She replies with a fine but proper distinction: she is 'maskelles' but not 'makeles', not unique. It is one of the differences between earth and heaven (like the different value attached to 'more' and 'less': cf. 601) that the Lamb can have countless brides (the 144,000 of the Apocalypse is not a figure of limitation but of perfection). We are now firmly in the Apocalyptic realm of thought. If the poet has chosen to read St John's *virgines* as female it is because all Christian souls can be represented as brides of the Lamb (845-6). The location of the New Jerusalem of the bridal feast on the hill of Zion will recall the earlier, less specific reference to that holy hill which only the pure could ascend (678-9), and so the poet links the two parts of his poem (Jerusalem, the city of Peace (*Visio Pacis*) is David's city, and Christ's)—just as the Epistle to the Hebrews does:

But ye are come unto mount Sion, and unto the city of the living God, the heavenly Jerusalem, and to an innumerable company of angels, to the general assembly and church of the first-born, which are written in heaven, and to God the judge of all, and to the spirits of just men made perfect. . . .

(Heb. 12:22-3)

Though only once alluded to (896: 'city of God'), these verses are the veritable basis of much of the poem's theology, and a pointer to its development here onwards. They read, to be sure, like an adumbration of the Apocalypse itself; it is on the hill of Zion that St John will see the Lamb standing. And the maiden now identifies *her* bliss with this Lamb (whilst the Dreamer had called *her* '*his* bliss' in 372), who is *her* dear jewel (the suggestion being that she had gladly given up all worldly goods for the Lamb). The poem is steadily moving towards a state in which all is Pearl, or conceived of in terms of jewel or pearl—*margarita*; and this will accord with the full manifestation of *Jerusalem caelestis*, the city of precious stones. Hence when the maiden sets forth—very much in her own terms—part of the prophetic allegory of Isaiah 53, her added reference to Christ's judgement in the (old) Jerusalem (804) sufficiently interprets it. The language here breathes the reciprocity of love: as the Lamb had called her 'my lemman swete', and unspotted (763–4), so she now calls *Him* 'my lemman fre', and guiltless (796–9). Hence too she can weave into the Gospel Passion phrases from Isaiah's prophecy: one of them—'he toke on hymself oure carez colde' (808) (he bore our griefs and carried our sorrows) points to the remedy for the Dreamer's own obsessive sorrows.

In medieval thought John the Baptist—witness the North Porch of Chartres—stands next in order (except for Simeon) to the prophets Isaiah and Jeremiah, a link between prophecy and fulfilment. Hence his appearance now, when he is actually given the words of Isaiah (ll. 825–7 representing Isa. 53: 6–8) ('The Lord hath laid on him the iniquity of us all . . . who shall declare his generation?'). But St John figured here for other reasons as well. He is the Baptist (cf. 817–18) and the power of the sacrament of baptism is fundamental to the maiden's discourse. John's proclamation—'Lo, Godez Lombe'—stands at the centre of the Canon of the Mass, and once this has been quoted, the eucharistic association will remain vivid for Dreamer and reader alike—to be clinched and confirmed in the very last lines of the whole work.

The image of the sacrificial *lamb* is now linked with the earlier theme of the *spotless* pearl by reference to the white wool of the Apocalyptic Lamb who is united to all who wear the Pearl (844–52). The union is that of the true love 'which to divide is not to take away'. The maid's 'the more the merrier, so God me bless' (850) is not merely a vivid, homely, reassuring touch: it is a fervent prayer that all may share this bliss. The Brides of the Lamb (and the figure as applied to *all* the Redeemed reminds one that it *is* a figure, that we are beyond the corporeal) have that direct knowledge of God ('thurghoutly . . .

cnawyng', 859) that comes from the beatific vision: they know even as they are known. The Lamb once and for ever slain (860) delights them at his *mes*, his marriage supper, the feast which the mass prefigures.

As the maiden has previously adduced all ranges of Scripture from the Prophecies to the Gospels and the Epistles, so now in the closing movement of her discourse she appeals to the book of the Last Things—the Apocalypse. In retelling the great Apocalyptic scenes she is herself illustrating the doctrine that the elect, regardless of age or intellect, do indeed have 'thurghoutly . . . cnawyng'. Once again—though for the last time—the Dreamer takes his wonted stance, compounded now of curiosity, doubt, humility (901–24). His alliterative formulas—'mokke and mul' (905), 'bustwys as a blose [? churl]' (911) (contrasting with 'thou so rych a reken [fresh] rose' (906))—underline his humility, but also suggest that he is still in some sense earthbound, just as his question about the housing situation in the New Jerusalem ('I se no bygyng [dwelling] nawhere aboute' (932)) indicates that he is still thinking of it as much like David's city, and reveals an irremediable matter-of-factness, a jeweller's concern for a proper setting. So the maiden must needs set forth the traditional distinction: Jerusalem is *Visio Pacis*; on earth the city in which peace was made by the blood of the Lamb, and man was reconciled to God; in heaven the place where 'is noght bot pes to glene' (955), a striking image, suggesting not only the August scene of the opening stanzas but also the essentially different nature of earthly and heavenly activity. The maiden has now become the mouthpiece for all the faithful for whom God has prepared a city, all who desire a better country (Heb. 11: 16), all who *press* to the mark of Christ's high calling (Phil. 3: 14). The line 'that is the borgh that we to pres' (957) represents a pregnant fusing of these two Pauline passages.

In medieval devotion, to speak of Jerusalem was to stir this longing for its peace—for those *sancta sabbata* that Abelard so memorably hymned. But the Dreamer's desire is expressed in more personal terms: 'let me se thy blysful bor [bower]' (964). It is an inordinate demand, suggesting that his gaze is still fixed on the maiden, not on the Lamb. She appears to yield so far as to allow him a view as a *spectator ab extra* ('outwith', 969), but in fact her full 'knowing' includes prescience of his desire: she has procured for him the special favour of a 'ghostly sight'.

This revelation involves a change—and as regards the reader's interest it comes just in time—from discourse to movement. To behold the city the Dreamer has to advance up to the head of the stream. Even so St John was led up the mountain to see the New

Jerusalem coming down from heaven (Rev. 21: 9–27). The new vantage point gives him a visionary glimpse—distinguished from that which St John had, for John 'hit sygh wyth syght' (with his very eyes, 984). And as a jeweller he can embellish St John's catalogue of the foundation stones: so jasper 'glente grene in the lowest hemme [edge]'; chalcedony appears clear and pale; emerald is 'grene of scale [surface]', beryl 'clear and white', topaz 'twynne-hew', amethyst 'purple blended with indigo blue'. To those versed in lapidary lore these stones may well have carried moral significance, but the poet's prime purpose (as the elaborate rhetorical variation in the two stanzas suggests) is to enhance the richness of the sight. Indeed he betters St John by providing the city with houses ('wonez', 1027) adorned 'with all kinds of precious stones'. It is as if he is interpreting the reference in St John's Gospel ('In my Father's house are many mansions', John 14: 2) with characteristic literalness. Further, he attributes to the walls a transparency that allows him to see, and see through, these houses (1048–50).

Each gate, as in Scripture, is a perfect pearl—because Purity is the only means of access: 'there shall in no wise enter into it anything that defileth' (Rev. 21: 27) (cf. 1067–8). Of this city the divine radiance that far eclipses sun, moon, and the other stars is the only light (there seems a hint of ambiguity in the form 'lombe light', 1046). The river of life that proceeds from God's throne is not simply 'clear as crystal' (Rev. 22: 1); it is brighter, 'sweeter' than sun and moon, and rolls in flood through the streets (just as the Angers artist depicts it). For the last time here *expolitio* takes over to enrich the theme (1057–68) and is capped by a rhetorical excursus on the spotty surface of the moon ('to spotty ho is, of body to grym'—perhaps because its shadows, in Dante's phrase, tell the tale of Cain). No inhabitant of the sublunary world can gaze upon this radiance (no *man* can see God and live). The dreamer who had at first stood 'as hende as hawk in halle' (184) now stands 'as stylle as dased quayle' (1085).

Suddenly, yet silently—as the 'maynful' moon rises unnoticed whilst the sun is still in the sky (1093–4), a fine stroke that uses the link-line device to prepare us for a return to the natural world—the city is thronged with a hundred thousand 'virgins' clothed like Pearl. They have no place in St John's account at this point, but they represent the multitude clothed in white who have come out of great tribulation (Rev. 7: 9–14), as well as the four and twenty elders who, in an earlier chapter (4: 10), cast down their crowns of gold before him that sat upon the throne and fell down before the Lamb (5: 8). If these are as 'mylde as maydenez seme at mas' (1115), it is not because they are virgins of the female sex (line 1119 precludes this) but because—as the Pearl had long ago insisted (404)—'meke arn alle that wonez hym nere'. Likewise, the legions of angels (1121: the phrase is from Matt. 26: 53) owe their presence here to Rev. 7: 11, though their incense is that of the golden vials of the elders (5: 8), and their song is the elders' song (5: 9). There is a bold fusion here of scenes distinct in Scripture—a fusion perhaps prompted by the omnipresence of censing angels in representations of the Apocalypse. The universal acclamation ('steven') that in Rev. 5: 13 rises from every creature in heaven, on earth and under the earth, and in the sea here is assigned to the angelic order of Virtues, and is given a vivid and weighty phrase—it *strikes* through earth to hell (a similar idea is found much later in Henryson, who makes his Cupid summon the gods by a bell 'that men might hear from heaven unto hell').

The Lamb ('that gay juelle', 1124) who is the object of the adoration is pictured much as in Rev. 5: 6. Yet not altogether. For here he leads the throng, his white garments are 'as praysed perlez' (1111), and blood wells from his pierced side, though his 'glentez' (glances) are 'gloryous glade' (1144). Now at last the Dreamer's attention is fixed on this Lamb. There is a faint vestige of his persistent naïvety in his rhetorical question 'Alas ... who did that spyt?' (1138). But it represents the tone of a devotional lyric rather than a failure to identify the suffering Lamb with Christ.

Absorbed in the scene, he has not noticed that his Pearl, his 'lyttel quene' (1147), has slipped away to rejoin the virgin company and is making merry with them again. It is a re-enactment, though with a difference, of the opening scene of loss—there associated with 'luf-daungere' (11), as here separation stirs his 'luf-longyng'—but in 'gret delyt'. The poem offers no more dramatic effect than this, and, like the deliberate 'solemnité' that the preceding verses record, the echo prepares us for the climax. As the Pearl takes up her former place, so does the Dreamer move to the edge of the severing stream, and makes a bid to cross it: he would 'swymme the remnaunt, thagh I ther swalte [were to die]' (1160). That last phrase bears more than its face value. He seems indeed eager to die if he can share these joys. But the very violence of his impetuous action breaks his dream. Vision poets always pay attention to this aspect of dream psychology. But here the waking reinforces the brief comment in the first link-line of this last section: 'Hit watz not at my Pryncez paye [pleasure]' (1164). It is not the disclosure itself that is significant, but the terms of it. The Lamb has now become '*my* Prince'. The jeweller is obedient not to his Pearl, but, like her, to the Prince whom they both worship. But this is retrospective—the reason why he is thwarted is not disclosed within the dream.

He comes to himself—in both senses (cf. 1163, 'out of that caste I watz bycalt')—in the 'erber' where he had lain down. Stretching himself, he feels at first such awe ('affray') as Dunbar experiences when he wakes from his Good Friday dream of the Passion. But if he sighs as he says submissively 'Now al be to that Pryncez paye', the sigh denotes submission to God's will not as regards his Pearl but as regards his own abrupt banishment from that fair region. The term 'outfleme' (exile, fugitive) carries all the overtones of the exile that is the fate of all banished children of Eve. For what he has been vouchsafed in the 'veray avysyoun' (1184)—it is a doubly emphatic phrase, far stronger than 'sweven' or even 'visioun'—he is duly grateful, even if a flicker of congenital doubt runs over his last address to his absent Pearl: 'if hit be veray [true] ... So wel is me in thys doel-doungoun' (1185–8). Again the crucial words are in the link-line (which is to bind up and round off the whole poem, since in the last line of the last stanza it modulates into a variation on the first line of the first). It betokens the fact that the dreamer has at last come to accept the 'prynces pay' as the *summum bonum*. In this regard, in this sense, he is in communion (of worship) with his Pearl.

The tenor of the penultimate stanza is not completely clear to me, and may seem contradictory. He would have liked to see more of God's mysteries—is he alluding to the Apocalyptic mysteries (cf. Rev. 1: 20, etc.) or to the other mysteries of the kingdom (cf. Mark 4: 11) or to the 'mystery' of Resurrection (1 Cor. 15: 51)? Mingled with his acknowledgement that man is prone to ask for more than his due is the implicit acknowledgement that his Pearl was right—'Lord, mad hit arn that agayn the stryven' (1199; cf. 290). If this seems somewhat subdued, a diminuendo after the *Visio Pacis*, that is part of the pattern of waking after dreams, in literature as in life. And the last verse briskly and beautifully restores the balance. Now he is speaking in the perspective of Christian experience, now he can call the Prince not only God and Lord but 'a frende ful fyin' (1204). Having learnt meekness he can be counted as one of his *mykez* (572), his friends: it is the term used by the Lord of the Vineyard addressing his *hyne*, his *familia*, and the poet recalls that parable and its continuing pertinence in the penultimate line—'He gef us to be his homly hyne'; we are bond servants of Christ.

The poem, the dream, had begun in grief for a lost pearl. Christ in his goodness has granted the dreamer the good fortune (*happe* 1195; *lote* 1205) of a vision that leads him to leave his Pearl, without repining, in God's hands. The *Visio Pacis* he cannot enjoy while in the body. But the eucharist presents daily to him and to us the *Agnus Dei*. Thus the poem that has revolved around the sacraments of baptism and penance concludes with the greatest of all sacraments, which unites the Church on earth with the Bride in heaven. 'In the forme of bred and wyn' is an orthodox formula, but here it recalls the last glimpse vouchsafed the dreamer of the Lamb whose 'blod outsprent' (1137).

The final lines turn—as the poet-dreamer has done—away from the merely personal into petitionary prayer that embraces all Christians, all who labour in God's vineyard: all, after death, will become Christ's precious pearls. 'Precious' is the pre-eminent and pervasive epithet throughout the poem, and the poet's *pearl* is now precious in a far deeper sense than when first so called, for it has become for him the means of salvific vision. But it is the very last phrase that 'caps, clears and clinches all'. They are jewels to *His* pay. It is not our own happiness that we must seek, but His.

Once awake, the dreamer never questions the veracity of his dream experience. We sense that it has been the means of revealing to him the operations of divine grace; so that the poem, like Dante's greater epic, represents the journey of a soul from grief and ignorance to gladness and knowledge. And as in Langland and Dante, the soul of the dreamer in learning the ways of grace learns also self-understanding.

The comparison with Dante is not far-fetched, for the Pearl's role resembles Beatrice's. But Dante's concerns are different, and vaster. It is possible, however, that both the Italian and the English poets were drawing, consciously or not, on a work widely diffused in Latin and French versions throughout Europe—the tale of *Barlaam and Josaphat*, versions of which found their way into several English Legend collections, some earlier in date than *Pearl*.

In this strange tale Josaphat, when tempted to break his vow of virginity, prays for help so continuously that at last out of weariness he falls asleep and is transported into a delightful meadow, full of flowers and fragrant trees, with benches of fine gold and precious glittering stones, and watered by streams that rejoiced the eyes. In the midst was a splendid walled city crenellated with gold and precious stones, whence issued songs that mortal ears could never hear. And a voice said: 'Here is the repose of the just, the place of joy for those pleasing to our Lord.' When Josaphat's escort makes to lead him away, he begs to be allowed to stay and pass his life in some little corner of this city. But that cannot be: only after painful effort and combat can he attain to it. Now he is led away to a place of mist and darkness and the fire that consumes the sinful. When brought back to his starting point, he finds that his face is wet with tears.

Much later in the story, when Barlaam, Josaphat's mentor, dies and is buried, Josaphat whilst in a deep sleep is 'ravished in spirit' and led across a marvellous plain to a city gleaming with celestial brightness. As he reaches its threshold angels bearing crowns of light approach. He asks who is to wear them, and is told that one is his, for his work in saving souls, the other for his father (who owes his salvation to his son). 'Why should he, who has suffered little, be rewarded like me, who have suffered much?' questions Josaphat, much as the dreamer questions Pearl. Whereupon Barlaam appears, to reproach him for showing chagrin instead of joy. Begging forgiveness, Josaphat asks to see Barlaam's present abode. It is in the glorious city, but the time has not yet come for Josaphat to enter it: if he perseveres to the end he will share his mentor's felicity and they will be companions forever.

Here the emphasis on virginity, the presentation of the holy city in terms of gold and precious stones, the refusal of access, the crown of light, the questioning of equality of reward—are all elements that link the tale with *Pearl*. But the tone and flavour are throughout ascetic to the point of Manichaeism. If the English poet knew it he has done no more than adopt and adapt its pattern.

7

Prose

(i) *The Peterborough Chronicle*; Early Middle English Sermons; *Ancrene Wisse*; The 'Katherine Group'

Religious prose was produced in abundance throughout the whole of this period; surviving examples of secular prose on the other hand are few, and limited to the latter part of the fourteenth century, with the solitary exception of the work with which we begin our survey. This—the later part of *The Peterborough Chronicle*—has a direct and interesting relationship with pre-Conquest literary culture, for it is a continuation of that remarkable achievement of Old English learning, *The Anglo-Saxon Chronicle*. After the Norman Conquest, a continuation of this was kept up at Worcester, a famous traditional centre of learning, but only up to 1080. At the monastery of Peterborough, however, a text of *The Anglo-Saxon Chronicle* was continued over the years from 1121 to 1154, and the events of post-Conquest history were recorded in it. It is usual to distinguish two 'continuations'—the 'first', covering the years 1122–31, and the 'final continuation' for the years 1132–54—both of which are believed to have been composed as well as copied at Peterborough. The value of this part of the text for historians of the English language is inestimable; it affords a wealth of information on changing sounds, inflexions, and vocabulary (it is here, for instance, that the new form of the feminine personal pronoun 'she' emerges, spelt *scæ*). Its historical and literary interest is not at first glance so obvious. 'Disappointingly brief and provincial in outlook' is the verdict of one modern historian.* It is certainly true that it cannot compete with contemporary histories written in Latin, such as the *Historia Ecclesiastica* of Ordericus Vitalis, which records the turbulent deeds of the Normans with vivid detail and gives in addition a remarkable panoramic view of Anglo-Norman society and its wider European relationships, or the even more distinguished *Gesta Regum Anglorum* of the scholar William of Malmesbury, whose erudition is accompanied by a power of incisive analysis and a remarkable awareness of men's motives and the workings of self-interest. Even

---

* Antonia Gransden, *Historical Writing in England* c.*550*–c.*1307* (London, 1974), 186.

considered as a work of 'local history', it cannot match the slightly later *Chronicle* of Jocelin of Brakelond with its marvellous portrait of the redoubtable Abbot Samson of Bury St Edmunds, which was to inspire Carlyle. But *The Peterborough Chronicle is* a local history in a period in which relatively little local history survives, and the fact that it does not share the aristocratic prejudices of some other chronicles enables it to present the sufferings of ordinary people with considerable sympathy—the final continuation particularly has a warmth of tone, and seems to be making use of personal knowledge. For the student of English literature, its interest is not simply that of an isolated and unique document.

The events from the Conquest to 1121 are recorded in the style of *The Anglo-Saxon Chronicle*, and in late Old English. The matter is exciting enough—the conquest itself, and the establishment of Norman authority against various enemies and dissidents. We hear of the incursions of Swein of Denmark, and later (1085) of the rumour that his son Cnut was planning to invade, and of the doings of Hereward and his band. But, it must be said, it is not the world of *Ivanhoe*: already in 1073 William is leading an army of English *and* French into Maine. Monastic troubles are recorded—the burning of the monastery at Peterborough (1070) through the carelessness and drunkenness of the monks, and the discord at Glastonbury (1083), where the abbot brought in a band of armed laymen. It is a period of violence, plot, and counterplot; devastations, exactions, plagues, famine, and portents (comets, two moons in the sky, etc.) abound. The years 1086–7 provoke the chronicler to an exclamation: 'Eala!' (alas!) he says, 'how wretched and how unhappy the times were then!' In his account of the Conqueror (d. 1087) he records 'both the good and the evil'—William was a man of wisdom and strength, but stern without measure to those who withstood his will. He includes a rather bitter poem about his fierce rule and exactions. The death in 1099 of William Rufus, portrayed as harsh, cruel, and an oppressor of the Church, is presaged by blood coming out of the ground.

In the account of the years 1122–31 we can see marked differences in the language. In a fine scene in the deer park at Woodstock, the King (Henry I) is riding with the bishop of Salisbury and the bishop of Lincoln. Suddenly the latter sinks down in his saddle, and the chronicler records (or invents) his words: 'Laferd kyng, ic swelte' (Lord king, I am dying). Here the first two words (= OE *hlaford cyning*) clearly indicate a change. Yet the old word for 'die' is still used (and we may note that the King's liegemen in Normandy are still called his 'theignas' and that 'durance vile' is imitated as 'on ifele bendas'). The many disasters that occurred in these years, violent winds, earthquakes, huge floods, failures of crops, murrain of cattle and pigs, the burning of the monastery at Gloucester (1121), and the deaths of great men are relentlessly recorded, so that the impression is for all the world like that of a modern television epitome of the year's news. Again, it is the plight of the poor and oppressed ('thet ærme folc') that excites sympathy. In 1124, 44 thieves were hanged, but, adds the chronicler, many true men said that many of them were executed unjustly. Our Lord, from whom no secrets are hidden, sees the poor deprived of their goods, and then slain. This was, the chronicler says, a 'full heavy year'—he who had any money was deprived of it by taxes and exactions, and he who had none died of hunger. Also, a strong 'local' interest begins to develop. The chronicle records the monks' indignation at the installation of Henry of Poitou as abbot (he was related to the King, and was already abbot of St Jean d'Angély). It was done *earmlice* (despicably); Henry was like a drone, and did nothing for the monastery but took all that he could. As soon as he arrived there was a significant portent—the Wild Hunt (cf. p. 140 above) was repeatedly seen in the deer park:

Tha huntes wæron swarte and micele and ladlice[1], and here[2] hundes ealle swarte and bradegede[3] and ladlice, and hi ridone[4] on swarte hors and on swarte bucces[5] . . .

[1] *the huntsmen were black and large and horrible*   [2] *their*   [3] *broad-eyed*
[4] *they rode*   [5] *goats*

and the monks could hear them sounding their horns all through the night. He was driven out finally by the nobles and the monks.

The chronicle of the years 1132–54 continues the standard form of a year by year account, but here the individual entries are often extended and give to the whole more of a sense of continuous narrative. Tribulations do not cease—any more than the schemings of the wicked ex-abbot. He tries to subject the monastery to Cluny, and, when he is thwarted, attempts to make his nephew abbot—'oc Crist it ne uuolde'—but Christ did not wish it. National events take a turn for the worse. The death of Henry I in 1135—a good man, and a king who 'made peace for man and beast' so that no one dared harm a traveller bearing gold and silver (something of a topos, but none the less a real test of a medieval king's rule)—ushers in a period of terrible anarchy. 'The traitors' (various noblemen and high ecclesiastics), realizing that King Stephen was a 'milde man', 'and softe and god', broke their oaths and perpetrated dreadful crimes. The chronicler gives us a famous description:

. . . ævric[1] rice[2] man his castles makede and agænes him heolden; and fylden the land ful of castles. Hi suencten suythe[3] the uurecce[4] men of the land mid castelweorces[5]; tha[6] the castles uuaren maked, tha fylden hi mid deovles[7] and yvele men. Tha namen hi tha men the[8] hi wenden[9] that ani god hefden, bathe be nihtes and be dæies, carlmen[10] and wimmen, and diden heom[11] in prisun and pined[12] heom efter[13] gold and sylver untellendlice pining[14]; for ne uuæren nævre nan martyrs swa[15] pined alse hi wæron. Me[16] henged up bi the fet and smoked heom mid ful smoke. Me henged bi the thumbes other[17] bi the hefed[18] and hengen bryniges[19] on her[20] fet. Me dide cnotted strenges abuton[21] here hæved[22] and uurythen[23] it that it gæde to the hærnes[24] . . .

[1] each	[2] powerful	[3] they afflicted greatly	[4] wretched
[5] building of castles	[6] when	[7] devils	[8] who	[9] thought
[10] men	[11] put them	[12] tortured	[13] in order to get	[14] with
unspeakable torture	[15] so	[16] one	[17] or	[18] head
[19] mail-coats	[20] their	[21] around	[22] head	[23] twisted
[24] entered the brains			

and continues thus in horrified fascination for a further ten lines before he brings it to a rhetorical conclusion: 'I ne can ne I ne mai tellen alle the wunder [atrocities] ne alle the pines that hi diden wrecce [unhappy] men on this land.' He describes the extraction of 'protection money', plundering and burning, robbing of church and churchyard—'every man robbed his neighbour . . . if two men or three came riding to a village all the inhabitants fled for fear of them, thinking that they were robbers'. He gives (at least, for the area he knows) a picture of total devastation:

War sæ me tilede[1], the erthe ne bar nan corn, for the land was al fordon[2] mid suilce[3] dædes. And hi sæden openlice that Crist slep[4] and his halechen[5].

[1] wherever one tilled	[2] ruined	[3] such	[4] slept	[5] saints

In the midst of all this, the abbey seems to have found in Abbot Martin a figure almost as powerful and successful as Jocelin's Samson. He 'provided everything necessary for the monks and the visitors', and carefully defended the revenues by tying the incomes to particular offices. He extended the church and had it roofed, and 'brought the monks with great ceremony into the new church on St Peter's day' (1137). Probably a whole historical novel lies hidden under the cryptic statement that he recovered monastery lands which 'great men held by force. . . From William Malduit, who held the castle of Rockingham, he won Cottingham and Easton [Maudit], and from Hugh of Waterville he won Irthlingborough and Stanwick, and rent of sixty shillings each year from Aldwinkle. . . .' The chronicle continues with the great and violent events of national history—the strife between the King and Ranulf, Earl of Chester, the escape of the Empress Matilda from Oxford castle, and many others. One may detect an increasingly sardonic tone—Eustace, the King's son, married the sister of the King of France, and 'thought to gain Normandy by this—but he prospered little, and rightly so too, for he was an evil man . . . she was a good woman, but she had little bliss with him'. This remarkable chronicle is brought to an abrupt close with a prayer for the new abbot William, who 'has made a good beginning'.

In early religious prose of the homiletic and didactic variety the connections with the pre-Conquest past are equally strong. Old English homilies (including those of Ælfric, which have sometimes been thought to influence later religious writing) were in fact being copied up to and during the twelfth century, the time at which the first collections of Early Middle English homilies begin to appear. These early collections—in MS Bodley 343, MS Lambeth 487, and MS Trinity College Cambridge B. 14. 52—are in general without much interest for the student of literature. The reader of *The Peterborough Chronicle* will notice an occasional reference to the world at large— No. x in the Trinity collection touches on the virtues of a good king, and remarks that if he neglects its precepts his land will suffer continually by war, famine, disease, tempests, and wild beasts ('ye on heryunge, ye on hungre, ye on cwalme, ye on uniwidere, ye on wilde deoran'). There is an occasional 'example' or similitude which stirs the interest. No. xxxi in the Trinity collection says there is a kind of adder 'ut in other londe' which has a precious gem on her head. Men therefore hunt it, but she has devised a remarkable way of protecting herself. She seeks out a stone and puts one ear to it, and stops up the other ear with her tail, so that she does not hear their speech or their song, and thus saves her life—so ought we to do against the devil. Life is often seen as a defensive war against the strength and the wiles of the devil. He (in Trinity No. xxxiii) is a hunter in the wilderness of the world, and sets snares for men who are his prey. Very few men are 'tamed' says the homilist; most share the wiles of wild animals and can therefore be properly compared to, say, a fox, a wolf, a bear, or a lion. And just as in the 'wilderne' the big animals oppress the little ones, so in the world of men, the rich oppress the poor. The devil's four snares are Play (with the snare of Idleness), Drink, Market (trickery, by both buyers and sellers), and Church (the snare of pride for both laity and clergy). The exposition of this last in detail becomes extraordinarily convoluted and unconvincing, a fault often found in these early homilies. By the thirteenth century traditional homiletic methods and language would no doubt have seemed outdated, especially to any preacher familiar with developments on the continent. By 1200 French prose had increased in variety and vigour and overtaken English. Chronicles and memoirs abounded. The four books of Kings had been rendered into splendid prose; and about 1170 a Parisian preacher, probably Bishop Maurice of Sully, had produced a collection of sixty-seven mass-homilies, the oldest original prose in French. It reflects the Victorine influences so powerful in the School of Paris in Maurice's time. Yet though predominantly patristic in its method of exegesis, it avoided the subtleties of the schools in favour of expositions and applications intelligible to the layman. Usually only the opening words of the Gospel for the day are cited in Latin—the rest is rendered in close paraphrase, preparing the way for the complete version of the Scriptures that was accessible a century later.

It is hardly surprising that the only English version of any of these sermons was made in Kent, open as that region was to continental influences. It *is* surprising that it was evidently not made till some fifty years after Maurice's death.* The English translator follows the French almost word for word, usually replacing French terms by English, though retaining (e.g.) *sergant* for 'steward' and admitting an occasional gallicism; the original cadences, said to echo the antiphonal quality of liturgical chant, do not, it need hardly be said, survive in translation. But the English versions retain the closing Latin (episcopal) benediction of the original. Most of them are brief, and simple in plan. The Gospel text is rendered carefully into the vernacular and the 'signefiance' follows at once. Typical is the homily on the Parable of the Vineyard, which was to be applied more poetically in *Pearl*. The good man is God, who sent forth first patriarchs, then prophets (Moses and Aaron), and finally his Son. The penny is the bliss of heaven, the vineyard, Christian faith, the hours of the day are the ages of the world, but also the ages of man. Only once does the English preacher expand on the French: in rendering Matt. 25:13 (cited towards the close of the sermon) he adds a popular native (and alliterative) proverb, found also in *Ancrene Wisse* and the *Ayenbite*: 'Man mai longe lives wene [expect], and ofte him legheth se wrench [the trick deceives him]'. Already we can see the workmanlike quality of the prose sermon, a characteristic of very many examples from the following centuries. The aim is to instruct and to edify, and the characteristic style is one of unaffected plainness and simplicity, with (as Robert South was later to say) 'no affected scheme, or airy fancies, above the reach or relish of an ordinary apprehension'.

The conception of life, the feelings displayed and appealed to in the early thirteenth-century *Ancrene Wisse* are so foreign to the modern

* The unique manuscript of these Sermons also contains Anglo-Norman versions of others in the French collection, possibly made by the same English translator, for a different congregation.

European world— in which all Churches have embraced an activist form of religion, leaving contemplation largely to Zen Buddhists—that it is now necessary to insist on the centrality in the Christian tradition of the devotional and ascetic practices that the work describes. It is not a quaint, local, obscurantist piety that is here displayed, but rather a distinctively English manifestation of a spirituality that had its prime source in that great and commanding figure of the twelfth century, St Bernard of Clairvaux—though it is Peter the Venerable, Abbot of Cluny, whom the compiler more closely resembles in his tone and outlook. Bernard's great series of Sermons on the Canticles popularized the 'mystical' reading of that book, which is constantly cited in the English work. His courtly similitudes likewise find a likeness there.

The English writer's description of such characters as the back-biter, 'who casts down his head, sighs, and talks round his subject for a long time with a woeful countenance, the better to be believed, and then says "Alas that so-and-so has fallen into disrepute. I did my best . . . but now, it's so well known that I can't gainsay it" '—this passage, anticipating the vivid 'characters' of the seventeenth century, has been singled out as showing his 'astonishing power'. In fact such passages often follow closely St Bernard or other spiritual writers. For Bernard's asceticism did not prevent him from employing all the resources of rhetoric with its elaborate figures and questions which the English writer will likewise adopt, as, for instance, in the aposiopesis and rhetorical question: 'Yef thi luve nis nawt to yeovene, ah wult thet me bugge hire—buggen hire hu?' (If thy love is not to be given, but you wish it to be bought—how should one buy it?) That the English master's deployment of such devices is deliberate is clear from his use of the terms 'hypallage' and 'antonomastice'; whilst the very organization of the work into *distinctiones* is proof of some scholarly expertise—even if the warmth of his feeling sometimes blurs the steps of his argument. To say that he presents 'at once the finest academic and worldly culture' is to make too high a claim; yet certainly there is a pervading sense of good breeding, an absence of the pedagogic, a kindly spirit. He identifies himself with those whom he instructs: 'Nu me thuncheth [it seems to me] *we* beoth icumen in to the seovethe dale [part].'

Everywhere a saving sanity and discretion shows through. 'Best is ever mete' (moderation is best). It was the axiom of Abbot Serlo of Gloucester, cited by William of Malmesbury* when describing the

* *De Gestis Pontificum Anglorum*, ed. N. E. S. A. Hamilton (RS 52, 1870), 293.

considerate rule (*religionis discretio*) practised in that abbey, 'which the weak may embrace and the strong not despise'. This Master repeats it: 'Wisdom and measure are the measure and nurse of all good practices.' But, he goes on, true wisdom is to put health of the soul before bodily health and to choose bodily hurt first. The doctrine is that of a Latin epistle sent by Ailred of Rievaulx about 1160 to his recluse-sister; and Ailred may be accounted amongst our Master's closest English precursors. Anselm's *Similitudines* are as miniature allegories similar to *Ancrene Wisse*'s 'forbisne'. The Carthusian *Consuetudines* of Guigo also offer some parallels, e.g. in their prescription about sleeping in belted garments and in their instancing of the Virgin Mary as an exemplar of the solitary life. In matter, even in style, there is in fact little that is new in the *Wisse*. It is the dominant tone that gives the work its lasting appeal.

It suits the purpose of the anchoresses' master and counsellor to see the *sponsa* of the Canticles ('that sweet book of love') as 'the clean soul': cleanness implying not only physical chastity but that 'schirnesse [purity] of heorte' which is 'al the strengthe of all religiuns [religious professions], the end of alle ordres'. And since the Canticles were read as a sequence of invocations to the Beloved, he presents Christ as appealing to the soul in the same terms, if enriched with rhetoric: 'Nam ich thinge feherest [am I not the fairest of all things], nam ich kinge richest, nam ich hest icunnet [of noblest kin], nam ich weolie wisest [wisest of rich men], nam ich monne hendest [most gracious of men], nam ich thinge freoest [most generous]. . . . Nam ich alre thinge swotest and swetest?' (pp. 202–3).* Christ's love surpasses all the chief kinds of love that are found on earth. *Amor vincit omnia*. However Chaucer's pilgrims read the Prioress's inscription, for the true recluse it denoted the love of Christ the wooer of the soul. Compared with this discovery of the sweetness, the demandingness, of Christian love, the invention of 'amour courtois' was a mere incident in literary history: for the love that Bernard preached soon issued in the humanizing of the Blessed Virgin, the poignant presentations of the Crucifixion, which mark a revolution in European sensibility, and one not confined to the courtly classes. Yet the appeal is by no means solely to the emotions. The twelfth century had given logic, reason, dialectic a place in Christian thought that they were not to lose. So in the *Ancrene Wisse* Christ will say: 'thus alle the reisuns hwi me ah to yeove [one ought to give] luve thu maht ifinden in me' (203). The term *reason* itself

---

* Page references are to the edition of J. R. R. Tolkien (EETS ccxlix, 1962).

(like *prove* in its modern sense) first appears in English form in the *Wisse*, where it is in constant use.

It is evident that the anchoresses addressed were literate. They must have known at least the Latin of their liturgical prayers; whether they could construe the classical and later Latin that is sometimes left untranslated is another matter. They can copy Latin Hours and orisons. The writer finds it necessary to gloss some technical terms by their vernacular equivalents: e.g. 'distinctiuns that ye cleopieth [call] *dalen* [parts]'. They sometimes are to pray in their 'own tongue'. Everything suggests that they were of good birth, and educated in one of the convents that were the finishing schools of the day. The social pattern appealed to is that of the castle, not that of the cottage. The anchoress is 'leafdi of heovene' and the solitary life is that of *noblesse*; nobles and gentles don't carry packs and purses—that is what burgesses do. But they give largesse as an anchoress gives her prayers. Several notable *exempla* are drawn from knightly practice. They imply an acquaintance with the practice of *deboneirté* and with such customs as the hanging of a dead knight's escutcheon in church; one of them presents a vivid picture of a knight who has won the field ('place') strutting about in it. Yet in the thirteenth century, castle and manor were very much part of rural life and these gentle ladies are not too squeamish, to be shocked by plain speaking. They have seen the cock crowing on his dung-hill, the cook roasting meat in his kitchen.

The rules that the writer expounds have been thought to reflect the reduction of spiritual life to a regular art that was in vogue at Paris in the late twelfth century. Of the eight *distinctiones*, or 'dalen', the first (a collection of devotions to be regularly recited*) and the last (concerned with their domestic arrangements, clothing, hygiene, servants) treat of the 'Outer Rule': it is merely the frame for the Inner Rule, which is concerned with spiritual welfare, treating, in order, the Senses, the Heart (or emotions), Temptations (again inner and outer, meditations on the Passion being the chief safeguard), Confession, Penance, Love. A brief analysis of the section on Confession (Shrift), which though daunting in its divisions and subdivisions is enlivened by a series of images with a specifically English tone, may serve to indicate the character of the work as a whole.

* The only hint of mystical experience comes in a passage on the mass: 'Efter the messe-cos [kiss] hwen the preost sacreth [communicates], ther foryeoteth [forget] al the world, ther beoth al ut of bodi, ther i sperclinde [burning] luve bicluppeth ower leofmon [embrace your beloved]' (21); though the ideal that is set forth—'Your will and God's will be so united that you shall will all that He wills, and he all that you will'—is assuredly the condition of the true mystic.

Shrift is the standard-bearer in God's army. Reason sits as Dooms-man; but it is not in God's court as in the shire court, where a clever man can escape punishment. The *exempla* are equally effective: a widow when cleaning house sprinkles water to lay the dust; another woman lends a fine dress for a wake. Again it is ordinary domestic life that comes before our eyes, not the anchor–hold. And again there is a surprising emphasis on sexual sins, which in confession are not to be cloaked in veiled language: 'Biclute thu hit nawt' (don't wrap it up); 'Do awei the totagges' (tear off the trimmings)—strong phrases that show the Master exemplifying his own precepts. They must not be mealy-mouthed, but confess: 'I'm a foul stud mare, a stinking whore. I sinned with a priest, a cleric: or with a woman.' Has the Master here forgotten whom he is addressing? An anchoress who has to confess 'I joined in the ring dance in the churchyard, I watched the wrestling' cannot have had her heart in the right place. But she can hardly have had opportunity for more than dalliance. Ironically, the Master at this point cites Ovid's *Remedia Amoris* (l. 91), probably being ignorant of its source or its context.

And so we pass to penance. Life itself is a penance, a pilgrimage, a crucifixion. Here he adapts a sermon of St Bernard's, and a cognate text, the *Declamationes*,* and introduces a whole volley of rhetorical questions. Is not Christ our head, are we not his members? If the head sweats but not the members, is it not a bad sign? When the Devil sees one at ease he knows that the Castle of the Soul is his and that he can enter and set up his banners (precisely as he will do in Bunyan's Man-soul). Following Isaiah, the Master presents Christ as chastised by God, intervening between him and us as a mother puts herself between an angry father and his child. As he addresses himself to 'leoue mon and wummon' we pass beyond the anchorhold, and his 'essample' is of a man who when away from home is happier to know that his wife pines for him than that she 'gleowde and gomnede' (was having a jolly time). At this point comes in material from the recluse Ailred of Rievaulx, into which he inserts another *exemplum*, the story of the fastidious monk. An allusion to 'Measure' (moderation) prompts—by a scriptural linkage of *measure* and *weight*—a digression to Nicodemus's *measure* of bitter spices and so to the Three Maries, whose name bespeaks bitterness. The tomb they sought, prefigured in Mary's womb and Christ's narrow *cader* (a Welsh term for cradle), betokens the anchoress's narrow cell. The anchoresses need not worry if they are abused. The (Dominical) 'Lovest thou me?' is the key

* *Declamationes de Colloquio Simonis cum Jesu* (*PL* clxxxiv), often attributed to Geoffrey of Auxerre, a disciple of St Bernard.

question. If they do so love, they must show it—as does a man who wears a hair shirt and iron shirt of mail (though elsewhere they are warned against such rigours).

Purifying love is the whole theme of Part vii. Christ is depicted as a Lover-king, wooing the poor though noble soul, first by the sealed letters of the Old Testament, then by the letters patent of the New, written in his own blood. In an ampler *exemplum* that follows (modelled on the parable of Matt. 21: 37, etc.) the King sends first messengers, then an army, and at length comes himself. Neither his 'meistries' (feats) nor his beauty soften man's soul till he fights and dies as its champion, his shield pierced through. 'Could Christ have delivered us with less pain?' Yes, but 'one buys cheaply what one loves little'. The tenderness of this passage is matched only in Henryson's *Bludy Serk* but here the allegory goes further: the shield is of leather (Christ's body) and wood (the Cross), and painted with a coat of arms (Christ's blood).

There are Four Loves: love between friends, between man and woman, woman and child, body and soul. Slightly different divisions can be found in the twelfth century; and strikingly similar ones in Alexander of Bath's *Moralia*. The marks on Christ's pierced hands are like so many knots tied in a belt as a reminder of a love that excelled all others.

Christ's appeal to the soul is expressed in a long series of rhetorical questions that breaks off in an aposiopesis, to resume in a pledge: 'Wult tu castles, kinedomes, wult tu wealden [rule] al the world? Ich chulle [I will] do the bettere—makie the withal this cwen of heoveriche [heaven].' The passage grows a shade too rhetorical: this Christ compares himself to Caesar or Alexander and labels those who reject him the devil's whores; his burning love is likened to Greek fire 'made from the blood of a red man'.

In the end is the beginning. To say that evil men set not their heart aright is to say *Recti diligunt te*—the just shall love thee. The conclusion constitutes a hymn to the love of Christ, yet it is built up out of learned allegory, Augustinian and Victorine commonplaces, biblical glosses and alliterative wordplay—'Chearité is cherté [holding dear] of leof thing and of deore. Undeore he maketh Godd . . . that for ei [any] worltlich thing of his luve leasketh [forgoes his love].' The mellifluousness of these passages recalls St Bernard, *doctor mellifluus*, who was their ultimate inspiration.

Everywhere the writer's thought can be seen advancing by purely verbal rather than logical nexus. The man who misjudges one is a *file* ('or *lime* as the French say'). That term is enough to suggest the notion of the metal that is filed; metals include gold and silver; gold and silver suggest first cleansing fire, and then the hammering and beating that make them into such vessels as the chalice. The passage includes a submerged allusion to the text, 'Does the pot say to the potter, Why hast thou made me thus?', but then it breaks into an astonishing image of the world as God's smithy, with its fires, its bellows, its hammers. Imagery of a different sort pictures the hell-hound that comes 'snakerinde' (snuffling). Then the figure changes again. The Devil is bargaining for the soul that Christ bought: you must not let it become the Devil's whore: the sign of the Trinity, made by lifting three fingers, will save it. It is the materiality of such images—like that of later Emblems—that gives them power.

The last Part (viii), on The Outer Rule, divided into 'seven little sections', is for many readers the most attractive, being concerned primarily with daily living. It is a series of injunctions showing that the Master knew exactly how his 'dear sisters' conducted themselves—he can say 'Your meat and drink have often seemed to be less than I should wish'—though at the same time he warns them against lavish entertainment—for they have chosen Mary's part—and against dispensing largesse. He is rich in reasonableness and saving common sense, never niggling over details. They are not to trouble about their dress so long as it is plain and well-made. In summer they can go barefoot and wear softer garments. They must not inflict undue corporal penances on themselves without leave: 'Me is leovere [I would prefer] thet ye tholien [suffer] wel an heard word then an heard here [hair shirt].' Bloodletting and haircutting are left to their discretion but they must recall that 'Dirt is never dear to God'. They are not to fuss about their wimples—'some anchoresses sin in their style of wearing a wimple no less than ladies in the world'. They are to make and mend church vestments and poor folks' clothes, not coifs or purses. Such tasks will help to support them, and keep them out of the Devil's clutches—he'll think: 'No point in my trying to get at her if she's occupied.' But they must not chaffer: 'Ancre thet is chepilt . . . chepeth hire saule the chapman of helle'—an anchoress who is a businesswoman sells her soul to the merchant of hell. They must never degenerate into school teachers, yet should instruct, and if need be chastise their maids—pouring more soft oil than biting wine—a figure that might serve for his own practice. They may keep a cat, but not a cow: a cow will stray, and get impounded and the hayward will have to be flattered to get it out—a picture that is confirmed by the Harley lyric of the Man in the Moon (see above, pp. 21–2). They mustn't let people use the anchorhold as safe deposit for deeds or bonds or treasure in times of unrest.

Finally, they are to read from this Rule every day when they have leisure: he has given much time to it and would sooner set out for Rome than begin it all over again. In this part, in fact, he has covered the ground of the whole of St Benedict's Rule, though of course the scope of that was necessarily wider. It is surely likely that the writer knew the older Rule: one authority remarks that the figure of the ladder in Part vi is 'one of the very few reminiscences'.* But the very differences in some details may point to some adaptation of St Benedict: for instance, *Ancrene Wisse* says that the anchoresses are to sleep in a gown belted at the waist; the Benedictine Rule (ch. 22) says that monks are to sleep clothed and girt with girdles or cords; chapter 54 says the monk should not receive gifts without permission, whereas *Ancrene Wisse* says that the anchoress can accept things from good people. Steadfastness, stability, emphasized at the outset of *Ancrene Wisse*, is laid down in chapter 58 of the Benedictine Rule as one of the vows that a monk must take. There is the same emphasis on measure, moderation, and silence. We note too that the Benedictine Rule is called *magistra regula*—the lady rule, as in the *Ancrene Wisse*.

But the Benedictine Rule is but one of the many 'sources', some identified, some perhaps now unidentifiable (such as manuals for confessors), that the writer may have consulted when composing the 'Outer' Rule. His closing reference to the labour of composition must be taken seriously. He was compiling a document for use in a comparatively new context, and has to make his own balance between spiritual and disciplinary elements—much as Abelard had to do (*mutatis mutandis*) in writing his directions to Eloise. The *Ancrene Wisse* is not so much a compilation as an orchestration and if we read it intently we catch a persistent yet unobtrusive theme: 'the swete and swote heorte'—*dulcis et suavis*.

Critics who judge prose by its wealth of poetic imagery have sometimes overvalued the *Ancrene Wisse*. Its imagery is indeed varied and unusual. But much of it depends ultimately on the mode of exegesis long before established by St Gregory's *Moralia in Job*, a work popular in the twelfth century, and providing a model for the *Moralia Super Evangelia* now ascribed to Alexander of Bath, which has much in common with the *Wisse*. More typical than the chivalric image of Christ as the lover-knight is a passage on the remedy for the capital sin of lechery. Like Jacob in Genesis, the soul cries: 'Ah, Lord, heal me, for I am wounded: Reuben [= bloody thought], grow thou not.' This prayer, typically, suggests another: 'Deliver my soul from the sword;

* *Ancrene Wisse*, ed. G. Shepherd, Parts Six and Seven (London and Edinburgh, 1959), 34.

my darling from the power of the dog' (Ps. 21). The dog is the Devil, sneaking up, loaded with bloody flies of stinking thoughts. It is not enough to shoo him out, you must beat him with your crucifix, that is, pray with the Cross before your eyes, hide in Christ's wounds. Every sin, in fact, is related to the Passion: the anchoress who lets out an angry word is reminded that Our Lord allowed the Jews to shut his mouth with their fists.

The writer's cast of mind is essentially metaphorical, and his book is built on a metaphor chosen to appeal to anchoresses attended by servants: the Inner (Spiritual) Rule is the Lady, the Outer, concerned with daily life, is her handmaid ('thuften'). The rich symbolism ('bitac-nung') of the Canticles is adapted at every turn. If the anchoress hangs black cloth at her window it is because she is *nigra sed formosa*, scorched by the Sun of Grace. Even a plain and practical verse from St James will be interpreted *mystice*, with help from Canticles: 'To comfort the widows and the fatherless' is to comfort the widowed soul that has lost her spouse.

Many of the stylistic features of the *Wisse*, scriptural and Patristic as they are, can be found in contemporary sermons, and the structure of the work resembles at some points that of a homily. Like a sermon, it begins with a text (*Recti te diligunt*; Song of Songs 1: 3—the emphasis is to be on *recti*—those who love a *rule*), and like a sermon it opens and closes with the invocatory trinitarian formulas. The numerical division of the text is a preacher's mnemonic device, like the use of summarizing sentences and of *exempla* employed in the way that Jacques de Vitry had popularized: the English form *essample* is first found in this text. Some of these (e.g. the tale of a prisoner ransomed by the gift of a purse) are drawn from town life, others, like that of the lover-knight, carry the aura of romance: this parable with hidden meaning ('wrihe forbisne') being set firmly in the past—'as knights were in former days accustomed to do' ('as weren sumhwile cnihtes iwunet to donne'), though since it allegorizes man's redemption it is explored in every detail. And like a sermon the work was designed in the first instance to be read aloud (cf. e.g. 'as ye mahen *iheren*' (as you may hear) (p. 9)): hence the conversational tone, varying as it does according to the nature of the topic. Yet it is the nature of a Rule that it should be written down, and we never lose the sense of a book that the sisters could consult: the Master several times remarks that he has 'treated this above'.

If the rhetoric owes much to the *artes predicandi*, it owes even more to the Scriptures from which come the texts that form its warp and woof. It was the Gospels that provided the first and highest model for instruction, precedents for appeals to ordinary experience by parables and proverbial phrase ('siheth [sees] the gneat and swolheth [swallows] the flehe'); other parts of Scripture displayed the parallelism, antitheses, repetition of words and forms, that are likewise features of the style. What is novel is the extension of the use of alliterative patterns of phrase as formerly practised by Ælfric and Wulfstan. The West Midland writers of Saints' Lives and of *Sawles Warde* employ these patterns much as the Saxon sermon had done. But here we find new combinations developing—of balanced word groups, of rhyming elements ('eithurles beon ihoten eil thurles' (eye windows are called troublesome windows)). Alliteration may be extended ('for scheome slummi, sloggi and slaw' (p. 132)). Elsewhere the prose falls into parallel and antithetical structures (cf. 'Nam ich thinge feherest', etc., cited above).

In counterpoint to the patterning of such phrases is the deft colloquial dialogue that preserves the discourse from dullness. An imagined interlocutor is always breaking in—as when the three degrees of patience are being expounded. Some foolish creature interrupts: 'Oh, no, I would never complain if I had really deserved it.' 'So you would sooner be with Judas than with Jesus?' The inference seems unfair, but the dramatic effect is undoubted. Or again: 'My dear Master,' some one may say, 'is it so very bad, just to peep out?' 'Yes it is, for evil always comes of it.' 'But sir, someone better than I does.' 'You should follow the wise in their wisdom, not in their folly. If anyone had said to Eve, "Turn away", she should have answered, "Dear heart, what are you accusing me of?" ' Sometimes in the imagined scene only one voice is heard: 'Don't worry, my dear man, you are not the only one. . . .' The Master's own words to the sisters allow a colloquial ellipsis, and abound in phrases that carry a colloquial ring, and in echoic dialectal verbs such as 'gnudden' (rub) and 'glucchen' (gulp).

Thus, paradoxically, it is a work designed for the solitary anchorhold that first gives us the sense of casual talk at the street corner or the ingle-nook. There is even a snatch of popular song—'Eaver is the ehe to the wude lehe' (the eye is ever on the wood's glade) (p. 52). Images and proverbial phrases of secular life are constantly employed. The maidens are to follow Our Lady, not cackling Eve, nor be like the hen who cackles when she lays an egg, which a chough forthwith bears off: the chough being the Devil as he is elsewhere a hell-cat. The Devil has his 'privy men', who cover the hole in the privy, his 'eskibah' or cinder-jack who pudders in the cinders, blinding himself with ash as he writes his reckonings in them, his juggler, his manciple, whose heart is in pots, his life in the tun, and who comes before his lord 'bismuddet and bismulret'. The slothful man sleeps on the Devil's breast as his dear darling and the Devil 'leith his tutel [snout] dun to his eare ond tuteleth him al thet he wule'—one of numerous images that is expressed in terms of purely local currency, though the image itself is probably traditional: the Devil in the *Visio Tundali* has a long snout, and Titivillus, his messenger in *Mankind*, says, 'I shall go to his ear and titill therein' (similarly, the figure of devils who 'dustin' (thwack) the wrathful, 'ase a pilcheclut [like a piece of old fur] euch towart other' reappears in James Hogg's *Confessions of a Justified Sinner*: 'that's the man Auld Simmie [the Devil] fixes on to mak a dishclout o' '). This series of lurid vignettes is equalled only in Dunbar's *Dance of the Seven Deadly Sins*, where the very same figures reappear in the same guise.

Never does he speak more plainly than when warning against lechery, the sin that one would have thought least tempting to such dedicated sisters (and that Langland was to dismiss in a few lines). But in general the writer dwells on the remedies for temptations liable to beset them daily. He sees the Devil much as a later spiritual adviser was to depict him in *The Screwtape Letters*: one who 'sent [sends] mon other wummon the telle the an bi [about] the other sum suhinde sahe [painful story] thet suster schulde nat segge [say] bi suster'. Yet they will not be tempted beyond endurance. The Lord but hides himself in play, as a mother hides from her darling child, letting him look for her and cry 'dame, dame', till with outstretched arms she leaps forth laughing, embraces him, kisses him, and wipes his eyes: a far tenderer picture than that of Donne's *Deus absconditus* who disguises his face in clouds of anger. A similar image brings home the shadowiness of our knowledge of heaven and hell: we should not shrink from shadows as a horse shies from such shapes when crossing a bridge and so falls into the stream—or as children flee from a 'grisly' picture.

In singling out the immediately attractive features of the Master's style and thought we run the risk of ignoring his essentially medieval mentality, the product of a lifelong study of Scripture and patristic exegesis. Often Scripture is, so to speak, bestiarized before our eyes. Thus in Part iii, dealing with the Inward Senses, the traditional *significacio* of the pelican in the wilderness is linked with the dominical utterance about birds with nests and foxes with holes (Matt. 8: 20): the acquisitive anchoress is like the fox that boasts its virtues yet seizes geese and hens. The word 'foveas' (holes) suggests—doubtless thanks to some biblical concordance—the cave of David (1 Sam. 22 ff.); whilst 'nidi' (nests) prompts a comparison of the anchoresses who spread their wings 'cross-wise', but must needs sometimes seek their nests:

Job says *in nidulo meo moriar*. The *nocticorax* (night raven) of Ps. 101: 7 symbolizes the recluses who live under the eaves of the church, its *anchors*, who hold it firm by their prayers (a false etymology, but no worse than many of St Thomas's). 'Night' in turn suggests the anchoress's watchfulness, solitariness, secrecy. Of solitariness the supreme exemplars are in the Old Testament: Isaac, Moses, Elias; in the New Testament, John the Baptist, Our Lady and Our Lord, and their followers Benedict, Jerome, and the Desert Fathers, who fled the world. Eight reasons are now given why one should flee the world, and set forth with a variety of rhetorical devices and 'forbisnen'. One reason, curiously argued, is to show *noblesse* and *largesse*, another to ensure that prayers are 'quick'. The etymologies of scriptural names, Esther, Semei, Jerusalem, are allegorized; Jerusalem (usually *Visio Pacis*) being here also interpreted as 'chirche grith' (sanctuary): 'For who of you has not at some time stolen from God and so stands in dread of the gallows of hell?'

And in fact the lively imagery and the esoteric or strained exegesis are closely linked. The bestiarizing of Scripture is paralleled in the bestiarizing of the capital sins. Pride the Lion, Envy the Leopard, Wrath the Unicorn, Covetousness the Fox, Gluttony the Sow, Lechery the Scorpion—all these can be found elsewhere in pictorial form. But the Master gives them offspring that enable him to accommodate every aspect of the moral life within his scheme; incidentally providing memorable glimpses of anchoresses' foibles and fancies: their liking for the Best People, their proneness to take offence without cause—'Look at them sitting over there and talking me over'— their fondness for pleating their veils or plucking their eyebrows, their liability to superstitious trust in charms, dreams, and sneezes.

To a modern reader the assumptions, the exegesis, the connections will all seem forced, even bizarre. They must not obscure the writer's insistence throughout on the things that matter. 'The Lord had rather you do good to them that hate you than eat coarse bread or wear coarse haircloth.' 'Someone may say, "I'll love her soul willingly enough, her body in no wise." But soul and body make one person. What God has joined together let no man put asunder.' This ascetic is no Manichaean.

Of the 'Katherine Group'—a number of texts, found in MS Bodley 34 and elsewhere, that share linguistic and stylistic features with *Ancrene Wisse*—*Sawles Warde* is the most notable, though like its congeners it is closely dependent on a Latin original. The *De Custodia interioris hominis* was frequently ascribed to St Anselm and bears some of the marks of his style. We have already noted that Anselm's *De* *humanis moribus per similitudines* at some points anticipates *Ancrene Wisse*: it abounds in small-scale similitudes drawn from contemporary life: comparing (e.g.) the human heart to a mill the owner of which puts a servant in charge, bidding him grind only wheat, oats, and barley—and live off what he grinds; instead, the servant grinds either sand, which damages the works, or gum ('picem'), or chaff, from which no sustenance can be drawn.* Similarly the *De Custodia* allegorizes the body as the habitation of the soul, setting a pattern to be followed by St Bonaventura, by the author of the *Somme le Roi*—and by John Bunyan. The appearance of Prudence, Measure, Spiritual Strength, and Righteousness as four daughters of God who defend this habitation also adumbrates later allegories.

From the time of Prudentius, allegory had been a method of Christian teaching 'in defence of the Faith'. But in the twelfth century it became a means of expressing what was otherwise inexpressible, including (in the *Anticlaudianus* of Alan of Lille) the mystical experience of the vision of God. The *De Custodia* illustrates both functions, the first part being moral and didactic, the second mystical. The Latin text indeed has an importance that transcends its literary merit. It is a harbinger of a new mode, that was ultimately to affect secular as well as religious writing: there would have been no Allegory of Love had it not been for this earlier love of allegory.

It so happens that the allegory of the body as the habitation of the soul (*anima*), which is first developed in *De Custodia*, became immediately popular, to some degree replacing the earlier Macrobian conception of the body as a prison-house: it is present, for example, in St Bonaventura's *Itinerarium mentis in Deum*, in which *Anima* is a microcosm entered through the gates of the five senses; and Langland will make Anima a maiden in the care of Dowel in the castle of Caro (flesh), with the knight Inwit as keeper of the watch (*Piers Plowman*, B ix). In the very first chapter of that favourite medieval story-book, the *Gesta Romanorum*, the daughter of the wise and powerful king Pompey is committed to the custody of five soldiers, to wit the five senses, whose task it is to preserve the soul from the world, the flesh and the devil. In Hilton's *Scale of Perfection* (pp. 317–8 below), as in *Ancrene Wisse*, the text *Mors penetrat per fenestras nostras* (cf. Jer. 9: 21) is read as referring to the five senses 'by which the soul goes out and seeks pleasure'.

In tone and pattern the English version of the *Custodia* is more markedly homiletic than the Anselmian text. It ends with the Trini-

---

* R. W. Southern and F. S. Schmitt (edd.), *Memorials of St Anselm* (London, 1969), 53–4.

tarian formula that was mandatory in sermons, and begins with a text (Matt. 24: 43, corresponding to Luke 12: 39 in the Latin) that itself provides dominical warrant for the allegory: 'si sciret paterfamilias qua hora fur venturus esset, vigilaret utique et non sineret perfodi domum suum'.* The master of this house is Man's Wit (*animus rationalis*), to whom the English writer gives a wife, Will. He makes her a wilful housewife, much as Anselm in one of his similitudes makes Selfwill a queen joined adulterously to the Devil. He is concerned with 'wernches' (wiles) of the Devil rather than with the custody of the inner man. The house in the Latin is *conscientia*—the mind of man rather than 'the man himself', as the English has it; to *Will* are given the senses as servants and we soon hear of their 'murth and untohe bere' (unruly clamour)—a phrase of distinctly local flavour characterizing their noisiness. The Devil's followers become 'keis' (catchpolls), another local term, of Welsh origin.

It is a common homiletic practice (favoured by St Bernard) that this writer is following when he asks: 'Who are the servants of Wit?', the answer being: 'some [the five senses] serve outside, others within'. He envisages Wit as the constable of a Marcher castle (to whom Our Lord lends his four daughters), and makes Warschipe (Prudentia) the 'durewart' (porter) who keeps watch for approaching strangers; he glosses Meath (Temperance) with the alliterating French synonym 'measure'. The gruesome description of the messenger Fearlac (= Memoria Mortis) is new: 'lonc ant leane ant his leor [face] deathlich ant blac [pale] ant elheowet [of unearthly colour]'. The English transfers from *oratio obliqua* his opening words: 'Ne mei ich nowher speoken bute Ich habbe god lust. Lustnith me thenne. . . .' Amongst the new touches are the 'swarte smeale leattres' in which sins are written in the great book—as if the script had to be cramped to keep them on the page. The long set piece of *descriptio loci*—the account of hell—expands fifteen lines of Latin into 60 lines of English outdoing similar passages in *St Marherete* and the twelfth-century Homilies. It omits the feature of *ordo nullus* and the scriptural *fletus et stridor dentium*, but adds the palpable darkness of Exodus ('thosternesse thet me hire mei grapin' (darkness which one can touch)), and a dozen grim and grisly details. They are doubtless not wholly novel because such accounts figure in earlier texts, like the *Visio Pauli* and *Visio Tundali* (they will reach their apogee in *Portrait of the Artist as a Young Man*). Perhaps the Virgilian allusion to the thousand tongues of steel (*Aen.* vi. 625–7) was also part of common stock: it appears in the *Visio*

* 'If the good man of the house had known in what watch the thief would come, he would have watched, and would not have suffered his house to be broken up' (AV).

Tundali and in a later English sermon. A passage immediately following appears to derive from a *Visio Monachi de Eynsham*, set down in 1196
(so that *Sawles Warde* can hardly have been completed before 1200).
The climax comes in a powerful asyndetic alliterative apostrophe:

O helle, Deathes hus, wununge of wanunge, of grure ant of granunge, heatel
ham ant heard wan of ealle wontreathes, buri of bale ant bold of eavereuch bit-
ternesse, thu lathest lont of alle. . . .

(O Hell, Death's house, dwelling of lamentation, of terror and of groaning,
cruel home and bitter haunt of all sorrows, habitation of misery, and hall of
every bitterness, thou most loathsome land of all. . . .)

The dialogue between the Virtues that follows drops some of the
scriptural allusions in the Latin but introduces others such as Ps.
115: 15, which appears also in *St Juliene*, and James 4: 7 (cited in
Ancrene Wisse), which gives 'Etstont then feont [withstand the devil]
ant he flith ananriht'; the devil of 1 Peter 5: 8 becomes an 'iburst'
(bristling, raging) lion. 'Meath' is given a major role, with an emphasis
accordant with the emphasis on the mean found in *Ancrene Wisse*. The
account of the heavenly bliss given by the harbinger of Joy ('Murthes
sonde') adds or subtracts various details and scriptural allusions (e.g.
martyrs who 'lihtliche talden to [accounted] alles cunnes neowcins
[hardships]': cf. Rom. 8: 18). The penchant for alliterative patterns
shows in 'yarowe [ready] for to demen i the dei of dome kinges and
keiseres [emperors] ant alle cunreadnes [kindreds] of alles cunnes
ledenes [nations]'. A typical change from the Latin to the English is
the treatment of *Amor vitae eternae*, the messenger who in the Latin is
simply described as 'pulcher et hilaris'; this cheerful aspect is
emphasized repeatedly in the English—'swithe glead-icheret [happy-
looking], *feier ant freolich* [handsome] *ant leofliche aturnet* [beautifully
arrayed]'; his entry is dwelt on dramatically yet domestically:

Warshipe let him in, ant he gret Wit then laverd, ant al thet hird seothen with
lahhinde chere, ant ye yeldeth him his gretunge ant beoth alle ilihtet ant igleadet
ham thuncheth of his onsihthe, for al thet hus schineth ant schimmeth of his
leome

(Prudence lets him in, and he greets Reason the lord and all that household with
laughing expression, and he returns his greeting and all are lightened in spirit
and gladdened, it seems to them, by the sight of him, for all that house shines and
gleams with his brightness)

—this last being almost a 'romance' touch—though perhaps dependent only on images from the last chapters of Revelation (21: 23—the
glory of the Lord God did lighten it, and the Lamb is the light thereof).
Again, it is the English writer, with his strong sense of light and

dark, who, speaking of the vision of God, says that 'ayein the briht-
nesse ant te liht of his leor [face], the sunne-gleam is dosc ant
thuncheth [seems] a schadewe'; and who makes of *per speculum et in
aenigmate* (1 Cor. 13: 12) 'a *schene* schawere' (bright mirror) (omitting
the 'in aenigmate'). Later the Latin, again following Scripture, speaks
of Christ on whom the angels desire to look—*desiderant angeli pros-
picere*: the English has 'te engles ne beon neaver ful on him to
bihalden'—and makes Christ show his wounds to the Father 'to
cuthen [make known] hu he luvede us ant hu he wes buhsum [obe-
dient] to him the [who] sende him swa to alesen [deliver] us, ant
bischeth him a [ever] for moncunnes heale [salvation]'.

The devotion to the Virgin Mary that is so characteristic of the
twelfth century is reflected in the place the Latin gives to Mary—'in
throno mirabili sedentem': one might compare the passage in her
praise at the end of Book Five of the *Anticlaudianus*, the most influential allegorical poem of the twelfth century; but I do not know of any
source for the English account of her throne 'se swithe briht with
yimmes istirret [studded with gems], ant hire wlite [splendour] se
weoleful [glorious] that euch eorthlich liht is theoster [dark] ther-
ayeines'. In describing the beatific vision, the English writer specifies
that there are *nine* orders of angels and characteristically adds that to
describe them all 'were long to tellen'. In the Latin the apostles are
'prepared to judge all tribes and tongues': the English specifies that
they will in particular judge 'i the dei of dome kinges ant keiseres'. The
English enlargement of the section regarding the virgins is noteworthy
in view of the connection of *Sawles Warde* with the *Hali Meithhad*
group. The English emphasizes that they 'overgath [overcome]
flesches lahe [uses] ant overcumeth cunde [nature]'; and adds the bold
and striking comment that 'ayein hare bisocnen [their petitions] Godd
himseolf ariseth thet alle the othre halhen [saints] *sittende* ihereth
[listens to]'.*

Speaking of the beatific vision the English writer introduces the
Pauline phrase from 1 Cor. 13: 12—'then we shall see him face to face'
(*facie ad faciem*)—translating it as 'nebbe to nebbe'. Nothing in his
source at this point answers to that; but it has doubtless been suggested by the earlier allusion to this passage in the Latin. He also adds
the image of the blessed being 'alle ase lihte ant ase swifte ase

---

* Conquest of fleshly desires is said in the *Anticlaudianus* (v. 435 ff.) to be prerequisite. But he does not associate this specifically with virginity. He gives to Prudence
a glimpse of the heavenly mysteries (*in speculo deitatis singula cernens*). His poetic exploita-
tion of the theme of the angelic orders is characteristic of his century: the Cherubim are
said (v. 415) to know the mind of God, and the Thrones to know his *censura* (cf. *Sawles
Warde*'s 'dome').

sunne-gleam the scheot [which shoots] fram est into west as tin ehlid [thy eyelid] tuneth [closes] ant openeth'. There is no scriptural base for this image (found also in *Ancrene Wisse*) except for the last phrase, which is from 1 Cor. 15: 52: 'in ictu oculi'—but in a different context. Finally he brings us back to the opening parable of the household: 'Nu is Wil thet husewif al stille thet er wes so willesful'—a fine dramatic conclusion that is not found in the Latin.

Like other texts of the 'Katherine Group', *Sawles Warde* falls, at least intermittently, into rhythmic alliterative patterns resembling those found in Ælfric's *Lives of the Saints*. They are most evident in lyrical passages describing the joys of heaven and its saints: 'Se gleade ha [they] beoth of Godd thet al is hare blisse se muchel that ne mei hit munne [tell of] na muth, ne spealie [recount] na speche.' And the resonance of: 'Ha beoth sa wise thet ha witen alle Godes reades [counsels], his runes [secrets], ant his domes [judgements] the derne [secret] beoth ant deopre [deeper] then eni sea-dingle' struck the ear of a modern poet who himself practised the alliterative art. W. H. Auden begins a poem 'Doom is dark and deeper than any sea-dingle.' Such cadences and alliterative linkings do not necessarily prove continuity of Ælfrician prose. The Latin original of *Sawles Warde* employs similar cadences and decorative alliteration, whilst rhyme and rhythm were marked features of the Victorine writers. More significant in the 'Katherine Group' is the dense pattern of scriptural allusions: early readers would have recognized at once in the last phrase cited above a rendering of *judicia tua abyssus multa* (Ps. 35: 7). Many such texts are common to two or more of the group, probably deriving from a *florilegium* that was common property.

The theme of *Sawles Warde* has an abiding appeal. The subject-matter of the four texts with which it is linked in language, dialect, date, and assumptions is, on the other hand, one that seems remote to most modern readers and repellent to many. Virginity has never been less honoured than it is today, when even the Greek and Roman cults of Artemis and Diana are of purely historical interest. Yet the martyr-saints Katherine, Margaret, Juliana have a claim as champions of conscience on the interest of the most infidel of moderns. The legends in question were originally read as much as tracts against idolatry as in favour of virginity. If they seem to make the idolatrous persecutors of chaste maidens inhuman, no one at this point in the twentieth century can deny the possibility of such inhumanity.

The legends belong to a period when idolatry was a present peril and persecution fearful. The English translations must at least be given the credit of realizing this, and not presenting us with plaster saints. In argument (and abuse) these saints give as good as they get; their courage and fearlessness is emphasized even more in the English than in the Latin.

Nowadays saints' lives are not everyone's cup of tea. But they were in the thirteenth century and in the fourteenth century. Chaucer thought it natural to provide *two* in *The Canterbury Tales*—the story of St Cecilia and the Marian Miracle of *The Prioress's Tale*; and though his Criseyde is found reading a romance, she thought that *as a widow* it would be more proper for her to read 'holy seyntes lyves' than to dance or do observance to May (*TC* ii. 118). Widowhood gave her a higher rank than wife, closer to the virgin martyrs. None of the three legends of the saints that we are concerned with is now accepted by the Church or thought to be authentic. They are all late compilations, and the compilers were indifferent to history or the laws of probability. Much of the imagined speech and action is bizarre. St Margaret urges her executioner to get on with the job which will win him heaven. It is impossible for us to recapture the state of mind with which such edifying tales were read. The authors probably regarded the stories first as a means of bringing home to ordinary people the conditions of the Church in the persecution period; second as a frame for a series of set prayers which they put in the mouths of the martyrs, and which could be put to other uses; and third as a means of spreading a cult.

The cult of these three virgin martyrs would clearly recommend itself to the audience of *Ancrene Wisse* and *Sawles Warde*, both of which place so much emphasis on virginity. And the legends contained just enough action, however horrendous, to serve as recreational reading for nuns or anchoresses, providing the authentic *frisson* that Gothic novels later developed. Jacobus de Voragine collected many more such vernacular stories in his *Golden Legend* though he found the story of the Dragon swallowing St Margaret too much to swallow himself.

Of the legend of St Margaret there are several Latin texts and no less than six Anglo-Norman verse versions before 1300—perhaps testifying to genteel audiences in fashionable convents. In 1222 Margaret's Feast Day—20 July—was made a major feast of the English Church by the Council of Oxford; and the English version is careful to name the day and the month, 'July in Latin'—'that o ure ledene [tongue] is ald Englisch *Efterlith* inempnet [named]'—a revealing phrase, showing how archaic and isolated the language of the texts and their area was. For the word is not found again. I suggest that the establishment of the saint's day in 1222 gives a *terminus a quo* for the text—putting it close in date to *Ancrene Wisse*. Our text was clearly intended to be read on the day—cf. 'thet eadie [blessed] meiden the we munneth [commemorate] todei'. This has no equivalent in the Latin. The Latin begins with an account of how one Theotimus came to write the life, and ends with his account of his burying her body. These are reproduced in the English—a trifle awkwardly inasmuch as elsewhere the English bears the marks of a homily. The English is addressed not to 'virgines' but to 'widewen with tha iweddede ant te meidnes nomeliche [especially]', bids them listen how they are to love the lord and *live in maidenhood*. It must then have been meant for a congregation of women (for whom these three categories represented degrees of excellence).

In a few passages added in the English version the influence of St Bernard, so obvious in the other texts, can be detected. Thus *Marherete* describes maidenhood as 'blostme brihtest in bodi the hit bereth', and similarly she addresses Christ as 'blostme iblowen ant iboren of meidenes bosum', a favourite symbol of St Bernard and Richard of St Victor. But I see no traces of Bernard's mysticism in them. Strictly speaking, however evident their outpourings, these saints have no mystical experience at all. It is for their constancy and chastity that they were valued, and for their prowess in the war against the World, the Devil, and not least the Flesh. It is the English text that describes them as 'ikudde kempen' (renowned warriors) in this warfare. And indeed these meek maidens speak the abusive language of soldiery when confronting a would-be husband or the Devil—'heateliche hund' (wicked dog), 'scheomelese schucke' (shameless fiend)—and so forth. The demon will confess the 'mihte of meithhad' which (in the Virgin Mary) has 'deprived us of all we possessed'.

The English text is basically a translation with some vivid bravura enrichments and extensions. The examples always quoted are the rendering of the Latin phrase that describes the dragon's eyes as shining like pearls, which becomes 'shining steeper (i.e. more brilliantly) than stars and ten gemstones broad as basins, on his horned head on either side of his high hooked nose'. 'Broad as basins' is probably a traditional phrase and equally 'steeper than stars' may well be traditional too; perhaps Chaucer uses a variation of it in his description of the Friar, whose eyes 'twinkled in his head', like stars. Similarly, where the Latin says of the demon *suscepit eum terra*, the English has 'he rarinde rad ruglunge [rode roaring backwards] into helle' which has been rightly compared with the grotesque terrors of the Mystery Plays. Less spectacular but equally effective is the translation of *mortua esset* as 'wes iwend the wei thet worldliche men [mortals] alle schulen wenden'.

An addition of another kind is a brief passage in which Marherete

reproves the beholders for grieving instead of rejoicing over her suffering. This appears to be suggested by a similar passage in *St Katherine* (2318 ff.) for which there *is* authority in the Latin text. Most
striking is the long insertion in which the demon repeats the ways in
which he lures a pure man or woman to sin: he lets them begin 'talkin
of Godd and tevelin of godlec [contend about goodness]', then shoots
unawares at their hearts till they 'with plohespeche [amorous words]
sputte [incite] to mare, se longe thet ha toggith and tollith togederes
[they embrace violently and grasp closely]'.

The Latin life itself is a carefully cadenced piece, and the English
writer may be seen as trying to show that whatever the Latin can do the
vernacular can do better. He had the precedent and model of Ælfric's
Saints' Lives, likewise based (generally) on Latin texts and written in
the same rhythm with alliterative prose. But he employs alliteration
more lavishly—most obviously in alliterative combinations of various
kinds (sometimes glossing a native word with a new word from French
or Old Norse). Characteristic are pairings of near synonyms: 'gleo and
gledunge', 'hehen and herien' (extol and praise), 'toggith and tollith'.
Some of these alliterative phrases were tenacious of life and doubtless
part of everyday speech, for instance 'windes and wederes' (Bunyan
has 'come wind, come weather' in 'Who would true valour see'), or 'of
stanes and of stockes' (for the *idola muta et surda et ceca* of the Latin).

Juliene presents much the same picture. It begins with exactly the
same invocation of the Trinity, but adjures 'ealle leawede men [lay
folk]' who cannot understand Latin to hearken to the life of a maiden,
which has been translated into the English tongue. There is no suggestion of a congregation of women. Nor is Juliana's feast day mentioned. It did not have the prominence of St Margaret's. The story has
the basic ingredients of the other lives: the Christian virgin who
refuses to marry a heathen hound, her tortures, her prayers, a dialogue
with a demon, further tortures, final death. But the embroidering of
each narrative is different. Juliana's wooer Eleusius is presented as a
thirteenth-century romantic lover who 'felt himself wounded in the
heart with the arrow that love lets fly so that it seemed to him that he
could nowise live without the healing of her love'. Beholding her
beauty he heaves a sigh like a man sore wounded; his heart is inflamed
and his bones melt as the rays of love penetrate his limbs. In the Latin
his father swears by the pitiful gods Apollo and Diana. The corresponding English expressions are far more intense: 'For the drihtfule
[noble] godd Apollo, mi laverd [lord], ant mi deore leafdi, the deore-
wurthe [precious] Diane, thet ich muche luvie' (all the English embellishments of the Latin are heavily alliterative). Juliana, on the other

hand, prays for guidance in keeping her virginity unspotted from intercourse with man—as in the other texts virginity is *per se* a priceless virtue. As in the other texts too, the martyr becomes Jesus Christ's 'leofman'. Her ripostes to her wooer are absolute: 'However angry you be, whatever you do it's no use unless you believe in the Trinity.' In vain her father points out the advantages of the match: 'It's no little thing, the reeveship of Rome; you could be chief lady of the city and of all its lands.' But the more he urges the more determined she grows, for she is already wedded to someone very different. 'Indeed,' says her father. 'Who might that be? No one I'm acquainted with.' 'The more's the pity.' The end of this first dialogue is a beating that draws blood and opens a rich stream of alliterative rhetoric: 'Beat as much as ye may, ye beadles of Belial. I'll never bow to the maumets [idols] that are the fiend's vessels. The more you mar me the brighter will be my crown. My death will be dear to God [a motif common to the group] whilst you sink down deep into hell.' But Eleusius still plays the lovelorn role. *Videns pulchritudinem eius* says the Latin—which becomes 'As he ... biheold hire lufsume leor [beautiful face], lilies ilicnesse and rudi ase a rose'—he heaves a sigh like a creature sore wounded. He tries persuasion, but Juliana sees him as a craven, frightened to gainsay a wicked emperor. It is now his turn to torture and Juliana's abuse rises to the occasion: 'Do, you limbs of the devil, all that the devil whose drudges you be, drives you to do.... Haldeth longe, ne leave ye neaver.' The next move is to pour boiling brass over her; but as St John (so the English writer notes) survived boiling oil, so Christ preserved his bride, who felt it no more than water. The miracle is the occasion for a long set prayer, full of biblical allusions and alliterative tags: 'Laverd, godd almihti ... lead me thurh this lease [deceptive], this lutle leastinde [short-lasting] lif to the havene of heale [salvation].' The immediate result is the appearance of a demon of hell disguised as an angel of light who purports to give her leave to yield. But heaven warns her of the trick, and Belial soon reveals his true nature and chronicles his own crimes, confessing that he is bound in durance vile to Beelzebub, 'the balde thurs [bold demon] of helle'. Belial becomes very sorry for himself but all he gets from Juliana is a sound thrashing—'heo leide on se lutherliche [severely] thet wa wes him o live'. This is sheer comedy, and doubtless intended as such, as similar scenes in the Mystery plays suggest (indeed the lively dialogue could be adapted for the stage). It reaches its climax when Belial begs Juliana not to let men treat him shamefully—to no avail. She drags him 'eaver endelong the cheping [market] chapmen to hutung [derision], ant heo [they] leiden to him, sum with stan, sum with ban, ant sleatten [egged on] on him hundes'. The light relief is like that of a Renaissance St George picture in which the maiden leads the dragon along like a poodle. 'Where did you learn such tricks?' asks Eleusius. 'Heathen hound, it's not my doing but Christ's. Ever be accursed, colt of such kind. Thy sorry soul and thy sorrowful ghost shall with such play-fellows play in hell.' Now comes torture on the wheel (described in almost loving detail). But an angel breaks her bonds, and 'fish-whole', and as though she had felt no hurt, she gives thanks in another elaborate prayer with a brief run-through of the Old Testament and the Gospels. Five hundred bystanders are converted in a trice. Maximian duly beheads them all and so makes blissful martyrs of them, whilst Eleusius gets a good fire going. But an angel quenches it, reducing him to frenzy, 'as eaver ei [any] iburst bar [bristly boar] thet grunde his tuskes'. He resorts to boiling pitch; but Juliana takes this like a warm bath whilst it spills over and fatally burns seventy-five of the attendants. Nothing now remains but beheading. Belial reappears to urge them on but a mere glance from Juliana makes him blench and cower as if shot by an arrow. He makes a last comically despairing speech, and Juliana, before offering her neck to the executioner, improves the occasion by preaching to the spectators just as the narrator is doing—'Lusteth [hearken] me leove men, ant litheth [listen] an hwile.' This world runs away like water, vanishes like a dream, is as false as wind, etc. This is a stock homiletic matter introduced by the English writer to improve the occasion. It is rounded off by a prayer; and as she gives up the spirit flights of angels sing her to her heavenly rest.

St Katherine is the first version of the Legend of this saint in English. It gives us a little more history than the others, by way of introduction before we come to the typical characterization of Katherine as steadfast and of true belief, of good family (though she took no account of being 'called lady' and loved no 'lihte plohen [games] ne nane sotte songes . . . ne nane luve-runes [secret love-runes]'). And there is more sheer story in the rest of the narrative which shows her reaction to enforced idol worship and her discourse with the Emperor has more content than similar speeches in the other lives. Even the alliterative passages, though built out of units found in the other texts, have an individual ring:

The feont . . . bimong alle his crokinde creftes with neaver an ne keccheth he creftiluker cang men . . . then that he maketh men . . . to make swucche maumez of treo other of stan. . . .

(The fiend, among all his hooking tricks with never one catches foolish men more craftily than by causing men to make such idols out of wood or stone.)

In the main body of the work there is a completely different emphasis from that of *Marherete* and *Juliene*. She is the learned lady, and it takes no less than fifty philosophers to combat her. When they insist that she shall 'set sickle forth' (i.e. set about it) she treats them in the same superior tone that Marherete and Juliene adopt towards their wooers, dismissing 'Homeres motes' (arguments) and 'Aristotles turnes' (artifices) and all their successors as 'idel yelpes' before she gives a brief outline of Christian theology with special references to the Incarnation (when Christ 'schrudde and hudde [clothed and concealed] him . . . mid ure fleschliche schrud [garment]'), and to the Trinity—a doctrine that these philosophers find contrary to natural law since it involves God undergoing death. So she has to explain the doctrine of the Two Natures and Divine Impassibility ('ne mahte his heovenliche cunde [nature] . . . *felen* nowther sar ne sorhe upo the cruche [cross]'). But by virtue of his hidden humanity he 'schrenchte [tricked] then alde deovel'. This high-toned argument is a welcome change from the thaumaturgy of the other lives. It is noteworthy that these argumentative passages are not markedly alliterative, or rather the stock alliterative formulas are rare. There was no native alliterative model for such discourse. Some sections of the Latin text are disregarded entirely, as if too great a strain on the writer's verbal resources or his listener's attention.

With some reason Katherine can claim to have unknotted some of the 'knotty knots' of theology. In fact the philosophers are converted on the spot, to the Emperor's understandable annoyance. They suffer the baptism of fire, but they lay with so 'lufsume leores [faces] . . . se rudie ant se reade ilitlet [coloured], eavereuch leor as lilie ileid to rose' that they seemed to be but in a sweet slumber—the alliterative lilt takes over again at such high points. Maxentius tries once more to woo Katherine but of course she avows her heavenly 'leofmon' who has wedded her 'meithhad [virginity] mit te ring of rihte *bileave*' (an appropriate expansion of the Latin *indissociabili federe*). Her subsequent fortunes follow the usual pattern and are described in the usual terms. An ecstatic description of heavenly joys is based on the Apocalypse rather than the Latin and brings about the conversion of one Porphynus, who immediately becomes a mouthpiece for Christianity. A prefect—the 'deovles budel'—proposes torture by the wheel—and you can guess the rest.

Of all the texts that make up the so-called 'Katherine Group', *Hali Meithhad* is the most uncongenial to modern taste, yet the most original in style and substance, and the most insistent in its mode of argument. What distinguishes *Hali Meithhad* is not its encomiums on maidenhood but its scorn and ridicule of the married state. The contemptuous and abusive tone allows no room for those touches of humanity and common sense that make *Ancrene Wisse* so attractive. There is not the slightest reason to attribute the two works to the same hand. Yet the spiritual director who felt it necessary to warn the anchoresses, of all women, against lechery, could hardly have found this text unsympathetic. Certainly, Peter Damian would not have done; and one must admit that even in the thirteenth century the ideals of Peter Damian, coloured by late Hellenistic dualism, still had a following; the tenets of extreme monasticism, that condemned marriage as intrinsically evil, were widely held.* *Hali Meithhad* accepts the ideas of three degrees of perfection: Virginity, and beneath it Widowhood, and, finally and lowest, Matrimony.

The whole intention of the work is to deter a maiden from matrimony. Every possible argument is enlisted in what is treated as a struggle with the Devil, to whom Virginity is loathsome because through its beginner, the Virgin Mary, he lost the rule over mankind. It is because the writer sees marriage as a devilish temptation that his language is so intemperate. He is no Manichee: he does not despise the body as such, rather he urges that virginity will be to 'thi flesches halschipe [integrity], for thi licomes [body's] luve, ant ti bodies heale [health]' (p. 17).†

The ideal of Christian marriage has been of slow growth and we can hardly be patient of the grotesque constructions this writer put on wedlock unless we take account of post-Conquest conditions, which made English gentlefolk socially inferior, and disadvantaged: 'Gentlewomen cannot be provided with dowries and so must marry beneath them'—a fate that to some may really have been worse than death. Certainly there is a gross confusion of ideals here. But a greater grossness was that of twelfth-century society: a society that, as St Bernard thought, could be regenerated only by the sacrifice of human affection: hence he persuaded his brother to leave his wife (who entered a convent) so that he could join him at Clairvaux.

St Bernard's spiritual teaching can be traced here and there in *Hali Meithhad*. This world, it says, 'is icleopet [called] lond of unlicnesse [dissimilarity]' (p. 6), translating his *regio dissimilitudinis*. Intercourse makes of men less than witless beasts, 'dumbe ant broke-rugget [with bent back] ibuhe [bowed down] towart eorthe, thu thet art i wit [reason] iwraht [made] to Godes ilicnesse [likeness] and iriht [erect]

---

* See R. Bultot, *La Doctrine du mépris du monde*, IV, *Le XIe siècle*, 1 *Pierre Damien* (Louvain and Paris, 1963); and G. Sitwell, *MÆ* 33 (1964), 218–20.

† Page references are to the edition by Bella Millett, EETS cclxxxiv, 1982.

bodi up, and heaved [head] towart heovene' (p. 13): the figure of man deformed by sin from his true posture is essentially Bernardine. But this writer goes further. Such men are worse than beasts, for beasts 'doth hare cunde [mate naturally] . . . in *a* [one] time of the yer; moni halt him to *a* make [mate], ne nule efter thet lure neaver neomen other' (p. 12) (they have one season for begetting, and often have only one mate, taking no other after its death). So Kind, Nature, has a role in this ethic. Elsewhere a maiden claims that she will keep herself uncorrupt, 'as cunde me makede' (whereas in *Sawles Warde* such maidens must *conquer* Kind).

The controlling conception is one of spiritual warfare. The maidens who overcome the Devil are to be rewarded with a warrior's crown ('kempene crune'). Wit (Intelligence, the shield of the Soul) fights against Will (Desire), who shoots with the Devil's arrows ('flan'). The most vivid images are those of evil, resembling the lurid pictures of the Capital Sins in *Ancrene Wisse*. As in that text, the Devil has his *fyrd*, so here he has his *here*, his invading army; both terms are Old English. The sorry wretches who wallow in the dung-heap unwed are the wagon-horses ('eaveres') of the Devil, who rides them and spurs them on. The writer is here expanding a text from Joel 1: 17: 'Devil's coach-horses' is a later dialectal term for black beetles, so the wretches are to be thought of as diminutive creatures bred out of dung. Elsewhere we glimpse devils dancing and clapping their hands over a maiden's shame. Much of this discourse takes the form of imagined dialogue, as thus:

'But, you will say, it is not filthy. Man's support ("elne") is of much worth, and one needs his help "to fluttunge and te fode" (to provide for one's needs). Association of man and wife bring happiness, and the begetting of bonny children delights the hearts of older folk. Not so—whatever these joys, they will end in sorrow. And why should you worry about your livelihood when you are the beloved of the Lord of all? Once married, you'll be worse than a drudge—and any posses-sions you have will be prey to moth, or plague. And what if you get no pleasure from it, but must grind your teeth in "westi wahes" (bare walls) and bring up your children in poverty? Or your husband grows detestable to you, so that you dread his return? He may chide and "chew" you or beat you as a lecher does his whore or a thrall he's bought. How will you get on in bed then? Even those who love each other often quarrel in bed though no sign of it may show the next morning. Or willy-nilly you'll have to put up with his foul practices in bed, because, be he "cangun" (fool) or cripple, you're stuck with him. If you're pretty you won't be able to guard yourself against slander. If he's indifferent you'll soon be making poisons or love-potions, or bribing witches. If you can't bear him children you'll be called barren. If you can, it will defile you and you'll suffer pain, perhaps death. Children bring more trouble than joy, and a misshapen child may bring both sorrow and shame. And what's the pleasure of pregnancy? Your face grows green and lean, your eyes grow dark, your breasts heavy, you suffer nausea, and then come the pains of childbirth and the shame-craft of old wives. (Mind you, I don't blame women for this suffering, I'm simply warning girls.) Then when the child is born it cries and you have to get up at midnight and clean the cradle. If you're rich and have a nurse, you've got to keep an eye on her.'

These, then, are the *tribulaciones carnis* of which St Paul speaks. The reference is to 1 Cor. 7: 28: 'If a virgin marries she does not sin: [but] she will have tribulation of the flesh.' It was on this verse that the whole structure of virginolatry was built, without regard to its context or to the Apostle's insistence that he voiced simply his own view. Each condemnation is shriller than the last: anyone who despite all this does not refrain from the act that causes it is harder than adamant, madder than madness, and his own worst enemy. Then, as if unable to halt, the writer turns back to the cradle. 'What if I ask about the wife who hears her child screaming as soon as she enters the house, sees the cat at the flitch, the dog at the hide, the cake burning, the calf sucking, the crock boiling over?' (p. 19.)

The effectiveness of this contained frenzy is undeniable. Jerome *Adversus Jovinianum*, the misogynist's *locus classicus*, or the Wife of Bath, who relied on it, can do no better (or no worse). Before we dismiss it as perversion we should re-read the admired Heloise's letters to Abelard in which, citing Jerome, she describes its woes in much the same terms as those just cited—a matter of squalling babies, domestic muddle, squalor; only riches make it bearable. And Heloise would have agreed that the 'love which brought us both to sin' should be called lust. The vernacular text, however, owes its power not to any literary source but to its particularity—those all too revealing glimpses of humdrum domestic life. Of spiritual nutriment the work offers little. The most that can be said is that, like *Ancrene Wisse*, it never lauds virginity as an end in itself. 'Though thou be virgin in body, and show pride, envy, wrath, or a weak will, thou makest thyself the devil's whore' (p. 20); 'Better a mild wife or a meek widow than a proud maiden, who is like a lamp without oil' (p. 22). Only the unspotted maiden should wed Christ, whose 'marheyeve' (morning-gift) is the kingdom of heaven.

Stylistically *Hali Meithhad* is a remarkable achievement. It leaves the constant impression of a speaking voice addressed to a 'seli meiden'. It rests largely on a single text, Ps. 44: 11: 'Audi, filia, et vide, inclina aurem tuam; et obliviscere populum tuum et domum patris tui' (Hearken, O daughter, and consider, and incline thine ear; forget also thine own people, and thy father's house)—interpreted in the Gregorian manner: *populum tuum* being 'the gathering within thee of fleshly thoughts that prompt to fleshly filths and marriage [*brudlac*]'. The Psalmist's vocative of address is retained throughout though the girl is sometimes given the right of reply—only to be quickly worsted.

The work shares with the other members of its group a common dialect, vocabulary and idiom, a fondness for native, not to say archaic, terms, constructions, and alliterative cadences. These last are more marked than in the *Wisse* and find their parallels chiefly in *Sawles Warde* and the Saints' Lives. But each of these texts has its distinctive nuances, its own blend of alliterative patterns and combinations; the prose is extraordinarily supple, yet fully controlled—as if alliterative patterns provided the same frame that the *cursus* did in Latin prose of the period. The alliterative pattern shows at its simplest in the pairing of near-synonyms and doublets: 'to fluttunge and te fode'; 'sorhin ant siken'; 'twinnin ant tweamen'; 'weorrith ant warpeth'. But it is the placing of the alliterative combinations that gives them their effect— e.g. at the close of a sentence: 'Nim yerne [take heed] hwet euch word beo *sunderliche to seggen* [means separately]' (p. 1); '*b*eo hit eanes [once] *f*orloren ne *b*ith hit neaver i*f*unden' (with alliterating alternate syllables; p. 5). Alliteration, again, binds a sentence together: 'ant mare beon idrechet [oppressed] then ei drivel [any drudge] i the hus' (p. 14). Sometimes elaborate interlacings are built up out of three or four consonant sounds:

ant sothes[1] yef thu thenchest, ant bihaldest on heh, towart te *m*uchele *m*ede[2] thet *m*eithhad a*b*ideth, thu wult *l*eote[3] *l*iht*l*iche ant a*b*eoren[4] *b*litheliche the *d*erf[5] thet tu *d*rehest onont[6] ti fleschliche wil ant ti *l*icomes[7] *l*ust thet tu for*b*erest her.   (pp. 8–9)

[1] *in truth*   [2] *reward*   [3] *estimate*   [4] *endure*   [5] *hardship*
[6] *sufferest in respect of*   [7] *body's*

Sometimes the pattern is varied by rhymed phrases: 'i gastelich [spiritual] este [joy] ant i breoste rest' (p. 14); or verb-rhyme is introduced, giving a more complex rhythm:

thus this worldes hweol[1] warpeth[2] ham abuten.
theoves hit steoleth ham
*r*eavers hit *r*obbith
*h*are over*h*erren[3] *w*itith[4] ham ant *w*reatheth[5].   (p. 15)

[1] *wheel*   [2] *whirls*   [3] *their superiors*   [4] *mulct*   [5] *harass*

Alliteration thus becomes less a stylistic device than a mode of thought, inherited, like the alliterative pattern, from Ælfric and Wulfstan, but with vitality enough to absorb new words like *reng* and *cader*, and new rhetorical devices, ranging from the rhetoric of self-answering question to the climactic sentence built up of variations on a basic pattern: 'thet wleatewille werc [disgusting deed], thet bestelich gederunge [intercourse], thet scheomelese sompnunge [union], thet ful [cup] of fulthe stinkinde, ant untohe [wanton] dede' (p. 4); 'thes cwenes, thes riche cuntasses, theos modie [proud] leafdis ... ha lickith honi of thornes' (p. 4). Or still more elaborately: 'with earmthe [misery] biwinneth hit, with fearlac [fear] biwiteth [keeps] hit, forleoseth hit with sorhe, swinketh to biyeotene [gain], biyeoteth for te leosen, leosith for te sorhin' (pp. 14–15)—where internal vowel-rhyme and verb-repetitions make an intricate pattern. As with St Bernard, an ascetic morality seems positively to encourage a rhetorical richness. But this could hardly have been achieved in the vernacular unless the writer had been bred in a tradition already well established. That this was the tradition of *Ancrene Wisse* and its congeners is evident from the distinctive vocabulary that it shares with one or other of those texts ('cangun', 'egede', 'healewi', 'nurth', 'schucke', 'schimminde'), as well as from distinctive combinations: 'luthere eie' (relentless anger), 'withuten ei etlunge' (without any consideration), and even distinctive adverbial 'fillers'—'me' (but, indeed), 'lanhure' (at least).

If it be agreed that at one point the writer drew on the *Moralia* now attributed to Alexander of Bath this work must belong to the first or second decade of the thirteenth century.[*] The argument for his knowledge of the *Moralia* would be unanswerable if the passage in question had included the comparison of the flesh of virgins to that of elephants, which follows in the Latin. Whether its omission shows that the Englishman had a sense of humour is a moot point.

(ii) Penitential and Homiletic Works: *The Ayenbite of Inwit*; *Jacob's Well*; Later Sermons

There be so many books and treatises of vices and virtues and of diverse doctrines that this short life shall rather have an end of any man than he may either study them or read them.

A modern reader is likely to accept that assertion of the translator of the *Horologium Sapientiae*[†] in a somewhat different sense from that

* Cf. E. J. Dobson, *The Origins of Ancrene Wisse* (Oxford, 1976), 429–30.
† *Anglia* x (1887), 328.

intended. Titles like *Ayenbite of Inwit*, *Prick of Conscience*, *Handlyng Synne*, *Le Somme des Vices et des Vertus*, *Le Livre de Seintz Medecines* have nowadays no immediate appeal, even though Rosemond Tuve has demonstrated the artistic interest of the imagery of the *Somme** and G. R. Owst has quarried these texts and a score of others for illuminating allusions to contemporary life and manners. Yet the medieval vogue of such works was not essentially different from the modern addiction to psychoanalysis, and in many ways more justifiable: it is simply that the couch has replaced the confessional. What the Church gave regularly to all gratis, the psychiatrist dispenses for a consideration to those near despair.

Penitential literature has an ancient history, but for our present purpose it may begin with the Decretals of Gratian and the Decrees of the Lateran Council of 1215 that were devised to ensure that every parish priest should regularly preach a homily and hear confessions. An early and important fruit of this movement—a movement at least as widespread in its effects as the Vatican Council of our own day—was the *Summa* of Raymund de Pennaforte (? *c*.1234), which remained a standard handbook for three hundred years. English bishops were eager to encourage their clergy to fulfil their duties of instructing the laity in doctrine, and especially in encouraging the practice of confession. Grosseteste of Lincoln wrote a manual for parish priests, the *Templum Domini*; Archbishop Pecham (or Peckham) in the Lambeth Council of 1281 issued a code for the clergy. Latin manuals for priests, such as the *Oculus Sacerdotis*, the *Regimen Animarum*, the *Memoriale Presbiterorum* and others, were soon followed by handbooks in English.† *The Ayenbite of Inwit*, a prose work of some 260 (printed) pages, written in his own hand by a Dan (Dom) Michel 'of Northgate' in 'English of Kent' for laymen to read, is one of the few texts of the fourteenth century that is firmly tied to a date (1340) and to a place ('the book-house of St Austin's of Canterbury'). To render the title literally, as 'Remorse of Conscience' is to suggest a work more rebarbative than it turns out to be. The term *inwit* occurs rarely in the text, there is little mordant about it, and much sound sense and moving exhortation. Admittedly these qualities can be traced to its French original, the *Somme des Vices et des Vertus*, compiled by Friar Lorens in 1279—a source that Dan Michel no more thinks it incumbent on him to disclose than Chaucer felt it necessary to signal his indebtedness to *Il Filostrato*. His concern is to provide sound ethical

---

* Rosemond Tuve, *Allegorical Imagery* (Princeton, New Jersey, 1966), ch. ii.

† On these works see W. A. Pantin, *The English Church in the Fourteenth Century* (Cambridge, 1955), 189–235.

and spiritual guidance for Everyman, to whom its sources were of no interest. And not only guidance, but a structure, a frame to which daily conduct could be related. Such frames are essential if religion is not to degenerate into mere inclination. A table of the 'capiteles', at the front of the unique manuscript—a novel feature in a vernacular text, helpful to a spiritual director—indicates that it is, in chief, an exposition of the Ten Commandments (treated in terms of offences against them); the twelve articles of the Creed; the seven Capital Sins (represented as the seven heads of the Beast in the Apocalypse but not pictured as they are in the French manuscripts and their numbered 'branches'). A chapter on how to distinguish good and evil is followed by a section on the Virtues set in the Garden of the Heart, into which is intercalated a long exposition of each of the seven petitions of the *Pater Noster* and a passage on the seven gifts of the Holy Spirit. The Virtues (more prominent in the *Somme* than the Vices) are similarly subdivided. The final pages of the work proper set forth the stages to Perfection. Thus though it is designed as a manual for easy consultation, its parts interlock. The colophon is followed by a contemporary rendering of part of the *De Custodia* of St Anselm, made independently of the version of that text found in *Sawles Warde*, and prefaced by a *Pater Noster*, *Ave*, and *Credo* that mark it off from the main text. A final page briefly sets forth the whole intent of the work, viz., to show that Man is distinguished from the beasts by thought and understanding—which is more than the title would lead us to expect.

On the face of it the classification is artificial, and the conception of sin implied may puzzle the modern mind. Thus under Avarice—treated largely from the lay viewpoint, as 'there are other books that clerics can consult'—falls the sin of those who for money call up the devil and make enchantments and 'make to look in the sword or in the thumbnail, to take thieves', and the sin of short measure 'as do these taverners that fill up the measure with froth'. Under Pride falls the sin of missing sermons. Lechery includes all five stages from 'foolish looking' through talking, touching, kissing, to 'the deed'. The social consequences of sin are always emphasized, and most classes of society put before our eyes: great lords so beguiled by Pride that they know not themselves; those who support Jews and 'caorsins' or usurers and are thus as guilty of usury as those moneylenders themselves; those who out of passion for tournaments put their lands and inheritance in pawn; merchants who by 'time-setting' bring knights to beggary; foolish women who walk 'with standing neck as a hart in the grove and look aside, like a horse of great cost'.

The imagery is predominantly feudal. Deadly sin is treachery to one's Lord and means thraldom to the Devil. Life is a knighthood—thus Dan Michel reads Job's *militia super terram*. A knight is eager to do courtesy, give generously, show his prowess, acquire fame (whilst a townsman wants to 'chaffer' and be honoured in his town). We are all companions, knights in Our Lord's Host. Just as there are tournaments in peacetime, so God tries his knights so that they may learn to use arms of virtue. And just as after a tournament the victorious knight goes home to rest, so the good heart 'comes again to itself and rests in God'. The habit makes not the monk, nor arms the knight, but the good heart, shown in deeds of prowess. Occasionally the imagery is more earthy: the busy or melancholic man is like him who looks for 'the crammels [crumbs] ine the russoles [rissoles]'. The chatterer is like a mill without a sluice; the wise man shuts the sluice to hold back the foolish words (a figure found elsewhere). But the whole homiletic armoury is drawn on for images and analogies; the Fathers (Augustine, Bernard, Anselm); Cicero, Seneca; the Ysopet (a collection of fables), and the Bestiary, as well as the farmyard: the sluggard is like the man frightened of a snail if it puts out its horns (an image that reappears in *Jacob's Well* and still later in a nursery rhyme of the four-and-twenty tailors frightened when the snail put out its horns 'like a little kyloe cow').*

Every page is thus securely anchored to the workaday world. But the binding ethic is equally important. Nature and Reason are the guiding forces: self-knowledge is the first step to perfection. In its modest way the manual synthesizes classical and Christian morality much as Dante had done. Righteousness ('prior in the cloister of the soul') lays out his work by line and rule, lead and level, taking first his 'pricke and his boune [rule]', but always looking to the end. Christian marriage means that man and wife are one body, 'so shall they be one heart by true love'. Those who ill-use the poor have blood on their hands. True nobility comes of the gentle heart. But no heart is gentle unless it loves God, and to see the face of Jesus Christ is the true *noblesse* that makes us God's children. The Beatitudes are the divine philosophy, and Christ is a great philosopher, who calls perseverance prowess. Virtue is the mean in marriage as in other things: so here comes in the apophthegm of Chaucer's Merchant: 'With his own sword a man may hurt himself, and sin mortally with his own wife.' Seneca is cited for the figure of Man as Emperor over himself (which Gower adapts), Cicero on *bonum commune* (147), 'a wise man' for the adage 'A man is never less alone than when he is by himself.' Thus

---

* See I. and P. Opie, *The Oxford Dictionary of Nursery Rhymes* (London, 1951), no. 496.

classical moralists are assimilated to the Christian tradition. The Pseudo-Dionysian figure of the soul as a mirror makes a brief appearance (158). But Charity, as St Paul conceived it, is the supreme virtue; and the *locus classicus*, 1 Cor. 13, here makes perhaps its first appearance in English prose (p. 89), a few years after Robert Mannyng had embellished it in verse.

It must be admitted that the monk of Canterbury is merely transmitting, and sometimes mistranslating, the far livelier French work of Friar Lorens. The difference between them is symbolized by the workaday character of the English manuscript and the elegance of contemporary copies of the French book. Dan Michel had no ear for prose rhythms, and he follows painfully French order and French idiom. Yet his remarkably consistent spelling gives us some indication of how Kentishmen spoke in the early fourteenth century and testifies to his eagerness to make the treatise available to lay folk. There is the germ of Screwtape in the Devil's servants reporting to him 'as he sat upon a faldstool' (239), to be soundly beaten when they did not come up to scratch. The *Ayenbite* itself never achieved popularity. But the numerous parallels it provides for Chaucerian and later apophthegms suggest that works of a similar kind provided important channels through which Christian allegory and Christian morality spread beyond the priestly, religious, and clerkly classes. It is with the *Ayenbite* that the conception of *la chevalerie celestienne* enters, if without flourishes, into our literature. Here too we find the doctrine of the 'Goods' of Fortune, Nature (or Study), and 'True Noblesse and Freedom', adapted from Augustine or Aristotle. Here Magnificence takes on something of the sense (including Perseverance) that it will have for Spenser. Dan Michel in his own modest way hopes like Spenser to fashion 'a virtuous and gentle discipline'. A later and more supple version of the *Somme*, the fifteenth-century *Book of Vices and Virtues*, has an undisputed place in the allegorical development that led to the *Faerie Queene*.

Jacob's Well (or *Fons Jacob*) is one of the latest works in the sequence of penitential prose (the manuscript is dated *c*.1440) but it earns a place here as proof that this tradition altered little in three centuries, though today only readers well versed in Scripture will take the point of its title and see its relation to the modern editor's subtitle: 'An Englisht treatise on the Cleansing of Man's Conscience'. The allusion is to the meeting of Christ and the woman of Samaria described in St John 4: 6 ff. The well is the basis of the allegory that provides a frame for the book, meticulously worked out in fifty chapters with the help of such verses as Ps. 68: 15 (p. 87*); one chapter including a similar allegorization of the pool of Bethesda (John 5: 2–6): the angel who troubles the waters being the preacher who stirs the conscience, its five porches the 'ghostly wits'. The well must be cleansed of the mire ('wose') of concupiscence by shovel and spade, by the scoop of penitence (p. 67) and the mattock of peace (p. 271) so that it can be filled with fresh water springing from the Seven Virtues, and be built round with stones that are the works of Faith. From such a spring the penitent soul may draw clear water, and the Lord may rest by it and be refreshed. The writer's learning (as he sometimes reminds us) is far from negligible, and he draws on more recent *auctores* than those cited by Dan Michel. Quotations left untranslated suggest that he had in mind a fully literate audience. He shows a trained canonist's familiarity with the Decretals, and with Councils and Constitutions (including Archbishop Peckham's, p. 19) of later date. Besides references to Pennaforte, Chrysostom, Gregory (the *Moralia*) there are quotations from less familiar, indeed fugitive, writers—including John Abbeville, 'Watertoun', or 'doctor filius matris'. He evidently had St Thomas's *Summa Theologiae* and *Summa Contra Gentiles* to hand, and Albertus Magnus also appears.

The doctrine, the divisions, the application of scriptural texts are familiar enough. The chapters are homilies addressed to 'freendys' and 'syres', delivered day after day and forming a continuum. At intervals there is a *resumé* of previous chapters, culminating in a *Recapitulacio totius operis*, a new feature of such works.

Fons Jacob begins with a detailed setting forth (some 60 pages) of all the crimes punishable by excommunication—a list brought up to date by the inclusion of Lollardy—and laced with technical terms of trade, condemning 'great men' who require Holy Church or the ministers to pay tolls ('pycage, murage, groundage, passage or guydage'), as well as false coiners. But soon we are in the full swing of trenchant injunction driven home by terse *exempla* enlivened by brisk dialogue: as in the story of the humble nun (ch. xii) or the unbending justice, Herkenbald of Bornayre (ch. xiv) who killed his nephew for attempted rape, 'for love of equity in my doom, and nought for hate', and was rewarded by a miracle. Tales from eremitical and monastic legend predominate—the *Vitas Patrum* provides Abbot Macarius's vision of fiends 'smale as chylderyn, blewe as men of Inde', but, whatever the source, they would make for an enlargement of mind and interest in hearers whose lives for the most part were bounded by their hedgerows and their

---

* Page references are to the edition by A. Brandeis, EETS cxv (1900).

fairs. Sometimes the *exemplum* functions like a dominical parable: such is the story of the Egyptian merchant who was willing to be hanged for his friend (p. 88). As always, Bestiary lore plays its part, Bartholomaeus Anglicus (ch. xiv) being cited to the effect that a harp strung with wolf's and sheep's gut will never keep tune 'because sheep and wolf are contrary in kind' (p. 90). Some of the issues considered belong to a wider, more troubled world: the nobility are instructed about restitution in an unlawful war; the clergy are told that a priest must not accept pillaged goods. Whatever the theme, the imagery and illustrations are simple and self-explanatory: 'Great fishes are taken in the net, small fishes escape and live.' Confession must be full: on a king's board is set whole bread, and not broken bread (p. 181). 'God biddeth thee rise and go to the church. Thy belly saith it is full and must take a rest, for the church is no hare, where men leave it they may find it' (p. 141). The idle man is fond of his soft feather bed or spends his time playing at the two-hand sword, at sword and buckler, at two-piked staff, and at the 'hurl-bat' (p. 105). Didactic intent shows at its plainest in the application of those parts of Canon Law that chiefly affect lay folk, e.g. tithes. But all is seen *sub specie aeternitatis*. In the Last Court the Steward of the Father of Heaven will not remit his tithes: 'thy pleading and thy usage shall not avail thee there but thou shalt be put out of thy tenement of heaven'. Thus dominical parables are reshaped in language that retains the simplicity and directness of the Gospels. We are never far from the world of wrestlings (that give opportunities for 'beckonings of nice signs'), marketings, bede-ales, bede-wines, and shootings (p. 291). The writer envisages his hearers as preoccupied with worldly affairs—'How should I come betimes to church that have so much to do?' (p. 261.) Household cares beset men even on their death-beds: 'My wife, my children, how shall they do and [if] I die? Who shall till that land, who shall milk those kine, who shall make my cheese and butter, now I may not do thereto?' (p. 305.) Typical of the many homely analogies is: 'as a cartwheel, dry and ungreased, crieth loudest of other wheels: so thou, dry and not greased with grace, grouchest loudest of all other' (p. 260). Yet, as in the *Ayenbite*, there is frequent resort to the knightly imagery that befits Christian warfare: nobleness of heart makes men to desire pains as knights desire jousts or tournaments (p. 288). The author's—or we should rather say the compiler's—learning shows itself not only in his scholarly references but also in his skilled handling of a text—such as the *Recogitabo tibi omnes annos* of Isa. 38: 15—where he adorns his exegesis by repeating the first three words each time that he adds to it a word or a phrase. He likes parallelisms, repetitions, and contrasts, and a phrase like 'I put this case' smacks of arguments in the Schools.

The moral doctrines of works such as these were presented in even more popular form in the vernacular sermons intended for lay audiences. The Church's insistence on prompt, regular, and thorough confession meant that a major part of the parish priest's duty was to induce his hearers to confess their sins, to explain what in the eyes of the Church that term covered, and to provide them with spiritual guidance and a scheme or 'form' of living. The sermon of John Gaytrige is simply a version of the instructions of Archbishop Thoresby, themselves based on the constitutions of Archbishop Peckham. In their task of instruction, the clergy were aided and advised by some of the works mentioned above, or humbler guides such as the verse *Instructions* of John Mirk, a canon of Lilleshall in Shropshire. This opens with the proverb: 'when the blind man leads the blind they both fall into the ditch', which is applied to ignorant priests. Priests should lead virtuous lives; they should not bear arms nor haunt taverns—and should not be so drunk that in conducting baptisms their tongues will not 'serve'. They are provided with a simplified and popularized summary of doctrine—when children should be baptized, which persons are cousins by baptism, what is an irregular marriage (or 'odd wedding'), etc. They should expound the *Pater Noster*, the Creed, the Ave Maria, the articles of the Faith, and the seven sacraments. There is a long section on how to hear confession.

The surviving sermons (and obviously many have been lost, or were never written down, or remain only in Latin copies) sometimes follow the 'modern' method of sermon construction, with its clearly marked divisions and logical construction (savoured no doubt by university audiences), but the older, less formalized patterns are still found. The popular sermon of the later Middle Ages was notable for its flexibility, a flexibility which allowed the quotation of brief verses to clinch a point or as a basis for moral expansion (see pp. 367–8 below), the use of *exempla* from all kinds of sources (the *Vitas Patrum*, the *Golden Legend*, miracles of the Virgin, stories from collections like those of Jacques de Vitry) which would catch the ear of the 'lewed folk'. The art of the preacher was to tinge both his theme and his *exempla* with local colour, phrase, or incident that would bring home his teaching to a (usually) miscellaneous and (often) restless audience. This could be carried to excess, and provoked criticism from both the orthodox and the unorthodox. Chaucer's Parson refuses to give his audience 'fables', and his austere view is echoed by the Lollards.

Preaching was widespread, and as varied as were the preachers. These included not only parish priests, but bishops, monks (Jocelin of Brakelond's Abbot Samson 'used to preach in English to the people, but in the speech of Norfolk where he was born and bred'), pardoners, and friars, who were especially celebrated for their popular vernacular sermons. Sermons were given not only in churches, but in open-air pulpits or at preaching crosses (the most famous of which was 'Paul's Cross' in the cemetery of St Paul's in London). Since medieval preachers were not slow to attack the vices and the wickedness of the great as well as the small, public sermons of this sort could easily touch on sensitive areas of ecclesiastical or political life. The best known example is probably that recorded by Froissart in 1381. There was, he says, a 'foolish priest' in Kent called John Ball, who used to preach in the cloister as the people were coming out of the minster, saying:

A ye good people, the maters gothe nat well to passe in Englande, nor shall nat do tyll every thyng be common; and that there be no villayns nor gentylmen, but that we may all be unyed toguyder, and that the lordes be no greatter maisters than we be. What have we deserved, or why shulde we be kept thus in servage? We be all come fro one father and one mother, Adam and Eve: wherby can they say or shewe that they be gretter lordes than we be? Savynge by that they cause us to wyn and labour for that they dispende. They ar clothed in velvet and chamlet[1] furred with grise[2], and we be vestured with pore clothe; they have their wynes, spyces, and good breed, and we have the drawyng out of the chaffe, and drinke water; they dwell in fayre houses, and we have the payne and traveyle, rayne, and wynde in the feldes; and by that that cometh of our labours they kepe and maynteyne their estates: we be called their bondmen, and without we do redilye them servyce, we be beaten. . . .*

    [1] *camlet (a costly Eastern fabric)*   [2] *grey fur*

Similarly, the Lollards, whose discourses, says the hostile chronicler Knighton, 'open with much sweetness and devotion but close with much subtle ill-will and detraction', realized the potential of popular preaching. William Swinderby (see p. 346 below), for instance, preached at Leicester and elsewhere, proving so attractive to his audiences that, Knighton says, 'he was revered as another god among them'. All agreed on the power of the sermon, illustrated by a favourite story concerning a wanton woman who was so moved by a preacher's words that she died, and when she was restored to life to make her confession the words 'Ave Maria' were found inscribed on her tongue.†

Many of the surviving Middle English sermons do not live up to such stories, nor indeed to the fictional example given by Chaucer to that immoral but persuasive preacher, the Pardoner. In general, they are less lively than didactic works like *Ancrene Wisse* or *Jacob's Well*.

* *The Chronicle of Froissart*, tr. Lord Berners, ed. W. P. Ker (London, 1901), iii. 224.
† G. R. Owst, *Preaching in Medieval England* (Cambridge, 1926), 57.

John Mirk's *Festiall* (i.e. a series of sermons to be preached on the festivals of saints) is more lively than most. It is full of vivid stories with extraordinary and melodramatic happenings made (more or less) realistic by direct speech—as (p. 142*) the woman so hungry during the siege of Jerusalem that she ate her own child: 'Then sayde the woman, "Here I have rostyd half my chyld forto ete; and yf ye woll not leve [believe] me, lo her that othyr halfe raw ayeynys [against] tomorou!" '
He can terrify his audience with a demon from hell (p. 238): 'Then the fende aperyd yn syght of all the pepull lyke a man of Inde, blak altogedyr as pich, wyth a scharpe nase and a lodely [horrible] face, wyth a berde downe to his fete, blake as soote, wyth een [eyes] brennyng as doth yern [iron] yn the fyre sparklyng on yche syde, and blowyng out hys mowth flamys of brenyng fure [fire]. . . .' And he is a born story-teller:

Ther was a man that had his howse by the chyrch-yeorde, so that the dure[1] openet toward the chyrche. Then had he a maner[2] that, als oft as he come other yede[3] over the chyrche-yeorde, he wold say a 'De Profundis' for all crysten soules. Then, on a day, hyt happonet so that he was pursewet wyth enmys, that he flogh[4] homward; but when he come ynto the chyrch-yeorde, he thoght: 'Now ys tyme forto say "De Profundys" ', and knelut adowne, and sayde. And anon therwyth[5] all the chyrch-yeorde rose full of bodyes, yche on[6] wyth an ynstrument yn hys hond of his craft, and dryven ayeyne[7] his enmyes. And when thay seen[8] that, thay cryed God mercy, and thes men and he allway aftyr were the more devot forto pray for the sowles. Thus devout prayer helpyth moch sowles. (pp. 269–70)

[1] *door*   [2] *habit*   [3] *or went*   [4] *fled*   [5] *straightway*   [6] *one*
[7] *back*   [8] *(the enemies) saw*

Altogether more sober is a collection (of varying date) in MS Royal 18 B. xxiii. Here the stress is on the duty of men to love and to obey God. The torments of the damned and the horrible shapes of demons are less emotively dwelt on, but there is some vivid exemplary detail—gluttons are always 'gulpande in as a gredy sowe in the draffe stoke [place with the swill]' (p. 101†); false friends are like hostellers who run gladly to pilgrims to pray them to come to their inns, and draw them by the hand and promise them many delicate things (p. 85), etc. And there are *exempla*—including the legend of Theophilus, the Faust-like monk, rescued from the devil by the Virgin Mary—or legendary matter—the description of Arthur's shield, which 'had in the innare parte . . . an ymage of Oure Lady Mary deprented, beryng a child in her armes, the wiche ymage he wold behold when that he was

* References are to the edition of T. Erbe, EETS xcvi (1905).
† Page references are to the edition of W. O. Ross, EETS ccix (1940).

werry [weary] in batell and feynte . . .' (p. 325). The sermons give clear and plain instruction in the basic tenets of the faith—the Ten Commandments are expounded, as is the *Pater Noster* ('This prayoure is every man and childe hold [beholden] to kunne [know] yif he passe vii yere olde . . .')—and there is a characteristic stress on the importance of penitence, which is the expression of our 'kindness' to Christ, who was so 'kind' to us.

(iii) Mystical Writings: Rolle; *The Cloud of Unknowing*; Hilton; Julian of Norwich

Of Richard Rolle* we know more than of almost any other English writer before Chaucer. If he is not the first English mystic—Ailred of Rievaulx might be so called—he is the first to pour out his joy and longing in his native language; and his Latin works carried his name far beyond our shores. They reached Central Europe almost as soon as those of Wyclif, and can still be found in libraries dotted along the main travel routes from the North to Italy: Ghent, Brussels, Trier, Metz, Basle. In Latin and in English they still leave the firm impress of a distinctive personality; and it is not surprising that biographical details were sought for and preserved (in an Office intended to promote his canonization). He thus has an early place in the history of English biography. For no other writer of his time have we so many biographical details or plausible inferences; and his Commentary on the Canticles—in his characteristic and highly ornamental Latin—includes a long justification of his eremitical manner of life as well as an account of his supernatural raptures.

That he was, or rather became, a hermit only added to his fame. Today that term connotes a total remoteness and removal from the world and worldly concerns. But such a condition was scarcely attainable in fourteenth-century Yorkshire, when the Scots were ravaging the lands of the Abbeys of Byland and Rievaulx and threatening York itself, the second capital of the country, where Parliament sometimes met and the Exchequer was for a time situated. John Dalton, with whose family Rolle was closely associated, was Constable of Pickering Castle when Edward III stayed at that strategic stronghold in 1334.

* Born *c*.1300 at Thornton Dale, near Pickering, Yorkshire; died 1349 at Hampole in the same county. He seems to have been sent to Oxford under the patronage of Thomas Neville, Archdeacon of Durham, but left at the age of 18 to become a hermit. Besides the English works discussed here, Rolle was the author of a number of Latin works—*Canticum Amoris, Judica Me Deus, Melum Contemplativorum, Super Lectiones Job*, and other commentaries, *Liber de Amore Dei, Incendium Amoris*, and *Emendatio Vitae*. See Hope Emily Allen, *Writings ascribed to Richard Rolle* (New York and London, 1927).

Moreover, Rolle had not always lived in the North. As a young man he evidently spent some years at Oxford and perhaps at the Sorbonne. He was familiar with scholastic learning and well-read not only in Scripture but in patristic commentaries thereon. His *Explanationes super lectiones beati Job* (a commentary on the passages from Job used in the Office for the Dead) was one of the first works issued by the Oxford Press (in 1483): and it was intended *ad studentium utilitatem*. However spare his manner of life, his cell must have been at least furnished with books and writing materials. The tension that Jean Leclercq describes in *The Love of Learning and the Desire for God*, so strong in St Bernard and Ailred of Rievaulx, is present in Rolle, as in Hilton. He owes to his reading in Augustine, Bonaventura, Peter Lombard, and others the very language in which he describes the joys and ardours of the solitary contemplative. His English prose, like his Latin, is ornate, even mannered, and has the rhetorical richness of his great spiritual masters—none of whom had despised the pagan *auctores*. So Rolle in his little *Moralitas* on the Bee will quote partly from the *Natura Animalium* attributed to Aristotle, partly from Gregory's *Moralia*, traces of which are found elsewhere in his thought and style.

But it is naturally the ascetic writers who, though unnamed, leave the greatest impress on his work. Two lyrics inserted into the *Ego Dormio*, a letter that takes its title from its opening text from the *Song of Songs*, provide good illustrations of his adaptations of such a writer. The first is a meditation on the Passion (a theme that was to draw so many contemplatives in this century), which merges into a characteristic expression of love-longing:

> My keyng[1], that watir grette[2] and blode swette[3];
> Sythen ful sare bette[4], so that his blode hym wette
>
> . . . .
>
> Ful fast thai gan hym dyng[5], and at the pyler swyng[6],
> And his fayre face defowlyng with spittyng.
>
> The thorne crownes the keyng; ful sare es that prickyng.
> Alas, my joy and my swetyng es demed[7] for to hyng[8]. . . .

[1] *king*   [2] *wept*   [3] *sweated*   [4] *then sorely beaten*   [5] *beat*
[6] *scourge*   [7] *condemned*   [8] *hang*

The first four stanzas of this lyric undoubtedly derive from two Latin meditations, *Respice in Faciem Christi*, and *Candet nudatum pectus*, both of which had been movingly rendered into English before Rolle's time (see below, p. 377).

A second lyric in the *Ego Dormio* is headed *Cantus Amoris*:

> My sange es in syhtyng[1], my lyfe es in langynge[2],
> Til I thee se, my keyng, so fayre in thi schynyng,
> So fayre in thi fayrehede
>
> . . . .
>
> When wil thou come, Jesu my joy,
> And cover[3] me of kare
> And gyf[4] me the, that I may se
> Lifand[5] evermare?

[1] *sighing*   [2] *longing*   [3] *rescue*   [4] *give*   [5] *living*

Here the closing lines owe much to *Jesu dulcis memoria*, one of the best-known poems of the entire Middle Ages and still familiar in a nineteenth-century hymn-version ('Jesu the very thought of thee'): 'Desiderate millies / Mi Jesu, quando venies?'(O my Jesu, desired a thousand times, when wilt thou come?). Again there is a Middle English version, of about the same date (see below, p. 369). But Rolle has made his own; and he makes another in *The Form of Living*, chapter viii, where he renders these lines 'When wil thou come to comforth me, and bring me out of care', etc. Indeed the Latin verses express the essence of his devotion and it is not surprising that reminiscences of them occur throughout his work. Thus when, in the Latin *Judica Me*, he writes: 'O dulce et delicatum gaudium, amare dei filium', he is recalling other lines from the same poem: 'O beatum *incendium* . . . / Amare Dei filium' (O blessed fire . . . to love the son of God). *Incendium Amoris* is the title of his chief Latin work.

In Rolle's *prose* we can trace affinities of a rather different kind, with the Victoriens: Hugh and Richard of the Abbey of St Victor. For him as for them it is the celestial joy of contemplation that counts. When in chapter xi of *The Form of Living* he speaks of the 'joy of a raysed thoght', the joy proceeding from elevated thought (= mind, almost imagination), he has in mind what Richard of St Victor, himself an Irishman, or a Scot, had called *mentis sublevatio*.* But there were also earlier works in *English* prose which would surely attract Rolle's notice if only by reason of their attention to the Passion and to the Name of Jesus, which bulks so large in his writings. When in the *Cantus Amoris* he sings:

> Jesu, my dere and my drewry[1], delyte art thou to syng,
> Jesu, my myrth and melody, when will thou come, my keyng?
> Jesu, my hele and my *hony* . . .

[1] *sweetheart*

* See H. E. Allen, *English Writings* (Oxford, 1931), 341-2.

he is using the same mode of almost erotic endearments that are found two centuries earlier in the prose *Wohunge of Ure Laverd*:*

Jesu, swete Jesu, my druth[1], my derling, mi drihten[2], mi healend[3], mi huniter[4], mi haleweie[5].

> [1] *love*   [2] *lord*   [3] *healer*   [4] *honey-drop*   [5] *balm*

The only difference is in the replacement of archaic forms like *drihten*, *healend*, *huniter*, by *hele*, *hony*, etc. It is the combination of native and Latin alliterative patterns as applied to expressions of ardent desire that produces the cloying effect of Rolle's poetic prose, and almost defeats his purpose. In Latin, as in English, it is often too fluent, too mellifluous.

The personal, individual note in Rolle's work, however, is so strong that it was comparatively easy for Miss Allen to establish the canon and even the relative chronology (as she showed in her life as well as in her work an intuitive sympathy with the ascetic experience). Taken as a whole, the canon presents a picture of the Divine transmutation of Rolle's life and consciousness, a religion centring in the name of Jesus, who granted him whilst in this present life a foretaste of the Song of Divine Love and of the sound of heavenly melodies.

He is not concerned to describe unique and personal mystical experiences, or discourses with the Lord or Apocalyptic visions. He gives little space to that theme of self-knowledge which bulks large in St Catherine's revelations. Nor does he preach the necessity of entering the Cloud of Unknowing. His God is not *deus absconditus*. From first to last it is the joyful sense of Divine Love that he is intent on communicating. And he sees the contemplative as concerned with more than private perfection. And the major English works show him putting this doctrine into practice. Whether it was originally disillusion or discontent that led him to withdraw from men, monks, and universities we cannot say: the fierce and wild allegations and reproaches of the earlier works might suggest as much. But whatever the cause, the outcome was and remains remarkable.

It is almost impossible to summarize the contents or outline the shape of Rolle's prose works: as well try to reproduce the bickerings of a northern burn, the plash of a northern 'force'. And their present titles, usually those supplied by Horstman, his first editor, convey little at first sight: whereas to a fourteenth-century reader the opening words *Ego dormio et cor meum vigilat* would at once suggest Rolle's association with those ascetic writers who from St Bernard on saw in the Canticles— *The Song of Songs*—the highest form of spiritual expression.

* Ed. R. Morris, *Old English Homilies*, EETS xxix (1868), 269.

It was as an allegory of Christ's love for the Church and the soul that Rolle—and everybody else—read it. So did George Herbert. And unless we accept this we have no key to traditional spirituality. (Curiously enough it was emphasized again in modern times by the most austere and literal of all sects, the Plymouth Brethren.)

His *English Psalter* may have been his first work in English. Besides the translation, it includes a long allegorical commentary. For Rolle, the Psalter is not a record of the Psalmist's fears and aspirations, it is a 'book of hymns of Christ' and his spouse (collectively Holy Church, individually, man-soul): it is 'heal of a sick heart, honey to a bitter soul'. He expounds it tropologically, and is the less concerned with minute accuracy in rendering the text itself. 'In the translacioun', he says at the close of an impressive Prologue, predominantly in native English phrase, 'I follow the letter als mekil [much] als I may, and thare [where] I fynde na propir Inglys I folow the witte [sense] of the word, so that thai that sal rede it, tham thar [they need] noght dred errynge.' He keeps the Hebraic parallelism, but he also often keeps the Latin word order: e.g. *Dormivi conturbatus* (Ps. 56) becomes 'I slepe druvyd [troubled]'. Rare Latin verbs or nouns are rendered literally: *incurvaverunt animam meam*: 'thai croked my soul'; *susceptor*: 'uptaker'. Compounds are given parallel English forms (*invocaverunt*: 'incald'). All of which makes for a certain stiffness, though Rolle sometimes conveys the power of the original, as in Ps. 120: 6: 'the sunn sall noght bren the no the mone be nyght'. In the Commentary on each verse, where he is following his own Latin original, the style is much more lyrical—and alliterative. He seizes and expatiates on verses that he reads as expressing his own devotion. Thus he renders *concaluit cor meum* (Ps. 38: 4) as 'my hert verily hetid with the fire of Cristes luf', and the *nomen tuum* of Ps. 9: 11 is read as the name of Jesus.

His exposition of the Seven Gifts of the Holy Ghost is, unexpectedly, of much more general application. Thus the gift of 'cunning' (intelligence) is to the end that one 'gather earthly goods only to the honour of God and to the benefit of other men more than himself': an application that chimes with the description of the Spirit's Gifts in *Piers Plowman* xix. Again 'consaile' (counsel) is defined as putting away worldly riches and all things that men may be 'tagild with' (encumbered). Wisdom is associated with contemplation: 'In this gyfte schynes Contemplacyone [i.e. is conspicuous] that es, Saynt Austyne says, a gastely dede [spiritual death] of fleschly affecyones, thurghe the joy of a raysede thoghte [the joy proceeding from elevated thought].' The medieval tradition associated a specific virtue with every gift of the Holy Spirit.

Of the English prose works, *The Form of Living* is probably the latest and certainly the most appealing. It is addressed to a young recluse, probably one Margaret Kirkby, at the beginning of her enclosure at East Layton—many miles away from her home at Skelbroke, not far from Hampole. The Latin rubric calls her 'suam dilectam discipu-lam'—suggesting that she may have become an anchoress under his influence; but enclosure was a quite common practice, from the twelfth century to the fifteenth; at a time when nunneries were often no more than finishing schools for the well-born, devout women were very likely to seek a more severe self-discipline. And perhaps there is some quality in the wide and empty Yorkshire moors that attracts soli-taries. I know of at least one hermit, a former Benedictine monk, who has set up his cell in the West Riding.

The twelve chapters of the *Form* constitute a guide for such devout souls. They fall into two parts, divided by a revealing rubric at the head of c. vii—*Amore langueo*—another allusion to the Canticles or 'buke of lufe', as Rolle here calls it, that would be seized at once. All that is of abiding appeal and applicability in Rolle's teaching is to be found in one passage or another of the *Form*. This is his prose at its best and most orderly. If it has less biographical interest than the Latin works and shows none of the expository power of his Scripture com-mentaries, it remains the best introduction to his work. For accounts of his raptures we must turn to the Latin works, and whether they can properly be described as ecstasies is still debated. He differs from some mystics in that he came to the view that the state of rapt contem-plation might be continuous. To the average layman he has nothing to say. But some of his spiritual counsels (as with other ascetics) would be acceptable to any devout soul. He gives us no reports of heavenly visions or direct communication with the Deity such as Julian of Norwich was to claim. His typical experience is the sense of a sudden, unusual, and 'merry' 'heat', followed by a melodious harmony, heaven-born. It is this that he calls a rapture, a foretaste of eternal sweetness. He makes no comparison with St Paul's classic account of ecstasy in 2 Cor. 12: 1–4.

The *Form* is none the worse for the absence of personal and auto-biographical reference. The (earlier) Latin works sometimes show a querulous self-justification that does not sit easily with Rolle's insis-tence on *caritas*. In them he seems almost too ready to brand his detractors as hypocrites, hateful to God. Like some other devout folk (though not like Hilton), he sometimes seems egocentric, and he is so ready to quote himself that the repetition of certain expressions is an all too easily distinguishable feature of his work. Along with this goes a willingness to attack the clergy that made it possible for his work to be read as Wycliffite. There is implicit—though not explicit—a certain drift towards a religion independent of formal observances. He has little to say about the sacraments, even the Eucharist.

The *Form* was deservedly popular, and soon rewritten in Southern dialects 'that it schulde the betir be understondyn of men that be of the selve countré', as MS Ii. iv. 9 in the Cambridge University Library puts it—though Miss Allen and the catalogues read the last two words as 'Selbe countré'. Passages were later incorporated into a compilation known as *The Poor Caitiff*, and in the *Speculum Spiritualium*: where the compiler keeps it in English 'because it seems to sound better in the mother tongue'. This was a work Carthusian in tone if not in origin, and it reminds us that the Carthusians—whose rule provided for solitary cells or houses—were to be the chief promoters of Rolle's kind of spirituality in the fifteenth century. The Carthusian house of Syon near Richmond was founded by north-country persons and Sheen, also Carthusian, also had northern conections. Syon had the autograph manuscript of the *Melum Amoris* (or *Melos*—Song of Love), and perhaps a copy of the *Office*. It was to play a major part in disseminating contemplative writings.

I have space to dwell on one aspect only of Rolle's spirituality. He was far from being the only begetter of the cult of the Holy Name. St Bernard had burst forth in praise of the name of Jesus in his fifteenth sermon on the Canticles, for which he took as his text 'Oleum effusum nomen tuum' (thy name is as oil poured out). But Rolle was the chief popularizer of the devotion in England and himself expatiated on this very text. He went so far as to claim that no one could attain ecstasy unless he showed special love to the name of Jesus and kept it constantly before him. Devotees (Rolle among them) quoted a passage in a fourth-century sermon by Peter Chrysologus that gives the clue to the cult: 'Si nomen tantum est, quanta potestas!' (If the name is so great, how great is the power.) It must not be thought of as a mechanical or magical incantation but as a vehicle for unspoken ineffable adoration. In the *Form* it is associated with the highest degree of ecstasy: 'the sawle that es in the thyrd degré ... es syngand *gastly* [spiritually] til Jesu, and in Jesu, and Jesu, *noght bodyly* cryand wyth mouth'. The Feast of the Holy Name survives in the Calendar of *The Book of Common Prayer*. The Jesus prayer current in pre-revolutionary Russia shows the persistence of this cult, and, if one of J. D. Salinger's novels is to be trusted, it had a certain vogue in America some years since.

In the *Form* as in all his other works, Rolle is preoccupied not with formal observances but with kindling the fire of Christ's love within the heart. It can never be achieved save by 'wilful povert', and turning away from the vain love that is 'ever wallowing'. Such poverty is an act of the *Will*, and the Will figures large in other English ascetic writings, as it had in St Anselm's.

Rolle's notion of the Contemplative life does not rule out 'good thewes', i.e. the occasions for Christian conduct: he envisages the recluse having opportunity to do deeds of charity. Ch. vi, the last chapter of the first part, is in fact largely concerned with outward conduct. Standard penitential material on the sins is here set forth in Rolle's very personal idiom: thus 'impatience' here figures as 'untholmodnes', excessive self-confidence as 'synguler witt'; 'flytyng' (contest in abuse), 'rusyng' (boasting), 'hethyng' (scoffing), polishing of words—all such sins are roundly condemned. The view of human equality before God that John Ball was to put into the rhyme of 'When Adam delved and Eve span' is given a new slant by Rolle: 'For all we are alike free before God's face unless our *deeds* make any better or worse than other.' Not all of this corrective matter seems appropriate to the state of a recluse who would surely be unlikely to practise witchcraft or 'lead caroles' or 'bring up new guise' (fashion in clothes) or (at prayers) 'rabble on and reck never but they be said', or have cause or opportunity to teach those who are not 'cunning' or to comfort those in prison. Yet precisely the same cautions are addressed to anchoresses in *Ancrene Wisse* and even earlier to the northern recluse to whom Ailred of Rievaulx wrote. It may be that Rolle was simply repeating injunctions that were traditionally given to recluses, but he would hardly have done so unless the dangers he warned against had been real and present.

It is less surprising that Rolle lays down no rules for penance: in the very next chapter he will affirm that those who have most of God's love, whether they do penance or not, shall be in the highest degree in heaven. The rubric of this seventh chapter, *Amore Langueo*, indicates that the rest of the book will have a very different direction. The special gift of the solitary is to love Jesus Christ till he or she feels 'joy, sweetness, and burning'. This *triad*, with its Latin variant—*canor, dulcor, calor*—is the sign-manual of all Rolle's utterances. The true lover of Christ (like Pope's rapt seraph) 'adores and burns'. The special gift will be granted if 'thou come with great travail in prayer and thinking . . .', and does not depend on 'how much thou sayest [in prayer] but how well'. With the progression from the stage of languishing for Love to the highest degree of love, as a burning fire, the prose itself becomes more fervent; and the third stage of love is presented as a burning fire: it is figured by the passionate nightingale 'that loves song and melody and fails for much love'. Soon Rolle himself breaks into a *cantus amoris*: 'When will thou come to comfort me and bring me out of care?'—heavily alliterative, like the Latin version of the same song in the *Melum Contemplativorum*, a strange work said by Hope Emily Allen to be 'the most extreme example of "polyphonic prose" ever attempted': its insistent alliteration, its barbarous Latinity and strained rhetoric combine with covert personal allusion to make it almost incomprehensible. But the prose of the *Form* has no such faults.

The key to the inner melody of Rolle's prose and verse is the name of Jesus: 'It shall be in thine ear joy, in thy mouth honey [hence the title *Melum*], and in thy heart melody.' One must *think* Jesus: 'that name wounds in love and fulfils of charity'. It opens heaven to the contemplative (though Rolle would also have him or her 'hail oft Mary, both day and night'). The contemplative has little need of books: 'Hold love in heart and in work, and thou hast all that we may say or write. For charity is fullness of the law. On that hangs all.' The passage echoes St Bernard on the Canticles and St Paul on *caritas*—not to mention that closing allusion to the dominical utterance of Matt. 22: 40. But Rolle's formulations have an individual inflection: 'If we give all that we have to *beggar-staff* and know as much as all men on earth, without love it is ordained sorrow and torment.'

As the spiritual eroticism of the prose deriving from the Canticles survives only in a Puritan sect, so Moody and Sankey and more recent revivalists on occasion curiously echo Rolle's tone and language:

> I came into the Garden alone
> When the dew was still on the roses . . .
> Oh, he walks with me and he talks with me
> And He tells me I'm his own
> And the joy we share as we tarry there
> None other has ever known.

Such verses do not usually figure in literary histories; yet perhaps they should, for however debased their rhythms, however obvious their sentiments, they give voice to emotions not basically different from Rolle's.

Rolle's activities remind us that mystics serve as personal spiritual guides to others, and this is not their least useful 'function'; indeed the only way in which ordinary men can judge them is by their value in this role. Not that they play a clinical or therapeutic part, but that their sanctity gives them a charismatic power, based on their own experience of spiritual conflict or development. They do indeed enable other men and women to gain a clearer vision of God (which Jung described as the function of all religious teachers).

About the author of *The Cloud of Unknowing* we know nothing, and he wished us to know nothing. But about the purpose and presupposi- tions of the book we can learn much from its rubric: 'Here bygynnith a book of Contemplacyon the whiche is clepyd the Clowde of Unknow- yng in the whiche a soule is onyd [united] with God.' The title at once establishes the affinities of the text with the *Mystical Theology* of 'Pseudo-Dionysius' (*c*.AD 500), which describes the ascent of the soul to union with God and avers that by ordinary ways of understanding one cannot come to know him who 'posuit tenebram latibulum suum' (who made the darkness his secret place) (Ps. 17: 12). So Moses had to enter into the *caliginem* or *nubem ignorantiae*—a term that the English writer avoided, doubtless because 'ignorance' in the sense of defective knowledge was not in question; it is the *via negativa*, the way of nescience, that he espouses. The spirit of the *Mystical Theology* the English writer has wholly absorbed and he may well have translated it, but to its content he owes little.

Certainly his opening paragraph accords with the tone of the earlier work. It enjoins anyone possessing a copy of the *Cloud* not to suffer it to be read, written, or spoken of except by one who purposes to be a perfect follower of Christ 'in the sovereignest point of contemplative living'. 'Fleshly janglers, open praisers and blamers of themselves or of any other, tiding-tellers and tutillers of tales [scandal-mongers] and all manner of pinchers [cavillers], cared I never that they should see this book'—nor 'these curious lettered or lewed men', either (*curiositas*, inordinate speculation, here as elsewhere figuring as the bane of the later fourteenth century). The book, in short, is intended only for professed contemplatives. Yet it at once concedes that good men (or women) living in the world may likewise feel an inward impulse towards 'the privy spirit of God' and implies that they too may from time to time attain the highest felicity of contemplation. It thus marks, almost unintentionally, a new development in ascetic thought, a breaching of the wall between the contemplative and the secular. But it promises no account of mystical ecstasy. There is only one reference to ravishment in the whole work, and no reference to the writer's own feelings or experience. Nothing could be further from the attitude of a Richard Jefferies, who because he described himself as 'rapt' and 'carried away' has been accounted a mystic.* The purpose of the

---

* See Cuthbert Butler, *Western Mysticism* (2nd edn., London, 1926), 229–32.

Cloud is simply to advise a young 'friend in God', a twenty-four-year-old solitary whose soul God has fastened by 'a leash of longing' for a 'more special state and form of living', a perfect degree that lies beyond the degrees he calls 'common' and 'special' and the third degree and manner of life, which is called 'singular'. Rolle had named the three degrees of love as insuperable, inseparable, singular, but gave no hint of a higher stage.

The young solitary must first learn to 'lift up the foot of his love': a figure deriving from Augustine's gloss on Ps. 9: 15, which Rolle had already adopted when interpreting Ps. 1: 1: 'He festid noght the fote of his luf in lykynge and joy of this werld.' The way to Perfection is complete self-surrender: 'God wil thou do bot loke on hym, and late Him al one [leave all to him]. And kepe thou the windowes and the dore for flies and enemies assailyng.' Again the clue to the figure is an Augustinian gloss, based ultimately on a text that had figured in *Ancrene Wisse*: *ascendit mors per fenestras nostras* (Jer. 9: 21), 'Death comes in through our windows.' Attention must be fixed, not on the words of God, but on God himself; no easy matter. At first one finds only a darkness, 'and as it were a cloude of *un*knowyng, thou wost never what, savyng that thou felist in thi wille a nakid entent unto God': a difference, this, from the Pseudo-Dionysius, who gives no such role to the will. It is not the kind of darkness felt when a candle goes out at night, but a 'lacking of knowing', a sense that what you thought you knew you do not know. Yet it reveals God rather than hides him: 'Yif ever thou schalt fele him or see him . . . it behoveth alweis be in this cloude and in this derknes.' This is the 'work', the experience, for which man was made, 'and alle thing for man, to help and forther him therto'. Once God is so felt, the sweet taste of the experience is never lost. The emphasis here is novel, and goes clean against the monistic or Manichaean drift of some interpretations of Neoplatonism. This *deus absconditus* is also the God of Kind (Nature), who will in no wise reverse 'the ordinel [regular] course'. Time is made for man, and not man for time; and hence God will not 'go before' (? anticipate) the stirring of Kind in a man's soul. The phrase is cryptic, but leaves no doubt that the writer is assuming the essential goodness of creation.

Intermittent imagined dialogue makes the *Cloud* more vivid, more readable than any treatise of Rolle's. The novice puts the very questions that rise in the reader's mind—and receives blunt answers. When he asks 'How schal I think on himself, and what is hee?' the reply is plain, and meant to stagger: 'I wote never'—God can be loved, but not imagined: 'By love may he be getyn [got] and holden, bot bi thought neither [not].' 'Smyte apon that thicke cloude of unknowyng with a scharp darte of longing love, and go not thens for thing [despite any-thing] that befalleth.' The firm clear utterance dispels any fear of obscurities, or obscurantism. There is nothing etiolated or fine-spun. Each of the short chapters marks a stage in a reasoned development. No difficulty is avoided, no hindrance overlooked. At one point (ch. vii) the nature of the dialogue alters and it becomes an interior argument with Thought—who is to play a similar part in *Piers Plowman* (B viii. 70). When Thought asks 'What sekist thou, and what woldest thou have?' it is answered: 'Him I coveite, him I seche, and nought bot him.' Here Thought embodies all the promptings that might distract from contemplation—including (even) recollection of the Passion or of the wonderful kindness of God. The intent can be lapped and folded in one simple monosyllable—'God', or 'Love': 'this worde schal be thi scheeld and thi spere, whether thou ridest on pees or on werre'. The absoluteness of all this is presented, reasonably enough, as puzzling the novice. So it is at once refined, and related to the two degrees, higher and lower, of the Active and Contemplative lives—not permanently or continuously exclusive of each other but differing inasmuch as what befits the one is irrelevant to the other. The highest form of contemplation excludes everything except 'a lovyng steryng [stirring] and a blinde beholdyng unto the nakid beyng of God himself only' (where 'blind' suggests the conditions of the *caligo ignorandi*). This is the *optimam partem* of Luke 10: 42: a key text, in its Vulgate form, for all contemplatives.

The prerequisite is humility; a true knowing and feeling of oneself as one is precedes a true knowledge and feeling of God. Yet contrition, confession, and amendment of life should not entail brooding on past sins. So Mary Magdalene, identified by strong if strange tradition with Mary the Contemplative, is to be thought of as sorrowing more for her lack of love than for sin: 'and have no wonder therof, for it is the condi-cion of a trewe lover that ever the more he loveth, the more him longeth for to love'. And the code of secular love will be applied again later. It is the condition of a perfect lover not only to love that thing he loves more than himself but also, 'in manner, to hate himself for thing that he loveth'. The erotic imagery of the *Canticles*, on the other hand, finds no place in the *Cloud*.

It was Mary's contemplation of the sovereign wisdom of the God-head in Christ that distinguished her from Martha—though Martha's 'busyness' was 'full good and full holy': which grants more to the active life than *Ancrene Wisse* does. The *unum necessarium* (Luke 10: 42) is that God be loved and praised for himself. The story of Mary, rapt in this love and in the cloud of unknowing as she sat 'full still' is here expounded with a delicacy equal to Augustine's, and perhaps follows Augustine in dwelling on Christ's repeated 'Martha, Martha'. As he spoke as advocate for Mary so will he answer for contemplatives, and prompt others to provide for their necessities—despite those who allege the proverb 'God sendeth the kow bot not by the horne' (i.e. helps only those who help themselves).

Beside the virtue of meekness is now put charity, with its two branches: love of God, now defined as a naked intent directed unto God for himself, and love of man for God 'even with thyself'. 'Naked intent' is a characteristic phrase, always marking purity of motive: 'in this werke a parfite prentis askith neither relesing of peyne, ne encresing of mede [reward] ne (schortly to sey) nought bot [God] himself'. As to the second or lower branch of charity, it is nowhere suggested that the contemplative should go out and do good to his fellows, though all men will seem alike akin to him. He wishes them as much good as he would to his homeliest (most familiar) friend, but he shows this by straining up his spirit for them, as Our Lord did his body on the Cross: it is the classic role of all those who in Langland's phrase 'in poverty and penance pray for all Christians'. At this point the terms *work* and *travail* begin to take on a special sense, and the soul is repeatedly required to 'do that in him is': a phrase that appears elsewhere at the time in scholastic contexts. The work is to suppress, with the help of Grace, all recollection of created nature. Then God will sometimes send out a beam of spiritual light that pierces the cloud and inflames with the fire of his love 'fer more then I kan telle thee, or may, or wile, at this tyme: for of that werke . . . dar I not take apon me to speke with my blabryng fleschely tonge'—even though this beam is not God himself, but a special sense of him.

In chapter lxx of *The Cloud* there is an appeal to 'Denis bookes' as authoritative, and there is a reference to 'Denis devinitie' in *The Book of Privy Counselling*, almost certainly by the author of the *Cloud*. These are grounds for attributing to the same pen the rendering of the *Mystica Theologia* of Pseudo-Dionysius that bears the title 'Dionise Hid Divinitie'. If the style of this short work differs from that of the *Cloud*— though likewise proceeding by question-and-answer—it is in part because the language of the *Mystica Theologia* (originally Greek) is highly technical and almost untranslatable. In the Middle Ages that book was the chief channel of transcendental teaching; and commentaries by Hugh of St Victor, Grosseteste, Albertus Magnus, and Aquinas (who contrived to accommodate its doctrine in his *Summa*, and commented on another work attributed to Dionysius, the *De Divinis Nominibus*) enhanced its prestige. The English translator assures us that he has followed not only the naked letter of the text but also the 'sentence' of the Abbot of St Victor, a 'noble expositor' thereof. He is referring to the glossed and expanded text of Thomas Gallus, a canon regular of the Congregation of St Victor, who became Abbot of St Andrew's, Vercelli (1219–46), a period, as it happens, during which a papal legate from Vercelli, Cardinal Guala, visited and stayed in Chesterton, Cambridge. The translator's text of Thomas Gallus may well have come direct from Vercelli, but for two chapters of the work he consulted another version, that by Johannes Sarracenus.

We have to do, then, with a writer who had access to libraries, and some learning. It takes a keen intelligence to follow Dionysian subtleties and it took some hardihood to transpose them into a language still woefully deficient in abstract vocabulary. It seems likely that he accomplished this whilst Chaucer was still working at his Boethius; and he deserves to rank with Chaucer and with Usk as a pioneer who deliberately forged a wholly new philosophical English, without precedent except in the French versions of Boethius and Aristotle, and with only Walton and Pecock for direct successors. We have to wait for the Cambridge Platonists to find a prose adequate for philosophical discourse of the kind that could consider the notions first made available in the *Hid Divinitie*. Even the title of the *Mystica Theologia* presented difficulties, implying as it does a theology dependent on Scripture interpreted *mystice*: the terms 'mystical', 'mysterious', 'mysterial' were as yet unknown. The translator's choice of 'hid' suggests an allusion to the central tenet of this theology, the *Deus absconditus*; by the same process of thought *mysticas visiones* will become 'blynde beholdynges'. An early passage will illustrate different difficulties:

et non negationes oppositas opinari esse affirmationibus, sed multo prius ipsam super privationes esse, quæ est super omnem et ablationem et positionem.

This appears as:

and not for to have it in opinyon that thees deniinges of thees being thinges ben contrary to the first affermynges of hem, bot fastliche for to holde in sight of byleve him for to be aboven alle doying awey of thees beyng or beable thinges, the whiche in himself is aboven alle, ye! bothe doyng away and affermyng of hem alle.

Here 'being thinges' represents the *existentia*, 'things existing', of an earlier sentence (*existences* in the required sense does not appear in English until 1605);* whilst 'beable' is an expansion of the text,

* In ME (e.g. *HF* 266) 'existence' = 'actuality', as opposed to appearance, though Lydgate has the word in a sense closer to the Latin, 'being or state of being': 'Thyng counterfetyd hath non existence'. 'Actuality', except for one example in Trevisa, is first found in Henry More and Glanvill.

a nonce-word, designed to cover all possibilities of existences. Similarly in the English version of the preliminary prayer we find 'first-heed', without any equivalent in the Latin, but representing the Platonic first cause, which is implicit in Dionysian theory. The Latin abounds in *super-* compounds: '*super*dea', '*super*bona', '*super*-ignotum', etc., the prefix which is neatly rendered as 'sovereyn' (e.g. 'sovereyn unknowen' = *superignotum*). *Inegressibilia* requires the coinage 'unpassyngliche' ('unpassingly' = without departing from itself).

The fifth and final chapter of the *Theologia* is a dazzling array of negative opposites, concluding: 'et super omnem ablationem est excessus ipsius ab omnibus absoluti et super omnia eminentis'—which sets the translator groping for an English expression of inconceivability: 'And his not-understondable overpassyng [*excessus*] is un-understondabely aboven alle affermyng and deniinge'; the Cambridge Platonist Glanvill (1661) was the first to hit upon 'inconceivableness' for this concept. This translator is in fact an interpreter and does not hesitate to introduce a simile of his own: visions have reason in subjection 'as the lady hath her maidens'. One striking figure in the Latin presents the 'work' of removing the inessential in order to perceive the Divine beauty as comparable to the sculptor's stripping away of material to reach the latent image—'the which cumbrous clog thus congealed of these innumerable diversities we must pare away'; and this Plotinian conception—it was to reappear in a sonnet of Michelangelo—is presented in terms of carving in wood:

Here is a man havyng a sounde stok . . . liing before hym and havyng withinne hym entent and craft to make an ymage of the leest quantitee, of that place of the wode, the whiche is, bi mesuryng of right lynyng, in the sentre or middes of that same stok. . . . Er he may com for to see that ymage bi cleer bodely sight of his outward iye[1] . . . the whiche he hath in hymself by cleer crafte of ymaginacioun . . . he most[2] algates[3] by craft and by instrumentes voide awey the outward partyes of that wode.

$$^{1}\ eye \qquad ^{2}\ must \qquad ^{3}\ always$$

This passage, if noteworthy for the role it assigns to 'imagination' is not, to be sure, of the sonorous kind that young men chant in Cambridge courts at midnight. Yet the *Denis* has its place—perhaps the earliest place—in the particular sequence of English prose that was to issue in *Religio Medici*. It is as near as English medieval thought will get to the high philosophy that informs the first canto of *Paradiso*. With the phrase 'dark night of the spirit' we may seem to approach St John of the Cross; but the figure is not developed. A few words and phrases bear the mark of the *Cloud*'s author: 'It is nothing thus: but thus it must be'; 'naked intent unto God'; 'listi' 'listely'. Indeed, it would be right to wrestle with the *Denis* before embarking on the *Cloud*: it is the intricate honeycomb from which the longer work has drawn much of its sweetness.

The Epistle of Discretion of Stirrings (i.e. 'about distinguishing between feelings') may also safely be credited to the author of the *Cloud*. Here is the same emphasis on 'blind stirrings of love', the same figure of the prick and the point, the same warnings against ape-like imitators. The 'stirrings' must come from within, not from without—not through the senses. Strict silence, singular fasting, solitary dwelling—these are not the true ends of our desire, only, for some men, the means. God is 'hid bitwix them' and may be found only by love, not by the 'ghostly' (the inner) eye of reason. 'Bot ever whan reson defaileth, than list love live and lerne for to plei.' Perfect knowledge of the self and of one's inward dispositions is learnt only in the school of God. It is the haven that the ship of the soul at last attains, wafted by the peaceable wind and soft 'weathers' of the Holy Ghost, through the which knowing the soul 'sitteth quietly in hymself as a king crouned in his rewme [realm], mightly, wisely and goodly governyng himself and alle his thoughtes and sterings, bothe in body and in soule'. This figure leads to that of the crown of life, with its gold (wisdom), its precious stones (discretion), and its 'toretes' of fleur-de-lis (the perfection of virtue): so the soul must

strongly rise and martir itself, with castyng doun of the owne wile [viz. its private desires] in alle soche sodein and singulere steringes, and sey scharply that it wil not folow soche steringes, seme thei never so liking, so heigh, ne so holy, bot if[1] it have therto the witnes and the consentes of som goostly techers (I mene soche as have ben of longe tyme experte in singuler levyng).

[1] *unless*

The passage illustrates the supple and relaxed nature of this prose. Elsewhere it is more carefully patterned. A basic statement is expanded by elaboration of alternatives that give it fullness and roundness. As thus:

And therfore speke when thee list[1] and leve whan thee list; ete whan thee list and fast whan thee list; be in companie whan thee list and by thiself whan thee list; so that God and grace be thi leder.

[1] *it pleases you*

Freedom of spirit is the keynote: singularities feigned under colour of holiness result in 'full and final destroying of the freedom of Christ'. Alliterative conjunctions of nouns play a central part in this prose ('a grace schal be lerner and leder', etc.). Though the paragraphs are carefully ordered and logical, the epistle breathes the inimitable air of a personal letter. The most attractive of all contemplative writings of the period, it has the further merit of being brief.

The Scale [or Ladder] *of Perfection*, ascribed to Walter Hilton, a Canon of Thurgarton, Notts., who in a Pepys manuscript is said to be of Oxford, and in the colophon to a York Minster manuscript is stated to have died in 1379 (not 1395, the date given by modern authorities), is substantially an original work; an early translation by Thomas Fishlake, a Carmelite, shows that its quality was quickly recognized. Like several other such books the *Scale*—or at least the first part—is addressed to a contemplative. The second, different in theme and treatment, appears to be meant for all 'souls' attempting to live the spiritual life: the content is doctrinal rather than devotional; and Baptism and Penance bulk large. In this second part, the Dionysian doctrine of the *Cloud* seems to be taken for granted: there are allusions to the secure *darkness* in which devout souls come through grace to the knowledge of themselves. Yet as regards such self-knowledge there is an apparent divergence. The *Scale* insists that to practise contemplation a man must first enter into himself, and know his own soul and the thoughts thereof. The *Cloud*, likewise (ch. lxviii), refers to this injunction, but only to scout it: 'When another man [?sc. Hilton] would bid thee gather thy powers and thy wits within thyself and worship God there, though he say full well and truly . . . *me* list not bid thee do so. Look on no wise that thou be within thyself.'

This divergence would make one chary of identifying Hilton with the author of the *Cloud*, even if Dionysian doctrine did not seem in general incompatible with the plainer teaching of the *Scale*, applicable as it is to many sorts and conditions of men. Hilton in fact enlarges on the necessity of self-knowledge more than any of his contemporaries, saying that there is a 'work' which is necessary: 'that is a man for to entere into hymself for to knowe his owne soule and the myghttes [powers] therof, the fayrenesse and the foulnesse of hir' (ch. xlii*). He soon adds, 'the soule of a man is a lyf [?living being], maed of thre myghttes—mynde [memory], reson and wille—to the ymage and the lyknesse of the blesside Trinyté' (ch. xliii). By the Fall, this likeness was perverted into an animal delight in ourselves and other creatures:

Thanne yyf thou wolt fynde hit [your own soul], wythdrawe thy body from alle bodyly thyng outward . . . and fro alle thy fyve wittes as moche as thou myght; and thenk of the kynde¹ of a resonable soule goostly² . . . the more clerly thou

* Quotations from the *Scale* are from the copy in MS Bodley 100; chapter references are to the modernized edition of Dom Gerard Sitwell (London, 1953).

myght thenken of the kynde and the worthynesse of a resonable soule, what hit is, and what is the kyndly werchynge³ of hit, the better seest thou thyself. . . . Alle gostly [things] beth seyen⁴ and knowyn by understondynge of the soule, naght⁵ by understondynge⁶. . . .

(II. xxx)

¹ *nature*   ² *spiritual*   ³ *natural function*   ⁴ *are seen*   ⁵ *not*
⁶ *imagination*

This is the language of the Schools rather than of the cell. It bears the impress of a clear mind; Hilton was not called *Magister* for nothing. But the conclusion goes to the heart of Hilton's faith: the more that the soul knows itself, through grace and by its vision of truth, and the less that it thinks it is loving God, the closer it comes to perceiving God's gift of his love for the soul. This love, he says in one of his most moving chapters (II. xxxv), is

freely had of the gracious yyft¹ of Jesu, after moche bodyly and gostly travele² goynge byfore. For ther beth³ summe lovers of God that maken hemself forto love God as hit were by here⁴ owne myght, for they steren⁵ hemself thorw gret vyolence. . . . A soule that hath yyft of love thorw⁶ gracious byholdynge of Jesu . . . he is naght besye forto streyne hymself over his myght. . . . Therfore preyeth he, and that desyreth he, that the love of God wolde touchen hym with hys blesside lyght, that he myghtte seen⁷ a litel of hym by hys gracious presence, for thenne ssolde⁸ he love hym; and so by thys way cometh the yyft of love, that is God, into a soule.

¹ *gift*   ² *travail*   ³ *are*   ⁴ *their*   ⁵ *strain*   ⁶ *through*
⁷ *see*   ⁸ *should*

The re-forming of the soul in faith and in feeling is the real plot of the work; and Evelyn Underhill did not err or exaggerate when she compared it with the purification and ascent in Dante's *Comedy*. Like Dante, Hilton has an eye for the homely and telling image:

Ryght as a costret¹ that is old, whan hit receyveth nuwe² wyn that is fressh and myghty, the costreth swelleth out and is in poynt forto³ cleven and barsten⁴, untille the wyn have boyled and spurged out alle unclennesse, but as sone as the wyn is fyned and clered, than standeth hit stille and the costret hool: ryght so a soule that is old thorugh synne, whanne hit receyveth a lytel of the love of God is in poynt forto cleven . . . hit barsteth out at the eyene⁵ by wepynge and at the mouth by spekynge . . . [but afterwards] . . . thanne is the love clere and stondeth still. . . .

(II. xxix)

¹ *large bottle*   ² *new*   ³ *is likely to*   ⁴ *burst*   ⁵ *eyes*

Hilton's prose has the same calm and clarity as settled wine. His modern editors have scarcely had to do more than regularize spelling and reduce inflections.

Eight 'Chapters on Perfection' that follow the *Scale* in several manuscripts hardly equal it in quality. They are said to have been 'founden in a book of Maister Lowes de Fontibus at Canterbrigge and turned into English bi Maister Walter Hilton of Thurgartoun'. The reference is evidently to an Aragonese Franciscan Lluis de Font, who was sent to read the Sentences at Cambridge in 1383; but no book by him is known. If the chapters are a translation we cannot credit Hilton with more than a facility in rendering the friar's account of the stages of perfection: tears of compunction; fervent desire; sweetness, softeness, gladness—'so that alle the lymes of the bodi and al the makyng of the world with alle the creaturis is as a melody of the harpe'; and finally the 'glymerynge of hevenly blis'.

Certainly Hilton would find himself in sympathy with much in these chapters—e.g. the answer to the question of what to do when the grace of devotion is withdrawn: 'the moore that thi tribulacion and thin afflicccioun is, the moore schal be thi cunfort whanne grace and devocioun is yovun [given] to thee. Preie thanne contynuely, redynge in the book of liif, that is the liif of Jesu Crist.' Charity is put before fasting, holiness before 'waking' (staying awake in vigil). There is a familiar caution against those who boast of visions and 'quaint feel-ings' or claim they may live as they list: even if these quote St Paul to their purpose ('Where the spirit of the Lord is there is liberty'), they mean not as St Paul meant. Other Pauline utterances provide a con-stant underweaving, strengthened by appeals now to 'Cato' (i.e. the *Disticha Catonis*), now to Jerome.

More unexpected are two whole chapters given to the perils of spiritual affection between a devout man and woman. They are in fact the most vivid in the book and they are traced with a knowing hand: 'Nedis thei mosten schewe outward sumtyme bi othere tokenes that semeth not myche [much] yvel, what the herte meneth.' Each says to the other that they mean naught but good; but 'may nether wordis ne touchingis ne handlyngis ne kissyngis ne bodili presence maken a ful seeth to her love'. (*Seeth* (satisfaction) is a favourite word of Hilton's.) The passage plays on the ancient topos of the *quinque lineae amoris*;* but it is also, perhaps, part of the *damnosa hereditas* of Abelard and Eloise.

Shorter but more noteworthy is a work of a few pages addressed to a 'dear brother in Christ' who wishes to know how angels' song may be perceived, felt, and versified. One good reason for assigning it to Hilton is the modesty of the writer, who owns that he cannot tell for

---

* See P. Dronke, *Medieval Latin and the Rise of European Love-Lyric* (Oxford, 1966), ii. 488.

certain the truth of this matter, though he insists that perfection consists in a true 'onehead' (union) of God and the soul by perfect charity.
This is attained when the mind is 'stabild sadly, withoutyn chaunge-
ynge and vagacion [a term here first found] in God and gastly things',
the reason is cleared of 'figure and fantasies of creatures', and will and
affection are purged from fleshly love and inflamed with burning love
of the Holy Ghost. Yet he does not completely condemn 'creatureli-
ness'. Rather, by virtue of charity, all that the senses offer may be
turned to comfort and gladness; 'sensuality' (in the Latin sense of
capacity for feeling) may receive new savour and sweetness in all
creatures, and man's lost dominion over creation be restored. When the
purified and ravished soul is filled with charity, then is heard, if our
Lord vouchsafe, the angels' song: an experience comparable with
Ezechiel's visions of God's privities 'in bodily imagination' (i.e. as
embodied in images). It cannot be described. Whoso hears it may
himself 'soothly sing a new song'—alluding, surely, to the new song
sung to the Lamb by the four and twenty elders (Rev. 5: 9). But this
experience is secondary to the joy in love of God for himself, and is to
be distinguished (as Rolle, too, emphasizes) on the one hand from the
devilish fantasies afflicting those who neglect prayers, Holy Writ, and
meditation on the Passion and seek 'by violence' to behold heavenly
things (a curious application of Matt. 11: 12); and on the other hand
from the delight derived from meditation on the Name of Jesus, 'who
makes his name as honey and as song'—a delight that is properly
expressed in the psalms and hymns and anthems of the Church, and is
not to be magnified into a special visitation. An awareness of the
dangers of subjective emotion shows all through this tract; and comes
to a head in its closing sentence: 'It suffices to me to live in truth prin-
cipally, and not in feeling'. If this is not Hilton's work, it may well be
by a disciple well-read in Rolle.

A work of a different order and consistently attributed to Hilton is
an Epistle on the 'mixed life' addressed to a lord who is both a parent
and a landowner, more pertinent to most modern readers than are his
strictly contemplative writings. It is a book of counsel for all whose
lives partake of both the active and the contemplative life, who take the
mid-path between secular and spiritual occupation, and so keep the
order of charity (*ordinavit in me caritatem*—for once a text from Canticles (2: 4) is given a practical gloss). The active life of penance or the
works of mercy could coexist with interior spiritual life. As in Part ii of
the *Scale*, a picture emerges of Hilton as a teacher desiring that all
should come to the love and knowledge of God, and a generosity of
spirit such as we rarely find in Rolle is suffused throughout the epistle,

together with a sense of the entanglements of ordinary life. The tone is usually that of talk, easy and relaxed. The mixed life involves self-knowledge, but attends to other matters. It does not fix the mind on the Passion whilst letting 'servants and tenants die for lack of care', 'unarrayed'. To tend them is to wash Christ's feet. Leah was fruitful, but 'sore-eyed', Rachel beautiful, but barren. One may wed both, as Jacob did. The good works of the Active Life are like sticks heaped on the coal of desire for God, that eventually spring into flame. Sometimes the note is more lyrical ('nother sownyng ne savourynge ne wondirfull lyghte ne aungells syghte . . .'), or more absolute ('lufe propirly es a full cuppillynge of the lufande and the lufed togedyre, as godde and a saule, in to ane. This cuppillyng may noghte be had fully in this lyfe bot anely in desyre and langynge thareto'). But the dominant accent is plain and pragmatic: 'If devocyone cum noghte with mynde of the passione, stryve noghte ne prese to mekill thareafter.' The sentences are supple, and not weighed down with scriptural allusion, admirably suited for the eye or ear of a 'temporal lord', and rich in saving common sense.

The *Stimulus Amoris*, an English version of which has been attributed to Hilton, is now seen to be a composite. To a central text once thought to be by Bonaventura but now identified as the work of a thirteenth-century friar, James of Milan, have been added nine chapters on the Passion and, at the end, meditations on the *Pater Noster, Ave*, and *Salve Regina*. James's work is itself derivative, and only partly about contemplation. The luxuriant rhetoric of the original (even when it has the authority of the Canticles) has been toned down—already we have a sense that English taste will suspect such extravagances—but left in the Meditations, and even added to in the Passion (e.g. the figure of Christ burnt and baked on the hard cross). More noteworthy is the way in which the author drives home the lesson of the Penitent Thief (ch. viii): remarking that we unnatural wretches will not receive our own brethren, better than we are, into our houses of clay, he bursts out: 'Be thou not too light to deem a man is a thief which thou knowest not; yea, and though he be a thief or an evil man, thy meed shall be never the less, but perchance the more. For why? All that thou dost, thou dost it to Christ.' We are here close to Langland's teaching that 'the most needy are our neighbours', and certainly to Hilton's constant assertions of the humanity of Christ. The Precious Manhood is the way, the mean, the bridge, and the door leading to the Godhead. It seems as though the high-flown Dionysian language of deification and mystic rapture that abounded in the original has not found favour. Passages that bespeak self-concern are also excised. The whole drift is now towards humility and moderation. He will add: 'Learn to hate thyself as thou hast made thyself and love that God has made' (ch. xv), or delete a dictum to the effect that a healthy body is not necessary for it is detrimental to the health of the soul. We feel that Hilton has made the book his own, a vehicle of his own ascetic teaching, consonant with his own experience.

Of the life and circumstances of Julian of Norwich, who stands first in rank amongst English writers on the spiritual life, we know little beyond what she occasionally alludes to in her book of *Revelations*. There she tells us that she had these 'showings' during an almost fatal illness in 1373, when she was thirty. She recovered, as if by miracle, to set down her visions in a form that she greatly expanded after years of meditation on their meaning. She was still living in Norwich in 1413, probably in an anchorhold: a Julian, anchoress, is named in several wills, from 1404; and if later references to an unnamed anchoress 'at St Julian', are also to her, she lived to be 86. For some, if not all of the time of her enclosure she had a servant, as anchoresses usually did. Norwich then as now was wealthy and populous. All four orders of friars had houses there, and the Franciscans maintained a *studium generale*, which attracted, amongst others, the future Pope, Alexander V. Though Julian was not mentioned by her local contemporary, the saintly Richard of Caistor-by-Norwich, her reputation for sanctity must have reached Lynn Episcopi (now King's Lynn): the indefatigable Margery Kempe of that town visited her in 1413, and received salutary advice. Margery alone names her as *Dame* Julian—a title implying gentle birth. At the beginning of her book Julian describes herself as 'a symple creature unlettyrde'; Margery too liked to refer to herself as 'this creature', but Julian's phrase is a literary formula of humility, a *captatio benevolentiae*. Almost every page testifies to her wide reading in the Vulgate and in spiritual writers. She assumes a knowledge of the context of scriptural phrases which she deliberately intertwines. The later, and longer text, which represents a deliberate revision and expansion after fifteen years or more of meditation on her visions, and so demands chief attention, is written in an assured and mature style that does not disdain rhetorical patterns and alliterative formulas. It doubtless reflects her reading in spiritual works over that period, including some, for instance *The Chastising of God's Children* and William of St Thierry's books, that were not always congruent with her own. Moreover, she alters the sequence of the visions as first described, and adds substantially to the description of the Passion as it had been revealed to her. Though the revelations were private, they had meaning for all Christians. Whilst Julian touches on theological subtleties, there is nothing arcane or esoteric in the teaching she transmits. She had many things in common with Walter Hilton, but neither her language nor her experience was Dionysian.

She tells us, at the outset, that she had asked for three gifts from God: first, remembrance of the Passion, so that she might share the sufferings of the Marys at Calvary; secondly, a sickness, 'nigh unto death', that by deepening her contrition would purify her and hasten her union with God (not, in the Middle Ages, an unusual understanding of the purpose of sickness); and thirdly, for three 'wounds', not physical, but interior—true contrition, kind compassion, wilful (voluntary) longing for God. The sickness, she says, was granted her in May 1373, when she was so ill that she hoped to die. She could not see even the gilt crucifix held before her. But the sight eased her pains and brought to mind the Passion: 'for I would that his paynes were my paynes'. Like St Paul—and Pauline locutions are to prove the very warp and woof of her narrative—she would suffer with Christ. The crucifix fades before a 'bodily sight' of the Passion itself. Of the blood trickling down from the garland of thorns she avers that Christ himself 'shewed it me without anie meane'. At the same time the Trinity filled her heart with joy: for Christ, who is both God and man, is likewise a member of the Trinity. She was doubtless thinking of those representations of the Trinity that show God the Father sustaining the cross on which the Son hangs whilst the Holy Spirit descends in the form of a dove. Remembrance of the Trinity as our maker and keeper, our everlasting lover, produces the waves of joy that alternate with grief throughout the book.

Forthwith she sees also—the doctrinal significance of this will become apparent later—Our Lady, 'ghostly in bodily lykenes' ('bodily' here may indicate simply that she had a clear sense of her as a living person, though the latest editors insist that the phrase means 'corporeally, but for a spiritual purpose'), 'a simple mayden and a meeke, yong of age, a little waxen above a chylde, in the stature as she was when she conceivede'. Mary's reverent beholding of her maker at his birth—Julian would think of miniatures of the Nativity in Books of Hours—connotes contemplation. And the image of 'homely loving' that she uses shortly after likewise suggests a Nativity scene: 'He is oure clothing that for love wrappeth us . . . and all becloseth us . . . for tender love.'

The image that follows is of a wholly different order:

He shewed a little thing, the quantitie of an haselnott, lying in the palme of my hand . . . and it was as rounde as a balle. I looked theran with the eye of my understanding, and thought, What may this be? And it was answered generaelly thus: It is all that is made.

The figure was perhaps suggested by a line in the *XV Oes*, a popular sequence of prayers: 'qui terram palmo concludis'. And the oblique form of answer suggests a dawning realization of the significance of the figure rather than a verbal explanation. So too she 'saw' (sensed) the nut's three properties: God made it, God loves it, God keeps it. The term *properties* suggests the encyclopedist's *De proprietatibus rerum*, but it is not physical qualities or characteristics that concern Julian. Nor is she thinking, like Blake, of holding infinity on the palm of the hand: the nut symbolizes the 'littleness' of all created things, which we must 'noughten', reduce to nought, if we would love and possess God, who is 'unmade' (Julian's equivalent for *increatum*). The language may seem Dionysian but the conclusion is Augustine's: 'It liketh God that we rest in him ... he hath made us only to himself.' We must come to him 'naked, plainly, and homely' (so, it is implied, he speaks through the homely image of the nut). Julian's prayer: 'God, of thy goodnes, geve me thyselfe', is more a response to this showing: it marks a stage in spiritual awareness for which her earlier devotional life must have been a preparation. Her later gloss on this prayer suggests its full meaning: 'His goodnes ... overpassith without end, for he is the endlesshead', where she is using Rolle's native calque on *infinitas* rather than Chaucer's 'infinité' (*Boece* V, pr. vi).

When she says that the Passion restores us to God, showing his love for the soul made in his likeness, she is following the traditional interpretation of *similitudinem nostram* in Gen. 1: 26 (cf. *Piers Plowman* v. 493). But she adds that both soul and body are clad in the goodness of God, as closely as the body is clad in cloth or the flesh in its skin, an assertion that is all of a piece with the role that is later assigned to 'Kind' (nature). Julian gives no hold to Manichaeism. The divine love is 'hygh, overpassyng, unmesurable' (she is surely alluding to Eph. 3: 19: *supereminentem ... caritatem Christi*). 'Oure *kyndely* wille is to have God, and the good wylle of God is to have us'—another appropriation of a Pauline text (1 Tim. 2: 4).

Such are the meditations prompted by the image of the little ball. But it has not displaced 'the bodily sight' of the Crucifixion: the bleeding head, the great drops of brown-red blood falling like pellets, as fast as raindrops fall from eaves and as round as herring scales (images not found in the first version). The sight is both hideous and sweet, dreadful and lovely—just as God is both dreadful and reverend, homely and courteous. On such paradoxes expressed in the rhetorical form of *oppositio*, Julian loves to dwell. Here she elucidates them by a simple *exemplum*, itself part of the 'showing': the 'homeliness' is the courtesy a great king shows to a poor servant: they are expressed in Jesus Christ, 'our brother and our saviour'; but not revealed in this life except by 'special showing' or by special grace, the reward of faith and hope and charity. Julian's own 'showing' stirs her at once 'in charity to my even-Christians', reflected in a desire that they might all see and know what she saw, 'for all this syght was shewde in generalle'—that is it was applicable to them too; she sets down her showings 'for their care and comfort'. And she insists that 'for the shewyng I am nott good, but if [unless] I love God the better'.

The crucifix (like the Rood in the Anglo-Saxon vision poem) has acquired a life of its own, and re-enacts the Passion, the spitting, and buffeting, and 'manie languryng paynes'. It changes in colour, with one half of the face covered with dry blood and then the other. But she sees it 'swemly' (fearfully) and darkly. Again we are in the presence of paradox: 'I saw him, and sought him, and I had him, and I wantyd [lacked] hym': a favourite balancing of opposites. Once, she says 'my understandyng was lett [in the Sloane manuscripts, 'led'] down in to the sea grounde and ther saw I hilles and dales grene semyng as it were mosse-begrowne with wrake [seaweed] and gravell'. It is perhaps the most mysterious of all the 'showings', and not to be accounted for by reference to Ecclesiasticus 24: 8 ('I have penetrated to the bottom of the deep')—was it suggested by tales of the buried foreshore of East Anglia? Its import is that even if a man were at the sea-bottom, and could have sight of God he would be safe. The water figures the foul blackness of our sins and so it makes her think of the Vernicle (the image of Christ's face on the handkerchief of St Veronica), which likewise changes 'colour and chere [aspect]' and which had become a popular cult object in her time. She draws the lesson that for the soul in travail seeking is as good as beholding. The nexus is not obvious and interpretation is not made easier by her account of the next showing: 'And after this I saw God in a poynte; that is to say in my understandyng, by which syght I saw he is in al thyng.' Here she is evidently presenting her sudden intellectual apperception of the omnipresence of God: 'in a point' perhaps representing the *in ictu oculi* of 1 Cor. 15: 52. Later (ch. lxiv) she will say that all our present life and longing is 'but a poynt'. Thus nothing is done by 'hap or aventure': God's fore-seeing wisdom ordains all.

In Julian's mind there is an illative connection between the doctrine of God in all things and the presence of Sin: 'He is in the myd poynt of all thynges and all he doth; and I was sewer [certain] that he doth no synne.' In this sense sin is no 'dede', has no actuality. The doctrine is basically scholastic, and applied later by Donne: 'as sinne is nothing, let it no where be'; whereas 'Rightfulhede' (Julian's unique expression for Divine Action) is both 'right' and 'full' (complete in itself), like all the works of God. 'All thynges wer sett in ordyr or [before] any thyng was made . . . and no manner thyng shalle feyle of that poynt. . . . The blessed Trynyté is evyr fulle plesyd in alle his workes.' Thus she applies two texts that constantly appear in medieval writing: 'vidit . . . cuncta quae fecerat, et erant valde bona' (and God saw everything that he had made, and behold it was very good) (Gen. 1: 31): and 'omnia in mensura et numero et pondere disposuisti' (Wisd. 11: 21).

It is tempting to isolate these passages of philosophical largeness from their scriptural origins, to consider them as the essential Julian. But always she reverts to the sight of the Passion. So now comes the Scourging, when the blood 'ranne out so plentuously that ther was neyther seen skynne ne wounde, but as it were all blode'. Julian has been touched by the contemporary cult of the Precious Blood. It is not a morbid or pathological obsession, but rather a logical fruit of meditation on the central event in World History, when Sin and God meet. God has made water plenteous to our service, but it pleases him better that we 'take full holsomly hys blessyd blode to wassch us of [from] synne . . . for ther is no lycour [liquor] that is made that lykyth hym [pleases him] so wele to yeve [give] us'. Herbert (in 'The Agony') was to use the same language:

> Love is that liquor sweet and most divine
> Which my God feels as blood, but I as wine.

Julian, in fact, is nowhere far from the ancient sources of Christian imagery. She sees the blood descending down into hell and bursting the bonds of those in Limbo, just as Langland saw it 'feeding our forefathers in darkness' (*Piers Plowman* v. 501). It flows also in heaven, 'enjoying [*sic*] the salvacion of all mankynd that be ther and shall be, fulfylling the number that faylyth' (i.e. the number of the 'elect', still to be made up).

It is the particularity of Julian's perceptions that produces unforgettable effects. St John (18: 18) indicates that the weather was cold on Good Friday morning, and the Bonaventuran *Meditations* enlarge on this. Julian sees Christ dying by inches in a dry, 'harre [keen] wynd', and 'wonder colde'. His 'swet body was so dyscolouryd, so drye, so clongyn [shrivelled] . . . as he had bene sennyght [seven nights] deed'; 'He was hangyng uppe in the eyer as men hang a cloth for to drye'—a variant of the simile that presents Christ as stretched out like a parchment. The flesh pressed by the garland of thorns was jagged in many places as a cloth, 'saggyng downwarde . . . rympylde [wrinkled] with a tawny coloure, lyke a drye bord'.

That the Maker of Kind itself should suffer thus is the core of the mystery of the Passion, comprehensible only if we accept the doctrine of *communicatio idiomatum*:* 'the unyng [unity] of the Godhed gave strenght to the Manhed, for love, to suffer more than alle man myght'. Thus the Cross manifests supreme love, not propitiatory sacrifice. Hence the truly mystical rapture of ch. xxii, when Julian's understanding is lifted to heaven. Christ tells her that if she can have joy in his sufferings he is well pleased. The wound in his right side is 'large inow for alle mankynde that shalle be savyd to rest in pees and in love'.

It was on the right side of the Cross that Our Lady was always represented as standing. So now Julian naturally calls to mind her truth, her wisdom, and her charity: 'wherby I am leernyd to know myself and reverently drede my God'. Common as the emphasis on self-knowledge is in the contemplatives, it rarely occurs in this context. Julian learns that it is one of the good effects of sin, which purges us and makes us know ourselves—and ask mercy. Thus it is that Julian can be assured that sin is 'behovely' (necessary). There is nothing novel in this doctrine, though some had looked askance at it; the Mass of Easter Day ('O necessarium Peccatum Adae') had enshrined it—hence Langland's acceptance of it (B v. 491). It would come naturally to mind in a paschal context. In our day, *Little Gidding* has made familiar its concomitant: 'but alle shalle be wele, and alle shalle be wele, and alle maner of thynge shalle be wele'. It is important to note that this affirmation is ascribed to Christ himself and that more than mere futurity is involved, *shall* implying the operation of divine prescience. Later this aspect is indicated in a careful *complexio*, involving repetition of initial and final words: 'I will . . . I shall . . . I may . . . I can / make all things well.' The Passion is the glorious 'asseth'—the atonement for men's sin 'more worshipful than ever was the sin of Adam harmful'—another restatement of an ancient assurance. It provides a leitmotif for the remainder of the work.

The power, skill, and purpose to make all things well represent the three aspects of the Trinity in Unity. As the Trinity created all things (Julian always gives due place to the dovelike Holy Spirit, and understands the significance of the plural *faciamus*: Gen. 1: 26) so it will bring about the restoration of all things; we are doubtless to think here

---

* i.e. The doctrine that 'while the human and Divine natures in Christ were separate, the attributes of the one may be predicated of the other in view of their union in the one Person of the Saviour' (*Oxford Dictionary of the Christian Church*).

not of universalism but of St Peter's *restitutio omnium* (Acts 3: 21), just as when Julian says that Holy Church will be shaken in sorrows and anguish and tribulation 'as men shakyth a cloth in the wynde', she has in mind the *tribulacio* of Matt. 24: 21 and of Rev. 7: 14 etc.: the scorn and persecution of that time are to be the purgative of pomp and pride.

Suddenly attention shifts from Christ's Passion to his compassion (ch. xxviii): 'Ech kynde compassion [the epithet indicates that the attribute is truly natural] that man hath on hys evyn-Cristen with charyté it is Crist in hym ... hys love excusyth us; and of hys gret curtesy he doth away alle our blame and beholdeth us with ruth and pytté as children innocens and unlothfulle.' The language here is limpid, the tone tender. And as the narrative proceeds, the dominical utterances take on a practical emphasis and pattern. The exalted Christ says:

I it am, I it am. I it am that is hyghest. I it am that thou lovyst. I it am that thou lykyst, I it am that thou servyst. I it am that thou longest. I it am that thou desyryst. I it am that thou menyste. I it am that is alle.

This is the rhetoric of the contemporary verse rendering of the answer to Isaiah's question (Isa. 63: 1): 'Who is he that cometh from Edom?' — *Quis est iste qui venit de Edom?*

> Ich[1] yt am, Ich yt am that ne speke bote[2] ryht,
> Chaumpyoun to helen[3] monkunde[4] in vyht[5]. (*SRL* No. 40)

[1] *I* [2] *but* [3] *heal* [4] *mankind* [5] *fight*

Julian's partiality for *repetitio* shows in a similar context some chapters later (ch. xxxiv): 'He is the grounde, he is the substannce, he is the techyng, he is the techer, he is the ende and he is the mede [reward] wherfore every kynde soule travelyth.'

Like Langland and other devout and thoughtful souls of her time Julian was much troubled about the salvation of righteous pagans (and of people who live unchristian lives). The only guidance vouchsafed is 'What is impossible to thee is not impossible to me. I shall save my word in all things . . .'; which she understands to mean that we must not concern ourselves with such priorities. Nowhere does she depart from the doctrine of the Church 'for he it is, holy Chyrch' (ch. xxxiv), and so she is content with the assurance that Mercy shall last as long as sin pursues souls.

Fundamentally, Julian's concern is not to describe her 'showings' — we had best avoid the term vision, which suggests the mystical and the arcane — but to interpret the Church's teaching in the light of them; in particular, its teaching on the remedies and forgiveness for sin. Hence she recalls those whose sin was turned to their honour: Mary Magdalene, Peter and Paul, St Thomas, and, inexplicably, John of Beverly. The rationale of petitionary prayer is established by the words that Eliot will put to his own purpose in *Little Gidding*: 'I am grounde of thy besekyng.'

Langland's Ploughman had averred that 'contemplatyf lyf or actyf lyf, Cryst wolde men wroughte' (*Piers Plowman*, vi. 251): whatever their vocation men should take it in earnest; which Julian reaffirms: 'it plesyth him that we werke in prayer and in good lyvyng by his helpe and his grace, resonably and with discrecion'. This medieval note of *measure* she strikes repeatedly, in contrast to some earlier and later women contemplatives, who do not strike it at all. 'And thus shalle we . . . in our owne meke continuall prayer come in to hym now, in this lyfe, by many prevy touchynges of swete gostly [spiritual] syghtes and felynges mesuryd to us as oure sympylhed may bere it.' Taking here and there a phrase from St Paul's hymn to love (1 Cor. 13) the prose flowers in rich rhythms and rhymes as it describes the bliss experienced after one dies 'in longing for love': 'And then shall we alle come in to oure Lorde, oure selfe clerely knowyng and God fulsomly havyng, and we endlesly be alle hyd in God, verely seyeng and fulsomly felyng, and hym gostely heryng, and hym delectable smellyng and him swetly swelwyng [swallowing]. And ther shall we se God face to face, homely and fulsomly. The creature that is made shall see and endlesly beholde God whych is the maker.' The figures here can be found in earlier treatises on contemplation, but nowhere else does a lyrical delight fuse them together.

Of self-knowledge, knowledge of our sins is a necessary part (for earlier ascetics it had been almost the whole). This we may reach by virtue of our 'high kind'—man's soul is made in God's likeness—and by 'speeding' of mercy and grace, but not completely. 'Oure faylyng is dredefull, oure fallyng is shamfull, and oure dyeng is sorowfull; but yet in all this the swet eye of pytté and love deperteth nevyr from us, ne the werkyng of mercy cesyth not.' Jeremy Taylor's tremulous prose never surpasses this. But when Julian writes that 'Oure lyfe is alle grounded and rotyd [rooted] in love, and without love we may nott lyve', part of her sentence bears, as so often, a Pauline impress (Eph. 3: 17). Flickering alliteration binds together a set of balanced phrases: 'We be all mercyfully beclosyd in the myldehed of God and in his mekehed, in his benygnité and in his buxomnesse.'

In the general lore and ordering of the 'showings' there is nothing homiletic. Yet more than once they take the form of that favourite device of the preacher, the *exemplum*, and notably in chapter li, where 'our courteous Lord' answers 'full mistily by a wonderful example of a Lord that hath a servant'. The sense of 'mistily' in this context is hardly subject to lexical analysis, for whilst Julian evidently does not mean to imply that the *exemplum* was obscure to her, she came to full understanding of its significance only after much meditation. It is indeed deep and double-sided, resting as it does on the recognition of Christ as the second Adam. The servant of this parable—and the tale is essentially parabolic, highly reminiscent of the *parabolae* of St Bernard—running to perform his Lord's will falls into a 'slade' (Christ will fall into the 'slade' or 'dell' of Mary's womb), and is unable to rise, being blinded in his reason and 'stonyd' (astounded, puzzled) in his understanding. But his lord counts his sufferings as arising from his love, and rewards instead of punishing him.

The points and 'properties' of this tale—the significance, for instance, of the Lord's garments ('wyde and syde [broad] . . . and blew as asure')—gradually grow clear to Julian (and to us). She was at first puzzled because some of the 'properties' might by no manner be directed to Adam 'single' (i.e. to Adam alone). She has to learn that in the sight of God one man is all men and all men one man. The allegory is susceptible of the threefold interpretation that we normally associate with scriptural exegesis. The servant is clearly the Christ who suffers for us, but also the first Adam who fell into sin. He is clothed in a white kirtle, single, old, defaced, dyed with the sweat of his body, strait-fitting, short, 'as it were an handfull beneth the knee'. It is the garb of a gardener who digs and ditches, sweating and turning the earth up and down. So did Adam, but so also, anagogically, did Christ. Mechtild of Hackeborn had said that 'Our Lord delved the earth in likeness of a gardener.' The figure expresses his humble obedience to the divine will. The fruit brought forth is mystical fruit. We here approach traditional interpretations of such texts as John 4: 6, and 6: 51–2: though Julian makes no explicit reference to the eucharistic reading of the latter verse here or elsewhere: few of the contemplatives are notable for devotion to the eucharist.

Though the anagogical reading of the parable is not always compelling, the particularity of description is of a piece with that in the earlier accounts of Christ's sufferings. And the abundant scriptural allusions enable the well-read reader to perceive the main drift readily enough. When the servant takes the role of the Son he stands before his Father 'in Adam's kyrtylle, all redy to sterte [start] and to rynne [run]': a fusion of Ps. 39: 7–9, as cited in Heb. 10: 7, and of Ps. 18: 5–7, traditionally applied to Christ as the strong man rejoicing to run a race. Pressing every point, Julian even perpetrates a poor pun: the servant stands on the left side, 'that the fader lefte his owne son wylfully in the manhed to suffer all mans payne'. It may be pardoned as a device to link up the *exemplum* with the earlier pictures of the Passion, now presented anew in the figure of the kirtle of flesh 'ragged and rent' by the rods and the scourges.

What at length emerges is a confidence that the 'kindness' of God assigns no blame to his chosen. In his endless love man's soul (that hidden treasure of Matt. 13: 44) is kept whole, and 'knit' to God by a subtle and mighty knot. The eventual bliss surpasses that we should have had if Adam had not fallen. It is a belief embraced by Langland, written out in the *Scale of Perfection*, and defended by St Thomas. Doctrine that is more characteristically mystical, Julian expresses by such figures as 'God dwelleth in our soul; our soul dwelleth in God'. 'I sawe no dyfference', she adds, 'betwen God and oure substance, but as it were all God.' The context, and Julian's essentially orthodox (Pauline) Christology, forbid us to interpret this pantheistically.

Gradually, attention shifts from the showings and the *exemplum* and the work turns into a sequence of lyrical, heightened (and sometimes cryptic) affirmations, expressed in language now reminiscent of Augustine and William of St Thierry, now of the scholastics (God is 'substantial kind unmade') but most often in Pauline terms: 'In the same poynt that oure soule is made sensuall, in the same poynt is the cytté of God, ordeyned to hym fro without begynnyng.' This city is the soul in which God takes up his dwelling, giving us the gifts enclosed in his Son till 'we be waxyn and growyn, oure soule with oure body and oure body with oure soule'. More remarkable here than the adaptation of Eph. 4: 13 ('till we all come . . . unto a perfect man, unto the measure of the stature of the fullness of Christ') is the incorporation into the *schema* of the concept of *kind*, Natura: *sensual* here carries no pejorative undertones. We are brought again by the motherhood of mercy and grace into our natural place, our '*kyndly stede*' (a phrase found in the Eagle's exposition of physics in *The House of Fame*), 'where that we ware in, made by the motherhed of kynd love, whych kynde love nevyr leevyth us'. The motherhood of Christ is a conception that can be paralleled in Mechtild, but here it introduces a new gentleness in the picture of a mother who knows the need of her child, and 'kepyth it full tenderly, as the kynde and condityon of moderhed will' (ch. lx). God is 'very fader and very modyr of kyndys', and 'of all kyndys that he hath sett in dyverse creatures by party [in part] in man is alle the hole [whole], in fullheed and in vertu, in feyerheed and in goodheed, in ryalté and in noblye, in alle manner of solemnyté, of preciousnesse and wurschyppe [honour]'. Neither Pico della Mirandola nor Hamlet could reach this height in glorifying what Julian's missal had taught her to think of as 'humanae substantiae dignitatem'. To that dignity man could be restored only by Grace. As Julian puts it: 'Grace was sent oute to save kynde . . . Grace is God, as unmade kynde is God.' All creation emanates from and returns to him.

We may seem to have come a long way from the sagging, dripping, figure on the cross. But the Christ who besprinkles us with his precious blood and whose visage was marred more than any man is both the suffering servant of Isa. 53 (and of the *exemplum*), and the Christ who 'quicked' us by taking of our kind, 'our very mother Jesu': 'Kyndly the chylde dyspeyreth nott of the moders love, kyndely the chylde presumyth nott of itselfe, kyndely the chylde lovyth the moder and eche one of them other.' *Repetitio* of this sort always marks the most emphatic of Julian's affirmations. And it comes as something of a shock to find her immediately afterwards recording (in the longer text only) a vision of a soul springing like a little child, 'whiter than the lily' out of a shapeless body, a pit of stinking mire. The departure of the soul to heaven is pictured thus in many a late medieval miniature, though in such pictures a devil fighting to possess it figures prominently. It is the last of the continuous series of showings. In the sixty-sixth chapter, Julian records that after it she felt that she would live longer. Yet at once her sickness returned, with a dryness which we must interpret as the spiritual dryness that other mystics have experienced after ecstasy. She had to be convinced by a 'religious person' (a Norwich friar?) that the sight of the bleeding crucifix had been real. Then she fell asleep: and 'me thought the fende [fiend] sett hym at my throte . . . with his pawes he helde me in the throte and woulde a stoppyd my breth and kylde me, but he myght not'. Later, she heard 'a bodely talkyng, as it had been of two bodyes, and both to my thyngkyng talked at one tyme, as they had holde a perlement with great besynes, and all was softe whystryn [whispering]'. The physicality of these presences is matched by the bodily speech with which—by God's grace—she comforts herself, and by the bodily sight that she has of the same crucifix that had brought her comfort before; in all of these passages 'bodily' apparently implies clear and precise perception or expression. But we move into a different area of experience when she avers that to her sense (though not to the bystanders) the fiend's heat and stench lingered after she awoke. It is hard not to think that this dream (Julian insists that the ugly showing was made 'sleeping', 'and so was none other') was prompted by such depictions of the departing soul as the previous chapter calls to mind. But for Julian the fiend represents the essential foulness of Evil; and most ecstatic experience is followed by a reaction that represents a new sense of the constraints of 'the body of this death'. Thanks to Our Lady, she comes to perceive that this fiend stands for all that is contrarious to love and peace, and the vision of the soul 'so large as it were an endlesse warde [? i.e. word, 'world'] and also as it were a blessyd kyngdom' returns with new power. There sits the Lord Jesus, God and Man, highest bishop, solemnest king, worshipfullest Lord; 'and the hyghest lyght and bryghtest shynyng of the sytté [city] is the glorious love of oure Lorde'. The penultimate chapters thus reflect the penultimate chapters of the Apocalypse.

The final chapters resume and rephrase the essential doctrine of the showings, at the same time introducing a distinction between the four different sorts of fear: dread of affray, dread of pain, 'doubtful' dread, reverent dread. 'Love and drede are bredryn [brethren] and they are rotyd [rooted] in us by the goodnesse of oure Maker.' The pages are dense with scriptural phrases, often freshly applied. There the Father's words: 'This is my beloved Son, in whom I am well pleased' (Matt. 3: 17) are converted into: 'the blessyd Trinité is fulle plesyd withoute ende in the makyng of mannes soule'. Sentences like these are everywhere linked by logical copulatives (*for* and *therefore*) to make a tight *catena*.

The assurance and firmness of Julian's prose (apart from a few passages that are perhaps editorial rewording) are the strongest testimony to her veracity. The careful consideration she gave when rewriting to balanced sentences and harmonious phrasing suggests not so much aesthetic sensitivity as a desire to make her experiences intelligible to all 'well-willing' Christians. Much of her theology (like that of *Ancrene Wisse*) has its roots in Augustine and Bernard; and whether or not she was familiar with the *Wisse* (it was addressed to women of the social rank to which she probably belonged) she seems to have been nurtured in a similar tradition of dignified and gracious discourse fortified by a training, by precept or example, in the rhetorical arts.* Her careful distinctions between the different sorts of showings reveal an analytical intelligence that would be quick to seize on scholastic refinements. Mindlessness is never an allowable synonym for mysticism, and however we appraise her experiences, the presence of a questing but reverent intelligence remains an indubitable feature of her book.

She lays no claim to special holiness or to that union with the Divine that Dionysian mystics expressed in such figures as 'annihilation', 'ecstasy', 'ingression into the divine shadow'. Though familiar

* Modernized versions usually fail to reproduce the inner harmonies of the prose.

with the 'mystical' reading of the Canticles, she never applies to her experience the erotic imagery to which Rolle and the author of the *Cloud* resort. Her spirituality cannot be dissociated from her visionary experiences. In the last resort it impresses because she herself has pondered over them and questioned their meaning. Her reliance on Pauline texts makes not only for a firm theology but for a sinewy prose that is in marked contrast to the mellifluous rhythms of a Rolle. By the same token she does not share the preoccupation with the sorrows of Mary that bulks large in much late medieval devotion: for her Mary at the foot of the Cross is the image of the Church at prayer.

To suggest that her book is no isolated phenomenon but comparable to the influential *Revelations* of St Bridget, or to 'The Book of Ghostly Grace' of Mechtild of Hackeborn (translated into English possibly before the turn of the century) is not to question the objectivity of her (or their) accounts. The number of women mystics in the fourteenth century is certainly remarkable. We cannot now reconstruct the cultural conditions that favoured the growth of particular forms of devotion in female recluses, though one may tentatively connect with this development the attachment of Julian to the unusual (though not unique) concept of the Divine Motherhood. Yet it is not unreasonable to suggest that in different circumstances (if, for instance, she had written in Latin) Julian might have become as widely known and read as her continental predecessors.

To a modern reader, at least, her sense of measure, of balance, her humility, her deep charity, her sane theology, displayed so unostentatiously, gives her an appeal greater than theirs. No bizarre legends attach to her as they do to Catherine of Siena. Like Langland, she is English yet not insular, and the quietism that so easily besets contemplatives has never taken root in England. Sir Thomas Browne, a later citizen of Norwich whose rhythmic prose still reverberates, has something in common with Julian, and the last page of *Urn Burial* shows that he would have taken her 'showings' seriously.

In the past perhaps too much has been made of the dramatic nature of these showings and of the eirenic quality of the divine affirmation as she received them. Close study of the text as now established reveals that almost every page is a tissue of scriptural phrases, often reworded in a sense accordant with traditional commentary, and as with St Bernard one such phrase will suggest to her another. The sheer scale of her book is as impressive as are those sentences that, separated from their context by a modern poet, have today given the work much of its *réclame*.

WYCLIF AND THE WYCLIFFITE WRITERS

(iv) Wyclif and the Wycliffite Writers

John Wyclif* was formerly enshrined as one of the 'fathers of English prose'. It is now clear, however, that the evidence for the ascription of any extant English text to Wyclif himself is so uncertain that even to allow him to survive as a shadowy 'Wyclif' presiding over a corpus of English sermons and treatises that seem to present or develop the ideas of the *doctor evangelicus* is dubious. Modern scholarship prefers to describe this material, together with the associated biblical translations, by the vaguer and safer term 'Wycliffite', which sufficiently indicates its indebtedness to the reformer. As a 'grete clerke', Wyclif probably deserves his reputation. He was one of Oxford's 'favourite sons'. His Latin works were numerous and substantial, and his later influence was profound. His local reputation rested chiefly on his role as a realist philosopher, partly on his views of ecclesiastical polity. But these are not features that bulk large in the extant English works that were once assigned to him. Any judgement of the latter must take account of the fact that no man's works were so deliberately destroyed after his lifetime, and it is perhaps unfair to hold him responsible for the monotony and wearisome iteration that characterize the polemical writings of his immediate followers, though it seems likely that they imitated these features, along with others. Wyclif cannot be dissociated from Lollardry, even if he would not have gone as far as some Lollards did: in argument they grew crude, pushing everything to extremes, eager to exaggerate every fault and shortcoming they could find in their opponents. In his opinionated and humourless argumentativeness, a well as in more fundamental ways, Wyclif anticipates the operations of what has come to be called the Nonconformist conscience.

Certainly, the 'Wycliffites' succeed generally in making their meaning plain. They are not ill at ease in English for they were used to hearing, or reading, vernacular sermons. But they are limited by their own polemical aims, which colour, if they do not control, everything they write. This is one reason why it is difficult to distinguish the Oxford clerk from his followers. He introduced a new tone, even a new language, into controversy. The chief difference between him and his successors is that they are more intemperate (and more aware that

* Wyclif seems to have come to Oxford *c*.1354, and to have spent most of his time there until 1381, although he held various ecclesiastical benefices. His teachings began to provoke official attacks from 1377. In 1382 ten heresies and fourteen errors were formally condemned; by that time he had withdrawn (1381) to his living at Lutterworth, where he died on 31 December 1384. Over a hundred works in Latin can be assigned to him.

they are not as other men are). As the true 'treasurers of Christ and his apostles' they will proclaim that the Church of England has been blind and leprous these many years by maintenance of proud prelacy, 'borne up with flattery of private religion'. The unmeasured invective and abuse of opponents does indeed foreshadow the Reformation, but in its worst aspects. 'Proud prelacy', 'fat benefices', 'feigned', 'nigromancy', 'privy falseness', 'the venomous dotaciun' (the Donation of Constantine)—these are the mildest of the abusive terms that bespatter Wycliffite tracts. Friars and religion are not only imperfect, they are in league with Satan. Readers nurtured on such polemic would acquire a querulous and critical vocabulary of sarcasm and abuse, and the effective use of contrast—the Pope is the most proud man of earth, Christ the most homely. The objectivity that now, rightly or wrongly, we associate with academic training finds no place in the minds of these writers. One rails against miracle plays of the Passion, saying that the players scorn God as did the Jews who 'bobbed Christ'; 'taking in play what He took in most earnest'.* The conception of *homo ludens* is foreign to this way of thinking, and the counter-arguments are dismissed as superficial. A superior tone of conscious rectitude characterizes every comment on topical issues. It is the stance of the seventeenth-century precisian and goes along with a contempt for display, for 'great churches' and 'gay windows'. Money spent on buying new ordinals and antiphoners would be better used to produce Bibles.†

In the literature of religious polemic, Wyclif developed one genre that was to have its successors in later centuries: the dialogue. He first tried his hand in this kind with a Latin *Dialogus*, which is really a monologue on the inequity of Church endowments: it presents little real argument and offers no characterization; its epilogue is in full scholastic form. The English version is only a little more tolerable. But his followers took up the form, and an argument on Church and State between a Clerk and a Knight who can cite Scripture to his purpose has some verbal liveliness.‡

Wyclif's faults, like his virtues, are those of an intellectual—of an intellectual who after years of academic study (there are parallels in our own time) weds himself to a doctrine and engages or becomes embroiled in the world of politics. As his views, theological and ecclesiastical, grew more extreme so, it seems, did his distrust of the

---

* *A Tretise of Miraclis Pleyinge* in *Selections from English Wycliffite Writings*, ed. Anne Hudson (Cambridge, 1978), 98–9.

† Wyclif, *Select English Writings*, ed. H. E. Winn (Oxford, 1929), 93.

‡ See Anne Hudson, 'A Lollard Quaternion', *RES*, NS xxii (1971), 435–42.

intellect—another paradox for which Protestant parallels might be adduced. In the Wycliffite *Epistola Sathanae ad Cleros* (*c*.1400), an adaptation of a common form of anti-clerical satire, a 'letter from Satan' (cf. the later *Screwtape Letters*), the devil notes that one stage in the friars' downfall was when friars 'went to school and began to savour of *our* learning'.* Yet Wyclif, a schoolman himself, never lost the habit of scholastic language: his doctrine of the Eucharist is unintelligible unless one knows the difference between 'accident' and 'subject'; and his followers struggle to adapt Latin scholastic language to vernacular use: 'habitudinal saying', in a sermon on the Eucharist,† represents his own scholastic term *praedicatio . . . habitudinalis*.

Wyclif's name has always been asociated with the translation of the Bible into English, but although the desire to make the Scriptures accessible in the vernacular accorded with his views, there is no clear evidence that he was directly involved in the work. Nor was such a translation quite the innovation that is often supposed. Much of the Vulgate had been rendered into Old English before the Conquest— here as in other departments of vernacular prose the English were certainly pioneers. Later there had been French and Anglo-Norman versions (whilst in Italy, Italian versions were circulating without let or hindrance). Most English preachers customarily translated for the benefit of their hearers at least the Gospel for the day—a custom well evidenced in the Wycliffite sermons themselves. The Wycliffite Bible translations were intended for the literate who had little Latin (and this class probably included many priests of the *mumpsimus* variety). There was nothing heretical in the versions themselves. It was the political situation, the fear that Lollards represented a threat to Church and State, which brought suspicion upon them.‡

The first Wycliffite version, the 'Early Version', sometimes associated with the name of Nicholas Hereford, is often almost unreadable in its literalness. If it sometimes seems to provide the basis of phrases and rhythms now (or till recently) familiar from the 1611 version, it may also incorporate traditional renderings that were common form in vernacular sermons. A typical passage, showing the translator's uncertainty about some (admittedly difficult) phrases in the Vulgate, is the beginning of Isa. 53:§

Lord, who leevede to oure heering? and the arm of the Lord to whom is it shewid? And it shal steyen[1] up as a quik heg [Vulgate *virgultum*] biforn hym, and as a roote fro the threstende[2] erthe; ther is not shap to hym ne fairnesse,

* Hudson, *Selections*, 91. † Ibid. 114.
‡ For the debate on biblical translations at Oxford in 1401, see *EHR* xc (1975), 1–18.
§ Hudson, *Selections*, 40–1.

PROSE

and wee seyen hym and he was not of sighte [Vulgate *et non erat aspectus*]. And wee desireden hym dispisid and the last of men; man of sorewis and witende[3] infirmyté. And as hid is his chere and dispisid; wherfore ne wee setten bi hym. Verreli oure syknesses he toc and oure sorewis he bar; and wee heelden hym as leprous and smyten of God and meekyd.[4] He forsothe woundid is for oure wickidnesses, defoulid is for oure hidous giltus, the discipline [Vulgate *disciplina*] of oure pes on hym, and with his wannesse[5] wee ben helyd.

> [1] *rise*   [2] *thirsting*   [3] *knowing*   [4] *humiliated*   [5] *paleness*

In the more idiomatic 'Later Version' this runs:

Who bilevyde to oure heryng? and to whom is the arm of the Lord schewid? And he schal stie as a yerde bifor him and as a roote fro thirsti lond; and nether schap nether fairnesse was to him and we sien him and no biholding was. And we desiriden him, dispisid and the laste of men; a man of sorewis and knowinge sikenesse. And his cheer was hid and dispisid; wherfor and we arrettiden[1] not him. Verily he suffride oure sikenesses, and he bar oure sorewis; and we arrettiden him as a mysel[2] and smytun of God and maad low. Forsothe he was woundid for oure wickidnessis, he was defoulid for oure grete trespassis, the lernyng of oure pees was on him, and we ben maad hool bi his wannesse.

> [1] *considered*   [2] *leper*

It will be seen that the advantage does not lie always with the second version, and that the 1611 text sometimes follows the *cursus* of the first. In continuous narrative (witness the book of Jonah) both the early and the later versions are generally more successful (Jonah 4: 7 offers an unexpected poetic embellishment of *ascensu diluculi in crastinum* as 'steying up of grey dai into morn'). Similarly the Gospels, where the Vulgate is following a clearer Greek text, and the translators would be familiar with renderings offered Sunday by Sunday in sermons on the Gospel for the day, generally run smoothly.

The quality of the renderings offered in Sermons on Gospel lections may be gauged from the example of the Parable of the Prodigal Son in the Wycliffite feria[1] sermons. Here the preacher does not follow the rendering of either of the Wycliffite biblical versions, but gives his own in the traditional (and readable) manner. The central passage runs:

'I schal rise and go to my fader, and seie to him "Fader, I have synned in hevene and bifore thee; now I am not worthi to be clepid[1] thi sone; make me as oon of thin hynen[2]".' And he roos and cam to his fadir. And yit whanne he was fer, his fadir saie[3] him and was moved bi mercy and, rennynge ayens[4] his sone, fel on his nek and kiste him.*

> [1] *called*   [2] *servants*   [3] *saw*   [4] *to meet*

> * Hudson, 52.

338

The capacity for literary organization that shows in the Prologue to the biblical translations shows also in the Wycliffite sermon-cycle, which in its most complete form contains no less than 294 sermons, providing a preacher with a gospel sermon and an epistle sermon for each Sunday, as well as sermons for some saints' days and specified weekdays. Most of the manuscripts containing the cycle are carefully, indeed handsomely, prepared and rubricated, suggesting that like the biblical translation they were produced by 'a well-organised and prosperous centre for the dissemination of Lollard texts'.*

If they seem plainer in style or construction than others of the period, it is because their authors deliberately eschewed devices such as snatches of verse or pointed *exempla*, favoured by the friars (though by no means peculiar to them). The connection with the friars is enough to earn an outright condemnation of the method: friars 'prechen lesyngus [lies] and japes plesynge to the peple ... thei docken Goddis word and tateren it bi ther rimes' so that the form that Christ gave it is hidden by hypocrisy. The academic or university type of sermon, with its careful structure and divisions, is also associated with the friars and 'the flourished words that they bring in': they shape their sermons by divisions and other 'japes' to please the people and make the people agree with them that sermons are nothing but their form (Winn, p. 80). The objection to elaborate form or extraneous titillating matter is of a piece with Wycliffite suspicion of all recreative literature: parents who teach their children 'jeestis of bataillis and fals cronyclis' not needful to their souls are berated as soundly as those who teach them to swear and fight. But there is also present a distrust of any speculative enquiry. The sermon on the calling of the disciples (Luke 5: 1) insists that there is no need 'to depe us in this stori more than the Gospel tellith, as it is no nede to bisie us what hight [was the name of] Tobies hound ... dreeme we not aboute newe pointes that the Gospel leveth, for this is a synne of curiousté, that harmeth more than profitith' (Arnold, i. 13†). St Bernard would have agreed.

The spiritual application of the text for the day is generally clear and orthodox, and the presentation of Gospel narrative may approach eloquence. Yet almost invariably the eloquence dwindles to a topical jibe. Dominical precedent is cited for such satire: 'and so ofte in Goddis lawe is scornynge well ment, as yif it were leveful [allowable], done on good manere' (Arnold, i. 114). But the argument scarcely excuses the abusive digressions or application to 'these stinking orders', 'these proud prelates' that too often leave little room for plain

---

* Hudson, 11.
† T. Arnold, *Select English Works of John Wyclif* (Oxford, 1869–71), 3 vols.

exposition. Dominical warrant is again claimed for the presentation of written sermons in the vernacular and in simple form: 'Of this dede of Crist [his reading from Isaiah] men taken that it is leveful for to write, and aftirward to rede, a sermoun, for thus dide Crist oure alther-maistir [the master of us all] . . . certes traveile of the prechour or name of havyng good witt shulde not be the ende of preching, but profit to the soule of the peple . . .' (Arnold, ii. 19). The objection is evidently to the rhetorical or scholastic display of learned sermons. But it is only hearers of such sermons, not the ordinary parishioner, who would take the point, or need the warning.

The sermon on the Good Samaritan exemplifies the style at its simplest and best. The exposition begins with the moral 'each should be to other neighbour in good will . . . for we came all of Adam and Eve' (Arnold, i. 32). But this depends on the traditional interpretation of the traveller as Adam. So the priest stands for the Patriarchs and the deacon for the Prophets. Another sermon treats the miracle of the loaves and fishes in the same mode: the two fishes represent 'thinking of God'; the baskets are the patristic glosses; five thousand is the number that shall be saved: 'for five is a round number that turneth without end in to himself' (Arnold, i. 121) (cf. the 'endless knot' in *Gawain*). Elsewhere in the sermons (Arnold, i. 307–8), the idea of the disciples as humble fishers is developed in a rather unexpected way: poor men are nearer the state of innocence. But why did Christ not make hunters better men than fishers, since 'it is more gentle craft'? In truth, men hunt in Lent, and gentle men—to have their game; but not so commonly does this befall in fishing. And fish are nearer the elements, and not so like to man's flesh; fish is nearer to the food that men will have in Paradise, and slaying of fish is further from slaying of men than is the slaying of earthly beasts—which leads to a still more curious digression on the new craft of killing (Friar Bacon's gun-powder)—'and friars without [abroad] say that men should most kill English'.

The sermons share the general view that the moral sense of Scripture is what counts. Readers of *Pearl* will find in the Sermon on the Parable of the Vineyard for Septuagesima Sunday (Arnold, i. 98–102) the tradi-tional 'mystical' (i.e. allegorical) interpretation. The sermon gives more attention than the poem to the nature of the work of the vine-yard—digging, dunging, covering the roots, pruning and 'availing' of the vine (the last falling, allegorically, to prelates who make the estates of men to stand in the bonds that God has ordained). To cultivate the vine is better than to grow 'coolwortis' (cabbage) and other 'weeds' that produce melancholy and sins. In fact most of the similes or enlargements of text in the sermons are of this rural kind. So the Parable of the Sower is in one sermon developed thus: 'And as wete somers nurishen siche tares, so lustful lyf of men . . . bryngith in siche lawes' (Arnold, i. 96), and in another (Arnold, ii. 35) the seed is sown on 'good hearts well defouled': land well ploughed and dunged is able to bear good fruit. Gospel references to the Pharisees are read as applying to the mendicants, who say (i. 28) 'that thei ben erberis [gardens] betir than comoun pasture, for erbis of vertue that growen in hem; certis makinge of erberis in a comoun pasture wolde distrie this pasture and lyf of the comouns, bothe for dichyng and hegging [hedging] and delvynge of tounes . . .'.

The exegesis of the New Testament is basically traditional. Thus the story of Nicodemus in John 3, the Gospel for Trinity Sunday, is read as referring to the doctrine of the Trinity, since it speaks of the need to be born of water and the Holy Spirit—'Crist is compendious in spekynge of his wordis'. The sermon admits that both the story and the doctrine are hard, 'as commonly is John's Gospel'. Indeed, this tight and allusive sermon would scarcely be comprehensible to the average congregation. A sermon on Matt. 24: 42 (*Vigilate, quia nescitis qua hora*) applies the text to the need to wake from sin: 'for that is the best wakynge, and this beste Lord spekith of beste thing' (Arnold, i. 248). But it at once refers to 'clerks' and their doctrine of the five wits or senses that, if hindered, allow deadly sleep to fall on man.

The sermon on the Nativity is one of the few that are wholly free from spleen or topical satire, and its emphasis on Christ's love of common poverty gives it a certain beauty. In describing the Virgin birth it resorts to a traditional image: 'for as he brak not Maries cloister whanne she was maad with childe, so he brak not his modirs wombe whanne he cam out of this cloister' (Arnold, i. 318). It is the homely, simple element in the Gospels that the sermons respond to. A comment on Matt. 4: 18 ff. says: 'Crist clepide [called] not thes two apostlis to his chaumbre to ete applis; but in the comun feld he clepide hem fro worldli traveil' (i. 301). Of John the Baptist in the desert it is said: 'other housis hadde he noon but this wildernesse and cope of heven' (ii. 3).

The Sermons are too often marred by forced application of the text to contemporary abuses—a besetting sin, to be sure, of preachers in all ages. Only occasionally does censure produce a pungent phrase or pregnant image, such as: 'O [one] leprous mai foule a flok and a flok mai foule a more [moor]' (Winn, 52). Still rarer is the note of yearning and of charity, as in the sermon for Palm Sunday: 'O Crist, thi lawe is hid yit. Whan will thou sende thin aungel to remove the stone and shewe thi treuthe to thi folk?' (Arnold, i. 129); or in the Sermon for Easter Day: the third virtue necessary to take this sacrament of the Eucharist is the virtue of charity, 'for that is ever nedeful, sith no man cometh to Cristis fest but yif he have this clothing' (i. 134; an application of the parable in Matt. 22).

Although the sermons are generally simple in language, they frequently resort to scholastic terms and themes. Almost every reference to the Eucharist includes the terms 'accident' and 'subject'. The comment on John 8: 58 ('Before Abraham was, I am') runs (i. 127): 'herfore seyen clerkes that ech creature hath beyng in his sample that is withouten eende' (= the Platonic *exemplaria* or original patterns in the divine mind, adopted by St Thomas Aquinas). On *sal terre* 'the salt of the earth' (Matt. 5: 13) we are referred to Aristotle's law of contraries; and the same sermon (i. 267) discusses the properties of light. Satan's fall from heaven is the occasion (i. 186) for an Aristotelian account of thunder and lightning, and earthquakes are explained in similar terms. The current disputes in the Schools on predestination, known to us (and to Chaucer) from the works of Bishop Bradwardine, are reflected in the description of Christ as the *granum frumenti* that 'bringith with him a grace that clerkes clepen predestynynge' (i. 179). Sometimes these allusions to scholastic philosophy are critical or contemptuous; errors in logic and 'kindly science' (natural philosophy) are duly noted. But in general the sermons are willing to invoke scholastic aids whenever Scripture is 'misty and dark': John 12: 24 is 'misty speech'—there is no suggestion that the writer means it must be read *mystice*. So there is a distinction made between 'open sight' and 'misty sight . . . as men seen bi shadewes and bileve' (ii. 8). We are not to doubt how belief may now be less and now be more: 'Such doubts we should send to the school of Oxenford' (i. 93).

The sermons have a notable unity of tone, partly doctrinal in origin, partly arising from the repeated satirical jibes at the usual targets. There is an interesting cross-reference in the second sermon on the parable of the householder (*Si fur venturus esset*): 'it is touchid bifore', says Sermon 82, referring to Sermon 76, 'how this theef is the fend [fiend]' (i. 277). In the latter sermon, it must be said, the writer develops the image effectively, and the exposition is for once completely homogeneous: 'For ech man and a fend ben couplid togider in a liste and fighten bothe night and dai . . . and so whanne the nyght of synne blindith men to knowun hemsilf, thanne is tyme to the fend to fighte fastist with his make [consort].' The development of the image in the earlier sermon is closer, initially at least, to that in *Sawles Warde*: the servants are the five senses, 'and wit withinne in mannis heed, that is God himself, mut move his out-wittis to worche as thei shulden' (i. 249).

In style and syntax there is little variation. Sentences are short and simple, beginning regularly with a copulative *And*—a result perhaps of continuous attention to the Gospel narratives, which employ it just as often; sometimes it does duty in as many as eight continuous sentences, to be relieved only by an adversative *But*. One persistent feature, common to Wycliffite preachers and Lollard pamphleteers, is the initial ejaculatory *Lord* ('Lord', says the tract *Of Dominion*, 'whether the lawe of Ynglond shal be now destried by fablis of heretikis contrarie to Goddis law?' (Winn, 66)).

Compared with Latimer, a later preacher of much the same creed and stance, these sermons come off poorly. The tone is monotonous, the accent austere. Latimer's are *preached* sermons, addressed, and very directly, to known audiences at known times; Latimer's habit of reminiscence, of owning to former errors, gives them a personal quality never found in Wyclif's followers. Yet the Cambridge man's homilies reveal that Reformation had removed few of the ills against which the Oxford man had fulminated: prelates were still worldly, clerics still sought secular office.

To treat of the English tracts and miscellaneous writings that have in the past gone under Wyclif's name is to launch out on the rough sea of fourteenth-century polemic. Their interest is slight in proportion to their bulk (they make up two stout volumes), but as they constitute the largest corpus of homogeneous prose before or about 1400 they cannot be passed over. They are the first Tracts for the Times ever to be published, but as with a more modern series they would be more accurately labelled tracts against the times, for they assert that 'hypocrisy reigneth among all states of Christian men'. It is not clear how widely they circulated, or for whom they were primarily intended, but the cumulative effect must have been considerable. Several of them are brief and most of them are tendentious and repetitious. One is reminded sometimes of the objurgations in *Lycidas*, sometimes of Edith Sitwell's young lady who always felt sick in the train—not once and again, nor again and again, but again and again and again. The Wycliffites knew nothing of the perils of 'overkill'. The shrill tone eventually deafens us, the abuse becomes formulaic, the jibes against friars, Rome-runners, prelates, popes, possessioners, pardoners, and pilgrimages, come to function simply as tags. None of the tracts bear the impress of a great intellect. The more substantial provide favourable samples of style and substance, but little new will be found outside them.

One of these longer works, on Clergy holding property (Matthew, 359–404*) is, in fact, more restrained than most of its congeners, and displays more sequacious thought (reflected in more elaborate sentence structure). It also has some unexpectedly lively touches and pungent phrasing: 'And wete [know] lordis well that if the clergi gete this swerde [of temporal rule] oonys fully in her power, the seculer party may go pipe with an yvy lefe'—the phrase Theseus uses in *The Knight's Tale*—'for eny lordeschipis that the clerks wille yeve hem ayen'; 'I wote wel that Gabriel schal blow his horne or [before] thai han prevyd the mynor [the minor clause in a syllogism].' This work is unusual in the names and number of authorities it cites: they range from Origen, Cyprian, Isidore, Bernard (*De Consideratione*), to a certain Odo, a 'Parisiensis' and Nicholas de Gorran or Gorham, a Dominican, Fellow of Merton (*ob.* 1295), author of a commentary on the Apocalypse. A reference to the *Polychronicon* illustrates the vogue of that work. Such citations are rare in other tracts: one to Hildegard of Bingen (Matthew, 11) is surprising, one to St (*sic*) Richard Fitzralph's *Defensorium* (Matthew, 128) is less so. *De Officio Pastorali*, another substantial tract formerly ascribed to Wyclif, may be taken as representative of English works that are based on Latin originals. Alongside this booklet may be placed that on 'The Church and her Members' (Arnold, iii. 338–65). It has been praised as superior in construction and expression to all the other controversial works, and to be sure it does contain some sharp strokes of irony, in paragraphs that set forth Wyclif's philosophic realism, as against the position of friars who 'hyen hem above Crist as yif thei wolden maken a newe world . . . but thes goddis varien' (i.e. differ among themselves), laymen who (in Milton's phrase) dying put on the weeds of Dominic 'ayens Cristis sentence . . . sewen an old cloute in newe cloith'—a favourite Wycliffite figure. The treatise in fact offers the usual blend of appeal to Scripture and denunciation of current practices.

As already suggested, the line of criticism that runs through most of the pamphlets is not altogether novel. Wulfstan had sometimes been as vehement, St Bernard and Grosseteste just as outspoken. What is new is the tone of contempt: worldly prelates with their 'fatte hors and precious pellure' (Matthew, 92) or their fourscore horses with harness of silver and gold are 'moldwarpis [moles] ful of symonye and heresie' (Matthew, 88). Those who 'feign dreams and miracles to please covetous clerks' are the devil's jugglers, and 'in stede of Cristis apostlis ben comen in viserid [visored] develis' (94, 99). New modes of Church

* F. D. Matthew, *The English Works of Wyclif hitherto unprinted* (EETS lxxiv, 1880, rev. edn. 1902).

music—'descant, counternote and organs' (77)—are a favourite target. Paintings of the Trinity that show the Father as an old hoar man, the Son as a crucified man, and the Spirit as a white dove, are condemned as the iconoclasts would have condemned them, for the Trinity is 'spirite and no creature' (Arnold, iii. 491).

Only at rare intervals do we glimpse the diurnal life of the four-teenth century that we know from Chaucer and Langland: friars as pedlars bearing knives, purses, pins, girdles, spices, or taking posts as stewards in hall, kitchen clerks, chamberlains, councillors, or studying 'on the holy day' witchcraft or vain songs and harping, gitterning, and dancing 'and other vain trifles to get the stinking love of damsels'; against which must be set the concession made in another passage (Matthew, 205–6), addressed to gentlewomen told, now that courtesy and 'gentilesse' are turned into vanity and nicety, to think on the example of the saints like St Margaret: 'Yonge wymmen may sum-tyme daunsen in mesure to have recreacion and lightnesse, so that [provided that] thei have the more thought on myrthe in hevene and drede more and love more God therby, and synge honeste songis of Cristis incarnacion, passion, resurexion and ascension' (one would like to know what these were, and when they were sung). Characters in Langland's prologue and Chaucer's come to mind when we are told that pardoners sell a fat goose for little or nought, but the garlic (for the stuffing, the seal of authorization) costs many shillings (Matthew, 82). Priests blabber out matins and mass as hunters (Matthew, 168), without devotion or contemplation. If the Host of the Tabard 'smells a loller in the wind' it is because the Parson, like the authors of these tracts, objects to swearing.

The appeal in the polemical tracts is always primarily to Scripture. So matins and evensong, *placebo* and *dirige*, are condemned as making men indisposed to study God's law, 'for akyng of hedis' (Winn, 90). Mistrust of the 'novelry' of song arises out of fear that it hinders the preaching of the Gospel, and that men do not follow the meaning of the words sung: 'For whanne ther ben fourty or fyfty in a queer [choir], thre or foure proude lorellis [good for nothings] schullen knacke the most devout servyce that no man schal here the sentence, and alle othere schullen be doumbe, and loken on hem as foolis. And thanne strumpatis and thevys preisen Sire Jacke or Hobbe, and William the proude clerk, hou smale thei knacken here motis . . .' (Winn, 91).

Rarely is the heavy body of polemic lightened by rhetorical ornament. Still rarer is the use of proverbial phrase: 'As dogge lokes ofer towarde Lincolne and litel sees theroff', so friars overlook the law of God (Arnold, iii. 236). Several tracts share with the sermons the stylistic features or mannerisms already mentioned: initial ejaculatory 'Lord', deadly strings of copulatives and rhetorical questions. 'It is great marvel' is a frequent tag; conclusions tend to be in the form of prayers: 'God almyghtty strengthe his litil flok ayenst thes foure whelis of Sathanas chaar [cart]' (Matthew, 262). Figures and similes are infrequent, but heretics are once likened to drunk men who look at moon or candle and see double (267). 'Of Faith, Hope and Charity' employs the figure of the secret seal (cf. *Piers Plowman*, iii. 145): 'As if thou haddist a lettre that thi kynge sent thee seelid with hiis privey seele . . . and hight thee greet eritage to be at his retenu and serve hym treuly, thou woldest do of thin hoode and kisse his seel for hope of rewarde. God is mich more than any lord of erthe; he sent a lettre to man by Moyses his messangere that is more worth than any pope or cardynal' (a typically gratuitous and invidious comparison). Alliteration, which satirists have regularly called in to aid their effects, is infrequent: 'lecherous lorelis [rascals] . . . knacke notis for many markis and poundis' is untypical.

It has been said that the Reformer and the writings he inspired had the gift of pointed, epigrammatical phrase; and one might cite in support of this such gnomic utterances as: 'Whoevere lyveth beste, he preieth best'; 'Croune and cloth maken no prest, ne the Emperours bischop with his wordis, but power that Crist yiveth'; 'Thus shulde the chirche draw to acord bi Crist, that ledith the daunce of love.' Such citations, however, are misleading if they suggest that Wycliffite works are studded with memorable sententiae: they represent careful gleanings in four closely printed volumes.

Foxe rightly incorporated in his *Book of Martyrs* the defences made by early Lollards to their accusers; indeed it is these accounts, like those of later trials, that give that tendentious work a lasting value. Some of those defences, like those of Swinderby, deserve a high place in the history of English prose and self-expression. The plain narrative is often moving, and sometimes breaks into eloquence: 'This land is full of ghostly cowardice, in ghostly battaile fewe dare stand. But Christ the comforter of all that falleth . . . against that fiend, the doughtie duke, comforteth us thus: "Estote fortes in bello: be ye strong in battaile", he saies, "and fight ye with the old adder. . . ." '*

(v) Later Secular Prose: Usk; Trevisa; 'Mandeville'

Prose no more than poetry advanced along predictable paths. Between the reigns of Stephen and Richard II we have no English

---

* John Foxe, *Acts and Monuments*, ed. S. R. Cattley, iii (London, 1837), 128.

prose that is not homiletic, devotional, didactic, or severely utilitarian. Of the two prose tales told by the pilgrims to Canterbury, Chaucer's own *Melibee* is unrestrainedly didactic, and *The Parson's Tale* is homily at its most comprehensive. The *Astrolabe* and perhaps the *Equatory of the Planets* are Chaucer's essays in *scientific* prose, of severely limited interest. His *Boethius* breaks new ground in attempting (as Alfred had done before him) to render a Latin philosophical text into a vernacular that had not hitherto seemed fitted for philosophical discourse. It cannot be said that Chaucer wholly succeeded, or that any other writer did for two centuries, though the ten copies surviving indicate that his version had some immediate appeal.

It has sometimes been presumed that it appealed in particular to Thomas Usk, a scrivener who became entangled in London politics, was imprisoned for treason, and was executed in March 1388. (His head was placed over Newgate, where Chaucer must have seen it.) Boethius himself had sought consolation from Philosophy when in similar danger; and political prisoners like James I of Scotland or Elizabeth I evidently packed a Boethius in the luggage they took to jail. In the turbulent London of Richard II, Usk, clerk to John of Northampton, draper mayor in 1381–2, was brought as a witness against his former master, who denounced him. He was imprisoned for some two months 'for wrathe of my firste medlinge', as he says; an event that would give rise to the despair reflected in the dialogue with Lady Love that forms the frame of his *Testament of Love*,* a work that is *inter alia* an apology for his conduct. It can hardly have been completed within that brief period of imprisonment; but his plight then must have brought to mind Boethius and the remedy Boethius provided.

Chaucer's cautionary verses to Adam 'his own scriveyn', give us some hint of a scrivener's task. It was not highly regarded, but could at least give to such a man as Usk an acquaintance with Chaucer's works that he might not otherwise have had. The apparent familiarity with the *Troilus* and the *Boece* that he shows in his *Testament* may be due simply to his general recollection of passages that he had copied. The interlocutor he provides for his persona, when touching on God's omnipotence and rightful punishment of evil, remarks that 'a treatise ... made of my servant Troilus by myne owne trewe servaunt, the noble philosophical poete in Englissh ... hath this mater touched, and at the ful this question assoyled [explained]' (123†): the allusion, if

---

* The identity of the author lay hidden until Henry Bradley in 1897 by rearranging a chapter discovered the acrostic 'MARGARETE OF VIRTW HAVE MERCI ON THIN USK'.

† Page references are to W. W. Skeat, *Chaucerian and Other Pieces* (*The Complete Works of Geoffrey Chaucer*, vol. vii, Oxford, 1897).

inexact, is unmistakable. She says further that this poet 'evermore him besieth and travayleth right sore my name to encrese (wherefore al that willen me good owe to do him worship and reverence both; trewly his better ne his pere in scole of my rules coude I never fynde). . . . In goodnes of gentil manliche speche, without any maner of nyceté [fool-ishness] of storiers [story-teller's] imaginacion, in witte and in good reson of sentence he passeth al other makers' (123).

The passage, which suggests that the writer had some acquaintance with Chaucer, can hardly be mere flattery. It anticipates by several years the greeting that Venus sends to Chaucer, 'my own poet', at the end of *Confessio Amantis*, and is thus the very first witness that we have to Chaucer's standing with his contemporaries. It is not altogether apposite or lucid, but it indicates what Usk valued in the *Troilus*. Some passages suggest that he also knew Dido's complaint in *The House of Fame*, though her sentiments acquire a different value when put on the lips of Lady Love, who has no personal cause to plead. Where Dido says 'We wreched women konne non wit', Love is more verbose: women 'con no more craft in queynt knowinge to under-stande the false disceyvable conjectements [devices] of mannes begyl-inges' (55). And where Dido complains that men change their love every year, for fame, friendship, delight, or 'singular profit', Love says that they change in a little while: 'for frendship shal be oon, and fame with another him list for to have, and a thirde for delyt; or els were he lost bothe *in packe and in clothes*' (55)—one of Usk's characteristically teasing phrases. But he does not draw on Chaucer's later characteriza-tion of Fame, which would have been equally to his purpose.

That Usk had *Chaucer's* version of Boethius (which cannot be precisely dated) at hand when writing is highly doubtful. Nothing save a certain stiffness of style requires us to believe that he took Chaucer's Boethius as a model for his prose, and several variations on the Latin text show him going his own way. Whatever his education, he would probably be more familiar with Latin than with English prose. How-ever, Boethius supplies the general frame of the *Testament*, though the Lady Love who replaces *Philosophia* is a more intangible figure. But Usk's adaptation of Boethius, beginning with the first *metrum*, varies from book to book. Love assumes the role of Boethius's Philosophy in the second chapter, and in the fourth the imprisoned narrator, whose role is that of the exiled Roman senator, praises her in terms derived from *De Consolatione*, ii, metrum 8. Later she points, like Philosophy, to the impermanence of Fame; but Usk introduces the notion of Virtue that wins everlasting fame in heaven (possibly with reference to Rom. 2: 7–8). Fortune and Providence play a minimal part. In general

Usk follows his own line, picking up here and there appropriate Boethian metaphors, or combining various apophthegms such as those on the nature of 'gentilesse':

gentilesse in kinrede maketh ɪ   gentil linage in succession, without desert of a mans own selfe. Where is now the lyne of Alisaundre the noble, or els of Hector of Troye? Who is discended of right bloode of lyne fro king Artour?

(52)

In fact his reliance on the Boethian frame is intermittent. Boethian arguments against the pursuit of worldly goods would certainly 'speak to his condition'; in the midst of an elevated discussion in the second book, he suddenly gives us an autobiographical excursus on himself: 'No wight in my administracion coude non yvels ne trechery by sothe cause on me putte' (84). At this point he seems almost to identify his past happiness with heavenly harmony; but perhaps he is intentionally playing the part of obtuse narrator. His defence against the charge of changing sides is something of a jumble: he is promised his freedom if he confesses; he thought he was helping the city; he was afraid to die in falseness; the Scriptures enjoin peace. Yet his disclosure of his own plight relieves the monotony of the dialogue.

It must be admitted that, quite apart from its stylistic difficulties, the dialogue is not easy reading; the narrator takes a long time to learn his lessons, and the theme shifts without warning. At first we see the Lady encouraging her interlocutor in his love-service for a 'Margaryte' whose name—as readers of *Pearl* would not need to be told—signifies a precious pearl and as such lends itself to a scriptural and spiritual interpretation. So Usk will explain in his closing pages that as manna was both bodily and spiritual meat and also signified Christ,

right so a jewel betokeneth a gemme, and that is a stoon vertuous or els a perle. Margarite, a woman, betokeneth grace, lerning, or wisdom of God, or els Holy Church. (145)

The transmutation is not unlike that in Dante's *Comedy* of the Beatrice who does not cease to be the Beatrice of Dante's earthly love when she becomes the vehicle and exponent of Grace. Usk's (un-identifiable) Margaryte may have been a real or at least an imagined woman. Such double meanings likewise abound in the *Roman de la Rose*, to which Love seems to allude when speaking of the mysterious 'intermelling' of two hearts at first sight:

Trowest thou, every ideot wot the meninge and the privy entent of these thinges. They wene, forsothe, that suche accord may not be, but [unless] the rose of maydenhede be plucked. Do way! Do way! They knowe nothing of this.

For consent of two hertes alone maketh the fasteninge of the knotte; neither lawe of kynde ne mannes lawe determineth neither the age ne the qualité of persones, but only accord bitwene thilke twaye. (40–1)

Whenever Usk touches on this 'knot' and on the law of Kind, his prose flows more clearly and surpasses Chaucer's. His conception of Kind seems (like Chaucer's) to be coloured by Alanus's, as found in *De Planctu Naturae*:

I wot wel myselfe that thilke jewel is so precious perle, as a womanly woman in her kynde. I leve that Kynde her made with greet studye. (94)

From Alanus too, whether at first or second hand, he may have taken the figure of the knot of love, though he sets it in new contexts.

His development of this figure of the knot* as an image of true felicity helps to tie his work together. He plays deliberately upon various senses of *knot*, both as noun and verb. Thus knowledge of understanding is 'nigh after eye, but not so nigh the covetyse of knittinge in your hertes' (78) (= ? the desire of lovers to be knit does not actually come so easily as other knowledge). There is 'ne power to chaunge the wedding ne the knotte to unbynde of two hertes that . . . togider accorden to enduren til deth hem departe' (40). 'Richesse, dignité and power ben not trewe way to the knotte, but as rathe by suche thinges the knotte to ben unbounde. . . . Shrewes shul not have the knotte. . . . Every wight, by kyndely reson, shrewes in knitting wol eschewe' (74). Fleshly beauty 'should be no way to the knot'; 'knitting' is associated with heavenly harmony:

Fayn wolde I and [if] it were your wil blisse of the knotte to me were declared. I might fele the better how my herte might assente, to pursue the ende in service as he hath begonne. 'Oh, (quoth she) and there is a melodye in heven whiche clerkes clepe [call] "armony"; . . . that is joyned by reson and by wysdome in a quantité of proporcion of knitting [the reference is to the unheard music of the spheres]: . . . This armony, this melody, this perdurable joye may nat be in doinge but betwene hevens and elementes or twey kyndly hertes ful knit in trouth of naturel understonding.' (77–8)

Still another appearance of *knot* is found in sentences like 'Of love . . . wol I now ensample make, sithen I knowe the heed-knotte in that yelke [yolk = centre]' (121–2). Ultimately, in a way hard to define, we come to a sense that the two symbols, the Margaret and the Knot, are one.

The moment of truth comes towards the end of Usk's third book,

---

* It was possibly a scriveners' term (an intricate design of crossing lines). Cf. *OED*'s quotation from Butler: 'As Scriveners take more pains to learn the slight / Of making knots, than all the hands they write.'

when the Lady, having bidden her interlocutor to 'thanke thy Margaryte of her grete grace that hiderto thee hath gyded' (137), and having pointed to 'wysdom and love in parfit charité' as the true glory, 'al at ones sterte into my herte: "Here wol I onbyde (quod she) for ever." ' Then the writer soberly threw up his eyes:

and hugely tho was I astonyed of this sodayne adventure . . . and anon al these thinges that this lady said, I remembred me by myselfe and revolved the lynes of myne understondinge wittes. . . .   (137)

He seems to be describing a revelation not unlike that promised by Truth in *Piers Plowman*, v. 615: 'Thow shalt see in thi-selve Treuthe sitte in thine herte / In a cheyne of charyté', and it is in his heart that Usk found, 'of perdurable letters wonderly there graven', the matters that he proceeds to name—in short, Love's testament. It is Usk (or his *persona*) who now himself enunciates the truths of Love, adapting terminology that St Anselm in his *De Concordia* had used for Justice: 'Wil wol not love but for it is lovinge, as Wil wol not rightfully but for it is rightful itselve' (137–8). But where Anselm equates 'rightfulness' with *lex dei*, Usk says that it 'maintayneth the lawe of Kynde' (139). Whether Usk quite knew what he was about when he took over St Anselm's arguments is another matter. (It is surprising that he should have known the work at all; he was perhaps in touch with London clergy who had been trained by Oxford Scotists, and thus became familiar with the saint's views on grace and free will.) Usk might have answered our queries with the Chaucerian phrase he used later: 'God and the Margaryte weten [know] what I mene' (140: echoing *TC* ii. 1561). To translate and adapt Anselm on free will meant introducing concepts like 'wil of commodité' that elude the ordinary reader, though there is no mistaking Usk's and Anselm's condemnation of 'the comune sentence of the people . . . that every thing after destenee is ruled' (142). We meet the conflict of free will and divine prescience (Usk's 'Goddes beforn-weting' (143)) more than once in Chaucer; and Troilus's view is like that which Usk attributes to the folk who say 'As it was destenyed of God toforn knowe, so it is thorow necessité falle, and otherwyse might it not betyde' (143).

The argument, so far as one can disentangle it from a cryptic and corrupt text, seems stronger when it comes to treat of the supreme good and to identify it with Love. Reason is given an essential part as the highway to this bliss, and in due course the virtue of the Margaret will be tested by it; increasingly, the form of argument smacks of the Schools, and Aristotle is openly or implicitly invoked.

The line of Usk's argument is too often obscured by rhetorical adornment and a covert justification of the activities that had brought him into disfavour. The rhetoric includes a large assortment of classical allusions, beginning with the identification of God and Jupiter and the introduction of the Isle of Venus, where the Margarite is revealed. Love's rhetorical questions to her obtuse interlocutor (who himself represents a favourite rhetorical device) blend Christian and pagan elements:

Hast thou not rad how kinde I was to Paris, Priamus sone of Troy? How Jason me falsed, for al his false behest? How Cesars swink[1], I lefte it for no tene[2] til he was troned[3] in my blisse for his service? What! . . . most of al, maked I not a loveday[4] bytwene God and mankynde, and chees[5] a mayde to be nompere[6], to putte the quarel at ende? (11)

[1] toil [2] vexation [3] enthroned [4] day of reconciliation [5] chose
[6] umpire

Just as Alfred had naturalized Boethius's *Ubi sunt ossa Fabricii?* as 'Where are now the bones of Weland?' (doubtless associating that smith—*faber*—with Fabricius), so Usk's Lady adds 'Where is now the line of Alexander? Who is descended by right blood of line from King Arthur?' (a pertinent question when England was still 'Brutus's Albion'). In another Boethian passage Usk pleasingly substitutes for Rome 'the glorious name of London'. If such passages delay the development of the argument, they lighten the tedium of the prose. They are as near as Usk comes to poetry, and serve something of the purpose of Boethius's metres as lyrical interludes. A passage on the constitution of Man, compounded of the four elements, achieves a similar effect: 'Now is his soule here, now a thousand myle hence . . . as fer in a moment as in mountenaunce [amount] of ten winter, and al this is in mannes governaunce and disposicion. Than sheweth it that men ben liche [like] unto goddes and children of moost heyght' (39). This is one of the many places where knowledge of Scripture shows through (cf. Ps. 88: 6). Elsewhere there is a queer medley of scriptural and classical language: 'trewly al hevenly bodyes with one voyce shul come and make melody in thy cominge and saye: "Welcome, our fere, and worthy to entre into Jupiters joye!" ' (40: cf. the scriptural 'enter into the joy of thy lord').

Usk constantly uses the terms and adopts the stances of the Schools: 'If I graunt contradiccion I shulde graunte an impossible; and that were a foul inconvenience' (61); 'After the sentence of Aristotle, every cause is more in dignité than his thinge caused' (61). He is perhaps trying to reproduce the formalism as well as the vocabulary of scholastic Latin, which may be the source of his unnatural word-order, his clipped phrases, and his indifference to prose rhythm. Yet he saw the virtues of language such 'as men do use'—at least, the virtues of such language in a lover's mouth. 'Thy wordes', says Love,

> may nat be queynt, ne of subtel maner understandinge. Freel-witted[1] people supposen in suche poesies to be begyled; in open understandinge must every word be used. 'Voice without clere understanding of sentence', saith Aristotel, 'right nought printeth in herte.' (134)
>
> [1] *thin-witted*

The unique, dismissive, use of *poesies* is revealing.

If we rarely catch the tone of actual talk, phrases and proverbs that smack of common use do occur: 'for every glittring thing is nat gold' (54–5); 'While men gon after a leche, the body is buryed' (134). Lady Love from time to time ejaculates 'Aha!' or 'What!' or 'Do way, do way!' Unexpectedly different is a passage on a negligent priest, which is introduced by a rough rhyme ('free herte is forsake; and losengeour is take'):

> For suche there ben that voluntarie lustes haunten in courte with ribaudye, that til midnight and more wol playe and wake, but in the churche at matins he is behynde, for yvel disposicion of his stomake; therefore he shulde ete bene-breed (and so did his syre). . . . His chalice poore, but he hath riche cuppes. No towayle[1] but a shete, there God shal ben handled; and on his mete-borde[2] there shal ben bord-clothes and towelles many payre. At masse serveth but a clergion[3]; fyve squiers in hal. Poore chaunsel[4], open holes in every syde; beddes of silke, with tapites[5] going al aboute his chambre. Poore masse-book and leud[6] chapelayn, and broken surplice with many an hole; good houndes and many, to hunte after hart and hare, to fede in their feestes. (51)
>
> [1] *towel* [2] *food-table* [3] *chorister* [4] *chancel* [5] *tapestries*
> [6] *ignorant*

Equally sharp is the bitter scorn born of personal experience, in 'Tho louteden blasours [then trumpeters bowed down]; tho curreyden glosours [flatterers curried favour]; tho welcomeden flatterers; tho worshipped thilke that now deynen nat to loke' (42). Apposition is his favourite, and most effective, device:

> I am servaunt of these creatures to me delivered, not lord, but defendour; not mayster, but enfourmer; not possessour, but in possession; and to hem liche[1] a tree in whiche sparrowes shullen stelen, her birdes to norisshe and forth bringe, under suretee ayenst[2] al raveynous foules and beestes, and not to be tyraunt them-selfe. (52)
>
> [1] *like* [2] *against*

Rather more gauche, and more typical of his style, but equally topical, is this passage (playing, incidentally, on the astrological sense of 'house'):

In heven on highe, above Saturnes sphere, in sesonable tyme were they lodged; but now come queynte counsailours that in no house wol suffre me sojourne, wherof is pité; and yet sayn some that they me have in celler with wyne shed; in gernere, there corn is layd covered with whete; in sacke, sowed with wolle; in purse, with money faste knit. . . .   (50)

A passage on the seasons (81), picked out by Skeat for special praise, is in fact conventional apart from one sentence: 'The same sees maketh smothe waters and golden sayling.'

Perhaps the Tudor readers for whom Thynne (supposing the *Testament* to be Chaucer's) printed it found its style or its philosophy more acceptable than we do. They were familiar enough with the kind of political treason and intrigue to which Usk alludes. And his similes and figures are just the kind that readers of *Euphues* might relish:

A marchaunt that for ones lesinge[1] in the see no more to aventure thinketh, he shal never with aventure come to richesse. So ofte must men on the oke smyte, til the happy dent have entred, whiche with the okes owne swaye maketh it to come al at ones. So ofte falleth the lethy[2] water on the harde rocke, til it have thorow-persed it. The even draught of the wyr-drawer maketh the wyr to ben even and supple-werchinge; and if he stinted in his draught, the wyr breketh a-sonder.   (135)

> [1] *losing, loss*   [2] *weak*

Idiosyncratic as the style and language often are, they may preserve genuine usages in such phrases as 'sleveless [vain] wordes of the people' (76); 'with superfluité of riches be a-throted [throttled]' (63); 'sperkelande [wandering] sheep' (11); 'playted [involved] praisings' (35).

Usk's final prayer, that Christ should grant to every manner of reader 'ful understanding in this leude pamflet to have', and that the Holy Ghost should lend 'of his oyntmentes mennes wittes to clere' is not supererogatory (he concedes that his work is 'not sufficiently' made). In it, he adds, again with justification, 'be many privy thinges wimpled and folde; unneth [scarcely] shul leude men the plites [folds] unwinde . . . for my dul wit is hindred by stepmoder of foryeting and with cloude of unconning, that stoppeth the light of my Margarite-perle' (144). Finally, like Chaucer, he desires not only a good reader but also a good book-amender, 'in correccion of wordes and of sentence' (145). The prose of the last pages grows suddenly more relaxed, and even reaches rhyme:

Charité is love; and love is charité. God graunt us alle therin to be frended! And thus the Testament of Love is ended.   (145)

Set against Dante's *Convivio*, a comparable vernacular prose treatise written some eighty years earlier, the *Testament* comes off poorly. Yet one must respect Usk's intention and his courage in trying to naturalize metaphysical and theological language. He stands with Chaucer, Langland, and Gower as an amateur of a kind not hitherto encountered in England. Is it mere coincidence that each of them at one time or another took on the role of slow-witted questioner? Usk's Lady goes so far as to say 'Me thinketh thee now duller in thy wits than when I first thee met. Although a man be lewed [unlearned], commonly for a fool he is not taken but if [unless] he no good will learn.' But Usk's 'lewedness' is part of his modesty. As he puts it:

> though my book be leude, the cause with which I am stered, and for whom I ought it doon, noble forsothe ben bothe. But bycause that in conninge I am yong, and can yet but crepe, this leude A.B.C. have I set in-to lerning. . . .
>
> (49)

One might regard the *Testament* as a first stumbling attempt at *Kunstprosa*; yet the stiff phrasing may be no more than a relic of the formal legal language with which a scrivener would be likely to be conversant. There is something amateurish and tentative about his style, as there is about his philosophy. The strained elliptical syntax of the work as we read it may be partly due to his printer; but the fondness for inversion must be his own.

'By Tre, Pol, and Pen ye may know the Cornishmen.' John of Trevisa was undoubtedly Cornish; and it is to two Cornishmen, John Cornwall and Richard Pencrich, grammar school masters, that he attributes the change from French to English as the medium of instruction in Latin, after the Black Death, which resulted in schoolboys knowing 'no more French than their left heel'. Like them, he was an Oxford man.* But it was whilst vicar of Berkeley, Gloucester, and chaplain to Thomas, Lord Berkeley that he undertook his translation of Higden's *Polychronicon* (1387) and of Bartholomew the Englishman's encyclopedic *De Proprietatibus Rerum* (1398). His versions of *The Gospel of Nicodemus*, and (possibly) of *De Regimine Principum* and Fitzralph's *Defensio Curatorum* testify to his remarkable versatility as a translator. His *Dialogue between the Lord and the Clerk on Translation* and his *Epistle to Lord Berkeley on Translation* which often precede the *Polychronicon* have some discussion of the translator's problems. His English *Dialogus inter Militem et Clericum* is a document of unique interest. It is a translation of a short *Disputatio* on the temporalities of the

---

* See A. B. Emden, *BRUO*.

Church, once ascribed to Ockham but probably by Peter of Blois. Trevisa evidently saw the topicality of the work (it touched on the absolute power of a king, as Langland does at the end of Passus xix). He was not completely at home with the complex syntax and difficult concepts of the Latin; but much of the Latin is based on the Vulgate and his *ad hoc* translation of biblical verses is of interest.

The encyclopedia of Bartholomaeus Anglicus, often identified with a friar Bartholomew of Glanville, represents the peak of a thirteenth-century encyclopedic movement, the direction of which is indicated by works with the title *De natura rerum*, or with a similar title, attributed to Thomas of Cantimpré and to Alexander Nequam (the latter also an Englishman). Hitherto Isidore of Seville's *Etymologiae* had been the standard work of reference; and Isidore's penchant for pseudo-etymology is still apparent in Bartholomaeus, who also follows Isidore's general arrangement. But his work owes its popularity largely to its inclusion of material made available by the twelfth-century rediscovery of Aristotle in Arabic versions, hence its vogue at Paris and its use by another English friar, Roger Bacon. As St Thomas adapted Aristotle to fit into the frame of Christian philosophy, so Bartholomew adapted Aristotelian texts to fit into the frame of Christian knowledge, both patristic and more recent. The variety of his sources suggests that he began it whilst a *baccalarius biblicus* at Paris: he remarks that whilst Athens was 'the modir of liberal artes and of lettres', now Paris 'bereth the prys' (Trevisa, 759*).

Like Nequam, Bartholomaeus was a compiler rather than (like his compatriots Grosseteste or Bacon) an investigator. But his name, like theirs, reminds us of the part Englishmen, and English friars, played in the cultural expansion of Europe. Part of his purpose was to provide a handbook for biblical scholars; and *proprietates* carries a meaning that Trevisa's *propirtees* does not fully convey today: the work is concerned to show not only the characteristic qualities of things but also the operations of Nature in a divinely ordained way. Its purpose is ultimately religious. As the proem says, in Trevisa's rendering: 'the unseye [unseen] thinges of God beth iknowe and undirstonde by thinges that beth iseye [seen]. . . . By cause hereof I profre this work to the edificacioun of the hous of oure lord that is God gloryous and hyghe and blessed withouten ende' (41). Hence it is with the divine *mysteria* that he begins. An early chapter is headed 'de proprietatibus divine essencie'. He was a friar and lector in theology before he was an encyclopedist. Though he finds in the world much to praise and avers

* Page references are to the edition of M. C. Seymour and others (Oxford, 1975).

that 'nothing in the schappe of the worlde is so vile nothir so lowe nothir partykel in the whiche schynyth noght praisinge of God in mater and in vertu and in schap' (444), he sees it also as a prison of spirits and 'most cruel exilinge of soules ande place and stede of ful meny wretchidnes and paynes . . . noyful to many men and profytable to fewe. He deceyveth and gyleth his lovers, for he byhoteth [promises] many thinges and payeth fewe at the laste' (446). The friar also shows through, in different fashion, in a passage on vegetable birds: 'it tokeneth . . . that the spirit of God gendreth by the tre of cros in the water of folwinge [baptism]' (136). In Book ix entries under Septuagesima and Quadragesima expound the doctrinal significance of these seasons of the Church; Book xiv is in effect a Dictionary of the Bible. But in general, Bartholomaeus eschews the older allegorical expositions. He presents *Natura* as the constant operative force, and the student of Chaucer will profit from his account of the planetary heavens, of the 'scale' of the bird-creation, of human physiology, of 'the lovers malady of Hereos' that Arcite suffered.

Trevisa's part was to bring this accumulation of popular scientific learning within the range of literate English laymen, such as his patron, Lord Berkeley. In so doing he bent (if he sometimes twisted) English to new uses. His version remained acceptable until Caxton's day, and indeed long after, though like some later encyclopedias, the book was by no means up to date even when first compiled. In presenting this large and comprehensive work to an English audience Trevisa was faced with the same problems that Usk and Chaucer confronted when translating Boethius. The complex syntax and the abstruse concepts of the Latin original are not easily rendered into English prose, which provided no precedent or model for such translation after the Old English period. Trevisa's style is hesitant, and his sentences are often obscure, e.g. 'the vertu of worching in case worcheth nothing parteliche or at the fulle'. 'Anima est substantia incorporea intellectualis, illuminationis a Primo ultima relatione perceptiva' says his text, which he renders as: 'A soule is an unbodili substance intellectual that fongith [receives] schinynge of the firste by the laste relacioun' (91).

Although Bartholomaeus cites Aristotle *de Caelo secundum novam translationem* (i.e. the translation direct from the Greek) at least once, he was largely unaffected by the Thomist synthesis. So in one sense Trevisa was setting the clock back by choosing this particular text for vulgarization. But it had the attraction of a logical order and a euphonious style. The rhythm Trevisa cannot reproduce, but he naturalizes the Latin wherever he can. Thus the Aristotelian term *vivacitas* gives 'liflichnesse', and the constellation Arcturus (Arthurus) becomes 'Cherlemaynes wayne' (the 'Charles' wain' of later verse). Some technical terms are given forms that Chaucer had already used: e.g. *fumosité, erratike sterris*; others keep their Latin form: e.g. *emigranea* (which was to become 'migraine'), and *mundus archetypus*. There is no place in such a rendering for colloquialisms. The nearest we come to them is in such phrases as 'wise and ware', 'his brag and his bost' (*arrogancia eius*), and 'the cofer or skepet [*archa sive cistata*] of resoun'. Trevisa is most at ease when rendering the chapters in Book vi that under such headings as *de puero* and *de nutrice* and *de viro* give vivid pictures of ordinary life.

He adds almost nothing of his own, not even under the entries *Britannia* or *Anglia*, and takes over the bizarre etymologies of the original. A passage on menstrual blood he keeps in the decency of the more learned language. The lyricism of the passage on the earthly Paradise derives from the original. He can find no English equivalent for the names of certain trees and herbs. He occasionally alters the force of a Latin phrase: thus where Bartholomaeus has *fantasiam sive imaginationem* he puts 'the fantastik ymaginacioun' (107).

Boccaccio had said with some justice that the English were defective in their knowledge of classical mythology, and though a few English friars had made some advances in this regard in the early fourteenth century, it certainly finds no place in Trevisa (or Bartholomaeus). Trevisa's handbook remained essentially a utilitarian work; it was one of the first books to be printed in English—by Wynkyn de Worde (*c*.1495)—but neither Wynkyn de Worde, nor Berthelet (1535), nor 'Batman' (1582) preserve the text in full. William Morris was one of the earliest to recognize its value as a proof that 'the people of that time were eagerly desirous for knowledge, and their teachers were mostly simple-hearted and intelligent men, of a diligence and laboriousness almost past belief'.

As Bartholomaeus had given a conspectus of the physical world as apprehended in the thirteenth century so in the fourteenth another Englishman, Ralph Higden, provided an all-embracing picture of human history. The only true predecessors of his vast *Polychronicon* are Otto of Freising's *Historia de duobus Civitatibus*—a title with Augustinian undertones—and the *Speculum Historiale* of Vincent of Beauvais. Higden divided this work into seven books, recalling the seven days of the first chapter of Genesis, and beginning with Creation as there described. But he essays far more than biblical history. For Greek history he has to rely chiefly on Dares, for Roman on Sallust, Livy (probably at second hand) and Valerius Maximus, for British on

Geoffrey of Monmouth. Amongst later legends Higden includes the suppositious story of Alfred's founding of Oxford, which thanks partly to Trevisa, who cites it in his *Dialogue* prefaced to the *Polychronicon*, was to have a long life. The *Polychronicon* was not only a quarry of historical information: it was a great treasury of *exempla*. As such it would appeal to preaching friars and clerics like Trevisa himself, and to the literate laity. On recent English history it is surprisingly weak. For that modern historians have to rely largely on the chronicles that were still being set down in French or Latin in monastic houses.

Trevisa's rendering of Higden is freer than his version of Bartholomaeus. Occasionally he differs from Higden—he is less sceptical about the historicity of Arthur; he adds little of his own, but that little, in particular, the passage on the change to English as the medium of instruction, has, thanks to literary historians, become the best-known part of the book. Readers of Wyclif and Langland have noted his views on the right of secular lords to take away superfluous property of 'possessioners'. His own continuation of the narrative till 1366 is said to have no great value.

'Sir John Mandeville' is rather more fictitious than the work attributed to him, which is saying a good deal. There can hardly be any doubt that no such knight was ever dubbed or that the name is a pseudonym devised by the clever compiler of the book of *Travels* that still goes under his name: a precursor of the larger collections of travellers' tales that the industrious Hakluyt was to put together two centuries later and of the more detailed and veracious accounts by foreign travellers on which Gibbon delighted to draw. The fourteenth-century book was originally written in French, possibly at Liège, and almost certainly by a Frenchman, who has sometimes been identified with Jean de Bourgogne, a physician, and sometimes with Jean d'Outremeuse, a notary. The English texts are simply plain renderings (sometimes misrenderings) of the French, diversions from the original being slight: the 'Cotton' version reveals an uncertainty about French idioms that suggests a translator unfamiliar with spoken French. A passage in the Prologue, important because it leaves the impression that the original writer was English, is actually an embellishment of a mistranslation: where the French text has 'I would have written this book in Latin for the sake of brevity; but because more people understand French than Latin I have written it in French', the English runs:

And yee schulle undirstonde that I have put this boke out of Latyn into Frensch and translated it ayen out of Frensch into Englyssch, that every man of my nacioun may understonde it.

The remainder of this Prologue, which includes a traditional *captatio benevolentiae*, illustrates the hesitant nature of the translator's style when he moves beyond matter of fact:

But lordes and knyghtes and othere noble and worthi men that conne not Latyn but lytyll and han ben beyonde the see knowen and understonden yif I seye trouthe or non. And yif I err in devisynge for foryettynge[1] or elles, that thei mowe redresse it and amende it. For thinges passed out of longe tyme from a mannes mynde or from his syght turnen sone into foryetynge, because that mynde of man ne may not ben comprehended ne withholden for the freeltee[2] of mankynde.

[1] *forgetfulness*   [2] *because of the frailty*

The 'Egerton' version was made by a different hand, and from the fifteenth century comes a verse rendering. The versions have a place in the history of English prose style only because they show that English had made little progress in this kind of writing since the accounts of Ohthere and Wulfstan's voyages were set down in Alfred's time. It is not the style but the tone and content of Mandeville's book that gave it an immediate appeal.

The appeal has been perennial, though the *Travels* are not now read for the same reasons as formerly. The work is primarily about the Holy Land and its environs, and in the fourteenth century the Holy Land was primarily a place of pilgrimage and devotion. Chaucer and Langland testify that Englishmen, and Englishwomen, regularly made their way to Jerusalem. In the following century, Margery Kempe was to set down a full account of her journey thither; yet until the fifteenth century there was, as far as we know, no guidebook in English except Mandeville's. But it is much more than a guidebook. It opens with pages on the Incarnation and the Passion that give the rationale for the later appeal to worldly lords to turn from bickering with their neighbours and lead the commons in another crusade to recapture the Holy Places.

The writer of the French text, born, as he says, at St Albans, had first crossed the sea on St Michael's Day 1322 and often visited Jerusalem as well as 'many diverse lands'. This last phrase points to the secondary attraction of the book. It caters for the same kind of curiosity that was whetted by Chaucer's picture of a far-travelled knight and by that knight's own account of a medieval tournament set in distant Athens: an account that happens to correspond to a passage in Mandeville's description of the Imperial Palace at Constantinople: 'therein is a fair place for justynges or for other pleyes and desportes; and it is made with stages and hath degrees aboute that every man may wel se and none greve other'. Similarly, the knight's opening allusions to the land of Femenye would be clarified by Mandeville's account of Amazoyne (ch. xvii), in which, *inter alia*, he tells us that the Amazons shot with 'bowe Turkeys' (just as Chaucer's Arcite did).

That we have to do with some travellers' tales less veracious than these we begin to suspect when, after describing the Crown of Thorns as made of 'jonkes [rushes] of the see' (a detail found in several accounts of the Passion), the writer adds: 'And I have one of the precious thorns that seemeth like a white thorn, and that was given me for a great specialty [favour].' Yet he is careful never to strain our credulity too far. He confesses that he has *not* seen the daughter of Ypocras, 'in form and likeness of a great dragon a hundred fathoms long', who awaits a transforming kiss—a bizarre embodiment of the Loathly Lady who figures in *The Wife of Bath's Tale* and Gower's Tale of Florent. He is astute enough to indicate that some of his information is by report, whilst in the same paragraph presenting himself in dialogue with his informants. For the rest, he anticipates scepticism by such dispassionate comments as the following (a specimen of the translator's plain style at its most successful):

And whoso that wole may leve¹ me yif he will. And whoso will not may leve also. For I wot wel yif ony man hath ben in tho contrees beyonde, though he have not ben in the place where the great Chane² duelleth, he schall here speke of him so meche³ merveylouse thing that he shall not trowe⁴ it lightly. And treuly no more did I myself til I saugh it. And tho that han ben in tho contrees and in the gret Canes houshold knowen wel that I seye soth. And therfore I will not spare—for hem that knowe not ne beleve not but that that⁵ thei seen—for to tell you a partie of him and of his estate that he holt⁶ whan he goth from contree to contree and whan he maketh solempne festes.

¹ *believe*   ² *Khan*   ³ *much*   ⁴ *believe*   ⁵ *except that which*
⁶ *maintains*

'Of Paradys', he says, 'ne can I not speken propurly, for I was not there. It is fer beyonde, and that forthinketh [causes me regret], and also I was not worthi'—which is not as naïve as it appears; he is speaking of the earthly Paradise, long sought, and carefully described in accounts of Alexander's journey to the East. At least one of the incredible claims in the English text, to the effect that the traveller had eaten of 'the vegetable lamb', is due to the Cotton redactor, who also adds, by way of stilling doubt: 'but that I knowe wel, that God is merveyllous in his werkes'.

The real art of the book consists in the original author's skill in weaving together passages from earlier, more authentic narratives and in conveying the impression that he himself had made the voyages he describes. The autobiographical element is never prominent, yet without it the book would lose much of its plausibility. The claim that the book had been examined and approved at the papal Court of Rome is a specious interpolation found only in the English version (and in a Latin manuscript of English provenance)—during the whole period of the supposed travels, as in the year 1366, given as the date when Mandeville put them in writing, the Pope was in Avignon. In an adjacent passage he alludes again to his knightly rank, insisting that he has been in many a full noble company and at many a fair deed of arms, 'all be it that I did none myself for myn unable insuffisance', a neat way of disarming the suspicions of any truly knightly readers; whilst a mention of his 'gowtes artetykes' (arthritic gout) induces sympathy. The final sentences, of high-sounding appeal to the Trinity, bring us full circle. They also indicate that the author envisaged the book's being read to those who could not read it for themselves: a mode of diffusing its contents that probably obtained for two centuries:

And I beseche almyghty God fro whom all godeness and grace cometh fro, that he vouchesaf of his excellent mercy and habundant grace to fullfylle hire[1] soules with inspiracioun of the holy gost in makynge defence of all hire gostly enemyes here in erthe, to hire salvacioun bothe of body and soule to worschipe and thankynge of him that is three and on withouten begynnynge and withouten endyng, that is withouten qualitee good, withouten quantytee gret, that in all places is present and all thinges conteynynge, the whiche that no goodness may amende ne non evell empeyre, that in perfyte Trynytee lyveth and regneth God be alle worldes and be all tymes. Amen. Amen. Amen.

[1] their

If the importance of the book in the development of English prose may be exaggerated, evidence abounds of its role in the history of popular culture. On the continent certainly, and probably in England, the book became part of the common stock of *colportage*, cheap books sold by pedlars, to such folk as Menocchio the naïve but irrepressibly curious North Italian miller whose opinions brought him into fatal conflict with the Inquisition.*

The sources of the French text range from standard universal histories (Peter Comestor's *Historia Scholastica*, Vincent of Beauvais's *Speculum Historiale* and *Speculum Naturale*, the *Aurea Legenda*, Brunetto Latini's *Li Livres dou Tresor*) to works dealing specifically with the Near East (e.g. Jacques de Vitry's *Historia Hierosolimitanae expeditionis*

* See Carlo Ginzburg, *Il formaggio e i vermi: il cosmo di un mugnaio del '500* (trans. J. and A. Tedeschi as *The Cheese and the Worms, the Cosmos of a 16th-century Miller* (London, 1980)), an absorbing study of a character that must have had medieval precursors.

and the Far East (the accounts of William of Boldensele and Odoric of Pordenone). Such names suggest that the compiler had access to a well-stocked library, possibly monastic, and probably French: an English writer would have drawn on Higden's *Polychronicon* (see p. 358 above). Though Marco Polo's *Il Milione* had first appeared in French, it is not certain that it was known to the creator of 'Mandeville'. Whatever the sources of his account of Prester John and his dominions, the pages devoted to him still retain their glamour; audiences that had listened to *The Squire's Tale* must have been captivated by them. Yet, as always, the glamour was not unmixed with dread. What some men called the 'Vale Enchanted', others, says Mandeville, called the Vale of Devils and others the Vale Perilous. He claimed that he had gone into it with thirteen others (including two friars), 'but at our going out we were but nine'.

The tales of wonder do not detract from the historical and geographical verities (including the roundness of the globe) that many of the pages painlessly conveyed. Other passages made for some understanding of Eastern sects and the Moslem faith. Like Langland, 'Mandeville' sees it as 'a gret sclaundre to oure feith and to oure lawe whan folk that ben withouten lawe schull repreven us and undernemen [reproach] us of oure synnes. . . . For the Sarazines ben gode and feythfull.' On the other hand, the vagaries of the Eastern Church—its denial of purgatory, the countenance it gave to fornication and usury, its sale of benefices—all are carefully set down: the last fault being found also near at home: 'For now is Symonye Kyng crouned in Holy Chirche, God amende it for his mercy.' Again the sentiments, and the imagery, are Langland's.

8

Lyrics

In the preceding pages we have occasionally come upon examples of songs or shorter 'lyrical' poems, such as the comic 'The Man in the Moon', the dialogue 'De Clerico et Puella', or the bird-debate 'The Thrush and the Nightingale'. We have seen that Richard Rolle was a writer of religious lyrics as well as of religious prose, that Robert Mannyng took from Langtoft's Chronicle topical satirical verses against the Scots, and that the Scots chronicler Barbour had an ear for the historical rhymes circulating in his country. These examples in themselves are sufficient to give some indication of a number of the most significant aspects of the surviving corpus of lyric poetry—that it is widespread; that it is closely related to, and often overlaps with, other literary forms; that it occurs in a variety of shapes and styles; that it is, in general, a humble kind of writing, meant to be used rather than to be admired for its self-conscious artistry; and that it is finally, a fugitive kind. These last two points in particular need to be stressed at the beginning of any survey.

It is not until the time of Chaucer and Gower that we find writers associated with the high courtly level of society producing lyrical poetry in the English vernacular—this is no doubt partly due to the cultural 'depression' of English in the earlier years of this period. Consequently, we do not find, as we would in continental Europe, famous, well-known lyric poets, who founded 'schools', and whose work is preserved in elegant manuscripts. We would look in vain for a Walther von der Vogelweide, a Cavalcante, a Dante, or even a Rutebeuf. We know the names of a few of the authors of the English lyrics, but rarely anything else about them. Our early lyric poets are, characteristically, anonymous craftsmen. It is also quite clear that much of the lyric poetry which was produced has not survived. The chances of survival for non-religious lyrics especially must have been extremely fragile. No doubt some popular songs were never written down at all. It is often only from chance references that we hear of them, as with the 'Com hider love to me' which Chaucer's Pardoner sings on pilgrimage. We would dearly like to know more about the 'rymes of Robin Hood' which Sloth alludes to in *Piers Plowman*, but

we have to wait until the fifteenth century to find surviving examples of
those. We are dependent on scraps: a famous early verse is recorded
by a chronicler in the twelfth-century *Liber Eliensis* (and attributed by
him to King Cnut):

> Merie sungen the muneches[1] binnen[2] Ely
> Tha Cnut ching[3] reu[4] ther by.
> Roweth cnites[5] noer[6] the land,
> And here we thes muneches sæng.

[1] *monks*   [2] *in*   [3] *king*   [4] *rowed*   [5] *men*   [6] *near*

Fragments are sometimes found jotted down on loose leaves or end-
papers of manuscripts. One manuscript, now in Worcester Cathedral,
has some scraps attributed to 'Robertus seynte Mary clericus':

> Ne saltou never, levedi[1],
> Tuynklen[2] wyt thin eyen . . .

[1] *lady*   [2] *wink*

and:

> Dore, go thou stille[1],
>   Go thou stille, stille
> That ic abbe[2] in the boure[3]
> Ydon[4] al myn uylle, uylle.

[1] *quietly*   [2] *have*   [3] *chamber*   [4] *done*

Another such tantalizing fragment is:

> So longe ich have, lavedy[1],
>   Yhoved[2] at thy gate
> That my fot is yfrore[3], faire lavedy,
>   For thy love faste to the stake[4].

[1] *lady*   [2] *waited*   [3] *frozen*   [4] *gate-post*

Such snatches often survive only because they are quoted by a moralist or a preacher. To one preacher we owe a specimen of a secular
lullaby (or part of it). He gives us a charming glimpse of domestic life
as well as a text which, though no doubt good advice for a girl when
she grows up, is notably and pleasingly less edifying than the religious
'lullabies' which survive in some numbers; women, he says, 'lull the
child with their foot and sing an old song', saying:

> Wake[1] wel, Annot,
>   Thi mayden boure;
> And get the fra Walterot,
>   For he is lichure[2].

[1] *watch*   [2] *lecher*

Such non-religious songs are sometimes quoted in order to be moralized. A famous example is:

> Atte wrastlinge[1] mi lemman[2] I ches[3],
> And atte ston-kasting I him forles[4] . . .

[1] *at the wrestling*   [2] *lover*   [3] *chose*   [4] *lost*

where the preacher explains that wrestling is fighting like a good champion against the world, the flesh, and the devil. Sometimes they are quoted to be parodied. We should never have had this little song:

> Alas, hou shold y synge?
> Yloren[1] is my playinge[2]:
> Hou shold y with that olde man
> To leven[3], and let[4] my leman,
> Swettist of al thinge?

[1] *lost*   [2] *pleasure*   [3] *live*   [4] *give up*

(the situation is that of the French *chanson de mal mariée*) if it had not been for the Franciscan Bishop of Ossory in Kilkenny, Richard de Ledrede, who did not wish the mouths of his clergy to be 'polluted by songs which are lewd, secular, and associated with revelry'. Believing with General Booth that the devil should not be allowed to have the best tunes, he produced pious Latin words (in the above case a prayer to the Virgin to help the sinner) for them to sing to these tunes at festivals. A number of the sixty Latin songs have scraps of English or French verse prefixed to them to indicate the tune. Mostly they are tantalizingly brief—'Have god day, my leman' or

> Gayneth me[1] no garlond of greene
> Bot hit ben of wythoues[2] ywroght

[1] *is suitable for me*   [2] *willow branches*

(perhaps, as in later folk-songs, the willow is associated with sorrowing or forsaken lovers). These scraps of popular song indicate not only the extent of what has been lost, but suggest that there was much more variety of type, form, and metre than is shown by the surviving examples.

The lyrics which have been lucky enough to be more carefully preserved are found in various kinds of manuscripts (nearly all of a humble kind). Some are embedded in sermons, others appear singly or in groups in manuscripts containing other kinds of matter. A number appear for instance in a Cambridge manuscript which contains works by Rolle; another group in the very large and extensive Vernon manuscript of the end of the fourteenth century. MS Harley 2253, which contains a celebrated series of both religious and secular lyrics—including 'The Man in the Moon'—also has a romance

(*King Horn*) and material (fabliaux as well as saints' lives) in Anglo-Norman and Latin. This miscellany was probably written in the fourth decade of the fourteenth century in the West of England (at Ludlow in Shropshire, it now seems likely). The intended owner must have been a man of varied and catholic taste. Other manuscripts contain material which can be used by preachers. An early specimen of one of these is Trinity College Cambridge MS 323 (B. 14. 39) of *c*.1255–60, which seems to come from the Worcester–Hereford area (where, as we have seen, the old traditions of devotional prose lived on long). It contains poems and *sententiae* apparently intended for preachers (possibly Franciscans). Once or twice religious lyrics are here given such rubrics as 'exemplum de beata virgine et gaudiis eius', 'aliud exemplum de eodem'; and the word 'exemplum' suggests that the compiler thought that such verses could be expounded or quoted in sermons. A famous preaching book of the fourteenth century is that of John of Grimestone, a Norfolk Franciscan, made in 1372. Among the preaching notes (arranged alphabetically under headings like 'De Abstinencia', 'De Morte') are found almost 250 lyrics or scraps of lyrics. This is a remarkable collection, and contains some of the best fourteenth-century religious verse. One or two are quite long—like an ABC poem on the Passion of nearly 200 lines, which begins with an exposition of the meaning of a child's ABC: the parchment nailed on wood is Christ's body; the five 'Paraffes' are his five wounds—but the majority are quite short and nearly all vivid and memorable in one way or another. Some are quite clearly mnemonic aids—to the preacher and to the congregation. This example, for instance, under the heading 'De Passione Christi' gives us four topics, and four ways to consider them:

> *Respiciamus*[1]:
>
> | | |
> |---|---|
> | *Oculis* | The rede stremes renning |
> | *Auribus* | The Jewes orible criiyng |
> | *Gustu* | Of Cristis drink the bitternesse |
> | *Tactu* | Of Cristis wondis the sarpnesse[2]. (W No. 191) |

[1] *Let us look* [*with eyes, with ears, with taste, with touch*]   [2] *sharpness*

Each heading could serve as the basis for exposition. Another, among similar examples, suggests a very imaginative sermon:

Crux est[1]:

> A barge to beren fro depe groundes,
> A targe to weren[2] fro detly woundes,
> A falle[3] to taken in the fend,
> And an halle to glathen[4] in a frend.   (W No. 51)

[1] *the cross is*   [2] *protect*   [3] *trap*   [4] *in which to entertain*

In another the Latin marginal words give the expositor's 'key':

> Wanne the sunne rist[1]:
> The day taket his lith[2],   *Misericordia*
> Theves taken here flith,   *Demones*
> The deu ginnet[3] springge . . .   *Gracia . . .*   (W No. 82)
>
> [1] *rises*   [2] *light*   [3] *begins*

A number list 'definitions' (e.g. statements about charity or cupidity), nearly always catchy and memorable:

> *Gloria mundi est*[1]:
>
> Als a se flouwende,
> Als a skiye[2] pasende
> Als the sadwe[3] in the undermel[4],
> And als the dore turnet on a quel[5].   (W No. 84)

[1] *The glory of the world is*   [2] *cloud*   [3] *shadow*   [4] *early afternoon*
[5] *wheel*

Sometimes a verse ingeniously uses systems of letters: 'Mors habet quatuor litteras, videlicet DETH, et possunt designari quatuor condiciones mortis. Nam per D . . .' (Death has four letters, namely DETH, and they can designate four qualities of death. For, by D . . .).

> Deth is a Dredful Dettour:
> Deth is an Elenge[1] hErbergour[2],
> Deth is a Trewe Tollere[3]
> And Deth is an Hardi Huntere.   (W No. 112)
>
> [1] *miserable*   [2] *hosteller*   [3] *tax-gatherer*

Sometimes it is proverbial (and often rather world-weary, in the way of proverbs)—e.g. on the instability and uncertainty of man's life:

> Nu is up, nou is doun;
> Nou is frend fo.
> Nou is out, nou is nout
> Nou is al ago[1].   (W No. 9)
>
> [1] *is gone*

It is a notable achievement of Grimestone's book that it is at the same time a useful preacher's guide and a splendid anthology in its own right.

The historian of the medieval English lyric has not only to worry about the great gaps in his records, he also has problems in dating the examples that have survived. Although it is possible to date the manuscript in which a lyric is copied, there is usually no certain way of knowing by how many years or decades that lyric will antedate the manuscript. Since it is virtually impossible to give a convincing 'chronological' survey, it will be more useful to treat our lyrics according to theme and general category, indicating which come from earlier or later manuscripts.

The religious lyrics, which survive in some number and which are often of high literary quality, lend themselves most easily to the historian's desire to arrange and to analyse. They share the attitudes and themes we have seen in the religious verse and prose already discussed. They are obviously in the main tradition of 'affective' spirituality that is associated with the great names of Anselm and Bernard, and which lies behind such treatises as the *Ancrene Wisse*. They too see the passion of Christ as the supreme act of love; they treat his human sufferings with the same intensity and tenderness. The accents of *Jesu dulcis memoria* which we heard in Rolle, recur in these poems:

> Swete Jesu, mi soule bote[1],
> In min herte thou sette a rote[2]
> Of thi love that is so swote[3],
> And wite[4] hit that hit springe mote[5].   (*CB XIII*, No. 50)

[1] *remedy*　　　[2] *root*　　　[3] *sweet*　　　[4] *protect*　　　[5] *may*

and, even more closely:

> Jesu, swete is the love of thee,
> Noon othir thing so swete may be;
> No thing that men may heere and see
> Hath no swetnesse ayens thee. . . .

> > (*CB XIV*, No. 89)

We find examples of the 'love longing' of Rolle and other mystics, of the 'homeliness' of Christ as perceived by Julian of Norwich. At the same time, the lyrics are part of the penitential and homiletic movements which produced manuals for confessors and for parish priests. Most of them are highly didactic, and many are conceived of as vehicles for instruction. As we have seen, they are frequently used in sermons. The preaching friars, who arrived in England in the earlier thirteenth century, seem sometimes to have had a particular interest in lyrics (in this, of course, they followed the example of St Francis and his *joculatores dei*). A number of manuscript collections were made by or are associated with friars, and a number of the known authors of the lyrics were friars. There is even one lyric which celebrates becoming a friar:

> Frer menur[1] I wil me make,
> And lecherie I wille asake[2];

To Jesu Crist ich wil me take[3]
And serve in holi churche,
Al in mi ouris[4] for to wake[5],
Goddis wille to wurche[6]. . . .   (*CB XIII*, No. 66)

[1] *minor*   [2] *renounce*   [3] *commit myself*   [4] *(canonical) hours*
[5] *keep vigil*   [6] *do*

But although these lyrics are very largely a product of the specifically religious culture of medieval England, they are also—like some of the prose treatises discussed earlier—close to ordinary life, and to popular literature and culture. Secular forms are adapted or parodied; popular proverbial lore is drawn on for instruction; vivid similitudes from ordinary experience are frequently found.

From the beginning there is considerable variety in form. We have seen examples of simple mnemonic or devotional sermon 'tags' like those in Grimestone's book—

Blissed moten[1] tho pappes[2] be
That Godes sone sok[3] of the   (W No. 36)

[1] *may*   [2] *breasts*   [3] *sucked*

and there are simple prayers as well. But alongside these, we find songs, meditations in verse (sometimes quite elaborate in form), and longer 'narrative' lyrics like that in MS Trinity 323 which tells of the coming of the three kings, or the more dramatic, ballad-like poem on Judas, close to popular lore (Pilate is 'a rich Jew'), which conducts its narrative through tense direct speech:

In him com ur lord gon[1] as is postles setten at mete[2]—
'Wou[3] sitte ye, postles, ant wi nule[4] ye ete?
Wou sitte ye, postles, ant wi nule ye ete?
Ic am aboust[5] ant isold to-day for oure mete.'

(*CB XIII*, No. 25)

[1] *in came our lord walking* [2] *his apostles sat at their food* [3] *why* [4] *will*
you not [5] *bought*

There is a great variety, too, in metrical form, ranging from simple couplets or quatrains to elaborate stanza patterns. There are experiments in macaronic writing, with Latin (and sometimes French) being used, though it is very rare to find the ease and mastery here that Langland shows. As with the prose writers, asceticism is sometimes accompanied by a liking for rhetorical ornament. Many poems are translated or adapted from Latin. Very early examples are the hymns or prayers of St Godric (d. 1170), who after a busy life as a merchant and traveller, settled as a hermit at Finchale near Durham. The rhythms are close to those of his originals with a pleasing simplicity of diction, and he adds a rather charming pun on his own name:

> Sainte Marie virgine
> Moder[1] Jesu Cristes Nazarene,
> Onfo[2], schild[3], help thin Godrich,
> Onfang[4], bring heghilich[5] with the in Godes riche[6].

[1] *mother* [2] *receive* [3] *shield* [4] *take* [5] *nobly* [6] *king-dom*

The music survives, and this is one of those cases where a simple lyric needs to be 'realized' in performance for its full effect to be felt. On the other hand, beside these poems which are very close to their ancestors in the central Latin devotional tradition, there are others which are more obviously English and original. But it is possible to distinguish two constant elements in the religious lyrics. They are practical, and meant to be used. They do not (typically) record the agonies of an individual soul, or grapple with problems of disillusionment or of faith. And, even at their most original, they are profoundly traditional—in idea, in image, and even in phrase. We shall consider them in two groups—firstly those which present and celebrate the scheme of salvation made real through the Virgin and Christ, and secondly those which show man how he may, by the imitation of Christ and by virtuous living, achieve salvation.

Mary has a central part in the lyrics which deal with the life of Christ. She is honoured particularly because her humble obedience allowed the doors of grace to be opened, when at the Annunciation:

> Gabriel, fram evene-king[1]
>   Sent to the maide swete,
> Broute thire[2] blisful tiding
>   And faire he gan hire greten[3]:
>   'Heil be thu, ful of grace a-rith[4]!
>   For Godes sone, this evene-lith[5],
>   For mannes loven
>   Wile man bicomen,
>   And taken
>   Fles[6] of the maiden brith[7],
>   Manken[8] fre for to maken
>   Of senne[9] and devles mith[10].'

> (*CB XIII*, No. 44)

[1] *king of heaven* [2] *brought these* [3] *greeted her* [4] *indeed*
[5] *light of heaven* [6] *flesh* [7] *bright* [8] *mankind* [9] *sin*
[10] *power of the devil*

This verse is the beginning of a flowing and eloquent translation of a very popular pious song 'Angelus ad Virginem' (which probably comes from the mid-thirteenth century: that it was still popular in the following century is indicated by the fact that it was sung by Nicholas, the clerk in Chaucer's *Miller's Tale*). This version is accompanied in the manuscript by the Latin words and the music, and is presumably meant for singing. Another thirteenth-century poem on the Virgin, 'On God Ureisun of Ure Lefdi' is quite different. It is a 'good prayer', a devotional and ecstatic meditation on Mary as the powerful queen of heaven; it is long, running to 171 lines, but it calls itself a 'song' and an 'English lay'. All men should honour Mary, says the poet,

> Vor thu ham havest alesed of deoflene honde[1]
> And isend[2] mid blisse to englene londe[3].   (*CB XIII*, No. 3)

[1] *For thou hast released them from the hands of devils*   [2] *sent*   [3] *land of angels*

The Virgin is exalted in Heaven, and the poet is enthralled by the magnificence of the scene:

> Heih[1] is thi kinestol[2] on-uppe[3] Cherubine
> Bivoren[4] thine leove[5] sune withinnen[6] Seraphine.
> Murie dreameth[7] engles bivoren thin onsene[8],
> Plieth and sweieth[9] and singeth bitweonen[10]. . . .

[1] *high*   [2] *throne*   [3] *above*   [4] *before*   [5] *dear*   [6] *among*
[7] *make music*   [8] *face*   [9] *make melody*   [10] *from time to time*

These are the angelic musicians we see in medieval paintings and sculptures. The Queen of Heaven gives generously to her servants and friends:

> Alle thine vreondes thu makest riche kinges
> Thu ham yivest[1] kinescrud[2], beies[3], and gold ringes

[1] *givest them*   [2] *royal garments*   [3] *bracelets*

and they stand around her in 'white ciclatoun' and golden crowns in an ecstasy of adoration, into which the poet himself is caught up as he addresses her:

> Mi lif is thin[1], mi luve is thin, mine heorte blod is thin,
> And yif ich der seggen[2], mi leove leafdi, thu ert min. . . .

[1] *thine*   [2] *if I dare say it*

If we take these two poems as representing the poles of 'song' and 'meditation', we can find between them an extraordinary variety of Marian lyrics. One from manuscript Harley 2253, usually entitled by editors 'An Autumn Song', begins with gloomy thoughts of mortality appropriate to that season:

> Nou skrinketh[1] rose ant lylie-flour
> That whilen ber[2] that suete savour
> In somer, that suete tyde;
> Ne is no quene so stark ne stour[3]
> Ne no levedy[4] so bryht in bour
> That ded ne shal by glyde[5] . . .   (*CB XIII*, No. 10)

[1] *shrinks*   [2] *once bore*   [3] *strong and powerful*   [4] *lady*   [5] *death shall not steal up on her*

before the poet's mind turns to Christ, with his pierced side. Then he boldly adapts a feature of secular lyric, the 'chanson d'aventure opening' (in which the poet rides out and sees or hears some strange or intriguing scene):

> From Petresbourh in o morewenyng[1],
> As y me wende o my pleyghyng[2],
>   On mi folie y thohte;
> Menen y gon my mournyng[3]
> To hire that ber[4] the hevene-kyng,
>   Of merci hire bysohte[5] . . .

[1] *a morning*   [2] *in my pleasure*   [3] *I made my lament*   [4] *bore*
[5] *besought*

and the rest is concerned with penitence, and the comfort which is available from Mary and Christ. Sometimes the phraseology is very close to that used in the secular lyrics in this collection when they speak of a lover's lady as a healer who can give soothing 'medicine'. Thus the poet remarks of Mary:

> Betere is hire medycyn
> Then eny mede[1] or eny wyn—
>   Hire erbes smulleth[2] suete—
> From Catenas into Dyvelyn[3]
> Nis ther no leche[4] so fyn[5]
>   Oure serewes[6] to berte[7]. . . .

[1] *mead*   [2] *smell*   [3] *Caithness to Dublin*   [4] *physician*   [5] *skilled*
[6] *sorrows*   [7] *assuage*

Another Marian poem which seems to have some secular undertones is a haunting little verse quoted in an *exemplum* on confession:

> At a sprynge-wel under a thorn,
> Ther was bote of bale[1]
> A lytel here a-forn';
> Ther by-syde stant a mayde,

Fulle of love ybounde.
Hoso[2] wol seche trwe love,
Yn hyr hyt schal be founde.   (*CB XIV*, No. 130)

¹ *remedy for sorrow*   ² *Whoso*

The explanation given is that the spring under the thorn is the great wound in the side of the crucified Christ (which is often called or compared to a fountain or a well), and that the maiden is the Virgin Mary (often pictured at the foot of the cross) who is ever ready to help the sinful. But it is hard not to think also of the springs and thorn-trees of romance and ballad (like the magical spring in *Ywain and Gawain*) beside which fairy ladies are often found. Yet another (longer) poem has a visionary, almost 'romantic' opening:

In a tabernacle of a toure,
    As I stode musyng on the mone¹,
A crouned quene, most of honoure,
    Apered in gostly² syght ful sone.
    She made complaynt thus by hyr one³
        For mannes soule was wrapped⁴ in wo:
'I may nat leve mankynde allone,
    Quia amore langueo.'   (*SRL*, No. 61)

¹ *moon*   ² *spiritual*   ³ *alone*   ⁴ *enveloped*

'Because I languish for love'—these passionate words from the Song of Songs are repeated as a refrain, as the crowned queen of heaven pleads with sinful man, remonstrating with him, urging him to repent, reminding him of the pain he has caused her 'kin'—

'My childe ys outlawed for thy synne,
    My barne ys bette¹ for thy trespasse . . .'

¹ *beaten*

and repeating, with growing intensity, her appeal:

'Why was I crouned and made a quene?
    Why was I called of mercy the welle?
Why shuld an erthly woman bene
    So hygh in heven above aungelle?
    For the, mankynde—the truthe I telle!
        Than aske mercy, and I shall do
That I was ordeyned, helpe the fro helle,
    Quia amore langueo.'

An earlier devotional lyric, this time a prayer to, and a celebration of the Virgin, creates its own kind of intensity by an easy and eloquent use of the macaronic form, neatly balancing the rhythms of the two languages:

> Of on that is so fayr and bright
> *Velud maris stella*[1],
> Brighter than the dayis light,
> *Parens et puella*[2],
> Ic crie to the, thou se[3] to me!
> Levedy, preye thi sone for me,
> *Tam pia*[4],
> That ic mote[5] come to the,
> *Maria*.   (*SRL*, No. 7)

[1] *as the star of the sea*   [2] *mother and maiden*   [3] *look upon*   [4] *so devoted*
[5] *may*

Sometimes it is the simplest poem, written in 'plain words which reach the heart', which achieves the highest art. An apparently simple prayer to the Virgin, beginning

> Levedie, ic thonke the
>   Wid[1] herte suithe[2] milde
> That god that thou havest idon me
>   Wid thine suete childe   (*SRL*, No. 56)

[1] *with*   [2] *very*

has an exquisite melody and precision of diction. Adjectives like 'milde' suggest those attributes central to Marian devotion, where Mary is both a great lady, and yet homely and simple, a mother eager to help. The lyric's final stanza

> Moder, loke one me
>   Wid thin suete eye:
> Reste and blisse gef[1] thou me,
>   Mi levedi, then[2] ic deye[3]

[1] *give*   [2] *when*   [3] *die*

fuses the two aspects—the loving look is that of a mother, and also that of a beloved lady in courtly literature, just as Beatrice looks at Dante 'with eyes full of the sparkling love and so divine' (*Paradiso*, iv. 139–40).

In the lyrics, the Virgin's motherly qualities are emphasized in two scenes from the life of Christ—when she 'lulls' him as a baby, and when she stands sorrowing beneath the cross. The first scene is vividly evoked at the abrupt visionary opening of a poem in Grimestone's book:

> Als I lay upon a nith[1],
> I lokede upon a stronde[2],
> I beheld a mayden brith[3],
> A child sche hadde in honde.

Hire loking was so loveli,
Hire semblant[4] was so suete,
Of al my sorwe sikerli[5]
Sche mithte[6] my bales bete[7].   (*CB XIV*, No. 58)

| [1] night | [2] shore | [3] bright | [4] demeanour | [5] certainly |
| [6] could | [7] assuage my sorrows |

The poet 'wonders', and the aged figure of Joseph, with 'hoar' head, who is sitting beside the Virgin, tells him the story of the Nativity. Sometimes the Virgin is given a lullaby in which there is a prophetic note of sorrow for her son's sufferings yet to come. In one or two cases it is difficult to say whether the speaker is Mary or the poet-meditator—or both. In Grimestone's book there is a powerful example in 'Lullay, lullay litel child, child reste the a throwe' (*CB XIV*, No. 65), where the speaking voice has a particularly sombre tone:

Child, it is a weping dale that thu art comen inne,
Thi pore clutes[1] it proven wel, thi bed mad in the binne[2];
Cold and hunger thu must tholen[3] as[4] thu were geten[5] in senne[6],
And after deyyen[7] on the tre for love of al mankenne[8]
   Lullay, lullay litel child, no wonder thou[9] thu care[10],
   Thu art comen amonges hem that thi deth sulen yare[11].

| [1] rags | [2] manger | [3] suffer | [4] as if | [5] begotten | [6] sin |
| [7] die | [8] mankind | [9] though | [10] weep | [11] will prepare |

On the other hand, the notes of joy and exultation which are characteristic of the fifteenth-century carols on the Nativity can be heard in a vigorous fourteenth-century example of the kind, in its recurring 'burden' or refrain, which alludes to those joyful ring-dances or *caroles* (like that mentioned in *Handlyng Synne*, pp. 41–7 above) which are the background of the literary carol:

Honnd by honnd we schulle ous take,
And joye and blisse schulle we make,
For the devel of elle[1] man hath forsake,
And Godes sone ys maked oure make[2]!

(*CB XIV*, No. 88)

| [1] hell | [2] companion |

The scene in which Christ died on the cross for the love of all mankind is treated in a variety of ways, and with great tenderness and intensity of devotion.

When y thenke on Jesu ded
Min herte overwerpes[1],

Mi soule is won[2] so is the led
For mi fole[3] werkes . . .   (*CB XIII*, No. 84)

¹ *is cast down*   ² *pale*   ³ *?wanton*

says one poet; another puts it in a less personal way:

The minde[1] of thi passiun, suete Jesu,
The teres it tollid[2],
The eine[3] it bolled[4],
The neb[5] it wetth
In herte sueteth[6].   (*CB XIII*, No. 56)

¹ *memory*   ² *draws*   ³ *eyes*   ⁴ *swells*   ⁵ *face*   ⁶ *brings*
sweetness

It is a scene of suffering and of triumph, which evokes both sorrow and joy.

One very effective way of treating the Passion is to produce a succinct, simple 'scene' or 'kernel' for meditation. These scenes are often based on Latin originals. Thus some urgent, nervous lines from a meditation of John of Fécamp:

Candet nudatum pectus. rubet cruentum latus. tensa arent viscera. decora languent lumina. regia pallent ora. procera rigent brachia. crura dependent marmorea. et rigat terebratos pedes beati sanguinis unda

are transformed into a more static and visual 'speaking picture', which acts as the focus for all the emotions associated with the scene:

Wyth[1] was hys nakede brest
And red of blod hys syde,
Bleyc[2] was his fair andled[3],
His wnde[4] dop[5] ant wide;

And hys armes ystreith[6]
Hey upon the rode;
On fif studes[7] on his body
The stremes ran o blode.   (*CB XIV*, No. 1)

¹ *white*   ² *pale*   ³ *face*   ⁴ *wounds*   ⁵ *deep*   ⁶ *stretched*
out   ⁷ *places*

A remarkable example of suggestive understatement is found in the quatrain that is quoted in the *Speculum Ecclesiae*, a long meditative work by St Edmund of Canterbury (d. 1240). The sorrowful moment and the scene with its two figures are austerely and impressively isolated by the voice of an onlooker. The only 'comment' is a simple expression of human compassion. The echoing repetition perhaps suggests the techniques of folk poetry. The words are all extremely simple and 'homely', but there is an artful association of Sun and Son (Christ the Son of God is the true Sun):

> Nou goth sonne under wod:
> Me reweth[1], Marie, thi faire rode[2].
> Nou goth sonne under tre;
> Me reweth, Marie, thi sone and the.   (*CB XIII*, No. 1)

> [1] *I pity*   [2] *face*

Other lyrics, however, are more elaborate. There are songs, extended meditations and lyrics which have a narrative structure, dealing with the events of the Passion in succession. These easily lose force and vigour, but there are one or two which have some interesting variations. One, 'Jesu that hast me dere i-boght' (*CB XIV*, No. 91) marks the significant moments with the request to Christ to 'write in my heart':

> Write in my hert with speches swete,
> Whan Judas the traytour can[1] the mete—
> That traitour was ful of the feende,
> And yit thou caldest hym thy frende.
> Swete Jesu, how myght thou soo
> Cal hym thy frend so fel and foo[2]. . . .

> [1] *did*   [2] [*who was*] *so fierce and hostile*

And so each moment is lovingly considered. Sometimes the intensity of the devotion of the 'onlooker' carries us with him. This is the case with a fine lyric in the Cambridge Rolle Manuscript, which combines rhyme and alliterations:

> My trewest tresowre sa trayturly[1] was taken,
> Sa bytterly bondyn[2] wyth bytand bandes[3],
> How sone of thi servandes was thou forsaken,
> And lathly[4] for my lufe hurld[5] with thair handes.

> (*CB XIV*, No. 79)

> [1] *treacherously*   [2] *bound*   [3] *biting bonds*   [4] *hatefully*   [5] *thrust*

It continues with this energy and intensity of personal emotion, culminating in a moving scene which alludes to the idea (which we have seen in *Ancrene Wisse*) of Christ as the lover-knight:

> My fender[1] of my fose, sa fonden[2] in the felde,
> Sa lufly lyghtand[3] at the evensang tyde;
> Thi moder and hir menyhe[4] unlaced thi scheld—
> All weped that thar[5] were, thi woundes was sa wyde.

> [1] *defender*   [2] *well-tried*   [3] *alighting*   [4] *company*   [5] *there*

In general, however, it is the lyrics which adopt a more dramatic structure which are the most successful. The two most usual forms are an imagined dialogue between the crucified Christ and his mother beneath him or a lament or an appeal directly addressed by the crucified Christ to the 'onlooker'. A good example of the former is 'Stond wel, moder, ounder rode' based on a Latin sequence 'Stabat iuxta Christi crucem' (*CB XIII*, No. 49), which occurs in a number of manuscripts.

This is conducted in a series of terse and tense exchanges:

> 'Stond wel, moder, ounder rode[1],
> Bihold thi child with glade mode[2],
> Moder blithe[3] might thou be.'
> 'Sone, hou may ich blithe stonde?
> Ich se thine fet and thine honde
> Inayled[4] to the harde tre . . .'

> [1] *cross*   [2] *heart*   [3] *happy*   [4] *nailed*

in which Christ attempts to convince his mother of the necessity for the torments which rend her heart, and of the joy which will result from this great sorrow. Both participants speak with genuine anguish:

> 'Moder, do wei[1] thine teres
> Thou wip awey the blodi teres,
> Hy[2] doth me worse thene mi deth.'
> 'Sone, hou mightte ich teres werne[3]
> I se thine blodi woundes erne[4]
> From thin herte to thi fet.'

> [1] *put away*   [2] *they*   [3] *restrain*   [4] *run*

The poet is most successful in exploiting dramatically both the strained human emotions and the theological paradoxes of the scene.

Laments by the crucified figure of Christ are treated with considerable variety. One very effective example in Grimestone's book (*CB XIV*, No. 74) is a simple expansion of a verse in *Lamentations* (1: 12) 'Is it nothing to you, all ye that pass by? Behold and see if there be any sorrow like unto my sorrow.' It concludes with the precise and stark visual details (carefully selected for emphasis and to serve as a focus for meditation) often found in the shorter Passion lyrics:

> Ye that pasen be the weyye,
> Abidet a litel stounde[1]!
> Beholdet, al mi felawes,
> Yef ani me lik is founde.

To the tre with nailes thre
Wol² fast I hange bounde,
With a spere al thoru mi side
To min herte is mad a wounde.

¹ *time*   ² *very*

Sometimes Christ speaks as the lover-knight. In one poem, 'Men me rent on rode' (*CB XIV*, No. 51), there is a bold identification of the cross with the knight's palfrey (and the 'gore' (robe) that Christ wears rather than a loin cloth may emphasize the parallel); the irony is bitter and yet full of tender emotion:

Biheld mi side,
Mi wndes¹ sprede so wide,
Restles I ride.
Lok up on me! Put fro ye pride.
My palefrey is of tre²,
Wiht³ nayles naylede thwrh⁴ me.
Ne is more sorwe to se—
Certes noon more no may be.

Under mi gore
Ben wndes selcowthe⁵ sore.
Ler⁶, man, mi lore⁷;
For mi love sinne no more. . . .

¹ *wounds*   ² *wood*   ³ *with*   ⁴ *through*   ⁵ *wondrously*
⁶ *learn*   ⁷ *doctrine*

In another (*CB XIV*, No. 78) the Christ-Knight appeals to his beloved. She must, like a real knightly lady, 'unlace' his armour (as Christ's mother and her company did in the lyric quoted above, p. 378, which is found in the same manuscript), and commit his arms 'prively' to the safest and most secret part of a castle, the 'treasury' (the parallel with the secret recesses of the heart of a true lover is very delicately made). The scene is an intensely personal one. Here there are no passers by the way; only the solitary figures of the knight (as alone as he would be in a romance) and of his beloved:

. . . take myne armes pryvely
And do tham in thi tresory,
In what stede¹ sa thou dwelles,
And, swete lemman, forget thow noght
That I thi lufe sa dere have boght,
And I aske the noght elles.

¹ *place*

Another (*CB XIV*, No. 68) makes the verse 'Behold I stand at the door and knock' (Rev. 3: 20) the basis for a lover's plea:

> Undo thi dore, my spuse dere!
> Allas! wy stond I loken out here?
> Fre am I thi make[1].
> Loke mi lokkes and ek[2] myn heved[3]
> And al my bodi with blod beweved[4]
> For thi sake. . . .

> [1] *consort* [2] *also* [3] *head* [4] *covered*

Sometimes the appeal becomes a reproach. Centuries later Herbert was to use the *Improperia* or 'reproaches' of the Good Friday liturgy (a series of contrasting statements of God's grace shown to man in the Old Testament, and of man's cruel responses to Christ in the Passion). Already in the fourteenth century these had been turned into English:

> 'Ich delede[1] the see vor the;
> And Pharaon dreynte[2] vor the;
> And thou to princes sullest[3] me.
> My volk[4], what habbe y do the
> Other[5] in what thyng toened[6] the
> Gyn nouthe[7] ond onswere thou me. . . .'

> *(CB XIV, No. 15)*

> [1] *divided* [2] *drowned* [3] *sellest* [4] *people* [5] *or*
> [6] *afflicted* [7] *begin now*

They perhaps lie behind a fine complaint of Christ (*CB XIV*, No. 126) which is built on a series of sharply ironic contrasts between the sufferings of Christ and the beautiful array and carefree behaviour of a gallant:

> 'Thyn hondes streite[1] gloved,
> White and clene kept;
> Myne with nailes thorled[2],
> On rode, and eke my feet.
>
> A-cros thou berest thyn armes,
> Whan thou dauncest narewe[3]
> .   .   .   .   .
> Myne for the on rode,
> With the Jewes wode[4],
> With grete ropis to-draw[5]. . . .'

> [1] *tightly* [2] *pierced* [3] *?keeping the feet close together* [4] *mad*
> [5] *pulled*

All these different tones are united in the most remarkable of all the laments, a poem which, like that discussed above (p. 374), has the refrain *Quia amore langueo* (*SRL*, No. 43). It has perhaps the most arresting and imaginative opening of all the lyrics:

> In the vaile of restles mynd
> I sowght in mownteyn and in mede,
> Trustyng a treulove for to fynd.
> Upon an hyll than toke I hede,
> A voise I herd (and nere I yede[1])
> In gret dolour complaynyng tho,
> 'See, dere soule, my sydes blede,
> *Quia amore langueo*.'

> [1] *I went nearer*

The poet finds a wounded man sitting under a tree on a 'mount' (like a sorrowing lover such as the Man in Black in Chaucer's *Book of the Duchess*). Although he is wounded from head to foot, he is 'a semely man to be a kyng', and when he announces himself as 'treulove, that fals was never', the lover of man's soul, another more devotional traditional image begins to emerge, that of the seated figure of Christ 'in misery' covered with wounds, and crowned with thorn ('I crownyd hyr with blysse, and she me with thorne' he says in the manner of the Reproaches). The poet develops the sharp ironic potential of the lament of the lover-knight—'this blody surcote she hath on me sett'; 'Thes gloves were geven me whan I hyr sowght; / They be nat white, but rede and wan, / Embrodred with blode (my spouse them bowght!)'; she has 'buckled' his feet with sharp nails. The rapidly flowing images are not only given powerful visual force, but are developed in detail in the boldest way. He has made his body the 'bait' for her heart; he has made a 'nest' for her in the wide wound in his side. This traditional image is developed further—this is her 'chamber', where she may rest, where 'she and I may slepe in fere [together]', where she may wash. Another traditional image is used most evocatively: the lover-knight will wait patiently and eagerly for his love—'if she be dawngerouse' (a word full of the connotations of courtly love), 'I will her pray. . . . Myn armes ben spred to clypp [embrace] hyr to.' (St Bernard and others were fond of the idea that Christ's arms were stretched out on the cross as if to embrace, and his head lowered as if to kiss.) Then there is a sudden transition in a line with a strange visionary quality:

> I sitt on an hille for to se farre,
> I loke to the vayle; my spouse I see. . . .

The lover-knight is a kind of Hound of Heaven:

> Now rynne she awayward, now cummyth she narre[1]
> 'Yet fro myn eye-syght she may nat be. . . .'
>
> [1] *nearer*

In the intense, urgent pleading that follows the poet uses not only the words of the Song of Songs, but seems to be able to recreate its spirit:

> My swete spouse, will we goo play?
>   Apples ben rype in my gardine;
> I shall clothe the in new array,
>   Thy mete shall be mylk, honye, and wyne . . .

not least its haunting changes of tone:

> My spouse is in hir chambre, hald yowr pease,
>   Make no noyse, but lat hyr slepe.
> My babe shall sofre noo disease,
>   I may not here my dere childe wepe. . . .

'True love' brings his monologue to a close with an appeal for endurance and fortitude in adversity:

> Spouse, shuld I alway fede
> With childys mete? Nay, love, nat so—
> I preve thi love with adversité. . . .

He will be ever present to support her:

> Than dere soule, go never me fro!—
>   Thy mede[1] is markyd[2] whan thow art mort[3],
> *Quia amore langueo.*
>
> [1] *reward*   [2] *destined*   [3] *dead*

In its range of tone and emotion, this is certainly one of the most ambitious and most successful of the religious lyrics.

Those lyrics which set out to teach men and women how to achieve the salvation made possible by Christ are often at their best when they express a positive response to the appeals of Christ the lover-knight we have just been considering. These are songs of 'love-longing', some of them by Richard Rolle, sometimes inspired by him:

> Lufe es the swettest thyng that man in erth hase tane,
> Lufe es goddes derlyng, lufe byndes blode and bane[1];
> In lufe be owre lykyng,[2] I ne wate[3] na better wane[4],
> For me and my lufyng[5] lufe makes bath be ane[6].
>
> I sygh and sob bath day and nyght for ane sa fayre of hew,
> Thar es na thyng my hert mai light bot lufe that es ay new

. . . .

Of Jesu mast lyst me[7] speke that al my bale[8] may bete[9];
Me thynk my hert may al to-breke when I thynk on that swete,
In lufe lacyd he hase my thoght that I sal never forgete;
Ful dere me thynk[10] he hase me boght with blodi hende[11] and fete.

(*CB XIV*, No. 84)

[1] *bone* [2] *delight* [3] *know* [4] *dwelling* [5] *loved one*
[6] *one* [7] *most delights me* [8] *sorrow* [9] *remedy* [10] *it seems to me* [11] *hands*

The idea expressed in this poem:

> Bot fleschly lufe sal fare as dose the flowre in May,
> And lastand be na mare than ane houre of a day

is sometimes expanded or made into a complete lyric. One such begins 'All other love is like the moon'. Another more elaborate example is the thirteenth-century 'Love Ron' of Friar Thomas de Hales (*CB XIII*, No. 43). He wrote it, he says, at the instance of 'a mayde Cristes'; he sends it to her in the form of a roll, to be read and learnt, and when she sits 'in longing' to be sung 'with sweet voice'. It is a praise of virginity as *Hali Meithhad* (see pp. 286–91 above)* is, but it is much less rebarbative in its treatment. The world's love is fickle and unstable, but it is not the horrors of the married state which the friar uses as a persuasion, but the mutability of our life on earth which is reflected in human love. He is moved to an eloquent *Ubi Sunt* (see p. 53 above)—and it is interesting to note that he seems to expect his (real or fictitious) nun to be familiar with romantic fiction (like the author of *Cursor Mundi* (see pp. 35–41 above), he is sensitive to the appeal of secular literature):

> Hwer is Paris and Heleyne
> That weren so bryht and feyre on bleo[1]?
> Amadas and Dideyne[2],
> Tristram, Yseude, and alle theo[3],
> Ector with his scharpe meyne[4],
> And Cesar, riche of wordes feo[5]?
> Heo beoth iglyden ut of the reyne,
> So the schef is of the cleo[6].
> Hit is of heom also hit nere[7]
> Of heom me haveth wunder itold[8].
> Nere hit reuthe for to heren[9]
> Hw[10] hi[11] were with pyne[12] aquold[13],
> And hwat hi tholeden[14] a-lyve here?

[1] *appearance* [2] *Idoine* [3] *those* [4] *fierce strength* [5] *mighty in*

* The phrase 'luve runes' appears in the Katherine Group, in *St Katherine*, where it translates *amatoria carmina*.

worldly possessions   [6] *they have glided from the kingdom (of earth) like the sheaf from the hillside*   [7] *It is as if they had never been*   [8] *marvellous things have been told of them*   [9] *were it not piteous to hear*   [10] *how*   [11] *they*   [12] *pain*   [13] *killed*   [14] *suffered*

Even a man as powerful as 'Henry our king' (Henry III) or as hand-some as Absolom will come to nought at the end ('it will not be worth a herring'). The idea of a 'king' leads the poet into a 'persuasion to love':

> Mayde, if thu wilnest after leofmon[1]
> Ich teche the enne treowe king.[2]

> [1] *lover*   [2] *I tell thee of a faithful king*

He gives an enthusiastic eulogy of the qualities and beauties of 'this child' (i.e. young man, probably here with romance connotations):

> He is feyr and bryht on heowe[1],
> Of glede chere, of mode[2] mylde,

> [1] *hue*   [2] *spirit*

true, and faithful, and the most powerful of all (Henry, King of England, renders obedience to him) and he has entrusted to the maiden a treasure better than gold. It is the precious jewel called maidenhood:

> He is idon[1] in heovene golde
> And is ful of fyn amur[2].

> [1] *set*   [2] *exquisite love*

The friar cleverly uses the terminology of secular love literature in his persuasion to the love of Christ: he concludes by saying that her choice is clear—no one given a choice between two lovers will 'take the worse and let the better go'.

There are many more obviously instructional and didactic lyrics—on the Ten Commandments, the seven deadly sins, and so on—which rarely find their way into anthologies, but it is necessary to remember the very practical nature of the medieval religious lyric. And there are some penitential and moral lyrics which deserve the attention of the modern reader. Even such an undistinguished song of penitence to the Virgin as this (*CB XIII*, No. 65) has an interesting experimental metri-cal and rhythmical quality:

> Hayl Mari!
> Ic am sori,
> Haf pité of me and merci,
> Mi levedi,
> To the I cri.
> For mi sinnis dred[1] am I

Wen I thenke that I sal bi[2]
That I haf mis idon[3]
In worde, in worke, in thoith[4] foli.
Levedi, her[5] mi bon[6]!

[1] *afraid*   [2] *must pay for*   [3] *done amiss*   [4] *thought*   [5] *hear*
[6] *prayer*

And one little lyric, based on a passage of St Augustine, makes a moving and personal statement of remorse for being slow to repent:

Loverd, thu clepedest me
An ich nagt[1] ne ansuarede the
Bute wordes scloe and sclepie[2]:
'Thole[3] yet! thole a litel!'
Bute 'yiet' and 'yiet' was endelis,
And 'thole a litel' a long wey is.   (*CB XIV*, No. 5)

[1] *nothing*   [2] *slow and sleepy*   [3] *suffer*

There is an interesting series of moral poems in the Vernon manuscript. Nearly all have rather memorable refrains, which give some idea of their edifying nature: 'Suffer in time and that is best', 'Ever more thank God of all', 'Truth is best', 'Charity is no longer cheer', 'Mercy passes all things', 'Tarry not till tomorrow' (which includes a traditional warning against trusting your executors), 'Against my will I take my leave' (the message of which is, predictably, that one should be prepared for the exit from this mortal stage) or (embodying a devotional topic we have met previously, see p. 56) 'Each man ought himself to know'. A poem on the earthquake of 1382 (*CB XIV*, No. 113), when

Chaumbres, chimeneys al tobarst[1],
Chirches and castels foule gon fare,
Pinacles, steples to grounde hit cast;
And al was warnyng to be ware

[1] *shattered*

takes it to be—along with the pestilence and the rising of the commons—a sign of the great vengeance that will come to pass because of sin. The best of these Vernon poems are those which deal with the instability of the world. One, which has the refrain 'think on yesterday' (*CB XIV*, No. 101) produces an image of the brevity of man's life which is as vivid as anything we have met in the prose treatises or sermons:

I have wist, sin I cuthe[1] meen[2],
That children hath bi candel liht
Heor[3] schadewe on the wal isen[4],
And ronne[5] therafter al the niht;

Bisy aboute thei han ben
To cacchen hit with al heore miht[6],
And whon thei cacchen hit best wolde wene[7],
Sannest[8] hit schet[9] out of heor siht[10];
The schadewe cacchen thei ne miht[11],
For no lynes[12] that thei couthe lay.
This schadewe I may likne a-riht[13]
To this world and yusterday.

[1] could   [2] ?speak   [3] their   [4] seen   [5] run   [6] might
[7] would best expect   [8] most quickly   [9] vanishes   [10] sight
[11] could   [12] cords (for snaring birds)   [13] indeed

And there is a remarkable reflective poem (*CB XIV*, No. 106) with the refrain 'this world fareth as a fantasy', based on the book of *Ecclesiastes* which echoes its melancholy and scepticism. Man's reason is small, and cannot comprehend the mysteries of the universe. Man himself is of no account, and dies as beasts die:

Whuch is mon, ho wot[1], and what,
Whether that he be ought or nought?
Of erthe and eyr groweth up a gnat,
And so doth mon whon al is souht[2];
Thaugh mon be waxen gret and fat,
Mon melteth awey so deth a mouht[3].
Monnes miht[4] nis worth a mat[5],
But nuyyeth[6] himself and turneth to nought.
Ho wot, save he that al hath wrought,
Wher mon bicometh[7] whon he schal dye?
Ho knoweth bi dede[8] ought[9] bote bi thought?
For this world fareth as a fantasye.

[1] who knows   [2] sought out   [3] moth   [4] man's strength   [5] ?mat
[6] harms   [7] what becomes of man   [8] death   [9] anything

This poem is in a long ascetic tradition of *contemptus mundi*. It is easy to find similar examples of a profoundly gloomy view of man's life. One of Grimestone's world-weary verses (W 166) reads:

With a sorwe and a clut[1]
Al this werd[2] comet in and out.

[1] shroud   [2] world

A very remarkable expansion of this idea is a lullaby (*SRL*, No. 82):

Lollai, lollai, litil child, whi wepistou so sore?
Nedis mostou wepe, hit was iyarkid the yore[1]
Ever to lib[2] in sorow, and sich[3] and mourne evermore,
As thin eldren[4] did er this, whil hi alives wore[5].

Lollai, litil child, child lolai, lullow,
Into uncuth[6] world icommen so ertow[7]!

[1] *prepared for thee long since*   [2] *live*   [3] *sigh*   [4] *parents*   [5] *while*
they were alive   [6] *unknown, strange*   [7] *thus art thou come*

It gives an extraordinarily bleak view of the hostile fate which awaits
the unfortunate Child. The adjective 'uncuth' evokes all the terrors of
existence: later in the poem the traditional image of man as a pilgrim
passing through the world is used, but only to be gloomily rejected—
'child, thou nert [art not] a pilgrim bot an uncuthe geste':

Child, thou nert a pilgrim bot an uncuthe gest,
Thi dawes beth itold[1], thi jurneis[2] beth ikest[3];
Whoder[4] thou salt wend North other Est,
Deth the sal betide with bitter bale[5] in brest.
Lollai, lollai, litil child, this wo Adam the wroght,
Whan he of the appil ete, and Eve hit him betoght[6].

[1] *days are reckoned*   [2] *days*   [3] *ordained*   [4] *whether*
[5] *pain, sorrow*   [6] *gave*

Medieval penitential teaching stresses that in the midst of life we
are in death, that the fear of death should move us to repentance and a
virtuous life. Perhaps not surprisingly, most of the best lyrics which set
out to instruct man on the best way to live are concerned with death. In
them we may see links with the past—with Old English expressions of
contemptus mundi—and with the future—with the 'macabre' stress on
decomposition, graves, and skeletons. They use the grim images of the
preacher—both king and queen must drink death's draught; they cannot escape his grasp, his 'wither-clench'; 'derne [secret] deth':

ay prickes and prokes[1]
Til he unclustri[2] al the lokes[3]
That liiff ligges[4] under

.   .   .   .   .   .

deth dinges[5] o thi dore
That nedes[6] schal be thi neighebore,
And fett[7] the to fen-fore[8]
Foule under fete.   (*CB XIV*, No. 27)

[1] *prods*   [2] *unfasten*   [3] *locks*   [4] *lies*   [5] *beats*   [6] *of neces-*
sity   [7] *fetches*   [8] *trench in the earth*

The most succinctly expressed verses are usually the most telling.
There is a strange riddling poem on the topic 'dust thou art and unto
dust shalt thou return':

Erthe toc[1] of erthe erthe wyth woh[2],
Erthe other erthe to the erthe droh[3],

> Erthe leyde erthe in erthene throh[4]—
> Tho hevede[5] erthe of erthe erthe ynoh[6].   (*CB XIII*, No. 73)

¹ *took*   ² *sin, injury*   ³ *drew*   ⁴ *earthen grave*   ⁵ *had*
⁶ *enough*

Some Latin lines from Pope Innocent's *De Miseria Conditionis Humanae*
('of the Wreched Engendrynge of Mankynde', as Chaucer calls it) are
in MS Trinity 323 turned into a neatly constructed, bitter, and
epigrammatic *memento mori*:

> Wen the turuf[1] is thi tuur[2],
> And thi put[3] is thi bour,
> This wel[4] and thi wite[5] throte
> Ssulen wormes to note[6]—
> Wat helpit the thenne
> Al the worilde wnne[7]?   (*CB XIII*, No. 30)

¹ *turf*   ² *tower*   ³ *pit*   ⁴ *skin*   ⁵ *white*   ⁶ *shall be useful*
  to worms   ⁷ *world's joy*

Sometimes the penitential verses on the 'Signs of Death' or *Proprietates
Mortis* (based on ancient medical lore turned to homiletic use in the
Middle Ages) have the same epigrammatic quality. In the following
example (*CB XIII*, No. 71) the short lines drive on and on until we are
finally brought to our end with a disenchanted proverb, suggesting
perhaps a kind of total disillusionment, comic and bitter at the same
time:

> Wanne mine eyhnen[1] misten,
> And mine eren sissen[2]
> And mi nose koldet[3],
> And mi tunge foldet,
> And mi rude slaket[4],
> And mi lippes blaken[5],
> And mi muth grennet[6],
> And mi spotel rennet[7],
> And min her riset[8],
> And min herte griset[9],
> And mine honden bivien[10],
> And mine fet stivien[11]—
> Al to late, al to late
> Wanne the bere[12] ys ate gate.
>
> Thanne y schel flutte[13]
> From bedde te flore,
> From flore to here[14],
> From here to bere,

From bere to putte[15],
And te[16] putt fordut[17].
Thanne lyd[18] min hus uppe min nese[19]—
Off al this world ne gyffe ic a pese[20].

[1] *eyes*	[2] *ears become deaf*	[3] *becomes cold*	[4] *colour fades*
[5] *grow pale*	[6] *grins*	[7] *spittle runs*	[8] *hair rises*	[9] *heart*
trembles	[10] *shake*	[11] *become rigid*	[12] *bier*	[13] *go*
[14] *shroud*	[15] *pit*	[16] *the*	[17] *shut up*	[18] *lies*	[19] *house*
upon my nose	[20] *pea*		

As we have already seen, secular songs and lyrics are often recorded only by chance, or in fragmentary form. It is much more difficult than in the case of the religious lyric to arrive at any kind of coherent 'picture' from the fraction that has survived. But it is clear, firstly, that there is considerable variety in type and in form, and secondly, that there is much work of excellent literary quality. 'The Man in the Moon', that splendid comic lyric, so close to folklore, which is so unlike anything in the more courtly lyric collections from France, perhaps looks slightly less isolated and odd when we put beside it a fine early verse charm against a wen, which literally talks the offending growth out of existence:

Wenne, wenne, wenchichenne,
Her ne scealt thu timbrien, ne nenne tun habben;
Ac thu scealt north heonene to than nihgan berhge,
Ther thu havest, ermig, enne brother.
He the sceal legge leaf et heafde.
Under fot-volmes, under vether earnes,
Under earnes clea, a thu geweornie!
Clinge thu alswa col on heorthe,
Scring thu alswa scerne a wage,
And weorne alswa weter on anbre!
Swa litel thu gewurthe alswa linset-corn,
And miccli lesse alswa anes hand-wurmes hupe-ban;
And alswa litel thu gewurthe thet thu nawiht gewurthe!*

Or this lyric (*CB XIII*, No. 21), an exchange between the speaker and a mysterious 'wight in the broom':

Say me, viit[1] in the brom,
Teche me wou[2] I sule don[3]

* 'Wen, wen, wen-chicken [i.e. little wen], you shall not build here, nor have a dwelling; but you must go north from here to the nearby hill where, wretch, you have a brother. He shall lay a leaf at your head. Under the soles of [the eagle's] feet, under the eagle's wing, under the eagle's claw, ever may you wither! May you waste away like a coal in the hearth, may you rot away like dung on the wall, and dry up like water in a pitcher! May you become as little as a grain of linseed, and much littler than a handworm's hip-bone; and may you become so little that you become nothing!' (trans. *OBMEV*, No. 2.)

That min hosebonde
Me lovien wolde'

Hold thine tunke[4] stille
And hawe[5] al thine wille.

[1] man   [2] how   [3] bring it about   [4] tongue   [5] have

The Wife of Bath would have approved of the result promised by this
proverbial lore, if not of the method it advocates. Or there is this later
onomatopoeic masterpiece (Sisam, p. 169), a complaint against black-
smiths (who did work at night, as we see in Chaucer's *Miller's Tale*)
which seems at the same time to be almost a parody of the alliterative
style:*

Swarte smekyd[1] smethes smateryd[2] wyth smoke
Dryve me to deth wyth den[3] of here dyntes[4].
Swech[5] noys on nyghtes ne herd men never:
What knavene cry[6] and clateryng of knockes!
The cammede kongons[7] cryen after 'col[8], col!'
And blowen here bellewys[9], that al here[10] brayn brestes[11]:
'Huf, puf!' seith that on; 'haf, paf!' that other.
Thei spyttyn and spraulyn[12] and spellyn[13] many spelles;
Thei gnauen and gnacchen[14], thei gronys togydere[15],
And holdyn hem hote[16] wyth here hard hamers.
Of a bole-hyde[17] ben here barm-fellys[18];
Here schankes[19] ben schakeled for the fere-flunderys[20];
Hevy hamerys thei han[21], that hard ben handled[22],
Stark[23] strokes thei stryken on a stelyd stokke[24];
Lus, bus! las, das! rowtyn be rowe[25].
Swech dolful a dreme the devyl it todryve[26]!
The mayster longith a lityl, and lascheth a lesse[27],
Twyneth hem tweyn[28], and towchith a treble[29].
Tik, tak! hic, hac! tiket, taket! tyk, tak!
Lus, bus! lus, das! swych lyf thei ledyn
Alle clothemerys[30]: Cryst hem gyve sorwe[31]!
May no man for brenwaterys[32] on nyght han hys rest!

[1] black smoky   [2] begrimed   [3] din   [4] blows   [5] such
[6] shouting of the menials   [7] snub-nosed misshapen rascals   [8] coal
[9] bellows   [10] their   [11] burst   [12] sprawl about   [13] tell
[14] grind and gnash their teeth   [15] together   [16] keep themselves hot
[17] bull-hide   [18] leather aprons   [19] legs   [20] gartered to protect them
against the fiery sparks   [21] have   [22] wielded   [23] strong
[24] anvil made of steel   [25] they beat in turn   [26] May the devil destroy such a
wretched noise   [27] ?the master smith lengthens a little piece and beats it smaller
[28] joins two of them together   [29] strikes a treble note   [30] mare-clothers (i.e.
smiths who make horse-armour)   [31] sorrow   [32] water-burners

* It is notable that in this period unrhymed alliterative verse seems (judging from the
surviving corpus) never to have been usual as a form for lyrics.

A number of the secular lyrics which have survived are topical verses on political events or satirical statements or complaints. These are usually neglected by modern critics, perhaps because they do not conform to late Romantic ideas of the Lyric, but in our period lyrics were meant to be used, and were used for complaint or vituperation as well as for prayer or persuasion to love.

Satirical poems on the various estates of society seem to have been popular throughout the Middle Ages. There is a good light-hearted example (apparently written in Ireland) which consists of a series of mock greetings:

> Hail Seint Cristofre with thi lang stake[1]!
> Thou ber ur Loverd[2] Jesus Crist over the brod lake[3].
> Mani grete kunger[4] swimmeth abute thi fete.
> Hou mani hering to[5] peni at West Chep in London?
> This vers is of Holi Writte
> It com of noble witte. . . .*

[1] staff   [2] bore our lord   [3] broad stream   [4] conger-eels   [5] for a

The poet is here almost certainly thinking of the popular depictions in wall-paintings of the huge St Christopher standing in waves out of which peep fishes of various kinds. That he is indeed a man of 'noble wit' is not only shown by the way he adapts this well-known image to the price of fish, but by such a vignette as that of the butchers:

> Hail be ye bochers with yur bole-ax[1]!
> Fair beth yur barmhatres[2], yolow[3] beth yur fax[4]
> Ye stondith at the schamil[5], brod ferlich bernes[6],
> Fleiis[7] yow folowithe, ye swolowith ynow[8]. . . .

[1] pole-axe   [2] aprons   [3] yellow   [4] hair   [5] meat-stall
[6] wondrously wide fellows   [7] flies   [8] enough

Merchants, bakers, hucksters also come under his fire, as do the friars, that favourite butt of late medieval satirists:

> Hail Saint Franceis with thi mani foulis[1],
> Kites and crowis, revenes and oules,
> Fure and twenti wild gees and a poucok[2]!
> Mani bold begger siwith thi route[3].
> This vers is ful wel isette[4]
> Swithe furre hit was ivette[5].

> Hail be ye freris with the white copis!
> Ye habbith a hus[6] at Drochda[7] war[8] men makith ropes.
> Evir ye beth roilend[9] the londis al aboute;

* W. Heuser, *Die Kildare-Gedichte* (*Bonner Beiträge zur Anglistik*, xiv, Bonn, 1904), 154; *OBMEV*, No. 62.

Of the watir daissers[10] ye robbith the churchis.
Maister he was swithe gode[11]
That this sentence understode. . . .

[1] *birds*   [2] *peacock*   [3] *follows your train*   [4] *composed*   [5] *it was*
brought from very far away   [6] *house*   [7] *Drogheda*   [8] *where*
[9] *roaming*   [10] *?sprinklers*   [11] *he would be an excellent scholar*

We are even further from the ideal chaste and pious friar of the lyric mentioned earlier (see p. 369) in this satirical piece, with its sarcastic opening:

Preste ne monke ne yit chanoun[1]
Ne no man of religioun
Gyfen hem[2] so to devocioun
As done thes[3] holy frers.
For summe gyven ham[4] to chyvalry,
Somme to riote and ribaudery[5];
Bot frers gyven ham to grete study,
And to grete prayers

.   .   .   .   .

Men may se by thair contynaunce[6]
That thai are men of grete penaunce,
And also that thair sustynaunce
Simple is and wayke[7].
I have lyved now fourty yers,
And fatter men about the neres[8]
Yit sawe I never then are these frers,
In contreys ther thai rayke[9].   (*HP*, No. 65)

[1] *canon*   [2] *give themselves*   [3] *these*   [4] *themselves*   [5] *debauchery*
[6] *demeanour*   [7] *poor*   [8] *kidneys*   [9] *wander*

They have all the vices of Chaucer's friar Hubert; and the initials of their four orders—Carmelites, Austins, Jacobins, Minors—indicate their true founder, Caim (i.e. Cain).

Complaints about contemporary wickedness are often very general ones, and the modern reader sometimes wonders whether there has ever been a year or a society which did not demonstrate these 'abuses of the age'. But a verse such as the following:

Bissop lorles[1],
Kyng redeles[2],
Yung man rechles[3],
Old man witles,
Womman ssamles[4].
I swer bi hevenkyng,
Thos beth five lither[5] thing (*HP*, No. 56)

[1] *bishop without learning*   [2] *without counsel*   [3] *careless*   [4] *shameless*
[5] *wicked*

could be given some sharp and particular point by the context in which it was used, while its generality would still serve as a protection. Of the two 'letters' associated with John Ball (*HP*, Nos. 17, 18), one is simply a verse list of generalized 'abuses' ('Now raygneth pride in price / Covetise is holden wise' etc.), while the other is deliberately enigmatic in the manner of popular prophecies ('Johan the mullere hath ygrounde smal, smal, smal. / The kynges sone of hevene schal pay for al . . .'). The famous couplet 'When Adam delved and Eve span / Who then was the gentleman' sounds like a proverbial verse being put to particular political use. Some such verses, however, are given a topical reference in their own text:

> Man be ware and be no fool:
> Thenke apon the ax, and of the stool[1]!
> The ax was scharp, the stool was hard,
> The iiii yere of kyng Richard.   (*HP*, No. 16)

[1] *executioner's block*

And there are longer songs and poems on political events such as the battle of Lewes (1264) or the death of Edward III (1377). One interesting series of such poems gives us the author's name—Laurence Minot. He celebrates the victories of Edward III in France and in Scotland with gusto:

> A litell fro that forsaid toune,
> Halydon Hill that es the name,
> Thare was crakked many a crowne
> Of wilde Scottes and alls[1] of tame. . . .

[1] *also*

Another poem (*HP*, No. 9) on this battle of Halidon Hill (1333) sees it as a personal revenge by the King for the defeat of Bannockburn. Minot uses the minstrel's alliterative formulas to achieve a note of exultation that makes us think of the anti-Scots poems of Skelton:

> Skottes out of Berwik and of Abirdene,
> At the Bannokburn war ye to kene[1];
> Thare slogh[2] ye many sakles[3], als[4] it was sene,
> And now has king Edward wroken[5] it, I wene.
> It es wrokin, I wene, wele wurth the while[6];
> War ye with[7] the Skottes, for thai er ful of gile.
> Whare er ye, Skottes of Saint Johnes toune[8]?
> The boste[9] of yowre baner es betin all doune.

> When ye bosting will bede[10], Sir Edward es boune[11]
> Forto kindel[12] yow care and crak yowre crowne.
>> He has crackked yowre croune, wele worth the while;
>> Schame bityde the Skottes, for thai er full of gile. . . .

[1] *bold* [2] *slew* [3] *innocent* [4] *as* [5] *avenged* [6] *happy the time* [7] *beware of* [8] *Perth* [9] *pride* [10] *offer* [11] *ready* [12] *increase*

His voice reaches a crescendo in the violent and gloriously excessive abuse of a 'flyting':

> Rughfute riveling[1], now kindels thi care,
> Berebag[2] with thi boste, thi biging[3] es bare. . . .

[1] *rough-shoed rascal* [2] *bag-carrier* [3] *lodging*

But it is rare, for poems such as these, however topical in their own time, to live on to engage the interest of later readers.

We should turn now to a more familiar tradition of lyric. It is one which is closer to French fashions, yet still very distinctive; the examples are rare, but of fine quality. In a commonplace book associated with Reading Abbey, among some musical pieces in French and Latin, there appears what is (deservedly) the most famous of the early secular lyrics:

> Sumer is icumen in,
> Lhude[1] sing, cuccu!
> Groweth sed[2] and bloweth med[3]
> And springth[4] the wde[5] nu.
>> Sing, cuccu!
>
> Awe[6] bleteth after lomb,
> Lhouth after calve cu[7],
> Bulluc sterteth[8], bucke verteth[9].
> Murie[10] sing, cuccu!
>> Cuccu, cuccu,
> Wel singes thu, cuccu,
> Ne swik[11] thu naver nu!
>
> Sing, cuccu, nu! Sing, cuccu!
> Sing, cuccu! Sing, cuccu, nu!   (*CB XIII*, No. 6)

[1] *loudly* [2] *seed* [3] *the meadow blooms* [4] *comes into leaf* [5] *wood* [6] *ewe* [7] *cow lows for calf* [8] *leaps* [9] *breaks wind* [10] *merrily* [11] *cease*

It is apparently composed to fit the tune, a splendid (and quite complicated) round, and the whole is exhilarating in performance. This is an example of what would in French lyric be called a 'reverdie' or welcome to spring, but it is unique and fresh. Its extraordinary vivacity comes as much from the sprightly syntax, with its series of present tenses punctuated by imperatives, as from the simple and rustic details which are singled out as examples of the surging life of spring-time. Another 'reverdie' (*CB XIII*, No. 8) seems typically English in its insistent alliteration, but that the poet was familiar with lyric tradition is shown by the allusive way in which he treats the conventional opposition of joyful spring and sorrowful lover:

> Foweles[1] in the frith[2],
> The fisses[3] in the flod[4],
> And I mon waxe wod[5]:
> Mulch sorw[6] I walke with
> For beste of bon and blod[7]. . . .

[1] *birds*   [2] *wood*   [3] *fishes*   [4] *water*   [5] *must grow mad*
[6] *great sorrow*   [7] *i.e. for the fairest creature alive*

A different season is splendidly and plangently recorded in this song:

> Mirie it is while sumer ilast[1]
>   With fugheles[2] song;
> Oc nu necheth[3] windes blast
>   And weder strong[4].
> Ei! ei! What[5] this nicht is long!
> And ich with wel michel wrong[6]
>   Soregh[7] and murne and fast.

[1] *lasts*   [2] *birds'*   [3] *But now approaches*   [4] *rough*   [5] *how*
[6] *most unjustly*   [7] *sorrow*

'Now springs the spray' (*CB XIII*, No. 62) is an early carol which uses the favourite French 'chanson d'aventure' opening:

> Als[1] I me rode this endre[2] dai
>   O mi pleyinge[3]
> Seih I hwar[4] a litel mai[5]
>   Bigan to singge. . . .

[1] *As*   [2] *other*   [3] *pleasure*   [4] *where*   [5] *maid*

We would expect the song to be of love, happy or sorrowful, but the little maid's song begins with an English directness—'the clot him clingge' (may the clod shrivel him). As her final stanza—an answer to the poet's inquiry—shows, she is having trouble with her man, but does not intend to take it lying down . . .

> Than answerde that maiden swote[1]
>   Midde[2] wordes fewe:
> 'Mi lemman[3] me haves bihot[4]
>   Of lovve trewe;
>   He chaunges a-newe.

Yiif[5] I mai, it shal him rewe[6]
Bi this dai!'

¹ *sweet*   ² *with*   ³ *lover*   ⁴ *has promised*   ⁵ *If*   ⁶ *he shall rue it*

Perhaps the fact that in the preceding stanza the poet has referred to the 'mirie note' of this 'mirie' maiden suggests that he is an observer with an almost Chaucerian incomprehension. In delicate counter-point to all this is the love-melancholy of his own repeated burden:

Nou sprinkes the sprai,
Al for love icche[1] am so seeke[2]
That slepen I ne mai.

¹ *I*   ² *sick*

One of the miraculous survivals of early lyric is a single strip of vellum (now in MS Rawlinson D. 913 in the Bodleian Library) which possibly once was a small roll. On it can still just be read a number of songs, which in the eyes of the Bishop of Ossory would have qualified as 'lewd, secular, and associated with revelry'. One is a splendid drunkard's song:

Hay! Robyne, Malkin,
Suster, Walter, Peter!
Ye drunke al depe,
Ant ichulle eke[1].
Standeth alle stille,
Stille, stille, stille,
Standeth alle stille,
Stille as any ston.
Trippe a lutel[2] wit thi fot
Ant let thi body go!

(*SL*, No. 117; *OBMEV*, No. 70)

¹ *And I will also*   ² *little*

This remarkable monologue with its wavering rhythms is more suc-cessful than many of the hearty 'literary' drinking-songs that were to follow it. 'The Irish Dancer'—who presumably let her body go in a more orderly way—entranced W. B. Yeats:

Ich am of Irlaunde,
Ant of the holy londe
Of Irlande.
Gode sire, pray ich the
Of saynte charité,
Come ant daunce wyt me
In Irlaunde.   (*SL*, No. 15; *OBMEV*, No. 67)

LYRICS

And it is in this leaf that we find a full text of that tantalizing song
'Maiden in the Moor Lay' (the Bishop of Ossory thought that a pious
version was more suitable for his clergy; twentieth-century moralists
have attempted to de-secularize it, but without success):*

Maiden in the mor lay[1]
    In the mor lay,
Sevenyst[2] fulle, sevenist fulle,
Maiden in the mor lay,
    In the mor lay,
Sevenistes fulle ant a day.

Welle was hire mete[3];
    Wat was hire mete?
The primerole[4] ant the—
The primerole ant the—
Welle was hire mete;
    Wat was hire mete?
The primerole ant the violet.

Welle was hire dryng[5];
    Wat was hire dryng?
The chelde[6] water of the—
The chelde water of the—
Welle was hire dryng;
    Wat was hire dryng?
The chelde water of the welle-spring.

Welle was hire bour;
    Wat was hire bour?
The rede rose an te—
The rede rose an te—
Welle was hire bour;
    Wat was hire bour?
The rede rose an te lilie flour.

(*SL*, No. 18; *OBMEV*, No. 68)

[1] *dwelt*   [2] *seven nights*   [3] *food*   [4] *primrose*   [5] *drink*
[6] *cold*

There is no doubt that the most substantial and significant group of
love-lyrics before the end of the fourteenth century consists of those in
MS Harley 2253, the so-called 'Harley Lyrics' (though it must be
remembered that they form only a small part of the contents of that
manuscript). They are not always easy reading. The language can be
difficult—a fondness for alliteration is perhaps responsible for some
recondite words, and the syntax sometimes seems jerky when read on

* See S. Wenzel, *Speculum* 49 (1974), 69–74.

the page. It is essential to remember that these lyrics are still close to an oral tradition, and are probably meant to be performed whether by reading aloud or by singing (there is no music in the manuscript but this itself is not conclusive). Two stanzas from 'Weping haveth myn wonges wet' (B No. 6), if read aloud, will illustrate the intricate sound patterns that the authors of some of these lyrics were undoubtedly striving for:

Weping haveth myn wonges[1] wet
 For wikked werk ant wone[2] of wyt;
Unblithe[3] y be til y ha bet[4]
 Bruches broken[5], ase bok byt[6],
Of levedis love, that y ha let[7],
 That lemeth[8] al with luefly lyt[9];
Ofte in song y have hem set[10],
 That is unsemly ther hit syt[11].
  Hit syt and semeth noht[12]
   Ther[13] hit ys seid in song;
  That y have of hem wroht[14],
   Ywis[15] hit is al wrong.

Al wrong y wrohte for a wyf[16]
 That made us wo[17] in world ful wyde;
Heo rafte[18] us alle richesse ryf[19]
 That durfte us nout in reynes ryde[20].
A stythye stunte hire sturne stryf[21],
 That ys in heovene hert in hyde[22].
In hire lyht[23] on ledeth lyf[24],
 Ant shon thourh[25] hire semly syde.
  Thourh hyre side he shon
   Ase sonne doth thourh the glas;
  Wommon nes[26] wicked non
   Sethe[27] he ybore[28] was.

[1] cheeks   [2] lack   [3] sad   [4] have atoned for   [5] broken transgressions (i.e. which have been committed)   [6] as the Book bids   [7] abandoned   [8] shines   [9] beautiful hue   [10] placed them   [11] sits, i.e. is   [12] is not seemly   [13] where   [14] composed about them   [15] certainly   [16] because of a woman   [17] sorrowful   [18] she deprived   [19] abundant   [20] who did not need to ride us in reins   [21] an excellent woman stopped her violent strife   [22] ?concealed in the heart of heaven   [23] alighted in her   [24] one who brings life   [25] through   [26] was not   [27] since   [28] born

We have here not only a rather demanding rhyme-scheme and very heavy alliteration, but an elaborate system of concatenations which is maintained throughout the poem, which links one stanza to the next, and also what is in effect the 'wheel' (as in *Sir Gawain*) to the main body of each stanza (ll. 8–9 and 20–21). This internal concatenation is embellished by a complicated pattern of reversal and echo ('. . . unsemly . . . syt / . . . syt . . . semeth'). As in *Pearl* or *Gawain*, these emphasized words often have thematic value ('wrong', 'seemly', etc.). There is occasionally (and more frequently in some other lyrics) further rhetorical decoration—the phrase 'bruches broken' nicely plays with two etymologically related, as well as alliterating, words. This writer can be allusive (in the second stanza he refers, successively, to Eve, to the story of Aristotle—a wise man made a fool by love— being ridden by a girl, the Virgin Mary, and to the common image of Christ entering her womb like light through glass—this last being boldly and imaginatively treated), but the argument is not complex, nor the thought profound. In this he is similar to other poets in the series. This combination of very elaborate decoration combined with a fairly simple series of statements, ejaculations, and the like, is one which may irritate a *reader*. In performance, though, it makes more sense. What we have here, if it is not the difficult *trobar clus* of the troubadours, is very far removed from the plain and simple style of the majority of religious lyrics which is designed to reach the heart by being quickly and profoundly understood. Poets like this one delight rather in constructing elaborate verbal and melodic artefacts; it is a 'formal poetry' rather than a meditative poetry.

We may find examples of this throughout the collection, different though the individual lyrics are. 'The Fair Maid of Ribblesdale', for instance (B No. 7), is largely a formal rhetorical eulogy of the beloved's appearance, similar in outline to many others. She has the fashionable grey eyes, long 'lefly' hair, brows that are 'bend an heh', red lips, teeth of the purest white, an exquisitely long neck, elegant arms and fingers, etc. All of this traditional material is given life through sometimes unexpected detail (her chin is 'chosen' (excellent); her nose 'ys set as hit wel semeth'), or through similes which range from the learned and the courtly to homely, country images like those used by Chaucer in the portrait of Alisoun in *The Miller's Tale*—she is as peerless as the phoenix; her speech is compared to spices, her teeth to whale's bone (highly prized for its whiteness), and her complexion to a rosebush, while her sides are 'soft as silk' and 'whiter than the morning milk'. The various levels are nicely combined in:

> Hyre tyttes aren anunder bis[1]
> As apples tuo of parays[2].

[1] *under the fine linen*   [2] *Paradise*

But her excellence is not demonstrated simply through comparisons.

The poet shows a liveliness of perception and an imaginative participation in the description:

> Hire hed when ich biholde apon,
> The sonnebeem aboute noon
> Me thohte that y seye[1] . . .
>
> [1] *I would think that I saw*

or he uses metaphorical compression—she has a 'swan's neck'—or he
will suggest movement or action or some kind of situation—her grey
eyes are beautiful 'when she smiles on me'; she has a merry mouth 'to
mele' (speak). It is far from the static and lifeless catalogues that are
found in some fifteenth-century lyrics.

The opening of the poem:

> Mosti[1] ryden by Rybbesdale,
> Wilde wymmen forte wale[2]
> Ant welde[3] whuch ich wolde
>
> [1] *if I could*   [2] *choose*   [3] *possess*

—where 'wilde' probably has the sense 'wanton' (perhaps as in the
later song concerning 'wild, wild women')—rather suggests that this is
a dream girl, an imaginary creation. Whether or not this is so is really
immaterial, for the poet breathes so much life into his creation and his
relationship with her that it sounds both 'real' and 'personal':

> Me were levere kepe hire come[1]
> Then beon[2] pope ant ryde in Rome,
> Stythest[3] upon stede
>
> [1] *I would rather wait for her coming*   [2] *be*   [3] *most powerful*

or as in the splendid hyperbole at the end:

> He myhte sayen that Crist hym seye[1]
> That myhte nyhtes neh hyre leye[2],
> Hevene he hevede[3] here.
>
> [1] *looked favourably on him*   [2] *who could lie by her at night*   [3] *had*

This pick of the wild girls of Ribblesdale is quite a high-class lady—
her admirer envisages her reading romances—and she is well turned-
out, with a golden girdle adorned with precious gems. Like Alisoun's
dress in *The Miller's Tale*, this item of clothing is made as erotic as her
body. A note of the faintest comedy in the hyperbole, which we may

have detected earlier in the juxtaposition of the lover's exquisite melancholy and his lady's seemly nose—

> Hire neose ys set as hit wel semeth;
> Y deye[1], for deth that me demeth[2] . . .
>
> [1] *die*　　　[2] *condemns*

—is perhaps confirmed here by the way he enthuses upon the gem (with its traditional 'virtue' and its associations with 'maiden head') set in the buckle of her girdle:

> Ther withinne stont[1] a ston
> 　That warneth[2] men from wo;
> The water that hit wetes yn[3]
> Ywis[4] hit wortheth[5] al to wyn[6],
> 　That seyen[7], seyden so.
>
> [1] *stands*　　[2] *protects*　　[3] *it is dipped in*　　[4] *certainly*　　[5] *becomes*
> [6] *wine*　　[7] *those that have seen it*

There is a playfulness in the creation of this gorgeous erotic object, as well as in the rhetorical construction of his poetic artefact, but it co-exists happily within the main and 'serious' drift of the poem which is a joyous celebration of the beauty of a lady who is —traditionally—the source of all the lover's 'bliss', and the light (cf. stanzas 1 and 2) which shines through all lands, opposed to, and yet the source of the sorrow which seems (even in an ecstatic poem such as this) never to be too far from 'bliss'.

Similar celebrations of a lady's beauty are found in other lyrics in the collection. 'A Wayle Whyt ase Whalles Bon' combines an intricate metrical and rhetorical structure with a directness of writing which brings new life to traditional topics of the European lyric:

> Ich wolde[1] ich were a threstelcok[2],
> A bountyng other a lavercok[3],
> 　Swete bryd[4]!
> Bituene hire curtel[5] ant hire smok
> 　Y wolde ben hyd.
>
> [1] *would*　　[2] *thrush*　　[3] *a bunting or a lark*　　[4] *sweet little bird*
> [5] *gown*

Skelton is to play with this idea in his *Phyllyp Sparowe*. Similarly, 'Blow, Northern Wind' has a simple lyrical burden (which some think is the refrain of a different, popular *carole* that has been attached to this poem):

> Blow, northerne wynd,
> Sent[1] thou me my suetyng!

> Blow, northerne wynd,
> Blou! blou! blou!
>
> [1] send

whereas the stanzas praising the lady are sometimes flamboyant in their ornament and rhetorical display:

> Heo[1] is coral of godnesse,
> Heo is rubie of ryhtfulnesse,
> Heo is cristal of clannesse[2],
>   Ant baner of bealté[3].
> Heo is lilie of largesse[4],
> Heo is parvenke[5] of prouesse[6]
> Heo is solsecle[7] of suetnesse,
>   Ant ledy of lealté[8].

[1] *She*   [2] *purity*   [3] *beauty*   [4] *generosity*   [5] *periwinkle*
[6] *excellence*   [7] *marigold*   [8] *fidelity*

An extraordinary elaboration of this topic is found in 'Annot and John' (B No. 3) where in five stanzas (each rhyming aaaaaaaabb, with alliteration in every line, as well as sundry other sound effects) the lady is compared to jewels, flowers, birds, spices, and a very recondite list of heroines and heroes. The idea here, emphasized almost unbearably by repetition, is that the lady is the jewel of jewels, flower of flowers, etc. She is here given a name in a riddling allusion: 'Hire nome is in a note of the nyhtegale / In Annote is hire nome.'

The same liveliness in the treatment of traditional forms and topics can be seen in the *pastourelle* 'In a fryht as y con fare fremede' or in the *reverdie* 'Lenten ys come with love to toune', where a direct lyricism celebrates the coming of spring, the regeneration of life, and the joy of nature:

> Lenten[1] ys come with love to toune[2],
> With blosmen[3] ant with briddes roune[4],
>   That al this blisse bryngeth.
> Dayeseyes[5] in this dales,
> Notes suete of nyhtegales,
>   Uch[6] foul song singeth.
> The threstelcoc him threteth oo[7];
> Away is huere[8] wynter wo
>   When woderove[9] springeth.
> This foules[10] singeth ferly fele[11],
> Ant wlyteth on huere wynne wele[12],
>   That al the wode[13] ryngeth.

[1] *spring*   [2] *the world*   [3] *blossoms*   [4] *birds' song*   [5] *daisies*
[6] *each*   [7] *the thrush chides continually*   [8] *their*   [9] *woodruff*
[10] *these birds*   [11] *wondrously many*   [12] *?warble about their wealth of joy*
[13] *wood*

Even the worms woo under the clod. There is an abrupt shift in the last three lines of the poem, where the speaker suddenly reveals his own involvement in love: if he does not have his will of one woman he will become a fugitive in the woods, abandoning all this 'wealth of joys'.

The best qualities of the collection can be seen in a single lyric, 'Alysoun':

> Bytuene Mersh ant Averil[1]
>   When spray[2] biginneth to springe,
> The lutel foul[3] hath hire wyl[4]
>   On hyre lud[5] to synge.
> Ich libbe[6] in love-longinge
> For semlokest of alle thynge[7]
> He[8] may me blisse bringe
> Icham in hire baundoun[9].
>
>   An hendy hap ichabbe yhent[10],
>   Ichot[11] from hevene it is me sent;
>   From alle wymmen mi love is lent[12],
>   Ant lyht[13] on Alysoun.

[1] *March and April* [2] *shoot* [3] *little bird* [4] *delight* [5] *her language* [6] *live* [7] *fairest of all creatures* [8] *she* [9] *I am in her power* [10] *I have had good fortune* [11] *I know* [12] *gone* [13] *alighted*

After some of our previous examples, there is something refreshingly direct in this opening, without their self-consciously intricate sound-patterns or rhetorical decorations. Although there is no music in the Harley manuscript, this lyric would seem supremely suitable for singing. There is no riddling concealment of the girl's name here: 'Alysoun' ends the refrain repeated after each of the poem's four stanzas. Alliteration, though frequently used, is more discreet. Formulaic phrases similar to those in the other lyrics ('semlokest of alle thynge', etc.) occur throughout the poem, set off by one unusual simile—'wery so water in wore' (?turbulent pool)—describing the lover's weariness from long vigils. This opening stanza succinctly opposes (in traditional manner) the joyful reawakening of the natural world to the solitary melancholy lover in his state of unsatisfied longing. The following two stanzas give a description of the lady, but it is not done in the formal rhetorical way we have seen elsewhere. In the second stanza only a few of the conventional details are singled out (hair, brows, eyes, slender waist) before it is interrupted, abruptly and dramatically, by the lover's outcry:

Bote he me wolle to hire take[1]
Forte buen[2] hire owen make[3]
Longe to lyven ichulle[4] forsake
Ant feye[5] fallen adoun

[1] *unless she will take me to her*   [2] *to be*   [3] *mate*   [4] *I will*
[5] *doomed to die*

and it is only resumed at the end of the third stanza with a rhetorical avowal of the inexpressibility of her goodness and beauty accompanied by one further detail:

In world nis non so wyter[1] mon
That al hire bounté[2] telle con;
Hire swyre[3] is whittore then the swon,
Ant feyrest may[4] in toune. . . .

[1] *wise*   [2] *excellence*   [3] *neck*   [4] *maid*

This curious and apparently artless technique is artistically very effective because it makes the relationship between lady and poet a much more dynamic (and interesting) one than it is in the other lyrics. It is matched, too, by a hint of a greater complexity in the treatment of love. We have the traditional situation of the lover poised between the extremes of bliss (love is a grace sent from heaven, etc.) and grief ('feye fallen adoun', etc.), but this poet is not afraid to emphasize the extremes, so that images of the worried, sleepless lover alternate with ecstatic praises of his lady's beauty and the recurring refrain with its tone of utter joy. It is all brought to a kind of unresolved balance at the end:

Betere is tholien whyle sore[1]
Then mournen evermore.
Geynest under gore[2],
Herkne to my roun[3].
An hendy hap ichabbe yhent. . . .

[1] *to suffer grief for a time*   [2] *most gracious under gown, i.e. most gracious of ladies*
[3] *speech*

The secular lyrics of Harley 2253 show a bold and distinctive handling of both English and French tradition. They are as remarkable a testimony to the vigour of local literary culture as are the poems of the *Gawain* manuscript. Whether they represent a taste that is more than local is uncertain. Metropolitan literature, and a tradition of courtly lyric connected with the royal court, and profoundly indebted to contemporary French fashions, can be seen developing at the end of the fourteenth century. Chaucer, who, according to Alceste in the Prologue to *The Legend of Good Women*, has made

Many an ympne for Loves halidayes
That highte balades, roundels, virelayes

has left us a remarkable series of lyrics—songs of love, philosophical lyrics, 'Horatian' epistles, and even a translation of a Petrarch sonnet (appropriately given to the tormented lover Troilus); his friend Gower was the author not only of French lyrics, but of a longer thoughtful lyrical poem on peace. English is now a vehicle for sophisticated and elegant lyric poetry.

9

Gower

About the life of John Gower, Chaucer's friend, little can be said with certainty. His family evidently had Yorkshire origins, but certain features of his language suggest a connection with Kent, where he purchased lands in 1378. In that year Chaucer, when setting out for Italy, gave power of attorney to Gower and a lawyer called Richard Forester. In his French poem, the *Mirour de l'omme* (21772–4), Gower says that he is not a 'clerk' but that he wears 'la raye mancé', the distinctive dress of serjeants at law and certain court officials; and other documents and allusions confirm the suggestion that he was a Londoner versed in the law, who was in touch with Kentish gentry, and had some knowledge of life at court. In the *Mirour de l'omme*, he confesses (27337 ff.) that in his youth he abandoned himself to 'foldelit et veine joye', and wrote 'fol ditz d'amours', songs and ditties such as those he was to attribute to Chaucer and to Amans in the *Confessio Amantis* (i. 2727), whom he represents as composing 'rondeal, balade and virelai'. Some of the fifty-one French balades that survive in the Trentham manuscript (now MS Egerton 2862 in the British Library) may represent these youthful poems: Machaut, Deschamps, and Froissart had made the *balade* a fashionable medium for love-poetry well before the death of Edward III (1377). In his Latin poem, the *Vox Clamantis*, he gives a mordant description of society in the following reign, including accounts of the Peasants' Revolt (1381) and of Richard II's reconciliation with the House of Commons (1392). The original (undated) Prologue and Conclusion to *Confessio Amantis* dedicate the poem to Richard, but about 1393 they were changed in favour of Henry of Lancaster, who in that year gave 'an esquire John Gower' the collar that is presumably the collar of SS shown on his tomb. Five weeks after his coronation Henry, as king, rewarded Gower with a grant of two pipes of Gascon wine for life. The untitled poem called by his editor, G. C. Macaulay, 'In Praise of Peace', belongs to this period.

By 1398, and perhaps for some time earlier, Gower was living in the Priory of St Mary Overy, Southwark. In that year the Bishop of Winchester granted a licence for his marriage to a fellow parishioner

Agnes Groundolf—whom he described in an epitaph as 'uxor amans humilis'. She outlived him.

In sending a copy of *Vox Clamantis* to Bishop Arundel about 1400, Gower described himself as *senex et cecus*; *senectus* could mean any age from forty to sixty and more, but other personal references in this *Epistola*, along with those at the end of the *Confessio Amantis*, suggest that he was nearing the later stage of *aetas decrepita* by the turn of the century. His will was proved on 24 October 1408.

Gower is remarkable in having written extensively and eloquently in three languages. The *Vox Clamantis*, prompted by the 'Peasants' Revolt', is the longest and most passionate of all Latin poems in the fourteenth century and of itself gives Gower a claim to a place in the history of European literature; whilst the *Mirour de l'omme*, three times as long as *Vox Clamantis*, tells us more about life in fourteenth-century London than Chaucer does; tells us indeed something about his father's trade—a lively vignette shows fine city ladies being cheated by a vintner and a druggist, who overcharges them for make-up. At other points it touches the *Confessio*. In particular it shows the same distaste for war: modern chivalry 'est vein et orguillous / et du pillage covotois'. The metre is as smooth as that of the English work, and far smoother than most fourteenth-century Anglo-French verse. Some of Gower's fifty French *balades* are more immediately attractive. Several allude to Ovidian tales in the *Confessio*, and in one he gives a new twist to the St Valentine's Day convention by attaching to it the story of Ceyx and Alcione, on which he lavished so much care in the *Confessio* (where the pair figure not only in the *exemplum* but also in the concluding vision, vii. 2647 ff.). Would that we might be birds, like them, is his conclusion. But it is with his long English poem that we are concerned here. As its name suggests, the *Confessio Amantis* is the confession of a lover (Amans) to Genius, priest of Nature. As Thomas Warton says, 'the ritual of religion is applied to the tender passion, and Ovid's *Art of Love* is blended with the breviary': the Confessor illustrates the Deadly Sins which threaten the Lover (and Love) by a large number of exemplary stories, many of them derived from Ovid, told with a delicate art.

For the indifference of most modern readers to Gower's poetic achievement Chaucer is partly, albeit innocently, responsible. No epithet has ever stuck more firmly than the 'moral' that he intended as encomiastic when he applied it to his friend, beseeching him to correct his *Troilus* (v. 1856–7). The fact that in *The Kingis Quair* Chaucer is praised in the same stanza as Gower for his 'moralitee' has not sufficed to counter the constant suggestion that the adjective is patronizing or sly. 'Sounyng in moral vertu' Gower certainly is; but he is more than a moralizer. He is a skilled poet—and in some respects more generous in his sympathies than Chaucer himself. But when Chaucer addressed him, he had published only his French and Latin works, to which Venus alludes in similar terms, at the end of *Confessio Amantis*:

> And tarie thou mi court no more,
> Bot go ther vertu moral duelleth,
> Wher ben thi bokes, as men telleth,
> Whiche of long time thou hast write.   (viii. 2925–8)

At the same point Gower delicately repays Chaucer's compliment when his Venus says

> And gret wel Chaucer whan ye mete
> As mi disciple and mi poete . . .

gently hinting at the same time that, like Gower himself, Chaucer is too old to write more love poetry of the sort that Amans's mistress dotes on—the *Troilus* that she loves hearing read aloud (iv. 2795).

Gower represents King Richard as commissioning the *Confessio*—much as he might have commissioned the Wilton Diptych: 'Som newe thing I scholde boke' (Prol. 51). We need not take this literally: it may be merely a variant of the modesty-formula still used by authors who claim that their friends have urged them to publish. But 'somme newe thinges' are just what Chaucer hopes to find in his journey in *The House of Fame*, a poem in the same metre as the *Confessio* and touching on some of the tales about false loves and the stellification of mortals that figure in Gower's poem. Gower is perhaps obliquely hinting at a friendly competition.

In telling the tale of Ceyx and Alcione, Gower is manifestly rivalling his friend Chaucer, who had used it as prologue to *The Book of the Duchess*. There the poet narrates the story as he found it in Ovid. It does not bring him the sleep he desires but Ovid's mention of Morpheus prompts him to make a decidedly quizzical vow, which does. For Gower's Amans, somnolence is a sin. When *he* retires to bed his heart remains with his mistress; he imagines her body, soft and warm, and when worn out he falls asleep, it is to dream of her. He would be content

> To meten evere of such a swevene[1]
> For thanne I hadde a slepi hevene   (iv. 2915–16)

> [1] *dream*

—a phrase that saves the passage from tedium.

Formally, the story that follows is but tenuously related to the general theme of love, though Gower inserts a typical motive not to be found in Ovid, or the *Ovide Moralisé* (which provided precedent for such *remaniement* as Gower practises, and on which Gower undoubtedly drew here and elsewhere): it is 'for the trowthe of love which in this worthy lady stod' that the gods transformed the pair into halcyon birds (iv. 3090). All the other changes that Gower makes are true to his poetic character. Thus Ceyx's voyage becomes a pilgrimage to procure a boon, and resolved on privately ('he thoghte in his corage') whereas in Ovid he at once broaches it to Alcyone. She now exacts from Ceyx a promise that he will return within two months; thus the speed of the narrative is quickened and the light octosyllabics convey this admirably. Ovid's ninety lines on the fatal storm are reduced to no more than:

> The tempeste of the blake cloude,
> The wode see, the windes loude. (3063–4)

The 'rainy cope' in which Iris descends, Ovid's *velamina mille colorum*, displays Gower's nice skill in epithets: elsewhere he says of the hypocrite feigning love-sickness that

> the colour of the reyni mone
> With medicine upon his face
> He set. (i. 692–4)

Ovid describes the branches of the tree near the cave of Sleep as 'non moti flamine rami', unmoved by breeze. Gower achieves the same effect differently:

> Ther stant no gret tree nyh aboute
> Wheron ther myhte crowe or pie[1]
> Alihte, forto clepe or crie (iv. 3000–2)

[1] *magpie*

—naming the birds that do not perch on small trees or bushes. The 'stille water' of the nearby brook answers to Ovid's echoic

> Rivus aquae Lethes per quem cum murmure labens
> Invitat somnos crepitantibus unda lapillis.*

He preserves the moody somnolence by such phrases as 'slepi eres', 'slombrende yhen [eyes]'. Fascinated as always by shape-shiftings, Gower gives ten lines to Morpheus, Ithecus, and Panthasas and

* *Met.* xi. In Dryden's *Fables* these lines appear as

> An arm of Lethe, with a gentle flow,
> . . .o'er the pebbles creeps,
> And with soft murmurs calls the coming sleeps.

assigns to the two last the visionary re-enactment of the fatal storm. But he preserves, or rather creates suspense by observing that such visions are 'otherwhile bot a jape' and Alcyone's maids assure her that dreams go by contraries.

To the actual metamorphosis, ignored by Chaucer, Gower devotes one fifth of his version—more, proportionately, than does Ovid himself. The birds' embraces become tokens of joy, and Alcyone shows as the true wife who serves her lord even though his shape has altered:

> Upon the joie which sche hadde
> Hire wynges bothe abrod sche spradde,
> And him, so as sche may suffise,
> Beclipte[1] and keste in such a wise,
> As sche was whilom[2] wont to do:
> Hire wynges for hire armes tuo
> Sche tok, and for hire lippes softe
> Hire harde bile, and so ful ofte
> Scho fondeth[3] in hire briddes forme,
> If that sche mihte hirself conforme
> To do the plesance of a wif,
> As sche dede in that other lif.   (iv. 3101–12)

[1] embraced   [2] formerly   [3] tries

Whether Gower had read *The Wife of Bath's Tale* before he set down his own version of the Loathly Bride is an open question. He claims to have read the story of Florent, whose bride turns out to be the daughter of the king of Sicily, in a chronicle, and there is no reason to doubt him. It has precisely the kind of transformation motif that attracted Gower to Ovid—the bride has been made into an ugly hag by a wicked stepmother. Florent is a victim of Fortune only because anyone who seeks knightly prowess runs risks. His *gentilesse* is of a sort superior to that of the Arthurian knight in Chaucer's tale. He never bewails his lot and keeps his word even though it means lying with this 'olde mone' (consort) in the blaze of torches.

What distinguishes Gower's narrative is a series of dialogues between the women of the tale and their victim. Extensive dialogue is rare in Gower, but here he handles it with assurance. It is crisp and varied, enlivened by records of visible responses: when Florent makes his promise the hag 'frounceth up the browe' (i. 1589). As the meditative, conscient knight he is cousin to Gawain and Troilus. We see him pondering the horns of his dilemma, 'casting his avauntage' (1575). He is a solitary, first as a prisoner (1424) and then as a 'knyght aventurous' (1522–3). In this too he is representative. Most of Gower's protagonists are shown in isolation. As Chaucer is the poet of society, his friend is the poet of solitude—which is why he puts his tales within the frame of private confession.

In contrast to Chaucer's 'outrageous' Arthurian knight, Florent takes his medicine—the figure is Gower's: 'his baldemoine with canele [gentian with cinnamon]' (1705)—like a man, or rather like a gentleman:

> He wolde algate his trowthe holde,
> As every knyht therto is holde
> What happ so evere him is befalle:
> Tho sche be the fouleste of alle
> Yet to th'onour of wommanhiede
> Him thoghte he scholde taken hiede.   (1715–20)

He actually goes beyond the terms of his pledge: setting the 'old mone' on his horse and making her as seemly as possible. His misery is expressed in a line that works with a beautiful economy:

> Florent his wofull heved[1] uplefte
> And syh this vecke[2] wher sche sat. . . .   (1674–5)

> [1] *head*   [2] *old woman*

The description that follows shows Gower exploiting to the full the topos of the Ugly Hag that appears in the *Roman de la Rose* (Elde) and *Gawain*. His similes are vivid: 'Sche loketh forth as doth a more' and 'lich unto the wollesak / Sche proferth hire'. Florent cannot bear to ride with her except

> as an owle fleth be nythe
> Out of alle othre briddes syhte   (1727–8)

—the one point of verbal identity with Chaucer's version. In the final scene, beautifully managed, two terms, 'purgatorie' (1776) and 'penance' (1799), give the clue to Florent's conduct. It is a religious test; and it is his sudden decision to go through with it to the point of fulfilling the marriage debt that works the miracle. Florent represents a wholly novel type of Romance hero, indeed he is unique; but Gower can properly put him alongside Tristram and Lancelot in his forty-third *Balade* because like them, though in radically different circumstances, he kept his pledge.

The unobtrusiveness of Gower's narrative art has also led to his poetic achievement being undervalued. In this unemphatic understatement he is typically English. He never raises his voice, nor do his characters. He seems to go out of his way to avoid surprise or shock. Of a false bachelor's miserable death he says merely 'that supplant hath his juise' (ii. 2781)—he got what was coming to him. When

Orestes sets out against Aegisthus the narrator comments 'I trowe
Egiste him schal repente' (iii. 2038). He is in fact to suffer a horrid
death. 'Cam non of hem to londe dreie' (ii. 1828) is Gower's way of saying that all were drowned. In the tale of Constance, when Alla receives
the forged letter about his child 'he maketh the messenger no chiere'
(ii. 991): we have to deduce his astonishment and grief. When his
wife's innocence had been strikingly proved by divine intervention he

> took it into remembrance
> And thoghte more than he seide.   (ii. 894–5)

'Thoghte more than he/she seide' is a tag found in at least one earlier
romance (*Kyng Alisaunder*, 7672) but in Gower it becomes almost a
refrain. His characters are meditatives. Ovid's Ceyx tells Alcyone
plainly that he will go to Delphi; Gower simply says:

> [He] thoghte in his corage
> To gon upon a pelrinage.   (iv. 2937–8)

His Rosiphelee

> stod al one stille
> To thenke what was in hir wille.   (iv. 1295–6)

The interior monologue as found in Chrétien or in Chaucer's *Troilus*
has no place here. It is as if the poet is insisting that none can know
'the privetes of mannes herte', except God:

> Thei speke and sounen in his ere
> As thogh thei lowde wyndes were.   (i. 2807–8)

Of a piece with this is his comment after Jason has seen Medea: 'I not
[know not] hou Jason that nyht slep' (v. 3403). And the refusal to con-
jecture, to particularize can result in flatness. The tale of Acis and
Galatea concludes with an allusion to Polyphemus:

> For his envie and for his hate
> Thei [the gods] were wrothe.   (ii. 199–200)

But how the gods showed their wrath he will not say.

Gower's humour is so muted that one easily overlooks it. It is a mere
glint, a flicker: as when Amans thanks Genius for telling him the tale of
tree-bound Daphne:

> Mi fader, grant merci of this:
> Bot while I se my ladi is
> No tre, but halt hire oghne forme
> Ther mai no man me so enforme[1].   (iii. 1729–32)

[1] *instruct*

The reticence goes with a simple style that professedly eschews elaborate rhetoric (though he shows knowledge of rhetorical figures in Book vii), claiming that

> I no Rethoriqe have used
> Upon the forme of[1] eloquence,
> For that is not of mi science;
> Bot I have do my trewe peyne
> With rude wordes and with pleyne
> To speke of thing which I have told.   (viii. 3064–9)

> [1] *so as to display*

We must not take such disclaimers too seriously. He is by no means a *naïf* and he abounds in commonplaces of literary origin. Thus in the Prologue we find the figures of the World Upside Down (see above, pp. 14–15) extended for several pages, of man the microcosm (946–7), of the 'mean' between 'lust' and 'lore' (18). The numerous incidental classical allusions to (e.g.) the fires of Etna and the gold of Croesus are also part of the *colores rhetorici*. But Gower prefers the gnomic to the elaborate, plain narrative to the picturesque. Genius speaks always in proverbial figures and expressions: 'Old senne newe schame' (iii. 2033), 'unknowe, unkist'; Sloth, he says,

> . . . liveth al upon his wisshes,
> And as a cat wolde ete fisshes
> Withoute wettinge of his cles[1]
> So wolde he do. . . .   (iv. 1107–10)

> [1] *claws*

That such phrases appear also in the Latin rubrics (e.g. *furatoque prius ostia claudit equo* at the beginning of Book iv*) is one reason for thinking that these are Gower's. They suggest that the poet had reached an age when he did not spurn the proverbial commonplace. One is constantly reminded of Crabbe, whose *Tales* E. M. Forster saw as essentially gnomic: a poet 'so slow-moving, yet so difficult to catch . . . a narrator whose narratives are seldom diversified by anything dramatic'; whose puns and epigrams—'those tiny dramas inside a sentence'—are not quite good enough; yet against them put his moral values, his judiciousness, his occasional surprises: 'He succeeds more frequently than could have been anticipated.'† As a narrator, Gower is, in fact, a Crabbe in octosyllabics managing his couplet just as deftly as Crabbe controls his. They both typify Reason and Restraint.

---

* Gower uses this proverb later in the book (ll. 901–3): 'for whan the grete stiede / Is stole, thanne he taketh hiede, / And makth the stable dore fast.'

† *The Listener*, 53 (1955), 1039.

Gower's rhymed octosyllabics allow little room for rhetorical flourishes, which would disturb their even flow, like that of the

> stille water, for the nones
> Rennende upon the smale stones   (iv. 3009–10)

which in the cave of Morpheus as he describes it 'giveth great appetite
to sleep'. The verses themselves are soporific only if we read continuously; medieval readers would perhaps have been satisfied with a tale
or two at a time. The element common to most of the tales is the
language of love, as popularized by the *Roman* and a hundred
romances. Amans is well nigh slain by Danger (i. 2443). Cupid shoots
with his golden arrow (i. 144). Orestes speaks of the draught (potion) of
love that deadens honorable feeling (iii. 2057). Lovers are 'poursuiantz
fro yeer to yere / In loves court' (ii. 239–40)—a recurrent image.
Amans vows perpetual service: 'I unto my lyves ende . . . wole hir
serven everemo.' (iii. 1734–5.)

But even these *courtois* sentiments are set down in simple terms
befitting the lightly moving couplets. The language is never rarefied,
often homely. Gower seems to have had a special liking for ships and
the sea and sailors' language. He pictures the Greeks withdrawing to
their ships before Troy:

> And crossen seil and made hem yare
> Anon as thogh thei wolden fare: (i. 1165–6)

'To cross sail', i.e. to set the sails across the yards, is a phrase not
found elsewhere before Berners. Gower is the first to use the phrase
'ride at anchor' (ii. 1136) after the *Beowulf* poet. When he specifies a
'galeie' (ii. 2542) it is because he associates that craft with the Medi-
terranean. Most of Gower's metaphors—they are few enough—are
nautical:

> . . . whanne he berth lowest the seil
> Thanne is he swiftest to beguile.   (i. 704–5)

Unusually elaborate is Genius' figure of Fals Semblant:

> Ther is noman so wys that knoweth
> Of thilke flod which is the tyde,
> Ne how he scholde himselven guide
> To take sauf passage there.
> And yit the wynd to mannes ere
> Is softe, and as it semeth oute
> It makth clier weder al aboute. . . .

The barge Envy ever holds off from the land:

> Wher Fals-Semblant with ore on honde
> It roweth, and wol noght arive,
> Bot let it on the wawes dryve
> In gret tempeste and gret debat. . . . (ii. 1882–907)*

It would be an exaggeration to call Gower an English Ovid, but he at least gives us more of Ovid in English than any other poet before the sixteenth century—Caxton's Ovid, only reconstructed in this century, being a prose version of a French text that drew heavily on a moralized version of the *Metamorphoses*. He is next in line to those fourteenth-century classicizing friars who had turned to classical mythology,† which is found allied with the exegesis of Ovid in Thomas Walsingham's commentary. Gower has a long excursus on classical divinities in Book v. But the medieval Ovid, Gower's Ovid, was not simply a storehouse of classical lore. He was praised as (*inter alia*) *sententiarum floribus repletus*—'full of high sentence'. The annotations to Sandys's edition of 1632 reflect that estimate.

Gower's role is Ovidian in another sense. Just as Ovid drew on earlier metamorphoses and various Greek and Latin *epyllia*, so Gower ranged beyond Ovid for some details of his stories, and like Ovid allowed himself digressions from the main theme. But that the main theme is love we are never able to forget. True, not all *metamorphoses* are love stories in the usual sense; yet they all appeal, if subconsciously, to a sexual element in the reader.

Even the purely topical allusions to Richard and his kingdom at the opening and closing of the Confessio have Ovidian antecedent in the closing lines of prophecy that 'when Augustus has given peace to the world he will turn his mind to civic justice, be a most righteous author of laws and guide morality by his own example'. These are the very terms that Gower applied to Richard. In the *Vox Clamantis*, as in the Prologue to the *Confessio* (37) he saw London as 'new Troy'; Britain and Rome had a common Trojan origin, and the manners and government of imperial Rome were a precedent to look to. Beyond all this there is a striking similarity of role and achievement: both the classical and the medieval poet present an all-embracing personal interpretation of classical mythology. The frames may sometimes crack at the joints but in general they both make out of the diverse elements of their fables a successful unity.

---

* Genius resorts to similar figures elsewhere; cf. i. 1064, ii. 2380, 2494.

† See Beryl Smalley, *English Friars and Antiquity in the Early Fourteenth Century* (Oxford, 1960).

Like Ovid, Gower provides a philosophical element or envelope
that is not obviously integrated into the main concerns of the poem.
Ovid's first 150 lines give an account of Creation and of the ages of
Gold, Silver, Brass, and Iron not unlike Gower's account in his
Prologue. In Ovid the strife of the elements is reconciled by God and
a kindlier Nature: 'hanc deus et melior litem natura diremit' (i. 21)—
where *deus* is the Zeus of the philosophers rather than the Jupiter of
Mythology. These are the two forces that Gower sees at work in all
the operations of the world.* Similarly Ovid's last book ends with
four hundred lines of Pythagorean speculation. Though Gower's
closing lines do not echo these, they do lift us in the same way
beyond the petty and impermanent human loves to the eternal
kingdom.

Yet in the Middle Ages the *Metamorphoses* was the least read of
Ovid's works. It was the *Ars Amatoria* and *Remedia Amoris* that were
glossed in a way to make them acceptable to popes and mystics. The
psychology of love inherent in the *Confessio* (and in the *Roman de la
Rose*) owes much indirectly to this 'amorous' Ovid. And like Chaucer,
Gower drew on the *Heroides*: his story of Demophon and Phillis
(iv. 731 ff.) is drawn partly on *Heroides* ii, and includes an allusion to
Ars Amatoria. In his version of Dido's tale she writes a letter to Aeneas,
just as she does in *Heroides* vii. More important, the *Heroides* were read
in the Middle Ages as an ethical work that could be shown to
commend that chaste and 'honeste' love that Gower approved. Such a
love is Penelope's for a husband who in Gower represents the sin of
Sloth, whereas Phillis's love for Demophon is foolish: *stultus amor*, as a
gloss on the *Heroides* epistle says. The contrast with Chaucer's treatment in *The Legend of Good Women* is striking.

Only one earlier vernacular poem offers likenesses to Gower's long
and wide-ranging composition. The *Roman de la Rose* has the same
professed theme, the same variety of learned and historical digressions, and likewise resorts to Ovid for its *exempla* (notably those of
Pygmalion, Medea, Narcissus, Phillis). And it is to the *Roman* that
Gower owes the figure of Genius, his priest-confessor. Yet whereas in
Jean de Meun his association with Nature is with the principle of
fecundity, of plenitude, for Gower he is the priest of 'charité', who tells
such a story as that of Constantine and Sylvester to show

> How charité mai helpe a man
> To bothe worldes. . . .   (ii. 3498–9)

---

* *Vox Clamantis*, vii. 525 ff. shows Gower applying to Adam the lines on the creation
of man in *Met*. i. 76–88.

He favours procreation, but within Christian marriage: a maiden
ought to marry young:

> Whyl sche the charge myhte bere
> Of children, whiche the world forbere
> Ne mai, but if it scholde faile.　　　　(iv. 1495–7)

The title of Gower's poem must be read as his contemporaries
would read it. The lover is a penitent who has committed six of the
capital sins relating to love. The traditional doctrine of penance called
for contrition, confession, and satisfaction. It had been promulgated
by the Church with increasing vigour ever since the Fourth Lateran
Council (1215) and every reader would take the point of Gower's adaptation. Handbooks had enjoined self-examination; the role of the
priest was not only investigative but therapeutic. This in itself provided a point of contact with the love-literature in which love figures
as a sickness. 'Tell thi maladie', says Venus at the outset: 'if thou feign-
est / I can do the no medicine' (i. 164 ff.) (cf. the rubric for the first
confession). Both passages are echoed at the close, where Venus
advises Amans:

> 'If thou thin hele wolt pourchace,
> Thou miht noght make suite and chace
> Wher that the game is nought pernable[1]'　　(viii. 2929–31)

[1] catchable

and where the poet takes his 'final leave':

> now for everemore
> Withoute makynge any more
> Of love and of his dedly hele,
> Which no phisicien can hele.　　(viii. 3153 ff.)

The resort to *exempla* to drive home the evils of particular sins we have
found in *Handlyng Synne* (see pp. 41–7 above), the *Ayenbite of Inwyt*,
and many other penitential works. Meanwhile the humble penitential
lover, seeking for grace, had appeared in Chrétien's *Lancelot* and
Andreas Capellanus's *De Amore*. Andreas converts the sins of the confessional into the sins of love: *avarice*, *chastity*, *envy*, *falsehood*, *pride*, etc.
In the *Roman de la Rose* Jean de Meun sets out the commandments of
love. But Jean's Genius is really the creation of Alanus, who in his *De
Planctu Naturae* had used the imagery of excommunication without the
faintest hint of parody. Natura's complaint has a counterpart in
Gower's Prologue, and his Venus refers to it when speaking of those
who act against Nature, 'wherof that sche ful ofte hath pleigned'
(viii. 2341). In short, Gower accepts Alanus's scheme of moral values,

whilst pursuing the possibilities of presenting Genius as confessor, making him very much a fourteenth-century priest, combining the offices of preacher and confessor, confidant, and didactic narrator. Secrecy was the very essence of the confessional, as it was of the courtly code; on the other hand the relation between priest and penitent was ideally as close as that between father and son. Confession in its religious as well as in its Jungian sense is based on the truth that we conceal things that are dark or stupid and attach guilt to them just because they are secret. It provides a release of suppressed emotion which in Jung's phrase has 'a wonderfully healing effect'. Of this Gower was instinctively aware.

Gower's nominalizing of the branches of the sins by giving (usually) five *species* to each has been described as pedantic. But it probably merely reflects contemporary feeling for numerology as we see it in Gawain's pentangle. Gower had used the same number-pattern in his *Mirour de l'omme* (where the Sins make a processional appearance).

Though the Capital Sins form a Christian category, they figure in pre-Christian literature, and Gower the Ovidian would note passages in which Sins are associated with wicked or unsuccessful love: Ovid's Aegisthus became an adulterer because he was slothful and lived in idleness (*desidiosus erat, Remedia Amoris*, 161–2). Gower does not so describe him; but he does make an *exemplum* on homicide, a branch of Wrath, out of the story (iii. 1906 ff.). There were moral as well as miraculous elements common to Ovid's tales and those that Genius told.

Though Gower's Genius first presents himself as Venus's priest, assigned to deal with matters 'touchende of love' (i. 236), he qualifies this at once:

> Bot natheles, for certein skile[1]
> I mot algate[2] and nedes[3] wile
> Noght only make my spekynges
> Of love, bot of othre thinges
> That touchen to the cause of vice.
> For that belongeth to th'office
> Of prest, whos ordre that I bere
>
> . . . . .
>
> It sit[4] a prest to be wel thewed[5],
> And schame it is if he be lewed.

[1] *reason*   [2] *must in any case*   [3] *of necessity*   [4] *is proper for*
[5] *virtuous*

Thus his didactic role is clear from the outset; and explains if it does not justify the long excursus in Book v on the religions of the world:

a topic eminently proper for a priest. When he describes the five senses (i. 296 ff.) he refers to the potential dangers to the soul before speaking 'in loves kinde' (i. 309). The decorum of the poem (like that of Chaucer's *Parlement*) forbids specifically Christian reference within the strictly confessional framework: the considered account of the Christian faith in Book v (where one notes the insistence that 'Crist wroghte ferst and after tawhte', v. 1825) is hung on the 'branch' of Avarice, besetting sin of the contemporary Church. But the ultimate appeal at all points is to 'the high God':

> men scholde obeie
> The hihe god which weldeth al
> And evere hath don and evere schal.   (v. 1630–2)

In Alanus Genius is associated with procreative Nature. But as a priest Genius stands for Measure and Reason. He is concerned with the vices in general as well as those to which lovers are prone. Thus he devotes some fifty lines to Avarice before turning to the penitent and enjoining him to 'Tell if thou farst *of love* so' (v. 59). Later *exempla* return to the theme of Avarice in an almost obsessive way, and are applied to Amans:

> My sone, loke thou despende,
> Wherof thou myht thiself amende
> Bothe hier and ek in other place [sc. heaven].
>
> (v. 399–401)

Likewise in Book iv, Sloth is made the occasion for a discourse on its corresponding virtue, Activity, and in particular intellectual and literary activity; the apparent digression being linked to the main theme by a reference to the learned poet Ovid, who taught (in the *Remedia Amoris*)

> if love be to hot
> In what manere it scholde akiele[1].   (iv. 2670–1)

[1] *cool*

In the relation between Genius and Nature, as Jean de Meun presents them, we have not so much a parody of Christian forms of religion as of the forms of the religion of love. Genius's role is indeterminate: he behaves almost comically yet his doctrine is seriously intended. Certainly he loses some of the dignity he has in Alanus's *De Planctu Naturae*. And Gower too, by making Genius the priest of Venus, whilst keeping his prime association with *Natura*, and at the same time making him the mouthpiece of a Christian code, shows him as ambivalent. Glossing the *exemplum* of Rosiphelee, Genius says:

> My ladi Venus, whom I serve
> What womman wole hire thonk deserve,
> Sche mai noght thilke love eschuie
> Of paramours, bot sche mot suie[1]
> Cupides lawe; and natheles
> Men sen such love sielde[2] in pes,
> That it nys evere upon aspie
> Of janglinge, and of fals envie,
> Ful ofte medlid[3] with disese;
> But thilke love is wel at ese,
> Which set is upon mariage;
> For that dar schewen the visage
> In alle places openly.   (iv. 1468–79)

> [1] *follow*   [2] *seldom*   [3] *mingled*

Nothing in the tale itself demands this gloss.

Equally innovative and equally striking is the role Genius assumes as the mouthpiece of Reason. He constantly appeals to the logical, the ratiocinative element in the lover: 'It is unreasonable to worship the elements, which are men's servants' (v. 761; cf. 837 and Latin headlink, 748).

> And if a man him wolde avise
> Of that befell to Vulcanus
> Him oghte of reson thenke thus:
> That sithe a god therof was schamed
> Wel scholde an erthli man be blamed.   (v. 720–4)

'Schame is it if [a priest] be lewed', Genius had said at the outset (i. 274). He praises 'thise olde wise' (iv. 2340) in terms strikingly similar to those of Chaucer at the opening of *The Legend of Good Women*. Wisdom is learnt in the Schools (iv. 2348), and scholastic learning is closely linked with Divinity:

> Of every wisdom the parfit
> The hyhe God of his spirit
> Yaf to the men in erthe hiere
> Upon the forme and the matiere
> Of that he wolde make hem wise;
> And thus cam in the ferste apprise[1]
> Of bokes and of alle goode. . . .   (iv. 2363–9)

> [1] *teaching*

The scholastic distinction between form and matter is according to Reason: a man may seem to be 'gentil' by birth:

> Bot nothing after the matiere
> For who that Resoun understonde,
> Upon richesse it mai noght stonde.   (iv. 2212–14)

As the gloss says, using similar scholastic phrases: 'cuius veritatem questionis Confessor *per singula* dissoluit'. Gentilesse grows

> after the condicion
> Of resonable entencion
> The which out of the soule groweth. (iv. 2269–71)

It is Reason that forbids us to worship the cruel and sinful Hercules as a god (v. 1101–2) or to call Diana the goddess of hills, trees, and wells (v. 1273 ff.). The Will acts well or badly according as Reason guides it: it is

> noght wel assised[1]
> Whan Wit and Reson ben aweie
> And that Folhaste is in the weie. (iii. 1866–8)

> [1] *placed*

So Donne will say of Ann Drury, in the *Second Anniversary*: 'reason still / Did not o'erthrow, but rectify her will'. If Alexander acted according to Reason, says Diogenes, he would not be so eager to conquer the world (iii. 1203 ff.). Amans admits that Reason demands that he should eschew the vice of envy (ii. 3155–6, cf. 3165). Reason sets a measure to love, and a man (or a god or a goddess)—Iphis (iv. 3517 ff.), or Cupid, or Venus (iv. 1414)—ignores it to his harm, or hers. It distinguishes man from beasts, whereas passion, jealousy, made Polyphemus dash about Etna

> As it were a wilde beste
> The whom no reson mihte areste. (ii. 161–2)

Gower's Genius is such a composite figure that he cannot be presented in wholly priestly terms; and this limitation, it must be admitted, affects also his presentation of Amans, and the very tone of the poem. Yet within the confessional framework there is much greater freedom and variety than might be expected. When, for example, Amans denies that he has ever been idle in love, Genius asks for proof positive of his *besischipe*, which prompts a revelation of his daily thoughts and actions. The nearest he ever gets to his mistress is when escorting her to mass (one thinks of meetings described in the Provençal *Flamenca*, which also has a church setting):

> Whan I, that mai noght fiele hir bare
> May lede hire clothed in myn arm:
> Bot afterward it doth me harm
> Of pure ymaginacioun . . .

> ... mi besi thoght
> Is torned ydel into nought
>
> .   .   .   .   .   .
>
> I pleie with hire litel hound,
> Nou on the bedd, now on the ground,
> Now with hir briddes in the cage. . . .   (iv. 1140 ff.)

It is a charming series of miniatures, and if we do not, like G. C. Macaulay, here see the mistress as a creature of flesh *and blood*, we at least have a sense of her fleshly presence.

And Amans can slide from the role of penitent to that of interlocutor. When Genius would pass over the genealogy of some of the gods because 'to long it were forto rime' (v. 1370), Amans agrees, yet would fain know more of Venus and Cupid 'which stant in alle mennes speche'. The sequel shows that Genius is in fact embarrassed because the pagan Venus had stood for lechery and prostitution, and Cupid for blind unreason. This is what the lover will eventually prove on himself:

> Lo, thus blindly the world sche diemeth
> In loves cause, as to me siemeth.
>
> (viii. 2385–6; cf. 3145–6)

Genius acknowledges that to believe in the pagan Venus is 'foul mescreance'. This may seem to put him in an anomalous position. But he will eventually make it clear both that his goddess is not the classical goddess of love (cf. viii. 2392) and that, in associating the classical goddess with sheer desire, the ancients were not wrong. Ultimately Genius's stance is congruous with belief in an over-ruling Providence. It is God who puts limits to Perseus's prosperity:

> For God, which alle thing hath bounded
> And sih the falshod of his guile
> Hath set him bot a litel while   (ii. 1754–6)

—and overthrows Capaneus:

> Godd tok himselve the bataille
> Ayein[1] his pride. . . .   (i. 2000–1)

[1] *against*

Surquidrie sin because he gives no thanks to God, 'which alle grace sendeth' (i. 1902: cf. i. 1235 ff.). Equally congruous is Genius's criticism of simony and other corruption within the Church and the four orders (*CA* i. 608 ff.).

Love *par amours*, now called 'courtly love', has its place in Genius's tales, but there is never the slightest hint that Amans is courting a married woman. 'Honest amour', which does not arise from lust or avarice and which issues in marriage and the begetting of children, is Gower's ideal in all his poetry: what is now called courtly love was for him *gallicum peccatum*, the French vice. The phrase marks a distinctively English attitude. Amans lives in a cool English climate, not the sultry heat of Boccaccio's Florence or Naples or Flamenca's Provence.

Peace, not Passion, is Gower's watchword. He devoted a lengthy and moving poem to it when a new king came to the English throne; but it is espoused at the very beginning of the *Confessio*. The Prologue to that work concludes with the *exemplum* of Arion and his harp taken from Ovid's *Fasti*. It foreshadows the pattern that the main poem will take. Arion's music made peace between wolf and lamb, hound and hare—would to God such a harpist could today bring peace! Gower is modestly hinting that this is part of his own purpose. He will return to the theme, speaking *in voce auctoris*, at intervals throughout the work. It was only when money came into use that

> wente pes out of the weie
> And werre cam on everi side
> Which alle love leide aside.   (v. 12–13)

The avaricious man does not, properly speaking, own wealth: 'For good hath *him*, and halt him teid' (property ties him down) (v. 52). Amans himself is seeking peace. When asked whether he has been guilty of Contek (strife), he confesses (iii. 1121 ff.) that the pangs of love have wrought strife within his heart 'whan I my wittes over-wende', and when Fortune turns her wheel the wrong way he grows desperate:

> And thus upon myself the werre
> I bringe, and putte out alle pes.   (iii. 1150–1)

Wit and Reason join forces against Will and Hope, in vain. The whole passage presents a typical thematic cluster, and Genius's ambivalent comment is equally characteristic: the law of love is indeed powerful, 'so miht thou thee the betre excuse'; none the less Desire must be governed by Reason: witness the tale of Pyramus and Thisbe—which, however, Genius retells with a rare intensity. Ovid has no equivalent to Thisbe's outburst:

> O, thou, which cleped[1] art Venus,
> Goddesse of love, and thou, Cupide,
> Which loves cause hast forto guide
> I wot now wel that ye be blinde. . . .   (iii. 1462 ff.)

[1] *called*

It is the very charge that earns Henryson's Cresseid the wrath of all the gods.

The themes that cluster together in the passage just cited belong to a group that is distinctly Gowerian, consisting of five concepts, often with their opposites: Love and Charité as opposed to Lust and Will (i.e. self-will, Jung's 'Libido'); Peace and Rest as opposed to War and Discord; Reason and Wit as against 'unreason'—folly and passion; Nature or Kind, and Mortality; Fortune and Necessity (but with Providence guiding them). Hints of these themes appear in the Prologue, though that is built mainly round the topos of the World Upside Down—hence there the priesthood is depicted as improperly concerned with war, and neglecting charity (212 ff.).* It is the lack of love and charity that is the occasion for the long excursus on the Empires of the World. The wheel that 'blinde Fortune overthroweth [i.e. turns]' (139) is later linked with 'Purveiance' (560 ff.) and Necessity (797). Death (due to the war of Nature's four elements, 'warring', in Marlowe's phrase, 'within our breasts for regiment') is ordained by Kind (978).

The presence of the theme of love hardly needs documenting. The *Confessio* is in one sense—though not in Ovid's, or Jean de Meun's (it assumes an audience less sophisticated, less cynical than theirs)—an *Ars Amatoria*. It reveals the lover's hopes and fears, but differs from the *Roman* in not registering his progress allegorically: indeed he makes no progress worth registering. His language is often Ovidian, more often 'courtois'. The priest describes the loves of Mars for Venus in contemporary terms:

> As he which was chivalerous
> It fell him to ben amerous   (v. 653–4)

whilst admitting that love 'makth curteis of the vilein' (iv. 2300).

For Gower peace is a very positive virtue, identified with the heavenly *Visio Pacis* in the Conclusion and in the tale of the Three Questions (i. 3275 ff.), in which the Virgin Mary's humility is named as the virtue that 'bodeth' peace. Amans is remarkable in his reluctance to spill heathen blood, urging dominical precept and practical reasons:

> This finde I writen, hou Crist bad
> That noman other scholde sle.
> What[1] scholde I winne over the se,
> If I mi lady loste at hom?
> Bot passe thei the salte fom

---

* The passage reflects the growing uneasiness at the interminable French wars.

To whom Crist bad thei scholden preche
To al the world and his feith teche.

. . . . .

A Sarazin if I sle schal,
I sle the soule forth withal,
And that was nevere Cristes lore². (iv. 1662–81)

¹ *why* ² *teaching*

And he proceeds (for once) to turn the tables on the Confessor by
citing the *exemplum* of Achilles and Polyxena (iv. 1694 ff.). Gower's
preoccupation with this virtue is constant, showing nowhere more
clearly than in the special colour he gives to *strife*, its antonym, which
becomes a doublet for trouble, pain, or distress: typical is the tale of
Dido, who commits suicide 'for to stinten al this strif'—to put an end
to her sorrow—'and thus sche gat hireselve reste' (iv. 132–6). Amans,
at his most desperate, says:

upon miself the werre
I bringe, and putte out alle pes . . .
So that of contek and of strif
I am beknowe. . . . (iii. 1150–5)

It is Gower's love of peace and quiet that makes him the poet of early
dawns and nights steeped in silence. He is drawn to stories like that of
Medea secretly gathering herbs by night, and tells that tale superbly
(v. 3241 ff.). He sees the Trojan horse under a night sky:

whan the blake wynter nyht
Withoute mone or sterre lyht
Bederked hath the water stronde,
Al prively thei gon to londe. (i. 1167–70)

Night too is the time for love's 'silence and coverte', the phrase in
Cephalus's moving prayer to Phebus (and Diana).

And thus whan that thi liht is faded
And Vesper scheweth him alofte
And that the nyht is long and softe,
Under the cloudes derke and stille
Than hath this thing most of his wille. (iv. 3208–12)

It is by night that Pygmalion's statue comes to life, that Iris and Iphis
make love, and Phillis watches for Demophon.

War, on the other hand, Gower depicts in the direst terms as the
worst result of the Fall: at the taking of Troy

thei that wende pees
Tho myhten finde no reles
Of thilke swerd which al devoureth. (i. 1187–9)

The implicit *moralitas* of the tale of the False Bachelor, in which the Emperor's young son goes off to the 'dedli werres' (ii. 2520 ff.), is that the desire for martial fame brings about death. 'To lead a land in peace' is to govern justly (cf. iv. 2046–7). Those who indulge in Contek, says Genius, 'knowe not the God of lif' (iii. 1107). He takes pleasure in the story of a war that does not take place because the disputants seek 'peace and grith' (iii. 1847). Private feuds and quarrels ('chestes') that 'maketh werre at beddes hedde', between husband and wife, are censured as severely as war.

Most pervasive is the theme of 'Kind'. The term itself, in its numerous senses and inflections, occurs, one would guess, more often than in any other poet except Alanus: it represents a dynamic force, even a grotesque force that is far removed from Wordsworth's placid Nature. It is the *vis*, the human energy, that is extinguished at death, when life loses its 'kindly hete' (ii. 2740). The law of Nature is ordained by God, the rule that Dame Nature imposes on her creatures to ensure that her procreative purposes are fulfilled.

Description of external Nature as the Romantics perceived it finds little place in Gower—or for that matter in Chaucer. Rosiphelee (iv. 1295) sees

> the swote floures springe,
> She herde glade foules singe.

But this account of a summer morning only becomes vivid when she sees 'the beasts in their kind', the buck and the doe, hart and hind, 'the madle [male] go with the femele'. What happens 'by way of kind' can hardly be altered: Constantine's leprosy is curable only because it 'of accidence and not be weie of kinde is falle' (ii. 3211).

The last of the threads that bind the poem, and Genius's *exempla*, together is that of Fate and Fortune. It was 'as fortune scholde falle' that Thisbe dropped her wimple (iii. 1395–6; cf. 'unhap', 1466). It was Fortune that led Midas to repent (v. 314). It was 'as hire infortune scholde' that Phillis granted Demophon his desires (iv. 769). Yet as in Dante (whom Chaucer followed) this fortune is executrix of Providence. Perseus in his *hubris* rides over the frozen Danube 'thurgh Goddes ordenance', whereupon

> the blinde whiel
> Which torneth ofte er men be war,
> Thilke ys which that the horsmen bar
> Tobrak   (ii. 1822–5)

—where the echoic verb is itself effectively broken off from the rest of the sentence. (It is noteworthy that Gower is the last poet of Southern

England to use OE *wyrd* (Fate, Destiny—or in the plural, the Fates): iii. 1819, iv. 2765.) The force of Fate is to be felt behind every instance of destinal 'shal' (a verb regularly coupled also with Fortune): 'May no man fle that schal betide' (ii. 2860: cf. iv. 1524).

As the poem develops Gower establishes a nexus between all his cherished themes. This is nowhere better illustrated than in the *exemplum* of the Wars and Death of Alexander (iii. 2438–80):

> Which hadde set al his entente,
> So as *Fortune* with him wente
> That *Reson* mihte him non governe,
> Bot of his *will* he was so sterne
> That al the world he overran
>
> . . . . . .
>
> And in such wise as he hath wroght
> In destorbance of worldes *pes*,
> His werre he fond thanne endeles,
> In which for evere desconfit
> He was. Lo now, for what profit
> Of werre it helpeth forto ryde
>
> . . . . . .
>
> For every lif which reson can
> Oghth wel to knowe that a man
> Ne scholde thurgh no tirannie
> Lich to these othre bestes die,
> Til *Kinde* wolde for him sende.

They are brought together also in the long final story of Apollonius of Tyre, that tale of violence, treachery, love, and 'pité' which is the source of Shakespeare's *Pericles*. When after all the storms, shipwrecks, separations, and vicissitudes of Fortune (which 'hath evere be muable'), the family is reunited in concord, the Confessor remarks:

> Lo, what it is to be wel grounded;
> For he hath ferst his love founded
> Honesteliche as forto wedde,
> Honesteliche his love he spedde
>
> . . . . . .
>
> And in ensample his lif was write,
> That alle lovers myhten wite
> How ate laste it schal be sene
> Of love what thei wolden mene.
> For se now on that other side,
> Antiochus with al his Pride,
> Which sette his love *unkindely*,
> His ende he hadde al sodeinly,

Set *ayein kinde* upon vengance,
And for his lust hath his penance.   (viii. 1993–2008)

These themes, appearing both in the priest's *exempla* and in his didactic discourses, give a unity to the whole work. They are woven
together in the long and weighty epilogue that runs for a thousand
lines. Amans is healed by Venus, and the fiery dart of love is removed.
He sees his face 'riveled' with age, and is told by Venus to go 'ther
moral vertu duelleth' (there is a marvellous moment of nostalgia and
melancholy when, lying in a swoon 'ne fully quik ne fully ded', he sees
Cupid with his music and all the companies of those lovers whose
stories, happy and unhappy, he has heard). But as the goddess rises to
the heavens, Amans goes 'homward' and prays for England, for
concord and peace in all estates.

10

Langland

It has taken a long time for the *Liber de Petro Plowman*, Langland's *Piers Plowman*, to come into its own—at least for it to come into its own as a poem: it has long been quoted by social and economic historians as illustrating fourteenth-century life with greater particularity than Chaucer does; and in the sixteenth century it attracted notice, and reached print, because its complaints, its satire, its predictions (notably in a messianic passage that was misread as justifying Henry VIII's role in the suppression of monasteries) seemed to anticipate the reformers' polemic. There is to be sure plenty of protest in this poem, but that does not make its author a Protestant before his time. Rather, in every sense he is the most Catholic of poets. No poet, not even Dante, drew so much on the teaching, patristic and other, of Holy Church. No poet, not even Traherne, cared so little for the 'dirty devices' of the world of men and so much for the phenomenal world of Nature, including the marvels of conception, which figure in the great vision of Middle Earth (ix. 315 ff.*). No poet, not even David Jones, found in the calendar of the liturgical year such a fit framework for his faith.† So *Piers Plowman* stands out as the greatest testament of faith in English. In this vernacular work the creative conceptions of medieval religion are more truly assimilated than they are in any other single theological or philosophical work. If it cannot strictly be called an epic—though to be sure E. M. W. Tillyard begins with it his study of English Epic—it is of epic proportions: Northrop Frye‡ cites it as the first major English treatment of 'contrast-epic', revolving round two opposite poles, Salvation and Resurrection, sombre judgement and Antichrist. These contrasts do appear at turning points in the narrative, but no single image will convey the articulation of the poem: it is *sui generis*.

Which is not to say that the poet—like the Blake of the Prophetic

---

* Unless stated otherwise, references are to the B text of the poem (ed. W. W. Skeat).

† W. H. Auden (*The Mint*, ii (1948), 4) claimed that Langland, Dante, and Pope, in that order, were the greatest influences on his work. But the influence only shows directly in Auden's fondness for the alliterative line. Of earlier poets, Skelton shows some relish for his satiric vein.

‡ Northrop Frye, *Anatomy of Criticism* (Princeton, 1957), 318.

Books—stands remote from the poetry of his time. The poetry of his time was often, like his, alliterative and, like his, often concerned with religious and social themes. The first version of *Piers Plowman* (the 'A text') was probably finished before Chaucer had written a line, and the second (the 'B text') before he had written any major work. Even more than Chaucer this poet is rooted in England, though his sense of Christendom saves him from ever being insular. He presents the dreamer of his opening lines as sleeping on Malvern hills, 'for mountains counted', as a later poet wrote: the properest place, Virginia Woolf perceived, to gain a panoramic vista of the coloured counties. But within the dream we are soon immersed in the noise and bustle of London streets, the busy hum and urgency of Westminster's court and parliament, alleys peopled by priests and piemen, Clarice of Cockslane, Godfrey of Garlickhithe, Cheapside scavengers: characters far more workaday than Blake's enigmatic Theotormon or Palamabron or the Bromion who makes 'Hampstead, Highgate, Finchley, Hendon, Muswell Hill rage loud', and closer to the Londoners of *Bartholomew Fair*. Though the earlier poet's world is, or merges into, a world of visions, he never loses sight either of that 'fair field full of folk'—the open field in which on a fine May morning he sees all the villagers at work—or of the Westminster that is the heart and centre of the realm: at the very end of the poem, darkly apocalyptic in tone as it is, we have a brief glimpse of folk making off to that city, still hoping to live there on borrowed money.

This juxtaposition of vision and actuality is, first and last, the unique feature of *Piers Plowman* and of the Christianity that it bodies forth: the visions themselves present actuality as much as they embody speculation and theological mysteries. This too is a specifically English trait, to be detected in such a typically English street as the Oxford 'High', where rich and formal buildings jostle with humble shops and houses, overarched by a spreading tree. But in poetry only Chaucer approaches this manifestation of a daily interweaving of the humdrum, or the sordid, and the sublime. For further parallel one must go to the serio-comic early chapters of *The Brothers Karamazov*, where the saintly elder listens to Ivan's subtle arguments on the relations of Church and State which his fool of a father constantly interrupts, whilst the elder blesses and counsels pilgrims rich and poor, telling the lady of rank that she should give up loving humanity and strive to love her neighbour, and so attain self-forgetfulness: 'But love in action is a harsh and dreadful thing compared with love in dreams. Active love is labour and fortitude and for some people too, perhaps, a complete science.' It is as if he were echoing the words of Conscience:

> 'For one Pieres the Ploughman hath impugned us alle
> And sette alle sciences at a soppe save love one[1]
> And no tixte[2] ne taketh to meyntene his cause,
> But *dilige deum* [*et proximum tuum*] . . .'

(xiii. 123–6)

[1] *alone* [2] *text*

—a text that will be the *titulus* and motto of the climactic passus. Such comparisons—and one could draw a similar one between Piers in his first epiphany and the Pierre of *Anna Karenina*, who learns to live for his soul and remember God—may serve to efface the stereotyped picture of Langland as the homely poet of the people, vigorous but crude, a gaunt melancholy figure muttering jeremiads or texts that he only half understands. For we must distinguish between the persona of the dream-narrator and the poet whom there is good reason to name as William Langland.* This persona is both a partly fictional character subject to impressions of the human and divine and also a vehicle conveying or embodying views, quests, questionings, which may or may not have been the poet's own, or those of some of his contemporaries. The poem is often called a spiritual autobiography; but this is a *simpliste* description, the ironical result of the very vividness of Langland's presentation of his dreamer. Thus at the end of the first and shortest recension (the 'A text'), as readers we feel the gulf implied between learning and salvation to be so great as to be unbridgeable; it was all too easy to suggest that the poet here cobbled up an ending, and then began again, at Passus XI in his 'B' text, when he had new light. That he halted at this point there is no doubt. But his problem may have been structural and aesthetic, not doctrinal and personal.

* A Latin note written *c*.1400 in a manuscript of the poem now in Trinity College, Dublin, states that the author was called William of Langland and was the son of Stacy de Rokayle of Shipton-under-Wychwood (Oxon). Later writers associate this William with Cleobury Mortimer (Salop), but this may be a mistake for Ledbury: the parish of Barton Colwall adjacent to Ledbury contains a field called Longland(s), from which the poet may have taken his name; it lies just north of the Malvern hills. The line ' "I have lyved in londe," quod I, "my name is Longe Wille" ' (xv. 148) appears to be a punning allusion to his name; and there are cryptic references to 'Wille' elsewhere. The poet-dreamer represents himself in the latest recension (the 'C text') as dwelling on Cornhill with 'Kytte', who figures as his wife, and a daughter 'Kalote' at B xviii. 426; as too weak and too 'long' to do manual labour and as earning a living by singing the offices of the Dead, i.e. as a cleric in minor orders. He may have had some connection with Great Malvern Priory, a sister house of Westminster. But numerous references show that he knew Westminster and the city of London well.

He was hardly formulating his beliefs or difficulties as he went along: the doctrines that emerge in the opening visions prove to be part of a coherent *Weltanschauung*, and he may reasonably be thought to have considered their relation to other doctrines before he 'meddled with making' and began to compose verse at all. It may be that, like a modern writer, Langland would have asked: 'How can I know what I think till I see what I set down?' But this does not justify us in assuming that when, for example, the Dreamer says

> Al for tene[1] of her tyxte trembled myn herte
> And in a were[2] gan I waxe and with myself to dispute
> Whether I were chosen or nought chosen . . .   (xi. 1102)

> [1] *vexation*   [2] *quandary*

the poet is recording a spiritual crisis that he experienced after a disputation with friars in later years. The poem, like Dante's, is certainly in one sense a Pilgrim's Progress—but hardly in Bunyan's sense; it describes not so much a spiritual journey (and *journey* was the dominant sense of 'progress' in Bunyan's day) as an unfolding, a development, stage by stage, passus by passus.

The allegory of a spiritual pilgrimage had taken impressive literary form forty years before Langland wrote, in a work that became immediately popular and remained so for three centuries. Guillaume de Deguileville had written his verse *Pèlerinage de la Vie Humaine* in 1331 and a revised and enlarged (indeed verbose) version had appeared in 1355. The seventy manuscripts (often illustrated) that survive testify to its popularity and accessibility, though evidently no English versions were made before the fifteenth century.* There is no proof that Langland knew this subtle and elaborate work (if it influenced Bunyan it must have been at several removes, and in simplified form). But we can hardly avoid noting that it proceeds by the device of didactic dialogue that Langland was to employ, and that some of its characters—e.g. *Reason, Anima*—appear in *Piers Plowman*, together with some of its distinctive features and images—e.g. the author who poses as a naïve narrator, or the barn which in *Piers* is Holy Church and in the *Pèlerinage* stands for Christ. These, like the figurative courts or castles that appear in Passus V and IX suggest that directly or indirectly Langland was influenced by the French tradition of didactic allegory.

But the Ploughman who gives his name to the poem and who appears in such diverse manifestations has no antecedent (or genuine

---

* See Rosemond Tuve, *Allegorical Imagery* (Princeton, 1966), ch. iii.

successor). When he first 'puts forth his head' to address the puzzled pilgrims in the fifth passus a new chapter opens in English literature, and rustic life takes on a new importance, a new value. Chaucer evidently took note: he presents a ploughman who is sufficiently well-to-do and independent to go on pilgrimage with his brother, a parish priest and a learned clerk. The Chaucer who at first sight seems so French and so courtly knew the vernacular poetry of his time, and his early verse, in dialogue, phrase, and narrative, owes much to it. And though Langland's concerns are broader, and his verse is a development of the native alliterative measure, he is not the product of a culture wholly distinct from Chaucer's. His opening lines, with their promise of 'a ferly of fairy', suggest the world of romance; Chaucer was to use the same dream-device. There is nothing rustic or even regional about Langland, and he writes for a literate audience, accustomed to read in private—as distinct, say, from the first audience of Chaucer's *Troilus*, or of *Gawain*. The complex structure, the sheer length, of *Piers Plowman*, the constant 'cross-references', point to an audience of 'clerks' with some university training or of laymen with at least some grammar school education. His concerns are those of thinking men in these classes of society—the 'clerisy', in Coleridge's phrase, of his day: e.g. the treatment of able-bodied vagrants (vi); the application of the scholastic doctrine of the Just Price (vii); the relation between the Active and the Contemplative Lives (viii ff.); the doctrine and practice of indulgences (vii); the nexus between Faith and Works; the function of the Papacy; the salvation of the heathen; the limits of theological enquiry. He was no Wycliffite, but some of these concerns overlapped with Wyclif's, and initially Wyclif drew his support from and appealed to the clerkly class. His scathing satire any audience would relish; but that directed against the friars of his day belongs to a tradition that goes back to the French clerk Rutebeuf. Yet at its most impassioned, his verse is vibrant with Franciscan feeling for the poor:

> Ac pore peple, thi prisoneres, Lorde, in the put of myschief,[1]
> Conforte tho creatures that moche care suffren
> Throw derth, thorw drouth, alle her dayes here,
> Wo in wynter tymes for wantyng of clothes,
> And in somertyme selde[2] soupen to the fulle—
> Comforte thi careful[3], Cryst, in thi ryche[4].

(xiv. 174–9)

[1] *pit of adversity*   [2] *seldom*   [3] *wretched ones*   [4] *kingdom*

No other poet was to touch this string till Henryson wrote his *Prayer for the Pest* and his fable of the Wolf and the Lamb. But the force of the last phrase should be noted; and the appeal concludes:

> For how thow confortest alle creatures, clerkes bereth witnesse
> *Convertemini ad me et salvi eritis.*

In no sense is this 'popular' poetry; rather it illustrates Langland's inclination not only to cite Latin but to think in Latin. He moved from the vernacular to Latin with ease and almost unconsciously.

In the decades before or during which Langland wrote the use of the alliterative mode is evidenced only from social, topical, and political poems. Three that show some similarities to his opening passus and that may have decided him to choose this mode are *Somer Sonday*,* written in stanzas similar to, though shorter than, those of *Gawain*, *Wynnere and Wastoure*, and the *Parlement of the Thre Ages*. The opening lines of *Somer Sonday* seem to be echoed in *Piers Plowman*, like some of its other phrases and situations. But it is not a dream-poem, and in its present form is only 132 lines long, concluding with the appearance of Fortune (who in Langland's poem also appears in dream) and a description of her wheel—a favourite fourteenth-century motif. From the account of the other two poems given above (pp. 50–5), it will be evident that dream-poems provide ideal opportunities for satire, debate, didactic discourse. It is in dream-poems that the literary movements of the Middle Ages come to their apogee: in Dante's *Commedia* (though nowhere described as a dream, it is presented as a narrative of experience befalling him in sleep); in the *Roman de la Rose*; in Chaucer's *Parlement* and *House of Fame*; and in *Piers Plowman*. Like so much in medieval literature these poems rested in part on classical foundations—on Macrobius's commentary on the *Somnium Scipionis* and Boethius's *Consolatio* (a vision of 'Philosophia'). The dream-poem was to the fourteenth century what epic was to the seventeenth.

Langland's choice of this form was not inconsistent with the deep scepticism about the interpretation of actual dreams that he shares with Chaucer. 'I have no savoure in songewarie [interpretation of dreams]' professes the poet-dreamer, 'for I se it ofte faille' (vii. 148). But it is this very reservation that allows him to stand aside, leaving his readers to interpret—'Devine ye, for I ne dar, bi dere God in hevene'—when in the opening vision he presents a political parable. Just because the dreams described *are* dreams, we are left free to attach our own assessment to them. Ordinary dream-experience is non-rational, fragmentary, disjointed, abrupt in its shifts and changes. It is these

---

* Ed. R. H. Robbins, *HP*, No. 38.

very features that Langland—as distinct from his continental predecessors, whose dream-narrative is continuous and regular to the
point of monotony—seizes on and exploits, linking the sequence of
visions by means of the Dreamer who is involved, and who comments,
in each of them. The shape and content of each may differ, but each
offers some continuum, some enlargement of the preceding dream.
What at first seem mere digressions or cryptic asides often turn out to
be foretastes, and take on a new significance in retrospect. This makes
for a tight interweaving, such as is lacking in Deguileville or Jean de
Meun. Thus every thread introduced in the first five hundred lines
forms part of an elaborate warp and woof, now showing brightly, now
subsumed. If there is any key word for the whole poem it is love,
caritas. It is wholly characteristic of Langland that it first appears
unobtrusively in the description of those who labour 'for love of owre
lord' (Prol. 26)—as distinct from the lawyers who plead 'nought for
love of owre lorde' (213)—and next in a cryptic reference to papal
powers: 'he left it with love as owr Lorde hight' and 'For in love and
letterure the eleccioun bilongeth' (Prol. 102, 110). When Holy Church
appears, she will speak of Love as manifest in creation—'Alle his
werkes he wroughte with love, as Him liste' (i. 148)—and supremely at
the Crucifixion, when God 'Loked on us with love, and lete his son
dye / Mekely for owre mysdedes, to amende us alle' (i. 165–6). The
sitio ('I thirst') of the Seven Last Words will later (xviii. 363 ff.) be read
as a cry not of anguish but of Love. The resurrection will be heralded
by a Love as lutanist (xviii. 423). At the very end of the first passus,
Christ himself is represented as interpreting *Date et dabitur vobis* as 'the
lok of love that unloseth grace', and Holy Church concludes that
'Love is leche of lyf', 'the graith gate' (direct road) to heaven. The
cluster of 'unliterary' images is as characteristic as the sudden swerve
in the next passus from sublimity to the sordid loveless marriage of
Meed. Not till the end of Passus III can Conscience predict that her
sway will at last yield to that of Love, Lowness, 'Lewté' (loyalty)
(iii. 289), and that Kind Love and Conscience will produce Love and
Peace among men (297). Then once again we are back in the sinful
world where men would do more for a dozen chickens or as many
capons or a 'seam' of oats than 'for love of our Lord'—the phrase is in
the nature of an oral formula, but its recurrence is illustrative not so
much of Langland's alliterative technique as of his abiding concern
with *caritas*. Seven hundred lines later the note is struck again, this
time in scripture Latin: *Qui manet in caritate, in deo manet* (v. 494). And
when the lesson of Redemption is applied in Passus VI to the plight of
the poor and needy, it concludes:

Conforte hem with thi catel for Crystes love of hevene:
Love hem and lene hem. . . .

(vi. 223–4)

The figure of pilgrim and pilgrimage, introduced, but almost incidentally, at the outset, and developed, not to say transmuted, in the fifth
and sixth passus, recurs in the closing lines of the whole work, in a
symmetry that can scarcely be accidental:

> 'Bi Cryste' quod Conscience tho, 'I wil bicome a pilgryme
> And walken as wyde as al the worlde lasteth . . .'

though there we recognize that Conscience's *peregrinatio* is to no
shrine, but rather to the celestial Jerusalem to which Chaucer's Parson
directs his hearers (*CT* x. 49–51).

The development of the poem is not linear, but neither is it, as
might sometimes seem, circuitous: it is that of a helix, or a corkscrew,
in which, at certain points of rest, the Dreamer looks back at earlier
scenes and views them in a new perspective; the simplifications or
exaggerations of earlier views are thus tacitly or explicitly corrected. It
is not altogether fanciful to regard the spiral as circling round four
crucial conceptions.

First, the field of folk, an image of the material world, which
narrows down to Piers's half-acre, widens again to be Middle-earth, is
reduced to the tree of Charity growing in a garden, and finally
becomes wholly spiritualized, ploughed by the four evangelists and
sown with seed of the Spirit.

Second, Holy Church as the repository of Truth: figured first as a
high-towered castle (i); then as an interior castle of the soul (v); then as
the Ark—the 'shingled ship' of Passus IX; finally as the barn of Unity
(Passus XIX).

Third, the theme of Pardon: introduced obliquely with the false
Pardoner of the Prologue; dramatized in Passus VII; linked with the
capital sins in the person of Haukin who questions the efficacy of his
priest's pardon; identified with the Christlike Piers (xix. 388).

Fourth, and in every sense crucial: the rood of the Crucifixion,
round which the whole work revolves: the symbol of Divine Love: so
presented in Passus I, by Holy Church; by Repentance in Passus V; as
the scene of Christ's duel with Death, from which he emerges as *Dux
Vitae* and *Rex Gloriae* in Passus XVIII. Central as the death of Christ is
to Langland's thought, the cross does not figure as the object of devotion, as it did in the art of his time, and in the meditative and mystical

writers—the scenes of agony that absorbed Julian of Norwich are compassed here in three lines:

> '*Consummatum est*', quod Cryst, and comsed[1] for to swowe[2]
> Pitousliche and pale as a prisoun[3] that deyeth;
> The Lord of lyf and of lighte tho leyed his eyen togideres.

(xviii. 57–9)

[1] *began*   [2] *swoon*   [3] *prisoner*

Langland's piety is spare, restrained, not affective.

Around this spiral treads the persistent figure of the pilgrim, the wayfarer. The Dreamer himself is such a figure, and he meets many others. At first a spectator, then an interlocutor, he gradually comes to participate in the dream-action. The involvement corresponds to his growth as a self-questioning, self-communing, Christian. Development in self-knowledge characterizes the protagonists, or the poetic personae, of the greatest fourteenth-century poems: Gawain similarly, engaged on a more knightly quest, will emerge as a penitent figure aware for the first time of his frailty. The allegorical figures that the Dreamer meets—Ymaginatif, Clergy, Study, Patience, represent qualities that he comes to value and even to assimilate. If at the close it is Conscience who becomes a pilgrim walking the world as the poet-dreamer does at the beginning, it is because only now is the Dreamer's Conscience fully apprised of the Person that he must seek.

It must be admitted that the articulation of the poem is not always clear. Langland's perceptions are greater than his powers to co-ordinate. David Jones said that the more impressive and perceptive the artist, so much the more is the architectonic ability required.* In *Piers Plowman* the diverse images and ideas are not, as they are in Dante, completely fused. Scenes are not only crowded but confused, characters (Piers himself, and the priest who impugns his pardon) enter unannounced and often have no marked exits; some of the personifications are so bodiless that an editor may be hard put to it when deciding whether to give them the dignity of a capital. At one point the poet will intrude to animadvert on benefactors who advertise themselves in church windows, at another the Dreamer (or the poet?) will admit that the castigation of ignorant priests has made him 'leap from' the theme of Poverty. Such anomalies produce initially the impression of a cloudy scene lit up by sudden flashes of sunlight— whilst differences in emphases in the three extant recensions suggest some dissatisfaction, or change of view, in the poet himself. Yet in this, as in so much else, the poem reflects the actualities of Christian

---

* *Epoch and Artist: Selected Writings by David Jones* (London, 1959), 282.

experience, the tension of an intensely serious and disturbed intelligence, rooted firmly in orthodox belief and practice yet alive to the disruption facing feudal society, and troubled by the failure of the Church and the religious orders to meet the crisis. If the poem is not spiritual autobiography, it does reflect the struggle and aspiration of the poet to provide some light in the darkness for his fellow Christians. And at the close (which is as compelling in its own fashion as the beginning) the reader has come to share, through the intermediacy of the Dreamer, his moods, his meditations, his exaltations. The Dreamer has allied himself to us by his very imperfections, his stubborn insistences.

The opening dream, by the side of a purling hillside stream on a warm summer morning, is of a field (with a tower on one side and a dungeon on the other) in which all sorts and conditions of men wander or work. Some of them make pacts to go on pilgrimage, others are enticed by the words of a false pardoner. The focus is soon on the state and function of the Church. From papal power it shifts to kingly. An angelic preacher exhorts that kingly justice must be mingled with mercy, and (in the B text) the problems of government for the common profit are particularized in a vivid topical application of the fable of the rats and mice who would bell the cat. The scene shifts again to the clamour of London shops and streets and courts. By the close of the Prologue our curiosity is aroused, and the opening of the first passus* promises some explanation. It is provided by Lady Holy Church, who comes down from a high tower in the form of a benign and beautiful Lady who might have stepped out of a niche or west portal of a cathedral where Ecclesia and Synagoga are seen juxtaposed. Her theme is that of the Redemptive Love which most men in the dale are disregarding. The pattern of her discourse is homiletic—it is replete with texts and biblical allusion—but she is not identified with the visible church except in so far as she reminds the Dreamer of his baptism. The mercy enjoined by the angel of the Prologue is here shown as an attribute of God himself, and of his Son, who would have mercy on his murderers. Thus the Passion makes its first appearance in the poem; at subsequent high points it will be pictured with increasing fullness—the Cross is the *kingbeam* on which the whole structure rests. Equally noteworthy is Holy Church's definition of *Truth*: 'a kynde knowyng ... that kenneth in thine herte / For to lovye thi

---

* The poem, in the 'B' text, has twenty passus, ranging from 200 to 650 lines. The unequal divisions suggest that they are intended to correspond to steps or stages in the internal development of the poem rather than (like the divisions of *The Knight's Tale* or *Gawain*) to suit the needs of reciters.

Lorde lever than thi selve', a sense, that is, implanted in man. Piers will say that he knows Truth 'as *kyndely* as clerke doth his bokes' (which is 'by heart', as we say), where 'kindly' means not simply 'naturally, instinctively', but 'intimately'. The Dreamer will ask Study 'to kenne [teach] me *kyndely* to know what is Dowel' (x. 146); and Patience will say that Contrition, Faith, and Conscience are '*kindly* Dowel' (xiv. 87): its very essence. Lady Church's withdrawal from the dream action—after she has warned the Dreamer of the false allure of a richly decked maid called Meed who is to be married by Liar's contrivance to one False—underlines the difference between her and the fourteenth-century Church, with its venal and self-indulgent priests and religious, who are to figure largely in the remainder of the work.

In the next three passus the Dream compasses the evils and the problems of contemporary society, and the sins of individuals—portrayed in vignettes done with unprecedented satiric force and brio. Coming after Holy Church's pronouncements, the emphasis may seem surprising: it amounts to saying that Man cannot advance in Christian perfection until he has settled the basis of society and his part in it. Elementary needs, elementary justice must be satisfied before he can grow in personal godliness. A King who has been involved in foreign wars, but is now governed by Reason and Conscience (Passus IV) finds no room for the Lady Meed that has almost overturned the rule of law. As the court moves to church to hear mass, the Dreamer wakes, only to dream again of the Field in which Reason, as a bishop, is preaching, as to the whole realm of England devastated as it is by storm and pestilence. Each estate of the realm is admonished and finally the pilgrims whom we have glimpsed in the Prologue are adjured to 'seek Saint Truth, for he may save you all'.

The capital sins now passed in review are—save for Pride and Luxury—characterized with a wealth of descriptive phrase that matches Chaucer: Envy, pale and looking like a leek that has lain long in the sun; Wrath, snivelling with two white eyes; Avarice 'bitelbrowed and baberlipped', cheeks lolling like a leather purse; Glutton, with guts that 'gunne to gothely [rumble] as two gredy sowes'; Sloth, 'all bislabered with two slymy eighen [eyes]'. Their confessions fill out these sketches with vivid vignettes: Envy, turning a covetous eye on Eleyne's new robe; Wrath, who admits to having been battered on the bare arse in the chapter house; Avarice, who thinks the French term 'restitution' means robbing; Sloth, who says he does not know his 'paternoster as the prest it syngeth' but rather 'rymes of Robyn Hood and Randolf Erle of Chestre'.

Yet all these seemingly depraved characters—composite in so far as they embody multifold manifestations of the sins—recognize the need of penitence, and know, or learn, the formulas of the Confessional. Thus it comes about that Repentance the priest can pray on their behalf the great Easter prayer that links the Creation with the Crucifixion, and can beseech God 'that art owre fader and owre brother, be merciable to us', That the prayer marks a turning-point is hinted by the sudden, if momentary, appearance of Hope, who seized a horn of '*deus, tu conversus*...' and blew it so that all the saints in heaven sang at once. Such heavenly song will not be heard again till the daughters of God 'carole' on Easter Day (Passus XVIII).

The folk who have made their Lenten penance are now fit to follow the bishop's injunction and seek Saint Truth. But they find no one to guide them. A palmer festooned with a hundred ampullae and many pilgrim signs, knows nothing of such a saint. It is at this critical point that a ploughman—who is more than a ploughman, but (like the Sinners) a composite figure, thrusts his head through a hedge. He represents the honest workman who can reasonably claim that he knows Truth 'kindly', for Conscience and Kind Wit have directed him to Truth's 'place'. The directions he gives are heavily allegorical—they are to pass through the Ten Commandments, to begin with—but after a liturgical allusion to the Virgin Birth and the Virgin's part in Redemption, they conclude with the revelation that Truth is to be found 'sitting in the heart'; it was in the heart that Holy Church had located the Kind Wit that teaches one to love the Lord more than oneself; but Holy Church had hinted that there is more to be learnt (i. 143–4).

We have sensed by now that a pilgrimage to Saint Truth will not be to a known place. Conscience and Kind Wit are internal monitors. If the pilgrims have to pass through the Commandments it is because Christ did not abrogate them: he had simply insisted that Love was greatest and 'If a man love me he will keep my words, and my Father will love him and we will come unto him and make our abode with him' (John 14: 23)—in Langland's words, will 'sit in thy heart'.

At the beginning of Passus VI, Piers offers to guide them to Truth himself, once he has sown his half-acre, and enlists their help in his task, first making his will (as any pilgrim would). But the only help some give is an alehouse song of 'how trolli-lolli'. We are faced with the problems, accentuated by the Black Death, of famine and of the poor. The 250 lines devoted to them here show that, for Langland, they are issues that no Christian can escape.

A desperate Piers calls in Hunger, and Hunger insists that everyone must work—but the work may be diking or delving *or* travailing in prayers. It is the same division of 'labour' found in the opening lines of the Prologue, but the kinds of life are here for the first time (in B) labelled Active and Contemplative; in the later (C) text they are introduced earlier in a scene suggested by the parable of the guests bidden to the supper (Luke 14: 16–24), in which the uxorious husband is named Active (he shows the weaknesses that will reappear in the character of Haukyn the Active Man in the B text) and Contemplative appears momentarily, vowing to follow Piers but ignorant of the way. The two kinds of Life are to figure more prominently in later passus.

It is concordant with the discovery that Truth is to be found in the heart that, in Passus VIII, Truth should bid Piers stay at home and till his field with the pilgrims' help, sending a complete pardon that makes pilgrimage superfluous. It has some features of a papal pardon—it is called a bull—but is glossed as a series of injunctions to all the grades of society so far considered, and 'dissolves' into a declaration by the poet himself, who relates it to the theme of the undeserving beggars and the care of the aged and the weak.

Not for the first time the boundary between comment and description grows blurred. We are dimly conscious of the poet-dreamer's presence and concern before he presents himself as looking over the shoulder of Piers and the priest who has asked to see the pardon. It is simply a clause of the Athanasian Creed (*Qui bona egerunt*), not the priest's idea of a pardon, still less that of the false pardoner in the Prologue. At this point—whether by accident or design is debatable—Piers tears the pardon, announcing at the same time that in future he will spend less time in ploughing and more in prayer and penance. The apparent dichotomy of Active and Contemplative here comes to the fore—but so also does the impetuosity of Piers, which issues in a slanging-match with the priest. He is becoming a many-sided, even a complex character. The noise of quarrelling wakes the Dreamer, 'meatless and moneyless on Malvern hills'. He ponders on the value of dreams and of pardons, and the Passus concludes with his exhortation to all Christians to pray for grace to *Do well*.

The poem might well have ended here: manuscripts of the C text add at this point an *Amen*. But it would leave us and the Dreamer a little at a loss as to what constitutes Dowel. He sets out in search of this figure, and at length meets two friars who claim Dowel's acquaintance, but of friars' teaching he is sceptical. Lying down again, this time under a linden tree, and listening delightedly to birdsong, he dreams another, and 'more marvellous' dream, in which Thought, Wit, Study, and Clergy all proffer descriptions of Dowel, Dobet, Dobest—and much else besides. It seems part of the poet's purpose to display these concepts in many different lights. 'Wit' in Passus IX shows Dowel dwelling in the Castle of Anima, who is served by Dobet, Dowel's daughter; Dobest, superior to them all, is 'a bishop's peer'. But the main theme of this Passus soon becomes Kind, Natura—not the Nature of Jean de Meun or Chaucer, but God the Creator. Kind is thus given a central place in the scheme of the poem, and its presence gives a new dimension to the allegory, extending it beyond the realm of the social, as of the spiritual.

Structurally Passus XI–XII are puzzling. The complexity of a dream within a dream strains the pattern: edges grow blurred as the poet (or his persona) launches into a digression from his professed theme of patient (i.e. voluntary) poverty. In the central vision of the mirror of Middle-earth the creative power of Kind is further displayed; and we are not surprised to learn that it was prompted by Ymaginatif. The Dreamer is led to perceive that the world of Nature is full of lessons that only 'Clergye' (a concept that includes Aristotle the great Clerk) can properly interpret. To discern these lessons is, in something of our modern sense, an imaginative act—if spiritual perception be taken as such an act: the dream had been the work of Ymaginatif. As so often in Langland, the dream offers a corrective to as well as an amplification of what has gone before. Thus in Passus XI the Dreamer was puzzled as to how birds learnt to build their nests or hide their eggs. Ymaginatif says that Kind (Nature) knows the answer (where we might use the word instinct). In the same Passus, when the Dreamer is in dialogue with Scripture on predestination, the Emperor Trajan, of all people, suddenly intervenes, with a 'baw for bokes' as if he had just escaped from hell (xi. 135), a heathen who had been saved without baptism. In Passus XII Ymaginatif explains why. His justification of Clergye (now placed above Kind Wit) is not without its wry humour: Clergy not only helps a man in danger of sin; it can save a clerk who knows his neck verse from the gallows (xii. 187–91)! Ymaginatif vanishes from the dream with a reference to the verse from Psalm 22 that the Dreamer had cited in Passus VIII: a reference so cryptic that he wakes almost out of his mind. In his next dream (xiii) Conscience comes to his aid, but the cleric who now figures as representing Clergy turns out to be a gluttonous friar and a winebibber. Conscience and Patience both try to extract from him a definition of Dowel. He gets no further—after taking a deep draught from his cup—than saying Dowel is not to do evil, or to do as clerks teach; Dobet is a teacher; Dobest is he who does what he teaches.

Conscience and Patience meet with a minstrel, Haukyn, the Active Man, who might seem to embody some aspects of Dowel but is in fact multifold in his actions and imperfections; Langland's most elaborate pictorial construction, he owns to all the sins tht have been scanned in Passus V. Now it is Patience that counsels him, in the very terms that Piers had used (cf. xiv. 33 and vii. 103). At this point the poem slackens, and falters in direction. The many-faceted *Anima* becomes a mouthpiece for general discourse culminating in a characterization of Charity that stirs the Dreamer to cry 'Would that I knew him!', only to be told that 'without help of Piers Plowman his person seest thou never'. Hence it is that when, in Passus XVI, Charity is figured as a tree where *Liberum Arbitrium* tends it under Piers's guidance, the Dreamer swoons at the mention of Piers's name. In a 'lone dream' Piers describes the tree as supported by three props figuring the Trinity. Yet the tree connotes other things as well. Its fruit is not only charity but three states of life of progressive value: Matrimony, Continence, Virginity. The Trinity for a time becomes the substantive theme of the poem but we are soon aware of another triad, *Fides*, *Spes*, *Caritas*, with *Spes* figured by the Abraham who on the plain of Mamre had entertained three angels unawares, and *Caritas* by the Samaritan who now dramatically appears in person, hastening to a joust in Jerusalem. Langland's enlargement of the terse dominical parable, though owing much to traditional exegesis, shows him deeply involved; but it also allows him to reaffirm the role of Holy Church (figured as the hostel where the Samaritan lodges the wounded man). The emphasis shifts from *Caritas* to Doctrine when the Samaritan himself delays his journey to expound the mystery of the Trinity (it evidently held a more central place in Langland's thought than the triad of Dowel, Dobet, Dobest on which critics have focussed attention).

Scripture (canonical and apocryphal) and liturgy continue to provide the frame for the last enlargement of the theme of Redemption, when it appears as keystone to the whole work, the climactic dream of Passus XVIII that gives to earlier images and actions their historical context and lasting significance. The Crucifixion as here presented recalls, and perhaps reflects, its enactment in the mystery plays. But the images used are those of single combat in knightly joust with death. For Repentance (in Passus V) *Verbum caro factum est* had meant that Christ did his doughtiest deeds in our *arms*—a purposeful *double entendre*. Now this concept is enriched as Christ on Palm Sunday enters Jerusalem, 'somdel like to Piers Plowman' (he is never to be named as Piers), like a knight-bachelor coming to be dubbed but sitting, like the Samaritan who prefigures him, on a simple mule; and barefoot, that is peaceably—and like the Christ earlier compared to a poor pilgrim—his only weapon *humana natura*. It is another knight-bachelor (Longinus) whose blindness, physical and spiritual, will be cured by the blood flowing from the wound his spear has made; and if the Jews are now called *caitiffs* it is because they treat the dead body unchivalrously. As the function of the Christian knight in Passus V was to redeem distress, so Christ as Knight-errant now harrows hell to free mankind. His cry of *Sitio* is now the cry of a tourneying knight, who in the romances finds fighting thirsty work; it is no cry of pain but of love, which Herbert (in *The Agonie*) will call 'that liquor sweet and most divine':

> And for that drynke today I dyde upon erthe.
> I faughte so, me threstes yet for mannes soule sake.'
>
> (xviii. 364–5)

On another, no less important level, the Harrowing is a legal argument—in equally traditional terms—with Lucifer as to his rights over man's soul; balanced by a scholastic disputation between the Four Daughters of God as to the Justice of Redemption. Lancelot Andrewes was to read the seminal verse from Psalm 84: 11 in the same fashion;* but no one gives them such gusty femininity. At their reconciliation Truth seizes a trumpet and Love her lute. The four 'carole' like the angels in Botticelli's *Nativity*:

> Tyl the daye dawed this[1] damaiseles daunced
> That men rongen to the resurexion. . . .   (424–5)
>
> [1] *these*

The bells that have been silent since Palm Sunday now wake the Dreamer. Of the import of this dream he has no doubt; and now for the first time his concern moves to others beside himself—to Kit his wife and Kalote his daughter. Together they kiss the cross that bore God's body and put the fiend to flight.

The term *cross*, here used of the Rood for the first time in the poem, prepares us for the dream of the next passus, wherein Piers, all bloody, enters armed with that same cross: his first actual appearance since he tore the Pardon. From what has been said of him we know that he now embodies perfected human nature. His field is now the World, his team are the Gospel-makers. With the wood of the cross will be built the manor-house of Unity with its barn for their harvest. Sloth, Pride, Hypocrisy will menace it: the last passus is heavy with the sense of urgency, of crisis. Conscience calls on Kind for support, but the Friars by their flattery succeed in penetrating

---

* See Lancelot Andrewes, *Sermons*, ed. G. M. Story (Oxford, 1967), 65–6.

the house, and cast a spell on the people. Conscience resolves to become a pilgrim:

> 'And walken as wyde as al the worlde lasteth,
> To seke Piers the Plowman that Pryde may destruye . . .'

(xx. 379–80)

and implores the help of Grace, the Holy Spirit. His words wake the Dreamer and the whole tenor of the poem leads us to think that the Dreamer—indeed the poet—makes these words his own. The time for dreams and discourse is over. The time of action has begun.

Medieval allegory at its most dynamic is not so much a literary genre as a mode of thought. Literary precedents for some of Langland's allegorical scenes can certainly be found: e.g. for the figurative highway and the castle of Truth moated with mercy and crenellated with Christendom (Passus V) and for the castle of Anima (Passus IX). Both seem to be patterned on the *Chasteau d'Amour*, a frigid allegory confidently ascribed to the great Grosseteste, whose powers are more finely demonstrated in his scientific and philosophical works. But Langland gives to the figure an unexpected twist: Truth is to be found not in the castle but sitting 'in thine herte / In a cheyne of charyté [= ? *vinculum amoris*]'; whilst the first recension has the cryptic claim that Truth 'may do with the day-sterre what him deore lyketh', the force of which is not evident till, in Passus XVIII, Truth, in the person of Christ, confronts *Lucifer* in Hell. The figure in Passus IX of the Body (*Caro*) as the house of the Soul (*Anima*) is more ancient—we have met it in *Sawles Warde* (see pp. 275–81 above). But Langland revivifies it by drawing on the romance associations of the lover-knight (see pp. 269, 380 ff.): Anima is in Passus IX a damsel whom a 'proude pryker of Fraunce' would carry off. The epithet is enough to indicate that Langland is here giving to the proud Lucifer a local habitation acceptable to readers for whom France was an ancient enemy. At once, however, he shifts to different ground. The protector of this damsel is Kind. In a Latin allegory Kind would figure as *Natura*, but Langland has given to the term a deeper value. For him it represents the creative power of the Trinity, signified by the *faciamus* of Gen. 1: 26.

The example may suffice to show that *Piers Plowman* is not so much an allegory as a series of allegories, of different kinds and substance. Langland was doubtless aware of the technical use of the term as applied in the fourfold exegesis of Scripture:

> litera gesta docet, quid credas allegoria;
> moralis quid agas, quo tendas anagogia.

446

His readers would be accustomed to exposition of texts at these levels, and in a poem in which the action begins with exposition of texts by Holy Church they would look for a deeper meaning than the literal. The abortive marriage of Meed and False (iii–iv), though set in fourteenth-century London, is easily interpreted allegorically as displaying the workings of cupidity in Church and State, morally as showing Conscience and Reason weaning the Soul from Cupidity, anagogically as (ultimately) announcing the victory of Divine Truth over Falsehood and Satan (iii, *ad fin.*). But it is implausible that Langland (or even Dante, who refers to these fourfold senses) constructed his entire poem with these senses in mind. He is too concerned with the complexities of life to be willing to accommodate them in a formal scheme. Even when he appears to be following literary models he will suddenly break off and introduce new elements. Allegorical characters move from one level to another; they are not confined to the frame of a particular scene. Thus Conscience, who figures as a knight returned from the French wars in Passus III, is Constable of Dowel's Castle in Passus IX (where he is called Inwit), and in the penultimate passus the counsellor of all Christian folk. The line between allegory and actuality is wavering and indistinct. Lady Meed, who in some aspects is Cupidity, in others Reward for services rendered, is first described in terms suggesting that she is modelled on Alice Perrers, Edward III's notorious mistress; the King who tries her case is very much a fourteenth-century English king, sitting in Council in Westminster. The Virtues and Vices personified throughout the poem lose their abstract nature by being localized in London streets, or the highways of southern England; Poverty could travel through the Pass of Alton (notorious for its robbers) without risk of robbery. Love mediates between God and man as the Lord Mayor of London mediates between King and Commons.

In fine, 'allegorical' turns out to be an inadequate description of this multiform work, in which the action is constantly located in Langland's England. Nothing could be further from the 'imposed' allegory of the contemporary *Ovide Moralisé*. Yet the realism resides in incidental touches rather than in characterization. The satiric vignettes of the sinners who make their confessions in Passus V abound in vivid touches, yet the sinners are mostly composite characters. Other personified figures are described far more briefly, if at all. *Spes* (as Abraham) figures in the guise of a herald who can identify Christ by his heraldic blazon, but all we are told of him is that he is 'hore as a hawthorn'. The spareness is that of the parabolic rather than the allegorical mode; and Langland's imaginative appropriation of the

Parable of the Samaritan in Passus XVII, though deriving from traditional interpretations, shows how deep was the impress of the pattern
of teaching set in the Gospels. Yet the world in which the Samaritan
can catch up with the Dreamer as he talks to *Spes*, and Faith (*Fides*)
can become a Forester who sets common folk on the right way to
Jerusalem, is a dream-world, and allows the Samaritan, hurried as he
is, to discourse piquantly on the difficulties of the spiritual life and the
trials of the flesh, which include those that Solomon speaks of—
contentious wife, leaky roof, smoky chimney:

> For smoke and smolder[1] smyteth in his eyen
> Til he be blere-nyed[2] or blynde, and hors in the throte,
> Cougheth, and curseth that Crist gyf hem sorwe
> That sholde brynge in better wode—or blowe it til it brende.

(xvii. 321–6)

> [1] *smoke from smouldering wood*   [2] *blear-eyed*

The domestic scene is vivid, but like those of the Parables it has
ulterior meaning:

> Ac the smoke and the smolder that smyt in owre eyghen,
> That is coveityse and unkyndenesse that quencheth Goddes mercy.

(xvii. 341–2)

To take another instance: the Samaritan's comparison of the Trinity
to the palm, the fist, the fingers of a hand (xvii. 138 ff.) is of ancient
lineage and Langland develops it to the full. But to drive home his
point about the sin against the Holy Ghost he adds another domestic
metaphor:

> Ac[1] hew fyre at a flynte fowre hundreth wyntre,
> Bot[2] thow have towe to take it with, tondre[3] or broches[4],
> Al thi laboure is loste. . . .

(xvii. 244–6)

> [1] *but*   [2] *unless*   [3] *tinder*   [4] *matches*

The use of such images brings Langland close to the pithiest of
contemporary preachers. And there is abundant evidence of his
familiarity with sermon techniques and homiletic devices. The political *exemplum* of the cat, the rats, and the mice inserted into the
Prologue in the 'B' text had been used by Bishop Brinton in a Latin
sermon, though for a rather different purpose, a year or so earlier,
and by others. The sermon preached by Reason, as a bishop, before
the Court (v. 10 ff.) follows the pattern of a *sermo ad status*, with a message for each grade of society, whilst with its insistence on penitence it
could also serve as a Lenten sermon to induce the confessions that

follow in the poem. Other allusions show that the poet had listened to the sermons (often controversial) regularly preached in London at Paul's Cross. He may owe some of his views and his readings of Scripture to such sermons, in English or Latin, though it is misleading to say that his poem is the quintessence of medieval preaching.

By the same token it is tempting to see in the *milieu* of the Prologue—with its tower of Truth on one side, a deep dungeon on the other—a reflection of some medieval theatre 'in the round' and in the presentation of the Harrowing of Hell the influence of the mystery plays in which that event regularly figured. But in fact no depiction of the Harrowing in the dramatic *corpus* compares with that in Passus XVIII; whilst a morality such as *Everyman*, aiming, a century or more later, at less complex effects, seems stiff and static by comparison with the poem. The relevance of the plays perhaps lies rather in the fact that they would dispose Langland's audience to accept his mode of presenting his arguments by means of the vigorous give-and-take of dialogue; though Langland also shows his familiarity with a more formal kind of *disputatio*—that of the Schoolmen. Ymaginatif argues with his Dreamer in good set terms (xii. 278–80); and when the Dreamer meets two Friars Minor, 'Masters [of the Schools]' and 'men of great wit', who claim that Dowel dwells with them, ' "*Contra*" quod I as a clerke and comsed to disputen . . .' (viii. 20). He disputes by citing Scripture, from the Vulgate. There is constant recourse in the poem to scriptural authority. The Vulgate, the Fathers, the Liturgy are the profoundest and most pervasive influences on Langland's thought and style. He thinks in Latin as easily as in English, and carries the macaronic practice found in earlier lyrics, which alternate Latin and English verses, a stage further, welding Latin and English into one alliterative line: 'And seide hem sothli, "*sepcies in die cadit justus*".' The Latin Liturgy of Easter gives resonance to Repentance's lyrical prayer at the climax to Passus V and patterns the presentation of the Crucifixion, the Harrowing of Hell, the Resurrection in Passus XVIII. Only David Jones (who read *Piers Plowman*) has so completely assimilated Latin to the vernacular:

> About the turn of the year, captain, when he sings out loud
> and clear from his proper: *in ligno quoque vinceretur*.
>
> (*Anathemata*, 165)

In fact, Langland's stylistic techniques are as novel as his uses of allegory. His alliterative line has its own distinctive quality. It corresponds more closely to the rhythms of speech than does that of *Wynnere and Wastoure* or the *Parlement of the Thre Ages*; it is freer, and looser. Each half-line normally contains two or more 'strong' (i.e. stressed) syllables, with two initial rhymes in these syllables in the first, and one in the second. Some lines do not conform to these requirements, or exceed them; but in the absence of a holograph one cannot be sure what liberties the poet, as distinct from his copyists, allowed himself. His readiness to interweave Latin phrases into a line suggests that he was not rigorous. He exploits to the full the potentialities of the alliterative line to yield pungent emphasis, as in 'And bad hym go pissen with his plow, forpyned schrewe!' (vi. 157). What is most evident is the fact that his metre, like his language, would offer no deterrent to readers in any part of England. Nearly two hundred years after he wrote a printer could produce an unmodernized edition with every hope of its being understood. Two hundred and fifty years later another edition found a reader in Byron, who thought Chaucer 'obscene and contemptible' in comparison.

To treat of Langland's style as if it were unrelated to his thought (or his theology) would be a meaningless exercise. Auerbach has shown how the dogma of the Incarnation, and the precedent of the Gospels, came to work against the ancient rhetorical rules that had governed the separation of styles into *sermo sublimis* or *sermo humilis*: 'In the world of Christianity ... the two are merged especially in Christ's Incarnation and Passion, which realize and combine *sublimitas* and *humilitas* in overwhelming measure.'* No poet was more seized of this truth than Langland. It is the clue to the infinite variety of his allegory, imagery, language, and idiom—and even to his choice of a native verse-form that will allow him to enmesh in an alliterative line phrases of scriptural and liturgical Latin. The very first time that he figures the Incarnation he displays his peculiar power of leaping from the sublime to the mundane image. Love, says Holy Church (i. 151 ff.), a plant of peace (cf. Isa. 53: 2), yearned to take its fill of earth, yet when it took flesh and blood it grew lighter than linden leaf, yet 'portatyf and persant as the poynt of a nedle'. At the same time its role as a mediator between earth and heaven is likened to that of a London mayor mediating between King and Commons: the fine (*amerciment*) that Christ imposes is no fine, but *mercy*. The poet has modified the term—*merciment*—to point to the play on *mercy*, which is to be the theme of the following lines. 'Wordplay' is an inadequate term for such ambiguities, which are the poet's constant means of conveying truth in a poem that deliberately exploits the ambivalence in the name Piers, the native form of *Petrus* (*id est Christus*)—itself the occasion of such

* E. Auerbach, *Mimesis*, tr. Willard R. Trask (Princeton, 1953), 151.

a word-play in the Gospels. The Dreamer's name is Will, and the faculty of Will has its part in the poem: the verb-form is repeated insistently to make a point (x. 116–34), just as *love*, noun and verb, is repeated seven times in seven lines (xii. 138–46). At a different level is the play on the name of Jordan, a well-known Dominican friar, in the line 'I shal jangle to this jurdan [pot] with his just wombe [pot belly]' (xiii. 83), which follows a favourite medieval punning application of the text 'periculum est in falsis *fratribus*'. The doublets *sute* and *secte* are pressed hard for every possible meaning when used of the Incarnation (v. 495–8).

Into the long alliterative line Langland packs words pregnant with meaning, or cryptic enough to arrest us—like Holy Church's French *portatyf*. When he later (xii. 141 ff.) returns to the paradox of sublime love taking humble form he employs a striking variation of the earlier metaphor:

> For the heihe holigoste hevene shal tocleve[1]
> And Love shal lepe out after into this lowe erthe
> And Clennesse shal cacchen it and clerkes shullen it fynde.

> [1] *cleave apart*

The passage alludes first to the Annunciation (as described in Luke 1: 35: 'The Holy Ghost shall come upon thee'); the verse is blended with Mark 1: 10, then to the (seven) leaps that Christ was said to have taken from heaven to earth and back, then to the Virgin birth (*cacchen* being perhaps suggested by the symbolism of the Unicorn that could be caught only by a virgin), and lastly to the Magi: *ibant magi ab oriente* is quoted two lines later, and given a characteristically topical, street-corner gloss:

> If any *frere*[1] were founde there, ich yif[2] the fyve shillynges;
> Ne in none beggares cote was that barne[3] borne,
> But in a burgeys place, of Bethlem the best

> [1] *friar*   [2] *give*   [3] *child*

where Langland (perhaps following Comestor) deliberately departs from the traditional conception. He further glosses the biblical narrative when he adds:

> Riche men rutte[1] tho and in here reste were
> Tho it schon to the schepherdes, a schewer of blisse.

> [1] *snored*

The emphatic *rutte* may owe something to St Bernard; but it takes us at once into the world of Chaucer's Reeve and Miller.

There is little that is consciously poetic in Langland's language or his imagery. A few of his similes (e.g. 'ded as a dore tre') will be found in other alliterative poems, but there is very little that is formulaic. Often the similes are less simple, more pregnant, than appears at first glance: 'chaste as a childe that in cherche wepeth' (i. 179) is meant to picture the innocence of a child the moment after baptism; 'lewde as a laumpe that no lighte is inne' (i. 187), the virgins of the parable who lack oil, i.e. love for the Bridegroom. Other similes (e.g. 'loked like a lanterne', 'hore as a hawethorne') smack of everyday use. The poet's vocabulary is equally plain, with just enough of the element of the unusual: 'renable' (loquacious) of tongue; 'mamely' (babble); 'preynte' (winked); 'sylinge' (gliding) in xviii. 304 (where the modern editors reject the Miltonesque 'seylinge'); the French 'chaude or plus chaud' is used with heavily ironic effect of labourers' diet (vii. 313).

On occasion he will give a noun verbal force ('cartesadel' (ii. 179) or transfer an epithet, with ironic effect ('And syngen ther for symonye, for silver is swete', Prol. 86). Contempt is packed into forceful lines: priests 'hakke after holynesse'; 'God is moche in the gorge [mouth] of thise grete maystres.' But the line may also be modulated to a lyrical lightness and tenderness: 'love is leche of lyf, and nexte owre Lorde selve'. Most notable is his penchant for kinetic verbs in an unexpected context: angels 'lopen out with Lucifer', light 'lepe oute' at the Harrowing and 'blewe alle thi blissed into the blisse of paradise' (v. 503–4). Action in this poem tends to be sudden, and violent, giving a new turn to the narrative. Piers pulls the Pardon in two. The Samaritan rides up 'rapely' and 'went away as wynde' (xvii. 350). But the poet never strains for a word, or a meaning. The sanity and saving common sense of his religion, its concentration on essentials, is reflected in the verbal organization of the whole work.

If Langland has no predecessor, he has likewise no successor. Only Spenser will approach him in scope and purpose; and the opening lines of *The Faerie Queene* are comparable to those of Langland's Prologue, which capture our attention at once with the figure of the narrator dressed like a hermit, looking for 'wonders', and finding one forthwith on the Malvern Hills. We never wholly lose sight of this figure; his questions become our questions, his puzzlement our puzzlement; they involve us in the action of the poem, much as Spenser's gentle knight does in the First Book of *The Faerie Queene*. To find a writer who shares Langland's social or spiritual (as distinct from poetic) concerns we must turn to Wyclif, different as his personality and purpose were. Though Wyclif's orthodoxy weakened, whilst Langland's remained unimpeachable, both saw the need of ecclesiastical reform, and came to see the friars as a danger; Langland even considered the disendowment that Wyclif favoured. But to read Wyclif, or the writings ascribed to him, is to see how unique was Langland's achievement in giving orthodoxy a dynamic power, restating it in human terms. There is nothing in the tenor of the work that cannot be confirmed from the Fathers—from Augustine or Bernard in particular or from Holy Writ: yet it continually arrests us by plain statement. The 'deification' of man by the Redemption has such warrant in Luke 18: 18 ff. But Holy Church puts it in startling form when she says that the man who pursues Truth 'is a god bi the Gospel, agrounde and aloft' (i. 90). St James had said that Faith without works is dead: Holy Church says it is as 'ded as a dore tre' (i. 185), adding that by the same token Chastity without Charity will be chained in hell. Yet formal doctrine does not bulk large. Much is taken for granted: the sacraments (the Eucharist figures only once), confessional practice, acquaintance with the liturgy and calendar of the Church.

A modern philosopher* (who recognizes as one ideal of human perfection that which conceives of man as finally becoming like God) speaks of 'a basic instability in the Christian account of relations between God and Man': 'If all human improvement is due to divine Grace, what is the point of moral effort? If men can improve themselves, God is superfluous.' In the century of Langland (and of Ockham) such antitheses would have appeared naïve; and central passages in *Piers* (xix) are devoted to depicting the role of Grace in a world where Man must 'do what in him is' (*Fac quod in te est* summarizes the teaching of many fourteenth-century theologians). The same philosopher complains that Christian views of the body oscillate between Gnostic extremes and their pantheistic opposites. But Langland's apprehension of the *magnum mysterium* of the Incarnation kept him from such extremes. He gives to generative Nature (Kind) a role like that she has in Chaucer's *Parlement*: there she is the 'Vicar of the Almighty Lord'; here she is linked with Reason, who follows all beasts 'in eating, in drinking, in engendering of kind' (ix. 327): marriage and procreation are affirmed as good (and *mariages de convenance* are scouted).

Oscillation there is in Langland in that the balance swings to and fro between a simple piety and high theology, between ploughmen and shepherds and such 'lewd sottes' who may 'pierce with a paternoster the palace of heaven', and Study, Clergy, 'the highest lettred out'. But Measure, Moderation, is the first principle that Holy Church enunciates: 'Mesure is medcyne' (i. 19–35). *Omnia in mensura et numero et*

---

* J. Passmore, *The Perfectibility of Man* (London, 1970), quoted *TLS* (1973), 29.

pondere disposuisti (Wisd. 11: 26) was a verse that had allowed the schoolmen to accommodate the Aristotelian doctrine of the Mean (as Dante does at *Purgatorio* xvii. 91 ff.), remote as it is from the Christian ideal of complete self-denial. That ideal Langland sees realized in the first friars, in contrast to those who unexpectedly emerge at the close of the poem to threaten Unity by their inordinate numbers, and to be condemned by Conscience for this reason:

> ye wexeth out of noumbre:
> Hevene hath evene noumbre[1] and helle is without noumbre.
>
> (xx. 267–8)

[1] *the right proportion*

The self-denial of ascetics is commended at the very outset of the poem, and at the end. But Langland does not conceive it as possible or even desirable for all Christians. When Grace, with Pauline warrant, distributes to men the treasure they are to live by, the weapons to fight Antichrist with, he names first those who use their intelligence in preaching or practising law, then merchants, labourers, mathematicians, artists ('to compas craftily and coloures to make', xix. 235), astronomers, philosophers, and those who execute justice. Those who live 'in longynge to ben hennes / In poverte and in penaunce to preye for alle Crystene' (xix. 242–4) come last in the file. And no class is to have greater status or prestige than the others; none has cause for pride. They are to be bound together in love. It is the monastic ideal transferred to the workaday world, and consistent with the tripartite division of Dowel, Dobet, Dobest set forth earlier in the poem.

It is pertinent to note that when after a long series of dialogues, disputes, and diatribes a definition of Dobest emerges, the first term of it is *Dilige* (love)—and it is put into the mouth of Patience, because 'Caritas suffereth long'. St Paul's hymn to love here takes on English form (xv. 160 ff.): Charité 'ne chaffareth noughte ne chalengeth', is 'as proude of a peny as of a pounde of gold': it 'leveth [? trusteth] and loveth alle that owre Lorde made'.

But if Love is the golden string, the clue to the whole poem, it is not a love that disregards the claims of Divine Justice. They are set forth, and met, in the debate of the Four Daughters of God (xviii; see p. 37 above); and earthly justice is shown at the outset to be likest God's when seasoned with mercy. The concern for a just ordering of society dominates the opening passus and reappears at the close. To Langland spiritual love and social justice were not a duality but two sides of the same coin.

Langland's ideal is the man who 'pursueth God *in doing*'. 'Contem-

platyf lyf or actyf lyf, Cryst wolde men *wroughte*' (vi. 251). The three
stages in the life of perfection, *Dowel*, *Dobet*, *Dobest*, have in common
the active verb. They are never strictly defined, but rather illustrated
or exemplified. The triad is of ancient origin. Threefold patterns can
be found for instance in the thirteenth-century Anglo-Norman *La
Lumière as lais* ('Light for the Layfolk'), which distinguishes three
levels of charity and three grades of perfection: (1) of 'religiun', (2) of
'prelacie', (3) of sanctity. Langland, though keeping the triadic pattern—it had scriptural precedent in the Parable of the Seed, which he
applies to Marriage, Widowhood, Virginity—alters the sequence so
that the 'best' form becomes the 'Mixed' Life, similar to that of a
devout and active bishop. Active and Contemplative are not juxtaposed, but balanced. In Passus XIX of *Piers*, the graces of the Spirit are
bestowed on the Active and the Contemplative alike.

The distrust of abstract scholastic speculation on such topics as the
Nature of the Trinity, which shows through elsewhere, is no more
than a suspicion of the intellectual vice of *curiositas* that had been stig-
matized by St Bernard, and was to be censured by Gerson, Chancellor
of the University of Paris—not to mention a contemporary poet,
evidently a scholar himself, who averred that

> The more we trace the Trinity
> The more we falle in fantasye. (*CB XIV*, p. 163)

Langland sees such speculation as diverting the learned from their
true work in the world. But the attention he gives to this same doctrine
of the Trinity shows that he was not content to rest in a simple fideism.

Balance and perspective, centrality, humanity—these are the terms
that come to mind when we look back on the work as a whole, obscure
though parts of it may remain. Here is none of the mawkish religiosity,
or of the intellectual slackness, that a century or so later were to let in
the flood tides of the Reformation: Reason has a high place in Langland's *schema*. He owes much to the ascetic tradition of St Bernard, yet
whilst recognizing the place of fasting, penance, celibacy, he keeps
them in proportion, and comes closer to the profundities of the
Gospel than many of the ascetics. Difficult as it is to pin him down, he
is in no sense eclectic. Like Dante, though not so deliberately, he
attempts to relate a Christian view of the Universe to the life, social
and political, of wayfaring man on earth.

Chronological Table

Political and Social History (Britain and Europe)	Cultural History (Britain and Europe)	English Literature
1066 Battle of Hastings. King Harold d.; succeeded by William the Conqueror (–1087)		
	1079–93 building of Winchester Cathedral	
	1083–c.1189 building of Ely Cathedral	
1087 William the Conqueror d.; succeeded by William Rufus (–1100)		
	1093–c.1128 building of Durham Cathedral	
	1093–1109 Anselm Archbishop of Canterbury	
	[late 11th century: first recorded troubadour, Guilhem of Aquitaine (1071–1127)]	
1099 Crusaders take Jerusalem		
1100 William Rufus d.; succeeded by Henry I (–1135)		
	1115 Foundation of Clairvaux; St Bernard first abbot (–1153)	
	[early 12th century: Oxford MS of *Chanson de Roland*]	

1135 Henry I d.; succeeded by Stephen (–1154)	1131 Gilbertine order founded at Sempringham	
	1134–c.1160 building of north and south towers of Chartres cathedral	
	?1135 Geoffrey of Monmouth's *Historia Regum Britanniae* completed in some form	
	?c.1140 AN *Mystère d'Adam*	
	1141 Ordericus Vitalis, *Historia Ecclesiastica*	
	1142 Abelard d.	
	1143 William of Malmesbury d.	
1147–9 Second Crusade		
1154 Stephen d.; succeeded by Henry II (–1189)	c.1150–c.1173 Bernart de Ventadorn	1154 end of *Peterborough Chronicle*
	c.1150–6 *Roman de Thèbes*	
	1155 Wace, *Roman de Brut*	
	c.1156 *Roman d'Enéas*	
	1159 John of Salisbury, *Policraticus*	
	c.1160 Benoit de Ste-Maure, *Roman de Troie*	
	Thomas, *Tristan*	
	c.1160–1200 Arnaut Daniel	
	?c.1165–80 Marie de France, *Lais*	
1170 Archbishop Thomas Becket murdered	c.1170 AN *Horn*	
	Chrétien de Troyes, *Erec*	
	1172 Wace, *Roman de Rou*	

457

Political and Social History (Britain and Europe)	Cultural History (Britain and Europe)	English Literature
	1174–5 Choir of Canterbury Cathedral built by William of Sens	?c.1175–80 *Ormulum*
	c.1177–81 Chrétien de Troyes, *Yvain, Lancelot*	
	1181 First Carthusian monastery in England (Witham)	
	c.1181–91 Chrétien de Troyes, *Perceval*	
	1182 St Francis of Assisi b.	
	1185 Rebuilding of Lincoln Cathedral begins	
1189 Henry II d.; succeeded by Richard I (–1199)		?1189–c.1220 *The Owl and the Nightingale*
1190 Beginning of Third Crusade	c.1190–1220 AN *Amadas et Ydoine*	
	1194–1260 Rebuilding of Chartres Cathedral	
	1198 Innocent III, Pope (–1216)	
1199 Richard I d.; succeeded by John (–1216)		?c.1200 Layamon, *Brut*
		?c.1200–c.1225 'Katherine Group'
		?c.1215–c.1225 *Ancrene Wisse*
	1215 Fourth Lateran Council (decrees on penance; auricular confession required)	
1216 John d.; succeeded by Henry III (–1272)	1216 St Dominic d.	
	1223 Gerald of Wales d.	

1224 Franciscans came to England		?.c.1225 *King Horn*
1237–42 Mongols invade Eastern Europe	1235–53 Robert Grosseteste, bishop of Lincoln	
	c.1237 Guillaume de Lorris, *Roman de la Rose* (unfinished)	
	1245–69 Rebuilding of Westminster Abbey	?.c.1250 *Floris and Blancheflour*
		1255–60 MS Trinity College Cambridge 323 (lyrics)
	1259 Matthew Paris d.	
	c.1260 *Manuel des Péchés*	
1262–3 Rising of Simon de Montfort's supporters at Gloucester		
	1264 Founding of Merton College, Oxford	
	1265 Dante b.	
1265 Battle of Evesham		
1272 Henry III d.; succeeded by Edward I (–1307)		1272–82 MS Digby 86 (*Fox and Wolf, Dame Sirith*, lyrics)
	1274 St Thomas Aquinas d.	
	c.1277 Jean de Meun completes *Roman de la Rose*	
	1280 Albertus Magnus d.	
	1284 Founding of Peterhouse, Cambridge	?.c.1280–c.1300 *Havelok*
	1292 Roger Bacon d.	
	c.1292 Dante, *Vita Nuova*	

459

Political and Social History (Britain and Europe)	Cultural History (Britain and Europe)	English Literature
	1298 Jacobus de Voragine (author of *Legenda Aurea*) d.	? c.1300 *Cursor Mundi*
		1303 Mannyng begins *Handlyng Synne*
1306 Robert Bruce crowned king of Scotland	c.1304–21 Dante writes *Commedia*	
1307 Edward I d.; succeeded by Edward II (–1327)		
1314 Scots defeat English at Bannockburn	1311 Feast of Corpus Christi made universal throughout the church	[early 14th-century romances, e.g. *Kyng Alisaunder, Sir Orfeo, Sir Landevale*]
1320 Declaration of Arbroath	1321 Dante d.	? c.1325 *Chronicle* of 'Robert of Gloucester'
1327 Edward II d.; succeeded by Edward III (–1377)		1330–40 Auchinleck MS (romances, etc.)
1329 Robert Bruce d.	1331 Deguileville, *Pèlerinage de la vie humaine*	MS Harley 2253 (lyrics)

1333 English defeat Scots at Halidon Hill
1337(–1453) Hundred Years War

1338 Mannyng's *Chronicle* completed
1340 Dan Michel, *Ayenbite of Inwyt*
c.1340 *Prick of Conscience*

1341 Petrarch crowned laureate poet on Capitol

c.1343–4 Chaucer b.

1346 English defeat French at Crécy
1349 Black Death reaches England

1349 Richard Rolle d.

c.1350–2 Boccaccio, *Decameron*
Higden, *Polychronicon*
Henry of Lancaster, *Livre de Seyntz Medicines*

1356 English defeat French at Poitiers
1358 Jacquerie—French peasant uprising

?1356–7 French version of 'Mandeville'

1359–60 Chaucer on service in France and captured

1361 Black Death reappears in England

1362 English used instead of French in lawcourts and Parliamentary proceedings

1364 Higden d.

1367–70 Langland, *Piers Plowman*, A text
1369–70 Chaucer, *The Book of the Duchess*

Political and Social History (Britain and Europe)	Cultural History (Britain and Europe)	English Literature
	c.1370 Wyclif begins teaching on theology	
		1372–3 Chaucer visits Italy
		? 1373–80 Chaucer, *The House of Fame*
1376 Black Prince d.	1374 Petrarch d.	1375 Barbour, *Bruce*
1377 Edward III d.; succeeded by Richard II (–1399)	1375 Boccaccio d.	? 1376–9 Gower, *Mirour de l'Omme*
	1376 Criticism of Wyclif begins	1377–9 Langland, *Piers Plowman*, B text
	1377 Machaut d.	1378 Chaucer visits Italy
	1378 Papal Schism	['later 14th-century' works, e.g. poems of *Gawain* MS, Alliterative *Morte Arthure*, *Sir Launfal*, *Siege of Jerusalem*]
	1378–1411 Rebuilding of nave of Canterbury Cathedral	? 1380–90 Chaucer, *The Parlement of Foules*
1381 Peasants' Revolt	1380 St Catherine of Siena d.	
1382 Turks capture Sofia	1382 Blackfriars Council condemns ten propositions of Wyclif as heretical	
	1384 Wyclif d.	
		c.1385–7 Chaucer, *Troilus and Criseyde*
		? c.1386–7 Langland, *Piers Plowman*, C text
		1387 Trevisa's translation of Higden's *Polychronicon*
		? c.1387 Chaucer begins writing *The Canterbury Tales*

1390-3 Gower, *Confessio Amantis*

1398 Trevisa's translation of Bartholomaeus, *De Proprietatibus Rerum*

1400 Chaucer d.
1402 Trevisa d.
1408 Gower d.

1388 Scots defeat English at battle of
Otterburn
1389 Turks defeat Serbians at Kossovo

1393 Bajazet subdues Bulgaria

1399 Richard II deposed; succeeded by
Henry IV (–1413)
1400 Richard II murdered

Select Bibliography

Fuller bibliographies may be found in the guides listed in Section A. Editions and studies of English works discussed are to be found in Section J.

A. BIBLIOGRAPHICAL GUIDES

The Cambridge Bibliography of English Literature, ed. F. W. Bateson (Cambridge, 1940), vol. i; vol. v. (Supplement, ed. G. Watson, 1957.)

The New Cambridge Bibliography of English Literature, ed. G. Watson (Cambridge, 1974), vol. i.

Renwick, W. L. and Orton, H., *The Beginnings of English Literature to Skelton* (London, 1939, 1962).

The Index of Middle English Verse, edd. C. Brown and R. H. Robbins (New York, 1943); *Supplement*, edd. R. H. Robbins and J. L. Cutler (Lexington, 1965).

The Index of Middle English Prose, edd. A. S. G. Edwards *et al.* (in progress); *Handlist*, vol. i, ed. R. Hanna III (Cambridge, 1984).

Jolliffe, P. S., *A Check-list of Middle English Prose Writings of Spiritual Guidance* (Toronto, 1974).

A Manual of the Writings in Middle English, originally ed. J. E. Wells (New Haven, 1916; with later supplements); new edn. in several vols., edd. J. B. Severs and A. E. Hartung (New Haven, 1967-) (*MWME*).

Utley, F. L., *The Crooked Rib* (Columbus, Ohio, 1949).

Annual bibliographies

The Year's Work in English Studies (The English Association, 1919-).

The Annual Bibliography of English Language and Literature (Modern Humanities Research Association, 1920-).

International Bibliography of Books and Articles on the Modern Languages and Literatures (Modern Language Association of America, 1969-).

Abstracts of English Studies (Boulder, Colorado, 1958-).

For medieval French literature:

Bossuat, R., *Manuel bibliographique de la littérature française du moyen âge* (Melun, 1951; with later supplements).

For folk tales:

Thompson, Stith, *Motif-Index of Folk Literature* (Bloomington, 1932–6; new edn., Copenhagen, 1955–8).

Aarne, A., *The Types of the Folk Tale*, ed. and trans. Stith Thompson (Helsinki, 1928).

For medieval Latin see below, Section E

B. DICTIONARIES

The Oxford English Dictionary, edd. J. A. H. Murray *et al.* (1884–1928; corrected reissue, 1933).

Middle English Dictionary, edd. H. Kurath and S. M. Kuhn (Ann Arbor, 1952–)

Glossary (by N. Davis) to *Early Middle English Verse and Prose*, edd. J. A. W. Bennett and G. V. Smithers (Oxford, 1966; 2nd edn. 1968) (*EMEVP*).

Glossary (by J. R. R. Tolkien) to *Fourteenth-Century Verse and Prose*, ed. K. Sisam (Oxford, 1921) (Sisam).

A Chaucer Glossary, edd. N. Davis *et al.* (Oxford, 1979).

Stratmann, F. H., *A Middle-English Dictionary* (revised and enlarged by H. Bradley, Oxford, 1891).

Dictionary of the Older Scottish Tongue, edd. W. A. Craigie and A. J. Aitken (London, 1937–).

Carter, H. H., *A Dictionary of Middle English Musical Terms* (Bloomington, 1961).

Whiting, B. J., *Proverbs, Sentences and Proverbial Phrases from English Writings Mainly before 1500* (Cambridge, Mass., 1968).

C. LANGUAGE

Brunner, K., *Abriss der mittelenglischen Grammatik* (5th edn., Tübingen, 1962); trans. by G. Johnston as *An Outline of Middle English Grammar* (Oxford, 1970).

Clark, J. W., *Early English* (London, 1957).

Huchon, R., *Histoire de la langue anglaise*, vol. ii (Paris, 1930).

Jordan, R. and Matthes, H., *Handbuch der mittelenglischen Grammatik* (Heidelberg, 1925, 1934); trans. by E. J. Crook as *Handbook of Middle English Grammar* (The Hague, 1974).

Luick, K., *Historische Grammatik der englischen Sprache* (Leipzig, 1914–40, 1964).

Mossé, F., *Manuel de l'anglais du moyen âge* (Paris, 1949); trans. by J. A. Walker as *A Handbook of Middle English* (Baltimore, 1952).

Strang, B. M. H., *A History of English* (London, 1970), ch. iv.

Particular topics and aspects

Benskin, M. and Samuels, M. L., edd., *So meny people longages and tongues: Philological essays in Scots and mediaeval English presented to Angus McIntosh* (Edinburgh, 1981).

Björkman, E., *Scandinavian Loan-Words in Middle English* (Halle, 1900).

Davis, N., 'Chaucer and Fourteenth-Century English', in D. S. Brewer, *Chaucer* (Writers and their Background; London, 1974), 58–84.

Dobson, E. J., *Early English Pronunciation 1500–1700* (Oxford, 2nd edn., 1968).

McIntosh, A., 'A New Approach to Middle English Dialectology', *English Studies*, 44 (1963), 1–11.

Mustanoja, T. F., *A Middle English Syntax*, vol. i (Helsinki, 1960).

Samuels, M. L., 'Some Applications of Middle English Dialectology', *English Studies*, 44 (1963), 81–94.

Sisam, K., 'The English Language in the Fourteenth Century' in Sisam.
Smithers, G. V., 'Early Middle English' in *EMEVP*.

D. HISTORY

1. Political and Social History

[See E. B. Graves, *A Bibliography of English History to 1485*, Oxford, 1975]

Barrow, G. W. S., *Robert Bruce and the Community of the Realm of Scotland* (London, 1965).

Bennett, H. S., *Life on the English Manor* (Cambridge, 1938; 3rd edn., 1948).

Bloch, M., *Feudal Society*, trans. by L. A. Manyon (London, 1961).

Coulton, G. G., *Chaucer and his England* (London, 1908, 1965).

—— *Social Life in Britain from the Conquest to the Reformation* (Cambridge, 1918).

Dickinson, W. C., *Scotland from the Earliest Times to 1603* (3rd edn., revised and ed. A. A. M. Duncan, Oxford, 1977).

Dobson, R. B., *The Peasants' Revolt of 1381* (London, 1971).

English Historical Documents, vol. ii, 1042–1189, edd. D. C. Douglas and G. W. Greenaway (London, 1953); vol. iii, 1189–1327, ed. H. Rothwell (London, 1975); vol. iv, 1327–1485, ed. A. R. Myers (London, 1969).

Fowler, K., *The Age of Plantagenet and Valois* (London, 1967).

Holdsworth, W., *History of English Law* (London, 1922–38, with later revisions), vol. ii.

Holmes, G. A., *The Later Middle Ages 1272–1485* (Edinburgh, 1962).

Jolliffe, J. E. A., *The Constitutional History of Medieval England* (London, 1937; 4th edn., 1961).

Keen, M., *England in the Later Middle Ages* (London, 1973).

McFarlane, K. B., *Lancastrian Kings and Lollard Knights* (Oxford, 1972).

Mead, W. E., *The English Medieval Feast* (Boston, 1931).

McKisack, M., *The Fourteenth Century 1307–99* (Oxford, 1959).

Myers, A. R., *England in the Late Middle Ages* (Harmondsworth, 1952).

Nicholson, R., *Scotland: The Later Middle Ages* (Edinburgh, 1974).

Pollock, F. and Maitland, F. W., *The History of English Law before the Time of Edward I* (Cambridge, 1895; revised edn., 1968).

Poole, A. L., *From Domesday Book to Magna Carta 1087–1216* (Oxford, 1951, 1955).

Powicke, F. M., *The Thirteenth Century* (Oxford, 1953, 1962).

Reynolds, S., *An Introduction to the History of English Medieval Towns* (Oxford, 1977).

Rickert, E., *Chaucer's World* (edd. C. C. Olson and M. M. Crow, New York, 1948).

Riley, H. T., *Memorials of London and London Life AD 1276–1419* (London, 1868).

Thrupp, S., *The Merchant Class of Medieval London* (Chicago, 1948).

2. Cultural History

General studies

Bolgar, R. R., *The Classical Heritage and its Beneficiaries* (Cambridge, 1954).
—— ed., *Classical Influences on European Culture AD 500—1500* (Cambridge, 1971).
Chaytor, H. J., *From Script to Print* (Cambridge, 1945).
Clanchy, M. T., *From Memory to Written Record: England 1066—1307* (London, 1979).
Coplestone, F. C., *A History of Medieval Philosophy* (revised edn., London, 1972).
Crump, C. G. and Jacob, E. F., edd., *The Legacy of the Middle Ages* (Oxford, 1926).
Huizinga, J., *The Waning of the Middle Ages* (English edn., London, 1924).
Keen, M., *Chivalry* (London, 1984).
Leff, G., *Medieval Thought: St Augustine to Ockham* (Harmondsworth, 1958).
Mathew, G., *The Court of Richard II* (London, 1968).
Morris, C., *The Discovery of the Individual 1050—1200* (London, 1972).
Painter, S., *French Chivalry* (Baltimore, 1940).
Poole, A. L., ed., *Medieval England*, 2 vols. (revised edn., Oxford, 1958).
Smalley, B., *English Friars and Antiquity in the Early Fourteenth Century* (Oxford, 1960).
Southern, R. W., *The Making of the Middle Ages* (London, 1953).
—— *Medieval Humanism, and Other Essays* (Oxford, 1970).

Religion

[See also Bibliography to Chapter 7, below, section J. 7]

Bultot, R., *La Doctrine du mépris du monde*, 4. 1. *Pierre Damien* (Louvain and Paris, 1963).
Charland, T. M., *Artes Predicandi* (Paris, 1936).
Coulton, G. C., *Five Centuries of Religion* (Cambridge, 2nd edn., 1929).
Delehaye, H., *The Legends of the Saints* (trans. by D. Attwater, London, 1962).
Gerould, G. H., *Saints' Lives* (Boston, 1916).
Gougaud, L., *Dévotions et pratiques ascétiques du moyen âge* (Paris, 1925).
Knowles, D., *The Monastic Order in England* (Cambridge, 1940; 2nd edn., 1963).
—— *The Religious Orders in England*, 3 vols. (Cambridge, 1956—9).
Lambert, M. D., *Medieval Heresy: Popular Movements from Bogomil to Hus* (London, 1977).
Leclercq, J., *The Love of Learning and the Desire for God* (trans. by C. Misrahi, New York, 1961).
——, Vandenbrouke, F., and Bouyer, L., *The Spirituality of the Middle Ages* (trans. by the Benedictines of Holme Eden, London, 1968).
Leff, G., *Heresy in the Later Middle Ages*, 2 vols. (Manchester, 1967).
Little, A. G., *Studies in English Franciscan History* (Manchester, 1917).
McFarlane, K. B., *John Wycliffe and the Beginnings of English Non-Conformity* (London, 1952)

Manning, B. L., *The People's Faith in the Time of Wyclif* (Cambridge, 1919).

The Oxford Dictionary of the Christian Church, edd. F. L. Cross and E. A. Livingstone (2nd edn., Oxford, 1974).

Pantin, W. A., *The English Church in the Fourteenth Century* (Cambridge, 1955).

Smalley, B., *The Study of the Bible in the Middle Ages* (Oxford, 1941; 3rd edn., 1983).

Southern, R. W., *St Anselm and his Biographer: A Study of Monastic Life and Thought* (Cambridge, 1961).

—— *Western Society and the Church in the Middle Ages* (Harmondsworth, 1970).

Wilmart, A., *Auteurs spirituels et textes dévots du moyen âge latin* (Paris, 1932).

Science

Carmody, F. J., *Arabic Astronomical and Astrological Sciences in Latin Translation: a Critical Bibliography* (Berkeley, 1956).

Crombie, A. C., *Augustine to Galileo: the History of Science AD 400–1650*, 2 vols. (London, 1952; 2nd edn., 1961).

—— *Robert Grosseteste and the Origins of Experimental Science 1100–1700* (Oxford, 1953, 1962).

Curry, W. C., *Chaucer and the Medieval Sciences* (New York, 1926; 2nd edn., London, 1960).

Duhem, P., *Le Système du monde*, 9 vols. (Paris, 1913–59).

Haskins, C. H., *Studies in the History of Mediaeval Science* (Cambridge, Mass., 1924; revised edn., 1927).

North, J. D., ed. and trans., *Richard of Wallingford*, 3 vols. (Oxford, 1976).

Sarton, G., *Introduction to the History of Science*, 3 vols. (Baltimore, 1927).

Singer, C., *A Short History of Science to the Nineteenth Century* (Oxford, 1941).

Talbot, C. H., *Medicine in Mediaeval England* (London, 1967).

Thorndike, L., *A History of Magic and Experimental Science*, 6 vols. (New York, 1923–58).

—— *The 'Sphere' of Sacrobosco and its Commentators* (Chicago, 1949).

White, L., *Medieval Technology and Social Change* (Oxford, 1962).

Education

Catto, J. I., ed., *The Early Oxford Schools* (*The History of the University of Oxford*, ed. T. H. Aston, vol. i, Oxford, 1984).

Emden, A. B., *A Biographical Register of the University of Oxford to AD 1500*, 3 vols. (Oxford, 1957–9) (*BRUO*).

—— *A Biographical Register of the University of Cambridge to 1500* (Cambridge, 1963) (*BRUC*).

Mallet, C. E., *A History of the University of Oxford*, 3 vols. (London, 1924–7).

Mullinger, J. B., *The University of Cambridge from the Earliest Times to the Royal Injunctions of 1535* (Cambridge, 1873).

Orme, N., *English Schools in the Middle Ages* (London, 1973).

Rashdall, H., *The Universities of the Middle Ages*, 2 vols. (Oxford, 1895).

Music

Harrison, F. Ll., *Music in Medieval Britain* (London, 1958; 4th edn., 1980).
New Oxford History of Music, vol. ii, *Early Medieval Music up to 1300*, ed. A. Hughes (Oxford, 1954; revised edn. 1955); vol. iii, *Ars Nova and the Renaissance*, edd. A. Hughes and G. Abraham (Oxford, 1960).
Reese, G., *Music in the Middle Ages* (New York, 1940).
Sternfeld, F., ed., *A History of Western Music*, vol. i (London, 1973).
Wilkins, N., *Music in the Age of Chaucer* (Cambridge, 1979).

The visual arts

Anderson, M. D., *Misericords* (Harmondsworth, 1954).
—— *The Medieval Carver* (Cambridge, 1935).
—— *Drama and Imagery in English Medieval Churches* (Cambridge, 1963).
Boase, T. S. R., *English Art 1100—1216* (Oxford, 1953).
Bond, F., *Gothic Architecture in England* (London, 1905, 1912).
—— *An Introduction to English Church Architecture from the Eleventh to the Sixteenth Century*, 2 vols. (London, 1913).
Brieger, P., *English Art 1216—1307* (Oxford, 1957).
Caiger-Smith, A., *English Medieval Mural Painting* (Oxford, 1963).
Evans, J., *English Art 1307—1461* (Oxford, 1949).
Gardner, A., *A Handbook of English Medieval Sculpture* (revised edn., Cambridge, 1971).
Harvey, J., *Gothic England* (London, 1947).
Mâle, E., *L'Art religieux du XIIe siècle en France* (Paris, 1947).
—— *L'Art religieux du XIIIe siècle en France* (Paris, 1948) (trans. by D. Nussey, *The Gothic Image*, London, 1961).
—— *L'Art religieux de la fin du moyen âge en France* (Paris, 1949).
Marks, R. and Morgan, N., *The Golden Age of English Manuscript Painting 1200—1500* (London, 1981).
Millar, E. G., *English Illuminated Manuscripts of the Fourteenth and Fifteenth Centuries* (Paris, Brussels, 1928).
Pritchard, V., *English Medieval Graffiti* (Cambridge, 1967).
Remnant, G. L., *A Catalogue of Misericords in Great Britain* (Oxford, 1969).
Rickert, M., *Painting in Britain in the Middle Ages* (Harmondsworth, 1954).
Rushworth, G. McN., *Medieval Christian Imagery as Illustrated by the Painted Windows of Great Malvern Priory Church* (Oxford, 1936).
Stone, L., *Sculpture in Britain in the Middle Ages* (Harmondsworth, 1955).
Tristram, E. W., *English Medieval Wall Painting: The Twelfth Century* (Oxford, 1944).
—— *English Medieval Wall Painting: The Thirteenth Century*, 2 vols. (Oxford, 1950).
—— *English Wall Painting of the Fourteenth Century* (London, 1955).
Woodforde, C., *English Stained and Painted Glass* (Oxford, 1954).

Scribes, books, libraries

Ker, N. R., *Medieval Libraries of Great Britain* (London, 1941; revised edn., 1964).
Parkes, M. B., *English Cursive Book Hands 1250—1500* (Oxford, 1969).
Powicke, F. M., *The Medieval Books of Merton College* (Oxford, 1931).
Wattenbach, W., *Das Schriftwesen in Mittelalter* (Leipzig, 1896).
Wright, C. E., *English Vernacular Hands from the Twelfth to the Fifteenth Centuries* (Oxford, 1960).

E. WORKS IN LATIN

Bibliographical guides and general studies

Manitius, M., *Geschichte der lateinischen Literatur des Mittelalters*, 3 vols. (Munich, 1911–31).
Medioevo latino: Bolletino bibliografico della cultura europea dal secolo vi al xiii, ed. C. Leonardi (Spoleto, 1980–).
Raby, F. J. E., *A History of Christian Latin Poetry from the Beginnings to the Close of the Middle Ages* (Oxford, 1927; 2nd edn., 1953).
—— *A History of Secular Latin Poetry in the Middle Ages*, 2 vols. (Oxford, 1934; 2nd edn., 1957).
Walther, H., *Versanfänge Mittellateinischer Dichtung* (Göttingen, 2nd edn., 1969).

Anthologies and collections of texts

Corpus Christianorum. Series Latina (Turnhout, 1953–); Continuatio medievalis (Turnhout, 1966–).
Dreves, G. M. and Blume, C., edd., *Analecta hymnica*, 55 vols. (Leipzig, 1886–1922).
Faral, E., *Les arts poétiques du XIIe et du XIIIe siècle* (Paris, 1924).
Patrologia Latina, ed. J. P. Migne, 221 vols. (Paris, 1844–) (*PL*).
Raby, F. J. E., ed., *The Oxford Book of Medieval Latin Verse* (Oxford, 1959).
Wright, T., ed., *The Anglo-Latin Satirical Poets and Epigrammatists of the Twelfth Century*, 2 vols. (RS lix, 1872).

Authors and texts (mainly those referred to in this volume)

Abelard, *Historia Calamitatum*, ed. J. Monfrin (Paris, 1967); *Epistolae duorum amantium*, ed. E. Könsgen (Leiden, 1974); (trans. by B. Radice, Harmondsworth, 1974).
Adelard of Bath, *Quaestiones Naturales*, ed. M. Müller, *Beiträge zur Geschichte der Philosophie des Mittelalters*, xxxi (1934–5).
Ailred of Rievaulx, *Opera omnia*, edd. A. Hoste and C. H. Talbot (*Corpus Christianorum, Contin. med.* 1– , 1971); *Letter to his Sister*, trans. by G. Webb and A. Walker (London, 1957) (ME trans. edd. J. Ayto and A. Barratt, EETS cclxxxvii, 1984); Walter Daniel's *Life of Ailred*, ed. and trans. F. M. Powicke, London, 1950.

Alanus de Insulis (Alain de Lille), *Anticlaudianus*, ed. R. Bossuat (Paris, 1955) (trans. by J. J. Sheridan, Toronto, 1973); *De Planctu Naturae*, in T. Wright, *Satirical Poets of the Twelfth Century*, vol. ii.

Alexander of Bath, *Moralia super Evangelia* (unprinted: see discussion in books of E. J. Dobson cited below, p. 483).

Alexander Nequam (Neckham), *De Naturis Rerum*, ed. T. Wright (RS xxxiv, 1863).

Andreas Capellanus, *De Amore*, ed. E. Trojel (Copenhagen, 1892) (trans. J. J. Parry, *The Art of Courtly Love*, New York, 1959).

Anselm, St, *Opera omnia*, ed. F. S. Schmitt, 6 vols. (Edinburgh, 1946–62); *Memorials of St Anselm*, edd. R. W. Southern and F. S. Schmitt (London, 1969) (contains *De Custodia interioris hominis*, pp. 354–60); Eadmer's *Life of Anselm*, ed. and trans. R. W. Southern (London, 1962; Oxford, 1972).

Bartholomaeus Anglicus (Bartholomew the Englishman), *De Proprietatibus Rerum* (no modern edn.; see Bibliography to ch. 7, below, section J. 7).

Benedict, St, *Regula*, edd. A. de Vogüé and J. Neufville, 7 vols. (Paris, 1972–7); (trans. by A. Gasquet, London, 1936).

Bernard, St, *Opera*, edd. J. Leclercq, C. H. Talbot, H. M. Rochais, 8 vols. (Rome, 1957–77).

Boethius, *De Consolatione Philosophiae*, ed. L. Bieler (*Corp. Christianorum*, Ser. Lat. 94, 1957); ed. and trans. H. F. Stewart and E. K. Rand (Loeb edn., 1918) (trans. V. E. Watts, Harmondsworth, 1976); see P. Courcelle, *La Consolation de philosophie dans la tradition littéraire* (Paris, 1967).

Bonaventura, St, *Opera omnia*, 10 vols. (Quaracchi, 1882–92).

Carmina Burana, edd. A. Hilka, O. Schumann, and B. Bischoff (Heidelberg, 1930–70).

Christina of Markyate, *Life*, ed. and trans. C. H. Talbot (Oxford, 1959).

Comestor, *see* Peter Comestor.

Fasciculus Morum (no modern edn.; see S. Wenzel, *Verses in Sermons: Fasciculus Morum and its Middle English Poems* (Cambridge, Mass., 1978)).

(?) Geoffrey of Auxerre, *Declamationes de Colloquio Simonis cum Jesu*, PL clxxxiv, 435–75.

Geoffrey of Monmouth, *Historia Regum Britanniae*, ed. A. Griscom (London, 1929) (trans. L. Thorpe, Harmondsworth, 1966); *Vita Merlini*, ed. J. J. Parry (Illinois Univ. Studies x. 3, 1925).

Gerald of Wales (Giraldus Cambrensis), *Opera*, edd. J. S. Brewer, J. F. Dimock, and G. F. Warner, 8 vols. (RS xxi, 1861–91); see R. Bartlett, *Gerald of Wales 1146–1223* (Oxford, 1982).

Gervase of Tilbury, *Otia Imperialia*, ed. G. G. Leibnitz, 3 vols. (Hanover, 1707–11).

Gesta Romanorum, ed. H. Oesterley (Berlin, 1872) (trans. C. Swan, London, 1905).

Gesta Stephani, ed. K. R. Potter (London, 1955; revised edn., Oxford, 1976).

Giraldus Cambrensis, *see* Gerald of Wales.

Glossa Ordinaria, PL cxiii–cxiv.

Gower, *Vox Clamantis, see* Bibliography to ch. 9 below, Section J. 9.

Gratian, *Decretum* (*Decretals*), ed. A. Friedberg (Leipzig, 1879).

Gregory the Great, St, *Moralia in Job*, edd. R. Gillet and A. Bocognano, 2 vols. (Paris, 1952–74).

Grosseteste, Robert, *see* Robert Grosseteste.

Guigo, *Consuetudines*, *PL* cliii. 631–759.

Higden, *Polychronicon*, *see* Bibliography to ch. 7, below, section J. 7.

Hugh of St Victor, *Opera*, *PL* clxxv–clxxvii.

Innocent III, Pope, *De Miseria Conditionis Humanae*, *PL* ccxvii. 701–46.

Jacobus de Voragine, *Legenda Aurea*, ed. T. Graesse (2nd edn., Leipzig, 1850) (trans. by W. Caxton, ed. F. S. Ellis, London, 1892).

Jacques de Vitry, *Exempla*, ed. T. F. Crane (London, 1890).

Jerome, St, *Adversus Jovinianum*, *PL* xxiii.

Jocelyn of Brakelond, *Chronicle*, ed. and trans. H. E. Butler (London, 1949).

John of Salisbury, *Metalogicon*, ed. C. C. J. Webb (Oxford, 1929) (trans. by D. D. McGarry (Berkeley, Los Angeles, 1962)); *Policraticus*, ed. C. C. J. Webb, 2 vols. (Oxford, 1909).

Knighton, *Chronicle*, ed. J. R. Lumby, 2 vols. (RS xcii, 1889–95).

Macrobius, *Commentary on the Somnium Scipionis*, ed. L. Scarpa (Padua, 1981) (trans. by W. H. Stahl, New York, 1952).

Malmesbury, William of, *see* William of Malmesbury.

Map, Walter, *see* Walter Map.

Martianus Capella, *De Nuptiis Philologiae et Mercurii*, ed. A. Dick (Leipzig, 1925; revised J. Préaulx, Stuttgart, 1978) (trans. by W. H. Stahl *et al.*, New York, 1971–7).

Matthew Paris, *Chronica majora*, ed. H. R. Luard, 7 vols. (RS lvii, 1872–83); *Historia Anglorum*, ed. F. H. Madden, 3 vols. (RS xliv, 1866–9); see R. Vaughan, *Matthew Paris* (Cambridge, 1958).

Monk of Farne, *The Monk of Farne: the Meditations of a Fourteenth-Century Monk*, ed. H. Farmer (with trans. by a Benedictine of Stanbrook, London, 1961).

Nigel Longchamps (Nigel Wireker), *Speculum Stultorum*, ed. J. H. Mozley and R. R. Raymo (Berkeley and Los Angeles, 1960) (trans. by J. H. Mozley, Oxford, 1961).

Ordericus Vitalis, *Historia Ecclesiastica*, ed. and trans. M. Chibnall, 6 vols. (Oxford, 1969–80) (see M. Chibnall, *The World of Ordericus Vitalis* (Oxford, 1984)).

Peter Comestor, *Historia Scholastica*, *PL* cxcviii. 1053–644.

Peter Damian, *Opera*, *PL* cxliv–cxlv.

Prudentius, *Carmina*, ed. M. P. Cunningham (Corp. Christianorum, Ser. Lat. cxxvi, 1966).

Raymund de Pennaforte, St, *Summa de Paenitentia*, ed. O.-A. Díez (Rome, 1976–8).

Richard of Bury, *Philobiblon*, ed. and trans. E. C. Thomas (Oxford, 1960).

Richard of St Victor, *Opera*, *PL* cxcvi.

Robert Grosseteste: *see* S. Harrison Thomson, *The Writings of Robert Grosseteste* (Cambridge, 1940).

Servius, *Commentarii*, edd. G. Thilo and H. Hagen, 3 vols. (Leipzig, 1878–1902).

Speculum Stultorum, see Nigel Longchamps.
Visio Monachi de Eynsham, ed. M. Huber (Erlangen, 1904) (trans. V. Paget, London, 1909).
Visio Pauli, ed. T. Silverstein (London, 1935) (trans. in M. R. James, *The Apocryphal New Testament*, Oxford, 1924, 1955).
Walter Map, *De Nugis Curialium*, ed. and trans. M. R. James (revised C. N. L. Brooke and R. A. B. Mynors, Oxford, 1983).
Walter of Wimborne, *Poems*, ed. A. G. Rigg (Toronto, 1978).
William of Malmesbury, *Gesta Regum*, ed. W. Stubbs, 2 vols. (RS xc, 1887–9); *Historia Novella*, ed. K. R. Potter (London, 1955).
Wyclif, *see* Bibliography to ch. 7, below, section J. 7.
Ysengrimus, ed. E. Voigt (Halle, 1884).

F. WORKS IN ANGLO-NORMAN AND FRENCH

Bibliographical guides and general studies

Bossuat: *see above*, p. 464.
Legge, M. D., *Anglo-Norman in the Cloisters* (Edinburgh, 1950).
—— *Anglo-Norman Literature and its Background* (Oxford, 1963).
Vising, J., *Anglo-Norman Language and Literature* (London, 1923).

Anthologies and collections of texts

Aspin, I. S. T., ed., *Anglo-Norman Political Songs* (Oxford, 1953).

Authors and texts (mainly those referred to in this volume)

Amadas et Ydoine, ed. J. R. Reinhard (Paris, 1926).
Aucassin et Nicolette, ed. W. Suchier (Paderborn, 1921); ed. M. Roques (Paris, 1925) (trans. P. Matarasso, Harmondsworth, 1971).
Benoit de Sainte-Maure, *Roman de Troie*, ed. L. Constans, 6 vols. (SATF xlix, 1904–12).
Bozon, Nicole, *Contes*, edd. L. T. Smith and P. Meyer (SATF xxvii, 1889).
Chandos Herald, *Life of the Black Prince*, edd. M. K. Pope and E. C. Lodge (Oxford, 1910).
Chanson de Roland, ed. F. Whitehead (Oxford, 1942) (trans. by D. D. R. Owen, London, 1972).
Chrétien de Troyes, *Sämtliche Werke*, ed. W. Foerster, 5 vols. (Halle, 1884–1932); *Yvain*, ed. T. B. W. Reid (Manchester, 1942) (trans. by W. W. Comfort, intro. D. D. R. Owen, London, 1975).
Jean Froissart, *Chroniques*, ed. Kervyn de Lettenhove, 25 vols. (Brussels, 1867–77) (trans. by Lord Berners, ed. W. P. Ker, 6 vols., London, 1901).
Gaimar, *Lestorie des Engles*, edd. T. D. Hardy and C. T. Martin, 2 vols. (RS xci, 1888–9); ed. A. Bell (Oxford, 1960).
Gower, *Balades, Mirour de l'omme, see* Bibliography to ch. 9, below, section J. 9.
Grosseteste, Robert, *Chasteau d'Amour*, ed. M. Cooke (London, 1852); cf.

K. Sajavaara, ed., *The ME Translations of Grosseteste's Chasteau d'Amour* (Helsinki, 1967).

Guillaume de Deguileville, *Pèlerinage de la Vie Humaine*, ed. J. J. Stürzinger (Roxburghe Club, 1895).

Henry of Lancaster, *Le Livre de Seyntz Medicines*, ed. E. J. Arnould (Oxford, 1940).

Histoire de Guillaume le Maréchal, ed. P. Meyer (Paris, 1891–1901).

Horn, see Bibliography to ch. 5, below, section J. 5.

Lai d'Havelok, see Bibliography to ch. 5, below, section J. 5.

Langtoft, *see* Bibliography to ch. 4, below, section J. 4.

L'Estoire Joseph, ed. W. Steuer (Erlangen, 1903).

Livere de Reis de Brittanie, ed. J. Glover (RS xlii, 1865).

Lorens, Frère (Laurent), *Somme des Vices et des Vertus* (*Somme le Roi*) (no modern edn.; see R. Tuve, *Allegorical Imagery*, Princeton, 1966, ch. ii).

Lumière as Lais, see Peter of Peckham.

Machaut, Guillaume, *Œuvres*, ed. E. Hoepffner, 3 vols. (SATF lv, 1908–21) (*Le Dit dou Vergier* is in vol. i).

Manuel des Péchés, see Bibliography to ch. 2, below, section J. 2.

Marie de France, *Fables*, ed. K. Warnke (Halle, 1898); *Lais*, ed. K. Warnke (revised edn., Halle, 1924); ed. A. Ewert (Oxford, 1944).

Ovide moralisé, ed. C. de Boer, 5 vols. (Amsterdam, 1915–36).

Peter of Peckham, *La Lumière as Lais* (no modern edn.; see Legge, *Anglo-Norman Literature*, 214–16).

Philippe de Thaon, *Bestiaire*, ed. E. Walberg (Lund, Paris, 1900).

Roman de la Rose, ed. E. Langlois, 5 vols. (SATF lxi, 1914–24).

Roman d'Enéas, ed. J.-J. Salverda de Grave, 2 vols. (Paris, 1925–31).

Roman de Renart, ed. E. Martin, 3 vols. (Strasburg, 1882–7).

Thomas, *Tristan*, ed. J. Bédier (SATF xliv, 1902, 1905); ed. B. H. Wind (Leiden, 1950) (trans. by A. T. Hatto, Harmondsworth, 1960).

Wace, *Roman de Brut*, ed. I. Arnold, 2 vols. (SATF lxxx, 1938, 1940); *Roman de Rou*, ed. A. J. Holden, 3 vols. (SATF xc, 1970–3).

G. MEDIEVAL LITERATURE: GENERAL STUDIES

Atkins, J. W. H., *English Literary Criticism: the Medieval Phase* (Cambridge, 1943).

Auerbach, E., *Mimesis* (Berne, 1946; trans. by W. Trask, Princeton, NJ, 1953).

Baldwin, C. S., *Medieval Rhetoric and Poetic (to 1400)* (New York, 1928).

Baugh, A. C., *et al.*, *A Literary History of England* (New York, 1948, 1967).

Bennett, H. S., *Chaucer and the Fifteenth Century* (Oxford, 1947, 1973).

Bennett, J. A. W., *The Humane Medievalist and Other Essays in Literature and Learning*, ed. P. Boitani (Rome, 1982; Cambridge, 1983).

—— *The Poetry of the Passion* (Oxford, 1982).

Bloomfield, M. W., *The Seven Deadly Sins* (Michigan, 1952).

Bolton, W. F., ed., *Sphere History of Literature in the English Language*, vol. i, *The Middle Ages* (London, 1970).

Burrow, J. A., *Essays on Medieval Literature* (Oxford, 1984).
—— *Ricardian Poetry* (London, 1971).
Chambers, E. K., *English Literature at the Close of the Middle Ages* (Oxford, 1945).
Coleman, J., *English Literature in History 1350—1400: Medieval Readers and Writers* (London, 1981).
Cornelius, R. D., *The Figurative Castle* (Bryn Mawr, 1930).
Crampton, G. R., *The Condition of Creatures: Suffering and Action in Chaucer and Spenser* (New Haven, London, 1974).
Curtius, E. R., *European Literature and the Latin Middle Ages* (Berne, 1948; trans. by W. R. Trask, London, 1953).
Daiches, D. and Thorlby, A., edd., *Literature and Western Civilization*, vol. ii, *The Medieval World* (London, 1973).
De Bruyne, E., *Études d'esthétique médiévale*, 3 vols. (Bruges, 1946).
Dronke, P., *Fabula* (Leiden, 1974).
—— *Medieval Latin and the Rise of European Love-Lyric*, 2 vols. (Oxford, 1965–6).
—— *The Medieval Poet and his World* (Rome, 1984).
—— 'Medieval Rhetoric', in Daiches and Thorlby (above) and in *The Medieval Poet and his World*.
—— *Women Writers of the Middle Ages* (Cambridge, 1984).
Everett, D., *Essays on Middle English Literature*, ed. P. Kean (Oxford, 1955).
Gradon, P., *Form and Style in Early English Literature* (London, 1971).
Gransden, A., *Historical Writing in England c.550—c.1307* (London, 1974).
Green, R. F., *Poets and Princepleasers: Literature and the English Court in the Late Middle-Ages* (Toronto, 1980).
Hieatt, C. B., *The Realism of Dream Visions* (The Hague, 1967).
Kane, G., *Middle English Literature* (London, 1951).
Ker, W. P., *English Literature, Medieval* (London, 1912; reissued as *Medieval English Literature*, Oxford, 1969).
Lawton, D., ed., *Middle English Alliterative Poetry and its Literary Background* (Cambridge, 1982).
Lehmann, P. J. G., *Die Parodie im Mittelalter* (Stuttgart, 1963).
Lewis, C. S., *The Allegory of Love* (Oxford, 1936).
—— *The Discarded Image* (Cambridge, 1964).
Loomis, R. S., ed., *Arthurian Literature in the Middle Ages* (Oxford, 1959).
Lord, A. B., *The Singer of Tales* (Cambridge, Mass., 1960).
Medcalf, S., ed., *The Later Middle Ages* (London, 1981).
Minnis, A. J., *Medieval Theory of Authorship* (London, 1984).
Murphy, J. J., *Rhetoric in the Middle Ages* (Berkeley, Los Angeles, and London, 1974).
Muscatine, C., *Poetry and Crisis in the Age of Chaucer* (Notre Dame, London, 1972).
Nykrog, P., *Les Fabliaux* (Copenhagen, 1957).
Oakden, J. P., *Alliterative Poetry in Middle English*, 2 vols. (Manchester, 1930–5).
Owst, G. R., *Literature and Pulpit in Medieval England* (Cambridge, 1933; Oxford, 1961).
—— *Preaching in Medieval England* (Cambridge, 1926).

Patch, H. R., *The Other World* (Cambridge, Mass., 1950).

Pearsall, D., *Old and Middle English Poetry* (London, 1977).

Peter, J., *Complaint and Satire in Early English Literature* (Oxford, 1956).

Pickering, F. P., *Literature and Art in the Middle Ages* (London, 1970).

Piehler, P., *The Visionary Landscape: a Study in Medieval Allegory* (London, 1971).

Salter, E., *Fourteenth-Century English Poetry: Contexts and Readings* (Oxford, 1983).

Scattergood, V. J. and Sherborne, J. W., edd., *English Court Culture in the Later Middle Ages* (London, 1983).

Schlauch, M., *English Medieval Literature and its Social Foundations* (Warsaw, 1956).

Spearing, A. C., *Criticism and Medieval Poetry* (2nd edn., Cambridge, 1972).

—— *Medieval Dream Poetry* (Cambridge, 1976).

Speirs, J., *Medieval English Poetry: the Non-Chaucerian Tradition* (London, 1957).

Traver, H., *The Four Daughters of God* (Bryn Mawr, 1907).

Turville-Petre, T., *The Alliterative Revival* (Cambridge, 1977).

Tuve, R., *Allegorical Imagery: Some Medieval Books and their Posterity* (Princeton, NJ, 1966).

—— *Seasons and Months* (Paris, 1933; Cambridge, 1974).

Warton, T., *History of English Poetry*, 3 vols. (London, 1774–81).

Wenzel, S., *The Sin of Sloth* (Chapel Hill, 1967).

Wilson, R. M., *Early Middle English Literature* (London, 1939).

—— *The Lost Literature of Medieval England* (London, 1952, 1970).

Wittig, K., *The Scottish Tradition in Literature* (Edinburgh, 1958).

Woolf, R., *Art and Doctrine: Collected Essays*, ed. H. O'Donoghue (London, 1985).

Yunck, J. A., *The Lineage of Lady Meed* (Notre Dame, 1963).

Zacher, C. K., *Curiosity and Pilgrimage* (Baltimore, 1976).

H. ANTHOLOGIES AND READERS

Bennett, J. A. W. and Smithers, G. V., edd., *Early Middle English Verse and Prose* (Oxford, 1966; 2nd edn., 1968) (*EMEVP*).

Bawcutt, P. and Riddy, F., edd., *An Anthology of Longer Medieval Scottish Verse* (Edinburgh, 1986).

Burrow, J. A., ed., *English Verse 1300–1500* (London, 1971).

Dickins, B. and Wilson, R. M., edd., *Early Middle English Texts* (London, 1951).

Gray, D., ed., *The Oxford Book of Late Medieval Verse* (Oxford, 1985).

Hall, J., ed., *Selections from Early Middle English*, 2 vols. (Oxford, 1920).

Hazlitt, W. C., ed., *Remains of the Early Popular Poetry of England*, 4 vols. (London, 1864–6).

McKnight, G. H., ed., *Middle English Humorous Tales in Verse* (Boston, 1913).

Mossé, F., ed., *A Handbook of Middle English* (trans. by J. A. Walker, Baltimore, 1952).

Sisam, C. and K., edd., *The Oxford Book of Medieval English Verse* (Oxford, 1970) (*OBMEV*).

Sisam, K., ed., *Fourteenth Century Verse and Prose* (Oxford, 1921) (Sisam).

Wright, T. and Halliwell, J. O., edd., *Reliquiae Antiquae*, 2 vols. (London, 1845).

I. PRE-CONQUEST ENGLISH TEXTS

Old English poems mentioned in this book—*Beowulf, Brunanburh, The Dream of the Rood, Finnesburh, Genesis B, Maldon, The Phoenix*—may be found in *The Anglo-Saxon Poetic Records*, ed. G. P. Krapp and E. V. K. Dobbie, 6 vols. (New York, 1931–42), as well as in separate editions. The prose works mentioned are available in the following editions: *Anglo-Saxon Chronicle*, ed. J. Earle and C. Plummer, 2 vols. (Oxford, 1899, 1929); Ælfric's *Homilies*, ed. B. Thorpe (London, 1845); ed. M. Godden (EETS, ss v, 1979); ed. J. C. Pope (EETS cclix–cclx, 1967–8); Ælfric's *Lives of Saints*, ed. W. W. Skeat (EETS lxxvi, lxxxii, xciv, cxiv, 1881–1900); Wulfstan's *Homilies*, ed. D. Bethurum (Oxford, 1957). There is an exhaustive bibliography: S. B. Greenfield and F. C. Robinson, edd., *A Bibliography of Publications on Old English to the end of 1972* (Manchester, 1980).

J. MIDDLE ENGLISH TEXTS AND GENRES

(arranged according to the chapters of this book)

1. Pastoral and Comedy

Dame Sirith, ed. *EMEVP*, No. vi (Caxton's version in R. T. Lenaghan (ed.), *Caxton's Aesop* (Cambridge, Mass., 1967), 208–10).

De Clerico et Puella, ed. *EMEVP*, No. xv.

Fox and the Wolf, ed. *EMEVP*, No. v, on the Reynard stories, see R. Bossuat, *Le Roman de Renard* (Paris, 1927); J. Flinn, *Le Roman de Renard dans la littérature française et dans les littératures étrangères au moyen âge* (Paris, 1963); K. Varty, *Reynard the Fox* (Leicester, 1967).

Land of Cokaygne, ed. *EMEVP*, No. ix.

Man in the Moon, ed. *EMEVP*, No. viii N; B No. xxx; see R. J. Menner, 'The Man in the Moon and Hedging', *JEGP* xlviii (1949), 1–14.

Owl and the Nightingale, ed. E. G. Stanley (London, Edinburgh, 1960); (parallel texts), ed. J. W. H. Atkins (Cambridge, 1922); facsimile of both MSS, with intro. by N. R. Ker, EETS ccli (1963); STUDY: K. Hume, *The Owl and the Nightingale: the Poem and its Critics* (Toronto, Buffalo, 1975); on debates, see H. Walther, *Das Streitgedicht in der lateinischen Literatur des Mittelalters* (Quellen und Untersuchungen zur lateinischen Philologie des Mittelalters, v. 2, 1920).

2. Verse, Didactic and Homiletic

(See *MWME* ii, 553–649 (Saints' Legends))

Bestiary, ed. R. Morris, EETS xlix (1872) (with text of Thetbaldus); ed. Hall, *Selections from Early Middle English*; (selections) *EMEVP*, No. xii; STUDIES:

F. McCulloch, *Medieval Latin and French Bestiaries* (Chapel Hill, 1960);
F. Klingender, *Animals in Art and Thought, to the end of the Middle Ages*, edd.
E. Antal and J. Harthan (London, 1971).

Cursor Mundi, ed. R. Morris, EETS lvii, lviii (1874), lxii (1876), lxvi (1877),
lxviii (1878), xcix, ci (1892–3).

Genesis and Exodus, ed. O. Arngart (Lund Studies in English, xxxvi, 1968).

Handlyng Synne, ed. F. J. Furnivall, EETS cxix, cxxiii (1901, 1903); see H. E.
Allen, *MP* xiii (1916), 743–4, for a prose translation of the *Manuel*; on the
Manuel see E. J. Arnould, *Le Manuel des Péchés* (Paris, 1940); Legge, *Anglo-
Norman Literature*, 213–14; on Mannyng, see *BRUC*. *Note*: A new EETS
edition by R. G. Biggar and S. Schulz is in preparation, which will
substantially increase our knowledge of this work. Dr Biggar (of Boston
College) has kindly sent the following communication: 'The interrelations
of the six major extant MSS of *Handlyng Synne* with each other and with
the 20 or so extant MSS of the AN *Manuel des Péchés* are obscured by
frequent scribal participation and by contamination from AN MSS of the
Manuel other than the one, or perhaps two, which Mannyng translated,
adapted, and added to. As a result of these processes, no single extant ME
MS of the poem is completely satisfactory. The best known version, found
in the three parchment MSS—Harley (the basis of Furnivall's edition),
Bodley, and Folger—is the most complete (especially Bodley, with its
12,638 lines) and blessed with accurate and conscientious scribes (especially Bodley); but it represents the work of a SE Midlands "Reviser",
who renders the poem into his dialect where possible, and adds redun-
dancy to assure the clarity of its moral message. His exemplar is also
probably at least two removes from Mannyng. The (generally later) paper
MSS—Cambridge, Yale, and Dulwich—are each individually unsatis-
factory in various ways, but together they give evidence of an earlier and
more authentic version of *Handlyng Synne*. The paper MS closest to the
"Revised" version is Dulwich, complete to l. 2894, including the Prologue,
in which there are two references to the title of the poem as *Handlyng of
Synne*, and a catchword at the end of the MS, indicating a fuller version
behind it. Although Cambridge is an excerpt, containing only the 2845
lines of the Ten Commandments, frequently and unexplainably omitting
couplets and having readings not shared by the other MSS, its unique
readings are often probably authentic, reflecting lines shared by all of the
MSS of the *Manuel*. The longest paper MS, extremely important because
of the northern forms both in the rhymes, a marked feature of all the ME
MSS, and also within the line, a characteristic unique to this MS, is Yale,
containing 8724 lines. It unfortunately has large gaps, beginning only at
l. 2501 and missing a full quire, several leaves, and the final 267 lines.
Many of its unique readings must be authentic: for example, it names the
twelve dancers in the Tale of the Dancers of Colbek, and it has the Tale
of the Drunken Priest who sees Two Candles, which is in the *Manuel*, but
not in the other English MSS. It is safe to conclude that the language of
Yale, like that of the Petyt MS of the *Chronicle*, represents Mannyng's

own language, a distinctly northern dialect with some features Mannyng may have acquired in Cambridge and Lincolnshire.

'There is, then, the question of which "Brunne" Robert of Brunne comes from. The northern nature of the Yale MS and of the vocabulary and rhyming sounds in all of the other MSS (-*and, kirk, es, ded* for 'death', etc.) suggests that it is the "Brunne" in the East Riding of Yorkshire (as Nunburnholme was called in 1280–6, when Mannyng would have been a youth there). Perhaps Mannyng calls the Lincolnshire "Brunne" (modern Bourne) "Brunnewake" or (Folger) "Bringwake" in order to make a distinction between his home town in Yorkshire and the local "Brunne" in Lincolnshire, the site of an Augustinian abbey where he may have spent 15 years.

'The MS of the *Manuel* which is closest to *Handlyng Synne* is MS Harley 4657, Furnivall's B, though some readings would indicate either a second manuscript, or a manuscript not now extant, in Mannyng's possession.'

Lutel Soth Sermon, ed. R. Morris, EETS xlix (1872), 186–91.

Mum and the Sothsegger, edd. M. Day and R. Steele, EETS cxcix (1936).

Northern Passion, ed. F. A. Foster, EETS cxlv (1913), cxlvii (1916).

Ormulum, ed. R. M. White, revised R. Holt (Oxford, 1878); on the date, see M. B. Parkes in E. G. Stanley and D. Gray (edd.), *Five Hundred Years of Words and Sounds* (Cambridge, 1983), 115–27.

Parlement of the Thre Ages, ed. M. Y. Offord, EETS ccxlvi (1959).

Poema Morale, ed. J. Hall, *Selections from Early Middle English*; H. Lewin (Halle, 1881).

Prick of Conscience, ed. R. Morris (The Philological Society's Early English Volume, London, Berlin, 1863); cf. R. E. Lewis and A. McIntosh, *A Descriptive Guide to the MSS of* The Prick of Conscience, *Medium Ævum* Monograph 12 (1983).

Quatrefoil of Love, ed. I. Gollancz in *An English Miscellany Presented to Dr F. J. Furnivall* (Oxford, 1901), 112–32.

Scots Lives of the Saints, ed. C. Horstmann, *Barbours des Schottischen Nationaldichters Legendensammlung* (Heilbronn, 1881).

South English Legendary, edd. C. D'Evelyn and A. J. Mill, EETS ccxxxv (1956), ccxxxvi (1957), ccxliv (1959); cf. M. Görlach, *The Textual Tradition of the SE Legendary* (Leeds, 1974).

Vision of Tundal, ed. A. Wagner (Halle, 1893); (Latin *Visio Tnugdali*, ed. A. Wagner, Erlangen, 1882); See H. R. Patch, *The Other World*.

Wynnere and Wastoure, ed. I. Gollancz (London, 1920).

3. Layamon

Ed. F. Madden (London, 1847); edd. G. L. Brook and R. F. Leslie, EETS ccl (1963), cclxxvii (1978) (in progress); (selections) ed. G. L. Brook (Oxford, 1963); ed. J. Hall (Oxford, 1924); STUDIES: F. L. Gillespy, *Layamon's Brut: a Comparative Study of Narrative Art* (Univ. of California Publications in Modern Philology, iii, 1916); H. Pilch, *Layamon's Brut: Eine literarische Studie* (Heidelberg, 1960); E. G. Stanley, 'Layamon's Antiquarian Sentiments',

MÆ xxxviii (1969), 23–37; Wace's *Brut*, ed. I. Arnold, SATF lxxx (1938–40); for Geoffrey of Monmouth, see p. 471 above.

4. History in Verse

Anonymous Short Metrical Chronicle, ed. E. Zettl, EETS cxcvi (1935).

Barbour's *Bruce*, ed. W. W. Skeat, EETS, ES xi, xxi, xxix, lv (1870–89) (reprinted as 2 vols., 1968, and in STS xxxi–xxxiii, 1893–4); ed. W. M. Mackenzie (London, 1909); edd. M. P. McDiarmid and J. A. C. Stevenson, STS 4th Series, xii (1980).

Mannyng's *Chronicle*, edd. (part i) F. J. Furnivall, 2 vols. (RS xlvii, 1889), (part ii) T. Hearne, *Peter Langtoft's Chronicle (as illustrated and improv'd by Robert of Brunne)*, 2 vols. (Oxford, 1725, 1810).

'Robert of Gloucester', ed. T. Hearne (Oxford, 1724, reprinted 1810); ed. W. A. Wright, 2 vols. (RS lxxxvi, 1887).

5. Romances

(Extensive bibliography in *MWME*, vol. i.)

Anthologies

French, W. H. and Hale, C. B., edd., *Middle English Metrical Romances*, 2 vols. (New York, 1930).

Schmidt, A. V. C. and Jacobs, N., edd., *Medieval English Romances*, 2 vols. (London, 1980).

Romances discussed in the chapter

Alexander and Dindymus, ed. W. W. Skeat, EETS, ES xxxi (1878); ed. F. P. Magoun (Cambridge, Mass., 1929).

Alliterative *Morte Arthure*, ed. E. Björkman (Heidelberg, New York, 1915); ed. (with Stanzaic *Morte*) L. D. Benson (Indianapolis, 1974); ed. V. Krishna (New York, 1974); (selections) ed. J. Finlayson (London, 1967); STUDIES: K. H. Göller, ed., *The Alliterative Morte Arthure: a Reassessment of the Poem* (Cambridge, 1981), W. Matthews, *The Tragedy of Arthur: a Study of the alliterative 'Morte Arthure'* (Berkeley, Los Angeles, 1960).

Apollonius fragment, ed. J. Raith, *Die alt- und mittelenglischen Apollonius-Bruchstücke* (Munich, 1956).

Arthur and Merlin, ed. O. D. Macrae-Gibson, EETS cclxviii, cclxxix (1973, 1979).

Athelston, ed. A. McI. Trounce, Phil. Soc. 1933, EETS ccxxiv (1950).

Avowing of Arthur, ed. C. Brookhouse, *Anglistica*, xv (Copenhagen, 1968); ed. R. Dahood (New York, London, 1984).

Awntyrs of Arthur, ed. R. Hanna III (Manchester, 1974).

Earl of Toulous, ed. G. Lüdtke (Berlin, 1881).

Emaré, ed. E. Rickert, EETS, ES xcix (1906).

Floris and Blancheflour, ed. F. C. de Vries (Groningen, 1966); French *Floire et*

Blancheflor, ed. M. Pelan (Publ. de la Faculté des Lettres de l'Université de Strasbourg, Textes d'étude vii, 1937, revised edn. 1956).

Gamelyn, ed. W. W. Skeat, *Complete Works of Geoffrey Chaucer*, vol. iv (Oxford, 1877).

Geste Hystoriale of the Destruction of Troy, edd. G. A. Pantin and D. Donaldson, EETS xxxix, lvi (1869, 1874).

Guy of Warwick, ed. J. Zupitza, EETS, ES xxv, xxvi (1875–6).

Havelok, ed. G. V. Smithers (Oxford, 1987); ed. W. W. Skeat, revised K. Sisam (Oxford, 1915); AN *Lai d'Haveloc*, ed. A. Bell (Manchester, 1925).

King Horn, ed. J. Hall (Oxford, 1901); AN *Horn*, ed. M. K. Pope, revised T. B. W. Reid, 2 vols. (Oxford, 1955–64).

Kyng Alisaunder, ed. G. V. Smithers, EETS ccxxvii, ccxxxvii (1952, 1957).

Lai le Freine, ed. M. Wattie (Smith College Studies in Modern Languages, x. 3, 1929); for French, see Marie de France, p. 474 above.

'Laud' *Troy Book*, ed. J. E. Wülfing, EETS cxxi, cxxii (1902).

Libeaus Desconus, ed. M. Mills, EETS cclxi (1969); French, ed. G. P. Williams (Paris, 1929).

Richard Coer de Lion, ed. K. Brunner (Vienna, Leipzig, 1913).

Siege of Jerusalem, edd. E. Kölbing and M. Day, EETS clxxxviii (1931).

Sir Amadace, ed. C. Brookhouse, *Anglistica*, xv (Copenhagen, 1968).

Sir Cleges, edd. French and Hale.

Sir Degaré, ed. G. Schleich (Heidelberg, 1929).

Sir Ferumbras, ed. S. J. Herrtage, EETS, ES xxxiv (1879).

Sir Gawain and the Green Knight, see Bibliography to ch. 6, below, section J. 6.

Sir Gowther, ed. K. Breul (Oppeln, 1886).

Sir Launfal, ed. A. J. Bliss (London, Edinburgh, 1960); for French, see Marie de France, p. 474 above.

Sir Orfeo, ed. A. J. Bliss (2nd edn., Oxford, 1960); STUDIES: D. Allen, 'Orpheus and Orfeo: the Dead and the Taken', *MÆ* xxxiii (1964), 102–11; J. B. Friedman, *Orpheus in the Middle Ages* (Cambridge, Mass., 1970).

Stanzaic *Morte Arthur*, ed. J. D. Bruce, EETS, ES lxxxviii (1903); ed. L. D. Benson (see Alliterative *Morte Arthure*).

Wars of Alexander, ed. W. W. Skeat, EETS, ES xlvii (1886).

William of Palerne, ed. W. W. Skeat, EETS, ES i (1867).

Ywain and Gawain, edd. A. B. Friedman and N. T. Harrington, EETS ccliv (1964); for French, see Chrétien de Troyes, p. 473 above.

General studies

Barrow, S. F., *The Medieval Society Romances* (New York, 1924).

Cary, G., *The Medieval Alexander* (Cambridge, 1956).

Chambers, E. K., *Arthur of Britain* (London, 1927).

Everett, D., 'A Characterization of the English Medieval Romances', *E&S* xv (1929), 98–121, reprinted in *Essays on Middle English Literature* (Oxford, 1955).

Hanning, R. W., *The Individual in Twelfth-Century Romance* (New Haven, London, 1977).

Loomis, R. S., ed., *Arthurian Literature in the Middle Ages* (Oxford, 1959).

Mathew, G., 'Marriage and Amour Courtois in Late Fourteenth-Century England', in *Essays Presented to Charles Williams* (Oxford, 1947).

Mehl, D., *The Middle English Romances of the Thirteenth and Fourteenth Centuries* (London, 1967).

Ramsay, L. C., *Chivalric Romances: Popular Literature in Medieval England* (Bloomington, 1983).

Stevens, J., *Medieval Romance* (London, 1973).

Tatlock, J. S. P., *The Legendary History of Britain* (Berkeley, Los Angeles, 1950).

Trounce, A. McI., 'The English Tail-Rhyme Romances', *MÆ* i (1932), 87–108, 168–82; ii (1933), 34–57, 189–98; iii (1934), 30–50.

Vinaver, E., *The Rise of Romance* (Oxford, 1971).

Wilson, A., *Traditional Romance and Tale* (Cambridge, 1976).

Wittig, S., *Stylistic and Narrative Structures in the Middle English Romances* (Austin, 1978).

6. The Poems of the Gawain Manuscript

(See *MWME* ii. 503–16, i. 238–43.)

Facsimile edn. of MS Cotton Nero A. x, intro. I. Gollancz, EETS clxii (1923); editions of all four poems by M. Andrew and R. Waldron, *The Poems of the Pearl Manuscript* (London, 1978) and of *Pearl* and *Gawain* by A. C. Cawley (London, 1962); STUDIES of the 'Gawain poet': A. C. Spearing, *The Gawain-Poet* (Cambridge, 1970); E. Wilson, *The Gawain-Poet* (Leiden, 1976); *Sir Gawain and Pearl, Critical Essays*, ed. R. J. Blanch (Bloomington, 1966). (A further poem, *St. Erkenwald* (ed. H. L. Savage (New Haven, 1916), ed. C. Peterson (Philadelphia, 1977)), has sometimes been associated with this group, but without general agreement.)

Patience, ed. I. Gollancz (London, 1913); ed. J. J. Anderson (Manchester, 1977).

Pearl, ed. E. V. Gordon (Oxford, 1953); STUDIES: I. Bishop, *Pearl in its Setting* (Oxford, 1968); D. Everett in *Essays on Middle English Literature*; P. M. Kean, *The Pearl: an Interpretation* (London, 1967); *The Middle English Pearl: Critical Essays*, ed. J. Conley (Notre Dame, Indiana, 1970); see also M. Manzalaoui, 'English Analogues to the *Liber Scalae*' *MÆ* xxxiv (1965), 21–35; on the Barlaam and Josaphat story, see D. M. Lang, *The Balavariani* (London, 1966); (Latin text, edd. and trans. G. R. Woodward and H. Mattingley (Loeb, 1914)).

Purity (Cleanness), ed. I. Gollancz (London, 1921); ed. R. J. Menner (Yale Studies in English, lxi, 1920); ed. J. J. Anderson (Manchester, 1977).

Sir Gawain and the Green Knight, edd. J. R. R. Tolkien and E. V. Gordon (Oxford, 1925; revised N. Davis, 1967); ed. T. Silverstein (Chicago, 1984); ed. R. A. Waldron (London, 1970); ed. J. A. Burrow (Harmondsworth, 1972); STUDIES: L. D. Benson, *Art and Tradition in Sir Gawain* (New Brunswick, 1965); M. Borroff, *Sir Gawain and the Green Knight: a Stylistic and Metrical Study* (New Haven, 1962); J. A. Burrow, *A Reading of Sir Gawain and the Green Knight* (London, 1965); G. L. Kittredge, *A Study of Sir Gawain and the Green*

Knight (Cambridge, Mass., 1926); D. Fox (ed.), *Twentieth-Century Interpretations of Sir Gawain and the Green Knight* (Englewood Cliffs, 1968).

7. Prose

For further bibliography, see A. S. G. Edwards (ed.), *Middle English Prose: a Guide* (New Brunswick, 1984); V. M. Lagorio and R. Bradley, *The Fourteenth-Century English Mystics: a Comprehensive Annotated Bibliography* (New York and London, 1981); *MWME* ii. 518–21 (Wycliffite Writings), 650–9 (Instructions for Religious).

Authors and Texts discussed in this chapter

Ancrene Wisse (Ancrene Riwle), ed. J. R. R. Tolkien, EETS ccxlix (1962) (Corpus Christi College, Cambridge, MS 402); (selections) ed. G. Shepherd (Parts vi–vii), (London, Edinburgh, 1959); *EMEVP*, No. xviii; (other MSS) ed. M. Day, EETS ccxxv (1952); ed. R. M. Wilson, EETS ccxxix (1954); ed. A. C. Baugh, EETS ccxxxii (1956); ed. F. M. Mack, EETS cclii (1963); ed. E. J. Dobson, EETS cclxvii (1972); ed. A. Zettersten, EETS cclxxiv (1976); (selections) ed. R. Dahood (Binghamton, 1984) (Introduction and Part i); modernized edn., M. B. Salu (London, 1955); French versions: ed. J. A. Herbert, EETS ccxix (1944); ed. W. H. Trethewey, EETS ccxl (1958); Latin version: ed. C. D'Evelyn, EETS ccxvi (1944); STUDIES: E. J. Dobson, *Moralities on the Gospels* (Oxford, 1975) and *The Origins of Ancrene Wisse* (Oxford, 1976).

Ayenbite of Inwit, see Michel of Northgate.

Cloud of Unknowing, ed. P. Hodgson, EETS ccxviii (1944).

Deonise Hid Divinite, ed. P. Hodgson, EETS ccxxxi (1955).

Gaytryge's Sermon, ed. G. G. Perry, EETS xxvi (1867, 1914).

Hali Meithhad, ed. B. Millett, EETS cclxxxiv (1982).

Higden, *see* Trevisa.

Hilton, Walter, *The Scale of Perfection*: EETS edn. by A. J. Bliss and S. S. Hussey in preparation; modernized edns. by G. Sitwell (London, 1953); L. Sherley-Price (Harmondsworth, 1957); *et al.*; *Eight Chapters on Perfection*, ed. F. Kuriyagawa (Keio, 1967), (modernized edn. in D. Jones, *Minor Works of Walter Hilton*, London, 1929); *The Goad of Love*, modernized edn. by C. Kirchberger (London, 1952).

Jacob's Well, ed. A. Brandeis, EETS cxv (1900).

Julian of Norwich, *A Book of Showings*, edd. E. Colledge and J. Walsh, 2 vols. (Toronto, 1978); modernized edns. by G. Warrack (London, 1901); C. Wolters (Harmondsworth, 1966); *et al.*

Kentish Sermons, see Sermons.

'Mandeville', Sir John, ed. M. C. Seymour (Oxford, 1967); ed. P. Hamelius, EETS cliii–iv (1919–23); ed. M. Letts (London, 1953); modernized edns. by C. W. R. D. Moseley (Harmondsworth, 1983); M. C. Seymour (Oxford, 1968); metrical version, ed. M. C Seymour, EETS cclxix (1973); STUDIES: J. W. Bennett, *The Rediscovery of Sir John Mandeville* (Oxford, 1954); M. Letts, *Sir John Mandeville, the Man and his Book* (London, 1949).

Michel of Northgate, Dan, *Ayenbite of Inwit*, ed. R. Morris, EETS xxiii (1866, 1965); revised P. Gradon, EETS cclxxviii (1979).

Mirk, John, *Instructions for Parish Priests*, ed. E. Peacock, EETS xxxi (1868, 1902); *Festiall*, ed. T. Erbe, EETS, ES xcvi (1905).

Peterborough Chronicle: The Peterborough Chronicle 1070–1154, ed. C. Clark (Oxford, 1958; 2nd edn. 1970); facsimile edn. of MS Laud misc. 636 by D. Whitelock (Copenhagen, 1954); cf. *Chronicle of Hugo Candidus*, ed. and trans. W. T. Mellows (London, 1949).

Rolle, Richard, *English Writings*, ed. H. E. Allen (Oxford, 1931); *Yorkshire Writers: Richard Rolle of Hampole*, ed. C. Horstman, 2 vols. (London, 1895–6); *The Psalter by Richard Rolle of Hampole*, ed. H. R. Bramley (Oxford, 1884); Latin works: *Incendium Amoris*, ed. M. Deanesly (Manchester, 1915) (trans. C. Wolters, Harmondsworth, 1972); *Melos Amoris*, ed. E. J. Arnould (Oxford, 1957); see H. E. Allen, *Writings Ascribed to Richard Rolle* (New York, 1927).

St Juliene, ed. S. R. T. O. d'Ardenne (Liège, Paris, 1936; reprinted EETS ccxlviii, 1961).

St Katerine, ed. E. Einenkel, EETS lxxx (1884); re-edd. S. R. T. O. d'Ardenne and E. J. Dobson, EETS, SS vii (1981).

St Marherete, ed. F. M. Mack, EETS cxciii (1934).

Sawles Warde, ed. R. M. Wilson (Leeds, 1938); ed. *EMEVP*, No. xix; for *De Custodia, see* p. 471 above.

Sermons: (MS Bodley 343) ed. A. O. Balfour, EETS cxxxvii (1909); (Kentish Sermons) ed. R. Morris, EETS xlix (1872); (selections) *EMEVP*, No. xvii; on Maurice de Sully, see C. A. Robson, p. 485 below; (MS Lambeth 487) ed. R. Morris, EETS xxix (1867); (MS Royal 18 B xxii) ed. W. O. Ross, EETS ccix (1940); (MS Trinity College Cambridge, B 14. 52) ed. R. Morris, EETS liii (1873); *see also* Mirk.

Trevisa, John: Translations of *De Proprietatibus Rerum*, edd. M. C. Seymour *et al.* (Oxford, 1975–); translation of Higden's *Polychronicon* in *Polychronicon Ranulphi Higden*, edd. C. Babington and J. R. Lumby, 9 vols. (RS lxxiv–lxxxii, 1865–86); (selections) Sisam, No. xiii; see also J. Taylor, *The Universal Chronicle of Ranulf Higden* (Oxford, 1966); *Dialogus inter Militem et Clericum*, Fitzralph's Sermon, etc., ed. A. J. Perry, EETS clxvii (1924); *Dialogue between a Lord and a Clerk upon Translation* in A. W. Pollard (ed.), *Fifteenth-Century Prose and Verse* (London, 1903); STUDY: D. C. Fowler, 'New Light on John Trevisa', *Traditio*, xviii (1962), 289–317.

Usk, Thomas, *Testament of Love*, ed. W. W. Skeat, *Complete Works of Geoffrey Chaucer*, vol. vii (Oxford, 1897).

Wyclif and Wycliffites: (*a*) Wyclif's Latin works, ed. for the Wyclif Society, 35 vols. (London, 1883–1922); *see* W. R. Thomson, *The Latin Writings of John Wyclif: an Annotated Catalog* (Toronto, 1983); STUDIES: K. B. McFarlane, *John Wycliffe and the Beginnings of English Nonconformity* (London, 1952); J. A. Robson, *Wyclif and the Oxford Schools* (Cambridge, 1961); H. B. Workman, *John Wyclif*, 2 vols. (Oxford, 1926).

    (*b*) Wycliffite Biblical Translations: *The Holy Bible translated by Wyclif and his Followers*, edd. J. Forshall and F. Madden, 4 vols. (Oxford, 1850); *The Earlier Version of the Wycliffite Bible*, ed. C. Lindberg (Uppsala, 1959–); *The Wycliffe Bible*, ed. S. L. Fristedt (Stockholm, 1953–); see also M. Deanesly (below).

(*c*) Wycliffite works in English: *English Wycliffite Sermons*, ed. A. Hudson, vol. i (Oxford, 1983) (in progress); *Selections from English Wycliffite Writings*, ed. A. Hudson (Cambridge, 1978); *Select English Works of John Wyclif*, ed. T. Arnold, 3 vols. (Oxford, 1869–71); *English Works of Wyclif hitherto unprinted*, ed. F. D. Matthew, EETS lxxiv (1880, revised 1902); *Wyclif: Select English Writings*, ed. H. E. Winn (Oxford, 1929); for studies *see* bibliography in Hudson, *Selections*.

General studies

Bethurum, D., 'The Connection of the Katherine Group with Old English Prose', *JEGP* xxxiv (1935), 553–64.

Colledge, E., ed., *The Medieval Mystics of England* (London, 1962).

Deanesly, M., *The Lollard Bible and other medieval Biblical Versions* (Cambridge, 1920).

Hodgson, P., *Three Fourteenth-Century English Mystics* (London, 1967).

Knowles, D., *The English Mystical Tradition* (London, 1961).

Mosher, J. A., *The Exemplum in the Early Religious and Didactic Literature of England* (New York, 1911).

Owst, G. R., *see* p. 475 above.

Pfander, H. G., *The Popular Sermons of the Medieval Friar in England* (New York, 1937).

Riehle, W., *The Middle English Mystics* (trans. by B. Standring, London, 1981).

Robson, C. A., *Maurice of Sully and the Medieval Vernacular Homily* (Oxford, 1952).

Shepherd, G., 'English Versions of the Scriptures before Wyclif', in *Cambridge History of the Bible*, vol. ii (Cambridge, 1969).

Sitwell, G., *Medieval Spiritual Writers* (London, 1961).

Tolkien, J. R. R., '*Ancrene Wisse* and *Hali Meiðhad*', *E&S* xiv (1928), 104–26.

Walsh, J., ed., *Pre-Reformation Spirituality* (London, 1966).

8. Lyrics

See *MWME* v. 1631–725 (poems dealing with contemporary conditions); vi. 1940–2081 (carols).

Anthologies and editions

Brook, G. L., ed., *The Harley Lyrics* (3rd edn., Manchester, 1964) (B).

Brown, Carleton, ed., *English Lyrics of the Thirteenth Century* (Oxford, 1932) *CB XIII*).

—— ed., *Religious Lyrics of the Fourteenth Century* (revised G. V. Smithers, Oxford, 1952) (*CB XIV*).

—— ed., *Religious Lyrics of the Fifteenth Century* (Oxford, 1939).

Davies, R. T., ed., *Medieval English Lyrics* (London, 1963).

Dobson, E. J. and Harrison, F. Ll., edd., *Medieval English Songs* (London, 1979).

EMEVP, No. viii.

Gray, D., ed., *A Selection of Religious Lyrics* (Oxford, 1975) (*SRL*).

Greene, R. L., ed., *The Early English Carols* (2nd edn., Oxford, 1977).

Heuser, W., ed., *Die Kildare-Gedichte* (Bonner Beiträge zur Anglistik, xiv, 1904).

Ker, N. R. (intro.), Facsimile edn. of MS Harley 2253, EETS cclv (1965).

Red Book of Ossory: poems, ed. R. L. Greene (Medium Ævum Monographs, NS v, Oxford, 1974), ed. T. Stemmler (Mannheim, 1975); ed. E. Colledge (Toronto, 1974).

Reichl, K., ed., *Religiöse Dichtung im englischen Hochmittelalter* (Munich, 1973).

Robbins, R. H., ed., *Secular Lyrics of the Fourteenth and Fifteenth Centuries* (Oxford, 1952; 2nd edn., 1955) (*SL*).

—— ed., *Historical Poems of the Fourteenth and Fifteenth Centuries* (New York, 1959) (*HP*).

Silverstein, T., ed., *Medieval English Lyrics* (London, 1971).

Sisam, No. xv.

Wilson, E., *A Descriptive Catalogue of the English Lyrics in John of Grimestone's Preaching Book* (Medium Ævum Monographs, NS ii, Oxford, 1973) (W).

Studies

Dronke, P., *The Medieval Lyric* (London, 1968; 2nd edn., 1978).

Gray, D., *Themes and Images in the Medieval English Religious Lyric* (London, 1972).

Moore, A. K., *The Secular Lyric in Middle English* (Lexington, 1951).

Stemmler, T., *Die englische Liebesgedichte des MS Harley 2253* (Bonn, 1962).

Weber, S. A., *Theology and Poetry in the Middle English Lyrics* (Columbus, Ohio, 1969).

Wenzel, S., *Verses in Sermons* (Cambridge, Mass., 1978).

Woolf, R., *The English Religious Lyric in the Middle Ages* (Oxford, 1968).

9. Gower

Ed. G. C. Macaulay, 4 vols. (Oxford, 1899–1902) (vol. i, French Works—*Mirour de l'omme, Cinkante Balades*, etc.; vols. ii–iii, English Works; vol. iv, Latin Works—*Vox Clamantis, Cronica Tripertita*, etc.); selections: ed. J. A. W. Bennett (Oxford, 1968); STUDIES: J. A. W. Bennett, 'Gower's "honeste love" ', in J. Lawlor, (ed.), *Patterns of Love and Courtesy: Essays in Memory of C. S. Lewis* (London, 1966); J. H. Fisher, *Gower: Moral Philosopher and Friend of Chaucer* (New York, 1964); C. S. Lewis in *The Allegory of Love*; A. J. Minnis, (ed.), *Gower's Confessio Amantis: Responses and Reassessments* (Cambridge, 1983).

10. Langland

Ed. W. W. Skeat: (A text) EETS xxviii (1867), (B text) EETS xxxviii (1869), (C text) EETS liv (1873), (parallel texts) (Oxford, 1886; reprinted with bibliography, 1954); ed. G. Kane (A text) (London, 1960); edd. G. Kane and E. T.

Donaldson (B text) (London, 1975); edd. G. Kane and G. H. Russell (C text) (forthcoming); ed. D. Pearsall (C text) (London, 1978); ed. A. V. C. Schmidt (B text) (London, 1978); edd. A. G. Rigg and C. Brewer, *Piers Plowman: The Z Version* (Toronto, 1983) (the text in MS Bodley 851, which it is claimed may represent an earlier version); selections: ed. J. A. W. Bennett (Oxford, 1972) (Prologue and Passus I–VII).

Studies

Baldwin, A., *The Theme of Government in Piers Plowman* (Cambridge, 1981).

Bennett, J. A. W., 'Chaucer's Contemporary', in Hussey (see below).

—— 'William Langland's World of Visions', *The Listener* (1950), 381–2.

Blanch, R. J., ed., *Style and Symbolism in 'Piers Plowman': a Modern Critical Anthology* (Knoxville, 1969).

Burrow, J. A., 'The Audience of *Piers Plowman*', *Anglia* lxxv (1957), 373–84.

Bloomfield, M. W., *Piers Plowman as a Fourteenth-Century Apocalypse* (New Brunswick, 1962).

Coleman, J., *Piers Plowman and the Moderni* (Rome, 1981).

Donaldson, E. T., *Piers Plowman: the C Text and its Poet* (Yale Studies in English, cxiii, 1949; reprinted, 1966).

Dunning, T. P., *Piers Plowman: an Interpretation of the A Text* (Dublin, 1957; 2nd edn., revised T. P. Dolan, Oxford, 1980).

Frank, R. W., *Piers Plowman and the Scheme of Salvation* (New Haven, 1957).

Hussey, S. S., ed., *Piers Plowman: Critical Approaches* (London, 1969).

Lawlor, J., *Piers Plowman* (London, 1962).

Norton-Smith, J., *Langland* (Leiden, 1983).

Salter, E., *Piers Plowman: an Introduction* (Oxford, 1969).

Stokes, M., *Justice and Mercy in Piers Plowman* (London, 1984).

Index

Main entries are in bold figures; figures in italics refer to the Bibliography. Characters and saints appearing in their own legends have not been included; nor have major biblical figures occurring *passim*. Information readily gleaned from the Contents is not repeated here.